Oxford Mathematics for the Caribbean

Nicholas Goldberg
with Neva Cameron-Edwards

1

FIFTH EDITION

With Companion CD

OXFORD

OXFORD
UNIVERSITY PRESS

Great Clarendon Street, Oxford OX2 6DP

Oxford University Press is a department of the University of Oxford.

It furthers the University's objective of excellence in research, scholarship, and education by publishing worldwide in

Oxford New York

Auckland Cape Town Dar es Salaam Hong Kong Karachi Kuala Lumpur Madrid Melbourne Mexico City Nairobi New Delhi Shanghai Taipei Toronto

With offices in

Argentina Austria Brazil Chile Czech Republic France Greece Guatemala Hungary Italy Japan South Korea Poland Portugal Singapore Switzerland Thailand Turkey Ukraine Vietnam

Oxford is a registered trade mark of Oxford University Press

in the UK and in certain other countries

First published 2010

British Library Cataloguing in Publication Data

Data available

ISBN 978 0 19 913917 0

20 19 18 17 16 15 14 13 12

Printed in India by Multivista Global Pvt. Ltd

Paper used in the production of this book is a natural, recyclable product made from wood grown in sustainable forests. The manufacturing process conforms to the environmental regulations of the country of origin.

Acknowledgements

Illustrations © Phill Burrows and Ian West.

Front cover photo Joseph Jones; **P1** Dylan Burrill/Crestock; **P4** Adnan Abidi/Reuters; **P10** AP Photo; **P15** Andy Clark/Reuters; **P16** Philip Brown/Reuters; **P17** Bragin Alexey/Shutterstock.com; **P22** Adnan Abidi/Reuters; **P25** Matthew Cole/Shutterstock.com; **P39** Roy Riley/Alamy; **P53** Martha Cooper/Photolibrary; **P58l** Drozdowski/Shutterstock.com; **P58r** Robin Graham/Art Directors & Trip Photo Library; **P63** AFP/Getty Images; **P74** Helene Rogers/Art Directors & Trip Photo Library; **P75** Pack-Shot/Shutterstock.com; **P76l** Edyta Pawlowska/Shutterstock.com; **P76r** Thomas Coex/AFP; **P79** Danny Moloshok/Reuters; **P81** Richard I'Anson/Lonely Planet Images; **P92** nito/Shutterstock.com; **P94** Jace Tan/Shutterstock; **P100** Stockbyte Stockbyte/Photolibrary; **P107** Rovenko Design/Shutterstock.com; **P112** Maksym Gorpenyuk/Shutterstock.com; **P121** Juliet Highet/Art Directors & Trip Photo Library; **P123** Lou Jones/Lonely Planet Images; **P125** ALIMDI.NET/Rgb Fotografie/Photographers Direct; **P132a** Maksim Toome/Shutterstock.com; **P132b** fritzkocher/Shutterstock.com; **P132c** Tomasz Mentel/Dreamstime; **P132d** Tischenko Irina/Shutterstock.com; **P136** c./Shutterstock.com; **P137** Amid/Shutterstock.com; **P140** Jewel Samad/AFP; **P143** Image Source/Photolibrary; **P148** Brasiliao/Shutterstock.com; **P155a** Cosmin Manci/Shutterstock.com; **P155b** Christin Gilbert/Photographers Direct; **P158** Planner/Shutterstock.com; **P161a** M.C. Escher's "Symmetry Drawing E28" © 2010 The M.C. Escher Company-Holland. All rights reserved. www.mcescher.com; **P161b** M.C. Escher's "Symmetry Drawing E85" © 2010 The M.C. Escher Company-Holland. All rights reserved. www.mcescher.com; **P161c** M.C. Escher's "Symmetry Drawing E70" © 2010 The M.C. Escher Company-Holland. All rights reserved. www.mcescher.com; **P162a** Marcio Goldzweig/Dreamstime; **P162b** M.C. Escher's "Symmetry Drawing E107" © 2010 The M.C. Escher Company-Holland. All rights reserved. www.mcescher.com; **P164** M.C. Escher's "Symmetry Drawing E87" © 2010 The M.C. Escher Company-Holland. All rights reserved. www.mcescher.com; **P177** Christopher Baker/Lonely Planet Images; **P178** Holger Leue/Lonely Planet Images; **P181** dyoma/Shutterstock.com; **P186** Ingram Publishing/Photolibrary; **P188** Peter Baxter/Shutterstock.com; **P199** Jeff Greenberg/Art Directors & Trip Photo Library; **P221** Hisham F Ibrahim/Photolibrary; **P228** Reuters Photographer; **P239** Manzrussali/Shutterstock.com.

Contents

About this book v

1 Number 1

1.1 The story of numbers 2
1.2 Adding and subtracting numbers 4
1.3 Multiples and factors 5
1.4 More about our number system 10
1.5 Division 12
1.6 Approximations and estimations 15
1.7 Using a calculator 17
1.8 Problem solving 19
Consolidation 21
Summary 22

2 Sets 25

2.1 Sets and their members 26
2.2 How to describe a set 26
2.3 Venn diagrams 28
2.4 Intersection of sets 30
2.5 Common factors, common multiples 32
Consolidation 35
Summary 36

3 Fractions 39

3.1 Showing fractions 40
3.2 Calculating fractions 41
3.3 Equivalent fractions 43
3.4 Fractions greater than '1' 48
3.5 Adding fractions 50
3.6 Subtracting fractions 51
3.7 Multiplying fractions 52
3.8 Dividing fractions 55
3.9 Problem solving 57
Consolidation 59
Summary 60

4 Decimals 63

4.1 Decimals 64
4.2 Two decimal places 65
4.3 Decimals and place value 68
4.4 Adding and subtracting decimals 70
4.5 Decimals and your calculator 72
4.6 Multiplying and dividing decimals by powers of ten 73
4.7 Multiplying and dividing decimals 74
Consolidation 78
Summary 79

Revision exercise 1 81

5 Angles 87

5.1 Lines and angles 88
5.2 Measuring angles 92
5.3 Drawing angles 96
5.4 Relations between angles 97
Consolidation 102
Summary 104

6 Solids 107

6.1 The cuboid or box 108
6.2 The cylinder 110
6.3 Prisms 111
6.4 The cone 112
6.5 The pyramid 112
6.6 The sphere 113
6.7 Properties of solids 114
6.8 Nets of solids 114
Consolidation 118
Summary 119

7 Measuring 121

7.1 Length 122
7.2 Mass 129
7.3 Time 132
7.4 Temperature 136
Consolidation 139
Summary 141

8 Shapes 143

8.1 Looking at triangles 144
8.2 Looking at quadrilaterals 147
8.3 Constructions 151
8.4 Symmetry 155
8.5 Reflection 158
8.6 Moving shapes 160
8.7 Investigating shapes 164
Consolidation 167
Summary 169

Revision exercise 2 171

9 Consumer arithmetic 177

9.1 Using money 178
9.2 Understanding percentages 181
9.3 Fractions, decimals and percentages 182
9.4 Finding percentages of amounts 186
9.5 Buying and selling 187
9.6 Loans and deposits 191
Consolidation 195
Summary 196

10 Representing information 199

10.1 Collecting data 200
10.2 Pictographs 201
10.3 Bar graphs 203
10.4 Pie charts 207
10.5 Looking at averages 209
10.6 Coordinate graphs 211
Consolidation 216
Summary 217

11 Area 221

11.1 What is area? 222
11.2 Comparing areas 222
11.3 Some units of area 226
11.4 Areas of rectangles and triangles 229
Consolidation 235
Summary 236

12 Symbols and patterns 239

12.1 Symbols 240
12.2 Adding, subtracting and multiplying symbols 241
12.3 Writing expressions 243
12.4 Writing equations 244
12.5 Solving equations 246
12.6 Looking for patterns 247
12.7 Arrow diagrams 251
Consolidation 255
Summary 256

Revision exercise 3 259

Glossary 265

Answers 267

Index 295

About this book

This edition of Oxford Mathematics for the Caribbean has been completely revised to cater more adequately to the changing needs of students in the Caribbean.

Particular attention has been made in Books 1–3 to the leading national mathematics curricula in the Caribbean as well as the *CCSLC*®. In order to deal with the curricula differences, there is some content overlap in the three texts. This overlap should allow schools to move at a rate that best suits them, while, at the same time, providing additional reinforcement material.

To bring the texts more firmly into the 21st century, technology boxes have been added. These boxes direct students to websites where there is copious review material or games that will enhance learning. Other such boxes give students the opportunity to engage in research or carry out ICT-related projects on mathematical themes. Each text also has its own CD that provides supplementary exercises, worked examples and animations.

The text has also been improved with additional investigation and activity boxes. These provide extension material for more advanced students while being accessible to all.

Some of the major features of the last edition have been retained:

- Check in boxes at the start of each unit to assess whether a student is ready to begin the unit.
- Worked examples throughout the texts.
- Graded exercises, generally easier questions are given in the earlier parts of an exercise with more difficult questions underlined.

  $\underline{1}$ A single underline will challenge the average student
  $\underline{\underline{2}}$ A double underline will challenge an able student

- Consolidation examples and exercises to give further practice; these have now been integrated into the text.
- Summary and check out; these provide quick review of the key points within the unit and enable the student to assess progress made.
- Review exercises provided every four units.

In this new edition two further features have been incorporated. First, at the start of each new unit a 'What's the point?' section has been included. This section provides a rationale for the inclusion of the topic in a real-world setting. Secondly, a glossary of terms introduced in the text has been provided to assist students when revising.

Finally, the texts have been completely redesigned in full colour with new pictures and photographs. It is hoped that the new design and the addition of colour will motivate students and help them see mathematics as an essential part of their world.

Nicholas Goldberg
Morne Jaune
Commonwealth of Dominica

Number

1

Objectives

- ✔ learn how the idea of place value makes calculations easier
- ✔ use properties of numbers such as compositeness and primeness to find factors, multiples, HCFs and LCMs
- ✔ use a variety of methods to multiply and divide numbers
- ✔ round off numbers so as to make good estimates of the results of calculations
- ✔ use a calculator

What's the point?

How many? Who has more? How much? Questions such as these led early man to develop number systems. Today, numbers are everywhere, from banks, to supermarkets, to airports.

Before you start

You should know ...

1 There are: 10 units in a ten
10 tens in a hundred
and 10 hundreds in a thousand.

2 Your multiplication tables up to 10×10.

Check in

1 **(a)** How many units are there in a hundred?
(b) How many tens are there in 50?
(c) How many hundreds are there in 700?

2 Write down the answers to:
(a) 2×7 **(b)** 3×6
(c) 8×4 **(d)** 5×4
(e) 9×7 **(f)** 9×8

1.1 The story of numbers

No one knows when man first started to use numbers. It probably began when people started to live in groups and keep animals.

One of the earliest users of numbers was the Mayan peoples of Mexico and Guatemala. Like the Egyptians they built pyramids. To do so they must have been excellent mathematicians. They were also among the first people to use zero as a number.

The symbols you use for numbers today came from the Hindu peoples of India. They used the idea of **place value** to show numbers. For example,

५९ for fifty-nine
५९० for five hundred and ninety
९०५ for nine hundred and five

Over the years, these numerals changed in shape, so that now the ten **digits** or symbols used to show numbers are:

0, 1, 2, 3, 4, 5, 6, 7, 8, 9

and:

59 is fifty-nine
590 is five hundred and ninety
905 is nine hundred and five

This way of writing numbers makes use of the position of the digits. This is called using **place value**. The digit 9 can mean nine or ninety or nine hundred depending on its place in the number.

In the number 486, the **face value** of the digit 8 is 8, while the **value** of the digit 8 is 80.

Example 1

What is the value of the digit 4 in these numbers?

(a) 94 **(b)** 481 **(c)** 4012

(a) four
(b) four hundred
(c) four thousand

Exercise 1A

1 Write down the value of the 4 in:
(a) 24 **(b)** 42 **(c)** 402
(d) 645 **(e)** 4132 **(f)** 49 206
(g) 14 873

2 Write each of these sets of numbers in order of size, smallest first.
(a) 9, 16, 2, 27, 81
(b) 29, 0, 308, 111, 99
(c) 401, 268, 41, 1001, 999
(d) 4132, 1234, 4321, 2413, 2134
(e) 3, 71 506, 6002, 8109, 610

3 Write down the number that is
(a) 1 more than 2499
(b) 10 more than 1090
(c) 2 more than 898
(d) 20 more than 10 980
(e) 1 less than 2500
(f) 10 less than 1001
(g) 20 less than 2012
(h) 2 less than 7101

4 Write down the largest number you can make using all four of these digits:

0, 0, 3, 1

5 Write down the smallest number you can make using all four of these digits:

7, 9, 8, 6

6 The Mayan religious calendar used twenty months each containing thirteen days. Using our numerals, the sixth day of the fourth month would be written 4.6. And ten days later would be 5.3, the third day of the fifth month.
How many days later than 4.6 is the date
(a) 4.9 **(b)** 5.1 **(c)** 5.6?

7 Write down the Mayan date that comes:
(a) 4 days after 4.6
(b) 9 days after 4.6
(c) 13 days after 4.6
(d) 26 days after 4.6
(e) 13 days before 4.6

8 (a) Find out about Roman numerals.
(b) How would you write
(i) 29 (ii) 92 (iii) 449
in Roman numerals?
(c) What are some of the difficulties in using Roman numerals?
(d) Where do you still see Roman numerals today?

Number systems

In our number system the position of the digits in a number is critical.

For example, the number 623 written in **expanded form** is

$623 = 600 + 20 + 3 = 6 \times 100 + 2 \times 10 + 3 \times 1$

while 263 would be

$263 = 200 + 60 + 3 = 2 \times 100 + 6 \times 10 + 3 \times 1$

Notice that each column is ten times the value of the previous column.

For example, 16 394 would be

10 000s	1000s	100s	10s	1s
1	6	3	9	4

or
$16\,394 = 1 \times 10\,000 + 6 \times 1000 + 3 \times 100 + 9 \times 10 + 4 \times 1$

Our number system is based on powers of ten (**base 10**) and is sometimes called the **denary** or **decimal** system.

Other number systems can be based on numbers different from 10. One example is the **binary** number system based on powers of 2. This system is used in computing. The processing unit in a computer is made up of millions of tiny switches that can either be ON or OFF. The digit 1 is used to represent ON and 0 represents OFF. In the binary system the first four column headings are

8s	4s	2s	1s

so the binary number 1101 is

8s	4s	2s	1s
1	1	0	1

$1101 = 1 \times 8 + 1 \times 4 + 0 \times 2 + 1 \times 1$
$= 8 + 4 + 1$
$= 13$ (base 10)

Exercise 1B

1 Write these numbers in expanded form.
(a) 27 (b) 106 (c) 271
(d) 914 (e) 1137 (f) 13 619

2 How many different numbers can be made using the digits
(a) 4, 6, 5
(b) 2, 1, 4, 7?

3 What number is represented by
(a) 6 tens 7 ones
(b) 16 tens 7 ones
(c) 5 hundreds 14 tens
(d) 6 hundreds 23 tens 6 ones
(e) 3 hundreds 12 tens 14 ones?

4 The number 132 can be represented as 12 tens 12 ones. What other ways can you find to represent the number?

5 You have \$100 and \$10 notes and \$1 coins.
(a) How can you pay out \$345?
(b) How many different ways can this amount be paid out?

6 David has 1 g, 2 g, 4 g, 8 g and 16 g weights (one of each weight only).
(a) What weights does he need to weigh an object with mass 22 g?
(b) What objects is he able to weigh?
(c) What objects is he unable to weigh?

7 (a) Find out more about the binary system. Why is it important?
(b) Write notes with examples showing how to convert a binary number to a decimal number and vice versa.

8 (a) What is the hexadecimal system?
(b) Find out where this system is used.
(c) Make a short presentation to your class on the hexadecimal system.

1.2 Adding and subtracting numbers

To add numbers you must line up their place values.

Example 2

What is $53 + 6 + 204$?

	H	T	U
		5	3
			6
+	2	0_1	4
	2	6	3

Subtraction is done in a similar way.

Example 3

Work out $205 - 34$.

	H	T	U
	$^{1}2$	$^{1}0$	5
−		3	4
	1	7	1

Exercise 1C

1 Add these numbers:
- **(a)** $3 + 27 + 4$
- **(b)** $62 + 39$
- **(c)** $615 + 4 + 14$
- **(d)** $1068 + 39 + 7 + 214$
- **(e)** $295 + 86 + 9$
- **(f)** $6 + 1009 + 219$

2 Work out:
- **(a)** $75 - 24$ **(b)** $69 - 5$
- **(c)** $63 - 25$ **(d)** $52 - 6$
- **(e)** $127 - 32$ **(f)** $101 - 9$
- **(g)** $253 - 64$ **(h)** $504 - 128$
- **(i)** $1024 - 9$ **(j)** $1111 - 222$

3 At Market School there are 93 students in Form 1, 105 in Form 2, 87 in Form 3, 79 in Form 4 and 81 in Form 5. How many students are there altogether?

4 Albert wants to buy a new bicycle for \$1000. He has saved \$824. How much more does he need?

5 Jamaica became independent in 1962. In which year will it celebrate its 50th anniversary of independence?

6 In test cricket tournaments in 2004, 2008 and 2009 Chris Gayle scored 105 runs, 197 runs and 165 runs respectively. How many runs did he score altogether?

7 In their test careers, Curtly Ambrose had scored 1297 runs compared to Carl Hooper's 4153 runs. How many more runs would Ambrose have needed to score to reach Hooper's mark?

8 18 years ago Chris was 5 years old. How old will he be in 16 years time?

9

(a) Arrange the numbers 3, 3, 3, 5, 5, 5, 7, 7, 7 in the square above so that each row, column and diagonal adds up to 15.

(b) Repeat for the numbers 1, 2, 3, 4, 5, 6, 7, 8, 9.

10 The number 24 has a digit sum of 6: $(2 + 4 = 6)$. 24 is exactly 4 times the sum of its digits: $(6 \times 4 = 24)$.

(a) Which other numbers are exactly 4 times the sum of their digits?

(b) Which numbers are exactly 2 times the sum of their digits?

1.3 Multiples and factors

Multiples

Activity

You will need 36 counters. You can use bottle tops or matchsticks or beans as your counters. You can work with a friend.

(a) Take two counters.

(b) Add two more counters to the group.

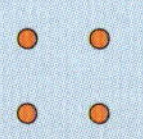

How many counters do you have?

(c) Add two more counters.

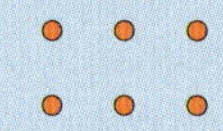

How many counters do you have?

(d) Continue adding two more counters until you have used all your counters.

(e) Write down how many counters you had each time you added two more.

The numbers you should have written down are:

2, 4, 6, 8, 10, 12, 14, 16, 18.

They are called multiples of two. They make up your two times table:

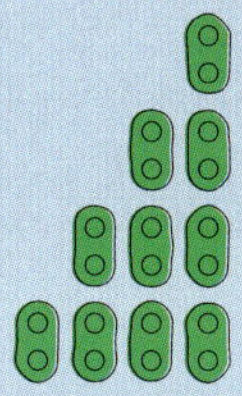

$1 \times 2 = 2$

$2 \times 2 = 4$

$3 \times 2 = 6$

$4 \times 2 = 8$

... and so on.

Repeat what you just did but this time add three counters each time.

- The **multiples** of a number are all the numbers from its times table.

  For example, the multiples of 3 are 3, 6, 9, 12, …

Exercise 1D

1 Use the method in the Activity to show the multiples of four.

2 **(a)** Write down the first six multiples of five.
(b) Write down the first six multiples of seven.

3 **(a)** What is the eighth multiple of six?
(b) What is the fifth multiple of twelve?
(c) What is the tenth multiple of nine?

4 Copy and complete:
(a) 4, 8, 12, 16, 20, □, □
(b) 9, 18, 27, 36, 45, □, □
(c) 12, 24, 36, 48, 60, □, □
(d) 16, 32, 48, 64, 80, □, □
(e) 63, 70, 77, 84, 91, □, □

5 Write down two numbers that are multiples of
(a) 2 and 3
(b) 3 and 5
(c) 4 and 6

6 How can you tell if a number is a multiple of 5?

7 What patterns can you find in the
(a) multiples of 9
(b) multiples of 6?

Investigation

Look at the number grid below. It has ten columns and ten rows. The multiples of 3 have been coloured.

1	2	3	4	5	6	7	8	9	10
11	12	13	14	15	16	17	18	19	20
21	22	23	24	25	26	27	28	29	30
31	32	33	34	35	36	37	38	39	40
41	42	43	44	45	46	47	48	49	50
51	52	53	54	55	56	57	58	59	60
61	62	63	64	65	66	67	68	69	70
71	72	73	74	75	76	77	78	79	80
81	82	83	84	85	86	87	88	89	90
91	92	93	94	95	96	97	98	99	100

(a) Describe the pattern made.

(b) What happens if you use a number grid with only 5 columns?

1	2	3	4	5
6	7	8	9	10
11	12	13	14	15
16				

or 3 columns?

1	2	3
4	5	6
7	8	9
10	11	

Make different number grids and colour the multiples of 3. Do they all make patterns?

(c) What happens if you colour the (i) multiples of 4 (ii) multiples of 5? Investigate.

(d) What if you coloured multiples on a triangular grid?

1
2 3
4 5 6
7 8 9 10

Factors

There are two ways of putting six counters in rows:

● ● ● ● ● ● 1 row of 6 = 1×6

● ● ●
● ● ● 2 rows of 3 = 2×3

The numbers 1 and 6, and 2 and 3 are called factors of 6.

- The **factors** of a number are all the whole numbers that divide into it.
  For example, 1, 2, 3 and 6 all divide into 6, so they are all factors of 6.

Example 4

Using counters, find all the factors of 12.

We can arrange a set of 12 counters in several ways like this:

● ● ● ● ● ● ● ● ● ● ● ● 1×12

● ● ● ● ● ●
● ● ● ● ● ● 2×6

● ● ● ●
● ● ● ● 3×4
● ● ● ●

There are no other row arrangements, so the factors of 12 are 1, 12, 2, 6, 3, 4.

Exercise 1E

1 Use counters to find all the factors of:
(a) 3 **(b)** 8 **(c)** 15 **(d)** 20
Write down how many different factors each number has.

2 Copy and complete the table started below, for all the numbers 1 to 20.

Number	Factors	Number of different factors
1	1	1
2	1, 2	2
3		
4		
5		
6	1, 2, 3, 6	4
7		

3 **(a)** For the number 7 there is only one arrangement that can be made from 7 counters.

● ● ● ● ● ● ● 1×7

What other numbers between 2 and 20 can be arranged in only one row?

(b) How many factors have these numbers?

4 Find three numbers bigger than 20 that have only two factors.

5 Which number has just one factor?

Investigation

Which number between 1 and 100 has most factors?

Prime numbers

In Question 3 of Exercise 1E you should have found that 2, 3, 5, 7, 9, 11, 13, 17 and 19 can be arranged in only one row.
They all have just two factors.

- A number with exactly two different factors is called a **prime number**.

Example 5

23 is a prime number.
It has exactly two factors: 1 and 23.
2 is a prime number.
It has exactly two factors: 1 and 2.

- A number which has more than two different factors is called a **composite number**.

Example 6

12 is a composite number.
It has 6 factors: 1, 2, 3, 4, 6, 12.

Exercise 1F

1 **(a)** **(i)** What are the factors of 35?
(ii) Is 35 a prime number?
(b) **(i)** What are the factors of 37?
(ii) Is 37 a prime number?

2 **(a)** Which numbers between 20 and 50 have just two factors?
(b) Write down all the prime numbers from 1 to 50.

3 Is 1 a prime number?
Explain.

4 Copy and complete these sentences.
(a) A number which has only two different factors, itself and 1, is called a ... number.
(b) A number which has three or more different factors is called a ... number.

5 For this question you will need red, green and blue pencils.
The following grid shows all the numbers from 1 to 100. Make a larger copy of the grid on squared paper.

1	2	3	4	5	6	7	8	9	10
11	12	13	14	15	16	17	18	19	20
21	22	23	24	25	26	27	28	29	30
31	32	33	34	35	36	37	38	39	40
41	42	43	44	45	46	47	48	49	50
51	52	53	54	55	56	57	58	59	60
61	62	63	64	65	66	67	68	69	70
71	72	73	74	75	76	77	78	79	80
81	82	83	84	85	86	87	88	89	90
91	92	93	94	95	96	97	98	99	100

(a) 1 is not a prime number. Shade it green.
(b) Is 2 a prime number? Shade it blue.
(c) Now look at the multiples of 2. Can you quickly tell whether they are prime numbers or composite numbers? Why? Shade them red.
(d) 3 is a prime number. Shade it blue.
(e) Are the multiples of 3 prime or composite? Why? Shade them continuing the colour pattern.
(f) Is 5 prime or composite? Shade it.
(g) What can you say about the multiples of 5? Shade them.
(h) Continue the process for the numbers that have not yet been shaded.

6 **(a)** In Question 5 which numbers were shaded blue?
(b) Do you agree that these numbers are all prime?

7 **(a)** Look at your grid for Question 5. How many times does a pair of primes occur together? Write down these primes.
(b) How many times do three primes occur together? Can you explain why?

8 3 and 5 differ by two and are both prime numbers.
(a) What is the next such pair?
(b) How many such pairs are there between 0 and 100?

9 (a) Is 613 a prime number?
How did you find out?
(b) Find out whether 4999 is a prime number.
(c) What about 30 031?

Investigation

The number 8 can be written as the sum of two prime numbers 3 and 5:
$3 + 5 = 8$
The number 9 is the sum of the primes 2 and 7:
$2 + 7 = 9$

(a) Can all the numbers between 5 and 20 be written as the sum of two primes?
(b) Copy and complete the table where possible.

Number	Two primes equal to number
5	2 + 3
6	3 + 3
7	
8	

(c) Can any number be written as the sum of two primes?
Which ones can? Which ones cannot?
Any rules?

Prime factors

The factors of a number that are also prime numbers are called the **prime factors** of that number.

For example, the prime factors of 15 are 3 and 5.

Any whole number can be written as the product of its prime factors.

For example
$12 = 2 \times 2 \times 3$
$14 = 2 \times 7$
$16 = 2 \times 2 \times 2 \times 2$

One of the easiest ways of finding the prime factors of a number is to use a factor tree.

Example 7

Find the prime factors of 126.

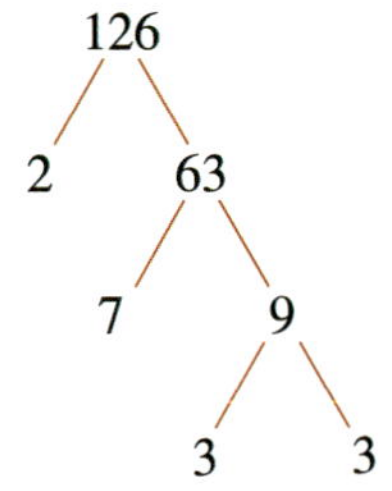

So $126 = 2 \times 3 \times 3 \times 7$

You can also find the prime factors of a number by repeatedly dividing it by primes.

Example 8

Find the prime factors of 126.

2 | 126
3 | 63
3 | 21
7

$126 = 2 \times 3 \times 3 \times 7$

Exercise 1G

1 Use a factor tree to find the prime factors of
(a) 12 (b) 16 (c) 24 (d) 36
(e) 46 (f) 48 (g) 64 (h) 65
(i) 72 (j) 84 (k) 136 (l) 196

2 Check your answers to Question 1 using the repeated division method.

3 A number has 2 and 3 as its prime factors.
What are the five smallest values it could take?

4 What is the smallest number with
(a) two different prime factors
(b) three different prime factors?

5 What is the smallest number greater than 144 with four different prime factors?

Highest Common Factor (HCF) and Lowest Common Multiple (LCM)

Look at the factors of 20 and 30.

Factors of 20 = **1**, **2**, 4, **5**, **10**, 20
Factors of 30 = **1**, **2**, 3, **5**, 6, **10**, 15, 30

The **common factors** of 20 and 30 are 1, 2, 5, 10.

The **highest common factor** (HCF) is 10.

- The highest common factor of two (or more) numbers is the common factor that has the greatest value.

To find the **lowest common multiple** (LCM) of two numbers, you need to look at their multiples.

For example,
Multiples of 6 = 6, 12, 18, **24**, 30, 36, 42, **48**, …
Multiples of 8 = 8, 16, **24**, 32, 40, **48**, 54, …

The common multiples of 6 and 8 are 24, 48, …
The LCM of 6 and 8 is 24.

- The lowest common multiple of two (or more) numbers is the smallest possible number into which all of them will divide.

You can find both the HCF and the LCM of a pair of numbers by writing them as a product of prime factors.

Example 9

Find the HCF and the LCM of 24 and 18.

Using repeated division

2	24	2	18
2	12	3	9
2	6		3
	3		

$24 = 2 \times 2 \times 2 \times 3$
$18 = 2 \times 3 \times 3$

The common factors are 2 and 3.

So the HCF $= 2 \times 3 = 6$.

To find the LCM, look for the highest product of each prime factor, and multiply them together.

$\text{LCM} = 2 \times 2 \times 2 \times 3 \times 3$
$= 8 \times 9$
$= 72$

Exercise 1H

1 **(a)** Write down all the factors of these number pairs.
(i) 12, 8 **(ii)** 18, 24
(iii) 36, 60 **(iv)** 48, 60
(v) 55, 80 **(vi)** 144, 108
(b) Find the HCF of each number pair.

2 **(a)** Write down the first eight multiples of these number pairs.
(i) 3, 5 **(ii)** 2, 7
(iii) 8, 12 **(iv)** 9, 12
(v) 12, 18 **(vi)** 8, 24
(b) Find the LCM of each number pair.

3 Use the method of repeated divisions to find the prime factors of the number pairs in Questions 1 and 2. Hence find the HCFs and the LCMs of these pairs.

4 Find the HCF and the LCM of
(a) 36 and 42 **(b)** 18 and 21
(c) 35 and 50 **(d)** 65 and 78
(e) 72 and 96 **(f)** 280 and 180

5 One athlete runs around a track in 65 seconds. The second athlete takes 70 seconds. If they both start together

(a) When will the first first 'lap' the second?

(b) How many laps will the first have completed when he 'laps' the second?

6 The HCF of two numbers is 12. What could these two numbers be? How many answers can you get?

Technology

Practise your skill at finding prime factors using a factor tree by visiting

www.mathgoodies.com/games

When you feel confident take the HCF and LCM practice game at

www.jamit.com.au/welcome

Need more practice or help? Visit

www.math.com

and click on the lessons dealing with factoring in the Pre-Algebra section.

1.4 More about our number system

To work with numbers efficiently you really need to learn your multiplication tables. This takes practice!

One excellent way of learning is to use some of the many interactive games on the internet.

Visit the website

www.woodlands-junior.kent.sch.uk/maths/timestable

for many great interactive multiplication games.

Some short cuts in multiplication

Th	H	T	U		Th	H	T	U
			8	× 10 →			8	0
		1	4	× 10 →		1	4	0
	2	6	9	× 10 →	2	6	9	0

Look at the table above. It shows a quick way of multiplying by ten. Each number moves into the column one place to its left.

It is also easy to multiply numbers by any multiple of ten.

Example 10

What is 24×70?

$$\begin{aligned} 24 \times 70 &= 24 \times 7 \times 10 \\ &= 168 \times 10 \\ &= 1680 \end{aligned}$$

Exercise 1I

1 Work out:

(a) 6×10 (b) 16×10

(c) 23×10 (d) 10×23

(e) 69×10 (f) 88×10

(g) 214×10 (h) 10×214

2 Use the method in Example 10 to work out:

(a) 3×40 (b) 12×40

(c) 37×40 (d) 17×90

(e) 80×24 (f) 90×87

(g) 100×21 (h) 120×44

3 A matchbox holds 50 matches. How many matches will there be in 47 such boxes?

Factors can be used to work out other multiplications quickly.

Example 11

What is 15×28?

$$\begin{aligned} 15 \times 28 &= 15 \times 2 \times 14 \\ &= 30 \times 14 \\ &= 10 \times 3 \times 14 \\ &= 10 \times 42 \\ &= 420 \end{aligned}$$

Exercise 1J

1 Do you think the method used in Example 11 is quicker than long multiplication?

2 Use the method of Example 11 to work out:

(a) 5×62	**(b)** 14×15
(c) 15×54	**(d)** 25×82
(e) 35×16	**(f)** 55×42
(g) 88×65	**(h)** 75×124

3 Use your knowledge of factors to find a quick way of working out $45 \times 65 \times 16$.

The distributive law

The drawing shows a set of counters.

There are two ways to find the number of counters in this set.

You could count them all or you could say there are 7 rows and 6 columns. So there are $7 \times 6 = 42$ counters.

Below is a set of black and white counters.

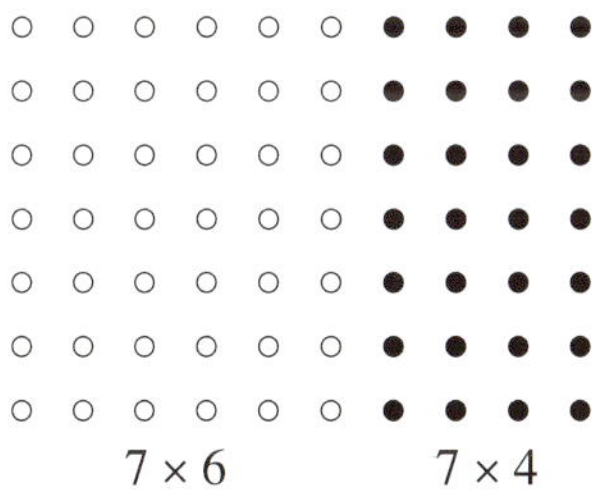

There are 7 rows. There are 6 white counters and 4 black counters in each row.

The total number of counters =
white counters + black counters.

This can be written as:
$7 \times (6 + 4) = 7 \times 6 + 7 \times 4$

Work out $7 \times (6 + 4)$ and $7 \times 6 + 7 \times 4$

Is the statement correct?

Exercise 1K

1 **(a)** Copy and complete the statement for these counters:

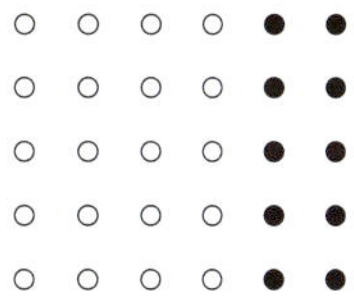

$5 \times (4 + 2) = 5 \times \square + 5 \times \square$

(b) Look at your statement. Work out the answers on both sides of the equals sign.

2 Repeat Question 1 for the following sets of counters.

(i)

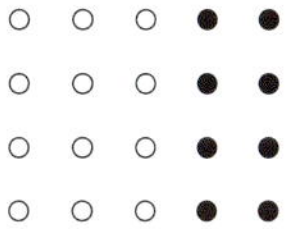

$4 \times (3 + 2) = 4 \times \square + 4 \times \square$

(ii)

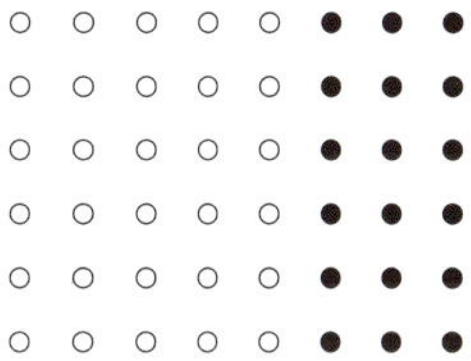

$6 \times (5 + 3) = 6 \times \square + 6 \times \square$

Look at the statements you completed in (i) and (ii). Can you see the pattern?

The statements in (i) and (ii) are examples of the **distributive** law.

You can use the distributive law to simplify multiplications.

Example 12

Use the distributive law to find
(a) 15×16 **(b)** 15×112

(a) $15 \times 16 = 15 \times (10 + 6)$
$= 15 \times 10 + 15 \times 6$
$= 150 + 90$
$= 240$

(b) 15×112
$= 15 \times (100 + 10 + 2)$
$= 15 \times 100 + 15 \times 10 + 15 \times 2$
$= 1500 + 150 + 30$
$= 1680$

Exercise 1L

1 Use the distributive law to write each multiplication in a different way. Then find the answer.

(a) 12×14 **(b)** 16×13
(c) 14×18 **(d)** 9×108
(e) 12×136 **(f)** 20×147

2 Check your answers to Question 1 using long multiplication.

3 $3 \times (6 - 2) = 3 \times 6 - 3 \times 2$

Work out the terms on each side of the equals sign to see if they are the same. Is the equation correct?

4 Copy and complete each equation. Then check if each equation is correct.

(a) $6 \times (8 - 4) = 6 \times 8 - \square \times \square$
(b) $10 \times (4 - 3) = \square \times \square - \square \times \square$
(c) $12 \times (8 - 5) = \square \times \square - \square \times \square$
(d) $15 \times (12 - 7) = \square \times \square - \square \times \square$
(e) $16 \times (8 - 2) = \square \times \square - \square \times \square$

5 Can you tell from Questions 3 and 4 whether subtraction obeys the distributive law?

6 Use the distributive law with subtraction to work out 17×19.

7 Use the method you used in Question 6 to calculate:

(a) 7×19 **(b)** 9×18
(c) 11×39 **(d)** 8×97
(e) 9×57 **(f)** 12×88

8 Work out 13×17 in as many different ways as you can. Compare your answers with some friends. Who found the most ways?

9 Work out 75×96 in four different ways. Which way is the quickest? Explain.

Technology

Practise your multiplication tables and division facts by playing the number invaders game at the site

www.mathplayground.com

Try and save the planet!

For additional practice check out number skills at

www.woodlands-junior.kent.sch.uk/maths

1.5 Division

The numbers 2, 4, 6, 8, 10, … are all divisible by 2. They are called **even** numbers.

The numbers 1, 3, 5, 7, 9, … are called **odd** numbers.

Numbers which end in 0, 2, 4, 6 or 8 are even numbers.

Numbers which end in 1, 3, 5, 7 or 9 are odd numbers.

For example, 84, 206, 1118 are all even numbers and are divisible by 2 without remainder:

$84 \div 2 = 42$
$206 \div 2 = 103$
$1118 \div 2 = 559$

Complete Exercise 1M to find other divisibility rules.

Exercise 1M

1 **(a)** Write down twelve multiples of 10.
(b) What do you notice about these numbers?
(c) What is the rule for divisibility by 10?

2 **(a)** Write down twelve multiples of 5.
(b) What do you notice about these numbers?
(c) What is the rule for divisibility by 5?

3 (a) Write down twelve multiples of 4.
(b) Divide these numbers by 2. What do you notice about your results?
(c) What is the rule for divisibility by 4?

4 (a) Copy and complete the table.

Multiple of 3	Digit sum
3	3
6	6
9	9
12	$1 + 2 = 3$
15	$1 + 5 = 6$
18	$1 + 8 = 9$
⋮	⋮
90	$9 + 0 = 9$

(b) What do you notice about the sum of the digits for multiples of 3?
(c) Write down five 4-digit numbers that are multiples of 3. What is the sum of their digits?
(d) What do you think is the rule for deciding if a number is divisible by 3?

5 Repeat Question 4 but this time look at multiples of 9.

6 $2 \times 3 = 6$
Use this fact to find the rule for divisibility by 6.

7 Look at multiples for other numbers.
What divisibility rules can you find?

If you completed Exercise 1M carefully, you should have found these divisibility rules or tests.

Divisibility test	
÷ 2	Number ends in an even number
÷ 3	Sum of digits is a multiple of 3
÷ 4	Last two digits divisible by 4
÷ 5	Number ends in 5 or 0
÷ 6	Any even number with digit sum a multiple of 3
÷ 7	No test!
÷ 8	The number when halved has its last two digits divisible by 4
÷ 9	Sum of digits is a multiple of 9
÷ 10	Number ends in 0

Divisibility tests can speed up calculations.

Example 13

Is 237 a prime number?

237 is odd, it is not divisible by 2.
237 has digit sum $= 2 + 3 + 7 = 12$, which is a multiple of 3.

So 237 is divisible by 3 and is not prime.

Exercise 1N

1 Use divisibility tests to find out if
(a) 1275 is divisible by 5
(b) 3141 is divisible by 9
(c) 21 648 is divisible by 8
(d) 43 572 is divisible by 6
(e) 38 520 is divisible by 18
(f) 512 617 is divisible by 9

2 Check your answers to Question 1 by seeing if the numbers have remainders when you divide.

3 Use the divisibility tests to find out which of these numbers are prime.
(a) 201 (b) 367 (c) 499
(d) 549 (e) 111 (f) 1313

4 Use the divisibility tests to help you complete factor trees for
(a) 448 (b) 729 (c) 6345
(d) 1024 (e) 12 640 (f) 72 144

Investigation

When you multiply a number ending in 5 by another number ending in 5 your answer also ends in 5.

For example
$1\mathbf{5} \times 2\mathbf{5} = 37\mathbf{5}$

What other endings have a similar property?

Long division

The multiplication 7×6 is really a repeated addition.

$7 \times 6 = 6 + 6 + 6 + 6 + 6 + 6 + 6$

In the same way, division can be thought of as a repeated subtraction.

For example $18 \div 6 = 3$ can be written as:

18		
− 6	1	6 can be subtracted from 18
12		three times until nothing remains.
− 6	1	
6		
− 6	1	
0	3	

You can speed up the process by subtracting multiples of the number you subtract.

Example 14

Work out $32 \div 4$

4	32		*Note:*
	− 20	5 fours	$5 \times 4 = 20$
	12		
	− 12	3 fours	$3 \times 4 = 12$
	0	8 fours	$8 \times 4 = 32$

8 fours can be subtracted from 32

So we can write the answer as:

$32 \div 4 = 8$

Example 14 could also be worked as:

4	32		
	− 16	4 fours	$4 \times 4 = 16$
	16		
	− 16	4 fours	$4 \times 4 = 16$
	0	8 fours	$8 \times 4 = 32$

Exercise 1O

1 Use repeated subtraction to work out:

(a) $6 \div 2$ **(b)** $12 \div 4$
(c) $24 \div 6$ **(d)** $30 \div 5$
(e) $36 \div 18$ **(f)** $56 \div 14$
(g) $72 \div 24$ **(h)** $96 \div 16$

2 Work out Example 14 another way.

3 Use the method of Example 14 to work out:

(a) $22 \div 2$ **(b)** $64 \div 4$
(c) $84 \div 6$ **(d)** $104 \div 4$
(e) $80 \div 5$ **(f)** $135 \div 5$
(g) $165 \div 15$ **(h)** $168 \div 14$

Question 3 (f) can be worked out in many ways. Here are two:

(i)

5	135	
	− 50	10 fives
	85	
	− 50	10 fives
	35	
	− 35	7 fives
	0	27 fives

(ii)

5	135	
	− 100	20 fives
	35	
	− 35	7 fives
	0	27 fives

The method in (ii) is the shortest. For large numbers you will have to subtract multiples of 10 and 100.

Example 15

$938 \div 14$

14	938		*Note:*
	− 700	50 fourteens	$50 \times 14 = 700$
	238		
	− 140	10 fourteens	$10 \times 14 = 140$
	98		
	− 98	7 fourteens	$7 \times 14 = 98$
	0	67	$67 \times 14 = 938$

So $938 \div 14 = 67$

Exercise 1P

1 Use the method of Example 15 to work out:

(a) $216 \div 12$ **(b)** $256 \div 8$
(c) $238 \div 14$ **(d)** $299 \div 13$
(e) $675 \div 15$ **(f)** $1558 \div 19$
(g) $1344 \div 21$ **(h)** $1767 \div 31$
(i) $1938 \div 19$ **(j)** $2834 \div 26$

2 Work out $544 \div 16$ in as many ways as you can.

3 Work out:
$656 \div 16$

4 Work out these divisions:

(a) $512 \div 13$ **(b)** $609 \div 14$
(c) $435 \div 17$ **(d)** $932 \div 15$
(e) $1244 \div 16$ **(f)** $1847 \div 24$
(g) $2089 \div 22$ **(h)** $2345 \div 36$
(i) $6148 \div 45$ **(j)** $7426 \div 43$

5 An egg box holds 12 eggs. How many boxes are needed to pack 8596 eggs?

6 All 623 students and their 36 teachers are going on a school trip. How many buses are needed if each bus holds 23 people?

1.6 Approximations and estimations

Often you do not need to work with exact numbers. For example, if 13 284 people attended a cricket match, you can say about 10 000 people attended. Such an **approximation** is called **rounding off**.

You can round numbers to the nearest 10, 100, 1000 etc.

Look at the number line below.

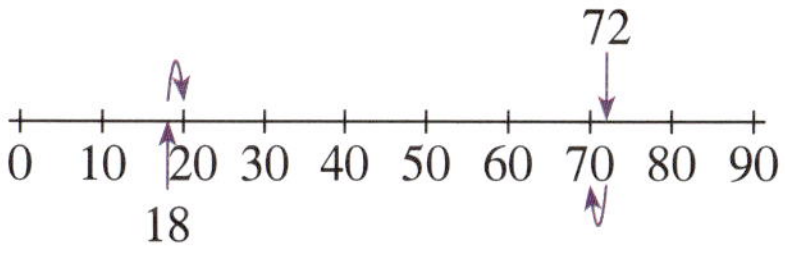

It shows multiples of 10.

Notice that 18 is closest to 20.
Notice that 72 is closest to 70.

You can write

18 = 20 (to nearest 10)
72 = 70 (to nearest 10)

18 has been rounded up to 20.
72 has been rounded down to 70.

In thc casc of a number ending in 5, for example 65, it is usual to round it up, so

65 = 70 (to nearest 10)

Rounding to the nearest 100 is done in a similar manner.

Example 16

Round off
(a) 729 **(b)** 483

to the nearest hundred.

Show the numbers on a number line marked in hundreds.

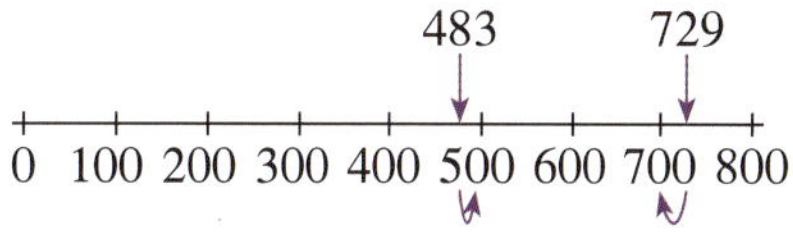

From the number line, you can see

483 = 500 (to nearest 100)
729 = 700 (to nearest 100)

Exercise 1Q

1 **(a)** Draw a number line from 0 to 100 marked in tens.
(b) Show the following numbers on your line.
(i) 8 **(ii)** 27 **(iii)** 42 **(iv)** 63 **(v)** 89
(c) Round each of the numbers to the nearest ten.

2 **(a)** Copy the number line below.

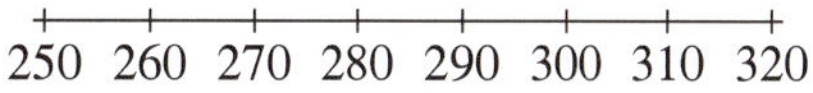

(b) Show these numbers on your line.
(i) 283 **(ii)** 255 **(iii)** 292 **(iv)** 306
(v) 319
(c) Round each of these numbers to the nearest 10.

3 **(a)** Draw a number line from 100 to 1000 marked in hundreds.
(b) Show these numbers on your line.
(i) 164 **(ii)** 375 **(iii)** 604
(iv) 429 **(v)** 781
(c) Round each of these numbers to the nearest 100.

4 **(a)** Copy the number line below.

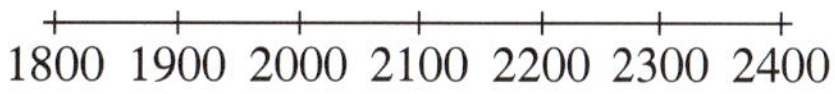

(b) Show these numbers on your line.
(i) 2003 **(ii)** 1917 **(iii)** 2189 **(iv)** 2362
(v) 2240
(c) Round off each of these numbers to the nearest 100.

5 By drawing a suitable number line round each of these numbers to the nearest 1000.
(a) 1402 **(b)** 3812 **(c)** 5617
(d) 949 **(e)** 33 609 **(f)** 45 113

6 Round off these numbers to the nearest 10.
(a) 76 **(b)** 105 **(c)** 846 **(d)** 1048
(e) 6142 **(f)** 7624 **(g)** 11 306
(h) 12 953

7 Round off the numbers in Question 6 to the nearest 100.

8 Round off the numbers in Question 6 to the nearest 1000.

9 

In his test match career to April 2009, Shiv Chanderpaul has scored 8502 runs. How many runs is this to the nearest
(a) ten **(b)** hundred **(c)** thousand?

10 649 is the largest whole number that when rounded to the nearest hundred gives 600. What is the smallest such number?

Estimation

Have you ever gone to buy things and found you didn't have enough money?

You can avoid this if you are able to make good **estimates**.

When you round off to the nearest ten, hundred etc, you are making a good estimate.

You can estimate the answer to a calculation by rounding off the numbers first.

Example 17

Estimate the result of
(a) $76 + 296 + 82$
(b) 69×84

(a) 76 is 100 (to nearest 100)
296 is 300 (to nearest 100)
82 is 100 (to nearest 100)
So $76 + 296 + 82$ is approximately
$100 + 300 + 100 = 500$
(b) 69 is 70 (to nearest 10)
84 is 80 (to nearest 10)
So 69×84 is approximately $70 \times 80 = 5600$

Exercise 1R

1 **(a)** You have \$20. What can you have for lunch?
(b) You have \$50 and have to buy lunches for three people. What can you buy?

2 Make good estimates for these calculations.
(a) $58 + 94 + 86$ **(b)** $213 + 789$
(c) $931 - 286$ **(d)** $1124 - 919$
(e) 16×54 **(f)** 29×104
(g) 314×69 **(h)** $16 \times 15 \times 21$
(i) $814 \div 24$ **(j)** $21\,336 \div 398$

3 A shirt costs \$79.55. Alan wishes to buy 14 such shirts. He has \$1000. Does he have enough money?

4 

A motorbike is priced at \$847.50. Johnson has \$5000. How many motorbikes can he buy?

5 A group of 215 cricket supporters wish to travel from Grenada to St Vincent to see a match.

They can charter a 48-seater plane for $23 172.

Give a good estimate for the cost of flying all 215 supporters.

Technology

For further lessons and tests on rounding off and estimations visit the website

www.aaaknow.com/est.htm

See if you can beat the clock when you play the countdown game or 20 questions.
Take care! Some of these are challenging!

1.7 Using a calculator

A calculator makes arithmetic easy and can save a great deal of time. However, unless you are careful it is still possible to make mistakes.

With a calculator, sums are done in the same order as they are written down.

Example 18

236 + 47

Press these buttons on your calculator

[2] [3] [6] [+] [4] [7]

The numbers 236 and 47 are now stored in the calculator ready to be added.
Next press [=]
The answer 283 now appears on the screen.

Exercise 1S

1 Use your calculator to work out:

(a) $36 + 45$	**(b)** $214 + 396$
(c) $472 + 109 + 218$	**(d)** $63 + 918 + 24$
(e) $6432 - 198$	**(f)** $716 - 692$
(g) 63×47	**(h)** 924×39
(i) 243×168	**(j)** $4816 \div 56$

2 **(a)** Repeat Question 1. Did you make any mistakes?
(b) What sort of mistake could you make?

3 **(a)** Add up all the numbers from 1 to 50 on your calculator.
(b) Did you get 1275 as your answer? If not, what sort of mistake did you make?

4 In each of the following calculations the operation sign is missing. Use your calculator to find which operation [+], [−], [×], [÷] should be used.

(a) 7 □ 6 = 42	**(b)** 23 □ 18 = 41
(c) 82 □ 19 = 63	**(d)** 72 □ 6 = 18
(e) 144 □ 4 = 36	**(f)** 114 □ 28 = 86
(g) 11 □ 17 = 187	**(h)** 18 □ 17 = 306
(i) 25 □ 21 = 525	**(j)** 25 □ 21 = 4

One way of reducing mistakes when you use your calculator is to make a good guess at the answer first. Your calculator answer should be similar to your guess.

Example 19

What is 52×8?

A good guess is about $50 \times 10 = 500$

[5] [2] [×] [8] [=] 416

The answer 416 is fairly close to the guess of 500. It is unlikely that a mistake has been made.

Exercise 1T

1 Copy and complete the table. For each question make a sensible guess and then use your calculator.

Problem	Guess	Calculator
29×8		
$216 - 82$		
$76 + 42 + 95$		
$256 \div 8$		
65×48		
96×98		
$966 \div 23$		
$4611 \div 87$		
143×37		
$2520 \div 56$		

2 Use your calculator to help you work out the missing numbers.

(a) $56 \div \square = 14$
(b) $\square \times 6 = 90$
(c) $72 \div \square = 18$
(d) $17 \times \square = 153$
(e) $136 \div \square = 8$
(f) $144 \div \square = 6$
(g) $18 \times \square = 414$
(h) $196 \div \square = 14$
(i) $882 \div \square = 21$
(j) $25 \times \square = 675$

Hint: Question 2 (j) could be set out as:

	Guess	*Calculator*
Guess 20		
$25 \times 20 = 500$	20	500
20 is too small, try 30		
$25 \times 30 = 750$	30	750
30 is too big, try 25		
$25 \times 25 = 625$	25	625
25 is too small, try 27		
$25 \times 27 = 675$	27	675

3 Use the method above and your calculator to find the missing numbers.

(a) $61 \times \square = 915$
(b) $46 \times \square = 828$
(c) $\square \times 56 = 1064$
(d) $\square \times 48 = 1104$
(e) $\square \times 23 = 529$
(f) $81 \times \square = 2835$
(g) $216 \times \square = 2808$
(h) $\square \times 192 = 2880$
(i) $29 \times \square = 2958$
(j) $53 \times \square = 5300$

4 **(a)** Work out
12×42 and 21×24
(b) What do you notice about your answers in part (a)?
(c) Repeat for
13×62 and 31×26
(d) What other such number pairs can you find?
(e) What patterns do you notice?

5 **(a)** Write down a three-figure number, for example 458
(b) Repeat the figures to get, for example, 458 458
(c) Divide this number by 13, then divide your answer by 11 and finally divide that answer by 7.
(d) What is your answer? What do you notice?
(e) Repeat with another three-figure number. What happens? Does this always happen? Why?

Investigation

Use a calculator to help you with this.

(a) How many different multiplications can you make using the numbers 1, 2, 3, 4? For example,
3×124, $1 \times 2 \times 3 \times 4$,
23×14, 43×21, and so on.

(b) Write down as many multiplications as you can.

(c) Which multiplication gives you the biggest answer? Can you be sure?

Activity

Work with a friend.
You may use only the operations

[+], [−], [×], [÷]

You may use only the numbers

2, 31, 5, 99, 248, 63

(a) The first player chooses two of the numbers, for example 5 and 31.

(b) The second player chooses an operation, for example [×].

(c) Both players guess the result of 5 [×] 31.

(d) Check the answer with your calculator. The player with the closest guess wins.

(e) Repeat the game until one player has won ten games.

1.8 Problem solving

A calculator will help you solve some of the problems in this section.

Exercise 1U

1 At rest Karen's pulse is 72 beats a minute.

(a) How many times will her pulse beat while she is asleep for 8 hours?

(b) When she runs to school, Karen's pulse increases to 96 beats per minute. For how long would she be running for her pulse to beat 1000 times?

2 A box of bananas weighs 38 pounds. How many boxes can a pickup truck hold if it can carry 1500 pounds of load?

3 127 students are planning a trip. For every 20 students, two teachers will go along. Five parents will also go. How many people will go on the trip?

4 Which pairs of numbers that have a sum of 40 have the largest product?

5 Find the missing numbers:

(a)
$$\begin{array}{r} 83 \\ +\ \square 9 \\ \hline \square 12 \end{array}$$

(b)
$$\begin{array}{r} 92 \\ -6\square \\ \hline \square 5 \end{array}$$

(c)
$$\begin{array}{r} 2\square \\ \times\ \ 7 \\ \hline \square 61 \end{array}$$

(d) $4\square 7 \div 3 = 1\square 9$

(e)
$$\begin{array}{r} 19 \\ 11\overline{)\square\square 9} \\ \underline{1\ 1} \\ 9\square \\ \underline{9\square} \\ - \end{array}$$

6 Using the numbers 3, 4, 5 and 6 only once, copy and complete

⬠ × □ + △ − ○ = 17

7 Copy and complete the patterns:

(a)
$1 \times 1 = 1$
$11 \times 11 = 121$
$111 \times 111 = \cdots$
$1111 \times 1111 = \cdots$

(b)
$1 \times 8 + 1 = \cdots$
$12 \times 8 + 2 = \cdots$
$123 \times 8 + 3 = \cdots$
$1234 \times 8 + 4 = \cdots$

8 Davis dropped his science book. It fell open.

He noticed that the product of the two open page numbers was 756. At which pages did it fall open?

9 A box contains more than 15 but fewer than 35 marbles.

When the marbles are counted in 3s there are two left over. When the marbles are counted in 5s there is one marble left over. How many marbles are in the box?

10 Use six 3s and any of the operations, $+, -, \times, \div$ to write an expression equal to 20.

11 The reverse of 253 is 352. The reverse of 126 is 621 and so on. Find the three-digit number which when added to its reverse is closest to 500.

Investigation

Look at the chain of numbers below:
$13 \rightarrow 40 \rightarrow 20 \rightarrow 10 \rightarrow 5 \rightarrow 16 \rightarrow ?$
It follows the rules:

(i) If the number is even, divide it by 2
(ii) If the number is odd, multiply it by 3 and add 1

(a) Can you complete the chain above?
(b) Start another chain with a different number. What happens?
(c) Try some more numbers. Does each chain end in the same way?
(d) Make another chain with some other rules. What happens?

1 Consolidation

Example 1

Work out:

(a) $17 + 3 + 6138$ **(b)** $904 - 83$

(a)

$$\begin{array}{r} 17 \\ 3 \\ +\,6138 \\ \hline 6158 \end{array}$$

(b)

$$\begin{array}{r} \overset{8}{\not{9}}\overset{1}{0}4 \\ -\quad 83 \\ \hline 821 \end{array}$$

Check: $821 + 83 = 904$

Example 2

(a) Write down the first three multiples of 7.

(b) What are the factors of 42?

(a) Multiples of 7 = 1 × 7, 2 × 7, 3 × 7 etc.
First three multiples of 7 = 7, 14, 21

(b) Factors of 42 = 1, 2, 3, 6, 7, 14, 21, 42

Example 3

Find the HCF and the LCM of 16 and 12.

Write the numbers as a product of prime factors.

$16 = 2 \times 2 \times 2 \times 2$

$12 = 2 \times 2 \times 3$ (see factor trees)

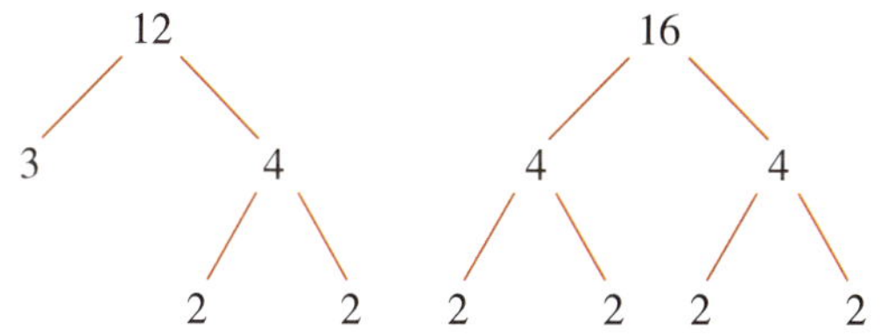

HCF of 16, 12 = 2 × 2 = 4 (factors common to both numbers)

LCM of 16, 12 = 2 × 2 × 2 × 2 × 3 = 48 (multiply factors that are repeated in both numbers)

Example 4

Use the distributive law to find

(a) 42×17 **(b)** 36×129

(a) $42 \times 17 = 42 \times (10 + 7)$
$= 42 \times 10 + 42 \times 7$
$= 420 + 294 = 714$

(b) $36 \times 129 = 129 \times (30 + 6)$
$= 3870 + 774$
$= 4644$

Example 5

Use repeated subtraction to calculate

(a) $132 \div 4$ **(b)** $259 \div 17$

(a)

$$\begin{array}{rr} 4\overline{)132} & \\ -40 & 10 \\ \hline 92 & \\ -40 & 10 \\ \hline 52 & \\ -40 & 10 \\ \hline 12 & \\ 12 & 3 \\ \hline 0 & 33 \end{array}$$

So, $132 \div 4 = 33$

Check: $33 \times 4 = 132$

(b)

$$\begin{array}{rr} 17\overline{)259} & \\ -\,170 & 10 \\ \hline 89 & \\ -34 & 2 \\ \hline 55 & \\ -34 & 2 \\ \hline 21 & \\ 17 & 1 \\ \hline 4 & 15\text{ R }4 \end{array}$$

So, $259 \div 17 = 15$ R 4

Check: $15 \times 17 + 4 = 259$

Exercise 1

1 Work out:

(a) 37 + 11 **(b)** 105 − 63 **(c)** 46 + 27
(d) 49 + 5 + 13 **(e)** 231 − 9
(f) 6138 + 9 + 104 **(g)** 694 − 588
(h) 1206 − 73 **(i)** 1061 + 789 + 6 + 29

2 Write down the first four multiples of:

(a) 6 **(b)** 13 **(c)** 23 **(d)** 37 **(e)** 48

3 List all the factors of:

(a) 24 **(b)** 36 **(c)** 27 **(d)** 54 **(e)** 112
(f) 96 **(g)** 108 **(h)** 144 **(i)** 256 **(j)** 1024

4 Find the HCF and the LCM of these pairs of numbers.

(a) 16, 8 **(b)** 14, 7 **(c)** 24, 20 **(d)** 18, 20
(e) 16, 24 **(f)** 20, 25 **(g)** 25, 30
(h) 36, 42 **(i)** 54, 28 **(j)** 72, 40

5 Use the distributive law to calculate:

(a) 17 × 13 **(b)** 33 × 14 **(c)** 36 × 24
(d) 18 × 29 **(e)** 54 × 13 **(f)** 27 × 27
(g) 47 × 38 **(h)** 342 × 37

6 Use repeated subtraction to calculate:

(a) 54 ÷ 3 **(b)** 72 ÷ 4 **(c)** 75 ÷ 5
(d) 108 ÷ 3 **(e)** 182 ÷ 13 **(f)** 224 ÷ 14
(g) 255 ÷ 15 **(h)** 456 ÷ 19

Check your answers.

7 Round off these numbers to **(i)** the nearest 10 **(ii)** the nearest 100.

(a) 24 **(b)** 37 **(c)** 138 **(d)** 206 **(e)** 314
(f) 749 **(g)** 813 **(h)** 1324 **(i)** 1068 **(j)** 1874

Application 1

8 Rainfall in the hurricane season on the island of St Peter is shown in the table.

Month	June	July	Aug	Sept	Oct	Nov
Rainfall in mm	30	50	78	104	68	93

(a) What was the total rainfall over the six months?

(b) If the total rainfall for the year was 613 mm, what was the total rainfall in the non-hurricane months?

9 Brian Lara's scores in 5 innings of the test matches against South Africa in 2005 were: 195, 4, 176, 13 and 4.

(a) How many runs did he score altogether in the series?

(b) Add up his scores and divide by the innings played to find his batting average for the series.

10 There are 624 students and 27 staff at the King Stevens school. The school wants to go on a day trip to Seaview Bay.

(a) How many people will go on the trip?

(b) How many buses should the school hire if a bus can hold 31 people?

(c) If the cost of transporting a busload of people is $225, what will be the total cost of the trip?

(d) How much should each person pay?

Companion CD

Want some extra practice? Go to Chapter 1 on your companion CD for further exercises, animations, and solutions.

Summary

You should know ...

1 How to write numbers using place value.

2 How to find multiples.

For example:

The first four multiples of 5 are

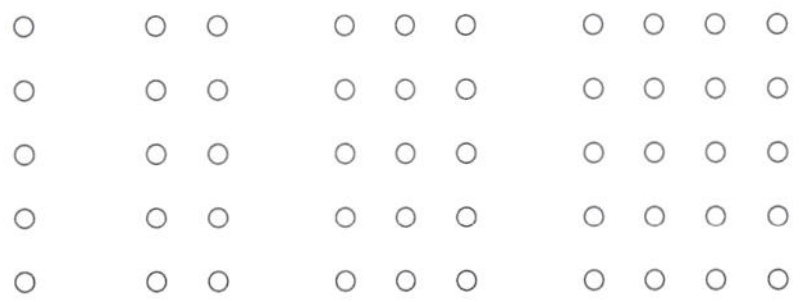

5 10 15 20

Check out

1 Write down the value of the 6 in:

(a) 46 **(b)** 64
(c) 624 **(d)** 26 751

2 **(a)** Write down the first five multiples of 3.

(b) Write down the first five multiples of 11.

3 How to find factors.

For example:

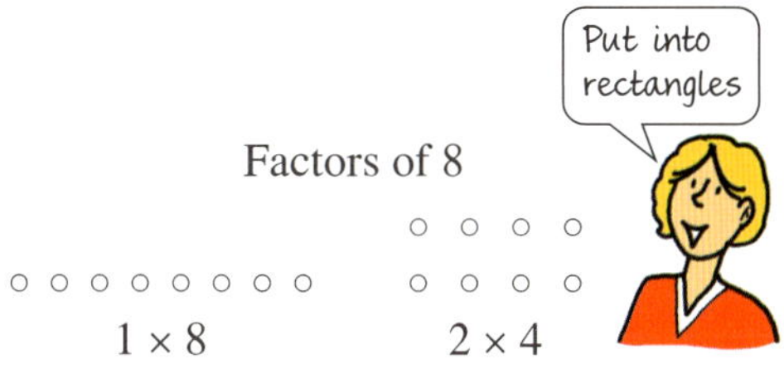

Factors of 8 are 1, 8, 2, 4.

3 Find all the factors of:

(a) 14

(b) 24

4 A prime number has exactly two different factors, one and itself.

A number which has more than two different factors is called a composite number.

4 State whether these are prime or composite numbers.

(a) 7 **(b)** 27

(c) 23 **(d)** 51

5 How to find prime factors of a number.

For example:

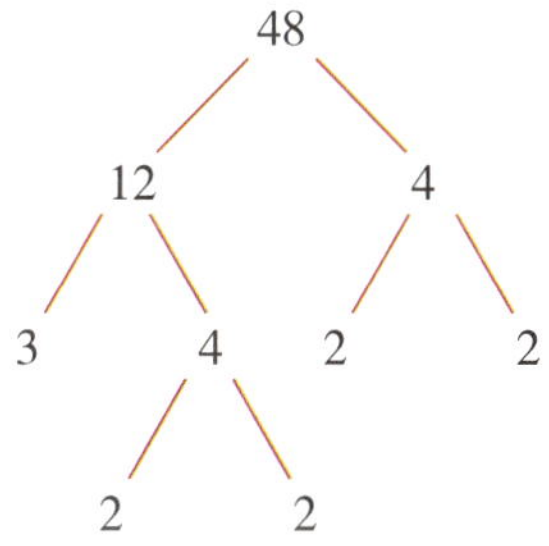

$48 = 2 \times 2 \times 2 \times 2 \times 3$

5 Write each of these numbers as a product of its prime factors.

(a) 24 **(b)** 72

(c) 168 **(d)** 255

6 How to find HCFs and LCMs.

6 Find the HCF and the LCM of:

(a) 16, 20 **(b)** 18, 27

(c) 36, 40 **(d)** 15, 35

7 The distributive law.

For example:

$$3 \times (6 + 5) = 3 \times 6 + 3 \times 5$$
$$= 18 + 15$$
$$= 33$$

7 Use the distributive law to find:

(a) 14×16 **(b)** 13×18

(c) 21×18 **(d)** 15×144

8 Long division is really repeated subtraction.

For example: 182 ÷ 13

13	182		*Note:*
	− 130	10	10 × 13 = 130
	52		
	−52	4	4 × 13 = 52
	0	14	14 × 13 = 182

182 ÷ 13 = 14

8 Use repeated subtraction to work out:

(a) 8 ÷ 2 **(b)** 40 ÷ 5

(c) 650 ÷ 15 **(d)** 1442 ÷ 14

9 How to round off numbers.

For example:

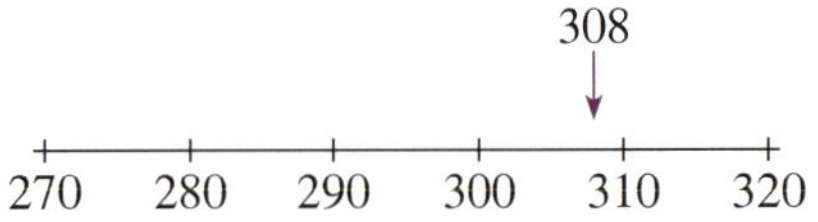

308 to the nearest 10 is 300.

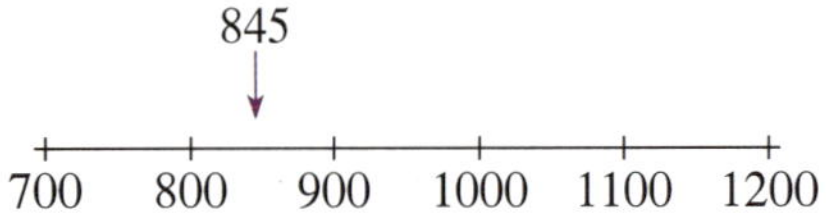

845 to the nearest 100 is 800.

9 Round off **(i)** to nearest 10

(ii) to nearest 100.

(a) 723 **(b)** 609

(c) 1109 **(d)** 1246

10 A calculator is only as good as its user.

Make a good guess of your answer before you work a problem.

For example: 23 × 39

10 Find the missing numbers using your calculator.

(a) 104 ÷ □ = 13

(b) □ × 18 = 198

(c) 425 ÷ □ = 17

Sets 2

Objectives

- ✔ understand the mathematical meaning of the word 'set'
- ✔ learn how ideas of sets and their notation assist in sorting and classification
- ✔ discover what a Venn diagram is, and how to draw and use one
- ✔ use Venn diagrams to find HCFs and LCMs

What's the point?

Sets are used in many areas of mathematics, so much so they are sometimes called the building blocks of the subject. Basic ideas about sets are used by many scientists to assist in sorting. Biologists use such ideas when they try to classify the 34 000 species of spider, which they sort into some 100 families!

Before you start

You should know ...	Check in
1 The even numbers are 2, 4, 6, 8, 10 … The odd numbers are 1, 3, 5, 7, 9 …	**1** Which of these numbers are **(a)** odd **(b)** even? 17, 28, 116, 215, 7, 30
2 The multiples of a number are the same as its multiplication table. *For example*: the multiples of 3 are 3, 6, 9, 12 …	**2** Which of these numbers are multiples of 5? 6, 15, 60, 103, 95
3 The factors of a number are the numbers that divide exactly into it. *For example*: the factors of 6 are 1, 2, 3 and 6.	**3** List all the factors of 12.
4 A prime number has exactly two factors: itself and one. A composite number has more than two factors.	**4** Which of these numbers are **(a)** prime **(b)** composite? 11, 15, 8, 20, 13

2.1 Sets and their members

- A **set** is a collection of things with a common feature.
  For example, a set of 4-legged animals.
- Each thing in a set is called a **member** of the set.
  For example, a pig is a member of the set of 4-legged animals.

Exercise 2A

1 Look at the drawings above. Write down what you see in each picture.

2 Look around your classroom. Write down five sets of things you can see.

3 Look at the drawings again.
How many members are in:
(a) the set of cattle
(b) the set of pineapples
(c) the set of steel drums
(d) the set of palm trees?

2.2 How to describe a set

To save time writing 'the set of' you can use curly brackets.
For example you write:
the set of cattle = {cattle}
or,
the set of whole numbers from 1 to 10
= {1, 2, 3, 4, 5, 6, 7, 8, 9, 10}.

Sometimes there are too many members in a set to list them all. You can still use curly brackets:

The set of even numbers between 4 and 20 000
= {even numbers between 4 and 20 000}

The set of students in Anil's school
= {students in Anil's school}.

To show that things belong to a set, you can draw a **loop** around them.
So a set of fruit could be shown as:

The set of whole numbers from 1 to 10 could be shown as:

Example 1

Describe these sets in your own words:
(a) {Alice, Ann, Alison, Anya}
(b) {35, 42, 49, 56, 63}

(a) A set of girls names beginning with A.
(b) The set of multiples of 7 from 35 to 63.

Exercise 2B

1 Using brackets, list the set of:
  (a) months of the year
  (b) Caribbean countries beginning with T
  (c) whole numbers between 10 and 20
  (d) even numbers between 10 and 14
  (e) odd numbers between 25 and 35.

2 Using a loop, show the set of:
  (a) names of people in your family
  (b) days of the week
  (c) subjects you study in school
  (d) odd numbers between 2 and 10
  (e) even numbers between 80 and 100.

3 For each set in Questions 1 and 2 write down the number of members it has.

4 Describe each of these sets in your own words:
  (a) {James, John, Judith, Jennifer, Joseph}
  (b) {Port of Spain, Castries, Kingston, Bridgetown, St George's}
  (c) {sandal, slipper, boot, shoe, clog}
  (d) {3, 6, 9, 12, 15}
  (e) {121, 132, 143, 154, 165}

5 Describe each of these sets in words.

(a)

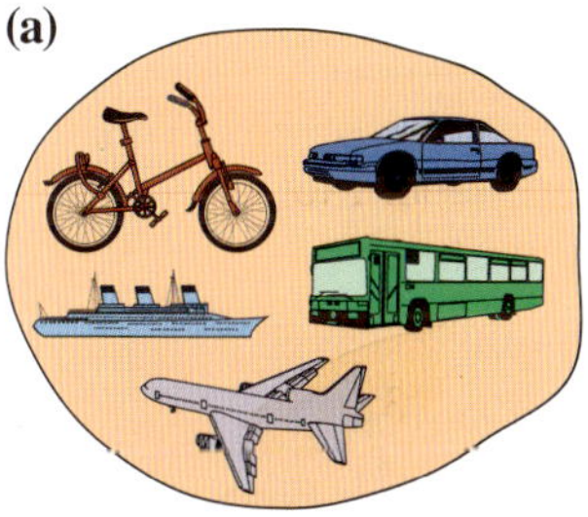

(b)

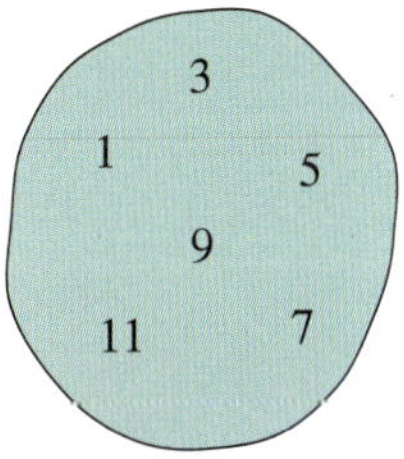

(c)

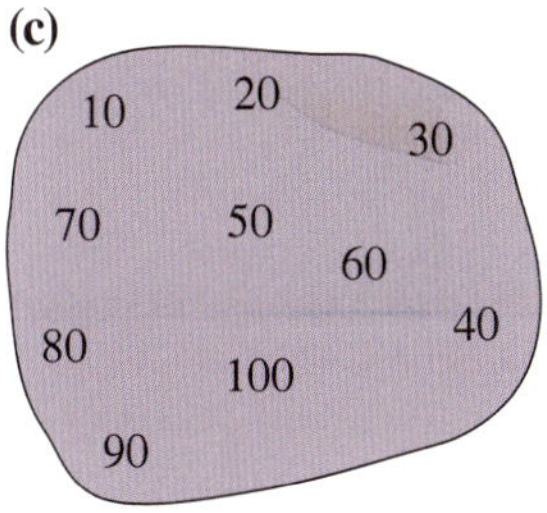

(d)

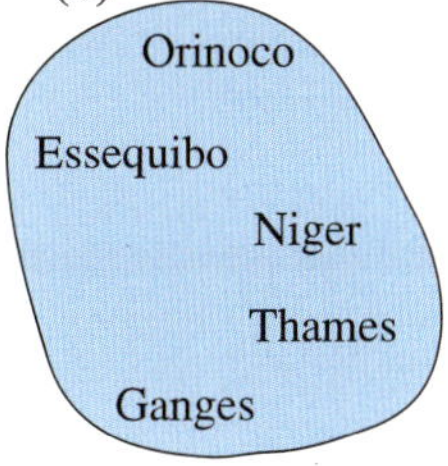

Using symbols

Look at the set {1, 2, 3, 4, 5}.
2 is a member of this set.

You can write this in a short way:
$2 \in \{1, 2, 3, 4, 5\}$.

- The symbol $\in$ means **is a member of**, or **belongs to**.

The empty set

Some sets have no members.
For example
{people with three heads}
or
{whole numbers between 1 and 2}.

- A set with no members is an **empty set**.
  The symbol for any empty set is { }.

Exercise 2C

1 Write in words:
  (a) 3 $\in$ {1, 2, 3}
  (b) blue $\in$ {blue, green, yellow, red, orange}
  (c) cricket $\in$ {cricket, football, tennis, badminton, volleyball}
  (d) 10 $\in$ {10, 20, 30, 40, 50}
  (e) 121 $\in$ {121, 132, 143, 154, 165}

2 Write using brackets and the symbol $\in$:
  (a) 36 is a member of {6, 16, 26, 36}.
  (b) A is a member of {A, B, C}.
  (c) St Lucia is among the islands Grenada, St Lucia, St Kitts, Trinidad, Puerto Rico.
  (d) 16 is one of the even numbers 10, 12, 14, 16, 18, 20

3 Using brackets, write these sets in a different way.
  (a) {0, 1, 2, 3, 4, 5, 6, 7, 8, 9, 10, 11, 12, 13, 14, 15, 16, 17, 18, 19, 20}
  (b) {1, 3, 5, 7, 9, 11, 13, 15, 17, 19, 21, 23, 25, 27, 29, 31}
  (c) {3, 6, 9, 12, 15, 18, 21, 24, 27, 30, 33, 36, 39, 42, 45, 48, 51}

4 Using brackets, list the members of each set.
  (a) {numbers between 1 and 101 that end in 0}
  (b) {numbers between 5 and 80 that are divisible by 3}
  (c) {numbers between 12 and 17 that are divisible by 9}

5 Which of these are empty sets?
- **(a)** {spiders that have twenty-four legs}
- **(b)** {whole numbers between 21 and 22}
- **(c)** {numbers ending in 1 that are divisible by 11}
- **(d)** {numbers between 0 and 500 that are divisible by 10}
- **(e)** {years with 370 days}
- **(f)** {boys' names beginning with A}
- **(g)** {days of the week beginning with X}
- **(h)** {rivers that run to the sea}
- **(i)** {months of the year ending with W}
- **(j)** {human beings with wings}

6 Make up five sets of your own. List each one, using brackets, then describe it in your own words.

7 Describe five empty sets of your own.

2.3 Venn diagrams

A labelled diagram like this is called a **Venn diagram**. It is named after the mathematician John Venn.

Months of the year

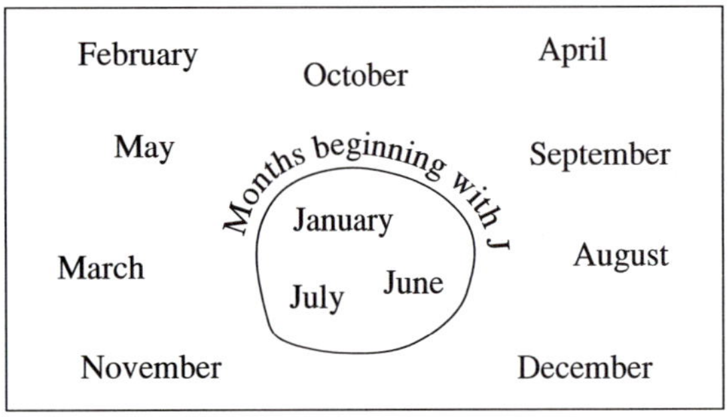

The rectangular box contains the whole set.

- The whole set is usually called the **universal set**.
- The smaller loop shows a **subset** of the universal set.
  All members of a subset are also members of the universal set.

Example 2

A Venn diagram has been started below.

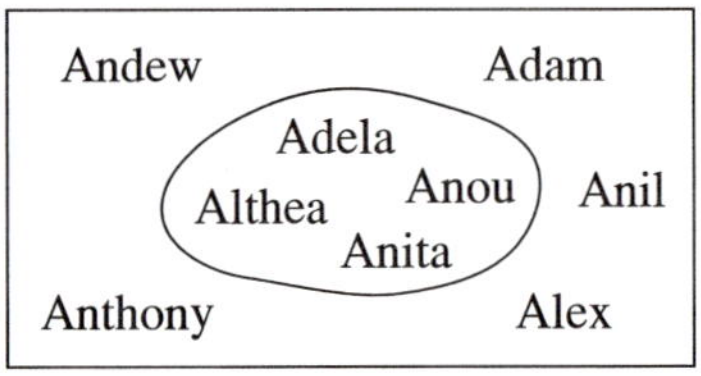

(a) Name the universal set and the subset.
(b) List, using curly brackets:
- **(i)** the universal set
- **(ii)** the subset.

(a) The universal set could be called 'Names beginning with A' and the subset 'Girls names beginning with A'.

(b) **(i)** The universal set is {Andrew, Adam, Anil, Anthony, Alex, Adela, Anou, Althea, Anita}
(ii) The subset is {Adela, Anou, Althea, Anita}

Exercise 2D

1 Copy this Venn diagram:

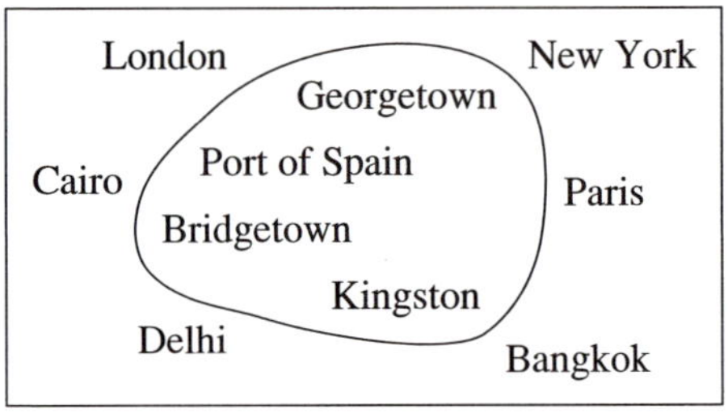

On your drawing label the universal set and the subset.

2 From Question 1 list, using brackets:
- **(a)** the universal set
- **(b)** the subset.

3 Using {1, 2, 3, 4, 5, 6, 7, 8, 9, 10} as the universal set, draw a Venn diagram showing the subset of even numbers. Label your diagram.

4 For the universal set {whole numbers from 1 to 20} draw separate Venn diagrams to show each of these subsets:
(a) multiples of 3
(b) multiples of 4
(c) multiples of 5
(d) factors of 20.
Which of these four subsets has fewest members?

5 A grid that shows information is called an **information matrix**.
Stephen asked eight of his friends about how they like to spend time. The information he found is shown in the information matrix. ✓ means *likes*. ✗ means *dislikes*. For example, Michael likes swimming but does not like reading.

Name	Swimming	Cricket	Movies	Reading	Drawing
Hugh	✓	✗	✗	✓	✗
Mohamed	✓	✗	✗	✓	✗
Donald	✗	✓	✓	✓	✗
Michael	✓	✓	✓	✗	✓
Greg	✗	✓	✗	✗	✓
Morris	✓	✓	✗	✓	✓
Winston	✗	✓	✓	✗	✗
Lawrence	✓	✗	✓	✗	✗

Using {eight of Stephen's friends} as the universal set, draw separate Venn diagrams showing the subsets of his friends
(a) who like swimming
(b) who like cricket
(c) who like reading and movies
(d) who like reading and drawing
(e) who like movies and drawing
(f) whose names begin with K
(g) who are male.
Label your diagrams.

The subset symbol

There is a quick way to show a subset of a set, without drawing a Venn diagram. You use the symbol ⊂.

- The symbol ⊂ means **is a subset of**.
  For example,
  {3, 6, 9} ⊂ {1, 2, 3, 4, 5, 6, 7, 8, 9, 10}

Exercise 2E

1 Using symbols, describe each Venn diagram. The first one can be described as {Monday} ⊂ {Monday, Tuesday, Wednesday, Thursday, Friday, Saturday, Sunday}

(a) The days of the week

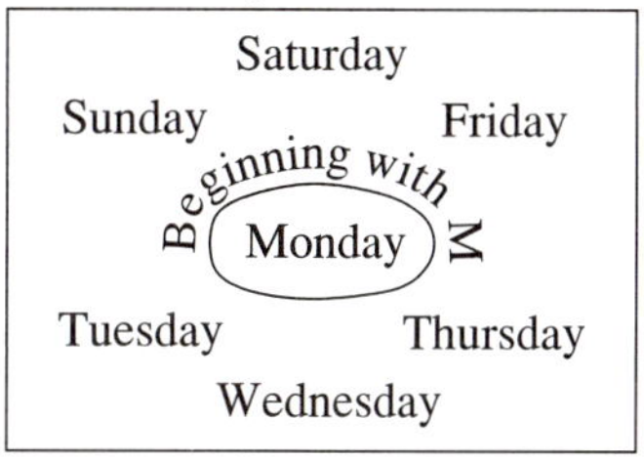

(b) A set of animals

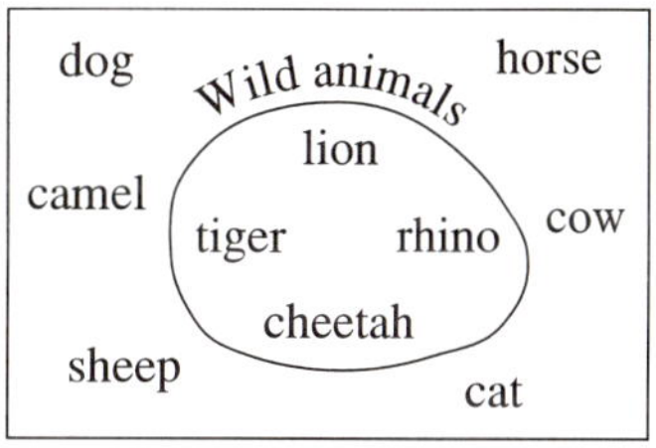

(c) Numbers between 0 and 11

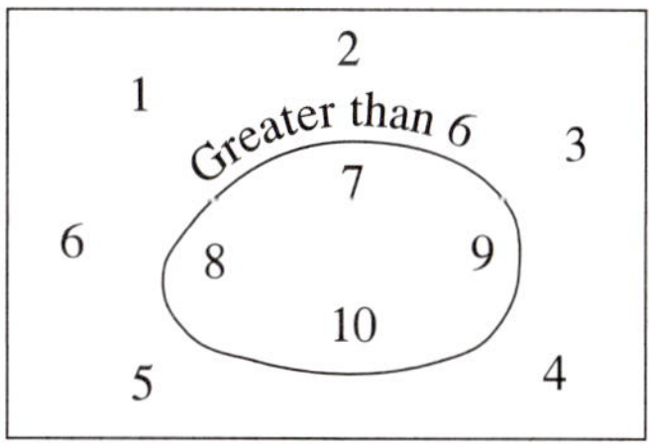

2 Show, with labels, these sets on Venn diagrams.
(a) {1, 3, 5, 7, 9} ⊂ {1, 2, 3, 5, 6, 7, 8, 9, 10}
(b) {2, 4, 6, 8, 10} ⊂ {1, 2, 3, 4, 5, 6, 7, 8, 9, 10}
(c) {3, 6, 9} ⊂ {3, 6, 9, 12, 15, 18, 21, 24, 27}

2.4 Intersection of sets

This set shows people whose photos appeared in today's *Daily News*.

Two subsets of the universal set are:

{people wearing glasses} = {Anita, Ratna, Charlie, Bernard}

and {people wearing a uniform} = {Claudia, Anita, Denis, Charlie}

Anita and Charlie are in both subsets. This can be shown on a Venn diagram:

People with photos in today's 'Daily News'

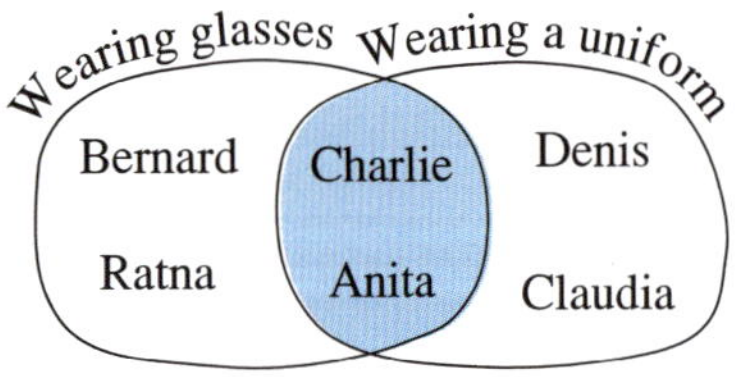

Anita and Charlie are both wearing glasses **and** wearing a uniform.
They make up the **intersection** of the two subsets.

- The intersection of two sets is made up of those members that are common to both sets.

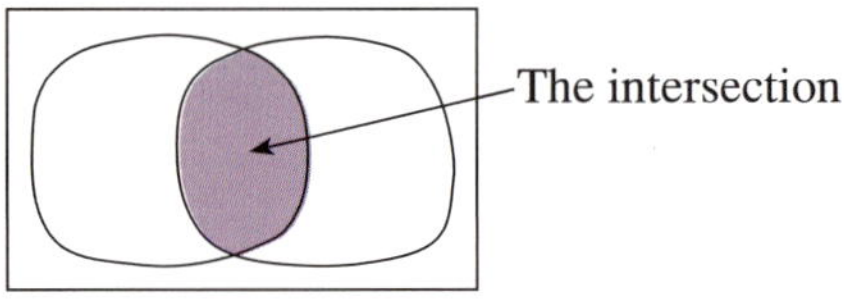

Exercise 2F

1 This is the set of names of Harry's friends.

Names of Harry's friends

Billy, Ratna, Rose, Regina, David, Michael, Roland, Ramsingh, Robert, Shirley, Raquel, Rocky, Janet

Using brackets, list the subset of these names that:

(a) are girls' names **(b)** begin with R.

2 **(a)** In Question 1, which names are girls' names *and* begin with R?

(b) Copy and complete the Venn diagram:

Names of Harry's friends

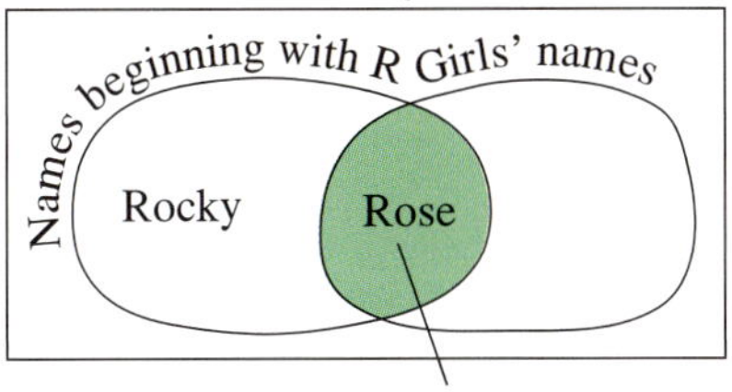

Rose is a girl's name and it begins with R.

3 In Question 2, are the names in the shaded region of the Venn diagram in part (b) the same as the names in your answer to part (a)?

4 The matrix below gives information about ten students in Form 1.
✓ means Yes. ✗ means No.

Name	Likes maths	Can swim	Owns a bicycle
Deo	✓	✓	✗
Wendy	✓	✗	✓
Ali	✓	✗	✗
Ramsingh	✗	✓	✓
Lorna	✗	✗	✗
Addie	✓	✗	✗
Bob	✗	✓	✓
Shirley	✓	✗	✓
Janice	✓	✓	✗
Rani	✗	✓	✗

List the subset of students who:

(a) like maths **(b)** can swim.

(c) Which students like maths *and* can swim?

(d) Copy and complete the Venn diagram. Remember to use all ten names.

Ten students in Form One

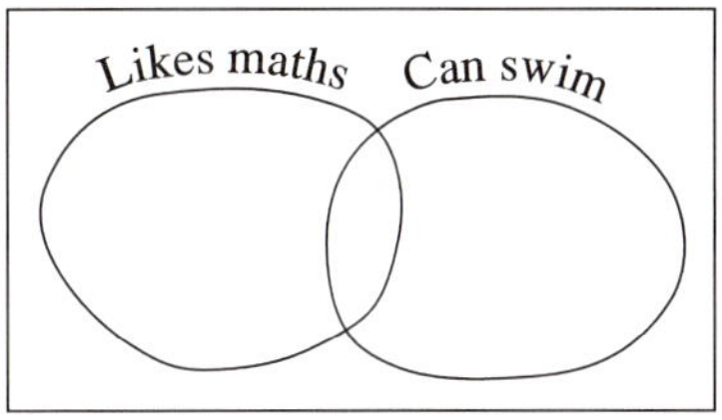

(e) Lorna's name appears outside both small loops in the Venn diagram you drew for part (d). What can you say about Lorna?

5 **(a)** Draw a Venn diagram using the students in the matrix in Question 4 showing:

(i) the subset of students who can swim

(ii) the subset of students who own a bicycle.

(b) Which students are in the intersection of the subsets?

(c) Which students *neither* own a bicycle *nor* can swim?

(d) Which students own a bicycle but can not swim?

6 From the Venn diagram list the subset of numbers from 1 to 20 which are:

(a) even

(b) multiples of 3

(c) even *and* multiples of 3

(d) even *but not* multiples of 3

(e) multiples of 3 *but not* even

(f) *neither* even *nor* multiples of 3.

Whole numbers from 1 to 20

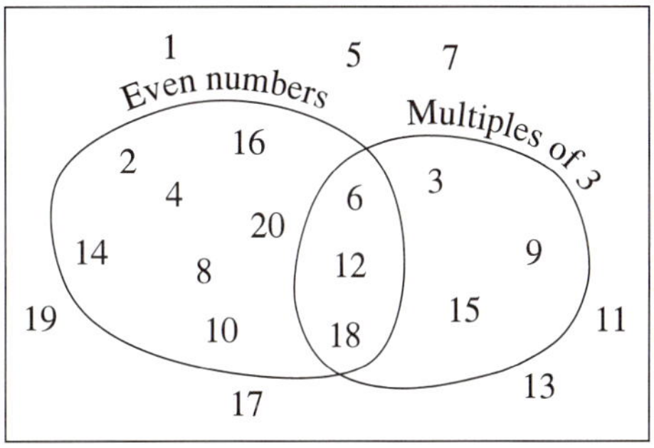

7 **(a)** Using {whole numbers from 1 to 30} as the universal set, copy and complete the Venn diagram:

Whole numbers from 1 to 30

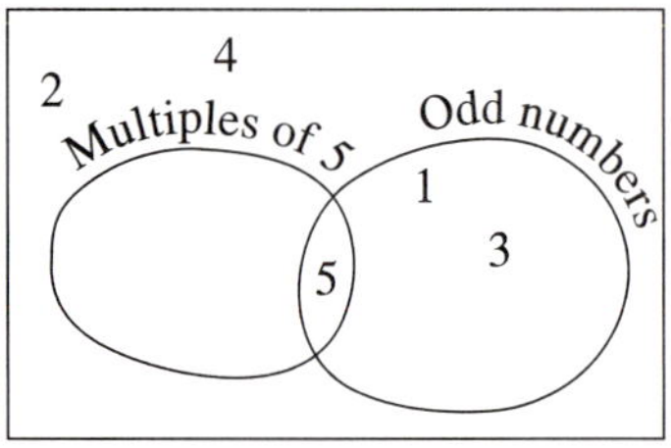

(b) Write down the subset of numbers from 1 to 30 which are:

(i) odd
(ii) multiples of 5
(iii) odd *and* multiples of 5
(iv) odd *but not* multiples of 5
(v) multiples of 5 *but not* odd
(vi) *neither* odd *nor* multiples of 5.

8 **(a)** Using the numbers from 2 to 25 as the universal set, show on a Venn diagram the subset of prime numbers and the subset of composite numbers.
(b) Which numbers are prime *and* composite?
(c) Which numbers are *neither* prime *nor* composite?

2.5 Common factors, common multiples

Set notation and Venn diagrams can give you another way of finding common factors and multiples.

Example 3

Draw a Venn diagram to show the factors of 6 and 9.

Factors of 6 = {1, 2, 3, 6}
Factors of 9 = {1, 3, 9}

Two of the factors, 1 and 3, are in both sets.
1 and 3 are **common factors** of 6 and 9.

A Venn diagram shows this well:

Whole numbers from 1 to 10

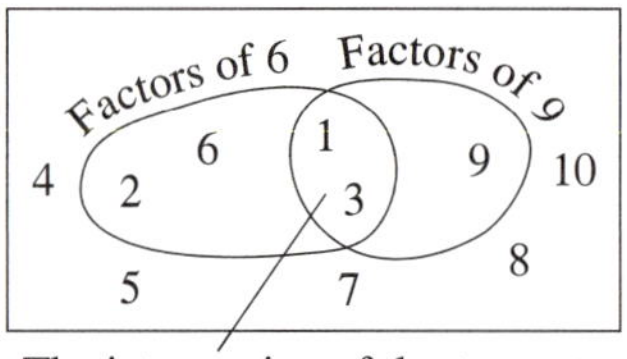

The intersection of the two sets shows the common factors.

Exercise 2G

1 **(a)** Write down the set of factors of 8.
(b) Write down the set of factors of 12.
(c) Copy and complete the Venn diagram:

Whole numbers from 1 to 15

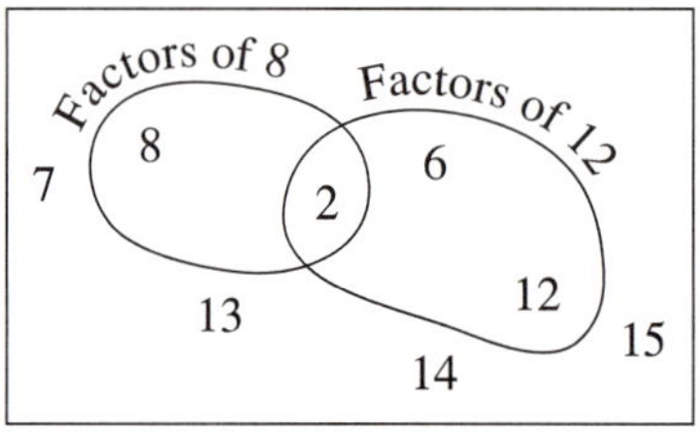

(d) Write down from the Venn diagram the set of common factors of 8 and 12.

2 **(a)** Write down the factors of 9.
(b) Write down the factors of 12.
(c) Copy and complete the Venn diagram:

Whole numbers from 1 to 12

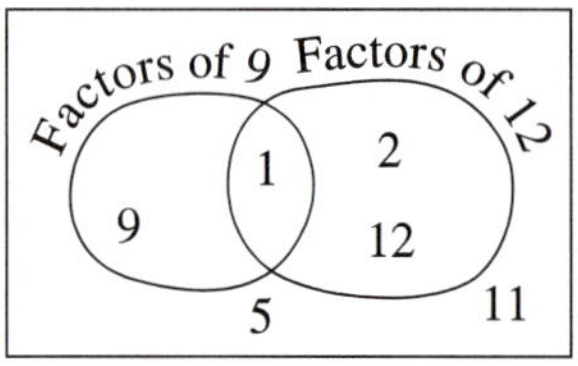

(d) Write down the common factors of 9 and 12.

3 Use Venn diagrams to find the common factors of

(a) 10 and 15 **(b)** 4 and 6
(c) 6 and 8 **(d)** 8 and 10
(e) 6 and 14 **(f)** 12 and 15.

It is now a short step to find the highest common factor (HCF) of two numbers using a Venn diagram.

Example 4

Use a Venn diagram to find the HCF of 18 and 24.

Factors of 18 = {1, 2, 3, 6, 9, 18}
Factors of 24 = {1, 2, 3, 4, 6, 8, 12, 24}

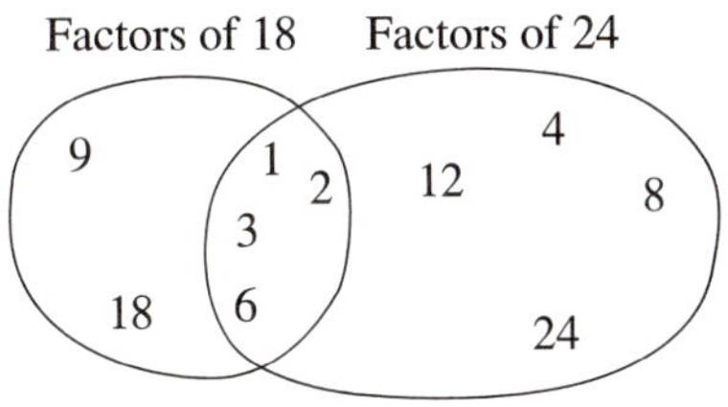

Common factors of 18 and 24 = {1, 2, 3, 6}
So HCF of 18 and 24 is 6.

Exercise 2H

1 Use the Venn diagrams you drew in Question 3 of Exercise 2G to find the HCF of
- **(a)** 10 and 15
- **(b)** 4 and 6
- **(c)** 6 and 8
- **(d)** 8 and 10
- **(e)** 6 and 14
- **(f)** 12 and 15

2 Use Venn diagrams to find the HCF of
- **(a)** 6 and 15
- **(b)** 10 and 15
- **(c)** 12 and 16
- **(d)** 24 and 30
- **(e)** 35 and 25
- **(f)** 28 and 42
- **(g)** 56 and 48
- **(h)** 36 and 54

3 List the elements of
- **(a)** {factors of 24}
- **(b)** {factors of 36}

Draw a Venn diagram to illustrate these sets and hence state the HCF of 24 and 36.

Common multiples

The set of the first eight multiples of 3
= {3, 6, 9, 12, 15, 18, 21, 24}

The set of the first six multiples of 4
= {4, 8, 12, 16, 20, 24}

12 and 24 belong to both sets.
12 and 24 are **common multiples** of 3 and 4.

A Venn diagram shows this:

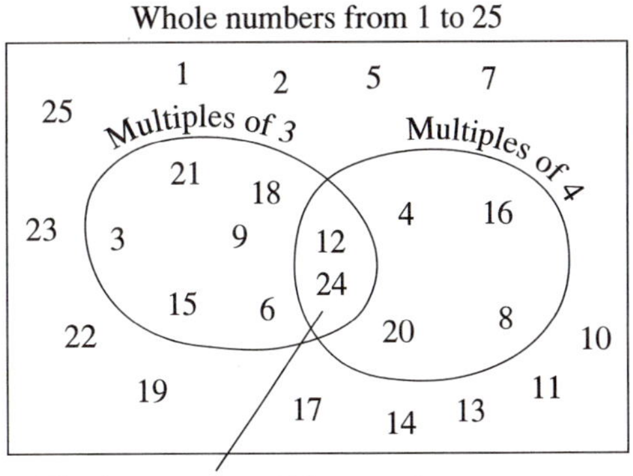

The intersection of the sets shows the common multiples.

Exercise 2I

1 **(a)** Write down the set of the first ten multiples of 2.

(b) Write down the set of the first four multiples of 5.

(c) Copy and complete the Venn diagram:

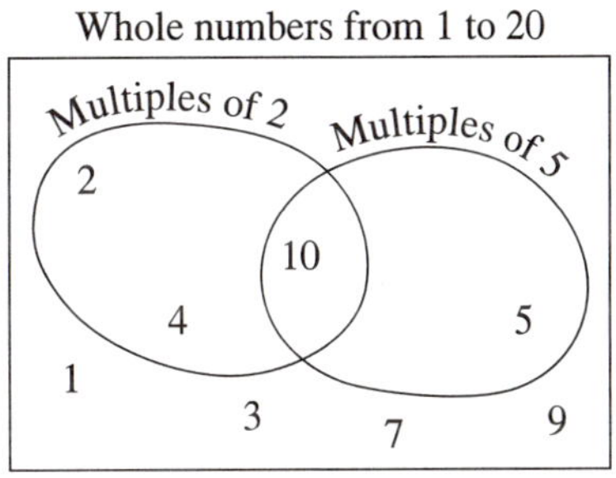

(d) Write down the set of common multiples of 2 and 5.

2 **(a)** Write down the first six multiples of 2.

(b) Write down the first six multiples of 3.

(c) Copy and complete the Venn diagram:

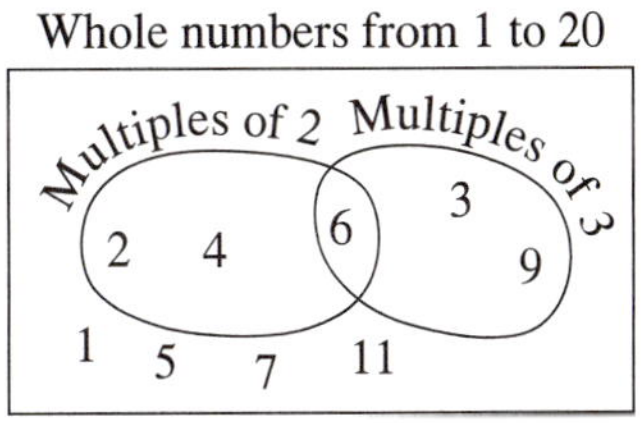

(d) Write down the set of common multiples of 2 and 3.

3 Use Venn diagrams to find the common multiples of
(a) 3 and 5 (b) 3 and 6
(c) 2 and 7 (d) 4 and 5
(e) 2 and 8 (f) 6 and 4

A Venn diagram can show the lowest common multiple (LCM) of a pair of numbers.

Example 5

Use a Venn diagram to find the LCM of 4 and 6.
The set of multiples of 4 =
{4, 8, 12, 16, 20, 24, 28, 32, 36, 40, 44, 48, 52, 56, 60, …}

The set of multiples of 6 =
{6, 12, 18, 24, 30, 36, 42, 48, 54, 60, …}

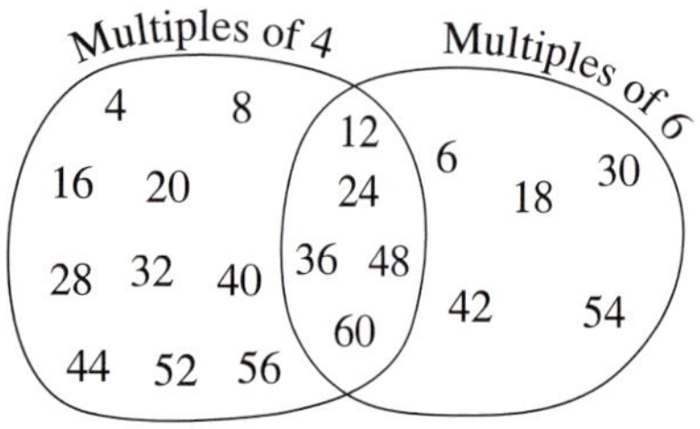

Common multiples of 4 and 6 =
{12, 24, 36, 48, 60, …}

So, LCM of 4 and 6 is 12.

Exercise 2J

1 Use the Venn diagrams you drew in Question 3 of Exercise 2I to find the LCM of
(a) 3 and 5 (b) 3 and 6
(c) 2 and 7 (d) 4 and 5
(e) 2 and 8 (f) 6 and 4

2 Use Venn diagrams to find the LCM of
(a) 2 and 3 (b) 4 and 8
(c) 3 and 4 (d) 2 and 4
(e) 2 and 9 (f) 5 and 10
(g) 5 and 7 (h) 8 and 12

Exercise 2K – mixed questions

1 Copy and complete using the correct symbol, ∈ or ⊂ in the space:
(a) physics … {science subjects}
(b) {April} … {months of the year}
(c) {knife, fork, spoon} … {kitchen utensils}
(d) 15 … {multiples of 5}
(e) {3, 6, 12} … {factors of 24}

2 Which of these are empty sets?
(a) {students in your class who like mathematics}
(b) {people over 150 years old}
(c) {students in your class with three legs}
(d) {prime numbers less than 20}
(e) {odd numbers with a factor of 2}

3 If $a \in \{3, 6, 9, 12\}$ and $a \in \{1, 2, 3, 4, 5\}$ find the value of a.

4 The Venn diagram shows the favourite sports of some students in 7B.

Students in 7B

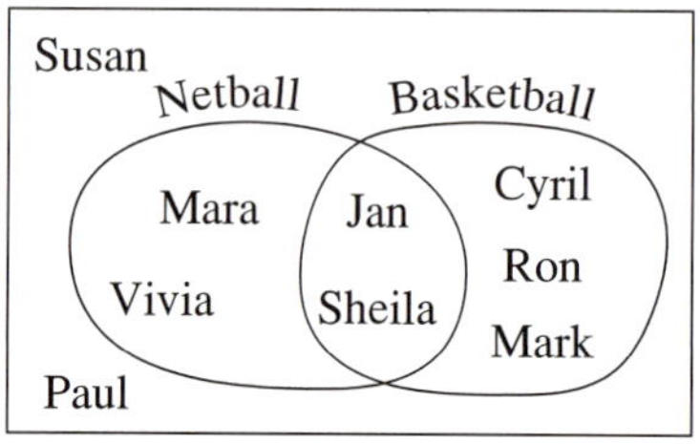

(a) List using brackets, the set of students who
(i) play basketball
(ii) play netball, but *not* basketball
(iii) play *neither* netball *nor* basketball
(iv) play *both* netball *and* basketball.
(b) How many students play either basketball or netball or both?

5 (a) Copy and complete:
The intersection of {factors of 6} and {multiples of 2 less than 10} is …
(b) Draw a Venn diagram to show the information in part (a).

6 (a) List the factors of 6.
(b) List the factors of 24.
(c) Draw a Venn diagram to show that {factors of 6} ⊂ {factors of 24}.

7 Use Venn diagrams to illustrate the HCF and the LCM of:
(a) 6 and 16
(b) 12 and 21
(c) 9 and 15

2 Consolidation

Example 1

Describe the sets.

(a)

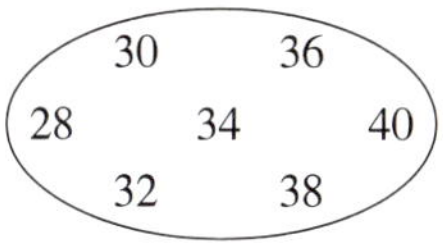

(b)

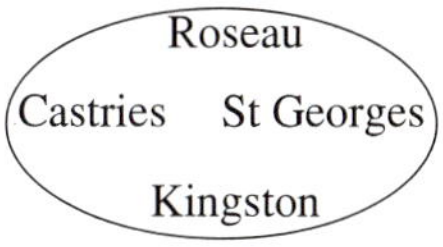

The set can be written as {28, 30, 32, 34, 36, 38, 40}

That is, the set of even numbers from 28 to 40.

The set can be written as {Roseau, Castries, St Georges, Kingston}.

That is, the set of Windward Island capitals.

Example 2

Draw a Venn diagrams to show

$$\{2, 4, 6\} \subset \{1, 2, 3, 4, 5, 6, 7\}$$

The symbol $\subset$ means **'is a subset of'**.

The Venn diagram to show the two sets is

Numbers between 1 and 7

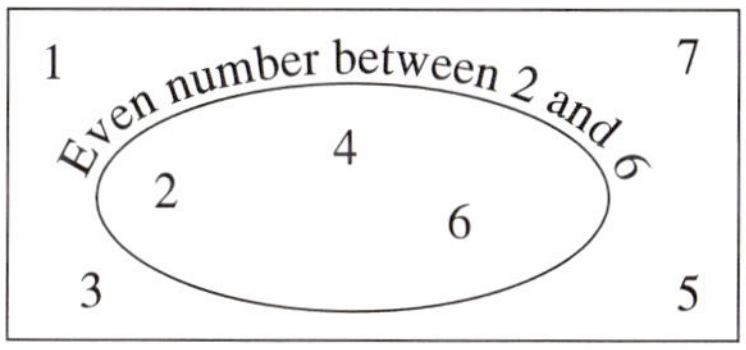

Example 3

Draw a Venn diagram to show the factors of 8 and the factors of 6.

Write down the intersection of the two sets.

Factors of 8 = {1, 2, 4, 8}

Factors of 6 = {1, 2, 3, 6}

The Venn diagram is

Numbers between 1 and 8

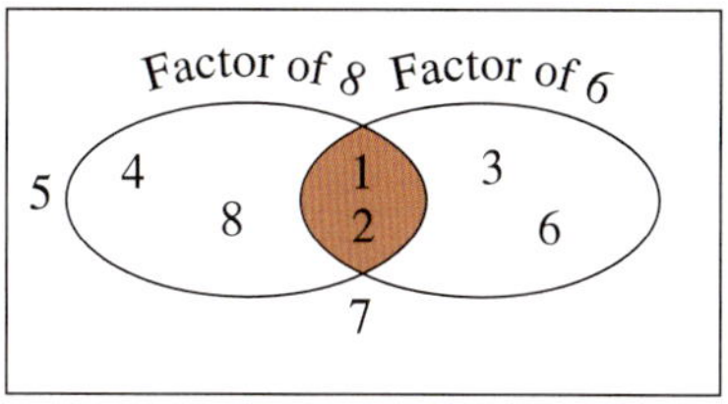

The intersection of the two sets is {1, 2}.

Exercise 2

1 Describe these sets:

(a)

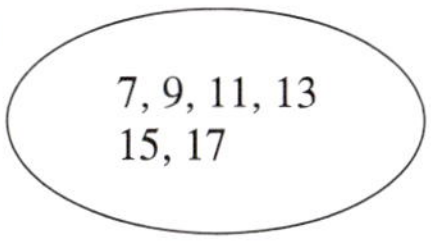

(b)

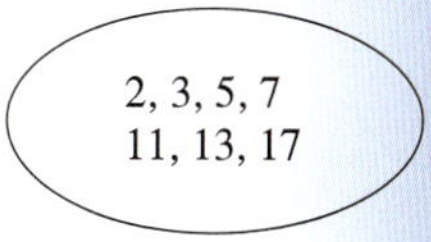

(b)

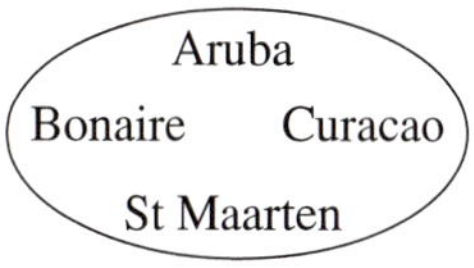

2 Write down five different empty sets.

3 Draw Venn diagrams to show

(a) $\{1, 3, 5\} \subset \{1, 2, 3, 4, 5, 6\}$

(b) $\{5, 10, 15, 20\} \subset \{5, 10, 15, 20\}$

(c) {Saturday, Sunday} $\subset$ {Days of the week}

4 Draw Venn diagrams to show

(a) factors of 4 and factors of 6

(b) factors of 12 and factors of 24

(c) factors of 9 and factors of 24

(d) factors of 36 and factors of 15

Write down the intersection of each of the pairs of sets.

5 **(a)** Using {whole numbers from 1 to 20} as the universal set, draw a Venn diagram to show {multiples of 3} and {odd numbers}

(b) Write down the subset of numbers from 1 to 20 which are:

(i) multiples of 3
(ii) odd
(iii) odd and multiples of 3
(iv) odd but not multiples of 3
(v) even and multiples of 3
(vi) neither odd nor multiples of 3

Application 2

6 **(a)** Draw a Venn diagram to show factors of 16 and factors of 24.

(b) List the members of the intersection of the two sets.

(c) What are the common factors of 16 and 24?

(d) What is the highest common factor (HCF) of 16 and 24?

7 Use the method you used in Question 6 to find the HCF of
(a) 12 and 18 **(b)** 36 and 27 **(c)** 36 and 60

8 Use a similar method to find the LCM of
(a) 3 and 5 **(b)** 2 and 6 **(c)** 7 and 15

Companion CD

Want some extra practice? Go to Chapter 2 on your companion CD for further exercises, animations, and solutions.

Summary

You should know ...

1 A set is a collection of things with a common feature.
For example: the set of even numbers between 1 and 11:

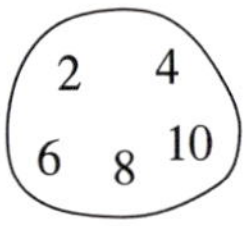

or {2, 4, 6, 8, 10}

2 The symbol ∈ means 'is a member of'.
For example: $r \in \{n, o, p, q, r, s\}$
A set with no members is an empty set, { }.
For example:
the set of girls with three heads = { }

Check out

1 **(a)** Use a loop to show the set of odd numbers between 6 and 16.

(b) Using brackets list the set of day of the week beginning with T.

2 **(a)** Rewrite the statement

'cod is a member of the set of fish' using the ∈ symbol.

(b) Rewrite the statement

'there are no birds with two heads'

using the symbol { }.

3 This is a Venn diagram:

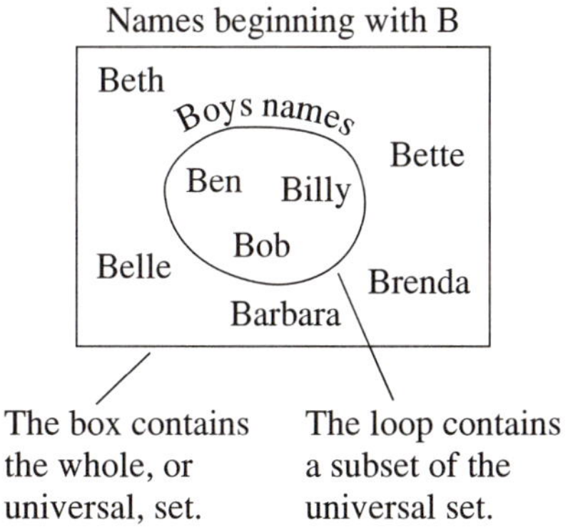

In symbols,
{Billy, Ben, Bob} ⊂ {names beginning with B}
⊂ means is 'a subset of'.

4 The intersection of two sets consists of members common to both sets.

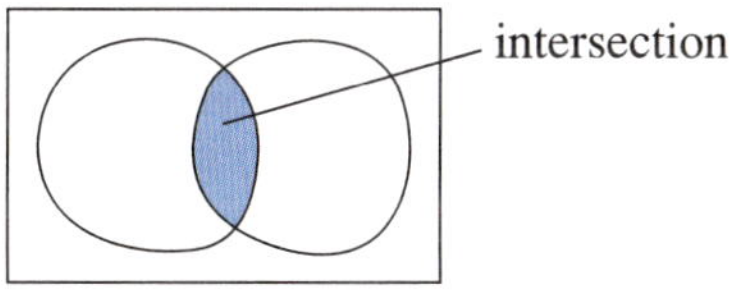

3 **(a)** Using {1, 2, 3 … 10} as the universal set, draw a Venn diagram to show the subset of prime numbers.
(b) Rewrite the statement 'Mary and Liz are girls names' using the symbol ⊂.

4 Copy and complete this Venn diagram:

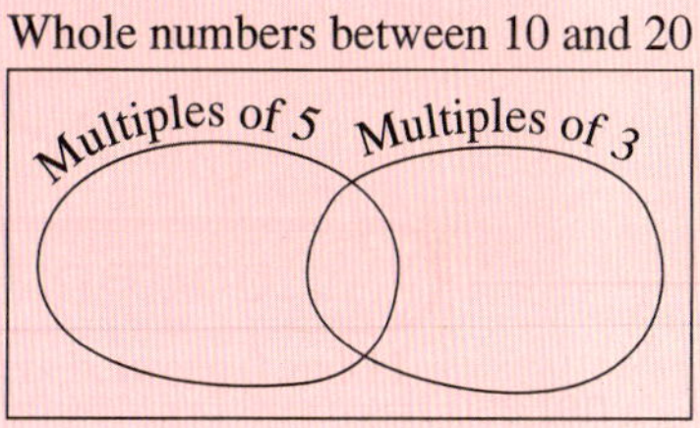

5 The highest common factor (HCF) is the largest factor common to two or more numbers.

For example: the HCF of 12 and 20 is 4.

The lowest common multiple (LCM) is the smallest multiple common to two or more numbers.

For example: the LCM of 3 and 5 is 15.

5 **(a)** Copy and complete the Venn diagram:

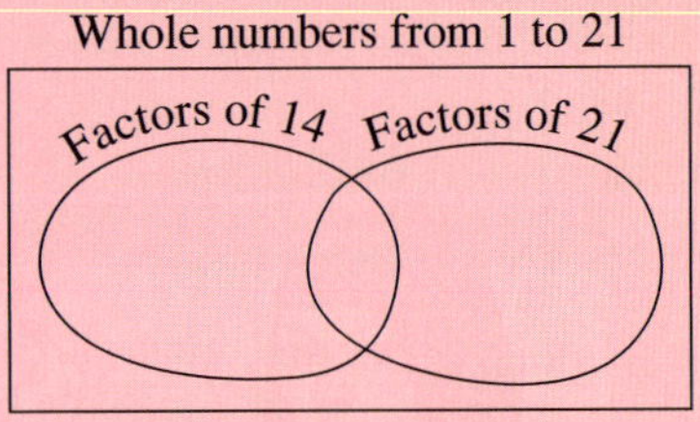

(b) Write down the HCF of 14 and 21.

(c) Draw a Venn diagram showing

(i) universal set = {whole numbers less than 25}

(ii) a subset of the multiples of 4

(iii) a subset of the multiples of 6.

(d) Find the LCM of 4 and 6.

Fractions

3

Objectives

- ✔ show fractions using diagrams
- ✔ calculate a fraction of a quantity
- ✔ find equivalent fractions
- ✔ work with fractions greater than 1
- ✔ add and subtract fractions
- ✔ multiply and divide fractions
- ✔ solve problems involving fractions

What's the point?

Fractions are used frequently in everyday life. How often do you say things such as 'I'd like half a glass', or 'Two-thirds of the class were sick'? Cooks use fractions all the time in their recipes: 'Take $2\frac{1}{2}$ cups of flour and mix in $\frac{1}{4}$ teaspoonful of salt …'

Before you start

You should know …

1 A **fraction** is the amount of each part when something is divided into equal sized parts.

For example:

One half ($\frac{1}{2}$)
Half an orange

One quarter ($\frac{1}{4}$)
One quarter of a pizza

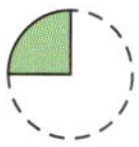

2 How to use numerals to describe fractions:

$$\frac{2}{3}$$

this shows how many parts you have — 2 is the numerator

this shows how many parts there are altogether — 3 is the denominator

Check in

1 **(a)** Janis shared a grapefruit equally between her and her sister. How much grapefruit did each get?

(b) Alan got half marks in a test out of ten. What was Alan's score?

2 Write down the numerator and denominator of these fractions.

(a) $\frac{3}{4}$ **(b)** $\frac{2}{3}$ **(c)** $\frac{5}{7}$ **(d)** $\frac{2}{10}$

3 How to use words to describe fractions:
$\frac{2}{3}$ is two-thirds.

3 Write these fractions as numerals.
(a) three-quarters
(b) two-fifths
(c) five-sixths

3.1 Showing fractions

You can show fractions using diagrams.

Example 1

What fraction of each shape is shaded?

(a)

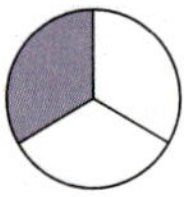

One part out of three equal parts is shaded so $\frac{1}{3}$ is shaded.

(b)

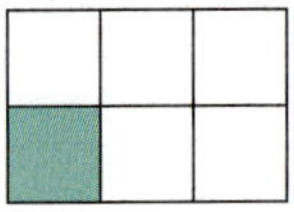

One part out of six equal parts is shaded so $\frac{1}{6}$ is shaded.

(c)

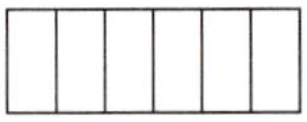

$\frac{1}{6}$

(d)

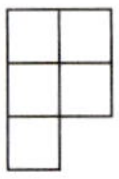

$\frac{1}{5}$

You can also show more than one part of a whole as a fraction for example:

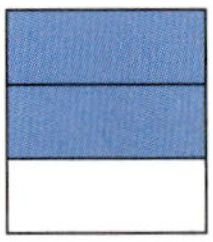

$\frac{2}{3}$ of a rectangle (two-thirds)

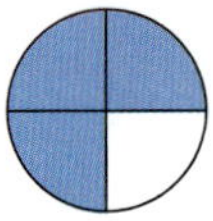

$\frac{3}{4}$ of a circle (three-quarters)

Exercise 3A

1 What fraction of each shape is shaded?

(a)

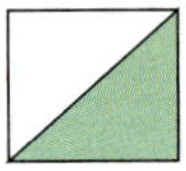

(b)

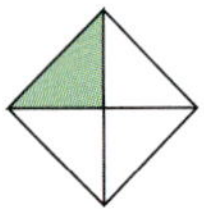

(c)

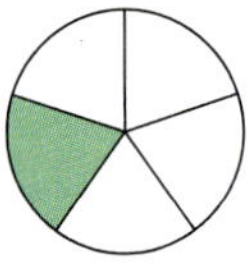

(d)

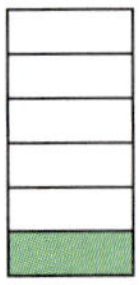

(e)

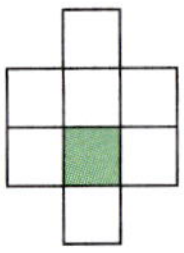

(f)

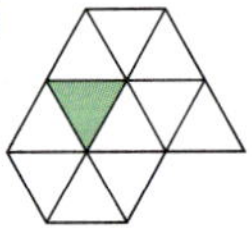

2 Copy the diagrams and shade the fractions shown.

(a)

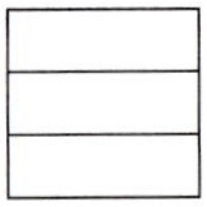

$\frac{1}{3}$

(b)

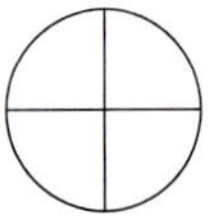

$\frac{1}{4}$

Exercise 3B

1 What fraction of each shape is shaded?

(a)

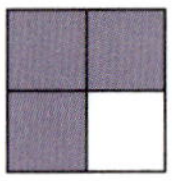

(b)

(c)

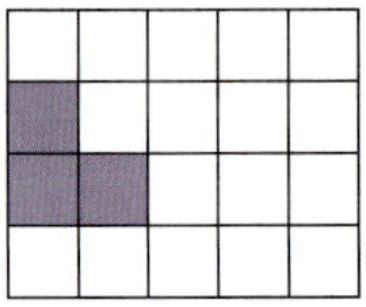

(d)

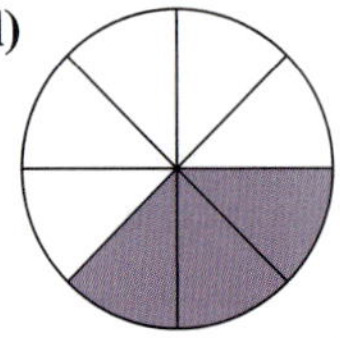

(e)

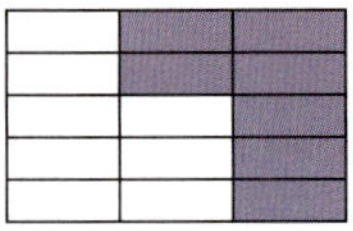

(f)

2 Copy each diagram and shade the fraction shown:

(a)

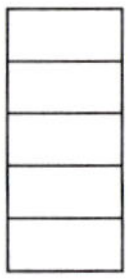

$\frac{3}{5}$

(b)

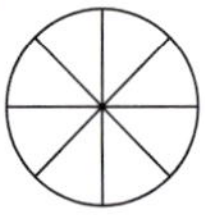

$\frac{3}{8}$

(c)

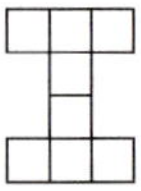

$\frac{3}{8}$

(d)

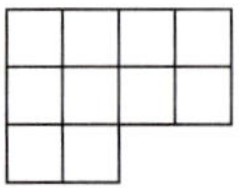

$\frac{7}{10}$

3 Using squared paper, show the fraction.
(a) $\frac{1}{7}$ **(b)** $\frac{4}{9}$ **(c)** $\frac{5}{11}$ **(d)** $\frac{2}{5}$ **(e)** $\frac{7}{10}$

4 The circle represents a jugful of fruit punch.

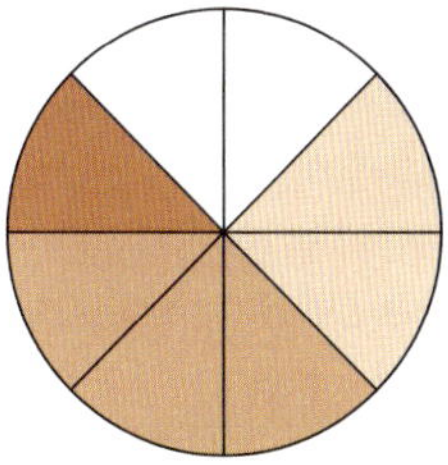

cane juice   orange juice
pineapple juice   water

What fraction of the punch is:
(a) pineapple juice **(b)** orange juice
(c) water **(d)** cane juice?

5 The rectangle below represents what Mr Olabode spent his wages on.

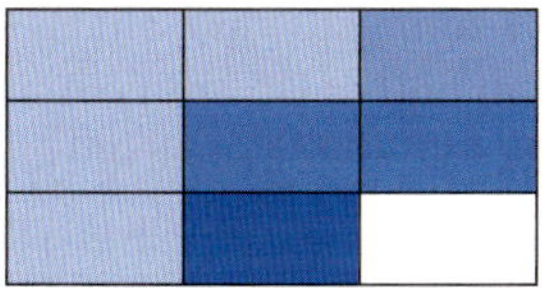

entertainment   food and fuel
new clothes   rent
savings account at the bank

(a) What fraction of his wages did he spend on
(i) food and fuel **(ii)** rent
(iii) entertainment **(iv)** new clothes?
(b) What fraction did he save?

6 Thomas Shabrai has a large farm. Here is how he uses his uses his farmland:
5 hectares for rice
5 hectares for timber
3 hectares for sugar cane
2 hectares for citrus fruits
1 hectare for yams
1 hectare left resting.
(a) How many hectares of farmland has Mr Shabrai?
(b) Use squared paper to represent Mr Shabrai's land. How many squares will you need? Using different shading, show what he does with the land. Remember to write a key to the shading you use.
(c) From your drawing, write down the fraction of land used each way.

7 Arthur Bentt was mixing concrete. He used 3 bucketfuls of sand, 2 bucketfuls of cement, 4 of gravel and 1 of water.
(a) How many bucketfuls of material did he use altogether?
(b) Write down the fraction of the total mixture that was:
(i) sand **(ii)** water **(iii)** cement
(iv) gravel.

Investigation

You can show $\frac{1}{2}$ on a square like  this

or like this  or even like this 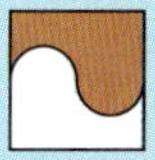.

How many different ways can you find of dividing up a square into two halves?

3.2 Calculating fractions

Fractions of a whole

To find a half ($\frac{1}{2}$) of an amount you divide by 2.

To find a third ($\frac{1}{3}$) of a whole amount you divide by 3, and so on …

To find $\frac{1}{3}$ of 12 you need to divide 12 into 3 equal parts.

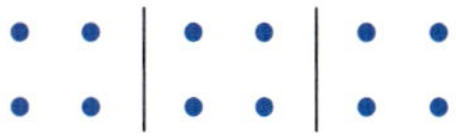

So $\frac{1}{3}$ of $12 = 12 \div 3 = 4$

Example 2

What is $\frac{1}{5}$ of \$30?

This means that \$30 is divided into 5 equal parts, so

$\frac{1}{5}$ of \$30 = \$30 ÷ 5 = \$6

Exercise 3C

1 Work out

(a) $\frac{1}{2}$ of 10 **(b)** $\frac{1}{4}$ of 20
(c) $\frac{1}{3}$ of 9 **(d)** $\frac{1}{5}$ of 15
(e) $\frac{1}{12}$ of 60 **(f)** $\frac{1}{15}$ of 90

2 What is $\frac{1}{3}$ of \$27?

3 Alicia's class has 36 pupils. One-third are girls. How many are boys?

4 Mr Largepocket earns \$8400 each month. He saves one-quarter of it. How much does he spend each year?

Other fractions of a whole amount can also be worked out in a similar manner.

Example 3

What is $\frac{3}{4}$ of 36?

$\frac{1}{4}$ of $36 = 36 \div 4 = 9$

$\frac{3}{4}$ of 36 is three times this, so

$\frac{3}{4}$ of $36 = 3 \times 9 = 27$.

A picture shows Example 3 more clearly.

$\frac{1}{4}$ of 36 • • • • • • • • •
$\frac{1}{4}$ of 36 • • • • • • • • • } $\frac{3}{4}$ of 36 = 27
$\frac{1}{4}$ of 36 • • • • • • • • •
$\frac{1}{4}$ of 36 • • • • • • • • •

Exercise 3D

1 What is:

(a) $\frac{1}{8}$ of 24 **(b)** $\frac{3}{8}$ of 24
(c) $\frac{1}{5}$ of 35 **(d)** $\frac{4}{5}$ of 35
(e) $\frac{1}{7}$ of 42 **(f)** $\frac{6}{7}$ of 42
(g) $\frac{1}{9}$ of 63 **(h)** $\frac{5}{9}$ of 63
(i) $\frac{1}{12}$ of 60 **(j)** $\frac{7}{12}$ of 60?

2 Draw pictures to show your answers to Question 1(b), (d), (f), (h) and (j).

3 Find

(a) $\frac{2}{3}$ of 18 centimetres
(b) $\frac{3}{4}$ of 24 students
(c) $\frac{7}{10}$ of 80 fishing boats
(d) $\frac{5}{8}$ of 64 lemons
(e) $\frac{3}{11}$ of 121 exercises
(f) $\frac{5}{8}$ of 96 minutes
(g) $\frac{3}{5}$ of 75 soldiers
(h) $\frac{5}{6}$ of 42 robbers.

4 (a) The circle represents the students of Form 2B, and shows how they get to school every day.

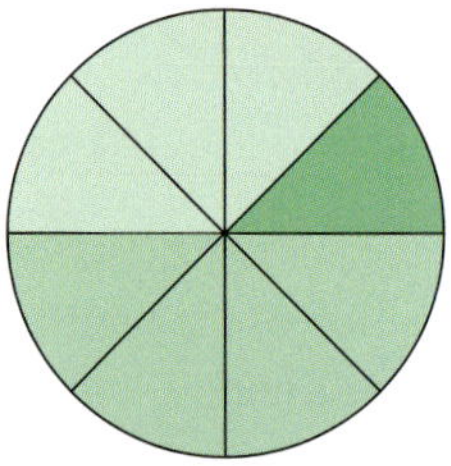

by bus
by car
walking

What fraction of the class comes to school
(i) by bus **(ii)** on foot **(iii)** by car?

(b) There are 48 students in Form 2B. Work out the *number* of students who come to school:
(i) by bus **(ii)** on foot **(iii)** by car.

5 The diagram represents the passengers on a flight between Barbados and Trinidad. The shaded part represents the female passengers.

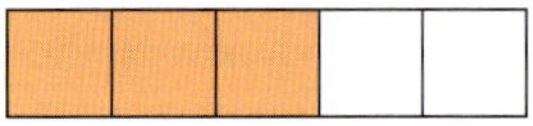

(a) What fraction does each square represent?
(b) What fraction of the passengers are female?
(c) There are 100 passengers on the plane. How many passengers does each square represent?
(d) How many of the passengers are female?

6 Two brands of soap powder, Cleano and Super wash, are both sold for \$15.95.

In a sales promotion:

$\frac{1}{3}$ box of Cleano, normal weight 720 g is given away free

and

$\frac{1}{4}$ box of Super Wash, normal weight 800 g is given away free.

Which brand of soap powder is the better buy during the promotion?

The whole from fractions

Sometimes you know the amount a fraction represents, but you need to find the size of the whole.

Example 4

The gas tank in Henry's car holds 4 gallons when it is $\frac{2}{3}$ full.

How much gas does the tank hold when full.

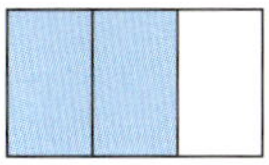

Tank is $\frac{2}{3}$ full

Gas tank

The shaded part ($\frac{2}{3}$) represents 4 gallons.

So each part represents $4 \div 2 = 2$ gallons.

There are 3 parts, so the tanks holds $2 \times 3 = 6$ gallons.

Exercise 3E

1 Find how much these gas tanks hold if

- **(a)** $\frac{1}{3}$ of the tank holds 20 litres
- **(b)** $\frac{1}{4}$ of the tank holds 16 litres
- **(c)** $\frac{2}{3}$ of the tank holds 24 litres.

2 The circle represents Form 1A.

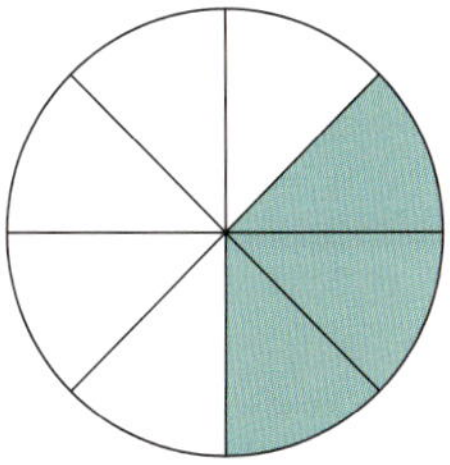

- **(a)** What fraction has been shaded?
- **(b)** The shaded part represents 15 students. How many students are represented by one part?
- **(c)** How many equal parts are there?
  How many students are in the class?

3 This drawing represents the teachers in a large school. The shaded part represents 30 teachers.

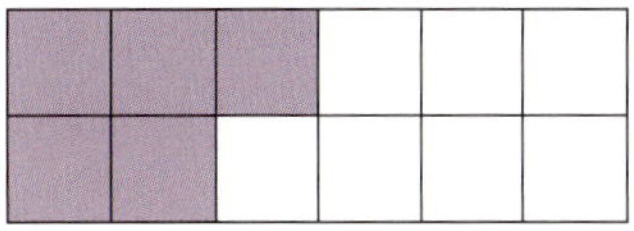

- **(a)** How many teachers are represented by one part?
- **(b)** How many teachers are in the school?

4 In the drawing the shaded part represents 49 litres.

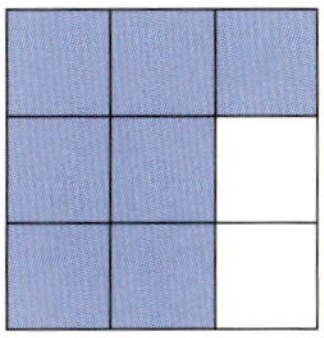

How many litres are there altogether?

5 Find the answer to Question 4, if the shaded part represents

(a) 7 litres **(b)** 21 litres **(c)** 35 litres.

6 12 men make up $\frac{4}{9}$ of a steel band.

- **(a)** Using squared paper, represent all the players in the steel band. Shade $\frac{4}{9}$ of it.
- **(b)** How many men does the shaded part represent?
- **(c)** How many men does one part represent?
- **(d)** How many men are in the steel band?

3.3 Equivalent fractions

In each of these circles one half is shaded.

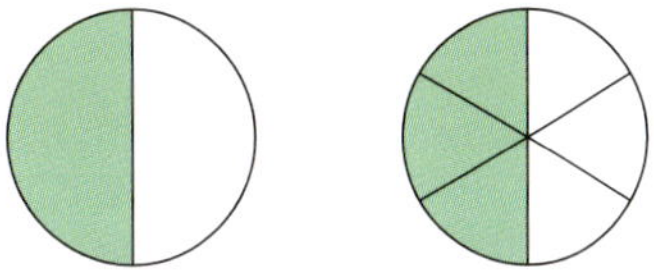

$\frac{1}{2}$ $\frac{3}{6}$

The same fraction is shaded so $\frac{1}{2} = \frac{3}{6}$.

$\frac{1}{2}$ are $\frac{3}{6}$ are **equivalent fractions.**

- Equivalent fractions show the same fraction, but use different numbers.

Exercise 3F

1 The diagrams show pairs of equivalent fractions. Use them to find the missing numbers.

(a)

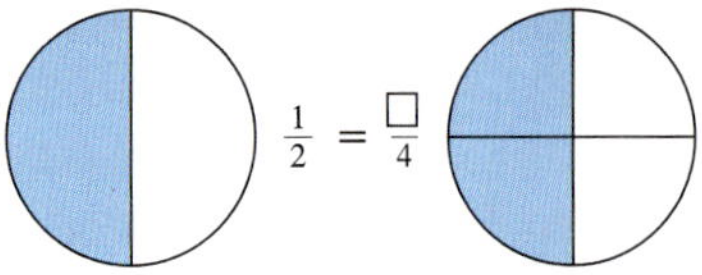

$\frac{1}{2} = \frac{\square}{4}$

(b)

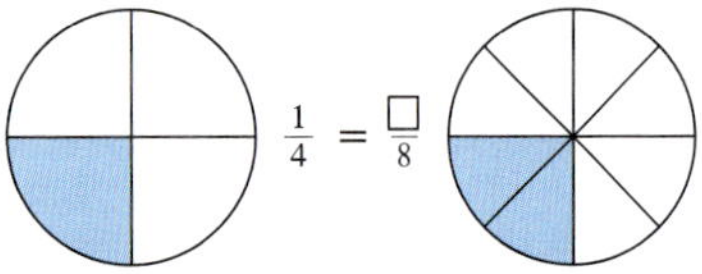

$\frac{1}{4} = \frac{\square}{8}$

(c)

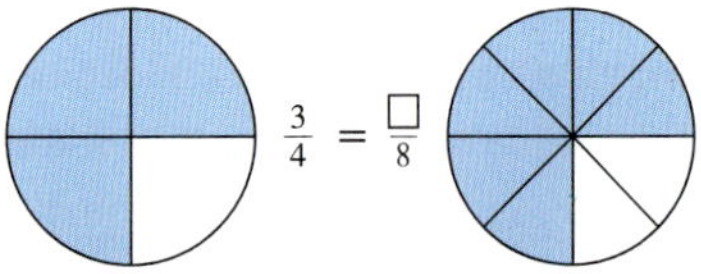

$\frac{3}{4} = \frac{\square}{8}$

(d)

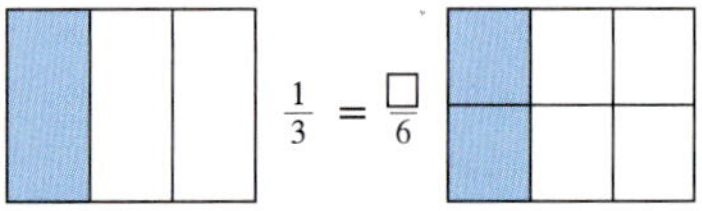

$\frac{1}{3} = \frac{\square}{6}$

(e)

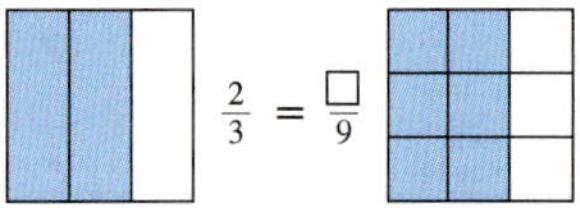

$\frac{2}{3} = \frac{\square}{9}$

(f)

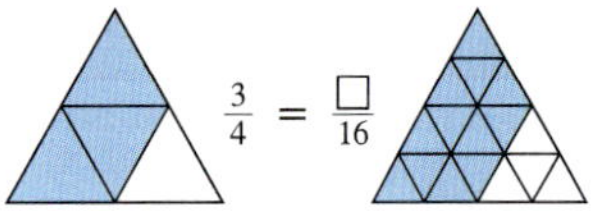

$\frac{3}{4} = \frac{\square}{16}$

(g)

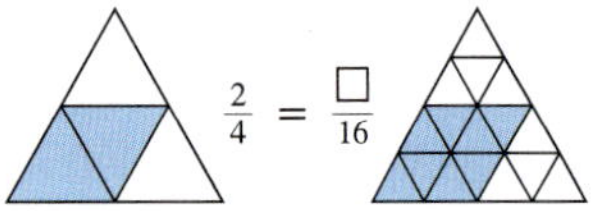

$\frac{2}{4} = \frac{\square}{16}$

2 On squared paper, draw rectangles to show that

(a) $\frac{1}{2} = \frac{2}{4}$ **(b)** $\frac{1}{3} = \frac{2}{6}$

(c) $\frac{3}{5} = \frac{6}{10}$ **(d)** $\frac{3}{4} = \frac{6}{8}$

(e) $\frac{4}{5} = \frac{8}{10}$ **(f)** $\frac{5}{6} = \frac{10}{12}$

3

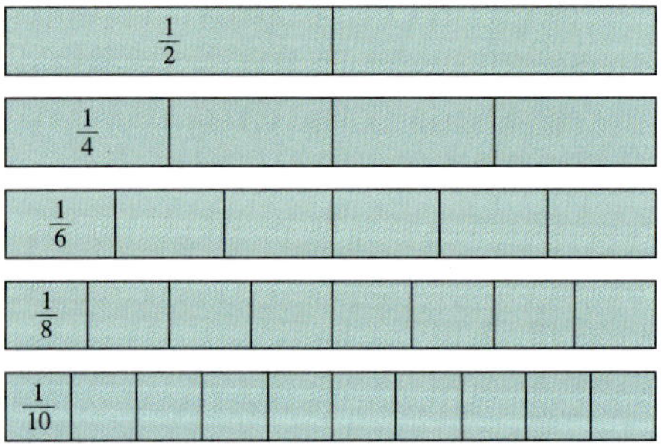

(a) The drawing above shows five strips of paper. Are all the strips equal in length?

(b) The first strip is divided into halves. The second strip is divided into quarters. The third strip is divided into sixths, and so on.

(i) How many halves are in the first strip?

(ii) How many quarters are in the second strip?

(iii) How many sixths are in the third strip?

(iv) How many eighths are in the fourth strip?

(v) How many tenths are in the fifth strip?

(c) Copy and complete:

$\frac{1}{2} = \frac{\square}{4} = \frac{\square}{6} = \frac{\square}{8} = \frac{\square}{10}$

Fraction walls

You can put the strips from Question 3, Exercise 3F together to get a fraction wall.

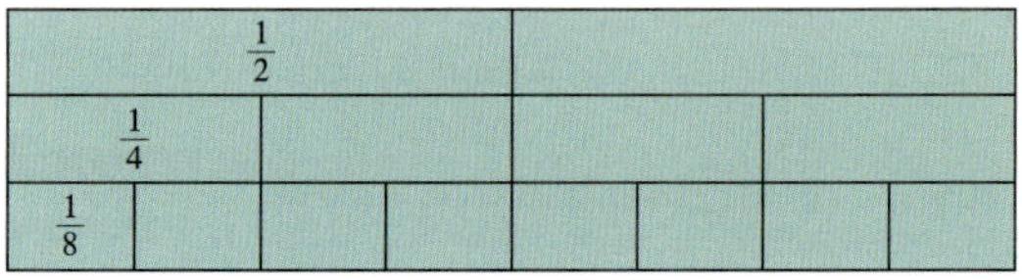

Fraction walls can help you find equivalent fractions.

Example 5

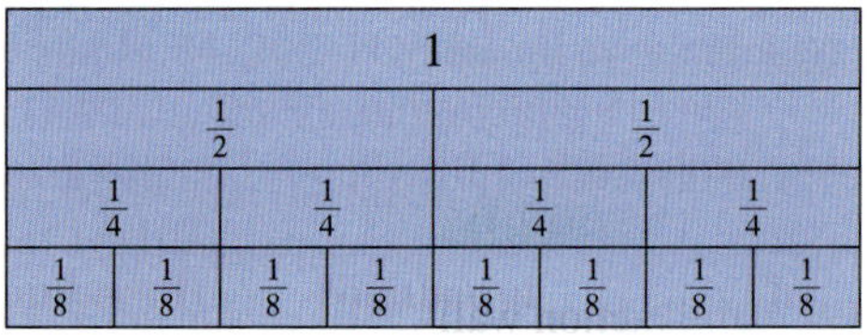

Use the fraction wall to

(a) write down a fraction equal to $\frac{3}{4}$

(b) write down two fractions greater than $\frac{1}{2}$.

The fraction wall can also be shown as:

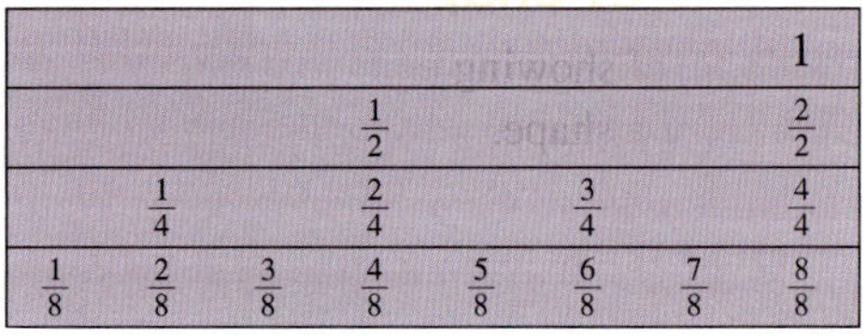

(a) You can see that $\frac{3}{4} = \frac{6}{8}$

(b) All the fractions to the right of $\frac{1}{2}$, that is $\frac{5}{8}, \frac{3}{4}, \frac{7}{8}$ etc are greater than $\frac{1}{2}$.

Exercise 3G

1

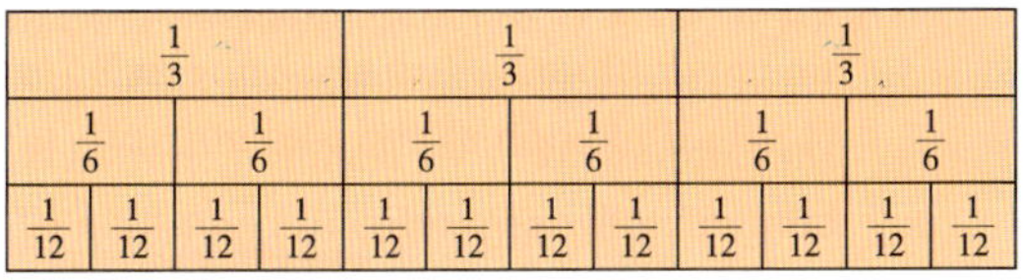

Use the fraction wall to write down:

(a) two fractions equal to $\frac{2}{3}$

(b) two fractions equal to $\frac{2}{6}$

(c) two fractions greater than $\frac{3}{6}$.

2

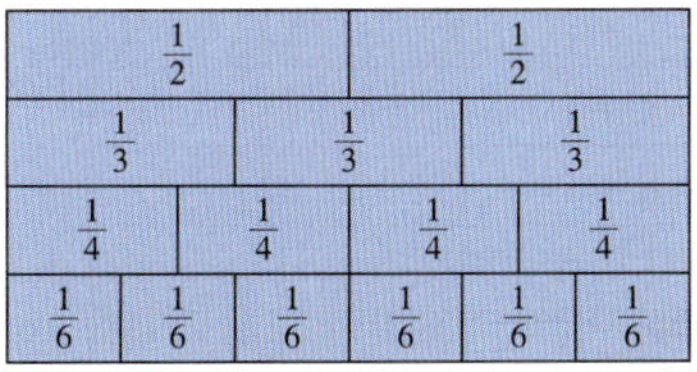

Use the fraction wall to write down:

(a) two fractions equal to $\frac{1}{2}$

(b) one fraction equal to $\frac{1}{3}$

(c) three fractions less than $\frac{3}{4}$.

3

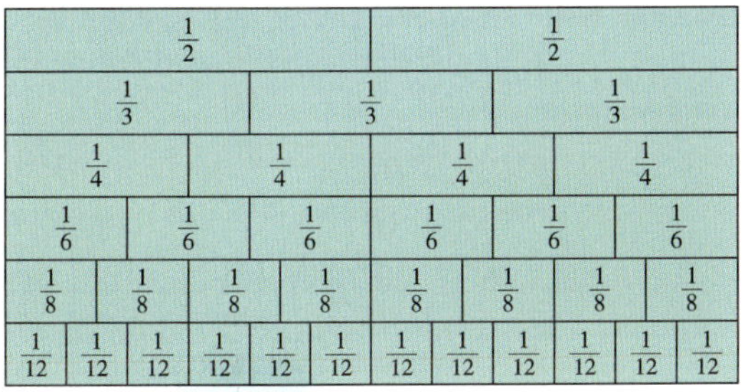

Use the fraction wall to copy and complete:

(a) $\frac{1}{3} = \frac{\square}{6} = \frac{\square}{12}$ **(b)** $\frac{1}{4} = \frac{\square}{8} = \frac{\square}{12}$

(c) $\frac{3}{4} = \frac{\square}{8} = \frac{\square}{12}$ **(d)** $\frac{3}{6} = \frac{\square}{8} = \frac{\square}{12}$

(e) $\frac{9}{12} = \frac{\square}{8} = \frac{\square}{4}$ **(f)** $\frac{4}{12} = \frac{\square}{6} = \frac{\square}{3}$

Fractions of shapes

Another way of showing equivalent fractions is to shade parts of a shape.

Example 6

(a) Shade $\frac{3}{4}$ of the shape.

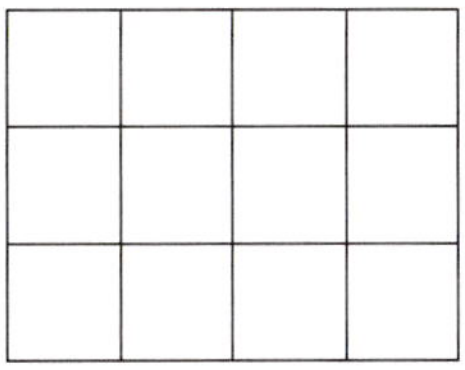

(b) Use your diagram to find a fraction equivalent to $\frac{3}{4}$.

(a) First, divide the shape into four equal parts, that is into quarters.

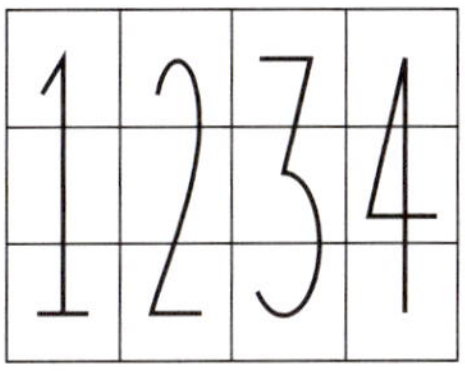

You want three of these quarters, $\frac{3}{4}$.

(b) 9 of the 12 small squares are shaded

So $\frac{3}{4} = \frac{9}{12}$

Exercise 3H

1 **(a)** Copy this shape on to squared paper.

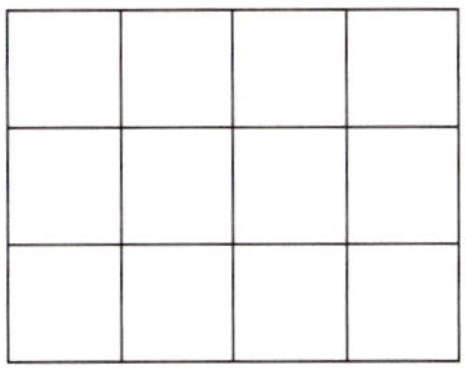

(b) What fraction of the whole rectangle is each small square?

(c) Divide the shape into three equal parts. What fraction of the whole rectangle is each of these parts?

(d) Look at one of the parts. How many small squares does it contain?

(e) Copy and complete: $\frac{1}{3} = \frac{\square}{12}$

2 (a) Copy this shape on to squared paper.

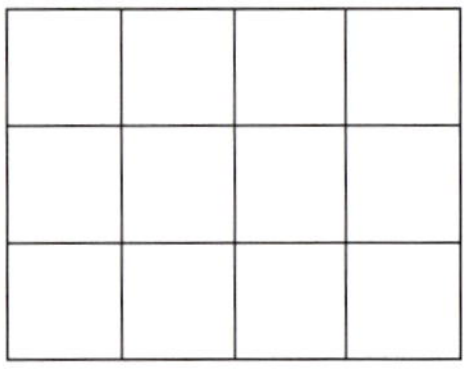

(b) Divide it into six equal parts.

(c) Shade $\frac{4}{6}$ of the shape.

(d) Copy and complete $\frac{4}{6} = \frac{\square}{12}$.

3 (a) Copy the shape on to squared paper

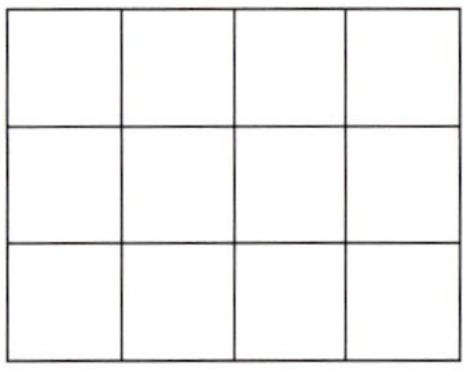

(b) Shade $\frac{5}{6}$ of the shape.

(c) Copy and complete $\frac{5}{6} = \frac{\square}{12}$.

4 (a) Copy the shape on to squared paper.

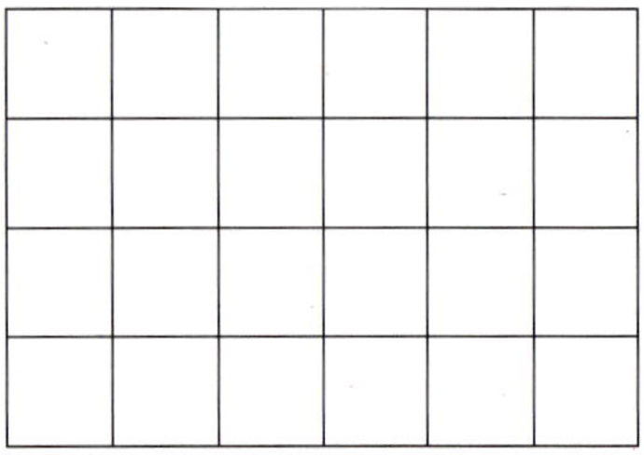

(b) Shade $\frac{2}{3}$ of the shape.

5 Repeat Question 4 for each of these fractions.

(a) $\frac{4}{6}$ (b) $\frac{6}{12}$ (c) $\frac{3}{8}$

(d) $\frac{6}{8}$ (e) $\frac{3}{4}$

6 Use your shaded shapes in Questions 4 and 5 to copy and complete:

(a) $\frac{2}{3} = \frac{\square}{24}$ (b) $\frac{4}{6} = \frac{\square}{24}$

(c) $\frac{6}{12} = \frac{\square}{24}$ (d) $\frac{3}{8} = \frac{\square}{24}$

(e) $\frac{6}{8} = \frac{\square}{24}$ (f) $\frac{3}{4} = \frac{\square}{24}$

Calculating equivalent fractions

There is a quicker way to find equivalent fractions than by drawing a picture. The Investigation will help you find out how.

Investigation

The fractions $\frac{1}{3}, \frac{2}{6}, \frac{3}{9}, \frac{4}{12}$ are equivalent fractions.

$\frac{1}{3} = \frac{2}{6} = \frac{3}{9} = \frac{4}{12}$

(a) Can you see how the fraction $\frac{2}{6}$ can be found from the fraction $\frac{1}{3}$?

(b) Can you see how the fraction $\frac{3}{9}$ can be found from the fraction $\frac{1}{3}$?

(c) Can you see how the fraction $\frac{4}{12}$ can be found from the fraction $\frac{1}{3}$?

(d) Can you write any other fractions equal to $\frac{1}{3}$?

You can write an equivalent for any fraction by multiplying its numerator and denominator by the same number.

$$\frac{1}{3} \xrightarrow{\times 2} \frac{2}{6} \qquad \frac{1}{3} \xrightarrow{\times 3} \frac{3}{9} \qquad \frac{1}{3} \xrightarrow{\times 4} \frac{4}{12}$$

(× 2, × 3, × 4 applied to both numerator and denominator)

Example 7

Copy and complete:

$$\frac{3}{4} = \frac{}{24}$$

$$\frac{3}{4} = \frac{}{24} \quad (4 \times 6 = 24)$$

24 is 4 multiplied by 6, so we multiply both numerator and denominator by 6.

$$\frac{3 \times 6}{4 \times 6} = \frac{18}{24}$$

Exercise 3I

1 Copy and complete:

(a) $\frac{1}{2} = \frac{\square}{4}$ (b) $\frac{2}{3} = \frac{\square}{6}$

(c) $\frac{3}{4} = \frac{\square}{12}$ (d) $\frac{3}{8} = \frac{\square}{24}$

(e) $\frac{5}{6} = \frac{\square}{24}$ (f) $\frac{5}{8} = \frac{\square}{32}$

(g) $\frac{4}{7} = \frac{\square}{14}$ (h) $\frac{3}{11} = \frac{\square}{55}$

(i) $\frac{6}{13} = \frac{\square}{52}$

2 You can work out a problem like

$$\frac{12}{36} = \frac{2}{\square}$$

by dividing instead of multiplying: 2 is 12 divided by 6, so we divide both numerator and denominator by 6.

$$\frac{12}{36} \underset{\div 6}{\overset{\div 6}{=}} \frac{2}{6}$$

Use the method above to complete:

$$\frac{6}{15} = \frac{\square}{5}$$

3 Copy and complete:

(a) $\frac{4}{8} = \frac{\square}{2}$ (b) $\frac{12}{24} = \frac{\square}{8}$

(c) $\frac{6}{9} = \frac{\square}{3}$ (d) $\frac{5}{15} = \frac{\square}{3}$

(e) $\frac{35}{40} = \frac{7}{\square}$ (f) $\frac{32}{40} = \frac{8}{\square}$

(g) $\frac{56}{84} = \frac{\square}{12}$ (h) $\frac{54}{63} = \frac{6}{\square}$

(i) $\frac{65}{91} = \frac{5}{\square}$

4 Copy and complete:

(a) $\frac{40}{100} = \frac{20}{\square} = \frac{\square}{25} = \frac{2}{\square}$

(b) $\frac{75}{90} = \frac{\square}{60} = \frac{25}{\square} = \frac{5}{\square}$

(c) $\frac{72}{84} = \frac{\square}{42} = \frac{\square}{14} = \frac{6}{\square}$

(d) $\frac{81}{189} = \frac{\square}{63} = \frac{9}{\square} = \frac{3}{\square}$

(e) $\frac{105}{135} = \frac{\square}{27} = \frac{7}{\square}$

Simplifying fractions

A fraction is in its **simplest form** when its numerator and denominator have no common factor.

The fraction $\frac{2}{5}$ is in its simplest form (2 and 5 have no common factors).

- To write a fraction in its simplest form you have to divide both parts of the fraction by their highest common factor.

For example, the HCF of 6 and 15 is 3, so

$$\frac{6}{15} \underset{\div 3}{\overset{\div 3}{=}} \frac{2}{5}$$

Example 8

Write $\frac{36}{48}$ in its simplest form.

The HCF of 36 and 48 is 12.

So

$$\frac{36}{48} \underset{\div 12}{\overset{\div 12}{=}} \frac{3}{4}$$

or you can simplify in steps:

$$\frac{36}{48} \underset{\div 4}{\overset{\div 4}{=}} \frac{9}{12} \underset{\div 3}{\overset{\div 3}{=}} \frac{3}{4}$$

Exercise 3J

1 Write each fraction in its simplest form:

(a) $\frac{3}{9}$ (b) $\frac{3}{12}$ (c) $\frac{8}{20}$

(d) $\frac{15}{21}$ (e) $\frac{24}{36}$ (f) $\frac{17}{51}$

(g) $\frac{28}{84}$ (h) $\frac{42}{54}$ (i) $\frac{48}{88}$

(j) $\frac{6}{58}$

2 Which fraction does not belong to the set of equivalent fractions?

(a) $\left\{\frac{1}{4}, \frac{3}{12}, \frac{12}{48}, \frac{20}{72}, \frac{23}{92}\right\}$

(b) $\left\{\frac{5}{55}, \frac{11}{121}, \frac{8}{98}, \frac{7}{77}, \frac{1}{11}\right\}$

(c) $\left\{\frac{2}{9}, \frac{14}{45}, \frac{6}{27}, \frac{18}{81}, \frac{40}{180}\right\}$

3 Explain why $\frac{195}{234}$ in its simplest form is not $\frac{65}{78}$.

4 Write these fractions in their simplest form:

(a) $\frac{504}{616}$ (b) $\frac{96}{216}$

(c) $\frac{576}{1444}$ (d) $\frac{441}{567}$

5 Express each of your answers as fractions in their simplest form.

(a) The towns of Hampton, Belles and Croft have populations of 700, 252 and 1568 respectively.

What fraction of their total population lives in **(i)** Hampton **(ii)** Belles?

(b) Dr Williams earned \$6350 last month. He paid \$1550 in tax and \$2450 on medical equipment. What fraction of his earnings went on (i) tax (ii) medical equipment?

6 Look at the fractions $\frac{2}{3}$ and $\frac{3}{4}$.
(a) Can you tell quickly which is larger?
(b) Copy and complete
$\frac{2}{3} = \frac{\square}{12}$, $\frac{3}{4} = \frac{\square}{12}$
(c) Now can you tell which fraction is larger?

Comparing fractions

Two fractions can be compared if they have the same denominator called a **common denominator**.

The common denominator is usually the lowest common multiple (LCM) of the two denominators.

Example 9

Which fraction is larger, $\frac{2}{5}$ or $\frac{1}{4}$, and by how much?

The denominators of the fractions are 5 and 4.
The LCM of 5 and 4 is 20.

$$\frac{2}{5} \xrightarrow{\times 4} \frac{8}{20} \qquad \frac{1}{4} \xrightarrow{\times 4} \frac{5}{20}$$

So $\frac{2}{5}$ is larger than $\frac{1}{4}$. It is $\frac{3}{20}$ larger.

Exercise 3K

1 (a) Write down the LCM of 4 and 6.
(b) Use it to find which fraction is larger, $\frac{3}{4}$ or $\frac{5}{6}$.
(c) By how much is it larger?

2 Use the method in Question 1 to find which fraction in each pair is larger, and by how much.
(a) $\frac{1}{3}, \frac{2}{7}$ (b) $\frac{2}{7}, \frac{1}{4}$
(c) $\frac{3}{4}, \frac{4}{5}$ (d) $\frac{2}{5}, \frac{3}{7}$
(e) $\frac{2}{3}, \frac{7}{10}$ (f) $\frac{8}{11}, \frac{2}{3}$
(g) $\frac{7}{9}, \frac{8}{11}$ (h) $\frac{7}{12}, \frac{11}{14}$
(i) $\frac{17}{20}, \frac{49}{60}$

3 $>$ means *is greater than* and $<$ means *is less than*.
Copy and fill in the missing sign ($>$, $<$ or $=$)
(a) $\frac{1}{3} \square \frac{1}{2}$ (b) $\frac{1}{6} \square \frac{5}{18}$
(c) $\frac{3}{4} \square \frac{9}{12}$ (d) $\frac{23}{24} \square \frac{11}{12}$
(e) $\frac{5}{6} \square \frac{7}{9}$ (f) $\frac{4}{15} \square \frac{3}{10}$
(g) $\frac{3}{7} \square \frac{4}{9}$ (h) $\frac{7}{12} \square \frac{9}{15}$
(i) $\frac{20}{100} \square \frac{5}{25}$

4 Find the largest fraction in each set.
(a) $\{\frac{2}{3}, \frac{4}{7}, \frac{5}{9}\}$
(b) $\{\frac{6}{9}, \frac{7}{10}, \frac{2}{3}\}$
(c) $\{\frac{4}{5}, \frac{5}{6}, \frac{17}{20}\}$

3.4 Fractions greater than '1'

Activity

You will need paper and scissors. Use something circular, like the rim of a cup, to draw six identical circles.

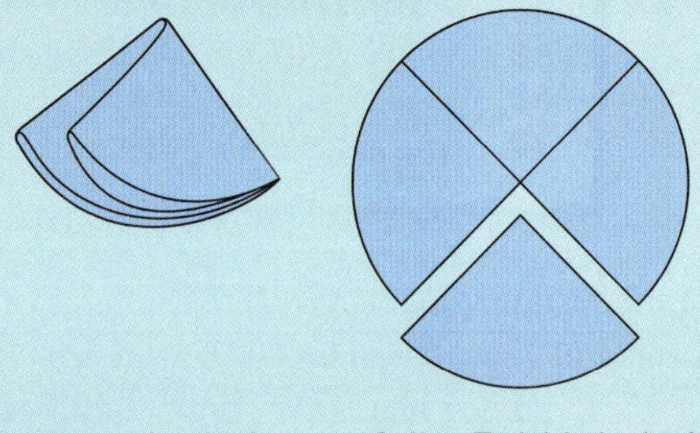

Cut out each circle carefully. Fold it in half, then fold it in half again. Cut along the fold lines. This will give you quarter-circles.

Take seven of your quarter-circles.
Put them together to make complete circles.
How many complete circles can you make?
What fraction of a circle is left over?

Keep your quarter-circles, you will need them again.

In the Activity, you should have made one complete circle, and had $\frac{3}{4}$ of a circle left over.

1 and $\frac{3}{4}$ is written $1\frac{3}{4}$.

- $1\frac{3}{4}$ is called a **mixed number** because it has both a whole number part and a fraction part.

The seven quarter-circles can also be written as the fraction $\frac{7}{4}$.

$$\frac{7}{4} = 1\frac{3}{4}$$

- Fractions like $\frac{7}{4}$ where the numerator is larger than the denominator, are called **improper fractions**. (Sometimes they are called 'top heavy' fractions.)
- Fractions like $\frac{3}{4}$, where the numerator is smaller than the denominator, are called **proper fractions**.

Exercise 3L

1 Copy and complete the table. Use your quarter-circles to help you.

Number of quarter-circles	As a fraction	As a mixed number
1	$\frac{1}{4}$	—
2	$\frac{2}{4}$	—
3	$\frac{3}{4}$	—
4		—
5	$\frac{5}{4}$	$1\frac{1}{4}$
6	$\frac{6}{4}$	
7	$\frac{7}{4}$	$1\frac{3}{4}$
8		
9		
10		
11		
12		

2 Here is a set of fractions.

$\frac{1}{3}$, $\frac{13}{2}$, $\frac{1}{9}$, $\frac{18}{5}$, $\frac{3}{3}$, $\frac{5}{2}$, $\frac{4}{11}$, $\frac{8}{8}$, $\frac{2}{7}$, $\frac{10}{3}$, $\frac{6}{6}$, $\frac{3}{2}$, $\frac{10}{10}$

Using brackets, write down:

(a) the subset of proper fractions,
(b) the subset of improper fractions,
(c) the subset of fractions equal to 1.

3 Here is a set of fractions and mixed numbers.

$2\frac{1}{3}$, $3\frac{1}{2}$, $\frac{1}{5}$, $\frac{7}{3}$, $\frac{10}{7}$, $\frac{3}{11}$, $2\frac{1}{5}$, $\frac{2}{9}$, $\frac{4}{15}$, $\frac{6}{5}$, $1\frac{1}{4}$, $\frac{8}{5}$, $4\frac{1}{3}$

Use brackets to write down:

(a) the subset of proper fractions,
(b) the subset of improper fractions,
(c) the subset of mixed numbers.

4 You can write the improper fraction $\frac{7}{6}$ as

$\frac{7}{6} = \frac{6+1}{6} = \frac{6}{6} + \frac{1}{6} = 1 + \frac{1}{6} = 1\frac{1}{6}$

Use this method to write $\frac{17}{6}$ as a mixed number.

5 Use the method given in Question 4 to change each fraction to a mixed number.

(a) $\frac{5}{3}$ **(b)** $\frac{7}{3}$ **(c)** $\frac{15}{9}$
(d) $\frac{17}{4}$ **(e)** $\frac{28}{11}$

6 From these examples:

$\frac{8}{5} = 1\frac{3}{5}$ $8 \div 5 = 1$ and remainder 3
$\frac{9}{7} = 1\frac{2}{7}$ $9 \div 7 = 1$ and remainder 2
$\frac{16}{7} = 2\frac{2}{7}$ $16 \div 7 = 2$ and remainder 2

(a) Can you spot the pattern?
(b) Can you see where the numerator in the mixed number comes from?
(c) Can you see a quick way to convert improper fractions to mixed numbers?
(d) Use your method to convert:
(i) $\frac{17}{7}$ **(ii)** $\frac{16}{5}$ **(iii)** $\frac{28}{3}$ **(iv)** $\frac{29}{4}$
(v) $\frac{37}{6}$ **(vi)** $\frac{46}{9}$ **(vii)** $\frac{91}{11}$ **(viii)** $\frac{87}{10}$
(ix) $\frac{121}{12}$ **(x)** $\frac{153}{20}$

7 From these examples:

$1\frac{1}{2} = \frac{3}{2}$ $(2 \times 1) + 1 = 3$
$3\frac{2}{5} = \frac{17}{5}$ $(5 \times 3) + 2 = 17$
$1\frac{5}{7} = \frac{12}{7}$ $(7 \times 1) + 5 = 12$

(a) Can you spot the pattern?
(b) Can you see where the numerator in the improper fraction comes from?

(c) Can you find a quick way to change mixed numbers into improper fractions?

(d) Use your method to convert:

(i) $2\frac{1}{2}$ (ii) $3\frac{1}{4}$ (iii) $4\frac{2}{5}$

(iv) $4\frac{7}{8}$ (v) $5\frac{2}{3}$ (vi) $6\frac{5}{11}$

(vii) $5\frac{9}{10}$ (viii) $4\frac{7}{9}$ (ix) $6\frac{5}{12}$

(x) $7\frac{9}{20}$

8 (a) Give three different ways to change the improper fraction $\frac{13}{5}$ to a mixed number.

(b) Give three different ways to change the mixed number $3\frac{2}{3}$ to an improper fraction.

(c) Which methods do you prefer? Give reasons.

Technology

You can get good practice with fractions by playing some fraction games.

The Woodlands Junior School website hosts some excellent fraction games.

Visit

www.woodlands-junior.kent.sch.uk

and see how good you are!

3.5 Adding fractions

Adding fractions with the same denominators

Exercise 3M shows you how to add fractions with the same denominator.

Exercise 3M

You will need the quarter-circles from the Activity on page 48.

1 (a) Take one of your quarter-circles.
Now add to it two more quarter-circles.
How many have you taken altogether?

(b) Copy and complete: $\frac{1}{4} + \frac{2}{4} = \frac{\square}{4}$

2 (a) Copy the rectangle on to squared paper. $\frac{3}{8}$ of it is shaded.
Now shade a further $\frac{2}{8}$ of it.
What fraction is shaded altogether?

(b) Copy and complete: $\frac{3}{8} + \frac{2}{8} = \frac{\square}{8}$

3 Draw rectangles on squared paper, and use shading to find the answers to the additions:

(a) $\frac{3}{10} + \frac{5}{10}$ (b) $\frac{1}{12} + \frac{4}{12}$

(c) $\frac{3}{16} + \frac{5}{16} + \frac{6}{16}$

4 Work out

(a) $\frac{7}{10} + \frac{2}{10}$ (b) $\frac{1}{6} + \frac{5}{6}$

(c) $\frac{5}{9} + \frac{3}{9}$ (d) $\frac{11}{20} + \frac{8}{20}$

(e) $\frac{9}{32} + \frac{6}{32}$ (f) $\frac{18}{50} + \frac{25}{50}$

5 Copy and complete:
To add fractions with the same ………, you add the ……… and put the answer over the original ……….

6 Calculate

(a) $\frac{3}{4} + \frac{3}{4}$ (b) $\frac{2}{3} + \frac{2}{3}$

(c) $\frac{5}{6} + \frac{1}{6}$ (d) $\frac{7}{12} + \frac{9}{12}$

(e) $\frac{3}{8} + \frac{5}{8} + \frac{1}{8}$ (f) $\frac{15}{16} + \frac{7}{16} + \frac{5}{16}$

Adding fractions with different denominators

- To add fractions with different denominators you must first use equivalent fractions to make the denominators the same.

Example 10

(a) $\frac{3}{5} + \frac{1}{10}$

$= \frac{6}{10} + \frac{1}{10}$

$= \frac{7}{10}$

$\left(\frac{3}{5} \overset{\times 2}{=} \frac{6}{10}\right)$ (×2)

(b) $\frac{3}{4} + \frac{2}{3}$

$= \frac{9}{12} + \frac{8}{12}$

$= \frac{17}{12} = 1\frac{5}{12}$

$\left(\frac{3}{4} \overset{\times 3}{=} \frac{9}{12},\ \frac{2}{3} \overset{\times 4}{=} \frac{8}{12}\right)$

(12 is the LCM of 4 and 3)

Exercise 3N

1 Copy and complete:

(a) $\frac{3}{5} + \frac{3}{10} = \frac{\square}{10} + \frac{3}{10} = \frac{\square}{10}$

(b) $\frac{1}{6} + \frac{2}{3} = \frac{1}{6} + \frac{\square}{6} = \frac{\square}{6}$

(c) $\frac{3}{4} + \frac{1}{8} = \frac{\square}{8} + \frac{1}{8} = \frac{\square}{8}$

(d) $\frac{5}{6} + \frac{1}{12} = \frac{\square}{12} + \frac{1}{12} = \frac{\square}{12}$

(e) $\frac{3}{8} + \frac{5}{16} = \frac{\square}{16} + \frac{5}{16} = \frac{\square}{16}$

2 Add these fractions.
Give each answer in its simplest form.

(a) $\frac{3}{10} + \frac{1}{5}$ (b) $\frac{2}{5} + \frac{1}{10}$

(c) $\frac{1}{5} + \frac{7}{10}$ (d) $\frac{1}{6} + \frac{5}{12}$

(e) $\frac{5}{6} + \frac{1}{12}$ (f) $\frac{2}{9} + \frac{2}{3}$

(g) $\frac{1}{4} + \frac{7}{16}$ (h) $\frac{5}{21} + \frac{3}{7}$

(i) $\frac{5}{9} + \frac{1}{3}$ (j) $\frac{5}{9} + \frac{5}{18}$

3 Copy and complete.

(a) $\frac{2}{3} + \frac{1}{2} = \frac{\square}{6} + \frac{\square}{6} = \frac{\square}{6}$

(b) $\frac{4}{5} + \frac{3}{8} = \frac{\square}{40} + \frac{\square}{40} = \frac{\square}{40}$

(c) $\frac{3}{8} + \frac{9}{12} = \frac{\square}{24} + \frac{\square}{24} = \frac{\square}{24}$

4 First find the LCM. Then do the addition.
Write the answer in its simplest form.

(a) $\frac{1}{3} + \frac{1}{2}$ (b) $\frac{1}{5} + \frac{5}{8}$ (c) $\frac{5}{8} + \frac{5}{12}$

(d) $\frac{1}{9} + \frac{5}{6}$ (e) $\frac{3}{5} + \frac{2}{7}$ (f) $\frac{4}{5} + \frac{2}{9}$

(g) $\frac{1}{4} + \frac{5}{7}$ (h) $\frac{1}{3} + \frac{6}{11}$ (i) $\frac{5}{12} + \frac{5}{9}$

5 (a) One-third of the students at Columbus School play cricket. Another quarter play football.
What fraction play either cricket or football?
(b) If the school has 240 students, how many play either cricket or football?

6 In a two-party election in the island of Sabrina, half of the electorate voted for the Democratic Party and two-fifths for the People's Alliance Party.
(a) What fraction of the electorate voted?
(b) What fraction did not vote?

3.6 Subtracting fractions

To subtract fractions with the same denominators, you subtract the numerators.

Example 11

Find: $\frac{7}{12} - \frac{5}{12}$

$$\frac{7}{12} - \frac{5}{12} = \frac{2}{12} = \frac{1}{6} \quad (\div 2)$$

When the denominators are different you have to make them the same using equivalent fractions.

Example 12

Work out: $\frac{3}{4} - \frac{2}{3}$
The denominators are 4 and 3
The LCM of 4 and 3 is 12

$$\frac{3}{4} - \frac{2}{3} \qquad \left(\frac{3}{4} \overset{\times 3}{=} \frac{9}{12}, \frac{2}{3} \overset{\times 4}{=} \frac{8}{12}\right)$$

$$= \frac{9}{12} - \frac{8}{12} = \frac{1}{12}$$

Exercise 3O

1 Copy and complete:

(a) $\frac{3}{5} - \frac{3}{10} = \frac{\square}{10} - \frac{3}{10} = \frac{\square}{10}$

(b) $\frac{2}{3} - \frac{1}{6} = \frac{\square}{6} - \frac{1}{6} = \frac{\square}{6}$

(c) $\frac{3}{4} - \frac{3}{8} = \frac{\square}{8} - \frac{3}{8} = \frac{\square}{8}$

(d) $\frac{5}{6} - \frac{5}{12} = \frac{\square}{12} - \frac{5}{12} = \frac{\square}{12}$

(e) $\frac{5}{8} - \frac{3}{16} = \frac{\square}{16} - \frac{3}{16} = \frac{\square}{16}$

2 Subtract these fractions.
Give each answer in its simplest form.

(a) $\frac{4}{5} - \frac{3}{10}$ (b) $\frac{3}{4} - \frac{1}{8}$

(c) $\frac{2}{3} - \frac{4}{9}$ (d) $\frac{5}{8} - \frac{1}{4}$

(e) $\frac{2}{3} - \frac{1}{6}$ (f) $\frac{7}{8} - \frac{3}{4}$

(g) $\frac{3}{4} - \frac{5}{12}$ (h) $\frac{5}{6} - \frac{1}{3}$

(i) $\frac{2}{5} - \frac{3}{20}$ (j) $\frac{7}{10} - \frac{2}{5}$

3 (a) Find the LCM of 3 and 4.
(b) Find equivalent fractions for $\frac{1}{3}$ and $\frac{3}{4}$ using the LCM as the denominator.
(c) Complete the subtraction: $\frac{3}{4} - \frac{1}{3} = \frac{\square}{12}$

4 Copy and complete:

(a) $\frac{1}{2} - \frac{1}{3} = \frac{\square}{6} - \frac{\square}{6} = \frac{\square}{6}$

(b) $\frac{2}{3} - \frac{1}{2} = \frac{\square}{6} - \frac{\square}{6} = \frac{\square}{6}$

(c) $\frac{1}{3} - \frac{1}{4} = \frac{\square}{12} - \frac{\square}{12} = \frac{\square}{12}$

(d) $\frac{3}{4} - \frac{2}{3} = \frac{\square}{12} - \frac{\square}{12} = \frac{\square}{12}$

(e) $\frac{5}{6} - \frac{3}{4} = \frac{\square}{12} - \frac{\square}{12} = \frac{\square}{12}$

5 Find the LCM of the denominators. Then do the subtraction.

(a) $\frac{1}{2} - \frac{1}{3}$ **(b)** $\frac{1}{4} - \frac{1}{8}$ **(c)** $\frac{1}{12} - \frac{1}{18}$

(d) $\frac{2}{3} - \frac{1}{2}$ **(e)** $\frac{5}{8} - \frac{3}{10}$ **(f)** $\frac{5}{6} - \frac{1}{4}$

(g) $\frac{5}{8} - \frac{5}{12}$ **(h)** $\frac{4}{5} - \frac{3}{8}$ **(i)** $\frac{5}{6} - \frac{2}{7}$

6 Leroy and Jake bought a pizza. Leroy ate $\frac{2}{3}$ of it. Jake ate $\frac{1}{5}$ of it. What fraction was left over?

7 After a project, Jackson had $4\frac{1}{2}$ bags of cement left. Delbert used $1\frac{2}{3}$ of these bags. How much cement did Jackson have left?

8 Find the value of $\otimes$ if

$$\frac{\otimes}{\otimes} - \frac{\otimes}{6} = \frac{\otimes}{12}$$

Investigation

A unit fraction is a fraction with a numerator of 1, for example:

$\frac{1}{2}, \frac{1}{3}, \frac{1}{4}, \frac{1}{17}, \frac{1}{26}$

The unit fraction $\frac{1}{2}$ can be written as the sum of two other different unit fractions:

$\frac{1}{2} = \frac{1}{3} + \frac{1}{6}$

Which other unit fractions can you write as sums of different unit fractions?

Are there any rules?

3.7 Multiplying fractions

You will need 24 identical quarter-circles, made from paper or thin card.

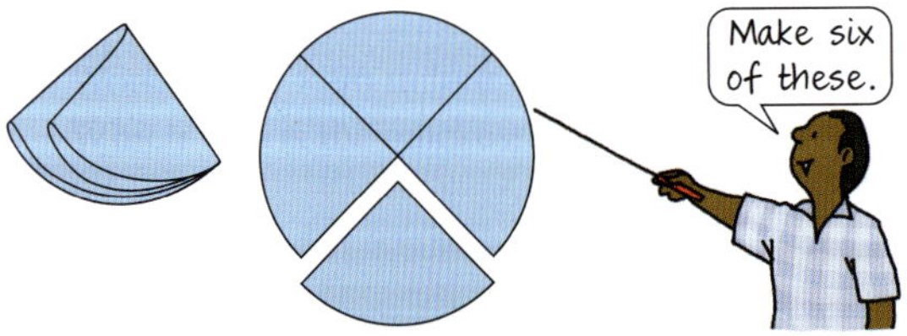

Multiplying fractions by whole numbers

Example 13

What is $3 \times \frac{3}{4}$?

Take three $\frac{3}{4}$-circles:

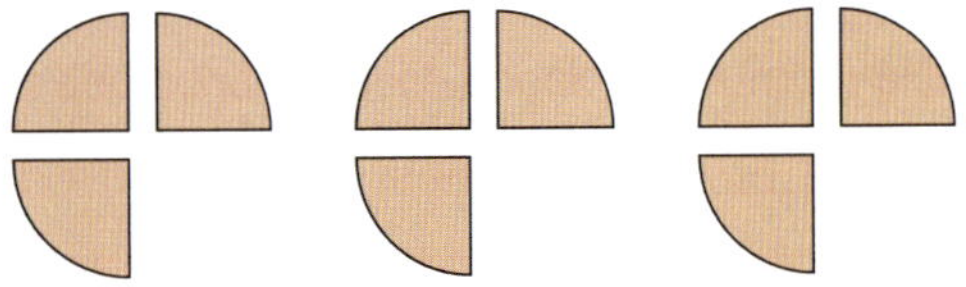

$\frac{3}{4}$ $\frac{3}{4}$ $\frac{3}{4}$

There are nine $\frac{1}{4}$-circles $= \frac{9}{4}$

so, $3 \times \frac{3}{4} = \frac{9}{4} = 2\frac{1}{4}$

Exercise 3P

1 **(a)** Take two $\frac{3}{4}$-circles. How many quarter-circles have you used?

(b) Copy and complete: $2 \times \frac{3}{4} = \frac{\square}{4}$

2 **(a)** Make up four $\frac{3}{4}$-circles. How many quarters have you used?

(b) Copy and complete: $4 \times \frac{3}{4} = \frac{\square}{4}$

3 Use your $\frac{1}{4}$-circles to make up $\frac{3}{4}$-circles.

(a) Copy and complete the table below.

Number of $\frac{3}{4}$-circles made	Number of $\frac{1}{4}$-circles used	The multiplication
1	3	$1 \times \frac{3}{4} = \frac{3}{4}$
2	6	$2 \times \frac{3}{4} = \frac{6}{4}$
3	9	$3 \times \frac{3}{4} = \frac{9}{4}$
4		
5		
6		
7		
8		

(b) Look at the last column in your table. Can you see a pattern?

(c) What numbers multiplied together give the numerator in the second fraction?

(d) What do you notice about the denominator in both fractions?

(e) Can you see a way of multiplying any fraction by a whole number?

- To multiply a fraction by a whole number you multiply the numerator by the whole number.

Example 14

Find (a) $\frac{3}{5} \times 4$ (b) $1\frac{3}{4} \times 4$ (c) $7 \times 5\frac{1}{3}$

(a) $\frac{3}{5} \times 4 = \frac{3 \times 4}{5} = \frac{12}{5} = 2\frac{2}{5}$

(b) $1\frac{3}{4} \times 4 = \frac{7}{4} \times 4$
$= \frac{28}{4}$
$= 7$

(c) $7 \times 5\frac{1}{3} = 7 \times \frac{16}{3}$
$= \frac{112}{3}$
$= 37\frac{1}{3}$

Exercise 3Q

1 Work out, using the method of Example 14:

(a) $\frac{1}{3} \times 4$ (b) $\frac{1}{4} \times 7$ (c) $\frac{1}{5} \times 9$
(d) $7 \times \frac{1}{3}$ (e) $\frac{1}{5} \times 6$ (f) $10 \times \frac{1}{8}$
(g) $\frac{1}{10} \times 12$ (h) $5 \times \frac{2}{3}$ (i) $7 \times \frac{3}{8}$

2 Work out:

(a) $\frac{1}{6} \times 13$ (b) $4 \times \frac{5}{8}$
(c) $\frac{4}{9} \times 3$ (d) $\frac{3}{11} \times 8$
(e) $6 \times \frac{7}{10}$ (f) $10 \times \frac{5}{12}$
(g) $\frac{2}{5} \times 14$ (h) $20 \times \frac{7}{12}$
(i) $\frac{4}{5} \times 72$ (j) $96 \times \frac{4}{17}$

3 Work out:

(a) $1\frac{2}{3} \times 6$ (b) $7 \times 2\frac{1}{6}$ (c) $5 \times 3\frac{1}{4}$
(d) $2\frac{1}{2} \times 8$ (e) $6\frac{1}{9} \times 12$ (f) $14 \times 5\frac{7}{8}$

4 Paula studies for $\frac{3}{4}$ hour each day.

How long does she study each week?

5 A box holds $1\frac{1}{2}$ kg of nails. What weight of nails do seven such boxes hold?

6

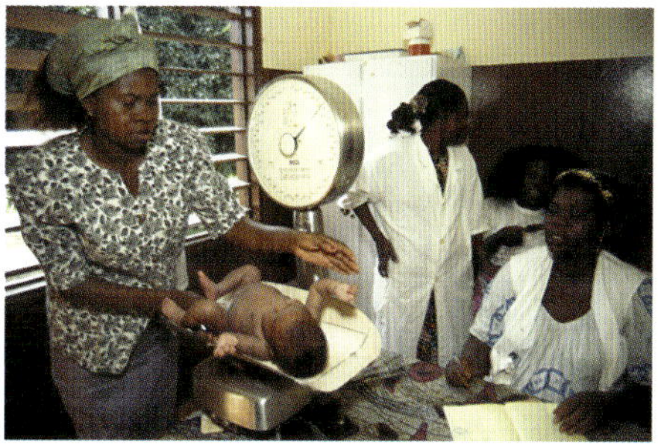

A kilogram is $2\frac{1}{5}$ lb. A baby weighs 6 kg. What is 6 kg in pounds?

7 Of 1800 voters only one-third voted in an election. How many did not vote?

8 What is the area of a rectangular yard that is $6\frac{1}{4}$ m long and 5 m wide?

Remember: Area of a rectangle = length × width.

9 Two-thirds of the children in a class are girls. Of these, $\frac{1}{4}$ wear glasses. If there are 24 children in the class how many girls wear glasses?

10 In the village of Lowcroft there are 630 people. Two-thirds of the villagers are under 16 and $\frac{4}{7}$ of these are girls.

(a) How many girls are under 16 in Lowcroft?

(b) How many boys are under 16?

Multiplying fractions by fractions

$\frac{3}{4}$ of this rectangle is shaded:

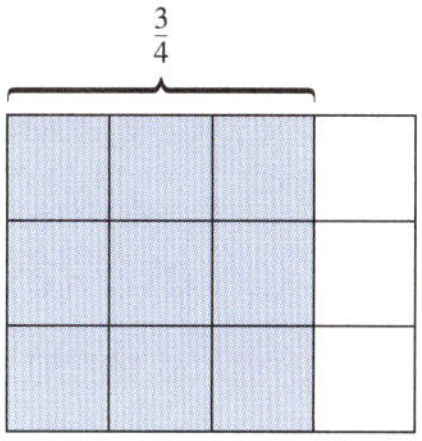

Now shade $\frac{1}{3}$ of the shaded part:

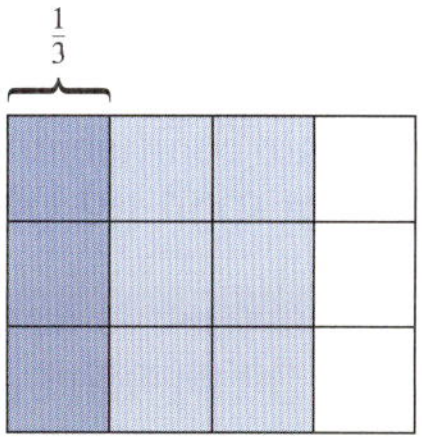

$\frac{3}{12}$ is shaded twice

so $\frac{1}{3}$ of $\frac{3}{4} = \frac{1}{3} \times \frac{3}{4} = \frac{3}{12}$

Exercise 3R

1 Use the diagrams to help you multiply the fractions.

(a) $\frac{1}{2}$

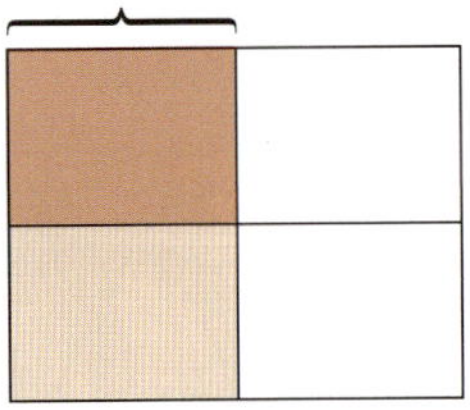

$\frac{1}{2}$ of $\frac{1}{2}$

(b) $\frac{1}{2}$

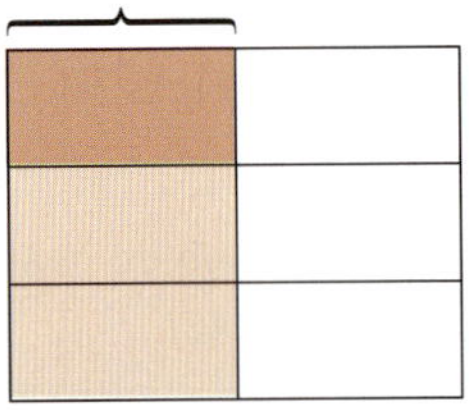

$\frac{1}{3}$ of $\frac{1}{2}$

(c) $\frac{2}{3}$

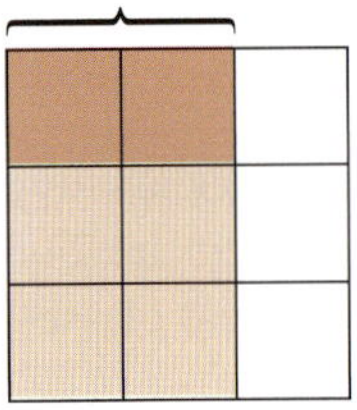

$\frac{1}{3}$ of $\frac{2}{3}$

(d) $\frac{3}{5}$

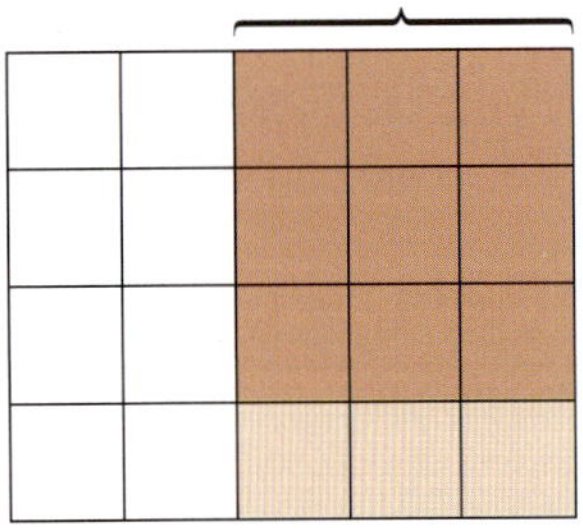

$\frac{3}{4}$ of $\frac{3}{5}$

(e) $\frac{1}{2}$

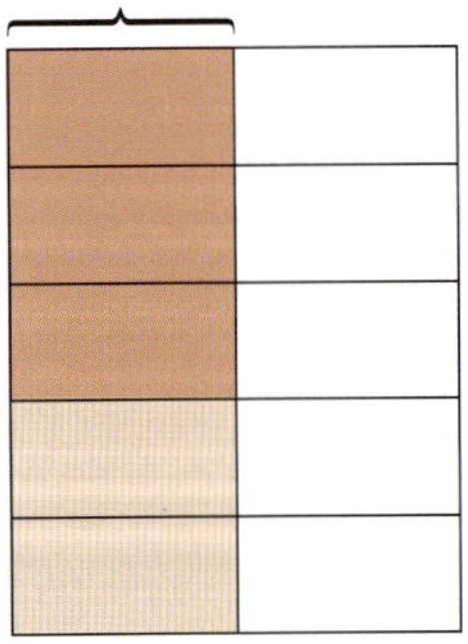

$\frac{3}{5}$ of $\frac{1}{2}$

Example 15

Work out $\frac{3}{4} \times \frac{2}{3}$

$\frac{3}{4} \times \frac{2}{3} = \frac{{}^{1}\cancel{3} \times \cancel{2}^{1}}{{}_{2}\cancel{4} \times \cancel{3}_{1}}$

$= \frac{1 \times 1}{2 \times 1}$

$= \frac{1}{2}$

Example 16

Work out

(a) $\frac{2}{3} \times 1\frac{2}{5}$

(b) $1\frac{3}{4} \times 2\frac{2}{3}$

(a) $\frac{2}{3} \times 1\frac{2}{5} = \frac{2}{3} \times \frac{7}{5} = \frac{14}{15}$

(b) $1\frac{3}{4} \times 2\frac{2}{3} = \frac{7}{4} \times \frac{8}{3}$

$= \frac{7 \times \cancel{8}^{2}}{{}_{1}\cancel{4} \times 3}$

$= \frac{14}{3}$

$= 4\frac{2}{3}$

Exercise 3S

1 Look for a common factor. Then do the multiplication.

(a) $\frac{1}{5} \times \frac{10}{19}$ **(b)** $\frac{3}{16} \times \frac{24}{27}$

(c) $\frac{4}{13} \times \frac{52}{60}$ **(d)** $\frac{11}{21} \times \frac{14}{17}$

(e) $\frac{5}{19} \times \frac{2}{15}$ **(f)** $\frac{4}{9} \times \frac{27}{28}$

2 Work out:

(a) $\frac{5}{9} \times 1\frac{1}{2}$ **(b)** $2\frac{1}{4} \times \frac{1}{3}$

(c) $4\frac{1}{3} \times \frac{2}{3}$ **(d)** $\frac{1}{5} \times 2\frac{4}{7}$

(e) $\frac{5}{8} \times 1\frac{3}{4}$ **(f)** $2\frac{2}{3} \times 1\frac{4}{5}$

(g) $2\frac{1}{2} \times 1\frac{1}{4}$ **(h)** $4\frac{1}{5} \times 2\frac{1}{3}$

3 Expressing your answers in their simplest form, work out:

(a) $\frac{5}{9} \times \frac{1}{3} \times 3$ **(b)** $\frac{6}{7} \times \frac{3}{11} \times 4$

(c) $\frac{8}{9} \times \frac{2}{5} \times 4\frac{1}{2}$ **(d)** $1\frac{1}{3} \times \frac{3}{4} \times \frac{5}{6}$

(e) $2\frac{3}{8} \times \frac{2}{5} \times \frac{1}{2}$ **(f)** $\frac{5}{7} \times \frac{1}{5} \times 3\frac{1}{2}$

4 A piece of cloth is $4\frac{1}{2}$ m long. Connie used $\frac{2}{5}$ of it. What length did she use?

5 It takes $3\frac{3}{4}$ hours to plaster a wall. One third of this time is spent mixing the plaster. How long does the actual plastering take?

6 It is $2\frac{1}{2}$ km from Frank's home to school.
Each day he walks one fifth of the way and takes a bus for the rest of the journey.
How far does he walk each week?

Investigation

Some things look wrong, even though they are correct:

For example:
$2 - \frac{2}{3} = 2 \times \frac{2}{3}$

(a) Is this correct?
(b) How about:
$5 - \frac{4}{5}$ and $5 \times \frac{4}{5}$?
(c) Can you find other fractions that work?
Any rules?

3.8 Dividing fractions

You will need the quarter-circles you used for the last section.

Dividing whole numbers by fractions

You can divide a number by a fraction.

For example:
what is $2 \div \frac{1}{4}$?

One way of working this out is to ask how many quarter-circles make 2 circles.

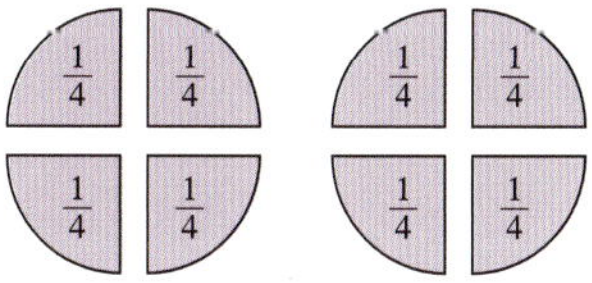

8 quarters = 2

So $2 \div \frac{1}{4} = 8$.

Exercise 3T

1 **(a)** Using quarter-circles, make up 6 circles.
How many quarter-circles are in 6 circles?
Copy and complete: $6 \div \frac{1}{4} = \square$

(b) From your 6 circles make $\frac{3}{4}$-circles.
How many $\frac{3}{4}$-circles can you make from 6 circles?
Copy and complete: $6 \div \frac{3}{4} = \square$

2 **(a)** Using quarter-circles, make up 9 circles.
How many quarter-circles are in 9 circles?
Copy and complete: $9 \div \frac{1}{4} = \square$

(b) From your 9 circles make up $\frac{3}{4}$-circles. How many $\frac{3}{4}$-circles can you make from 9 circles?
Copy and complete: $9 \div \frac{3}{4} = \square$

3 Look at your answers to Question 1.
$6 \div \frac{1}{4} = 24$
$6 \div \frac{3}{4} = 8$

(a) There are 24 quarter-circles in 6 circles.
What number could you have *multiplied* 6 by, to get 24?
Copy and complete:
$6 \div \frac{1}{4} = 6 \times \square = 24$

(b) What number should you *divide* 24 by, to find how many $\frac{3}{4}$-circles there are in 24 quarter-circles?
Copy and complete:
$6 \div \frac{3}{4} = \frac{6 \times 4}{\square} = 8$

4 Look at your answers to Question 2.
$9 \div \frac{1}{4} = 36$
$9 \div \frac{3}{4} = 12$

(a) There are 36 quarter-circles in 9 circles.
What number could you have *multiplied* 9 by, to give 36?
Copy and complete:
$9 \div \frac{1}{4} = 9 \times \square = 36$

(b) To find how many $\frac{3}{4}$-circles are in 36 quarter-circles, what number should you *divide* 36 by?
Copy and complete:
$9 \div \frac{3}{4} = \frac{9 \times 4}{\square} = 12$

5 Look at some of the answers to Questions 3 and 4:
$6 \div \frac{1}{4} = 6 \times 4 = 24$
$6 \div \frac{3}{4} = \frac{6 \times 4}{3} = 8$
$9 \div \frac{1}{4} = 9 \times 4 = 36$
$9 \div \frac{3}{4} = \frac{9 \times 4}{3} = 12$
Can you see the pattern?
Can you see a way to divide a whole number by a fraction? Explain.

- To divide a whole number by a fraction you turn the fraction upside down and multiply.

Example 17

Work out:

(a) $2 \div \frac{3}{4}$ (b) $6 \div 1\frac{1}{2}$

(a) $2 \div \frac{3}{4} = 2 \times \frac{4}{3}$
$= \frac{8}{3}$
$= 2\frac{2}{3}$

(b) $6 \div 1\frac{1}{2} = 6 \div \frac{3}{2}$
$= 6 \times \frac{2}{3}$
$= \frac{{}^{2}\cancel{6}}{1} \times \frac{2}{\cancel{3}_{1}}$
$= 4$

Exercise 3U

1 Copy and complete:

(a) $4 \div \frac{2}{3} = 4 \times \frac{3}{2} = \frac{4 \times 3}{2} = \frac{12}{2} = \square$

(b) $10 \div \frac{2}{5} = 10 \times \frac{5}{2} = \frac{\square}{\square} = \square$

(c) $10 \div \frac{4}{5} = 10 \times \frac{5}{4} = \frac{\square}{\square} = \square$

(d) $5 \div \frac{3}{4} = 5 \times \frac{4}{3} = \frac{\square}{\square} = \square$

(e) $8 \div 1\frac{3}{4} = 8 \div \frac{7}{4} = 8 \times \frac{4}{7} = \frac{\square}{\square} = \square$

2 Do the division and write the answer in its simplest form.

(a) $5 \div \frac{1}{9}$ (b) $4 \div \frac{3}{4}$ (c) $6 \div \frac{2}{3}$
(d) $8 \div \frac{5}{6}$ (e) $9 \div \frac{3}{4}$ (f) $7 \div \frac{7}{9}$

3 Change the mixed number to an improper fraction, then do the division.

(a) $6 \div 1\frac{1}{4}$ (b) $4 \div 1\frac{1}{2}$ (c) $9 \div 1\frac{5}{6}$
(d) $7 \div 2\frac{3}{8}$ (e) $10 \div 3\frac{4}{5}$ (f) $8 \div 2\frac{5}{11}$

4 How many half litre bottles of juice can you get from a $10\frac{1}{2}$ litre container?

5 I have 12 oranges.
How many people can I give $\frac{2}{3}$ of an orange to?

6 Andrew uses $\frac{2}{5}$ of a bag of fertiliser each week.
How long will one bag of fertiliser last?

7 Which is the better value:
$\frac{3}{4}$ kg of soap powder for $9
or $\frac{2}{3}$ kg of soap powder for $8?

Dividing fractions by fractions

- To divide a fraction by a fraction you turn the second fraction upside down and multiply.

Example 18

Work out $\frac{3}{4} \div \frac{5}{6}$

$\frac{3}{4} \div \frac{5}{6} = \frac{3}{4} \times \frac{6}{5}$
$= \frac{3 \times \cancel{6}^{3}}{{}_{2}\cancel{4} \times 5}$
$= \frac{9}{10}$

Turn mixed numbers into improper fractions before you divide.

Example 19

Find

(a) how many thirds in $1\frac{5}{8}$
(b) $2\frac{1}{2} \div 1\frac{1}{8}$

(a) $1\frac{5}{8} \div \frac{1}{3} = \frac{13}{8} \div \frac{1}{3}$
$= \frac{13 \times 3}{8 \times 1}$
$= \frac{39}{8}$
$= 4\frac{7}{8}$

(b) $2\frac{1}{2} \div 1\frac{1}{8} = \frac{5}{2} \div \frac{9}{8}$
$= \frac{5}{2} \times \frac{8}{9}$
$= \frac{5}{{}_{1}\cancel{2}} \times \frac{\cancel{8}^{4}}{9}$ (cancel)
$= \frac{20}{9}$
$= 2\frac{2}{9}$

Exercise 3V

1 Do the division.

(a) $\frac{1}{6} \div \frac{1}{4}$ (b) $\frac{3}{5} \div \frac{10}{11}$ (c) $\frac{3}{8} \div \frac{2}{5}$
(d) $\frac{2}{5} \div \frac{3}{8}$ (e) $\frac{1}{7} \div \frac{3}{4}$ (f) $\frac{6}{7} \div \frac{3}{8}$

2 Change the mixed number to an improper fraction. Do the division.

(a) $1\frac{2}{3} \div \frac{3}{4}$ (b) $3\frac{1}{5} \div \frac{2}{5}$ (c) $2\frac{4}{5} \div \frac{7}{11}$
(d) $2\frac{1}{4} \div 1\frac{2}{3}$ (e) $6\frac{1}{3} \div 1\frac{1}{2}$ (f) $\frac{7}{8} \div 1\frac{1}{4}$
(g) $\frac{3}{4} \div 6$ (h) $1\frac{5}{8} \div 7$ (i) $2\frac{1}{2} \div 5$

3 Find the number of twentieths in the fraction:

(a) $\frac{1}{2}$ (b) $\frac{3}{2}$ (c) $\frac{2}{5}$
(d) $\frac{1}{10}$ (e) $\frac{3}{10}$ (f) $\frac{7}{10}$

4 Find the number of eighths in the fraction:

(a) $\frac{1}{3}$ (b) $\frac{2}{3}$ (c) $\frac{1}{4}$
(d) $\frac{7}{8}$ (e) $\frac{9}{10}$ (f) $\frac{5}{12}$

5 Study this example.

$\frac{3}{5} \div \frac{2}{3} = \frac{9}{15} \div \frac{10}{15}$ $\quad (\frac{3}{5} = \frac{9}{15}, \frac{2}{3} = \frac{10}{15})$

$= \frac{9 \div 10}{15 \div 15} = \frac{9 \div 10}{1}$

$= 9 \div 10 = \frac{9}{10}$

(a) Use the method to work out:

(i) $\frac{3}{4} \div \frac{4}{5}$ **(ii)** $\frac{2}{3} \div \frac{1}{6}$ **(iii)** $\frac{4}{7} \div \frac{5}{8}$

(iv) $1\frac{3}{4} \div \frac{4}{5}$ **(v)** $1\frac{3}{4} \div 1\frac{4}{5}$ **(vi)** $2\frac{3}{7} \div 4\frac{2}{7}$

(b) Do you prefer this method of dividing fractions? Why?

(c) Do the divisions in Question 1 using this method. Did you get the same answers as before?

6 Janice bought $6\frac{1}{2}$ metres of cloth. She used $1\frac{1}{4}$ metres. What fraction did she use?

7 $7\frac{1}{2}$ kg of coffee are put into $\frac{1}{4}$ kg bags. How many bags will be needed?

8 A tin holds $5\frac{1}{2}$ litres of oil. How many $\frac{2}{3}$ litre cans can be filled from it?

9 A piece of wood is $4\frac{1}{3}$ metres long. How many $1\frac{1}{4}$ metre strips can be cut from it?

10 A man's work day is $8\frac{1}{2}$ hours. He spends $3\frac{1}{4}$ hours dealing with customers and the remaining time working in his office.

(a) What fraction of his day does he spend with customers?

(b) What fraction of his day is he in his office?

11 A man spends $\frac{2}{7}$ of his weekly wage on food and $\frac{2}{5}$ on rent. If he spends \$200 on food, how much does he spend on rent?

Technology

Need to review?

You can find a complete course on fractions at the website

www.aaaknow.com/fra.htm

Simply click on the section or sections that you need help on. There are also plenty of practice materials and opportunities to race against the clock!

Another good site is

www.coolmath.com/prealgebra

Have fun!

3.9 Problem solving

Solving problems involving fractions is very much like solving problems involving whole numbers. The stages are similar.

- Read the problem carefully.
- Work out what you are being asked to do.
- Draw a diagram or make a table or look for a pattern.
- Answer the problem.
  Check your answer makes sense.

Exercise 3W – mixed questions

1 How do you spend a school day?

(a) Write down all the things you do each school day: sleeping, playing and so on.

(b) Next to each activity put the number of hours you spend doing it.

(c) Make sure your total for all activities is 24 hours.

(d) Using a suitable key, copy and complete the rectangle below representing your day. You will need to make it larger.

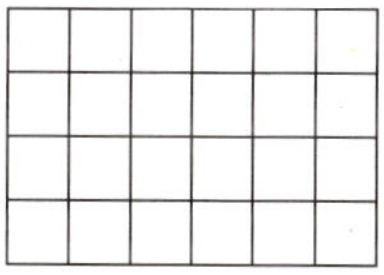

 represents 1 hour

(e) What activity takes up the largest fraction of your school day?

2 Repeat Question 1 for a Sunday.

3 **(a)** How many lessons do you have each week?

(b) Write down all the subjects you study in school.

(c) Next to each subject write down the number of lessons in that subject that you attend each week.

(d) Make sure your total in part (c) is the same as your answer to part (a).

(e) What fraction of your school week is spent on each subject?

(f) Draw, with a key, a diagram to show this information.

4 Here are three ways of dividing the number line between 1 and 2.

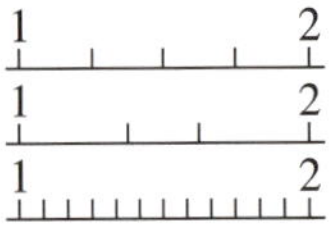

(a) Copy the lines and mark the positions of the numbers:
$1\frac{1}{2}$, $1\frac{3}{4}$, $1\frac{2}{3}$, $1\frac{7}{10}$, $1\frac{4}{10}$
Use the positions of the numbers to put them in order starting with the smallest.

(b) Draw two lines to help you decide which is greater, $1\frac{13}{20}$ or $1\frac{5}{8}$.

5 Draw a number line like this.

Mark in the approximate positions of the numbers: $\frac{1}{2}, \frac{1}{3}, \frac{3}{4}, \frac{2}{5}$

6 Peter scored 14 out of 20 in a maths test. He scored 20 out of 30 in an English test. Which was the better mark?

7 Mr Cenac saves $\frac{2}{7}$ of what he earns. What fraction of his earnings does he spend?

8

Beverly buys 28 grapefruits.
Her sister Ann-Marie takes half of them and her friend Patsy eats $\frac{1}{7}$ of the remainder.

How many grapefruits does Beverly have left?

9 When Albert had sold one-third of his fowls he had 18 fowls left. How many fowls did he have to start with?

10 **(a)** $\frac{1}{4}$ of Denise's weekly wage is spent on rent and $\frac{1}{3}$ on food. What fraction does she have left?

(b) If she has \$60 left over, what was her weekly wage?

11 A length of string is 35 cm long. It is cut into six equal pieces. How long is each piece?

12 A barrel of rum holds 50 litres.

How many bottles each holding $\frac{3}{4}$ litre can be filled from the barrel?

13 A plank of wood is $1\frac{1}{2}$ cm thick. How thick is a pile of 25 planks?

14 A book with 150 pages is $7\frac{1}{2}$ mm thick. How thick is each page?

15 A bag of flour weighs $50\frac{2}{3}$ kg. What is the weight of 10 bags?

Investigation

There are many ways of dividing fractions to give the answer $\frac{2}{3}$.

Here are two of the ways:

$$\frac{4}{9} \div \frac{2}{3} = \frac{2}{3}$$

$$\frac{3}{5} \div \frac{9}{10} = \frac{2}{3}$$

What other fraction pairs when divided give $\frac{2}{3}$ as an answer?

How many can you find?

Are there any rules?

Investigate further.

3 Consolidation

Example 1

What fraction of each shape is shaded?

(a) 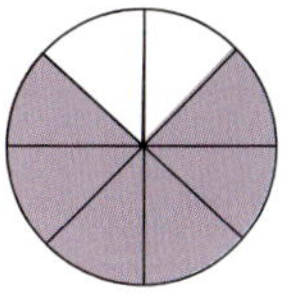 **(b)** 

(a) 6 parts out of 8 equal parts are shaded, so $\frac{6}{8}$ is shaded.

(b) 7 parts out of 12 equal parts are shaded, so $\frac{7}{12}$ is shaded.

Example 2

John has \$15 and spends $\frac{1}{4}$ of it on books.
How much does he have left?

$$\frac{1}{4} \times 15 = \frac{1}{4} \times \frac{15}{1} = \frac{15}{4} = 3.75$$

$$15 - 3.75 = 11.25$$

John has \$11.25 left.

Example 3

Write $\frac{32}{60}$ in its simplest form.

$$\frac{32}{60} = \frac{32 \div 2}{60 \div 2} = \frac{16}{30} = \frac{16 \div 2}{30 \div 2} = \frac{8}{15}$$

Example 4

Work out:

(a) $\frac{4}{9} + \frac{1}{3}$ **(b)** $\frac{3}{4} - \frac{2}{5}$ **(c)** $1\frac{1}{2} \times 2\frac{1}{4}$

(d) $1\frac{3}{5} \div 2\frac{1}{4}$

(a) $\frac{4}{9} + \frac{1}{3} = \frac{4}{9} + \frac{3}{9} = \frac{7}{9}$ (LCM of 9 and 3 is 9)

(b) $\frac{3}{4} - \frac{2}{5} = \frac{15}{20} - \frac{8}{20} = \frac{7}{20}$ (LCM of 4 and 5 is 20)

(c) $1\frac{1}{2} \times 2\frac{1}{4} = \frac{3}{2} \times \frac{9}{4} - \frac{3 \times 9}{2 \times 4} = \frac{27}{8} = 3\frac{3}{8}$

(d) $1\frac{3}{5} \div 2\frac{1}{4} = \frac{8}{5} \div \frac{9}{4} = \frac{8}{5} \times \frac{4}{9} = \frac{32}{45}$ (Note that $\div \frac{9}{4}$ is the same as $\times \frac{4}{9}$)

Exercise 3

1 Write down the fraction of each shape that is shaded.

(a) 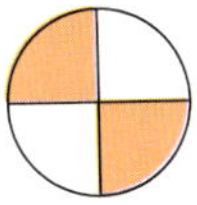 **(b)** 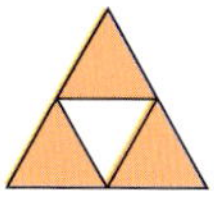 **(c)** 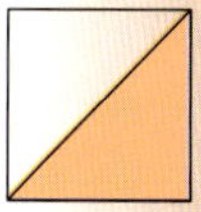

2 Calculate:

(a) $\frac{9}{10}$ of \$40 **(b)** $\frac{3}{4}$ of 28 gallons

(c) $\frac{7}{20}$ of 140 students **(d)** $\frac{2}{3}$ of 66 days

3 Copy and complete these equivalent fractions.

(a) $\frac{3}{4} = \frac{}{12}$ **(b)** $\frac{2}{5} = \frac{}{30}$

(c) $\frac{6}{10} = \frac{}{100}$ **(d)** $\frac{4}{25} = \frac{16}{}$

4 Calculate:

(a) $\frac{3}{4} + \frac{3}{4}$ **(b)** $\frac{3}{4} + \frac{2}{5}$

(c) $\frac{7}{8} + 1\frac{3}{4}$ **(d)** $2\frac{3}{4} + 1\frac{7}{8}$

(e) $\frac{3}{5} - \frac{1}{3}$ **(f)** $\frac{7}{8} - \frac{3}{5}$

(g) $1\frac{2}{3} - 1\frac{1}{2}$ **(h)** $2\frac{1}{3} - 1\frac{3}{4}$

5 Calculate:

(a) $\frac{2}{3} \times \frac{3}{5}$ **(b)** $\frac{4}{5} \times 1\frac{1}{2}$

(c) $2\frac{1}{4} \times 3\frac{2}{3}$ **(d)** $7\frac{1}{2} \times 1\frac{1}{3}$

(e) $\frac{2}{5} \div \frac{4}{5}$ **(f)** $\frac{3}{7} \div \frac{3}{5}$

(g) $1\frac{1}{3} \div 1\frac{1}{2}$ **(h)** $4\frac{3}{4} \div 2\frac{1}{3}$

Application 3

6 There are 260 girls and 240 boys at Weston High School. Calculate how many students each statement represents.

(a) $\frac{2}{3}$ of the boys come to school by bike.

(b) $\frac{3}{10}$ of the girls eat school dinners.

(c) All of the boys and $\frac{1}{5}$ of the girls wear ties.

(d) $\frac{3}{10}$ of the girls and $\frac{4}{10}$ of the boys play on a school team.

(e) $\frac{11}{100}$ of the students are left-handed.

7 Janice walked $5\frac{1}{2}$ km in $1\frac{1}{4}$ hours. What was her speed?

8 The drawing shows the fuel gauge in Ray's car. When full the fuel tank holds 120 litres.

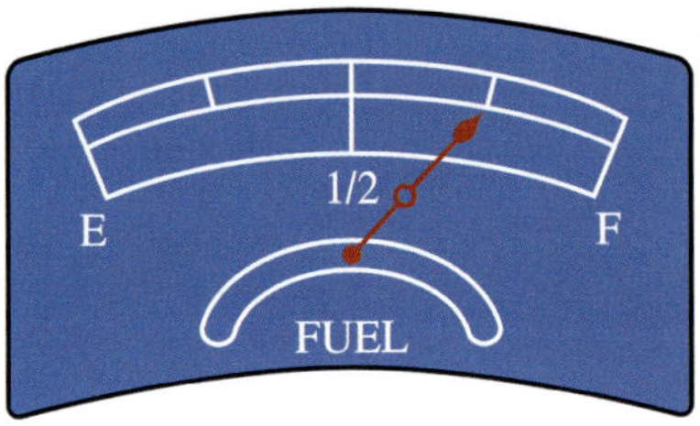

(a) How much fuel does the tank hold now?

(b) After travelling 80 km, Ray noticed his tank was half full. How much fuel did he use?

Companion CD

Want some extra practice? Go to Chapter 3 on your companion CD for further exercises, animations, and solutions.

Summary

You should know ...

1 You can show fractions using diagrams.
For example:

$\frac{3}{4}$ of the square is shaded

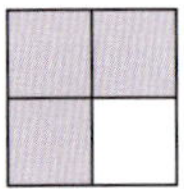

2 You can find a fraction of an amount by first dividing.
For example: to find $\frac{2}{3}$ of 15

$\frac{1}{3}$ of 15 = 15 ÷ 3 = 5

So $\frac{2}{3}$ of 15 = 2 × 5 = 10

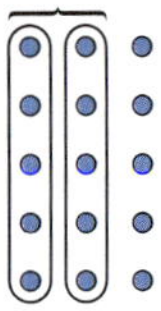

Check out

1 Write as a fraction the part of the shape that is shaded.

(a)

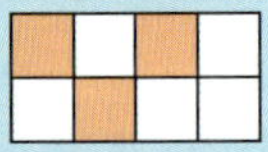

(b)

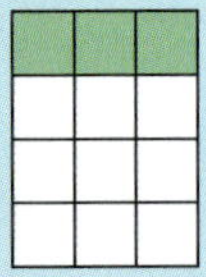

Draw a picture to show the fractions

(c) $\frac{2}{3}$ **(d)** $\frac{5}{6}$

2 Work out

(a) $\frac{1}{3}$ of 30 **(b)** $\frac{3}{4}$ of 28

(c) Sherry drank $\frac{2}{3}$ of a bottle of soft drink. The bottle held 360 ml. How much did she drink?

3 Equivalent fractions show the same fraction using different numbers:

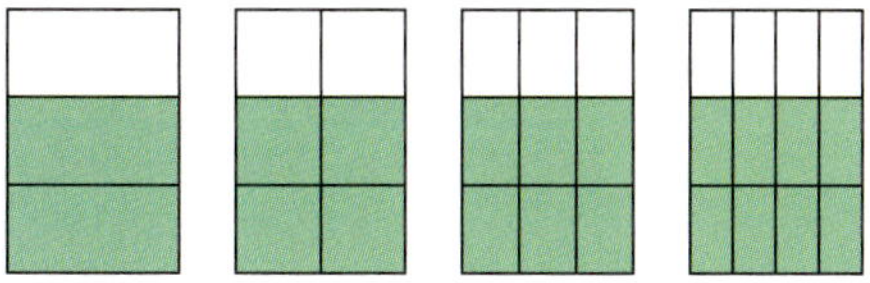

$\frac{2}{3} = \frac{4}{6}$ $\frac{6}{9} = \frac{8}{12}$

You can simplify some fractions by dividing:

$$\frac{48}{72} \overset{\div 4}{=} \frac{12}{18} \overset{\div 6}{=} \frac{2}{3}$$

2 and 3 have no common factor so $\frac{2}{3}$ is in its simplest form

4 A mixed number is made up of a whole number and a fraction.
For example: $2\frac{3}{4}$

An improper fraction has a numerator bigger than its denominator.
For example: $\frac{7}{4}$

The improper fraction $\frac{13}{5} = 2$ rem $3 = 2\frac{3}{5}$ (a mixed number).
The mixed number $3\frac{2}{3} = \frac{3 \times 3 + 2}{3} = \frac{11}{3}$ (an improper fraction).

5 You can add and subtract fractions when they have the same denominator.

When the denominators are different you have to make them the same using equivalent fractions.
For example:

$\frac{1}{6} + \frac{3}{8} = \frac{4}{24} + \frac{9}{24} = \frac{13}{24}$

The LCM of 6 and 8 is 24.

3 Copy and complete:
(a) $\frac{3}{4} = \frac{\square}{12}$
(b) $\frac{2}{3} = \frac{\square}{24}$
(c) Write these fractions in their simplest form:
(i) $\frac{16}{24}$ **(ii)** $\frac{25}{45}$

4 **(a)** Write as mixed numbers:
(i) $\frac{11}{3}$ **(ii)** $\frac{17}{5}$
(b) Write as improper fractions:
(i) $2\frac{1}{2}$ **(ii)** $4\frac{2}{5}$

5 Add these fractions:
(a) $\frac{1}{6} + \frac{5}{6}$ (b) $\frac{2}{5} + \frac{1}{10}$
(c) Sandra had half a cake.
Tessa ate one-third of it.
What fraction did Sandra have left?

6 How to multiply by fractions.

For example:

(a) $6 \times \frac{3}{4} = \frac{6 \times 3}{4} = \frac{18}{4} = 4\frac{2}{4} = 4\frac{1}{2}$

(b) $\frac{2}{7} \times \frac{3}{4} = \frac{2 \times 3}{7 \times 4} = \frac{6}{28} = \frac{3}{14}$

6 **(a)** Calculate:

(i) $3 \times \frac{1}{2}$ **(ii)** $6 \times \frac{2}{3}$

(iii) $\frac{3}{4} \times 8$ **(iv)** $\frac{2}{3} \times \frac{3}{4}$

(v) $\frac{3}{10} \times 1\frac{1}{2}$ **(vi)** $2\frac{1}{2} \times \frac{3}{5}$

(b) Kathy ate $\frac{3}{4}$ of a box of cornflakes. The box holds 152 g. What mass of cornflakes remains?

7 You should try to cancel your fractions before multiplying to save working.

For example:

$\frac{6}{25} \times 3\frac{1}{3} = \frac{6}{25} \times \frac{10}{3} = \frac{{}^{2}\cancel{6} \times \cancel{10}^{2}}{{}_{5}\cancel{25} \times \cancel{3}_{1}} = \frac{2 \times 2}{5 \times 1} = \frac{4}{5}$

7 Cancel, then work out:

(a) $\frac{2}{3} \times 1\frac{1}{2}$ **(b)** $\frac{3}{5} \times \frac{5}{6}$

(c) $2\frac{3}{4} \times \frac{3}{22}$ **(d)** $3\frac{1}{2} \times 2\frac{3}{7}$

8 To divide a fraction by a fraction, you turn over the second one and multiply.

For example

$$\frac{3}{4} \div \frac{2}{5} = \frac{3}{4} \times \frac{5}{2} = \frac{3 \times 5}{4 \times 2} = \frac{15}{8} = 1\frac{7}{8}$$

8 **(a)** Work out:

(i) $6 \div \frac{1}{2}$ **(ii)** $3\frac{1}{2} \div \frac{1}{2}$

(iii) $\frac{2}{3} \div \frac{3}{4}$ **(iv)** $3\frac{4}{5} \div 2\frac{2}{3}$

(b) How many $5\frac{1}{2}$ cm pieces of pipe can be cut from a pipe 66 cm long?

Decimals 4

Objectives

- ✔ write numbers as decimals
- ✔ represent decimals on a number line
- ✔ compare and order decimals
- ✔ add and subtract decimals
- ✔ multiply and divide decimals
- ✔ use a calculator to work with decimals

What's the point?

Decimals are used to make accurate measurements. When Usain Bolt broke World Records at the 2009 World Athletics Championships in Berlin his times were measured to two places of decimals.

Before you start

You should know ...

1 A fraction can be shown by a picture:

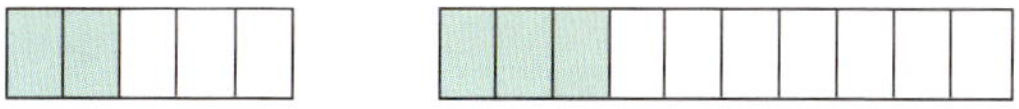

$\frac{2}{5}$ is shaded $\frac{3}{10}$ is shaded

2 Equivalent fractions are equal fractions.

For example,

$\frac{3}{4} = \frac{6}{8} = \frac{9}{12} = \frac{12}{16}$

3 How to add fractions:

$\frac{3}{5} + \frac{1}{10} = \frac{6}{10} + \frac{1}{10} = \frac{7}{10}$

Check in

1 **(a)** What fraction of each shape is shaded?

(i)

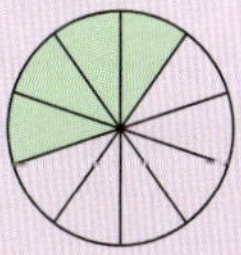

(ii)

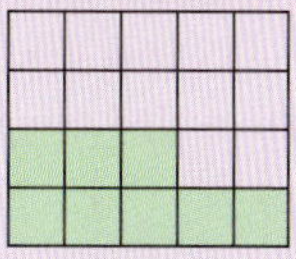

(b) Draw shapes to represent

(i) $\frac{2}{10}$ **(ii)** $\frac{16}{100}$

2 Copy and complete:

(a) $\frac{2}{5} = \frac{\square}{10}$ **(b)** $\frac{9}{10} = \frac{\square}{100}$

3 Work out:

(a) $\frac{3}{10} + \frac{5}{10}$ **(b)** $\frac{3}{10} + \frac{7}{100}$

4.1 Decimals

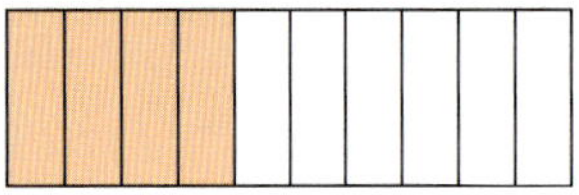

$\frac{4}{10}$ of the rectangle is shaded.
Tenths can be written a shorter way:

$\frac{4}{10}$ = 0 . 4

no units — decimal point — 4 tenths

0.4 is the **decimal form** for the fraction $\frac{4}{10}$.

The . is called the **decimal point**.
It separates the whole numbers from the tenths.

Example 1

Write as decimals
(a) $2\frac{3}{10}$ **(b)** $6\frac{7}{10}$

(a) $2\frac{3}{10} = 2.3$

(b) $6\frac{7}{10} = 6.7$

Exercise 4A

1 Write these fractions in decimal form.
(a) $\frac{3}{10}$ **(b)** $\frac{6}{10}$ **(c)** $\frac{9}{10}$ **(d)** $1\frac{2}{10}$
(e) $2\frac{8}{10}$ **(f)** $3\frac{4}{10}$ **(g)** $12\frac{1}{10}$ **(h)** $132\frac{5}{10}$

2 Write, first as a fraction, then as a decimal the part of each shape that is shaded:

(a)  **(b)** 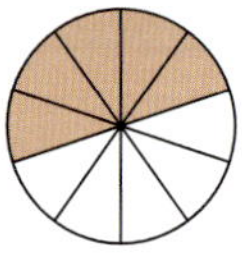

(c)  **(d)** 

3 Write in order of size, smallest first.
(a) 0.3, 0.6, 0.2, 0.8
(b) 0.9, 0.5, 1, 0
(c) 2.1, 0.6, 0.9, 1.8
(d) 9, 13.2, 0.2, 6.9

4 What number is $\frac{1}{10}$ more than
(a) 0.3 **(b)** 0.7 **(c)** 0.9
(d) 1 **(e)** 2.9 **(f)** 6

5 Four boys ran a 100 metre race.
Delbert ran the race in 12.3 seconds.
Jason was 1 tenth of a second slower than Delbert.
Fitzroy was 3 tenths of a second slower than Delbert.
Earlson was 5 tenths of a second faster than Fitzroy.
(a) Who won the race?
(b) How long did Earlson take?

Representing decimals on a number line

This number line has been divided into tenths.

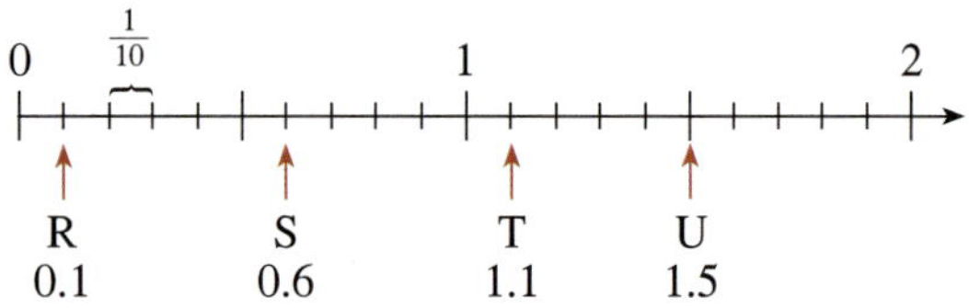

The distance between each division is **one** tenth.
The point R is one tenth from 0, R = 0.1
The point S is six tenths from 0, S = 0.6
The point T is one tenth from 1, T = 1.1
The point U is five tenths from 1, U = 1.5

Example 2

(a) Show the point 0.8 on the number line.
(b) Write the point X as a decimal.

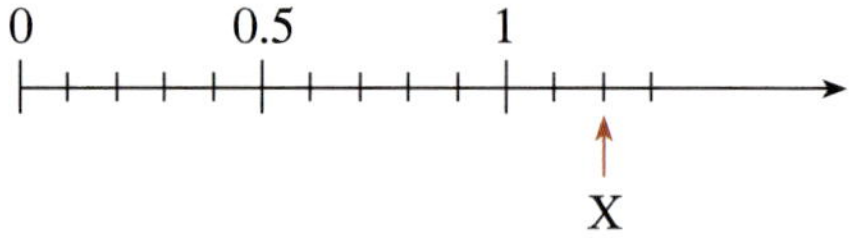

(a) 0.8 is eights tenths from 0

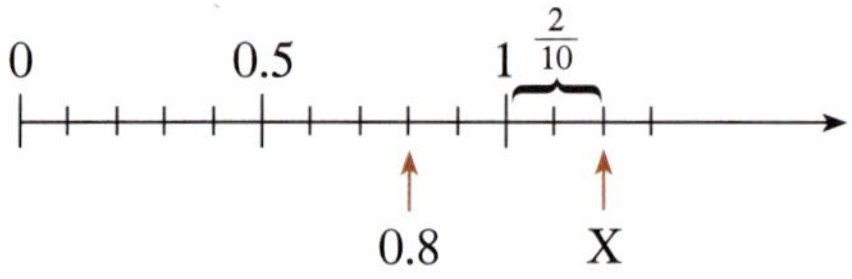

(b) The point X is 2 tenths from 1, X = 1.2

Exercise 4B

1 Copy the number line:

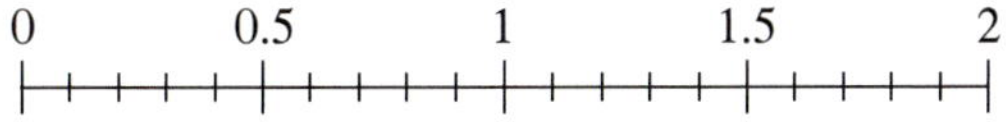

Show these numbers on your number line.

(a) 0.3 **(b)** 0.6 **(c)** 1.3
(d) 1.4 **(e)** 1.9 **(f)** 2

2 Write as decimals the letters marked on the number line.

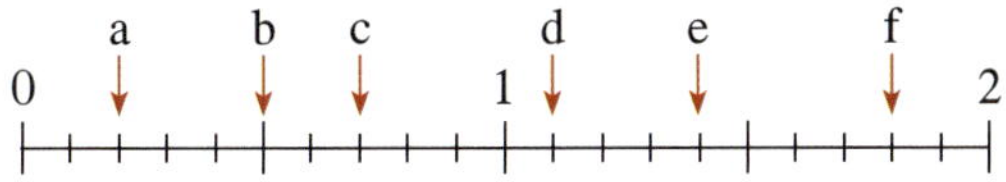

3 These scales are divided into tenths. What number is represented by the arrow?

(a)

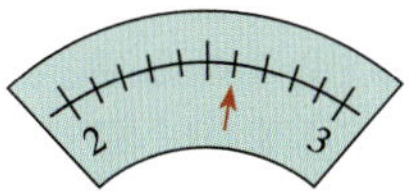

(b)

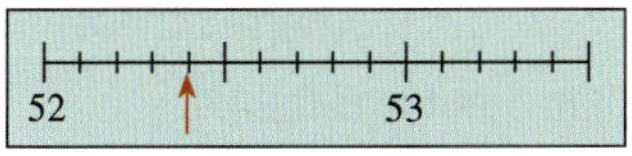

(c)

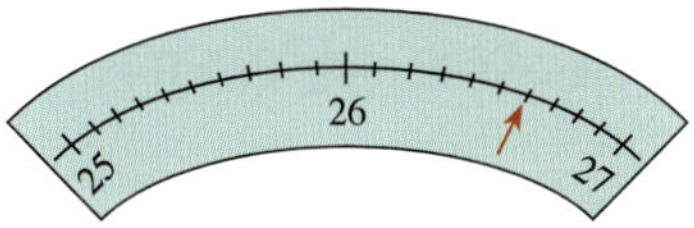

4 What is the temperature, in °C, on these thermometers?

(a)

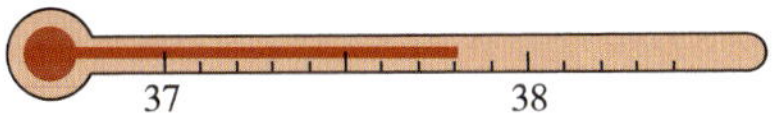

(b)

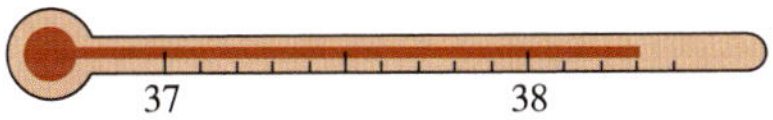

4.2 Two decimal places

You will need squared paper and scissors.

Cut out:

(a) four
10×10 squares
(A small drawing of a 10×10 square is shown.)

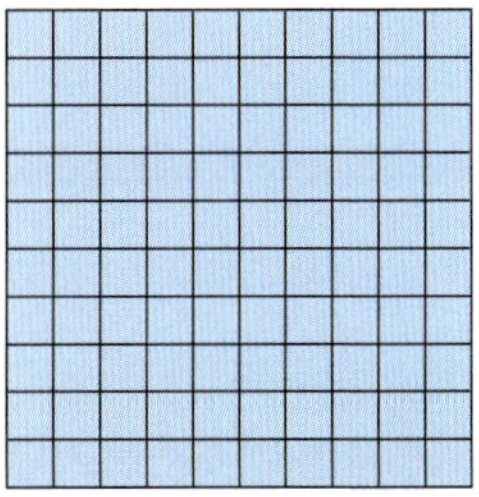

(b) twenty
10×1 rectangles

(c) twenty
1×1 squares

Do not throw the shapes away at the end of this section. You will need them again in a later section.

Activity

Use your cut-out squares and rectangles to work out:

(a) How many rectangles make a large square?

(b) How many small squares make a large square?

(c) What fraction of the large square is the rectangle?

(d) What fraction of the large square is the small square?

From the Activity you should be able to see that:

if 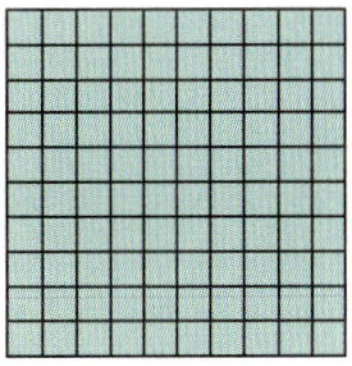 represents 1 unit

then  represents $\frac{1}{10}$ (one tenth)

and  represents $\frac{1}{100}$ (one hundredth)

Hundredths can be written a shorter way as decimals:

$\frac{1}{100}$ = 0 . 0 1

(no units; decimal point; no tenths; 1 hundredth)

You can use your cut-outs to show decimals.

Example 3

Show the decimals

(a) 0.3 **(b)** 0.25

using your cut-outs.

(a)

0.3

(b)

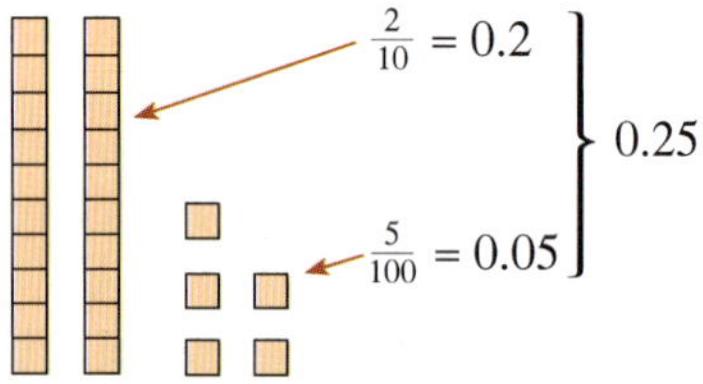

0.25

Exercise 4C

1 Use your cut-outs to show these decimals.

(a) 0.2 **(b)** 0.6 **(c)** 0.02
(d) 0.07 **(e)** 0.12 **(f)** 0.36
(g) 0.48 **(h)** 1.2 **(i)** 1.23

2 What decimals do these pictures represent?

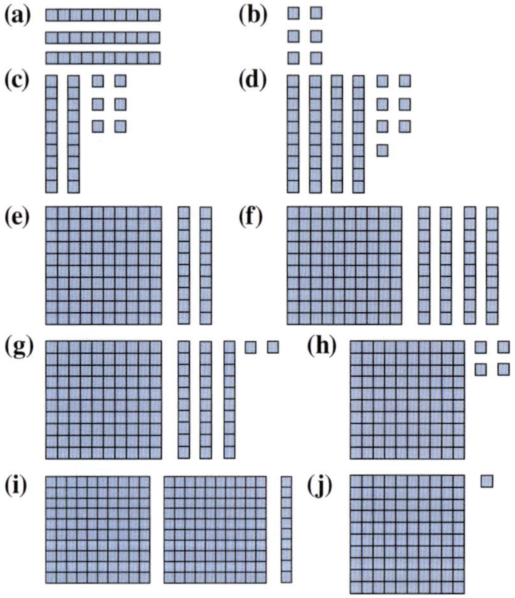

Your cut-outs are very useful when comparing decimals.

Example 4

Which is the larger decimal 0.19 or 0.2?

$0.19 = \frac{1}{10} + \frac{9}{100}$

$0.2 = \frac{2}{10}$

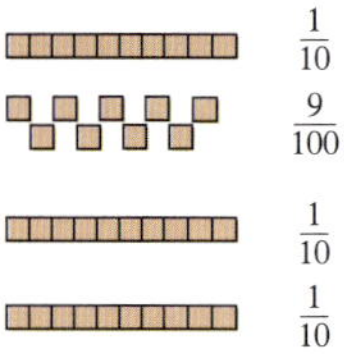

The rectangles show that 0.2 is larger.

Exercise 4D

1 Use your cut-outs to find which is larger:

(a) 0.3 or 0.5 **(b)** 0.7 or 0.2
(c) 0.03 or 0.06 **(d)** 0.32 or 0.45
(e) 0.4 or 0.39 **(f)** 0.06 or 0.1
(g) 1.2 or 1.13 **(h)** 1 or 0.98
(i) 1.02 or 1.3 **(j)** 2 or 1.64

2 Write down four numbers that are

(a) bigger than 3 but less than 4
(b) bigger than 3.4 but less than 3.6
(c) bigger than 0.6 but less than 0.7

Representing hundredths on a number line

You can divide a number line into hundredths to show two place decimals.

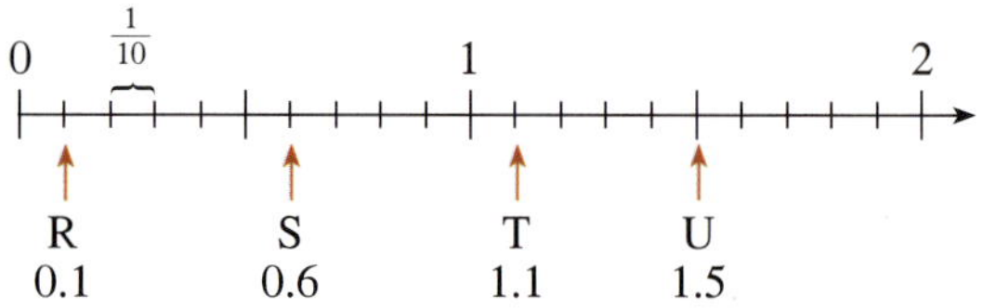

The number line between 0.5 and 0.7 becomes:

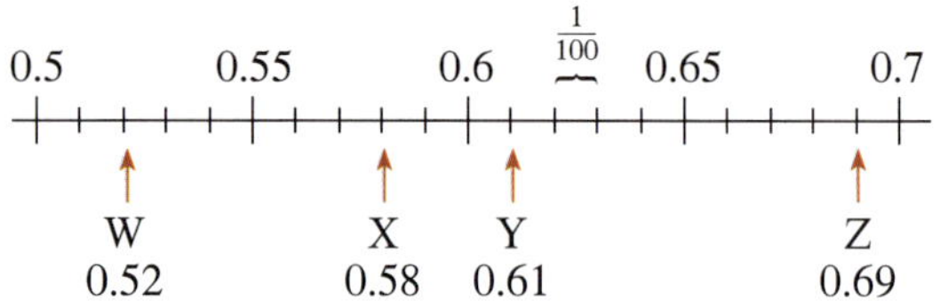

The point W is $\frac{2}{100}$ from 0.5, W = 0.52
The point X is $\frac{8}{100}$ from 0.5, X = 0.58
The point Y is $\frac{1}{100}$ from 0.6, Y = 0.61
The point Z is $\frac{9}{100}$ from 0.6, Z = 0.69

Example 5

(a) Show the point 1.68 on the number line.
(b) Write down the point Y as a decimal.

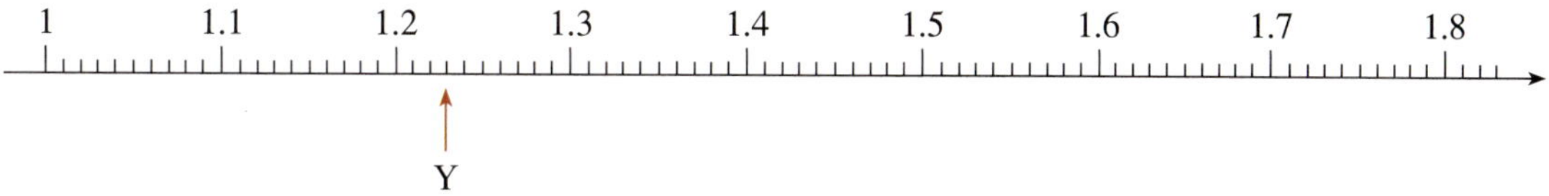

(a) 1.68 is $\frac{8}{100}$ from 1.6
(b) The point Y is $\frac{3}{100}$ from 1.2,
Y is the point 1.23

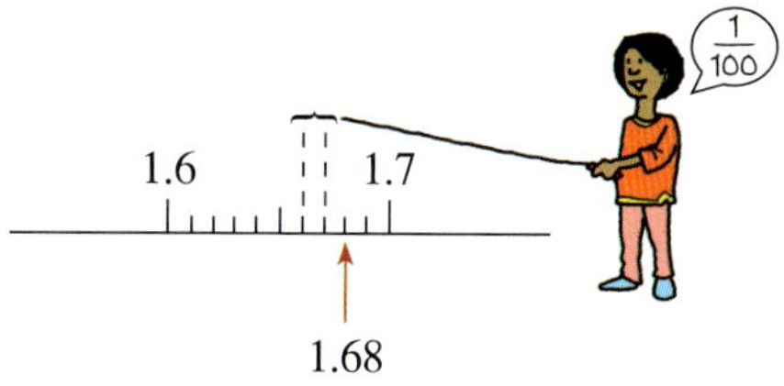

Exercise 4E

1 This number line has been divided into hundredths.

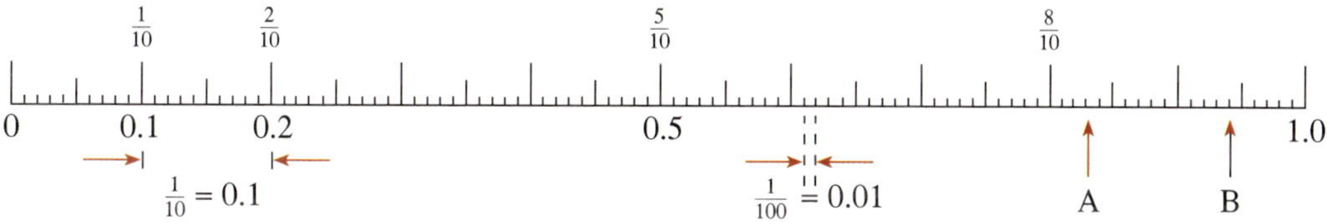

A is at $\frac{8}{10} + \frac{3}{100}$ or 0.83. Where is B?

2 Write down the positions of each of the letters on this number line:

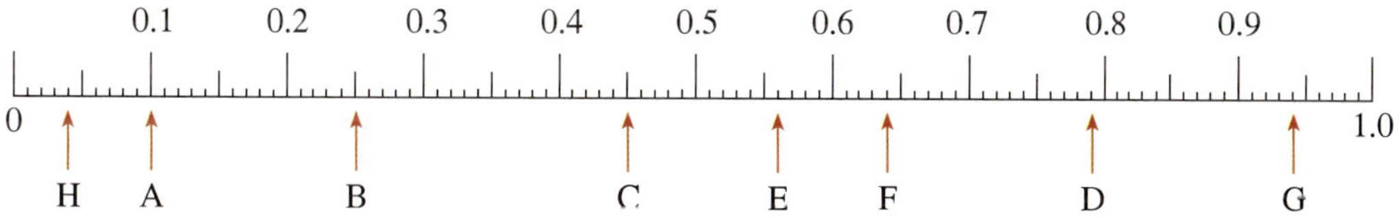

3 Copy this number line:

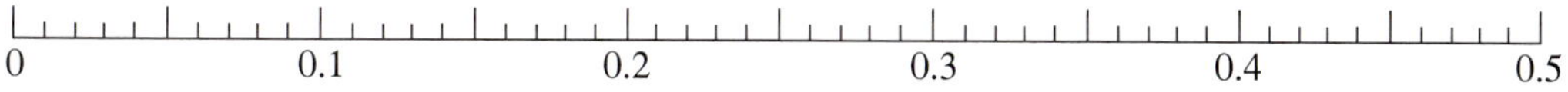

On your number line show the points:
A = 0.2, B = 0.25, C = 0.45, D = 0.40, E = 0.30, F = 0.05

4 Estimate the positions of the letters on this number line.

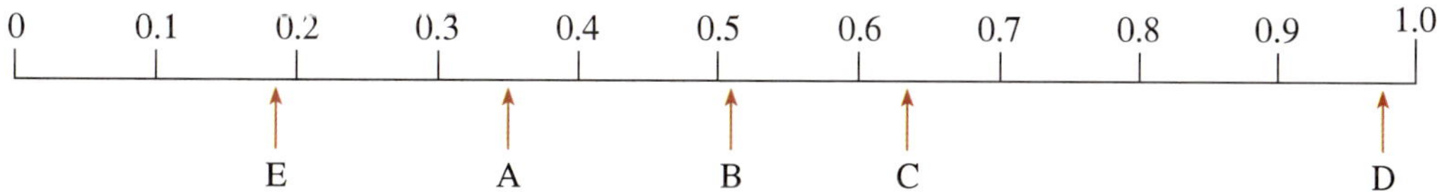

4.3 Decimals and place value

Column headings are often used to show place value.

For example, the number 618 can be shown as

Hundreds	Tens	Units
6	1	8

Columns to the right of the units column show the decimal parts.

For example, the numbers 276.38 is

Hundreds	Tens	Units		Tenths	Hundredths
2	7	6	.	3	8

The columns headings can be shortened:

H	T	U	.	$\frac{1}{10}$	$\frac{1}{100}$
2	7	6	.	3	8

Example 6

What is the value of the 3 in the decimal 46.34?
The decimal point tells you where the whole numbers end

4 6 . 3 4

The column headings are

H	T	U	$\frac{1}{10}$	$\frac{1}{100}$

Putting the column headings over 46.34 gives

H	T	U	. $\frac{1}{10}$	$\frac{1}{100}$
	4	**6**	**· 3**	**4**

The value of the 3 is $\frac{3}{10}$.

Exercise 4F

1 What is the value of the 3 in each number?
(a) 305 **(b)** 30.5
(c) 3.05 **(d)** 45.3
(e) 5.03 **(f)** 0.32
(g) 28.13 **(h)** 261.3

2 Write down the place value of the 2 in each number.
(a) 237 **(b)** 2.3
(c) 0.25 **(d)** 2541
(e) 0.02 **(f)** 28

3 Give the place value of the last digit in
(a) 241 **(b)** 241.3
(c) 8.6 **(d)** 3.02
(e) 5.21 **(f)** 6.32
(g) 0.5 **(h)** 0.04

Thousandths

Each column heading is one tenth of the one to its left:

$$\text{Th} \xrightarrow{\div 10} \text{H} \xrightarrow{\div 10} \text{T} \xrightarrow{\div 10} \text{U}$$

What happens if you divide the units column by 10?

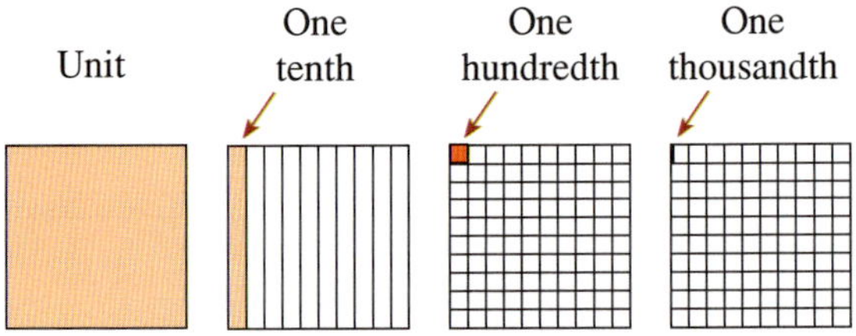

$$1 \xrightarrow{\div 10} \frac{1}{10} \xrightarrow{\div 10} \frac{1}{100} \xrightarrow{\div 10} \frac{1}{1000}$$

The column to the right of $\frac{1}{100}$ column is $\frac{1}{1000}$ column.

Thousandths can be written as decimals:

$\frac{1}{1000}$ = 0 . 0 0 1

0 → no units; first 0 after the point → no tenths; second 0 → no hundredths; 1 → 1 thousandth

The number 384.615 written with column headings is

H	T	U	. $\frac{1}{10}$	$\frac{1}{100}$	$\frac{1}{1000}$
3	**8**	**4**	**· 6**	**1**	**5**

Example 7

Give the value of each underlined digit.
(a) $0.\underline{2}7$ **(b)** $6.13\underline{4}$ **(c)** $\underline{2}8.1$

(a) Two tenths or $\frac{2}{10}$ or 0.2
(b) Four thousandths or $\frac{4}{1000}$ or 0.004
(c) Two tens or 20

Exercise 4G

1 Give the value of each underlined digit.

(a) $4.\underline{2}$ **(b)** $6.3\underline{8}$ **(c)** $0.\underline{5}$
(d) $\underline{1}3.3$ **(e)** $6\underline{2}.4$ **(f)** $12.8\underline{4}$
(g) $0.03\underline{2}$ **(h)** $1.24\underline{5}$ **(i)** $13.\underline{4}6$
(j) $\underline{3}847$ **(k)** $11.8\underline{0}4$ **(l)** $384.\underline{4}$

2 Write these numbers in order of size, smallest first.

(a) 0.3, 0.02, 0.4, 0.006
(b) 3, 30, 0.3, 0.003
(c) 36, 3.6, 0.36, 0.036
(d) 8, 800, 0.8, 0.008

3 Write down four numbers that lie between:

(a) 3 and 4
(b) 3.1 and 3.2
(c) 3.14 and 3.15
(d) 0.68 and 0.69

4 The batting averages of five international batsmen are shown in this table:

Kallis	54.66
Tendulkar	54.72
Gamber	56.00
Hussey	53.04
Ponting	55.67

Put them in order, starting with the highest average.

Writing decimals as fractions

Example 8

Write 0.63 as a fraction.
The column headings are:

	T	U	$\frac{1}{10}$	$\frac{1}{100}$
0.63 =		**0** ·	**6**	**3**

So $0.63 = \frac{6}{10} + \frac{3}{100}$

$= \frac{60}{100} + \frac{3}{100}\ \left(\frac{6}{10} = \frac{60}{100}\right)$

$= \frac{63}{100}$

In the same way:

	U	$\frac{1}{10}$	$\frac{1}{100}$	$\frac{1}{1000}$
0.236 =	**0** ·	**2**	**3**	**6**

$= \frac{2}{10} + \frac{3}{100} + \frac{6}{1000}$

$= \frac{200}{1000} + \frac{30}{1000} + \frac{6}{1000}$

$= \frac{236}{1000}$

Exercise 4H

1 Using the method of Example 8 write these decimals as fractions.

(a) 0.5 **(b)** 0.7 **(c)** 0.15
(d) 0.34 **(e)** 0.72 **(f)** 0.699
(g) 0.708 **(h)** 0.094

2 Compare each decimal in Question 1 with its corresponding fraction.

(a) If there is one digit after the decimal point, what is the denominator of the fraction?
(b) If there are two digits after the decimal point, what is the denominator of the fraction?
(c) If there are three digits after the decimal point, what is the denominator of the fraction?
(d) Can you see a quick way to write any decimal as a fraction? What is it?

3 Write as a fraction:

(a) 0.3 **(b)** 0.8
(c) 0.15 **(d)** 0.37

4 Write as a fraction:

(a) 0.9 **(b)** 0.4 **(c)** 0.14
(d) 0.46 **(e)** 0.07 **(f)** 0.05
(g) 0.04 **(h)** 0.149 **(i)** 0.237
(j) 0.097 **(k)** 0.062 **(l)** 0.051

5 Write as a mixed number:

(a) 1.7 **(b)** 2.5 **(c)** 3.54
(d) 9.27 **(e)** 5.114 **(f)** 11.438
(g) 8.005 **(h)** 21.009 **(i)** 9.422
(j) 14.803 **(k)** 16.002 **(l)** 15.077

6 Make up five decimals of your own, and change them to fractions.

7 $0.4 = \frac{4}{10} = \frac{2}{5}$

In the same way, write each decimal as a fraction in its simplest form.

(a) 0.2 **(b)** 0.6 **(c)** 0.8
(d) 0.5 **(e)** 0.25 **(f)** 0.75
(g) 0.125 **(h)** 0.375 **(i)** 0.625

8 $\frac{1}{2} = \frac{5}{10} = 0.5$

In the same way, write each fraction as a decimal.

(a) $\frac{1}{5}$ **(b)** $\frac{3}{5}$ **(c)** $\frac{9}{10}$ **(d)** $\frac{13}{20}$
(e) $\frac{7}{25}$ **(f)** $\frac{14}{25}$ **(g)** $\frac{3}{50}$ **(i)** $\frac{41}{50}$

Decimals and money

Money is written using decimals.

For example:

2 dollars and 25 cents is written \$2.25

39 cents is written \$0.39

3 dollars and 7 cents is written \$3.07

Exercise 4I

1 **(a)** How many cents are there in a dollar?

(b) Write 1 cent as a fraction of 1 dollar.

(c) Write this fraction as a decimal.

2 **(a)** Write 15 cents as a fraction of a dollar.

(b) Write this fraction as a decimal.

3 Write using the decimal point:

(a) 1 dollar 10 cents

(b) 2 dollars 25 cents

(c) 3 dollars 55 cents

(d) 5 dollars 5 cents

(e) 10 dollars 9 cents

(f) 100 dollars 5 cents

(g) 54 dollars 13 cents

(h) 1 dollar 50 cents

4.4 Adding and subtracting decimals

Adding decimals

Adding decimal numbers is similar to adding whole numbers. It is a good idea to use column headings.

Example 9

Find

(a) $3.7 + 1.5$

(b) $2.4 + 3.18$

(a)

U		$\frac{1}{10}$
3	.	7
1_1		5
5	.	2

(b)

U		$\frac{1}{10}$	$\frac{1}{100}$
2	.	4	
3	.	1	8
5	.	5	8

When adding decimals remember to put the decimal points one below the other. This makes sure that you don't add tenths to hundredths or units to tenths by mistake.

Exercise 4J

1 Work out:

(a) $3.7 + 1.2$ **(b)** $2.6 + 1.4$

(c) $9.1 + 0.8$ **(d)** $4.3 + 5.8$

(e) $2.3 + 8.7$ **(f)** $3.1 + 1.62$

(g) $0.03 + 3.2$ **(h)** $4 + 0.05$

(i) $6 + 0.4$ **(j)** $3.96 + 1.5$

2 Study this example:

What is $5.2 + 6 + 1.86$?

Remember that $6 = 6.0$

Write the sum vertically:

$$\begin{array}{r} 5.2 \\ 6.0 \\ +\ 1.86 \\ \hline 13.06 \\ \hline \end{array}$$

Use this method to work out $7.5 + 9 + 3.79$

3 Calculate:

(a) $3 + 0.6 + 0.24$

(b) $0.8 + 4 + 3.62$

(c) $17.3 + 200 + 0.08$

(d) $6 + 4.8 + 0.34$

(e) $0.01 + 0.1 + 10$

4 Look at this part of a page from Ann's exercise book:

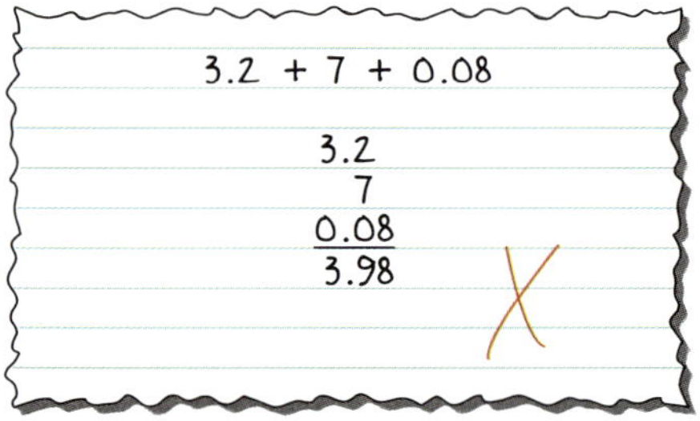

(a) What was Ann's mistake?

(b) Work out the addition correctly.

5 Bernelle buys an exercise book for \$1.50, a pen for \$3 and a ruler for \$1.75. How much did she spend altogether?

6 The times of four boys in a 4×100 metre relay race were:

Abdul	12.6	seconds
Wayne	13	seconds
Kenroy	12.4	seconds
Antoine	12.03	seconds

(a) Who ran the fastest leg?
(b) What was the team's total time for the race?

7 The example shows how you can add decimals by first changing them to fractions:

$$\begin{aligned}1.87 + 2.79 &= 1 + \tfrac{87}{100} + 2 + \tfrac{79}{100}\\ &= 3 + \tfrac{166}{100}\\ &= 3 + 1\tfrac{66}{100}\\ &= 4\tfrac{66}{100}\\ &= 4.66\end{aligned}$$

Use this method to calculate:
(a) $3.6 + 1.4$ **(b)** $6.2 + 1.24$
(c) $4.91 + 1.62$ **(d)** $7.28 + 3.79$

Subtracting decimals

Subtraction of decimals is exactly the same as subtraction of whole numbers, except that the decimal point is included.

Example 10

What is $3 - 1.4$?

Remember $3 = 3.0$. You write the difference vertically:

$$\begin{array}{r} {}^{2}\not{3}.{}^{1}0 \\ -\,1.4 \\ \hline 1.6 \\ \hline \end{array}$$

Study the next example carefully.

Example 11

What is $2.4 - 1.86$?

Remember $2.4 = 2.40$, so

$$\begin{array}{r} {}^{1}\not{2}\,.\,{}^{13}\not{4}\,{}^{1}0 \\ -\,1\,.\,8\,6 \\ \hline 0\,.\,5\,4 \\ \hline \end{array}$$

Exercise 4K

1 Work out:
(a) $2.8 - 1.6$ **(b)** $2.8 - 1.9$
(c) $3 - 0.4$ **(d)** $2 - 1.7$
(e) $13.6 - 9.4$ **(f)** $2.9 - 0.03$
(g) $7 - 0.25$ **(h)** $4.63 - 3$
(i) $2.9 - 1.46$ **(j)** $100 - 6.8$

2 In his exercise book, Hilroy wrote:

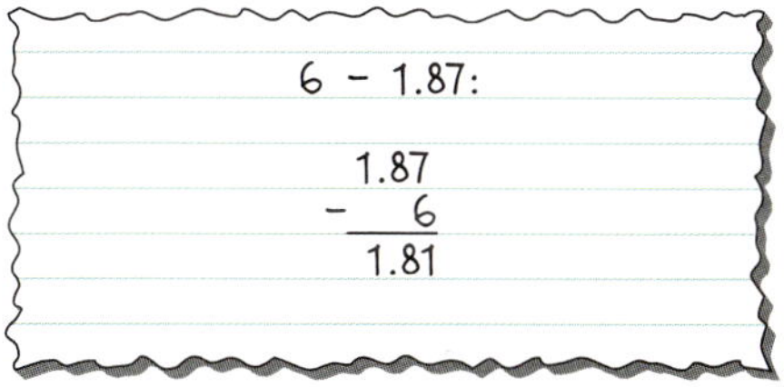

(a) What were Hilroy's mistakes?
(b) If you were Hilroy's teacher, how would you explain the subtraction to him?
(c) Work out $6 - 1.87$ correctly.

3 Rosa had a \$20 bill. She bought a packet of biscuits for \$4.95. How much change was she given?

4 The times of the first three girls in a 50 metre swimming trial were:

Cynthia	40.52 seconds
Marvlyn	41.6 seconds
Gretta	38.71 seconds

(a) Who came first in the trial?
(b) How many seconds was the third swimmer behind the winner?

5

In a 100 metre race shown on the television the commentator said:

... Roberts finishes 2 hundreths of a second behind Davis in a time of 10.41 seconds

... Johnson's winning time of 10.3 seconds is only 5 hundredths of a second outside the record...

(a) List the runners from first to third and their times.
(b) What is the record time?
(c) Copy and complete:
'Johnson beat Davis by _____ seconds'.

4.5 Decimals and your calculator

Decimal calculations are done very easily on a calculator. To display a decimal you must use the [·] button.

For example, to work out 3.6 + 2.62, press

[3] [·] [6] [+] [2] [·] [6] [=]

Exercise 4L

1 Use your calculator to check your answers to Question 1 in Exercise 4J.

2 Use your calculator to check your answers to Question 1 in Exercise 4K.

3 Use your calculator to find:
(a) 10×7.32 **(b)** 10×6.38
(c) 10×8.4 **(d)** 10×1.07
(e) 10×0.825 **(f)** 10×6.045

4 Work these out in the same way.
(a) 100×7.32 **(b)** 100×6.38
(c) 100×8.4 **(d)** 100×1.07
(e) 100×0.825 **(f)** 100×6.045

5 Copy and complete the table started below, for all your answers to Questions 3 and 4.

Number	Number × 10	Number × 100
7.32	73.2	732
6.38	63.8	
8.4		

6 Look at any number in the table. What happens to each digit when you multiply by 10?
What happens when you multiply by 100?

7 Use the pattern you discovered in Question 6 to write the answers to these multiplications, without working them out.
(a) 7.45×10 **(b)** 8.9×10
(c) 0.34×10 **(d)** 3.04×10
(e) 0.06×10 **(f)** 1.006×10
(g) 18.4×10 **(h)** 21.63×10

8 Repeat Question 7 but this time multiply each number by 100.

9 Use your calculator to find:
(a) $7.6 \div 10$ **(b)** $4.3 \div 10$
(c) $26.1 \div 10$ **(d)** $48 \div 10$
(e) $523 \div 10$ **(f)** $68.7 \div 10$
(g) $943 \div 10$ **(h)** $99 \div 10$

10 Work these out in the same way:
(a) $7.6 \div 100$ **(b)** $4.3 \div 100$
(c) $26.1 \div 100$ **(d)** $48 \div 100$
(e) $523 \div 100$ **(f)** $68.7 \div 100$
(g) $943 \div 100$ **(h)** $99 \div 100$

11 Copy and complete the table started below for all your answers to Questions 9 and 10.

Number	Number ÷ 10	Number ÷ 100
7.6	0.76	0.076
4.3	0.43	0.043

12 Look at any number in the table. What happens to each digit when you divide by 10?
What happens when you divide by 100?

13 Use the pattern you discovered in Question 12 to write the answer to each division without working it out.

(a) 7.8 ÷ 10 **(b)** 9.2 ÷ 10
(c) 27.3 ÷ 10 **(d)** 59 ÷ 10
(e) 947 ÷ 10 **(f)** 31.5 ÷ 10

14 Repeat Question 13, but this time divide each number by 100.

15 **(a)** What is 33 ÷ 5? Make a guess.
(b) Your guess should have been between 6 and 7. Was it?
(c) The correct answer must be six point something. Make a better guess.
(d) Use your calculator to find 33 ÷ 5.

16 Copy and complete the table below. For each question make a good guess and then use your calculator.

Problem	Guess	Calculator
26 ÷ 5		
19 ÷ 4		
27 ÷ 6		
57 ÷ 8		
96 ÷ 10		
13 ÷ 2		
6 ÷ 5		
21 ÷ 9		
17 ÷ 3		
1 ÷ 4		

4.6 Multiplying and dividing decimals by powers of ten

Look at the results you got in Question 5 of Exercise 4L.

7.32 × 1 = 7.32
7.32 × 10 = 73.2
7.32 × 100 = 732.

You should have noticed that when a decimal is **multiplied** by 10 each number in the decimal moves **one** place to the **right**.

When **multiplied** by 100 each number moves **two** places to the **right**.

Now look at Question 11 of Exercise 4L.

7.6 ÷ 1 = 7.6
7.6 ÷ 10 = 0.76
7.6 ÷ 100 = 0.076

Notice here that when a decimal is **divided** by 10 each number in the decimal moves **one** place to the **left**.

When divided by 100 each number moves **two** places to the left.

Example 12

Work out:
(a) 83.75 × 10 **(b)** 83.75 ÷ 100

(a) 83.75 × 10 = 837.5
(b) 83.75 ÷ 100 = 0.8375

Exercise 4M

1 Work out without a calculator:

(a) 6.35 × 10 **(b)** 6.35 × 100
(c) 71.4 × 10 **(d)** 71.4 × 100
(e) 0.318 × 10 **(f)** 0.318 × 100
(g) 0.076 × 10 **(h)** 0.076 × 100

2 Multiply each of these numbers by
(i) 10
(ii) 100
(iii) 1000

(a) 9.843 **(b)** 16.04 **(c)** 0.14
(d) 7.96 **(e)** 103.2 **(f)** 84.19

3 Work out without a calculator:

(a) 8.1 ÷ 10 **(b)** 8.1 ÷ 100
(c) 53.7 ÷ 10 **(d)** 53.7 ÷ 100
(e) 0.014 ÷ 10 **(f)** 0.014 ÷ 100
(g) 0.176 ÷ 10 **(h)** 0.176 ÷ 100

4 Divide each of these numbers by
(i) 10
(ii) 100
(iii) 1000

(a) 46.2 **(b)** 7.08 **(c)** 0.314
(d) 76.9 **(e)** 240.1 **(f)** 23.04

5 Write in cents:
(a) \$6.42 (b) \$19.06 (c) \$247.11

6 Write in dollars:
(a) 45 cents (b) 6 cents (c) 137 cents

4.7 Multiplying and dividing decimals

You can see how to multiply two decimal numbers by first turning them into fractions.

For example:

$$3.6 \times 1.4 = 3\frac{6}{10} \times 1\frac{4}{10} = \frac{36}{10} \times \frac{14}{10} = \frac{504}{100} = 5.04$$

Notice that
$36 \times 14 = 504$
while $3.6 \times 1.4 = 5.04$

Note there are 2 decimal places

As there are two decimal places in the product, there are two decimal places in the answer.

Example 13

Given that $32 \times 47 = 1504$
find (a) 3.2×4.7
(b) 0.32×0.047

(a) In 3.2×4.7 there are two decimal places.
So $3.2 \times 4.7 = 15.\underline{04}$
2 d.p.

(b) In 0.32×0.047 there are five decimal places.
So $0.32 \times 0.047 = 0.\underline{015\ 04}$
5 d.p.

Exercise 4N

1 Given that $12 \times 13 = 156$, find:
(a) 1.2×13 (b) 12×1.3
(c) 1.2×1.3 (d) 0.12×13
(e) 12×0.13 (f) 0.12×1.3
(g) 0.12×0.13 (h) 0.12×0.013

2 Given that $261 \times 54 = 14\ 094$, find:
(a) 2.61×5.4 (b) 26.1×5.4
(c) 261×0.54 (d) 26.1×0.54
(e) 0.261×54 (f) 0.261×5.4
(g) 0.261×0.54 (h) 0.261×0.054

3 Work out:
(a) 0.4×6 (b) 0.4×0.6
(c) 0.3×0.5 (d) 4×0.2
(e) 8×0.4 (f) 0.7×0.2
(g) 0.5×1.4 (h) 1.5×0.2
(i) 6.3×0.4 (j) 0.7×3.2

4 What is the cost of
(a) 14 pens at \$3.15 per pen
(b) 6 radios at \$47.25 per radio
(c) 24 sweets at \$0.45 per sweet
(d) 15 erasers at \$0.65 per eraser
(e) 42 oranges at \$0.75 per orange?

5 A car averages 8.4 km on one litre of gas. How far will it travel if the car's tank has 14.2 litres of gas?

6 What is the price of 0.34 kg of cheese, if cheese is sold for \$24.05 per kilogram?

7 Ashton can run 100 m in 14.6 seconds. How long should it take him to run 47.3 m?

8 The product of two numbers is 1.82. What are the two numbers if their sum is 2.7?

Dividing decimals by whole numbers

Division of decimals by whole numbers is similar to dividing whole numbers by whole numbers.

Example 14

Calculate $5.4 \div 4$

$$\begin{array}{r} 1.35 \\ 4\,\overline{)\,5.40} \\ \underline{4} \\ 14 \\ \underline{12} \\ 20 \\ \underline{20} \end{array}$$

You could also work this out using a 'short' division method.

$$\begin{array}{r} 1.\ 3\ \ 5 \\ 4\,\overline{)\,5.\,{}^{1}4\ {}^{2}0} \end{array}$$

Exercise 40

1 Without using a calculator work out:

(a) $2.4 \div 6$ **(b)** $3.6 \div 4$
(c) $0.28 \div 7$ **(d)** $0.72 \div 9$
(e) $2.56 \div 8$ **(f)** $0.128 \div 8$
(g) $3.75 \div 5$ **(h)** $0.064 \div 4$
(i) $3.61 \div 19$ **(j)** $0.27 \div 5$

2 Work out:

(a) $7.45 \div 5$ **(b)** $0.71 \div 5$
(c) $14.41 \div 8$ **(d)** $0.726 \div 12$
(e) $36.4 \div 8$ **(f)** $1.78 \div 12$

3 A 5 kg fish sells for \$86.40.
What is the price of the fish per kilogram?

4 A man walks 17.4 km in 4 hours.
What is his speed?

5 The cost of 12 handkerchiefs is \$29.52.
What is the cost of one handkerchief?

6 A 3 kg tub of soap powder sells for \$42.39.
What is the cost of 1 kg of soap powder?

7 Six boys shared \$53.40 equally among themselves.
How much money did each boy receive?

8 The result when dividing one number by another is 0.8. Write down five pairs of numbers for which this is true.

Dividing decimals by decimals

To divide a decimal by a decimal you need to turn the divisor into a whole number.

Example 15

Work out $6.3 \div 0.7$

$$6.3 \div 0.7 = \frac{6.3}{0.7} = \frac{6.3 \times 10}{0.7 \times 10} = \frac{63}{7} = 9$$

Sometimes you will need to multiply the divisor by 100 or a higher power of 10.

Example 16

Work out $142.8 \div 0.42$

$$142.8 \div 0.42 = \frac{142.8}{0.42} = \frac{142.8 \times 100}{0.42 \times 100} = \frac{14\,280}{42} = 340$$

Exercise 4P

1 Without using a calculator work out:

(a) $8 \div 0.2$ **(b)** $16 \div 0.4$
(c) $12 \div 0.5$ **(d)** $18 \div 0.6$
(e) $1.2 \div 0.5$ **(f)** $1.8 \div 0.6$
(g) $2.4 \div 0.08$ **(h)** $2.7 \div 0.03$

2 Given that $828 \div 23 = 36$
find:

(a) $8.28 \div 2.3$ **(b)** $8.28 \div 0.23$
(c) $82.8 \div 2.3$ **(d)** $82.8 \div 0.23$
(e) $0.828 \div 2.3$ **(f)** $0.828 \div 0.23$

3 Work out:

(a) $4.5 \div 0.09$ **(b)** $1.32 \div 0.11$
(c) $2.88 \div 0.12$ **(d)** $25.6 \div 0.16$
(e) $7.8 \div 0.013$ **(f)** $10.24 \div 3.2$

4 A piece of cheese weighs 0.54 kg and costs $17.50. What is the price of 1 kg of cheese?

5 In a test Pat wrote

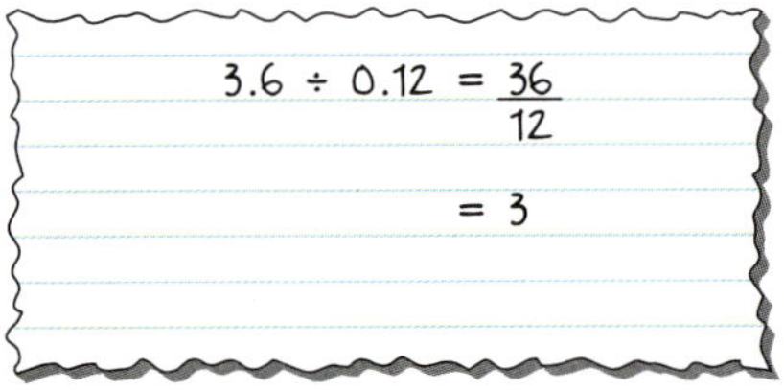

(a) What was Pat's mistake?
(b) Work out the division correctly.

6 How many pieces of ribbon 0.35 metres long can be cut from a roll of ribbon containing 14.5 metres?

7 How many 0.375 litre bottles of juice can be filled from a container holding 6.2 litres?

Technology

Without a calculator the four rules on decimal numbers can be hard work. Review what you've learnt and more by visiting the websites
www.aaamath.com/dec.htm
and
www.mathsisfun.com/numbers
Both sites give detailed revision and practice with decimals.

Calculator problems

Use your calculator to help you work out the problems in Exercise 4Q.

Exercise 4Q

1 Find the cost of 23 yards of cloth at $6.85 per yard.

2 Mrs Austrie buys 3 tins of milk at $1.98 a tin and 7 oranges at 25 cents each.

(a) How much money does she spend?
(b) How much change does she get from $20?

3 **(a)** How many exercise books at $2.30 can I buy for $100?
(b) How much change will I receive?

4 Look at the headline:

If the five members of the group share the money equally, how much does each member get?

5 A certified grower gets $8.24 for each box of bananas he sells. How much money does he make if he sells 43 boxes but pays the truck driver 60 cents per box carried?

6 A hotel charges \$127.30 a night for a double room. Evening meals are \$67.95 per person. How much will it cost a couple to spend 12 nights at the hotel with evening meals included?

7 Mr Alport earns \$6.45 per hour. He is paid \$7.95 for each hour he works over 40 hours in a week.
(a) How much is he paid for a 43 hour week?
(b) How many hours did he work if he received \$313.65?

8 Shelly-Ann Fraser set a national sprint record of 10.73s in 2009 for the 100m dash. What was her speed in kilometres per hour?
(1000 metres = 1 kilometre)

Activity

Work with a friend.
You may use only the operations
[+], [−], [×] and [÷]
You may use only the numbers 130, 7.2, 5, 6.2, 9.9, 426, 29.7, 15

(a) The first player chooses two of the numbers, for example 7.2 and 5
(b) The second player chooses an operation, for example [÷]
(c) Both players guess the result 7.2 ÷ 5 within ten seconds!
(d) Check the answer with a calculator. The one with the closest answer wins.
(e) Which of you is the first to win ten games?

4 Consolidation

1 Write these numbers as decimals.

(a) $\frac{3}{10}$ **(b)** $\frac{7}{10}$ **(c)** $\frac{49}{100}$

(d) $1\frac{6}{10}$ **(e)** $13\frac{9}{10}$

2 Copy the number line and place on these decimals.

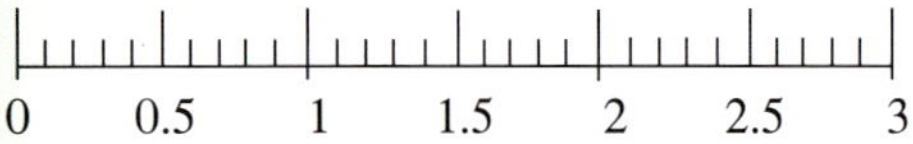

(a) 0.3 **(b)** 1.2 **(c)** 0.6 **(d)** 2.9
(e) 1 **(f)** 2.0 **(g)** 0.45 **(h)** 1.65

3 Use cut-outs to find the largest of these pairs of numbers.
(a) 0.2, 0.14 **(b)** 0.32, 0.4 **(c)** 0.1, 0.03

4 Write these numbers in order of size, smallest first.
(a) 0.3, 0.17, 0.2, 3 **(b)** 1.6, 0.07, 15, 0.8
(c) 0.48, 0.5, 1, 8.02

5 Write these decimals as fractions.
(a) 0.5 **(b)** 0.8 **(c)** 1.4 **(d)** 3.8

Application 4

6 On Wednesday, Anton bought a tie for $15 and a shirt for $47.99. He then went to the shop and bought a sweet for $0.15 and a lollipop for $0.75.

(a) How much did he spend on Wednesday in total?

(b) Anton left his house Wednesday morning with a $100 bill in his pocket. On Wednesday night, how much did he have left?

7 Read the value on each scale.

(a)

(b)

(c)

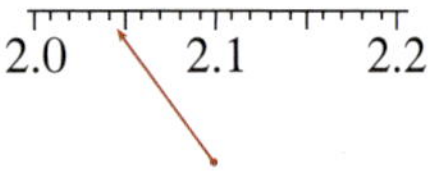

8 The times of the eight athletes in the women's 200 m race at the 2004 Olympic games in Athens, Greece, were

Lane 1	Kim Gevaert	Belgium	22.84 sec
Lane 2	Ivet Lalova	Bulgaria	22.57
Lane 3	Allyson Felix	USA	22.18
Lane 4	Veronica Campbell	Jamaica	22.05
Lane 5	Abiodun Oyepitan	Britain	22.87
Lane 6	Aleen Bailey	Jamaica	22.42
Lane 7	Muna Lee	USA	22.87
Lane 8	Debbie Ferguson	Bahamas	22.3

(a) Who won the race?

(b) Who came last?

(c) How much faster was Campbell than Felix?

(d) The World record in this race was held by Florence Griffith Joyner at 21.34 seconds. How far outside this time was the third place runner in 2004?

9 Which is better value for money:
a 0.35 kg piece of cheese that sells for $6.93 or
a 0.65 kg piece of cheese selling for $12.88?
Give reasons for your answer.

Companion CD

Want some extra practice? Go to Chapter 4 on your companion CD for further exercises, animations, and solutions.

Summary

You should know …

1 A decimal is a way of writing a number using place values of tenths, hundredths etc.

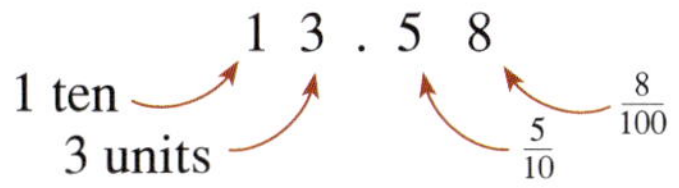

2 A decimal can be shown on a number line.

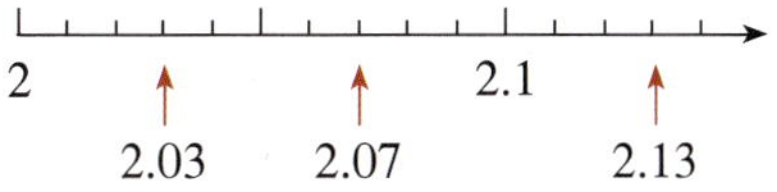

3 A fraction can be written as a decimal.

U	$\frac{1}{10}$	$\frac{1}{100}$
0 •	5	8

$\frac{58}{100} =$ (table above) $= 0.58$

4 A decimal can be written as a fraction.
For example: $0.74 = \frac{7}{10} + \frac{4}{100} = \frac{70}{100} + \frac{4}{100} = \frac{74}{100}$

5 You can use a number line to compare the size of two decimals.

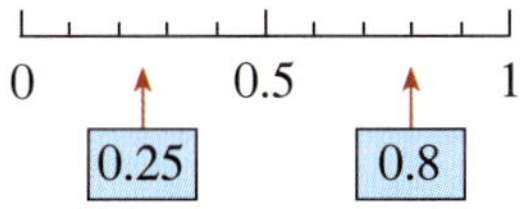

0.25 is smaller than 0.8

Check out

1 Write the value of the underlined digit.
(a) 0.$\underline{6}$8 **(b)** 3$\underline{2}$.61
(c) 0.0$\underline{7}$ **(d)** $\underline{4}$03.128
(e) 1.30$\underline{2}$

2 What numbers are represented by the letters A, B, C, D on the number line?

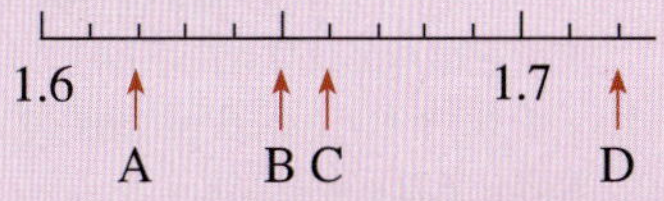

3 Write these fractions as decimals.
(a) $\frac{3}{10}$ **(b)** $\frac{6}{100}$ **(c)** $2\frac{5}{10}$
(d) $13\frac{7}{100}$ **(e)** $9\frac{17}{100}$

4 Write these decimals as fractions.
(a) 0.75 **(b)** 0.8 **(c)** 0.3
(d) 2.25 **(e)** 13.68

5 For each number pair, write the larger number.
(a) 0.3, 0.5 **(b)** 3, 1.6
(c) 0.3, 0.29 **(d)** 0.93, 1

6 To add or subtract decimals, write the numbers with the place values lined up.
For example: 26 – 0.4

$$\begin{array}{r} 26.0 \\ -\ \ 0.4 \\ \hline 25.6 \\ \hline \end{array}$$

6 Work out:
(a) $7 + 0.3 + 0.06$
(b) $6.3 + 7.78$
(c) $10 - 0.3$

7 How to multiply and divide decimals.
For example: 0.62×0.4
$0.\underline{62} \times 0.\underline{4}$ has 3 places of decimals.
Since $62 \times 4 = 248$
$0.62 \times 0.4 = 0.\underline{248}$ also has 3 places of decimals.

For example: $7.36 \div 0.04$

$$7.36 \div 0.04 = \frac{7.36}{0.04} = \frac{7.36 \times 100}{0.04 \times 100} = \frac{736}{4} = 184$$

7 Work out:
(a) 6.2×0.7
(b) 0.14×0.28
(c) $7.6 \div 0.04$
(d) $14.4 \div 0.012$

Revision exercise 1

Number

1 Copy and complete

(a) 11, 22, 33, 44, 55, □, □, □

(b) 17, 34, 51, 68, 85, □, □, □

(c) 23, 46, 69, 92, 115, □, □, □

(d) 76, 95, 114, 133, 152, □, □, □

2 Use the distributive law to calculate:

(a) 26×53 (b) 34×68

(c) 54×186 (d) 84×239

3 (a) A passenger bus holds 46 persons. How many people can fit into 17 buses?

(b) How many buses are needed for 1058 passengers?

4 Eggs are sold in boxes of six. How many boxes are needed to pack 4836 eggs?

5 (a) Mr Shillingford drives 32 kilometres to and from work each day. How many kilometres does he drive in 28 working days?

(b) How many days does it take him to travel 2208 kilometres?

6 The cost of 35 books is \$420. How much do 18 books cost?

7 Six men can pick grapefruit from 174 trees in one day.

(a) How many trees can ten men pick in one day?

(b) How many trees can 17 men pick in three days?

8 Seven men can build a house in 21 days. How long will it take:

(a) 3 men (b) 9 men?

9 What is the largest prime number less than 1000?

10 (a) What is the LCM of 18 and 12?

(b) What is the smallest number that can be divided exactly by 8, 13 and 24?

(c) What is the smallest number which has remainder 3 when divided by 5, 7, and 8?

Sets

11 Describe these sets in your own words:

(a) {7, 14, 21, 28, 35, 42}

(b) {u, v, w, x, y, z}

(c) {121, 129, 137, 145, 153}

(d) {2, 3, 5, 7, 11}

12 For the universal set {letters of the alphabet} draw Venn diagrams to show the subsets of letters which are:

(a) vowels

(b) consonants

(c) used in the word 'mathematics'.

13 Copy the Venn diagram below; then answer the questions.

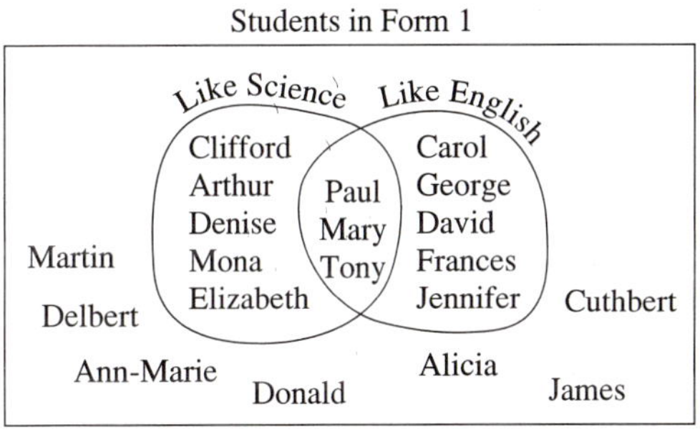

(a) How many students are there in Form 1?

(b) How many students like science?

(c) List the students who like English.

(d) List the students who do not like science or English.

(e) List the students who like both science and English.

(f) List the students who like English but do not like science.

(g) What can you say about {Clifford, Arthur, Denise, Mona, Elizabeth}?

14 Use Venn diagrams to find the HCF of:

(a) 14 and 63 (b) 18 and 42

(c) 72 and 64 (d) 84, 32 and 48

15 Use Venn diagrams to find the LCM of:

(a) 9 and 15 **(b)** 24 and 36

(c) 26 and 78 **(d)** 5, 12 and 20

16 Copy and complete the Venn diagram below.

Whole numbers from 20 to 40

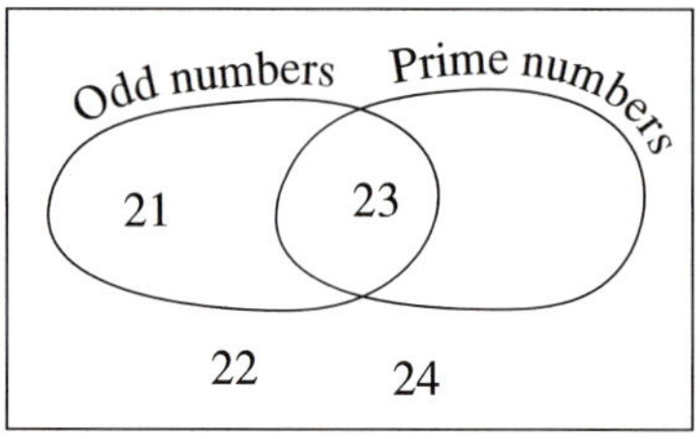

(a) List those prime numbers which are odd.

(b) Are there are odd numbers which are not prime?

(c) Describe the subset of numbers outside the two loops.

(d) Draw the Venn diagram again to illustrate the sets more appropriately.

17 Copy and complete the Venn diagram.

Whole numbers from 1 to 24

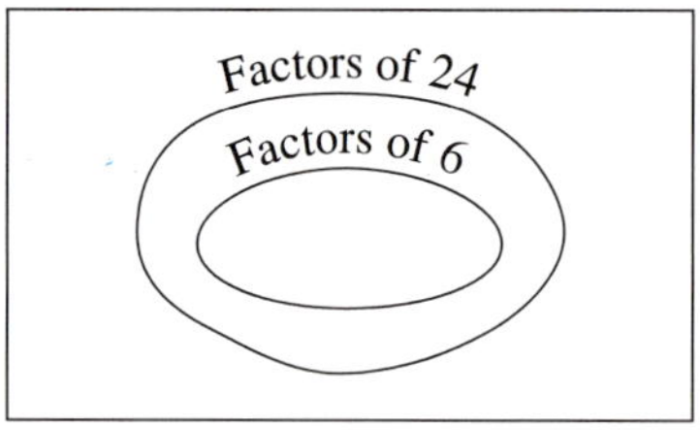

(a) Is it true to say:
{factors of 24} ⊂ {factors of 6}?

(b) Use the signs ⊂ or ⊄ (**is not a subset of**) to copy and complete:
{factors of 6}   {factors of 24}

(c) Draw another Venn diagram which shows the set of factors of: 6, 12, and 24.

18 Draw a Venn diagram with universal set {whole numbers from 1 to 30}.

On the same diagram show the subsets of {factors of 25}, {factors of 10} and {factors of 5}.

19 Write down **all** the subsets of:

(a) {1, 2} **(b)** {a, b, c}

(c) {2, 4, 6, 8}

Remember, both the universal set and the empty set are **subsets** of the universal set.

20 Look at the Venn diagram below.

Students in form 1

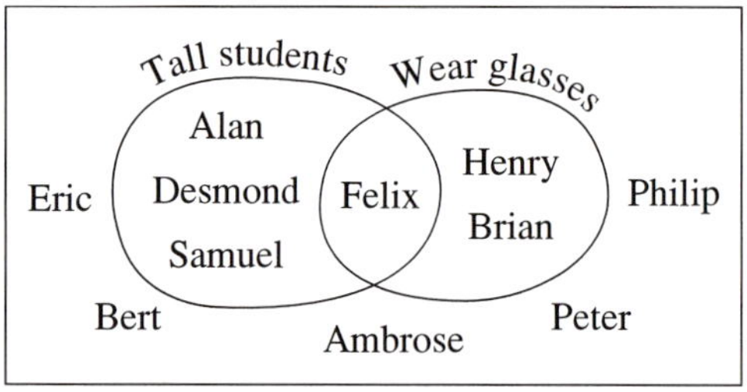

Henry is short and wears glasses. Describe:

(a) Felix **(b)** Alan **(c)** Eric **(d)** Brian

Fractions

21 Copy and complete:

(a) $\frac{3}{4} = \frac{6}{\square} = \frac{\square}{16} = \frac{21}{\square} = \frac{63}{\square}$

(b) $\frac{4}{7} = \frac{\square}{21} = \frac{24}{\square} = \frac{48}{\square} = \frac{\square}{63}$

(c) $\frac{12}{18} = \frac{\square}{21} = \frac{10}{\square} = \frac{28}{\square} = \frac{\square}{63}$

(d) $\frac{\square}{6} = \frac{25}{\square} = \frac{20}{\square} = \frac{\square}{42} = \frac{60}{72}$

22 Arrange these fractions in order of size, smallest first:

(a) $\frac{1}{3}, \frac{2}{9}, \frac{5}{18}$ **(b)** $\frac{3}{4}, \frac{2}{3}, \frac{7}{12}$ **(c)** $\frac{9}{15}, \frac{7}{12}, \frac{13}{18}$

23 A water container when a quarter full holds 320 litres. How much does the full container hold?

24 The petrol tank of a motor car holds 15 litres when it is $\frac{5}{12}$ full. How much petrol can a full tank hold?

25 Write these fractions in their simplest form:

(a) $\frac{32}{56}$ **(b)** $\frac{56}{6}$ **(c)** $\frac{114}{12}$

(d) $\frac{96}{112}$ **(e)** $4\frac{16}{28}$ **(f)** $12\frac{108}{144}$

26 The legs of a chair are $\frac{1}{3}$ metre long while the back is $\frac{2}{5}$ metre.
Find the height of the whole chair.

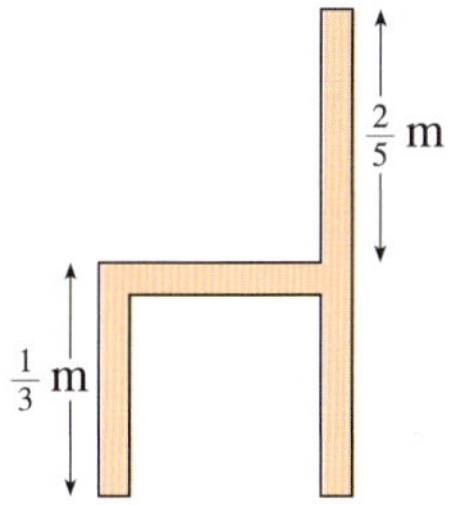

27 A metre ruler has $\frac{2}{7}$ metre cut off.
How much of the ruler is left?

28 Giselle spends $\frac{1}{3}$ of her day in bed, $\frac{1}{8}$ in front of the television set, $\frac{1}{4}$ at school, and $\frac{1}{12}$ eating.
What fraction of her day is left?

29 A typist can type six pages in $\frac{3}{4}$ hour.
How long will it take to type 72 pages?

30 Jayceline walks at $6\frac{3}{4}$ km/hr.
How far can she walk in 8 hours?

Decimals

31 Change to decimals:

(a) $\frac{3}{5}$ **(b)** $\frac{9}{20}$ **(c)** $\frac{19}{20}$
(d) $\frac{2}{25}$ **(e)** $\frac{13}{100}$ **(f)** $\frac{3}{100}$
(g) $\frac{33}{50}$ **(h)** $\frac{3}{250}$

32 Write as a fraction in its simplest form:

(a) 0.8 **(b)** 0.2 **(c)** 0.25
(d) 0.15 **(e)** 0.125 **(f)** 0.37

33 Write down the greater number:

(a) $\frac{1}{2}$, 0.2 **(b)** $\frac{1}{4}$, 0.4
(c) $\frac{1}{5}$, 0.5 **(d)** $\frac{3}{4}$, 0.34

34 Write down the number that is:

(a) $\frac{1}{2}$ of 0.1 **(b)** $\frac{1}{4}$ of 0.2
(c) $\frac{1}{2}$ of 0.4 **(d)** $\frac{1}{10}$ of 0.25

35 Draw a number line with divisions like this:

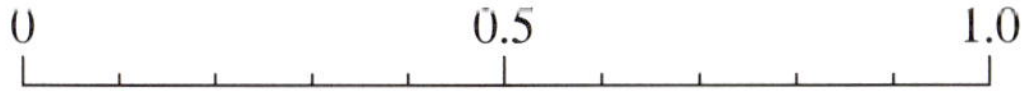

On your number line mark, as accurately as you can, the positions of the numbers:

(a) 0.3 **(b)** 0.8 **(c)** 0.15
(d) 0.75 **(e)** 0.43 **(f)** 0.06

36 Draw a number line with divisions like this:

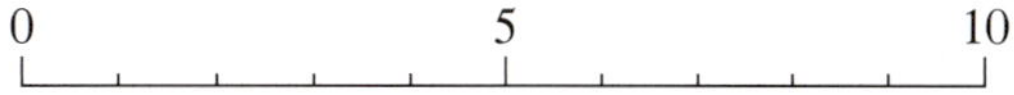

On your number line mark, as accurately as you can, the positions of the numbers:

(a) 3.5 **(b)** 6.4 **(c)** 9.1
(d) 1.25 **(e)** 4.8 **(f)** 5.99

37 What change would you get from \$10.00 if you spent:

(a) \$3.50 **(b)** \$3.05
(c) \$0.35 **(d)** \$0.03

38 Calculate:

(a) $3.2 + 4.8$ **(f)** 14×0.35
(b) $3.28 + 4.82$ **(g)** 2.8×0.04
(c) $3.62 - 1.72$ **(h)** $8.4 \div 7$
(d) $3.6 - 1.06$ **(i)** $14.4 \div 1.2$
(e) $8 - 0.32$ **(j)** $1.56 \div 0.13$

39 Here is a game you can try on a calculator or on a piece of paper. Put a number in the calculator, say:

This number is made up of 5 digits.
Can you eliminate it by subtracting 5 numbers?
Try some more.

40 Is $\frac{1}{6}$ the same as 0.16?
This number line shows 0.16:

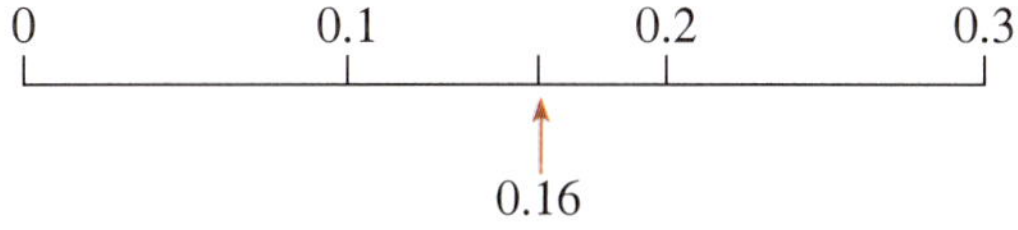

Find 0.16×6. Is it less than 1?
Find 0.16×7. Is it more than 1?
Is $\frac{1}{6}$ nearer 0.16 or 0.17?

Mixed questions 1

1 3 ④ 7 4 2
How many times greater is the circled digit than the underlined digit?
A 10 **B** 100 **C** 1000 **D** 10 000

2 Which of these is a multiple of 2, 5 and 7?
A 10 **B** 14 **C** 35 **D** 140

3 Which number has the most factors?
A 12 **B** 16 **C** 24 **D** 36

4 The smallest composite number greater that 45 is:
A 43 **B** 46 **C** 48 **D** 53

5 How many prime numbers are there between 70 and 80?
A 1 **B** 2 **C** 3 **D** 4

6 $14 \times (20 - 1)$ equals
A $14 \times 20 - 1$ **B** $20 - 14 \times 1$
C $280 - 14$ **D** $280 - 1$

7 In six years time Julie will be 17. How old was she five years ago?
A 28 **B** 23 **C** 6 **D** 13

8 A bus holds 14 persons. How many buses are needed to transport 189 persons?
A 10 **B** 12 **C** 13 **D** 14

9 The mileometer on a car shows

| 1 | 5 | 8 | 9 | 9 |

What will it show after the car has gone one more mile?

A | 1 | 5 | 8 | 1 | 0 | **B** | 1 | 5 | 8 | 9 | 10 |

C | 1 | 5 | 9 | 1 | 0 | **D** | 1 | 5 | 9 | 0 | 0 |

10 What is 326 rounded to the nearest 10?
A 400 **B** 330 **C** 320 **D** 300

11 Use the Venn diagram to determine which of the following statements is false.

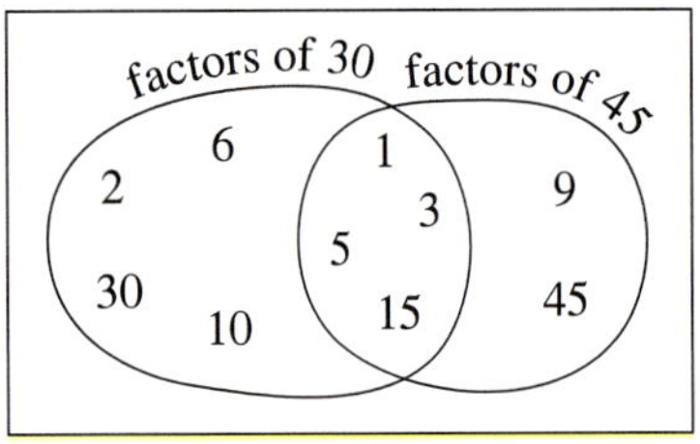

A {factors of 30} = {1, 2, 3, 5, 6, 10, 15, 30}
B {factors of 45} = {9, 45}
C {intersection of factors of 30 and factors of 45} = {1, 3, 5, 15}
D $5 \in$ {factors of 30}

12 The universal set is {cars in Jamaica} with subsets {red cars} and {sports cars}.
Which Venn diagram shows the most likely picture of this information?

A
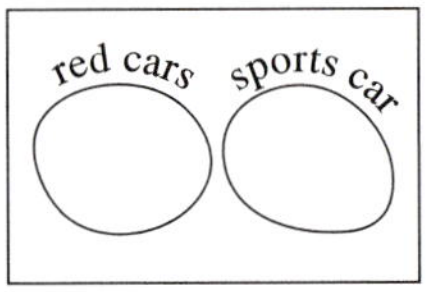

B
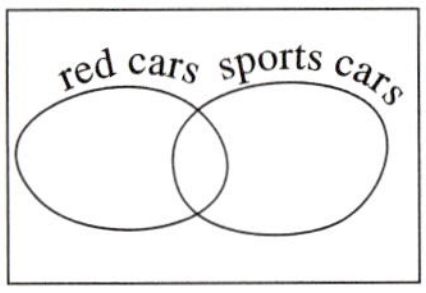

C
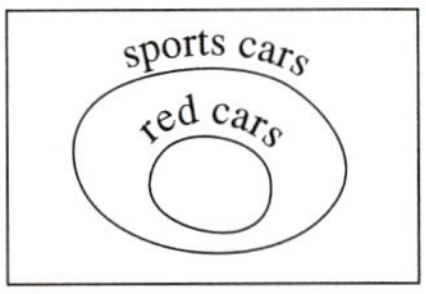

D
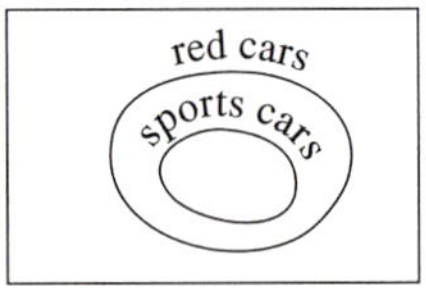

13
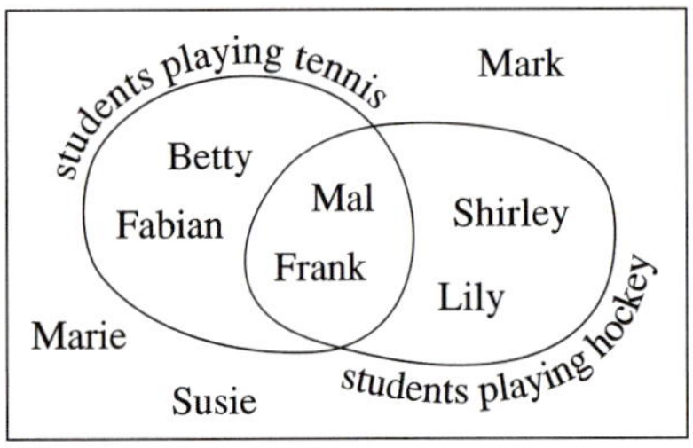

The set of students who play hockey is
A {Mal, Frank, Shirley, Lily}
B {Shirley, Lily}
C {Betty, Fabian}
D {Marie, Susie, Mark}

14 The statement that correctly shows that 1 is a member of the set of factors of 10 is
A $\subset$ {1, 2, 5, 10}
B {1} $\subset$ {1, 2, 5, 10}
C {1} $\in$ {1, 2, 5, 10}
D 1 $\in$ {1, 2, 5, 10}

15 Which of the following is an element of {odd numbers greater than 11}?
A 9 **B** 11 **C** 12 **D** 13

16 If {even numbers} $\subset$ {whole numbers} the diagram illustrating this is

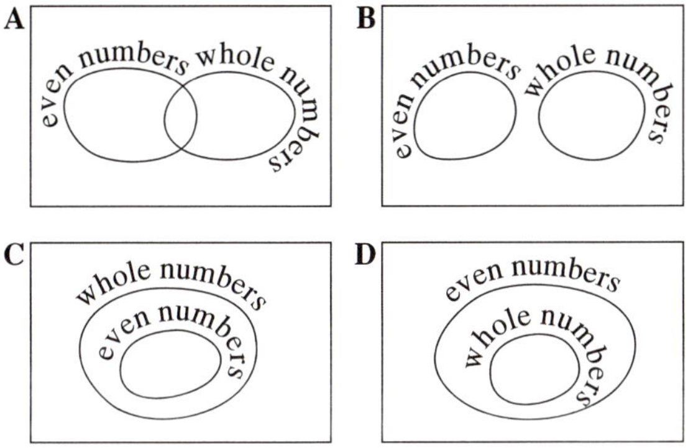

17

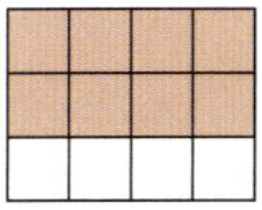

What fraction of the shape is shaded?

A $\frac{1}{2}$ **B** $\frac{4}{12}$ **C** $\frac{2}{3}$ **D** $\frac{3}{4}$

18

You are asked to erase $\frac{2}{3}$ of the X's in the diagram. How many must you erase?

A 3 **B** 4 **C** 8 **D** 10

19 What fraction lies between $\frac{1}{5}$ and $\frac{3}{5}$?

A $\frac{1}{2}$ **B** $\frac{1}{5}$ **C** $\frac{1}{10}$ **D** $\frac{7}{10}$

20 A bottle of juice holds $\frac{2}{3}$ litre. How much juice must Karen make to fill 27 bottles?

A 9 **B** 12 **C** 18 **D** 36

21 What is $1\frac{1}{8} \div \frac{3}{4}$?

A $\frac{15}{4}$ **B** $1\frac{1}{2}$ **C** 1 **D** $\frac{27}{32}$

22 A container when $\frac{3}{5}$ full holds 36 gallons. How much does the full container hold?

A 12 gallons **B** 40 gallons
C 60 gallons **D** 180 gallons

23 Which fraction is greater than $\frac{4}{7}$?

A $\frac{1}{3}$ **B** $\frac{1}{2}$ **C** $\frac{3}{5}$ **D** $\frac{4}{9}$

24 Ray lives $6\frac{1}{4}$ miles from school.
If a bus takes him $4\frac{1}{2}$ miles, how far is the bus stop from his home?

A $1\frac{1}{4}$ miles **B** $1\frac{3}{4}$ miles
C $2\frac{1}{4}$ miles **D** $10\frac{3}{4}$ miles

25 $2\frac{3}{4}$ equals

A $\frac{9}{4}$ **B** $\frac{12}{3}$ **C** $\frac{6}{4}$ **D** $\frac{11}{4}$

26

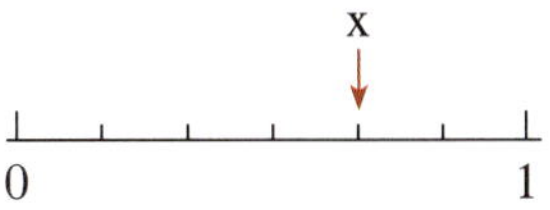

Look at the number line above.
What number does the letter x represent?

A $\frac{1}{2}$ **B** $\frac{2}{3}$ **C** $\frac{3}{4}$ **D** 4

27

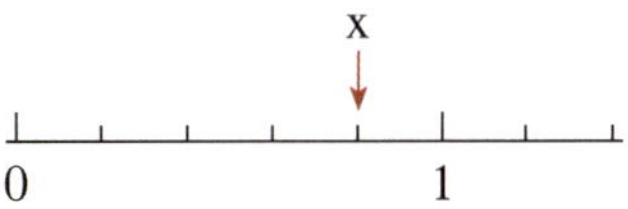

The number represented by the letter x is

A 0.4 **B** 0.8 **C** 1.1 **D** 1.2

28

Which number best represents the shaded region?

A 0.03 **B** 0.3 **C** 0.7 **D** 3.7

29 The fraction $\frac{3}{5}$ written as a decimal is

A 5.3 **B** 3.5 **C** 0.6 **D** 0.06

30 Which is the largest number?

A 0.3 **B** 0.29 **C** 0.301 **D** 0.4

31 $8 - 0.3$ equals

A 8.7 **B** 8.3 **C** 7.7 **D** 5

32 Sixteen dollars and twenty-eight cents can be written as

A \$16.28 **B** \$16.208
C \$1628 **D** \$16280

33 What is the cost of twenty books if each book costs \$1.25?

A \$250 **B** \$25
C \$2.50 **D** \$2.500

34 What is $8.4 \div 0.04$?

A 2.1 **B** 21 **C** 210 **D** 2100

35 Which number lies between 0.6 and 0.7?

A 0.5 **B** 0.55 **C** 0.63 **D** 0.8

36 The decimal 0.85 written as a fraction in its simplest form is

A $\frac{5}{8}$ **B** $\frac{85}{100}$ **C** $\frac{17}{20}$ **D** $1\frac{3}{5}$

37 What is the value of the 2 in 1.23?

A 2 **B** 20

C $\frac{2}{10}$ **D** $\frac{1}{2}$

38 What is 0.6 as a fraction?

A $\frac{3}{5}$ **B** $\frac{1}{6}$

C $\frac{10}{6}$ **D** 6

39 What number is between 0.4 and 0.42?

A 0.65 **B** 0.421

C 0.403 **D** 0.04

Angles

5

Objectives

- ✔ name angles and compare them
- ✔ measure and draw angles
- ✔ discover some relations between angles
- ✔ learn about angles in triangles and quadrilaterals

What's the point?

Wherever you look you will see angles, from the corners of your classroom to the angle made between the hands of a clock. Architects are just one group of professionals who use angles to good effect to design buildings.

Before you start

You should know ...

1 About whole turns, half turns, quarter turns, three-quarter turns, clockwise and anticlockwise.
For example:

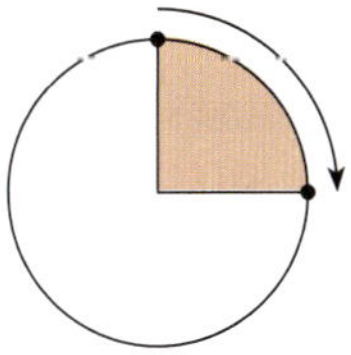

2 A right angle looks like this:

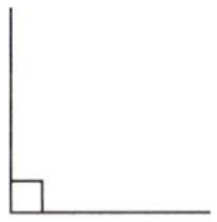

Check in

1 **(a)** After turning clockwise from P, a half turn, the arrow will point to □

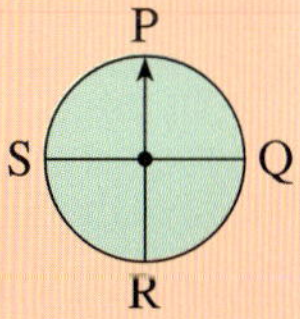

(b)

After turning clockwise from P	The arrow will point to
(i) a quarter turn **(ii)** a whole turn **(iii)** a three-quarter turn	

2 Which of these shapes contain right angles?

(a)  **(b)** 

(c)  **(d)** 

3 How to find missing numbers:
$20 + \square = 60$, 40 is missing
$150 + \square = 180$, 30 is missing.

3 Find the missing numbers:
(a) $10 + \square = 60$
(b) $190 + \square = 210$

5.1 Lines and angles

Lines can either be straight or curved.

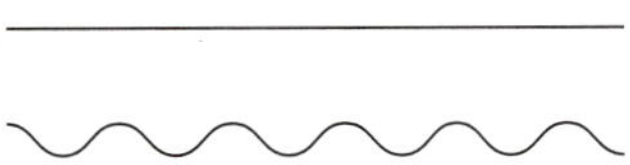
Straight line
Curved line

Two straight lines intersect in a **point**.

A straight line that extends from a point is called a **ray**.

ray

Two rays and the point where they meet form an **angle**.

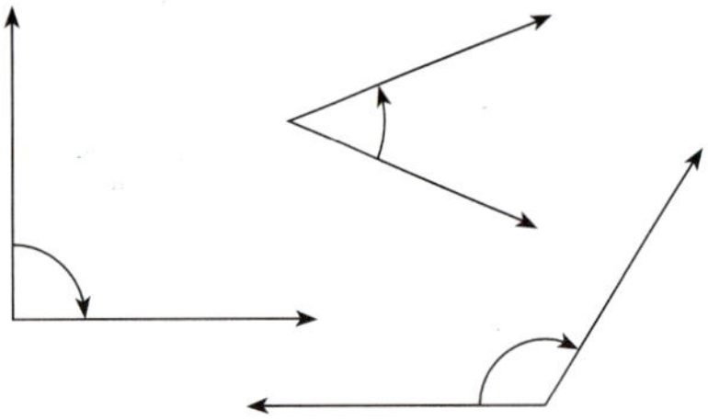

- An **angle** is a measure of turn.

Two rays that do not meet are called **parallel** rays.

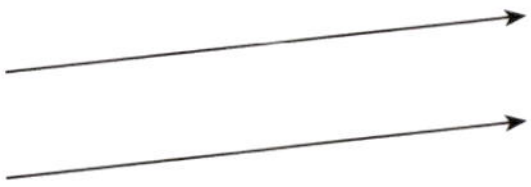

Exercise 5A

1 Look at each pair of rays below.
Is an angle formed? Explain.

(a)
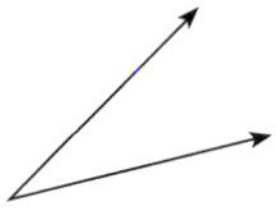
(b)
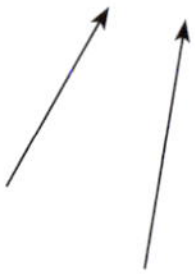
(c)

(d)
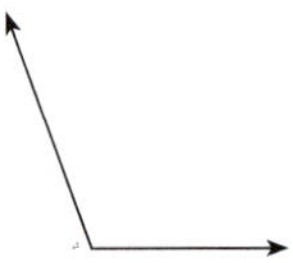

2 Write down the number of angles you can see inside each of these shapes.

(a)
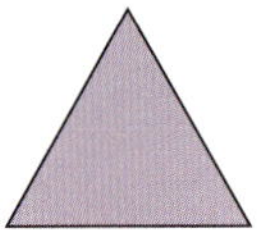
(b)

(c)

(d)
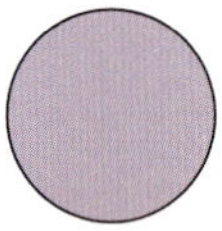
(e)

(f)
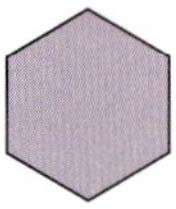
(g)
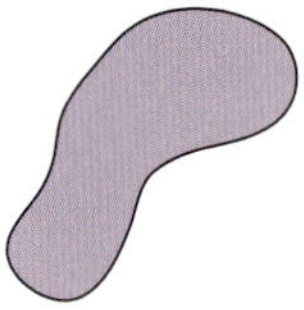
(h)

3 Write a list of twenty objects, from school and home, that contain angles.

Naming angles

The usual way to name a line is to write a letter at the end points of the line.

A line joining two such points is called a **line segment**.

The picture shows the line segment AB.

In the drawing below, the line segments AB and AC meet at the point A. An angle is formed.
A small curve is drawn between the lines to show the angle we mean.

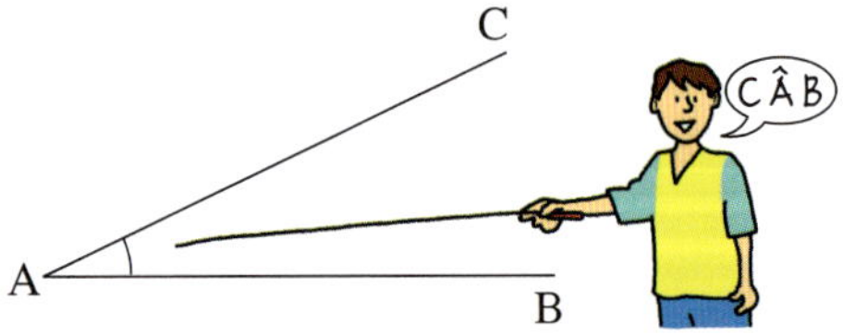

The angle is called *angle* BAC, or *angle* CAB.
The letter at the point always goes in the middle.
Angle BAC is usually written in a short way as $B\hat{A}C$.

In the drawing below, the lines XZ and YZ meet.
The angle we are looking at is $X\hat{Z}Y$, or just $\hat{Z}$.

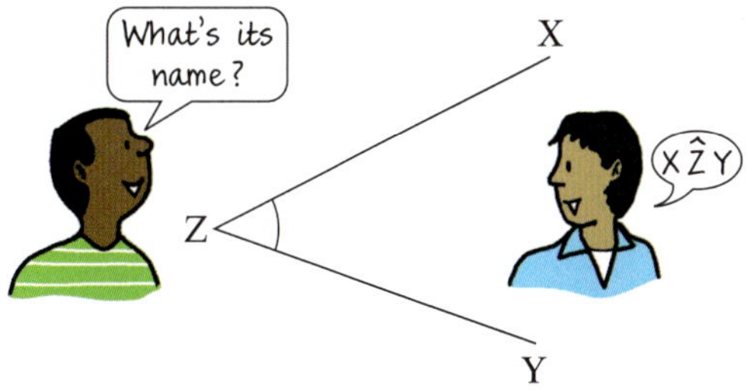

Exercise 5B

1 Which of these are correct names for the angle below?

(a) $Q\hat{R}P$ **(b)** $P\hat{Q}R$ **(c)** $R\hat{P}Q$
(d) $R\hat{Q}P$ **(e)** $P\hat{R}Q$

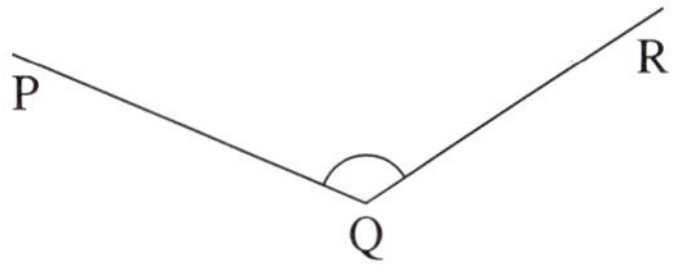

2 Write down the names of the lines that meet and the name of the marked angle in each diagram.

(a)
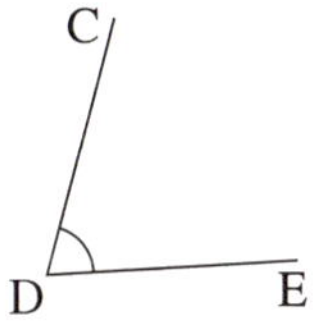

(b)
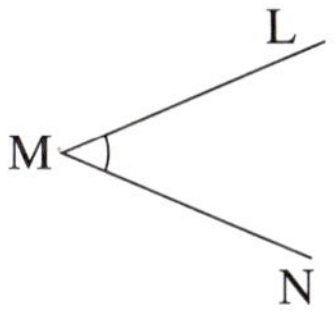

(c)
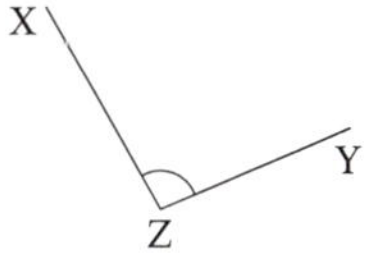

(d)
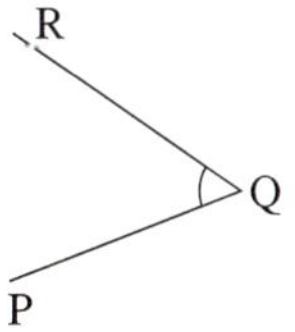

(e)
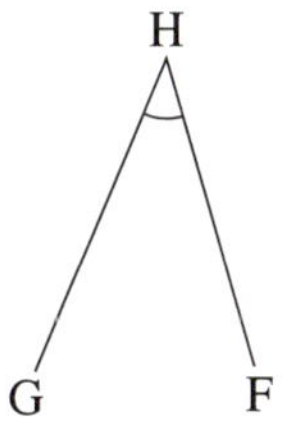

(f)
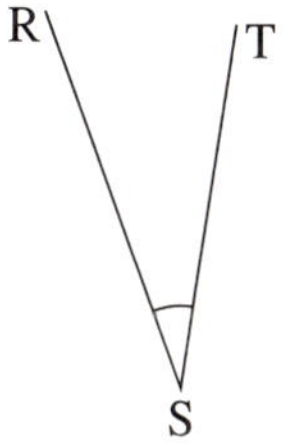

(g)
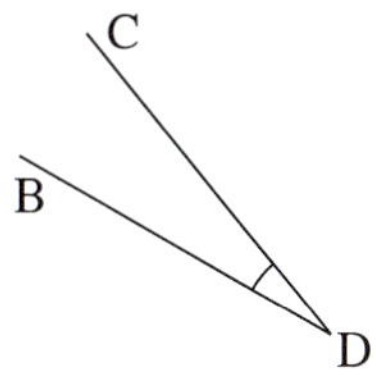

(h)
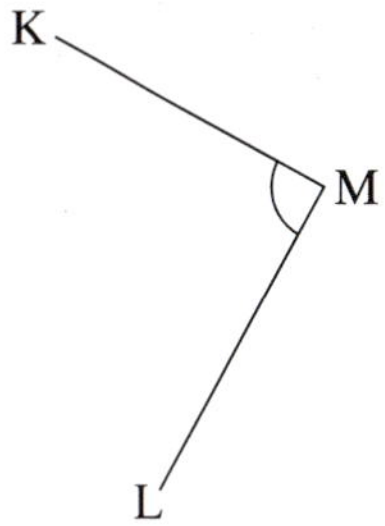

(i)
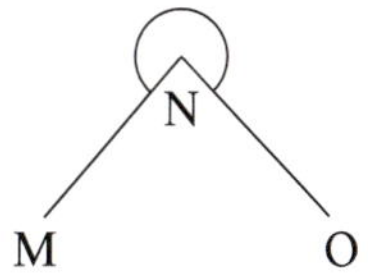

(j)
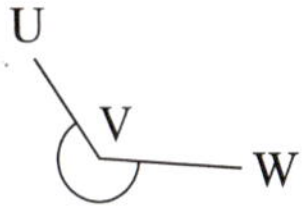

Comparing angles

To compare angles you make use of the idea of *turning*.

Activity

Make two cardboard strips, each $\frac{1}{2}$ centimetre by 10 centimetres. Fasten one end of each strip together with a paper fastener like this:

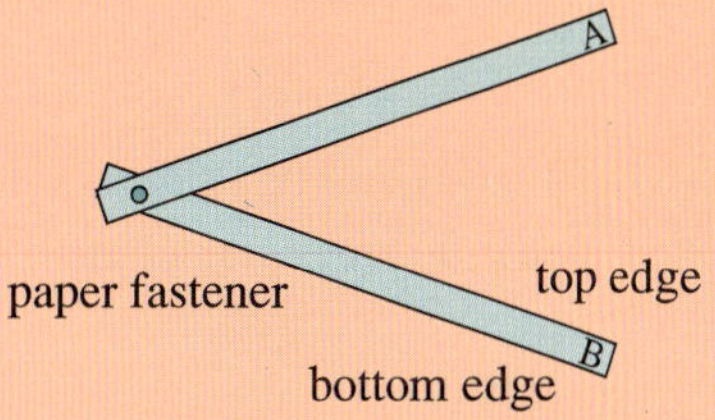

Write the letter A on the free end of one strip, and B on the free end of the second strip.
The point the paper fastener goes through is the point O.
Close the strips so that OA is on top of OB.

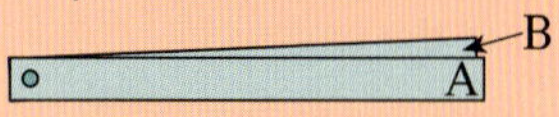

Now turn OA about O, so that it makes an angle with OB.

The larger the turn, the larger the angle AOB.

You will now use the strips to compare angles.

Example 1

Which of the two angles is larger?

(a)

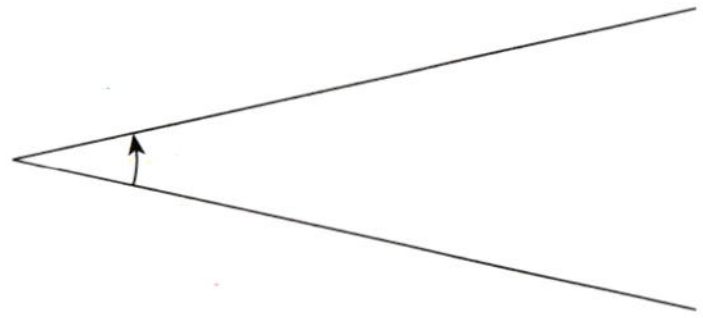

(b)

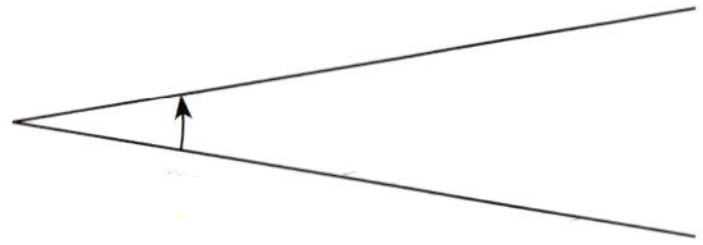

Open the cardboard strips. Place OB on the lower line and OA along the upper line of angle (a):

(a)

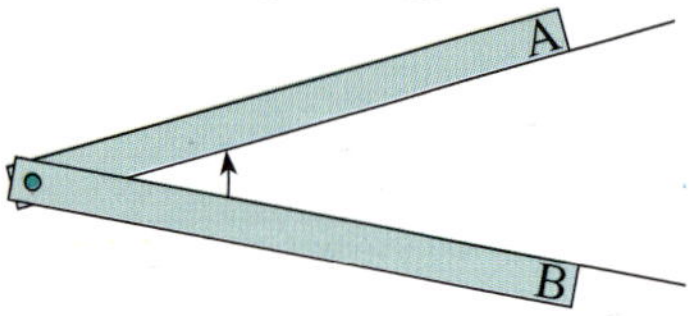

Without changing their position, place the strips on angle (b), so that the top edge of OB lies along the lower line of the angle:

(b)

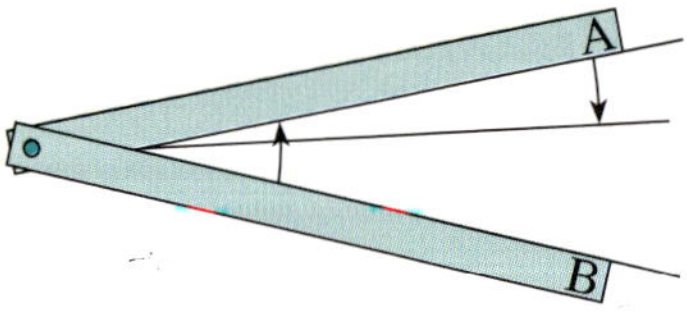

OA must be turned less to make the second angle.
So angle (a) is larger.

Exercise 5C

1 Use your cardboard strips to find out which angle is the largest in each of the following pairs.

(a) **(i)**

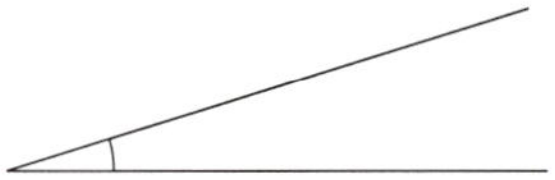

(ii)

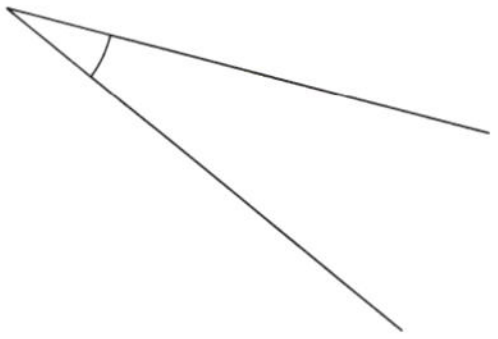

(b) **(i)**

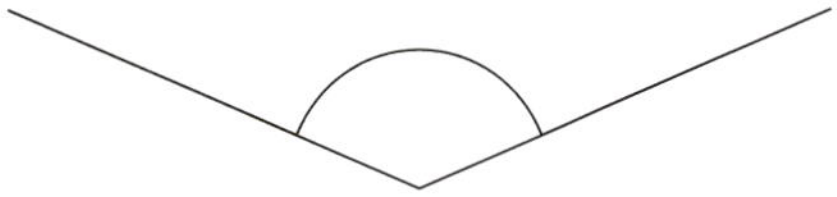

(ii)

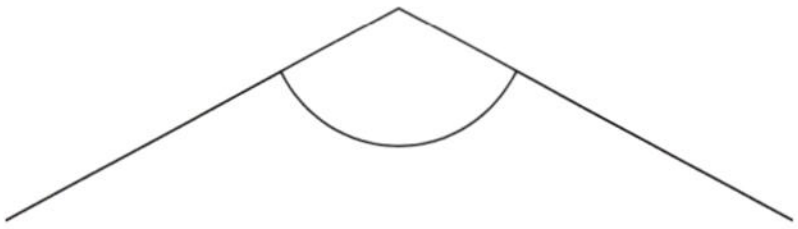

(c) **(i)**

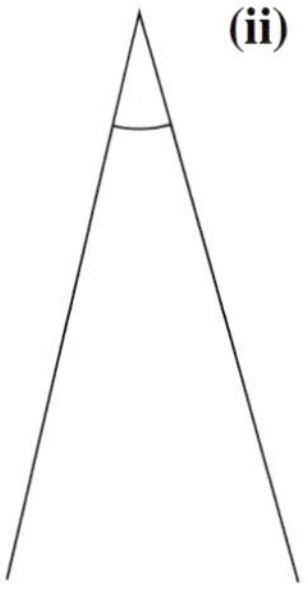

(ii)

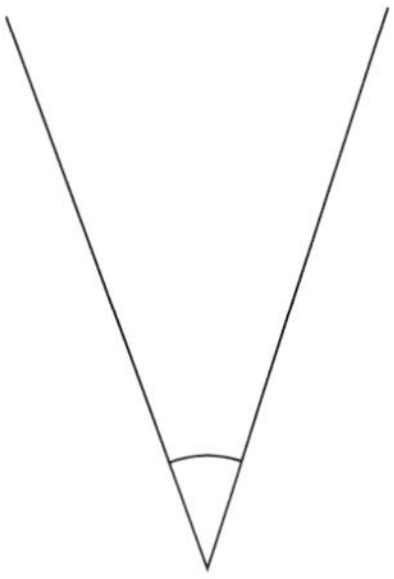

(d) **(i)**

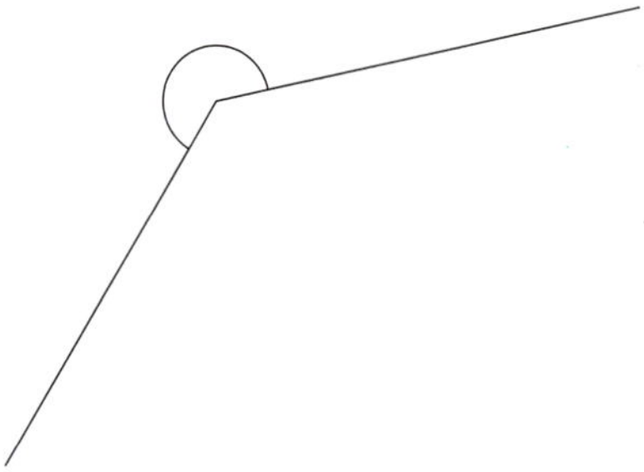

(ii)

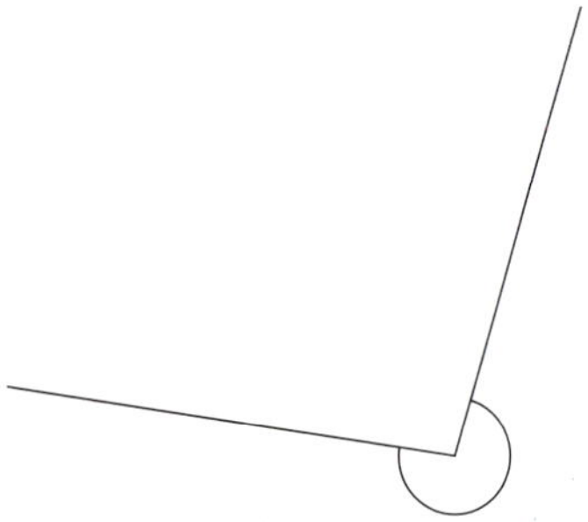

2 Look at these angles:

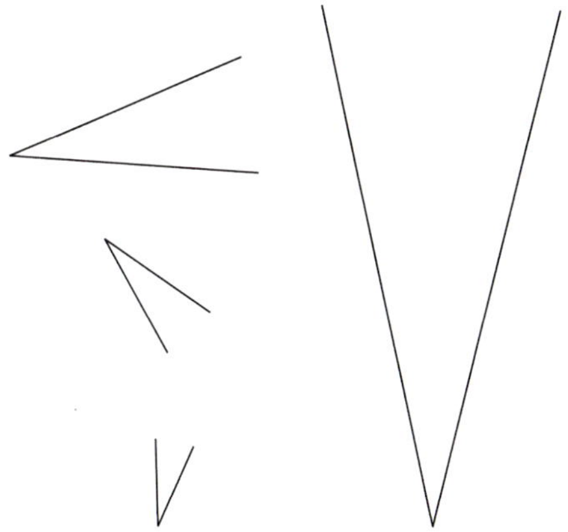

(a) What do you notice about the lengths of the lines?
(b) Use your strips to compares the angles. What do you notice?
(c) Do you think the length of the lines affects the size of the angle formed?

Some special angles

You can classify angles by the size of the turn:

A complete turn

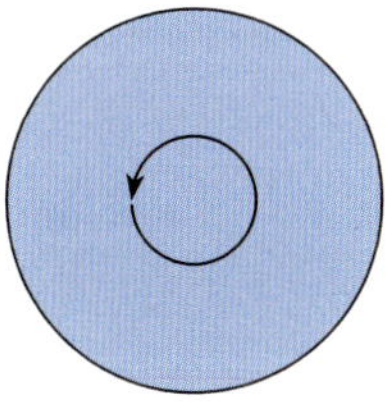

A $\frac{1}{2}$ turn is a **straight angle**

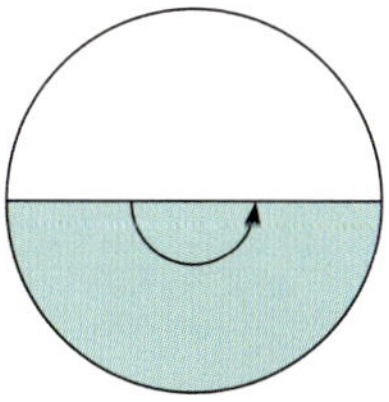

A $\frac{1}{4}$ turn is a **right angle**

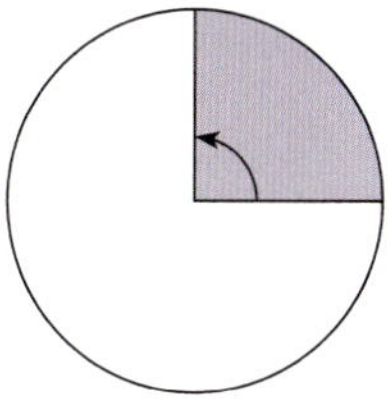

Less than a $\frac{1}{4}$ turn is an **acute angle**

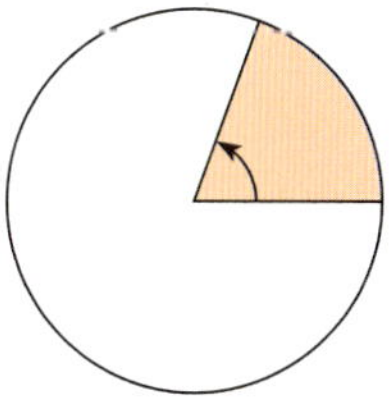

Between a $\frac{1}{4}$ and a $\frac{1}{2}$ turn is an **obtuse angle**

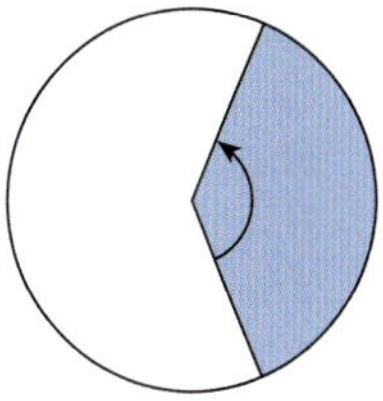

More than a $\frac{1}{2}$ turn but less than a whole turn is a **reflex angle**

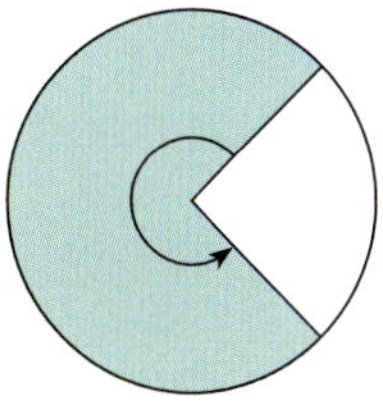

Activity

You can construct an angle maker like this:

1.

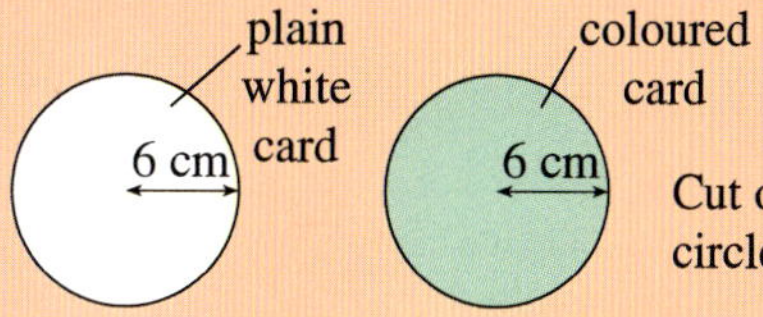

Cut out two circles.

2.

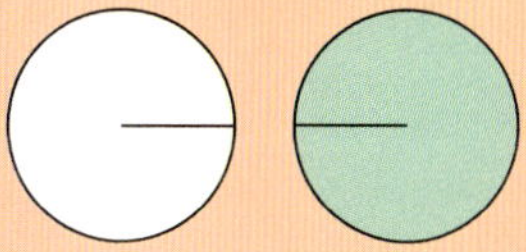

Cut a slit from the outside to the centre of each circle.

3.

Slide the circles together so the centres meet.

4.

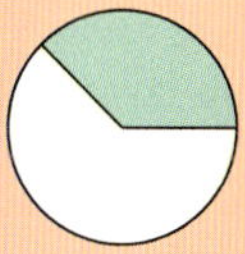

Rotate your angle marker to show different angles. Name each angle you make.

Exercise 5D

1 What is the name of the angle formed at the corner of this page?

2 Tear off a corner from a sheet of paper.

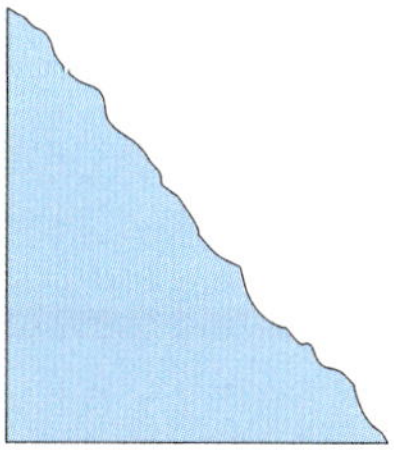

It forms a right angle.

(a) Use your right angle to identify 10 right angles in your classroom.

(b) Explain why you think right angles are important.

3 Use your square corner or right angle to find the number of right angles inside these shapes.

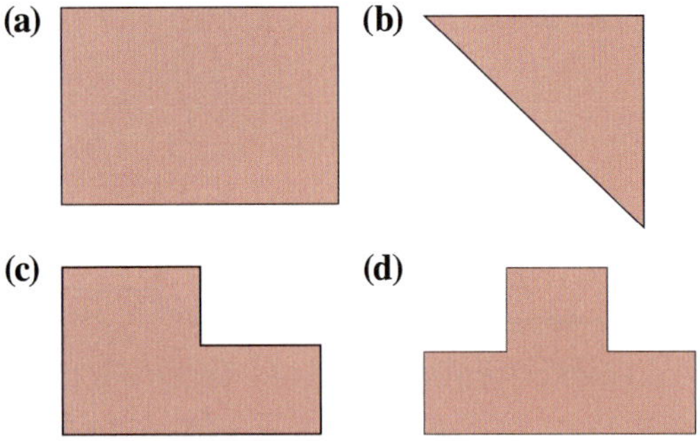

4 Draw four different shapes that have

(a) two right angles
(b) three right angles
(c) four right angles
(d) five right angles
(e) six right angles

5

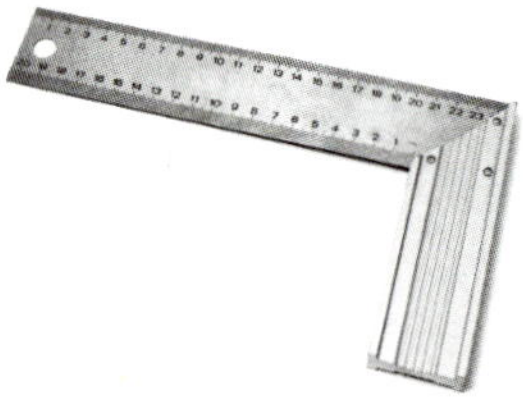

Use a set square to test whether the tables, chairs or other objects in your classroom have square corners or are straight.

6 When two lines meet to form a right angle, they are called **perpendicular** lines.
Look at the shapes. Identify the lines that are **(a)** perpendicular **(b)** parallel.

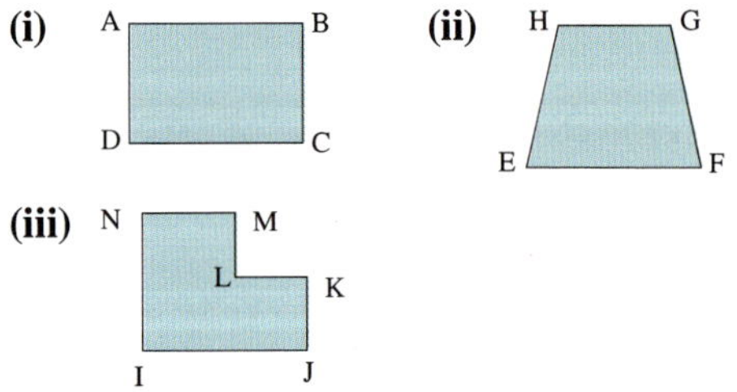

7 Look at the set of angles below.

(a) Which angles are right angles?
(b) Which angles are straight angles?
(c) Which angles are acute angles?
(d) Which angles are obtuse angles?
(e) Which angles are reflex angles?

A set of angles

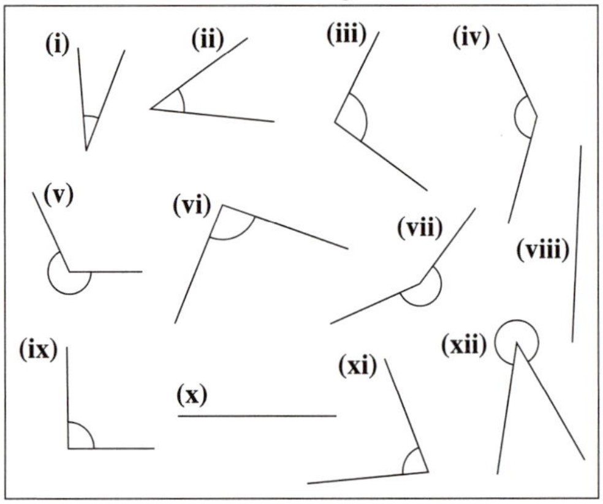

8 **(a)** Use your answers to Question 7 to copy and complete the Venn diagram below.

A set of angles

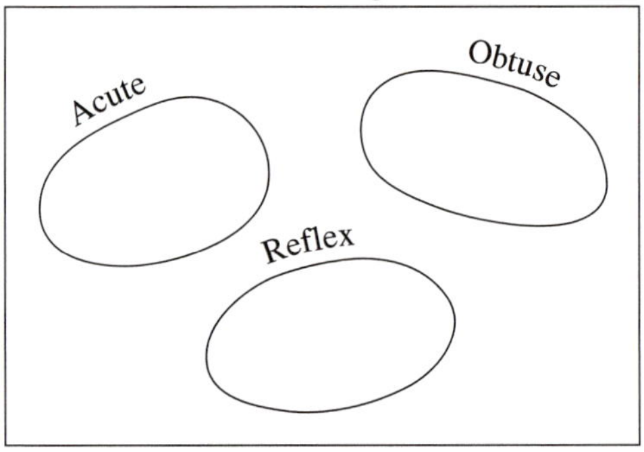

(b) Write down the names for the two sorts of angles which are outside the small loops in your Venn diagram.

5.2 Measuring angles

Before you measure an angle you should estimate its size:

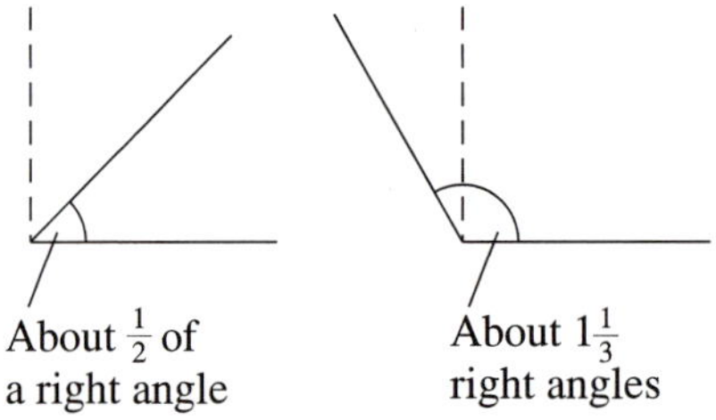

Exercise 5E

1 Estimate the size of each of these angles in the same way.

(a)

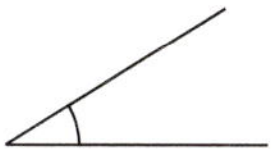

(b)

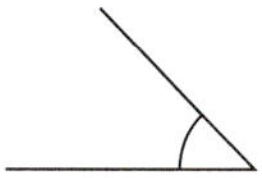

(c)

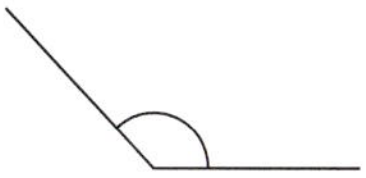

(d)

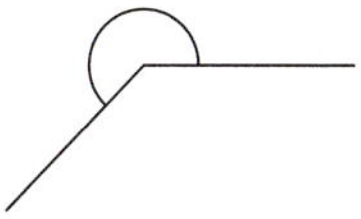

(e)

(f)

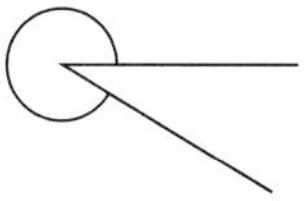

2 Compare your answers for Question 1 with those of a friend. Do you think the above method is a good one for measuring angles? Why?

The Babylonians, about 3000 years ago, thought of a better way to measure angles.
They divided a complete turn into 360 equal parts because they thought there were 360 days in a year.

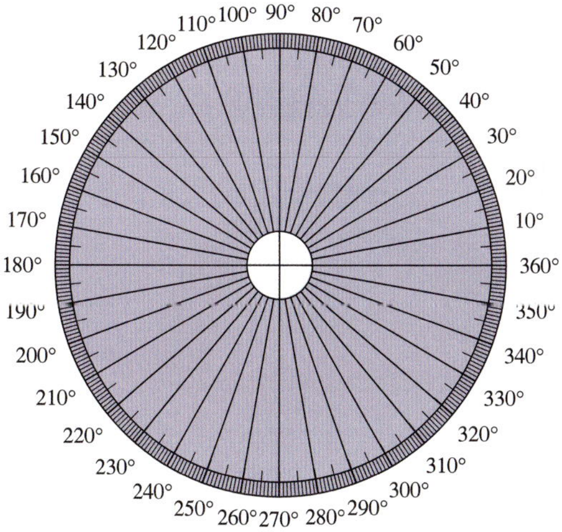

Each of these equal parts is now called a **degree**.
$\frac{1}{360}$ of a complete turn is a degree.
One degree is written as 1°.

•

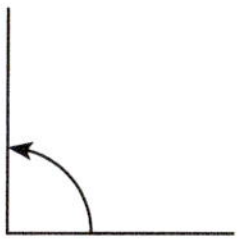

a quarter turn = 90°

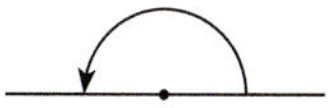

a half turn = 180°

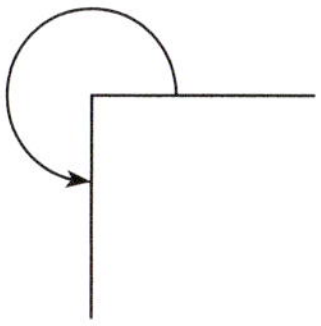

three-quarter turn = 270°

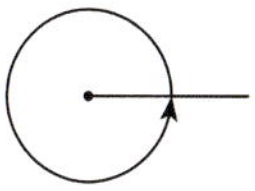

one whole turn = 360°

Dividing a complete turn into 360 equal parts helps you make better estimates of angle size.

Example 2

Estimate the size of these two angles.

(a)

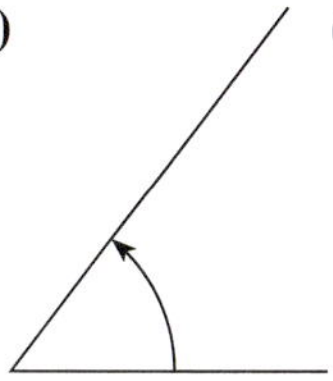

(b)

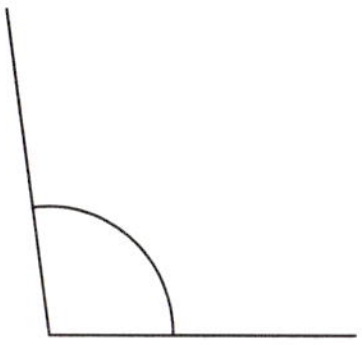

(a) This is less than a $\frac{1}{4}$-turn or 90°.
It is about 50°.

(b) This is more than 90°, but not much more.
It is about 100°.

Exercise 5F

1 How many degrees are in:

(a) a right angle
(b) a straight angle
(c) three right angles
(d) half a right angle
(e) one third of a right angle?

2 Estimate the size of these angles in degrees.

(a)

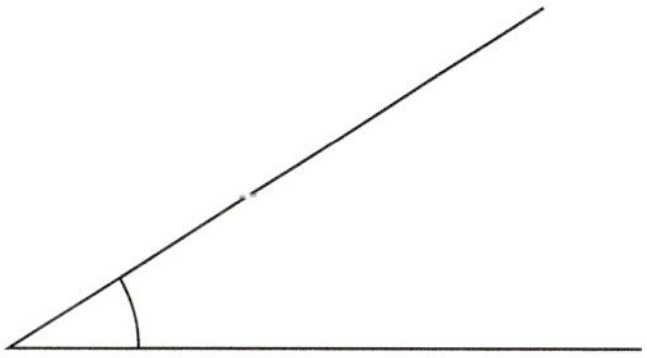

(b)

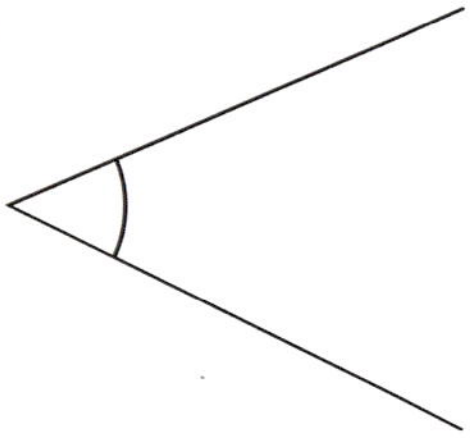

(c)

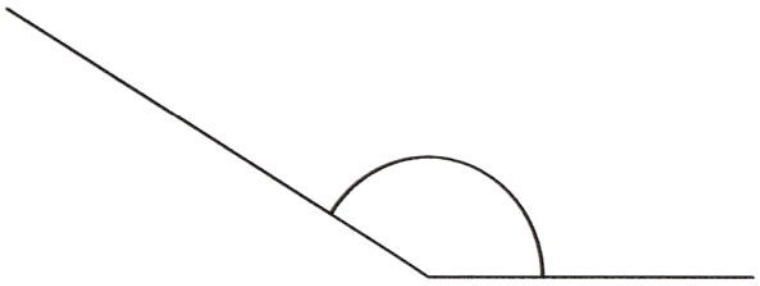

(d)

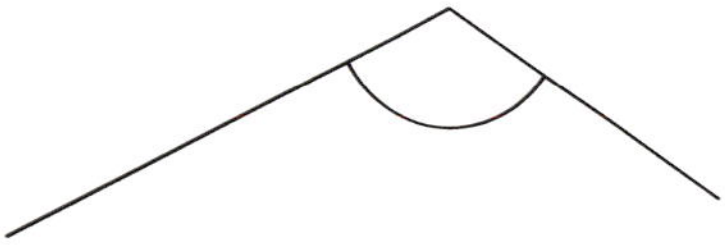

(e)

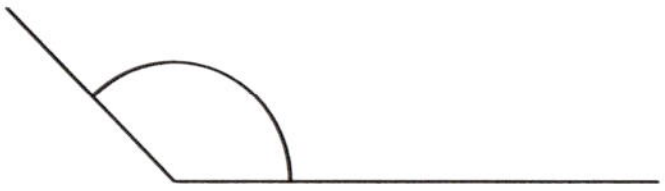

(f)

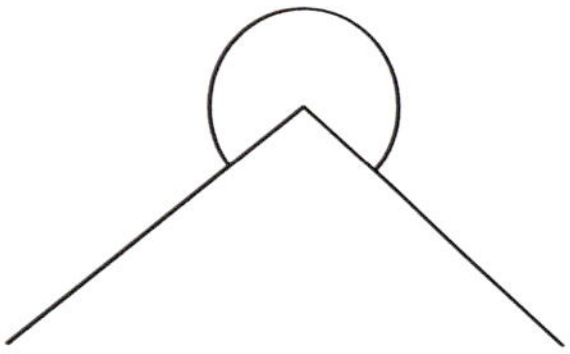

3 Copy and complete this table. All turns are clockwise from the first compass point to the second.

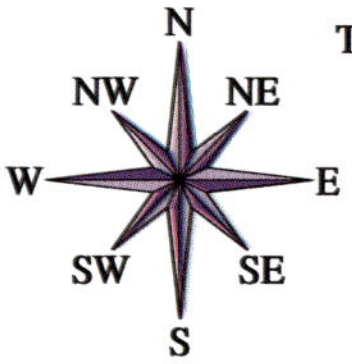

The compass

	Turning clockwise		Number of degrees	Kind of angle
	From	To		
(a)	N	E		
(b)	E	SW		
(c)	W	NW		
(d)	E	NE		
(e)	NW	SE		
(f)	SW	SE		
(g)	NE	S		
(h)	NE	W		
(i)	N	NW		

Technology

Forgotten all about angles? Have a go at the Kung Fu angles game in The Math Zone at the website

www.woodlands-junior.kent.sch.uk

Start at level 1. Level 3 is for experts!

If you prefer something easier try the alien angles game at

www.mathplayground.com

Measuring angles accurately—using a protractor

To measure angles accurately, we use an instrument with the degrees marked on it called a **protractor**.

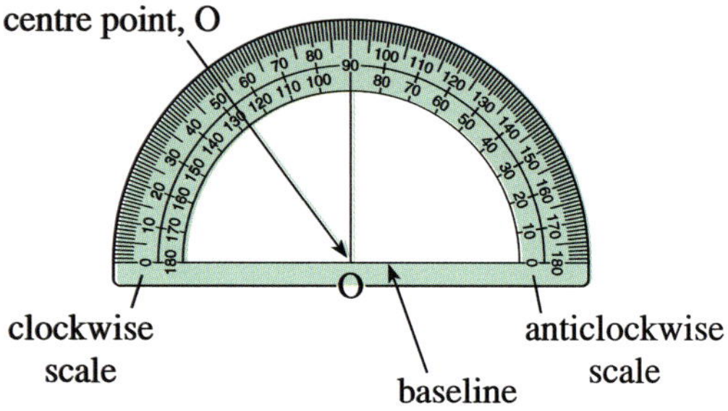

There are two scales; both read from 0 to 180°.

To decide which scale to read, check if the angle is larger or smaller than 90°.

Example 3

Measure the angle ABC.

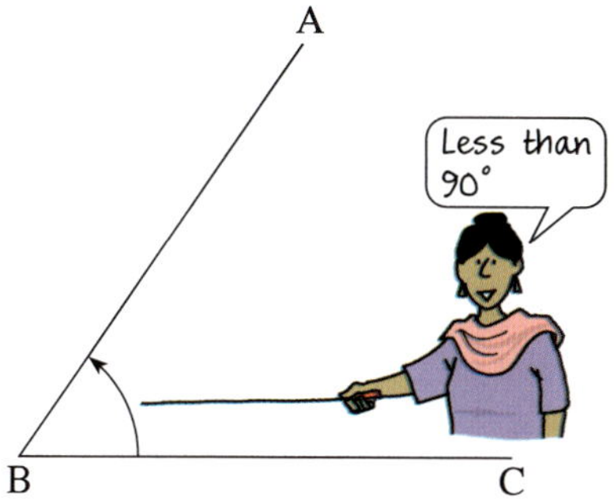

Put the protractor on the angle as shown. Make sure that the centre of the protractor, O, lies on the point B of the angle and that the baseline lies on BC.

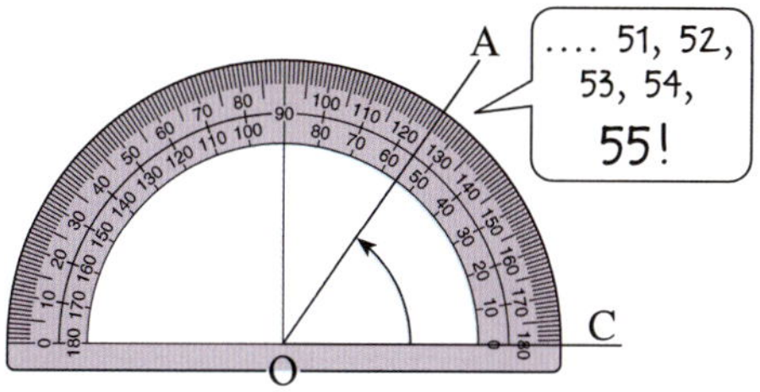

A$\hat{B}$C is less than 90°, so we can use the anticlockwise scale.

A$\hat{B}$C = 55°

The position of the angle does not matter:

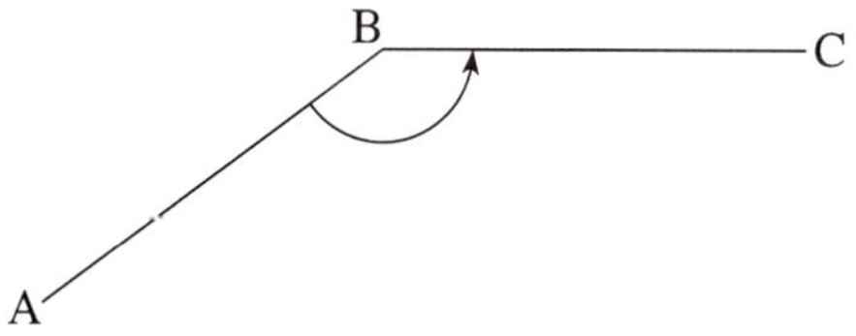

Just place the baseline on AB and make sure O lies on the corner of the angle B.

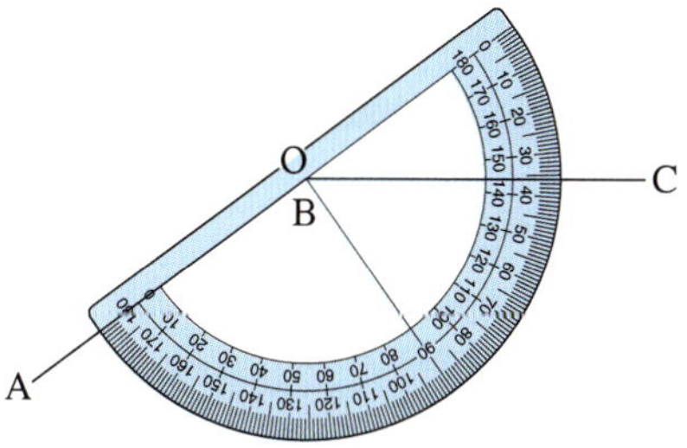

A$\hat{B}$C is larger than 90°, so we use the anticlockwise scale.

A$\hat{B}$C = 144°

(A clockwise scale reading would be 36°. This cannot be correct as the angle is larger than 90°.)

Exercise 5G

1 **(a)** Estimate, then measure the size of these angles.

(i)

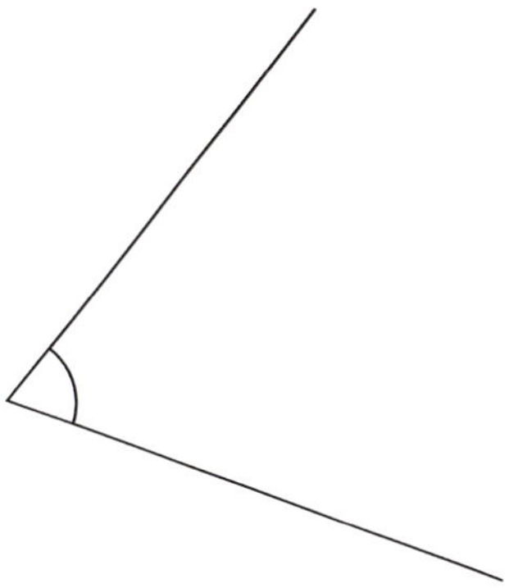

(ii)

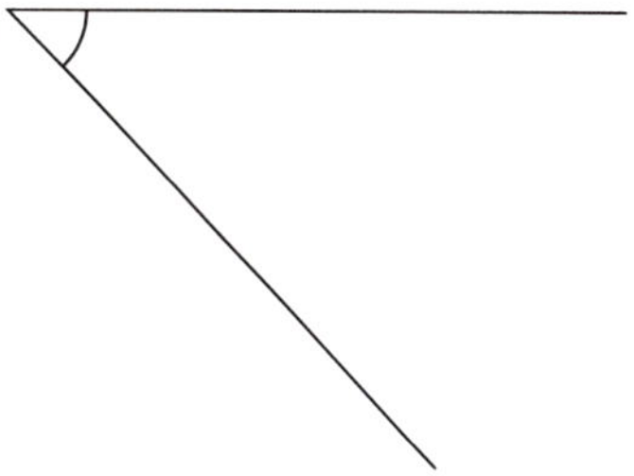

(iii)

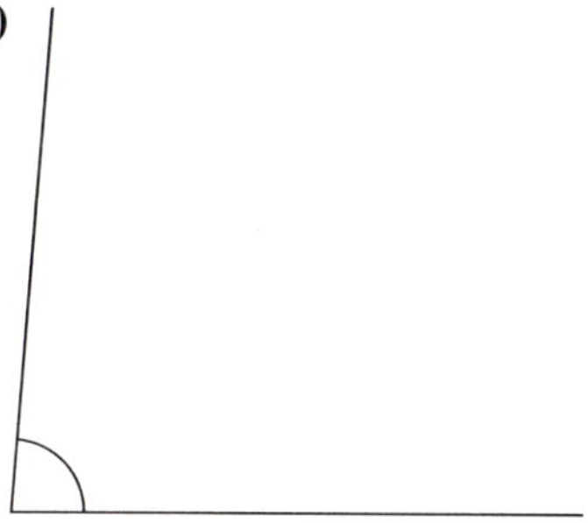

(iv)

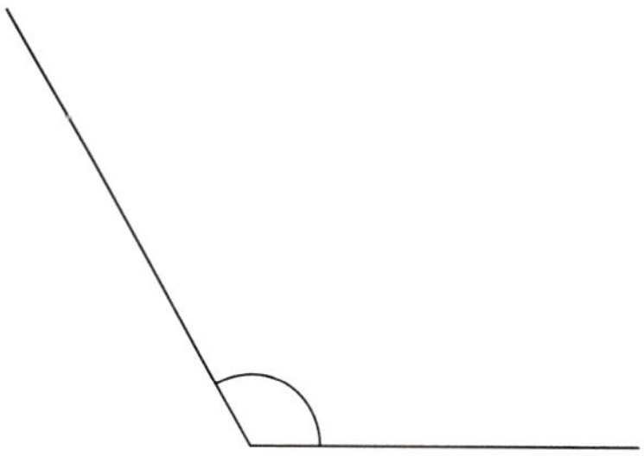

(b) Copy and complete the table for the angles in part (a).

Angle	Estimate	Actual size
(i)		
(ii)		
(iii)		
(iv)		

2 Repeat Question 1 for these angles.

(i)

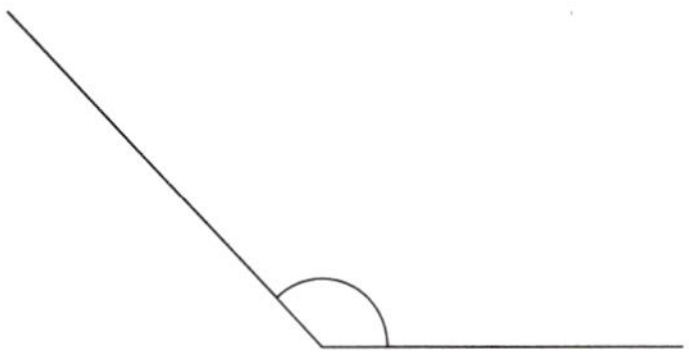

(ii)

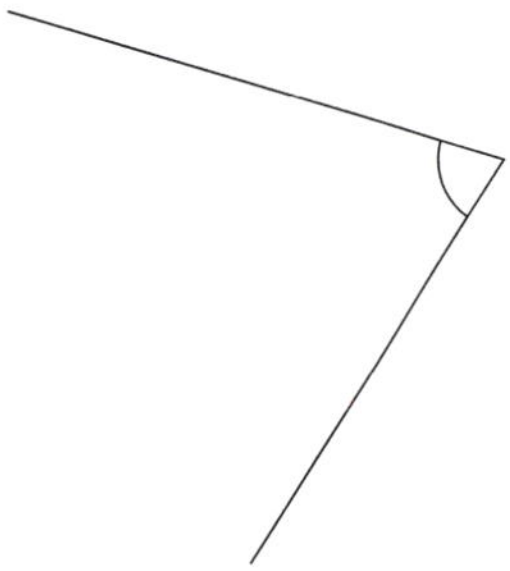

(iii)

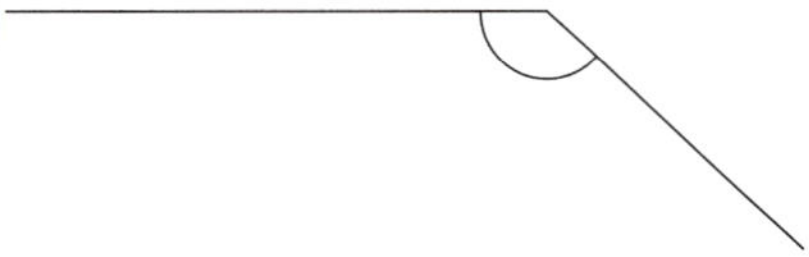

(iv)

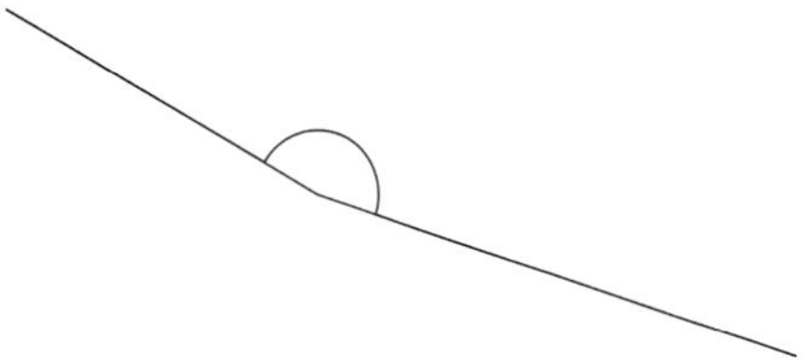

3 Using a ruler and pencil, draw an angle you think is:

(a) 10° **(b)** 30° **(c)** 60°
(d) 80° **(e)** 105° **(f)** 130°
(g) 145° **(h)** 170°

Now measure your angles. Did you guess well?

5.3 Drawing angles

A protractor can be used to draw angles as well as to measure them. You will need a protractor in this section, and a ruler.

Drawing an angle accurately is almost the reverse of measuring an angle.

Example 4

Draw the angle PQR = 55°.

The drawing of angle PQR is made up of the two lines PQ and QR which meet at Q.

First draw the line PQ.

P ———————————— Q

Place your protractor with its base line on PQ and its centre on Q, as shown:

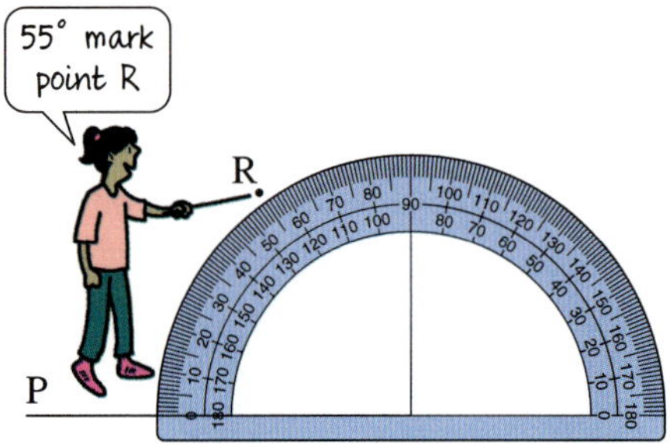

Start at 0°, on the clockwise scale, and move around until 55° is reached. Mark that point R.

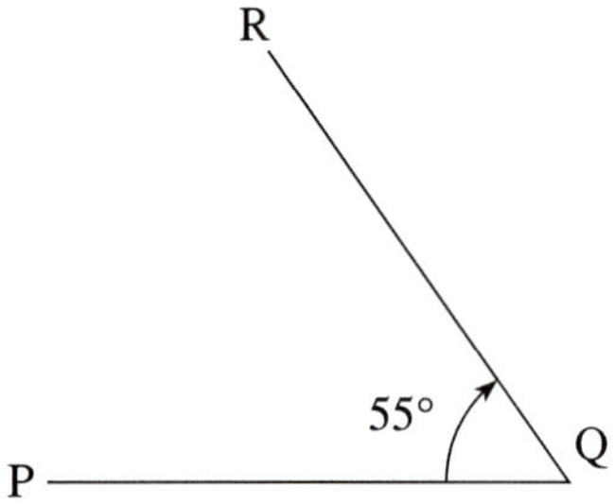

Finally join the point R to Q with your ruler.

Exercise 5H

1 **(a)** Draw the line XY, as shown below.

X ———————————— Y

(b) Now use a protractor to draw an angle $Z\hat{X}Y$ of 55°.
This time, where should you put the centre point O of the protractor?
Should you use the clockwise or anticlockwise scale?

2 For each of the following, decide whether it is acute or obtuse, then draw it.

(a) 60° **(b)** 78° **(c)** 35°
(d) 90° **(e)** 120° **(f)** 44°

3 Repeat Question 2 for:

(a) 177° **(b)** 10° **(c)** 12°
(d) 136° **(e)** 94° **(f)** 100°

4 **(a)** Draw the line PQ = $5\frac{1}{2}$ cm, as shown below.

(b) Draw a 30° angle at P.
Your drawing should look like this:

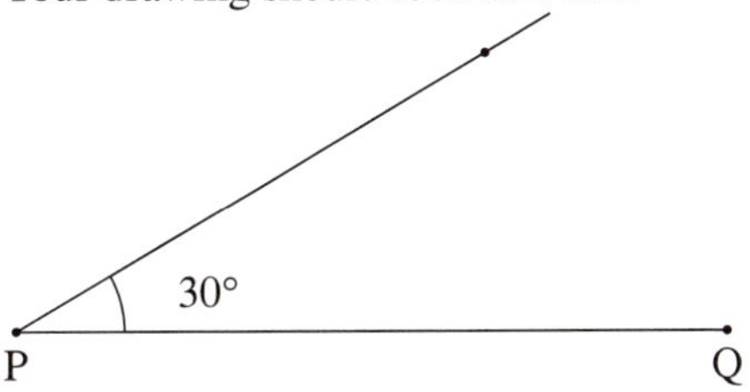

(c) At Q, draw a 40° angle.
Your drawing should now look like this:

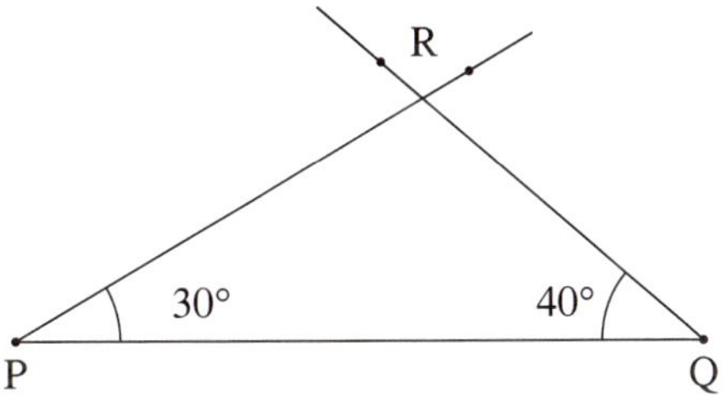

(d) Label the point where the two lines meet R.
You have drawn the triangle PQR with PQ = $5\frac{1}{2}$ cm, $\hat{P} = 30°$ and $\hat{Q} = 40°$.

5 Draw these triangles in the same way as you did in Question 4.

(a) Triangle PQR with PQ = 6 cm, $\hat{P} = 35°$ and $\hat{Q} = 50°$.
(b) Triangle XYZ with XY = 6 cm, $\hat{X} = 60°$ and $\hat{Y} = 60°$.
(c) Triangle ABC with AB = 4 cm, $\hat{A} = 90°$ and $\hat{B} = 37°$.

5.4 Relations between angles

A **corner** measures 90°.

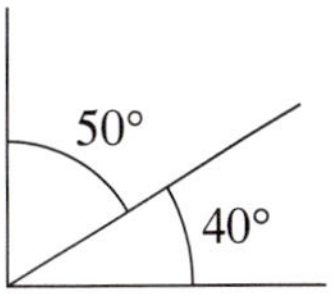

Angles that add to 90° are called **complementary**.
A **straight angle** measures 180°.

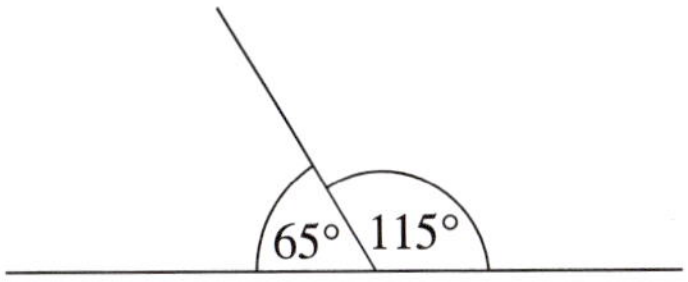

Angles that add up to 180° are called **supplementary**.

Exercise 5I

1 From the diagram, use your protractor to copy and complete:

(a) $A\hat{D}B = \square$
(b) $B\hat{D}C = \square$
(c) $A\hat{D}C = \square$
(d) $A\hat{D}B + B\hat{D}C = \square$
(e) $A\hat{D}B$ and $B\hat{D}C$ are called ☐

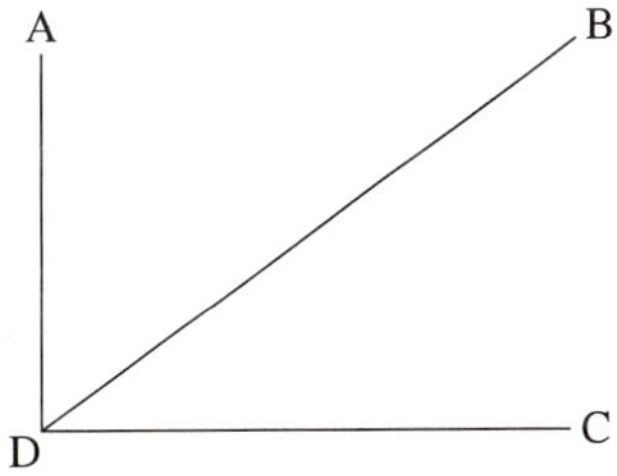

2 From the diagram use your protractor to copy and complete:

(a) $M\hat{O}N = \square$ **(b)** $L\hat{O}M = \square$
(c) $M\hat{O}N + L\hat{O}M = \square$
(d) $M\hat{O}N$ and $L\hat{O}M$ are called ☐.

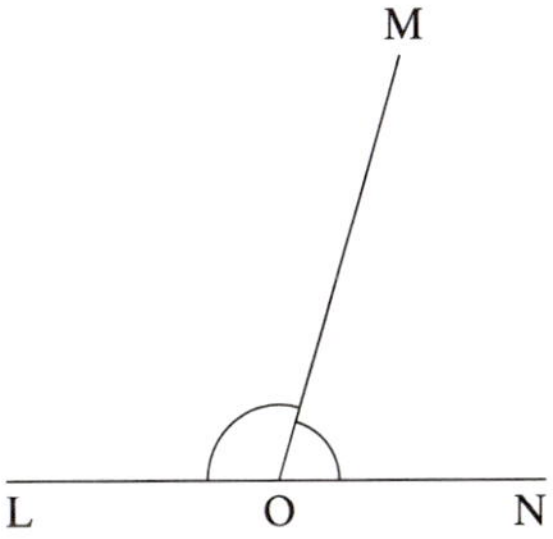

3 **(a)** Repeat Question 2 for these diagrams.

(i)

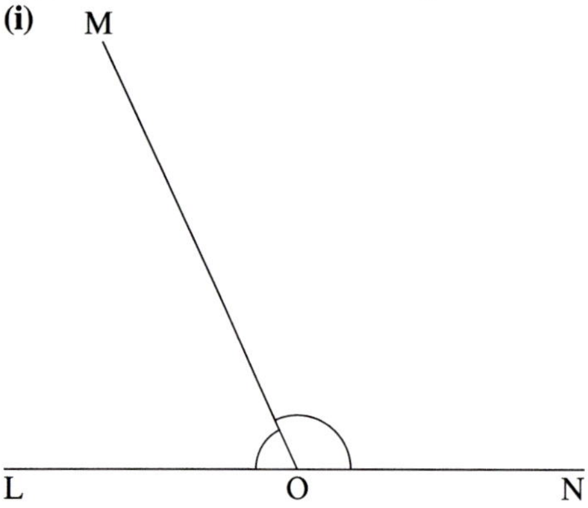

(ii)

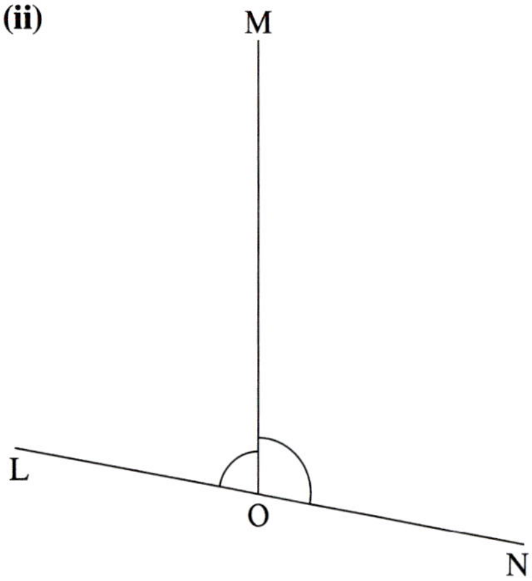

(b) Do you agree that: MÔN + LÔM = 180° in each diagram? Why should this be true?

4 From the diagram use your protractor to copy and complete:

(a) AÔD = □
(b) BÔC = □
(c) DÔB = □
(d) AÔC = □

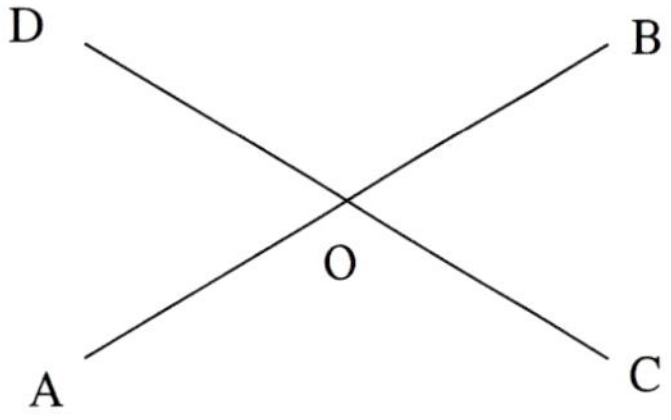

What do you notice about your answers?

5 Repeat Question 4 for these diagrams.

(i)

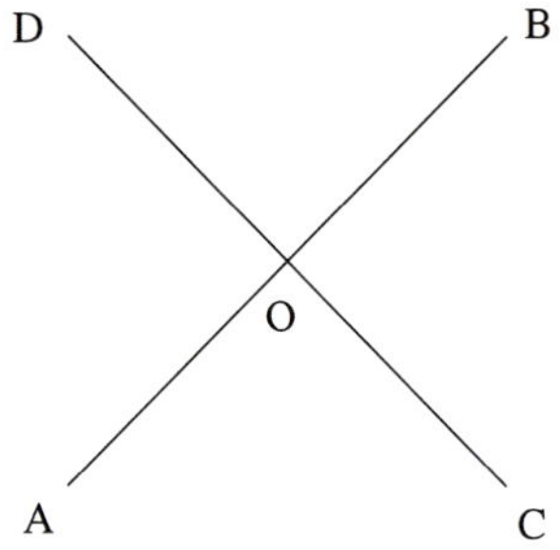

(ii)

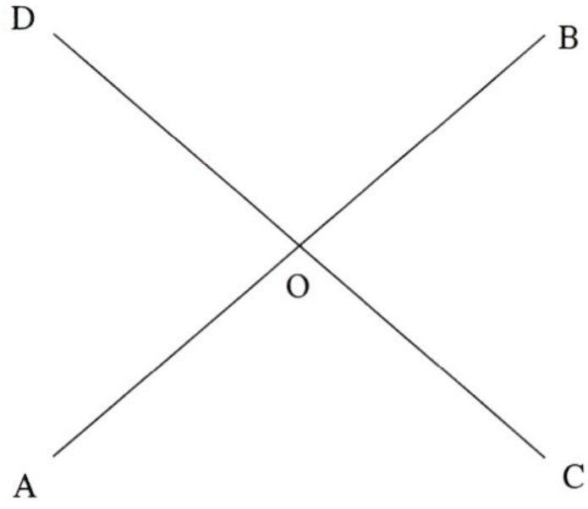

You should have found that

AÔD = CÔB

and AÔC = DÔB.

That is, **vertically opposite** angles are equal.

Calculating complementary and supplementary angles

You can find complementary and supplementary angles without measuring:

Example 5

Without measuring, write down the missing angle.

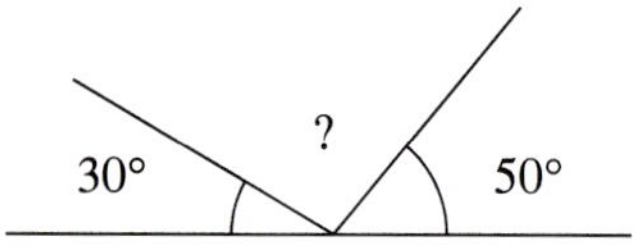

As the angles 30°, ?, 50° form a straight angle they add up to 180°.

That is 30° + ? + 50° = 180°

? = 100°

Exercise 5J

1 Without measuring, find the missing angles.

(a)

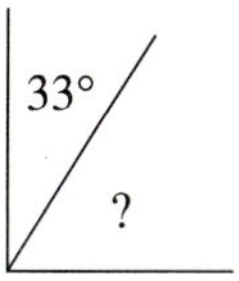

(b)

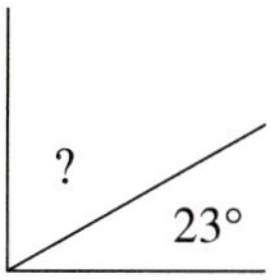

(c)

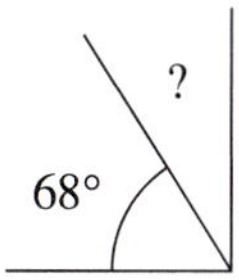

(d)

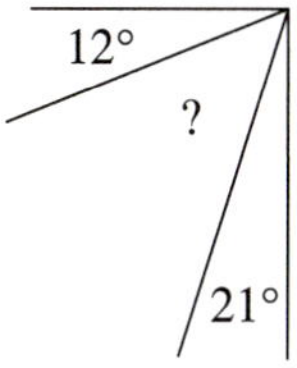

2 Without measuring, find the missing angles.

(a)

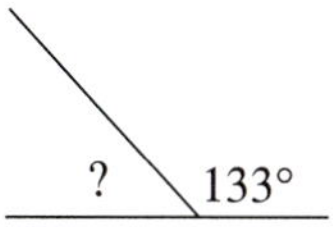

(b)

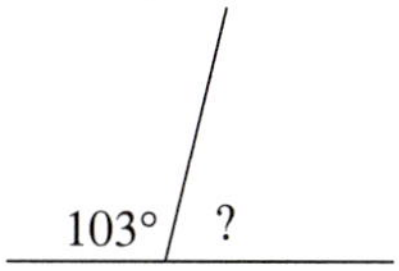

(c)

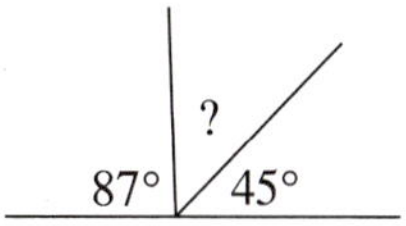

(d)

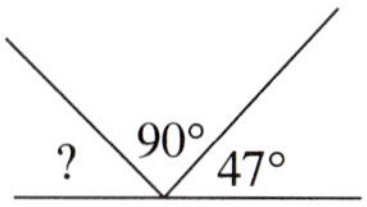

3 Without measuring, write down the missing angles.

(a)

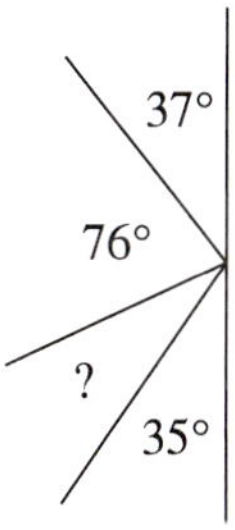

(b)

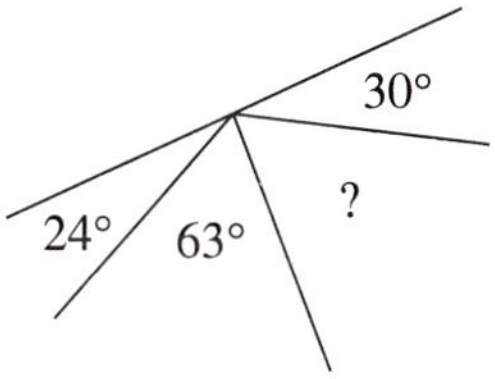

Angles in triangles and quadrilaterals

A triangle has 3 sides.
A quadrilateral has 4 sides.

Exercise 5K will help you find the sum of the angles in any triangle or quadrilateral.

Exercise 5K

1 **(a)** Use your protractor, to measure the angles in the triangle.

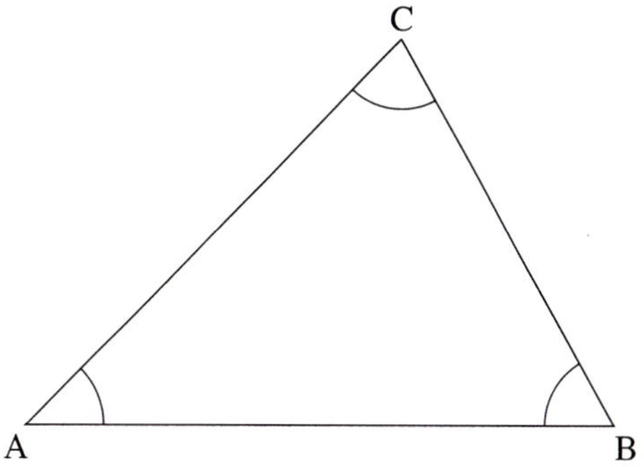

(b) Copy and complete:

$$\hat{A} = \square$$
$$\hat{B} = \square$$
$$\hat{C} = \square$$
$$\hat{A} + \hat{B} + \hat{C} = \square$$

2 **(a)** Draw four more triangles of your own. Repeat Question 1 for each of them.

(b) Did you find that $\hat{A} + \hat{B} + \hat{C} = 180°$?

3 **(a)** With a ruler and pencil, draw a triangle. Cut it out very carefully.

(b) Now colour or shade each angle differently.

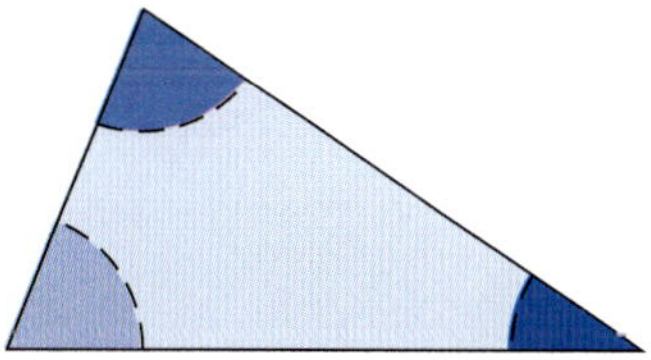

Cut off the angles along the dotted lines.

(c) Carefully fit the cut-out angles together. They should look like this:

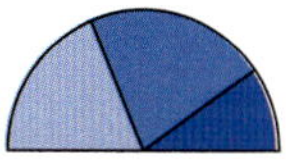

(d) What angle is formed by the three angles?

4 **(a)** In the four-sided figure ABCD measure each of the angles.

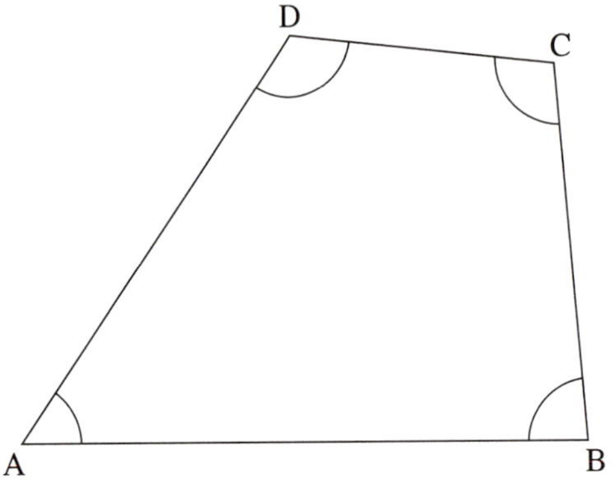

(b) Copy and complete

$\hat{A} = \square$

$\hat{B} = \square$

$\hat{C} = \square$

$\hat{D} = \square$

$\hat{A} + \hat{B} + \hat{C} + \hat{D} = \square$

5 **(a)** Repeat Question 4 for three different four-sided figures of your own.

(b) Did you find that $\hat{A} + \hat{B} + \hat{C} + \hat{D} = 360°$?

6 **(a)** With a ruler and pencil, draw accurately a four-sided figure. Cut it out carefully.

(b) Now colour or shade each angle differently.

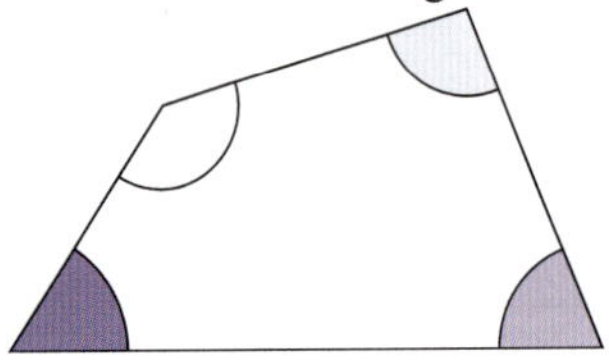

Cut off the angles along the dotted lines.

(c) Carefully fit the cut-out angles together. They should look like this:

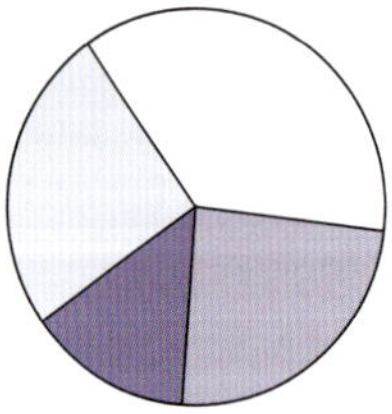

(d) What angle is formed by the four angles?

Investigation

Using a rectangular piece of paper can you make an angle of

(a) 45°

(b) 60°?

What other angles can you make?

Activity

Draw a large circle. Mark every 15° around the outer edge.
Using your ruler and a pencil join every point marked on the circle to every other point.
This is how you should start:

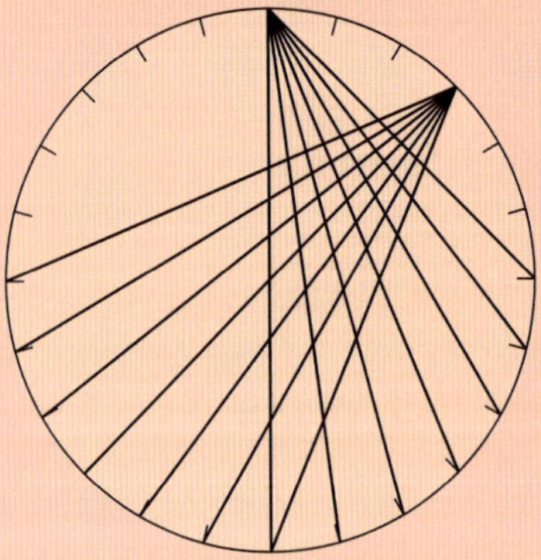

The finished pattern is called a Mystic Rose.

Exercise 5L – mixed questions

1 Here is a sketch of a building.
Copy the sketch and mark in the acute angles, obtuse angles and right angles.

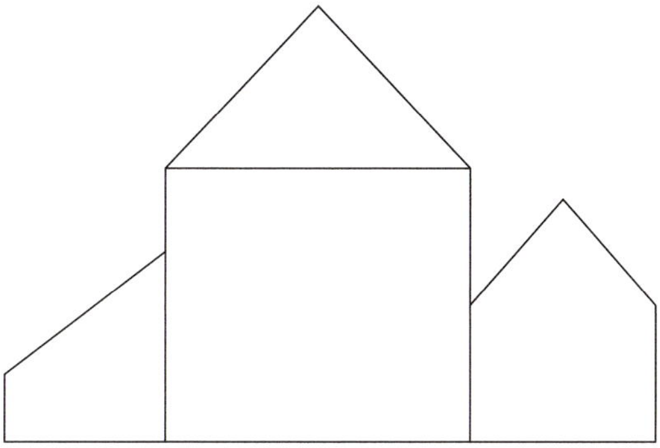

2 Estimate, then measure the size of these angles.

(a)

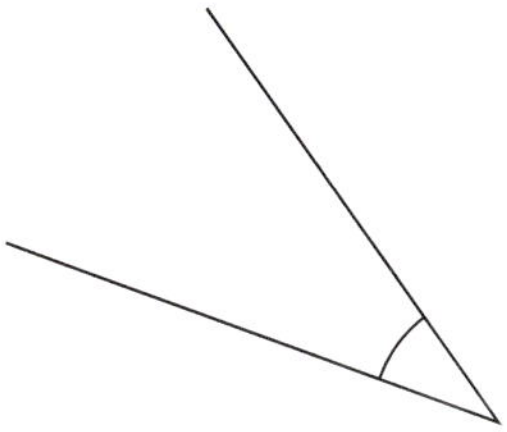

(b)

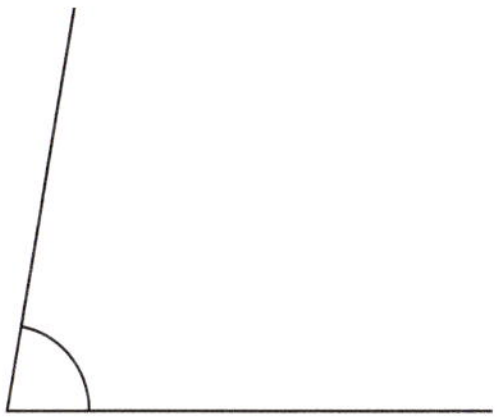

(c)

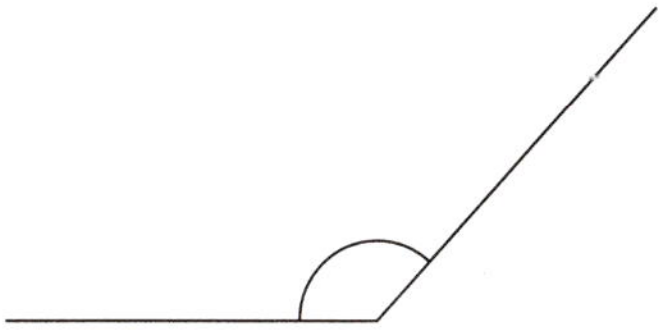

3 The diagram shows part of a bicycle frame.

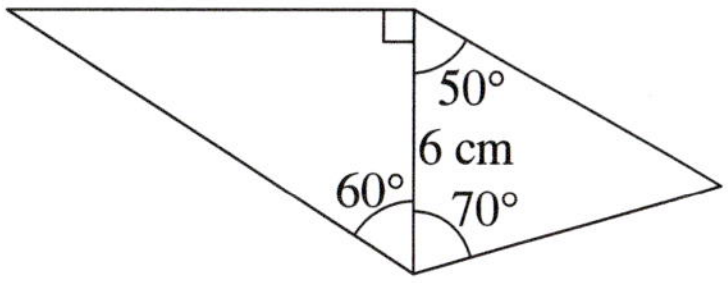

Make an accurate drawing of the bicycle frame diagram using the measurements on the diagram.

4 Without measuring, find the missing angles:

(a)

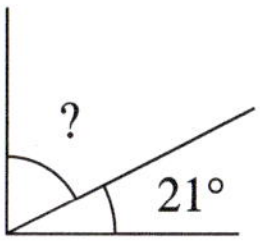

(b)

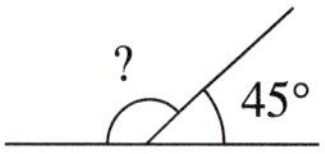

(c)

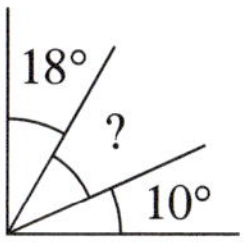

(d)

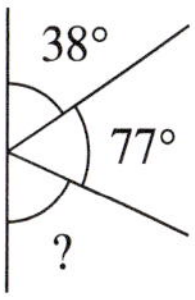

5 Find the missing angles:

(a)

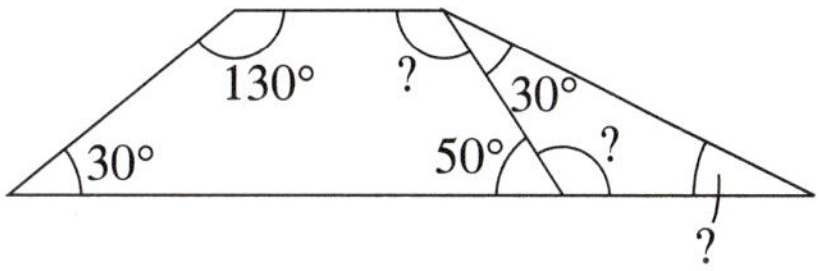

(b)

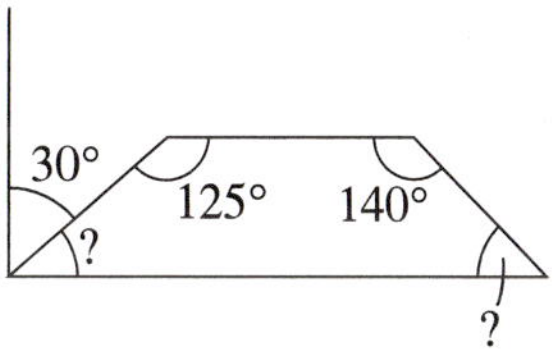

5 Consolidation

Example 1

(a) Estimate the size of the marked angles.

(i)

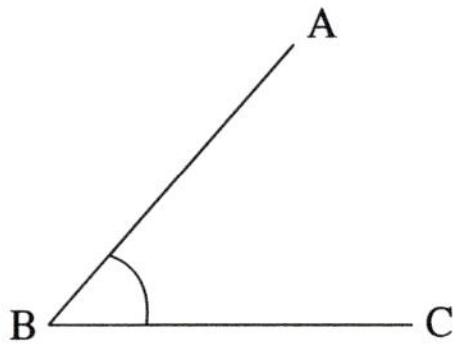

(ii)

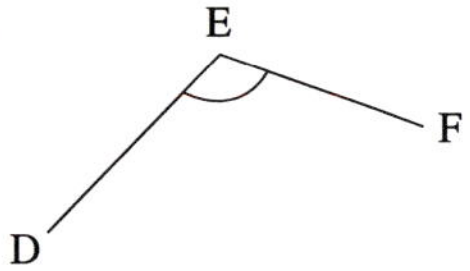

(b) Measure these angles with a protractor.

(a) **(i)** AB̂C is less than 90°, so estimate 40°.

(ii) DÊF is less than 180°, so estimate 120°.

(b) **(i)**

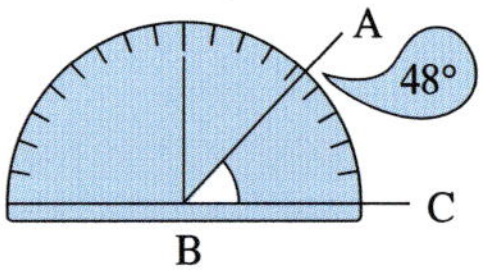

(ii)

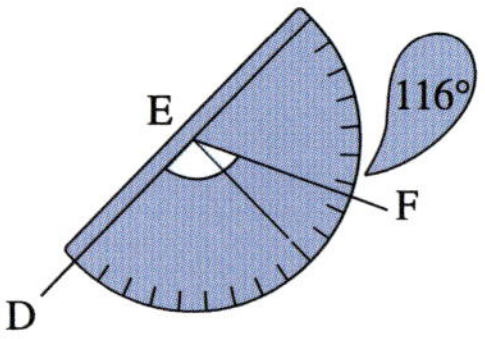

Example 2

Without measuring, find the missing angles.

(a)

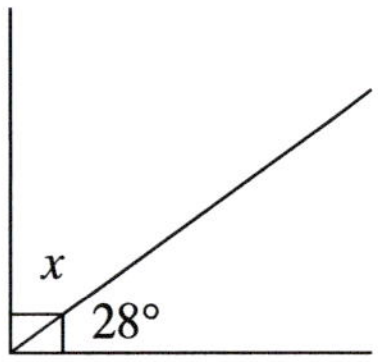

(b)

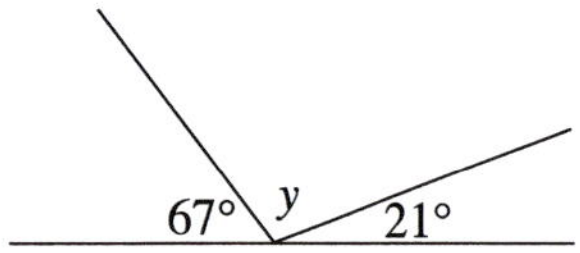

(a) The angles form a right angle.

Hence, $x + 28° = 90°$

$x = 90° - 28°$

$x = 62°$

(b) The angles form a straight line.

Hence, $67° + y + 21° = 180°$

$88° + y = 180°$

$y = 180° - 88°$

$y = 92°$

Example 3

Find the missing angles.

(a)

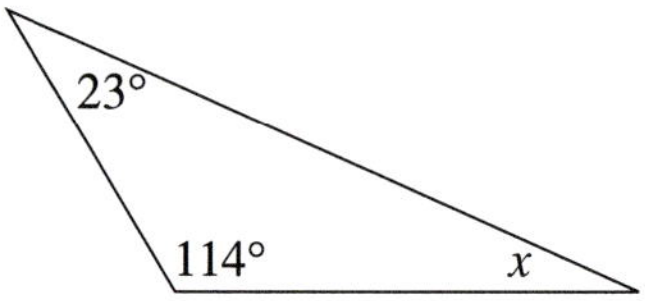

(b)

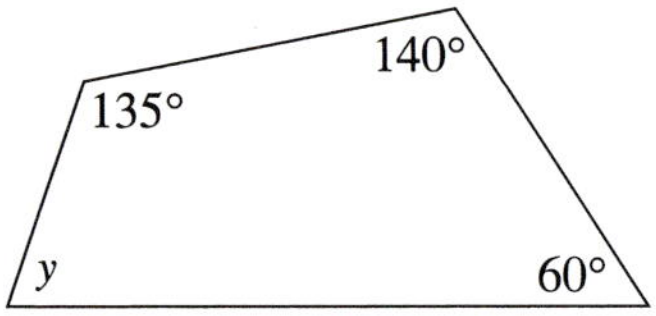

(a) Angles in a triangle sum to 180°.

$23° + 114° + x = 180°$

$137° + x = 180°$

$x = 180° - 137°$

$x = 43°$

(b) Angles in quadrilateral sum to 360°.

$y + 135° + 140° + 60° = 360°$

$y + 335° = 360°$

$y = 360° - 335°$

$y = 25°$

Exercise 5

1 **(a)** Estimate the size of the angles marked.

(i)

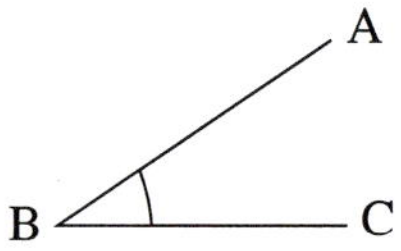

(ii)

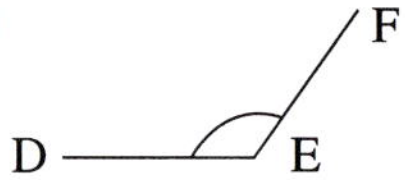

(iii)

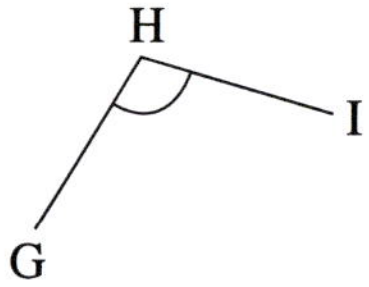

(b) Measure the angles above accurately with a protractor.
(c) How good were your estimates?

2 Use your protractor to draw angles of
(a) 30° **(b)** 37° **(c)** 52° **(d)** 100° **(e)** 169°

3 Without measuring, calculate the missing angles.

(a)
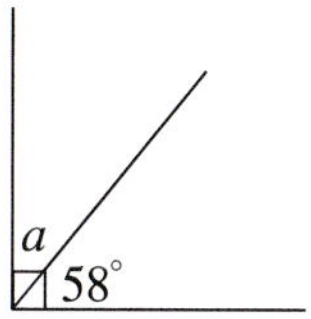

(b)
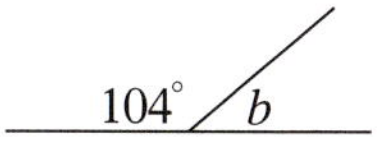

(c)
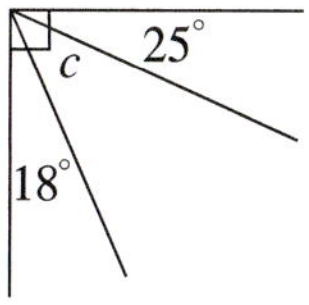

(d)
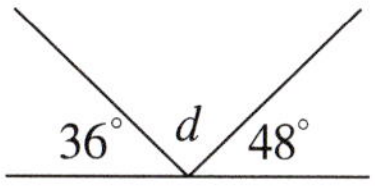

(e)
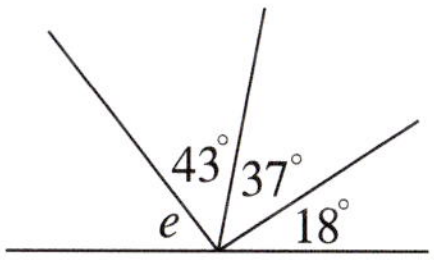

4 Calculate the missing angles.

(a)
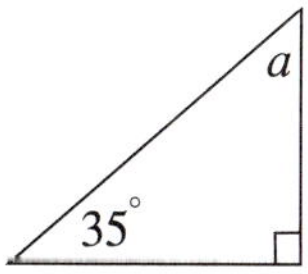

(b)
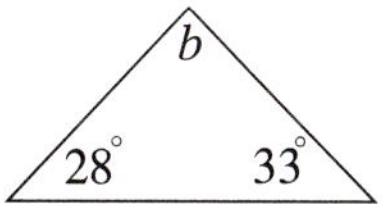

(c)
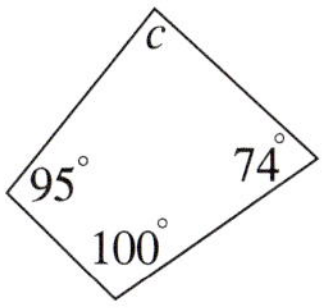

Application 5

5 Some experts advise that a hurricane-resistant house should have a roof with a $\frac{5}{12}$ slope.

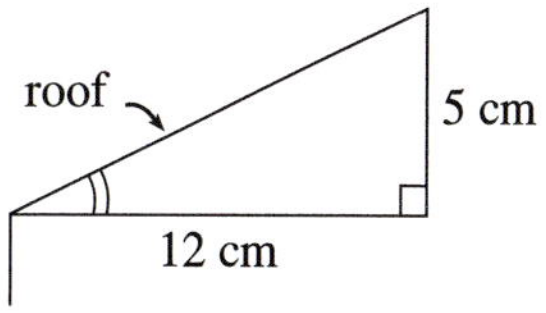

(a) Make an accurate drawing of the triangle above.
(b) Measure the angle marked to find angle of slope of the roof.
(c) Do you agree with the experts? Give reasons.

6 A bicycle wheel has 12 equally spaced spokes. What is the angle between the spokes?

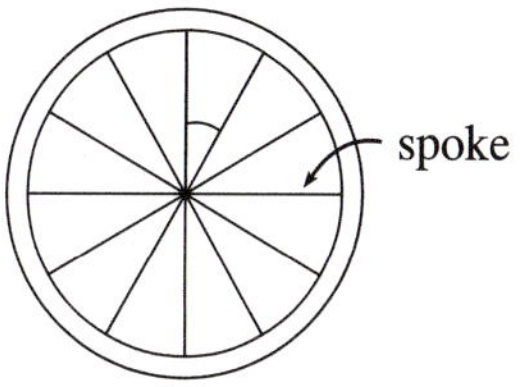

Companion CD

Want some extra practice? Go to Chapter 5 on your companion CD for further exercises, animations, and solutions.

Summary

You should know ...

1 You can use letters to name an angle:

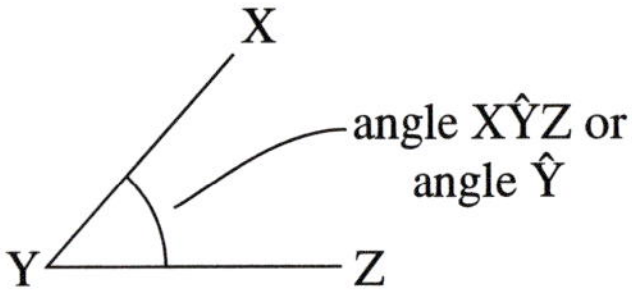

2 You can classify angles by the amount of turn:

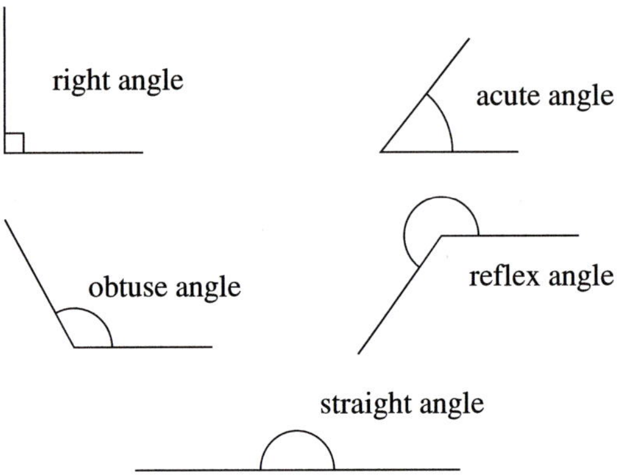

Check out

1 **(a)** Name this angle.

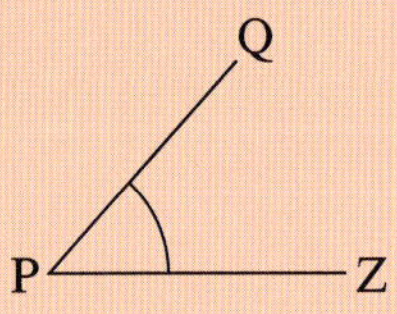

(b) Which is the largest angle?

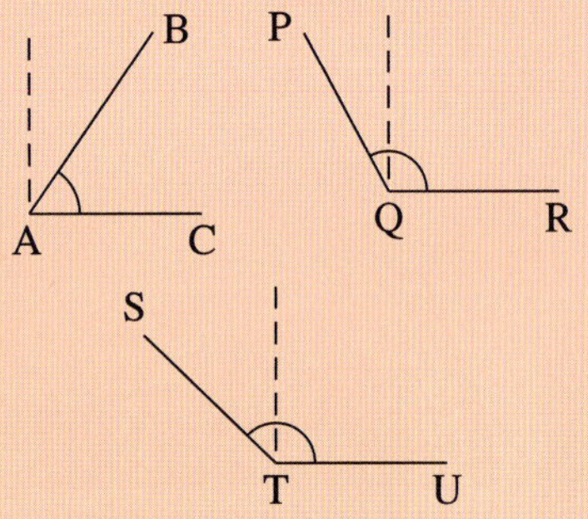

2 Classify these angles:

(a)

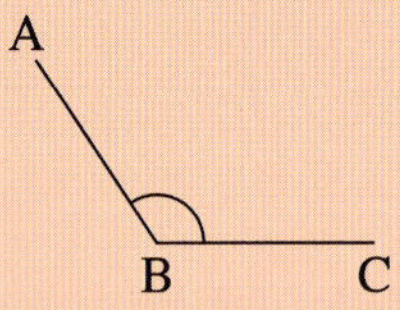

(b)

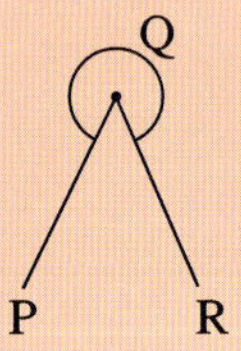

(c)

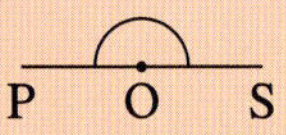

(d)

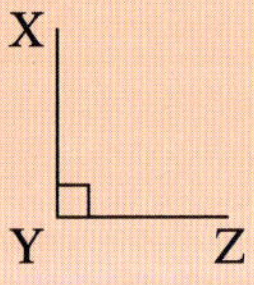

3 You can draw an angle using a protractor.

3 Draw the following angles using a protractor.
(a) 60° **(b)** 80° **(c)** 120° **(d)** 160°
(e) 200° **(f)** 270° **(g)** 180° **(h)** 150°

4 An angle can be measured in degrees, or ° for short.

You use a protractor to measure angles in degrees.

4 Use your protractor to measure these angles:

(a)

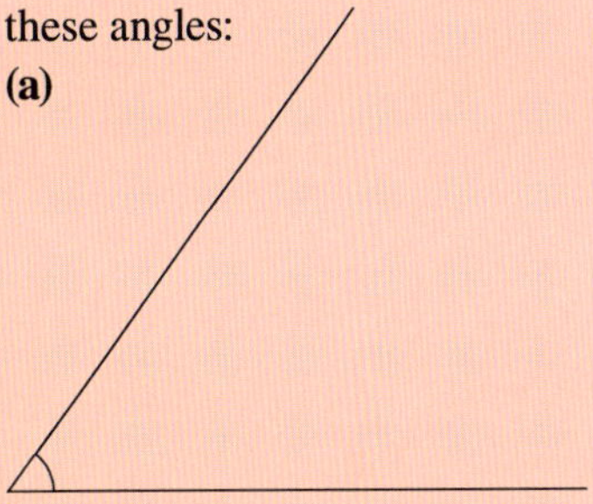

(b)

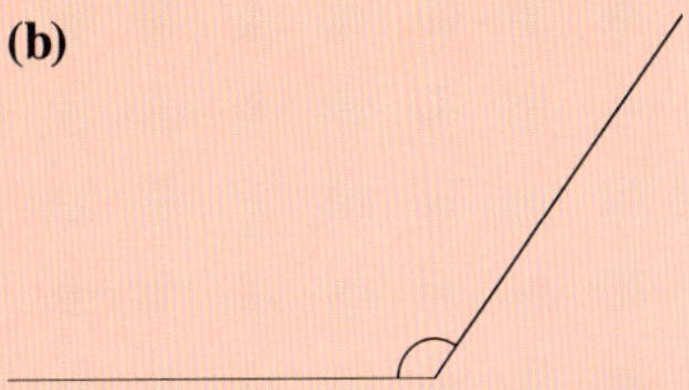

5 Complementary angles add to 90°.

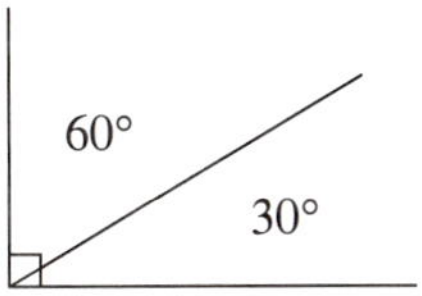

Supplementary angles add to 180°.

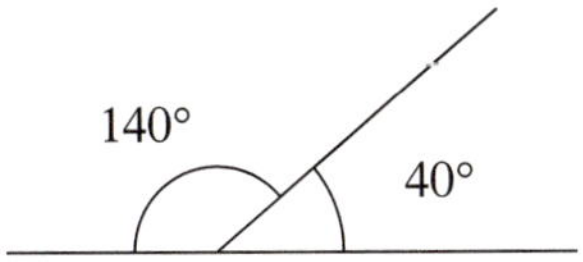

5 Find the missing angles.

(a)

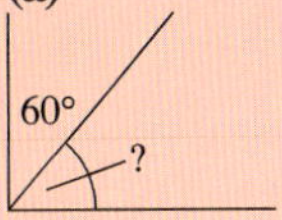

(b)

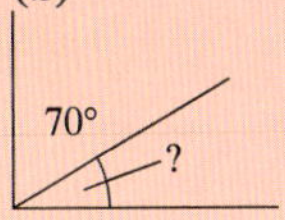

(c)

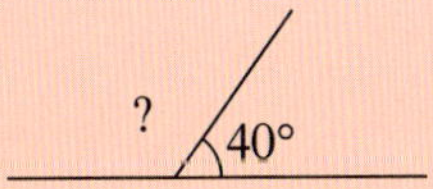

(d)

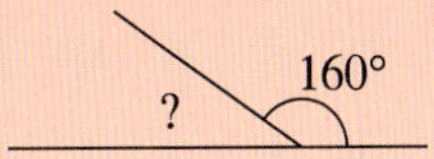

6 Angles in a triangle add to 180°.

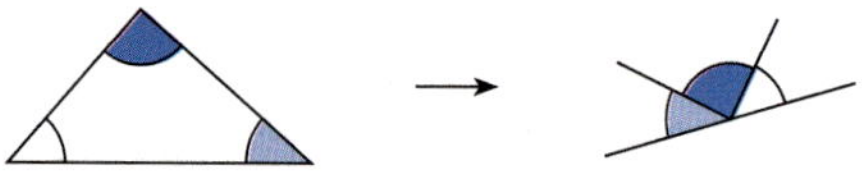

Angles in a quadrilateral add to 360°.

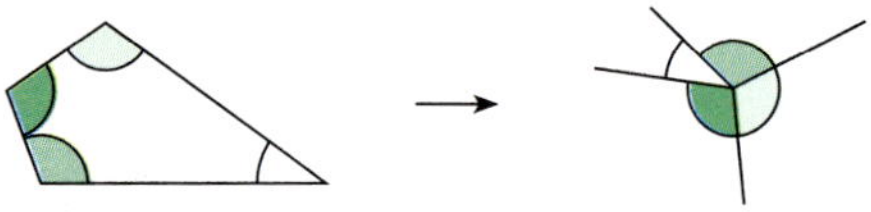

6 Find the missing angles.

(a)

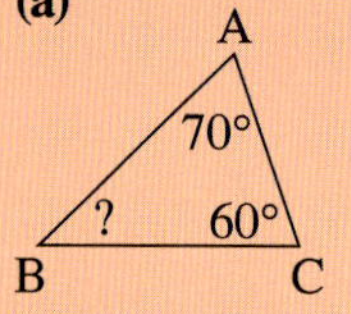

(b)

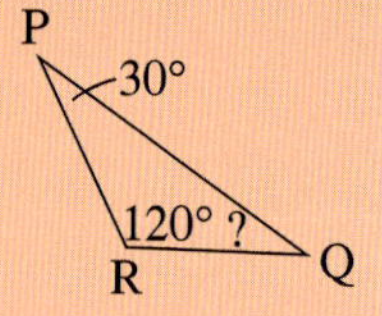

(c)

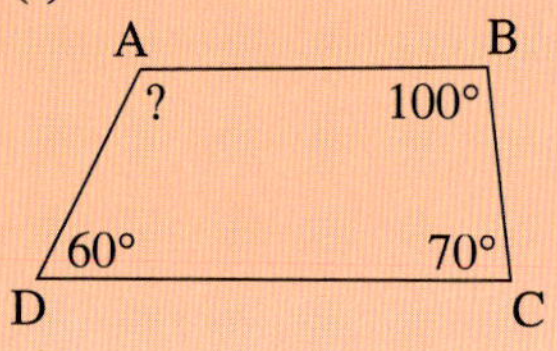

Solids

6

Objectives

- ✔ recognise the main properties of a cuboid, a cylinder, a cone, a sphere, prisms and pyramids
- ✔ draw the net of a solid
- ✔ construct a solid from its net

What's the point?

Shapes are all around us, from the boxes shoes are sold in, to the cans that hold soft drinks. Space and shape are key elements in the world of design and retail.

Before you start

You should know ...

1 The names of these solids:

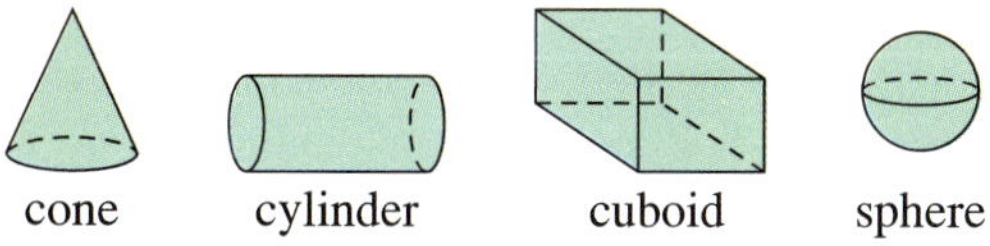

2 The terms: face, edge, corner.

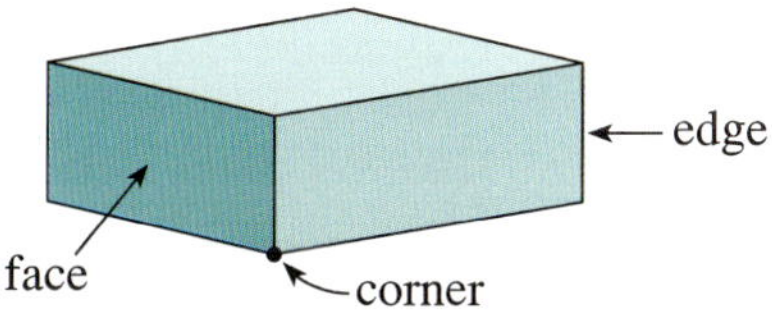

Check in

1 **(a)** Name these shapes.

(i) **(ii)** **(iii)**

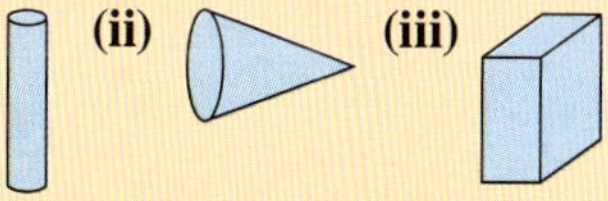

(b) What shape is

(i) a cricket ball

(ii) a drinking straw

(iii) a matchbox?

2 In a cuboid:

(a) How many corners are there?

(b) How many faces?

(c) How many edges?

3 A pentagon has 5 sides.
A hexagon has 6 sides.

3 Which of these shapes are
(a) hexagons **(b)** pentagons?
(i) **(ii)** **(iii)** **(iv)**

4 Parallel lines are always the same distance apart.

4 Which of these shapes have parallel lines?
(a) **(b)** **(c)** **(d)**

You will need

For this unit you need to bring to class the following sets of objects. (You can share with friends.)

Set **1**: a matchbox, a tea packet, a shoe box, a sugar cube, a toy building-block, some dice, and any other objects you can find, with the same shape as these.

Set **2**: an evaporated-milk tin, a powdered-milk tin, and other objects with the same shape as these.

Set **3**: an ice-cream cone, a paper ice-cream tub, a margarine tub made of plastic, a flower pot, and any other objects you can find, with the same shapes as these.

Set **4**: a table-tennis ball, a marble, a ball bearing, and other objects shaped like these.

6.1 The cuboid or box

Box-like solids are called cuboids. Their six faces are rectangular.

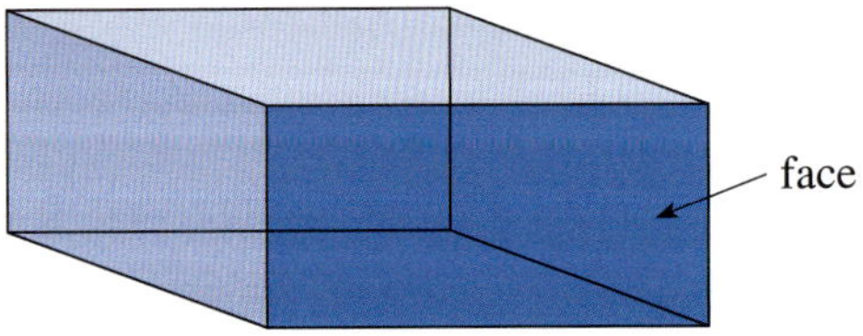

A matchbox is an example of a cuboid.

Exercise 6A

1 **(a)** Take your matchbox. Draw an outline of one of its faces on a sheet of paper.
(b) What shape is it?
(c) Repeat parts (a) and (b) for the other faces.

2 The objects in Set 1 are all cuboids.

Take each of the cuboids in turn. Count its faces. Copy and complete the table.

Cuboid	Number of faces
matchbox	6
dice	

3 How many faces has a cuboid?

4 Pick up the shoe box. Look at one face. (Call it face 1.) Is it a square or a rectangle?

Repeat for the other five faces of the shoe box.

5 Repeat Question 4 for each object in your set. Call the faces 1, 2, 3, 4, 5 and 6.
Using S for square and R for rectangle, copy and complete the table below, for all the objects in your set.

	Shape of the faces					
Cuboid	1	2	3	4	5	6
matchbox	R	R	R	R	R	R
dice	S					
shoe box						

6 Name five other objects that are cuboids.

7 Write down two reasons why things are usually stored in boxes.

The cube

Cuboids with all their faces square are called **cubes**.

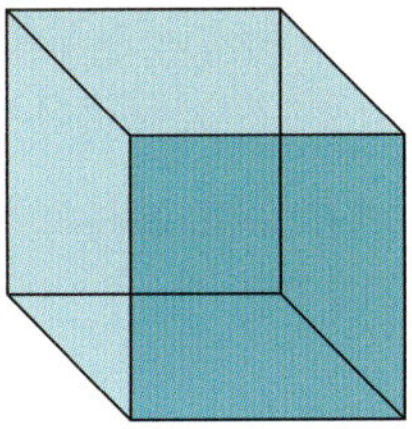

Sugar cubes, chicken stock cubes and dice are all examples of cubes.

Exercise 6B

1 How many corners has your
(a) tea packet
(b) sugar cube
(c) dice?

2 A corner, or pointed part, of a solid is called a **vertex**.
The plural of vertex is **vertices**.
How many vertices has a
(a) cuboid
(b) cube?

3 The line joining two vertices of a solid is called an **edge**.

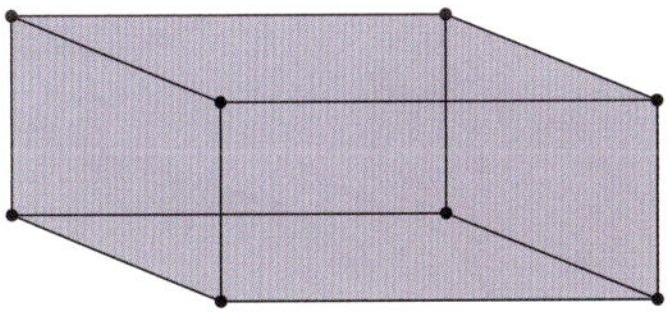

• = vertex
—— = edge

(a) How many edges does a cuboid have?
(b) How many edges does a cube have?

4 In the cuboid, the front face has been marked A. The face directly behind it (shaded in the diagram) has been marked B.

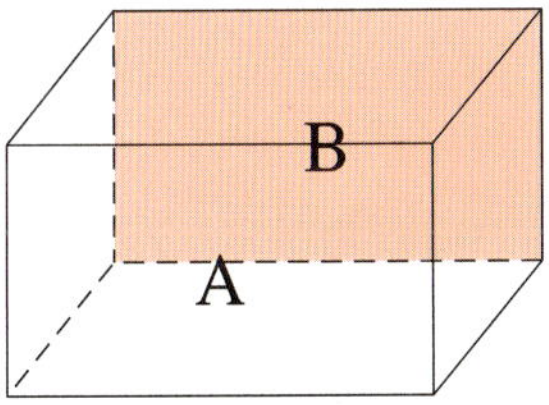

A and B are **opposite** faces.
How many pairs of opposite faces does a cuboid have?

5 Take one of your cuboids, for example the shoe box. Mark one pair of opposite faces A and B, as in the drawing for Question 4.
Mark the second pair C and D. Mark the third pair E and F.
Carefully cut out the faces. Fit face A on top of face B. What do you notice?
Repeat for the other two pairs of faces.

6 Make a list of all the properties you have discovered for a cuboid and a cube.

7 Which of these shapes are cuboids? Give reasons.

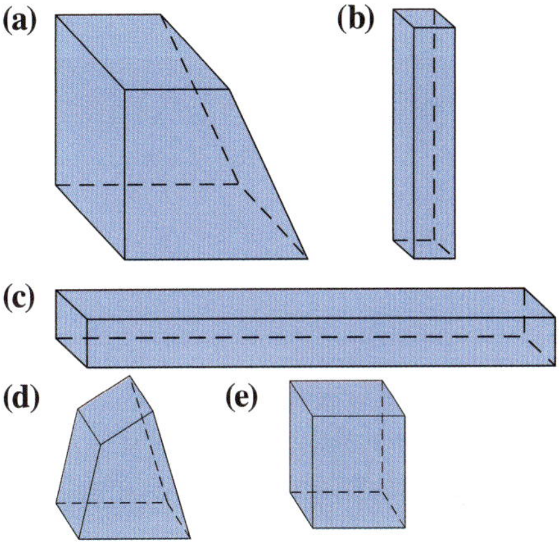

8 (a) Is a matchbox a cube?
(b) Is a sugar cube a cuboid?
Give reasons for your answers.

9 Are all cubes cuboids?
Are all cuboids cubes?
Give reasons for your answers.

Drawing and making cuboids

How to sketch a cuboid.
First draw one of its faces.

Then draw its opposite face. Make sure this face is some way away from the face already drawn.

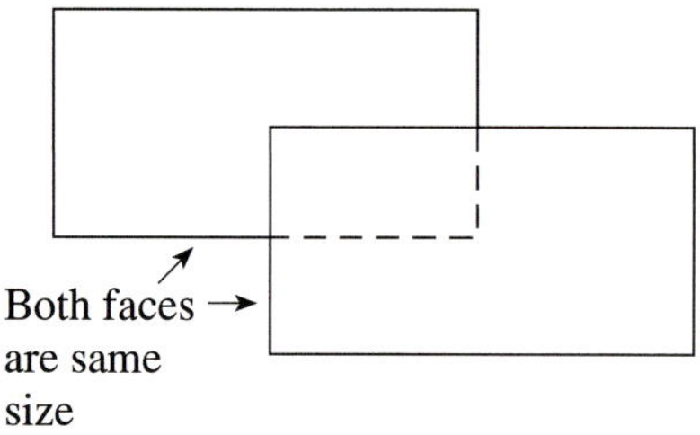

Finally join the vertices.

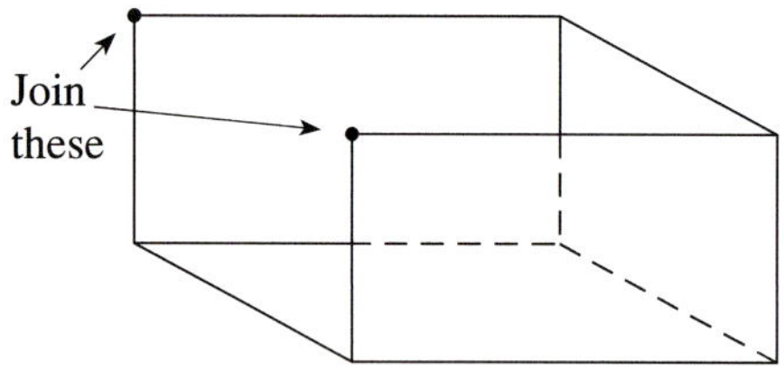

Exercise 6C

1 Make a sketch of
 (a) a matchbox
 (b) a shoe box
 (c) a sugar cube.

2 Sketch the cuboids in Question 7 of Exercise 6B.

Activity

Making a cube.

(a) Draw accurately a square with side 5 cm.

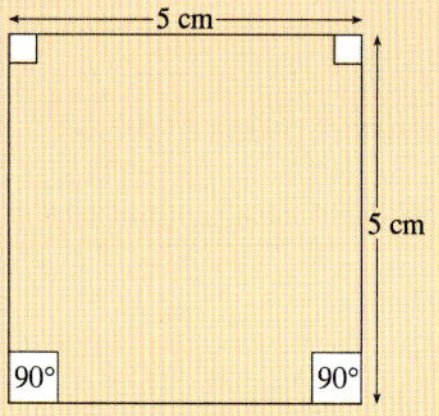

Use your protractor to make sure the angles in the square are 90°.

(b) Cut your square out.
On a piece of card, trace around your square to make the shape shown below, made up of six squares.

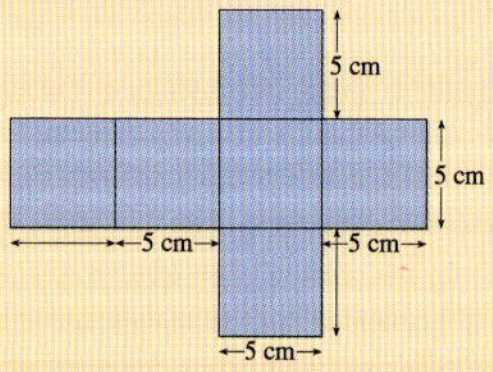

(c) This shape is called the **net** of a cube.
Cut out the net. Fold it along the lines. Stick the edges together with tape. You now have a cube.
You can make a stronger cube by attaching flaps to the outside of the net. You need to attach flaps only to every other edge.

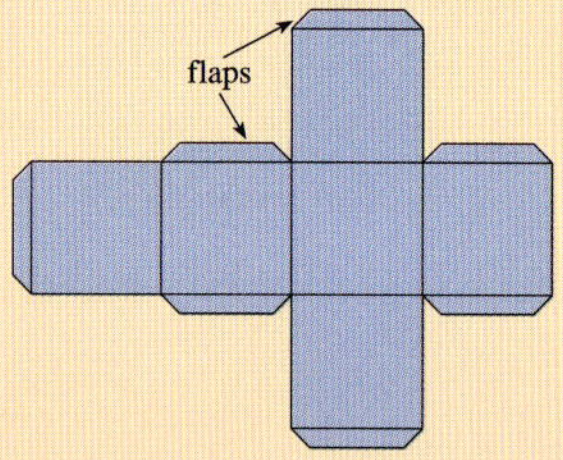

Fold the cube up as before. This time use glue to stick the flaps together.

6.2 The cylinder

The objects in Set 2 are cylinders.

Exercise 6D

1 Make a list of five other objects which are cylinders.

2 Look at the evaporated-milk tin.
(a) How many flat faces has it?
(b) How many curved faces has it?
(c) Are the flat faces opposite each other?

3 Repeat Question 2 for each of the cylinders. What can you say about the number of faces of a cylinder?

4 How many vertices has a cylinder?

5 Choose one of your cylinders.
(a) How many edges has the cylinder?
(b) Are the edges straight or curved?
(c) What shape are the edges?

6 Mark a T (for top) on one of the flat faces of a cylinder. Mark a B (for bottom) on the other. Stand the cylinder on face B. Draw the outline of the face. What shape is it?

7 Now place face T of the cylinder in Question 7 on the outline for face B. Does it fit? What can you say about the two faces of a cylinder?

8 Repeat Questions 6 and 7 for the other cylinders in your set. Do you get the same answers each time?

9 Write down all the properties you have discovered for a cylinder.

10 Look at each shape below. Is it a cylinder? Give reasons for your answer.

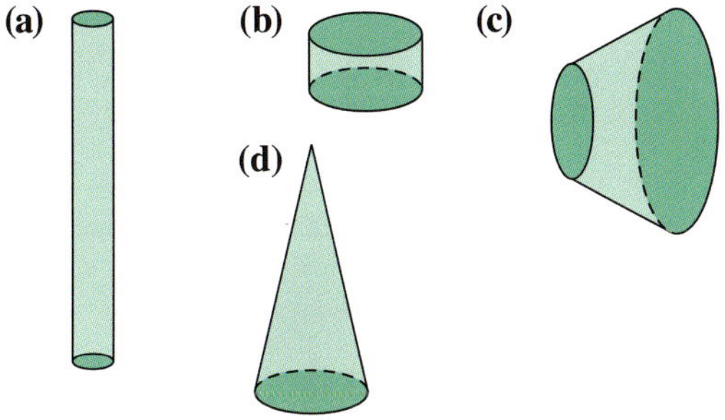

11 Look at a cylinder and a cuboid. Can you see any way in which they are alike?

6.3 Prisms

Cuboids are special kinds of **prisms**.

- A **prism** is a solid shape with constant cross-section.

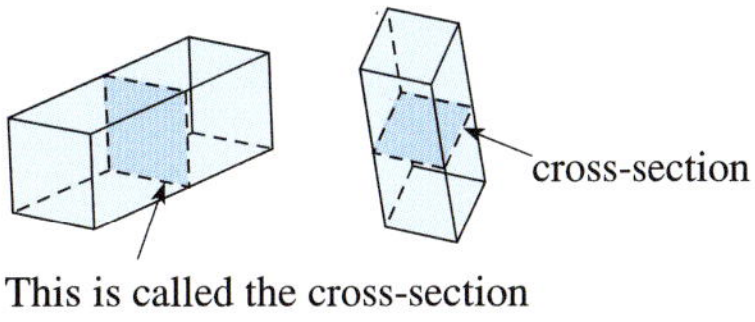

- You can identify and name a prism by the shape of its cross-section:

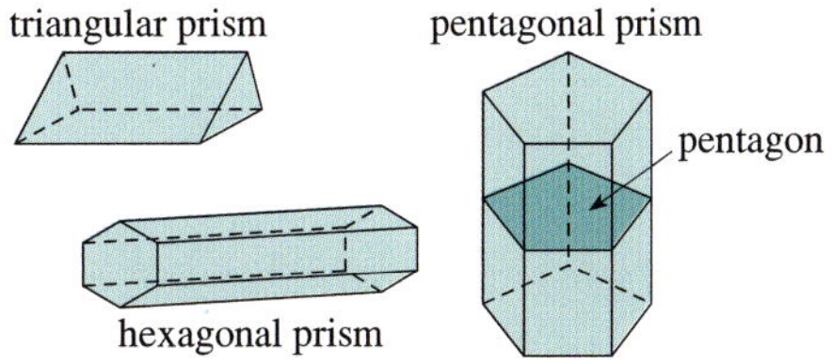

Exercise 6E

1 Here is a set of prisms.

A set of prisms

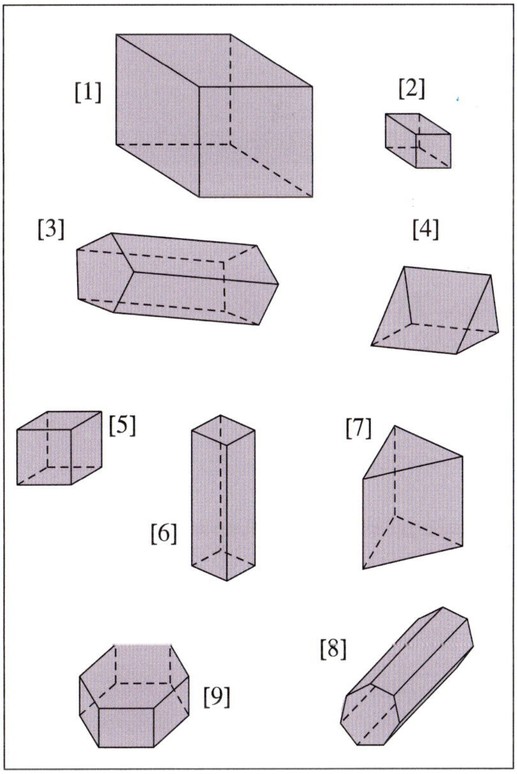

Using the numbers to represent the shapes, copy and complete the Venn diagram:

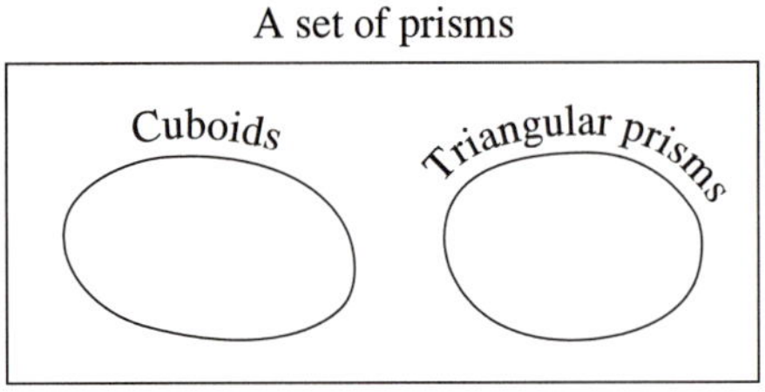

2 From the Venn diagram you completed:
(a) Are all the cuboids also prisms?
(b) Are all the triangular prisms also prisms?
(c) Do these two subsets intersect?

3 Are all cubes prisms?
Are all prisms cubes?
Give reasons for your answers.

4 (a) Copy and complete the table for the prisms in Question 1.

Shape	Number of vertices	Number of faces	Number of edges
1. cuboid	8	6	
2.			
3.			
9.			

(b) Is there any relationship between the numbers of vertices, faces and edges?

6.4 The cone

The objects in Set 3 are cones or truncated cones.
A cone looks like this:

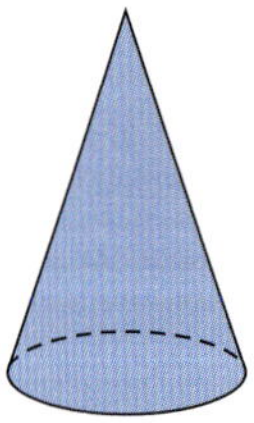

Exercise 6F

1 How many edges does a cone have?

2 Stand a cone on a sheet of paper. Carefully draw the outline of the edge. What shape is the outline?

3 (a) How many curved faces does a cone have?
(b) How many flat faces has it?
(c) How many vertices?

4 Make a list of the properties you have discovered for a cone.

5 Look at a cone and a cylinder.
(a) In what ways are they alike?
(b) In what ways are they different?

6 Make three different sketches of a cone.

7 Look at one of the objects in Set 3, which is not a cone, for example the ice-cream tub.
(a) Is its shape like a cone in any way?
(b) Can you see how it could be made from a cone?

8 Many of the objects in Set 3 are the shape of cone with the top cut off.
These are **truncated cones**.

Here is a sketch of a cone and a truncated cone.

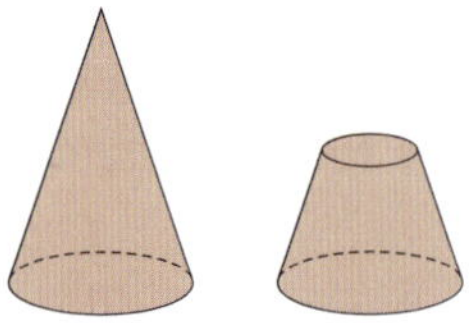

(a) Write a list of three objects, apart from those in your set, which are cones.
(b) Write a list of three objects, apart from those in your set, which are truncated cones.

6.5 The pyramid

The pyramids at Giza in Egypt were built some 4500 years ago. They are, of course, shaped like pyramids.

This shape is a pyramid.

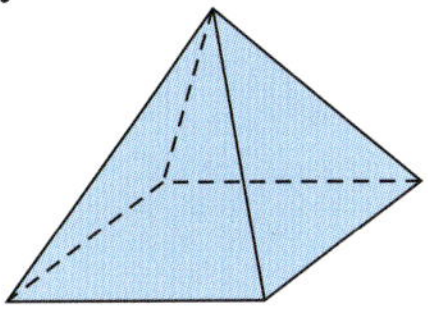

The base of this pyramid is a square.
It is called a **square-based pyramid**.

Here are some sketches of pyramids.
The base of each has been shaded.

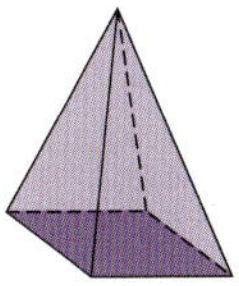

square-based pyramid

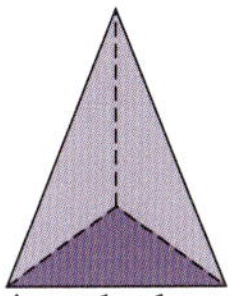

triangular-based pyramid

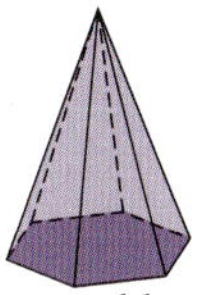

hexagonal-based pyramid

- You can name a pyramid by the shape of its base.

Exercise 6G

1 Which of these shapes are
  (a) pyramids
  (b) prisms?

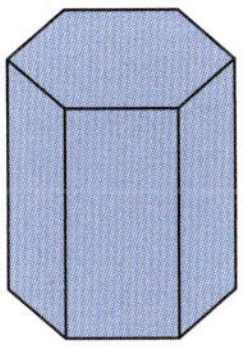

A

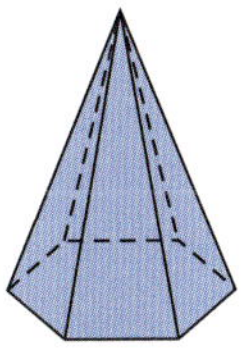

B

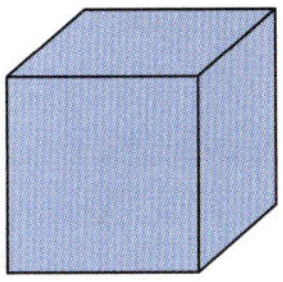

C

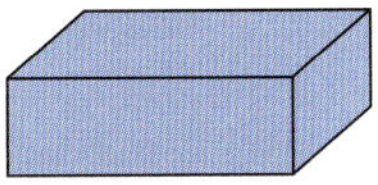

D

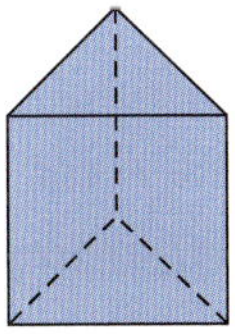

E

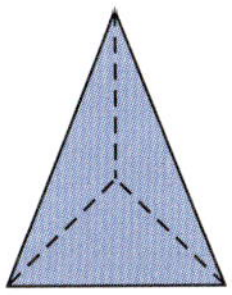

F

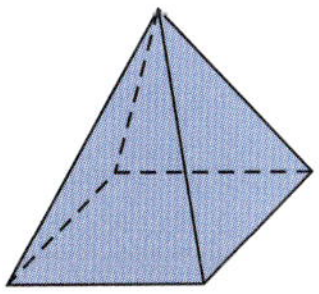

G

2 **(a)** Using the shapes from Question 1, copy and complete the Venn diagram.

3-D shapes

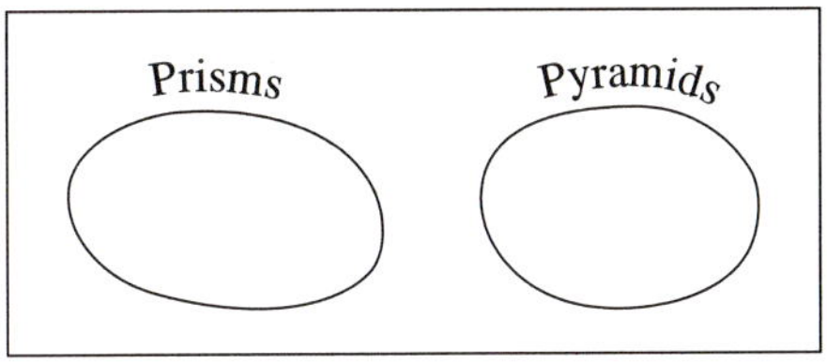

  (b) From your Venn diagram
    (i) Are all the prisms also pyramids?
    (ii) Do the two subsets intersect?

3 Which shapes in Question 1 have
  (a) more than 6 faces
  (b) more than 5 vertices
  (c) less than 12 edges
  (d) exactly 6 vertices
  (e) more than one triangular face
  (f) square faces?

4 **(a)** Copy and complete the table for the 3D shapes in Question 1.

Shape	**Number of vertices**	**Number of faces**	**Number of edges**
A		8	
G			

  (b) Is there any relationship between the numbers of vertices, faces and edges?

6.6 The sphere

The objects in Set 4 are called **spheres**.

- A sphere looks like a ball:

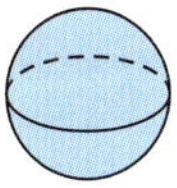

Exercise 6H

1 (a) Pick up the table-tennis ball. Look at its outline. What shape is the outline?
(b) Turn it around. Look at it again. Does the outline always look the same?

2 Make a sketch of the table-tennis ball.

3 Look again at the table-tennis ball.
(a) How many flat surfaces has it?
(b) How many curved surfaces has it?
(c) How many edges?
(d) How many vertices?

4 Repeat Question 3 for the other spheres in your set. Now write down the properties of spheres you have discovered.

5 Make a list of five objects, apart from those in your set, which are spheres.

6.7 Properties of solids

The table summarises the properties of the different solids:

Solid	Faces	Edges	Vertices
Cube	6	12	8
Cuboid	6	12	8
Cylinder	3	2	0
Triangular prism	5	9	6
Cone	2	1	1
Square-based pyramid	5	8	5
Sphere	1	0	0

Exercise 6I

1 Write down the name of any solid which:
(a) has a flat face (b) has a curved face
(c) has a flat face and a curved face
(d) has a pair of equal and opposite faces.

2 Write down the name of the shape of each object.
(a) a piece of chalk (b) an orange
(c) a drainpipe (d) a ten-cent coin
(e) this book (f) a broom handle
(g) a drinking glass (h) a globe
(i) a candle (j) a football

3 What shape is the object?
(a) a rocket nose (b) a tomato
(c) a church steeple (d) a record
(e) a bicycle pump (f) a steel drum
(g) the sharp end of a pencil
(h) a new pencil, before it is sharpened

4 Draw pictures to show a shape that has
(a) one vertex, one edge and two faces
(b) six square faces
(c) one curved face and no vertices
(d) four vertices, four faces and six edges
(e) one curved face and two edges.
Can you name these shapes?

6.8 Nets of solids

Factories use different shaped boxes for packing goods. They start with a **net**.

- A net is a flat shape that folds to make a solid.

Exercise 6J

You will need squared paper, card, scissors and glue or sticky tape.

1 (a) Make a larger copy of these nets on squared paper.

(i)

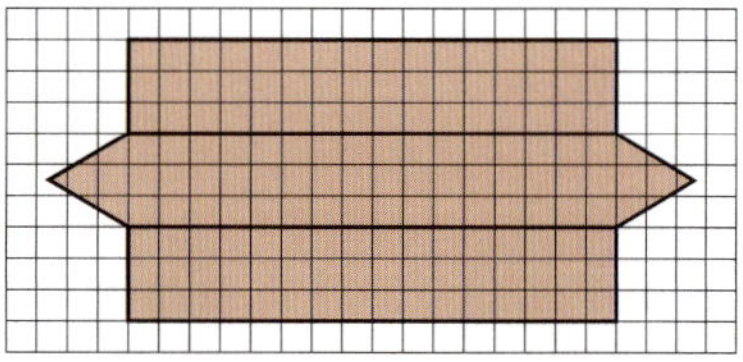

(ii)

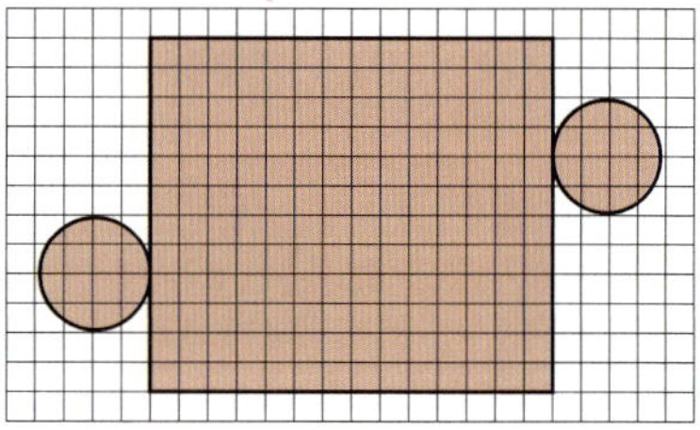

(iii)

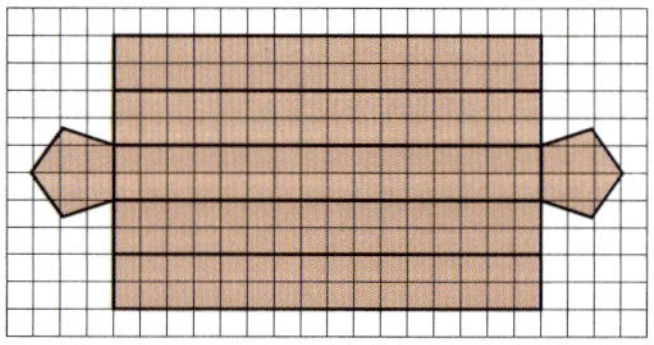

(b) Cut them out carefully.
(c) Fold them along the heavy lines.
(d) Stick the edges together with sticky tape.
(e) Name the solids you have made.

2 Copy each net on to squared paper. Cut it out and fold it. What shape does it make?

(a)

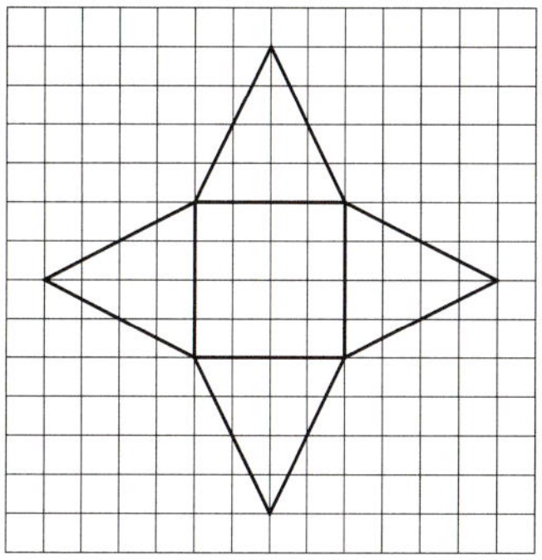

(b)

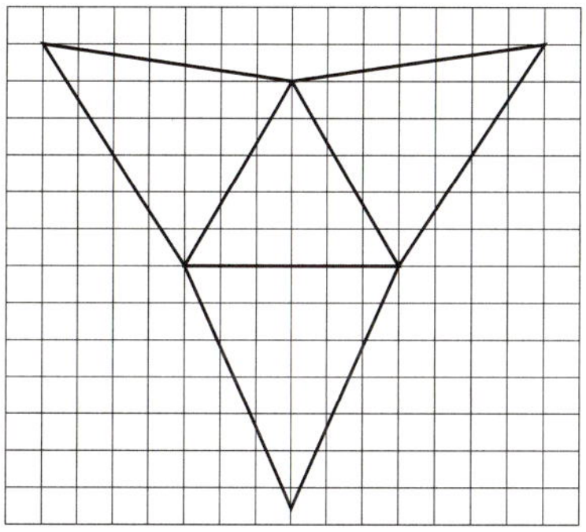

3 **(a)** Draw accurately this triangle.

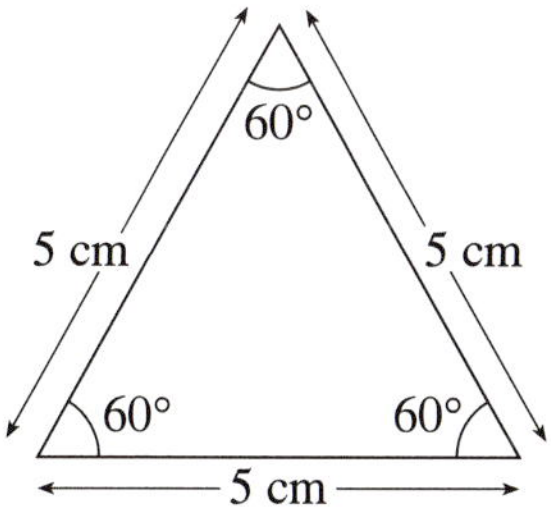

(b) Cut this triangle out. Trace around it on card to make this net:

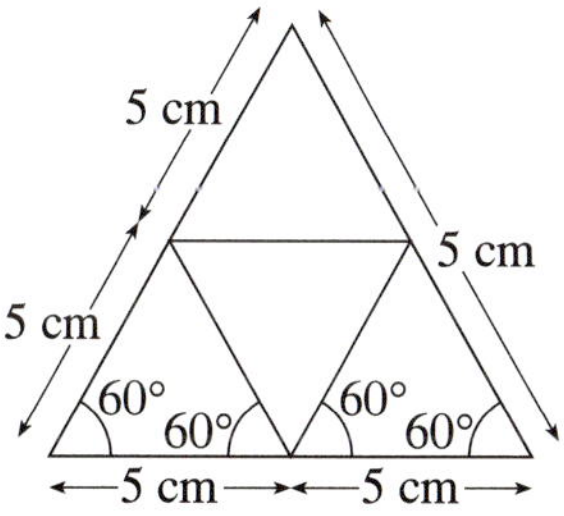

(c) Draw flaps on every other outside edge:

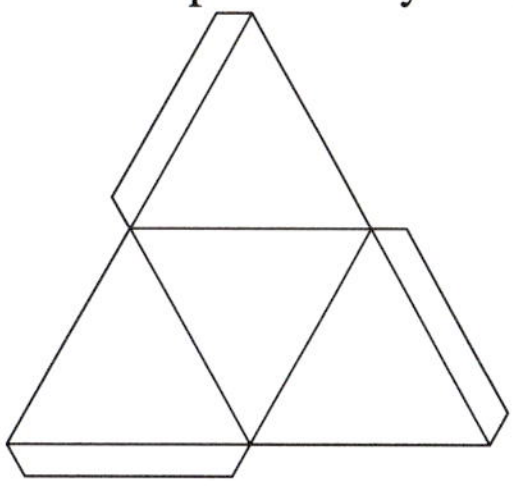

(d) Fold your net along the lines.
(e) Glue the flaps carefully.
Your completed solid should look like this.

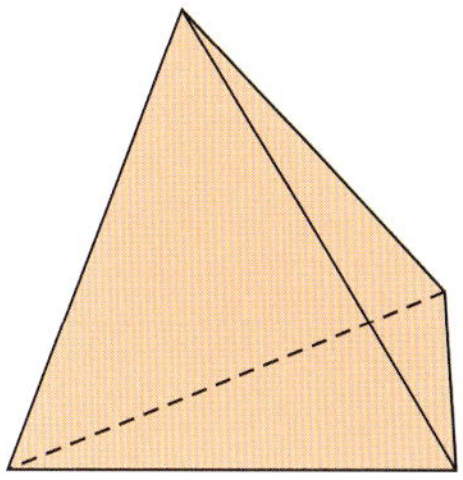

It is called a tetrahedron.
(f) Colour your tetrahedron.
(g) How many faces, edges and vertices does it have?

4 Repeat the steps in Question 3 to make solids from each of these nets.

(a)

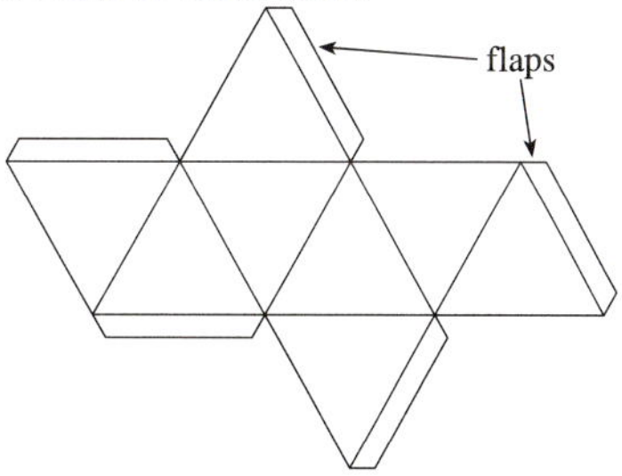

This solid has 8 faces. It is called an **octahedron**.

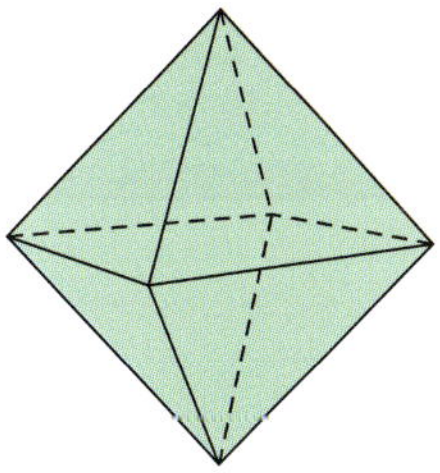

(b)

This solid has 20 faces. It is called an **icosahedron**.

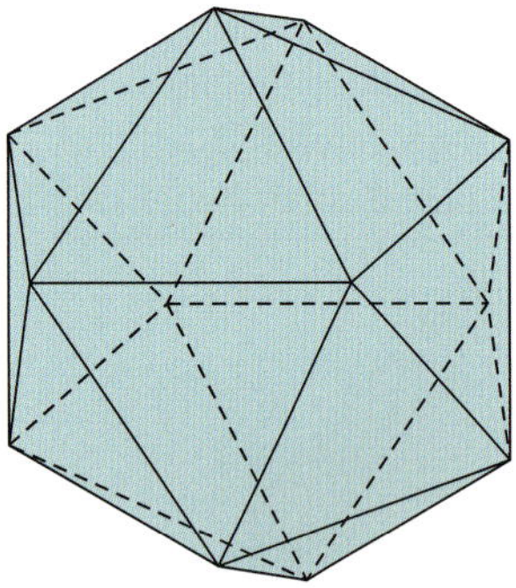

5 Another well-known solid is the **dodecahedron**.

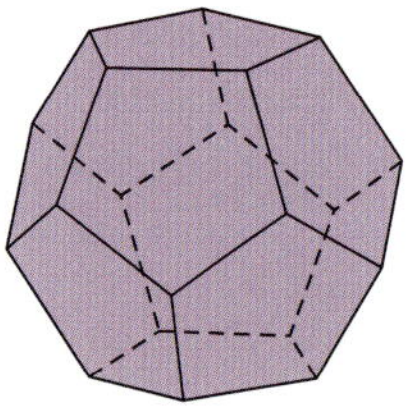

Its net consists of 12 five-sided shapes.

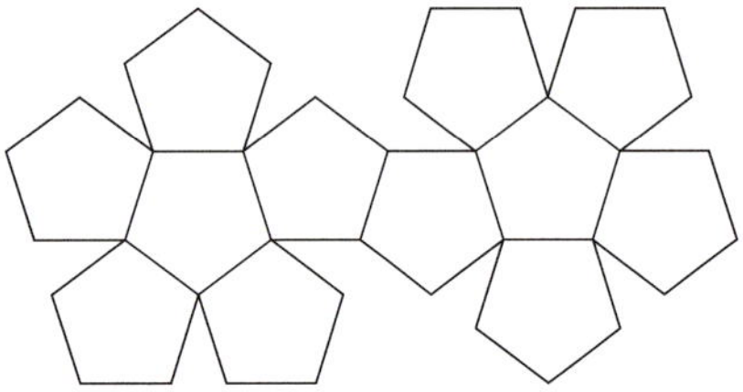

Make each five-sided shape with these dimensions.

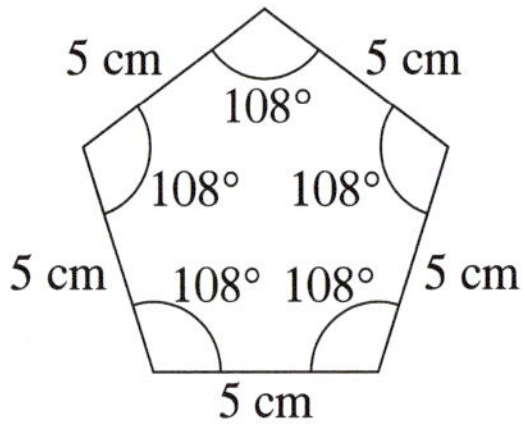

Investigation

(a) Why are these shapes not nets of cubes?

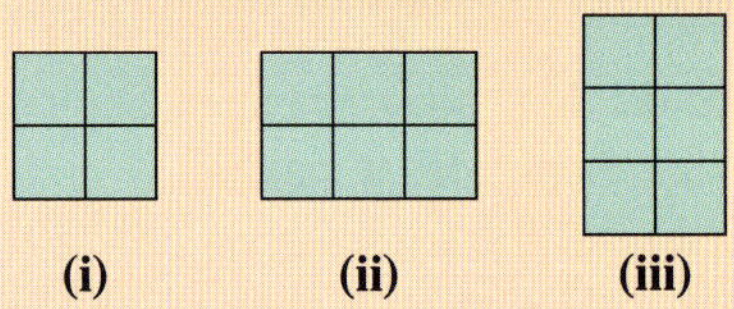

(b) A net of a cube must be made up of 6 faces. Which of these are nets of cubes?

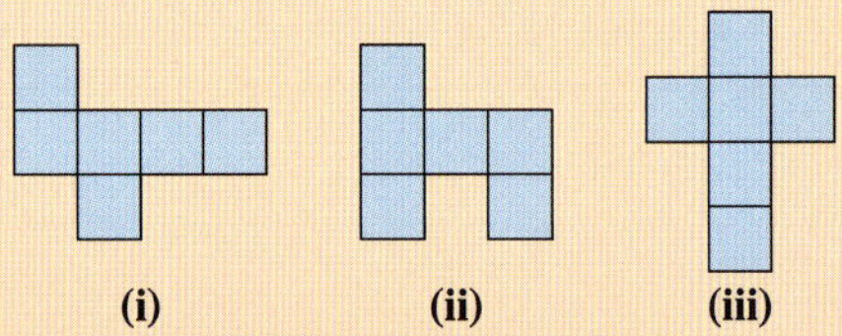

If you find this difficult, trace the shapes out and cut them out.
Do they fold to make a cube?

(c) Draw some more shapes made up of six squares.

(d) Which of the shapes you drew in (c) are nets of a cube?

(e) How many nets can you draw?

(f) Compare your answers with a group of friends. Can you add more nets to your list?

Investigation

Work in a group of four. Pick up the four cubes your group has made (they should all be the same size).

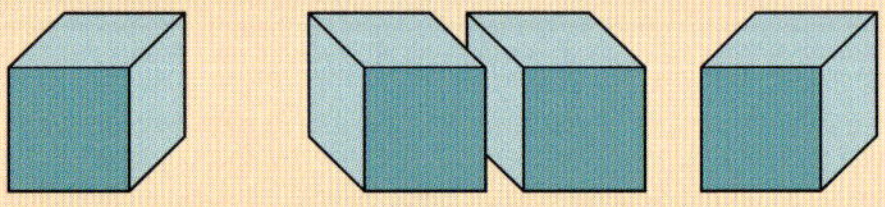

(a) See how many different solids you can make using these four cubes.

(b) Add a fifth cube to your set.
How many different solids can you now make?

Investigate further.

Activity

Cut out a strip of paper 20 cm long and 4 cm wide.

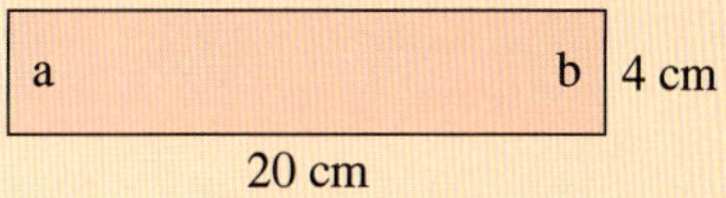

(a) How many faces does it have?

Now put a twist in the paper strip and glue the two opposite ends together.
This twisted band is called a **Möbius strip**.

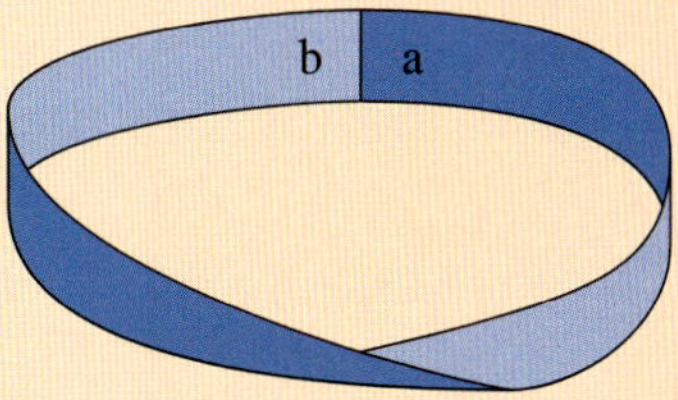

(b) How many faces does it have?

(c) Cut the band down the middle: what happens?

(d) Make a new strip, put two twists in it and join the ends to make a band. Cut it down the middle.
What happens?

6 Consolidation

Example 1

What are the names of these shapes?

(a) 

(b) 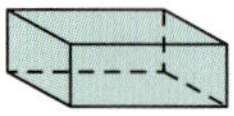

(c) 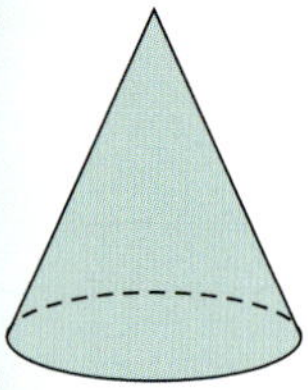

(d) 

(a) truncated cone
(b) cuboid
(c) cone
(d) cylinder

Example 2

Write down three properties of **(a)** a cube **(b)** a cylinder.

(a) A cube has **(i)** 6 square faces
(ii) 8 vertices
(iii) 12 edges

(b) A cylinder has **(i)** 2 flat faces
(ii) 1 curved face
(iii) 2 edges

Example 3

Which of these shapes are nets of a cube?

A 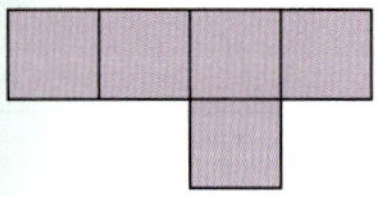

B 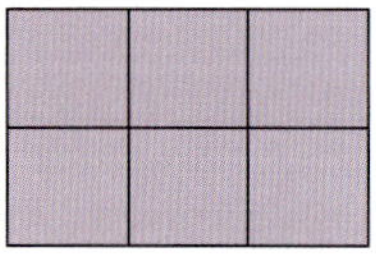

C 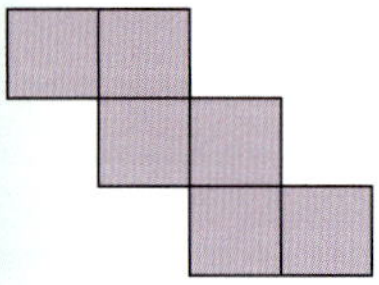

D 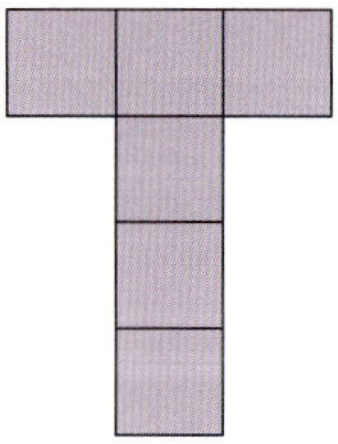

A is not a net because it has only 5 faces (squares).
B is not a net because it cannot be folded to make a cube.
C is a net because it has 6 faces and can be folded to make a cube.
D is a net, it has 6 faces and can be folded to make a cube.

Exercise 6

1 What are the names of these shapes?

(a) 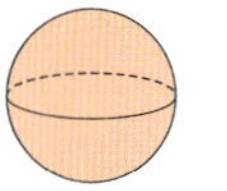 **(b)** 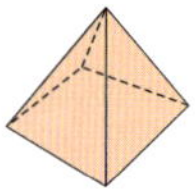 **(c)** 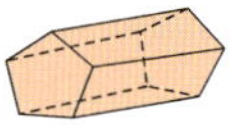

2 Make sketches of these shapes.
(a) cylinder **(b)** cone **(c)** triangular prism
(d) sphere **(e)** truncated cone
(f) truncated pyramid

3 Sketch and name a shape that has
(a) 2 curved edges **(b)** 2 flat faces
(c) 8 vertices **(d)** 1 curved surface
(e) 4 triangular faces **(f)** 9 edges

4 Write down the properties of a
(a) cuboid **(b)** square-based prism
(c) truncated cone **(d)** triangular prism
(e) square-based pyramid
(f) hexagonal-based pyramid

5 **(a)** Draw four different nets of a cube.
(b) Draw three different nets of a pyramid with a triangular base.

Application 6

6

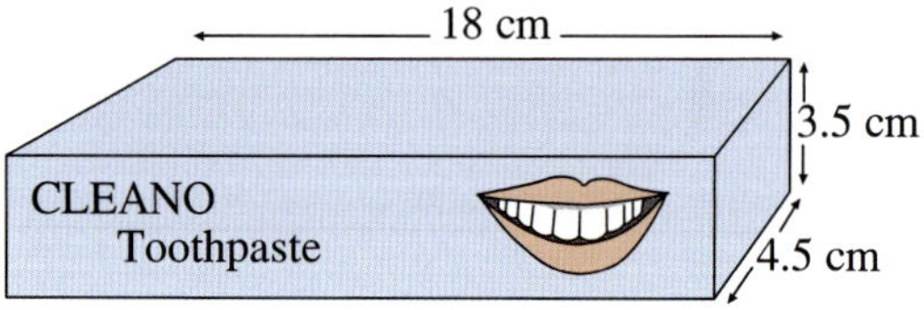

Cleano Toothpaste is packed in a box 18 cm by 4.5 cm by 3.5 cm.
(a) Make accurate drawings of each face of the box.
(b) Make an accurate drawing of the net of the box.
(c) Cut out the net in part (b) and fold to construct your own toothpaste box.

7 Tasty's packages its chocolates in triangular prism shaped boxes.

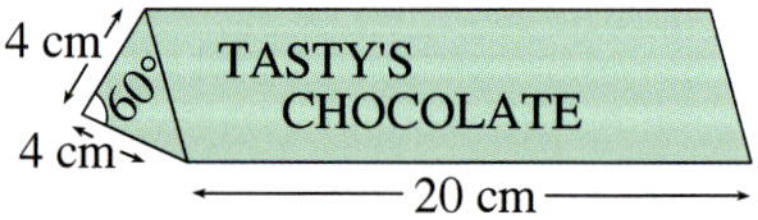

(a) Make an accurate drawing of each face of the box.
(b) How many rectangular faces does the box have?
(c) Make an accurate drawing of the net of the box.
(d) Draw a design for your own brand of chocolates on the net.
(e) Cut out the net and fold to construct your chocolate box.

Companion CD

Want some extra practice? Go to Chapter 6 on your companion CD for further exercises, animations, and solutions.

Summary

You should know ...

1 A cuboid is a solid with six rectangular faces:

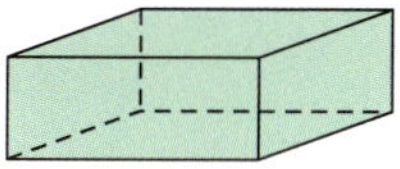

Properties: faces are rectangular
opposite edges are parallel and equal
it has 6 faces, 12 edges, 8 vertices

A cube is a special cuboid with six square faces:

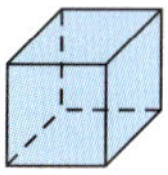

2 A cylinder is a solid with a circular cross-section:

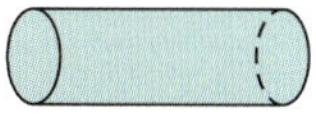

A prism is a solid with a constant cross-section:

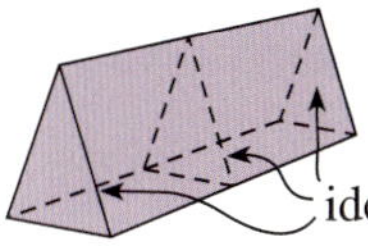

Check out

1 Write down two examples of
(a) a cuboid
(b) a cube.
(c) How are cubes and cuboids the same?
(d) How are they different?

2 **(a)** Write down two examples of a cylinder.
(b) Which of these shapes are prisms?

(i) 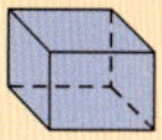 **(ii)** 

(iii)  **(iv)** 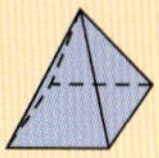

3 You can name a pyramid by the shape of its base:

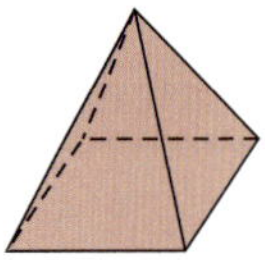

square-based pyramid

3 **(a)** Which of these shapes are pyramids?

(i)

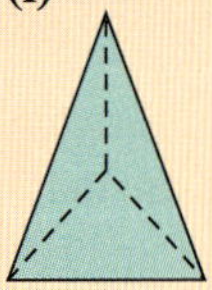

(ii)

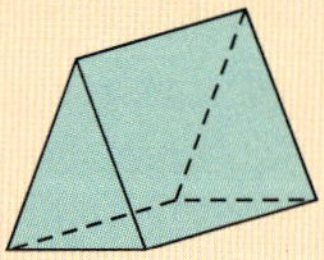

(iii)

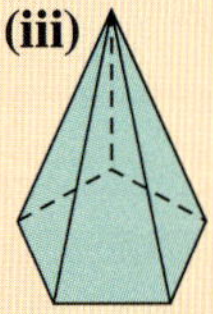

(iv)

(b) For each pyramid in part (a), give its full name.

4 A sphere looks like a ball:

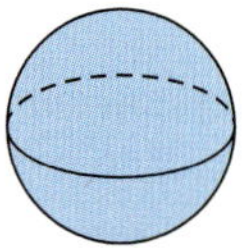

4 How many faces, edges and corners does a sphere have?

5 A net is a flat shape that folds to make a solid.

 is a net of a cube

5 Which of these are nets of a cube?

(a)

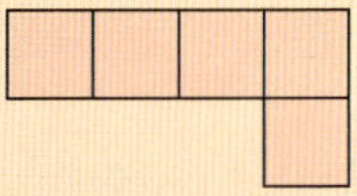

(b)

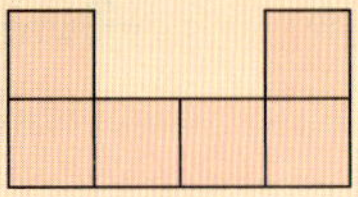

(c)

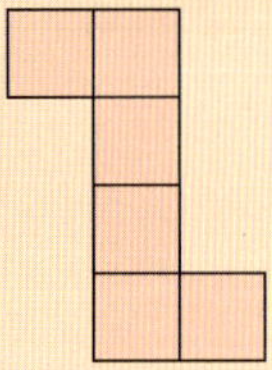

(d)

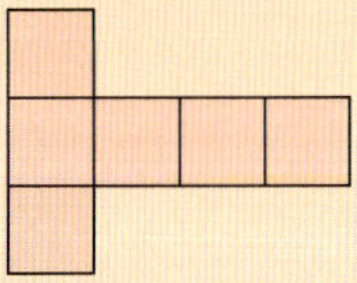

Measuring 7

Objectives

- ✔ find reasons for using standard units of measurement
- ✔ use standard units for length and mass
- ✔ understand the difference between mass and weight
- ✔ estimate and measure distance, mass, time and temperature using the appropriate units

What's the point?

You ask questions such as 'How far?' 'How heavy?' 'How long?', 'How hot?' on a daily basis. Masons and carpenters are groups of people whose livelihood depends on good measures.

Before you start

You should know ...

1 The relationship between a second, minute, hour, day, week, month and year.

2 For times before midday you use am. For times after midday you use pm.

Check in

1 **(a)** How many seconds are there in one minute?
(b) How many minutes in one hour?
(c) How many days in one week?
(d) How many hours in one day?
(e) How many months in one year?

2 Write down whether these times are in the morning, afternoon or evening:
(a) 11 am **(b)** 6 pm
(c) 2.45 pm **(d)** 3.25 am

3 How to multiply and divide by 10, 100 and 1000.

For example

To multiply by 10:

$$4.27 \times 10 = 42.7$$

decimal point moves one place to the right

To divide by 100:

$$320.6 \div 100 = 3.206$$

decimal point moves two places to the left

3 Find:

(a) 3.7×10 **(b)** 4.3×100

(c) 18×1000 **(d)** $2.33 \div 10$

(e) $1424 \div 100$ **(f)** $1424 \div 1000$

7.1 Length

Units of length

To answer the question 'How many oranges are there?' you can count. There are 7 oranges.

To answer the question 'How long is the rope?' you cannot count. You must **measure**.

To measure the rope you must first choose a unit of length.

Long ago, people used many different units for measuring the length of things.

For example:

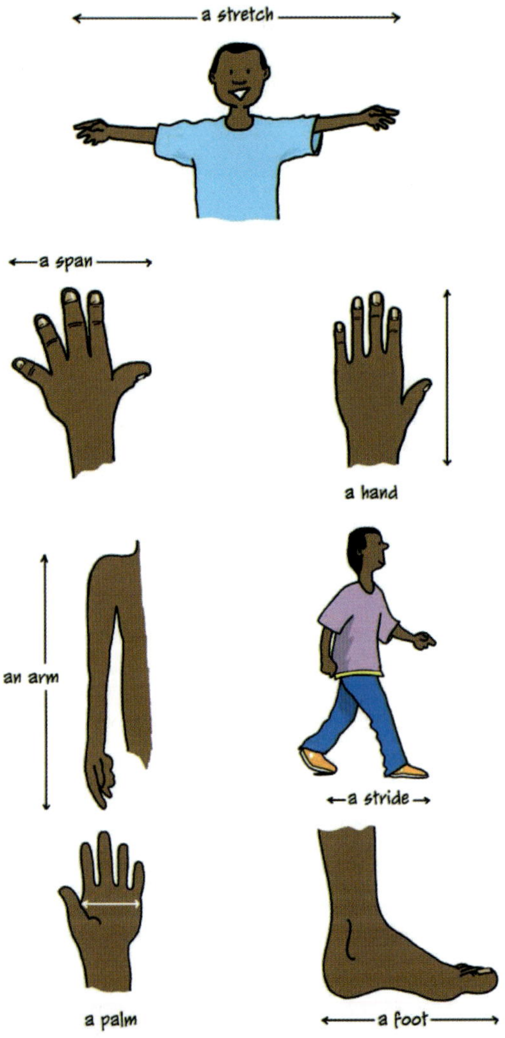

Exercise 7A

1 Which of the units above would be suitable for finding:
  (a) the width and length of a field
  (b) the width and length of a handkerchief
  (c) the distance round your classroom
  (d) the distance from your classroom to the school office
  (e) the distance round this page
  (f) the height of your best friend
  (g) the length of a necklace?

2 Deo and Tony sell the same cloth for $6 a stretch. From which of them would you buy cloth? Why?

3 Slim and Jojo each have a piece of farmland. Each one measured his land last Tuesday. Each said that his piece was 90 strides long and 40 strides wide.

Who do you think has the bigger piece? Why?

4 Look again at the units on page 122. Do you think that using them might cause problems? Why?

5 Write down four units of length that are used today.

SI units

The units on page 122 were not satisfactory to use, because not everyone's hands, arms, feet, and strides are the same.
You need to use standard units.

More and more countries, including your own, are using standard units based on the metric system, called the **Systéme International d'Unités**, or **SI** for short.

The metre

The SI unit of length is the **metre**, **m**.
A good estimate of a metre is one long stride.

Exercise 7B

You will need a metre rule and some string.

1 Use your metre rule to measure the
  (a) height of your classroom door
  (b) width of your classroom
  (c) length of your classroom.

2 Write down the name of an object that is about
  (a) 1 m long
  (b) 2 m long
  (c) 5 m long.

3 **(a)** Use your metre rule to cut a piece of string 1 metre long. With a pen, put a mark on the string every $\frac{1}{4}$ metre.
  You can now measure with this string.
  (b) Work with a friend to measure, to the nearest $\frac{1}{4}$ metre:
    (i) your stretch, when you stretch your arms out wide
    (ii) the length of your arm from shoulder to finger-tip
    (iii) your height
    (iv) your stride, when you take a large step.

4 Practise taking strides 1 m long. Now measure the length and width of your classroom by striding around the walls. Do you think this is an accurate way of measuring?

5 Measure the length and width of your classroom to the nearest $\frac{1}{4}$ m. Do your results agree with your answer to Question 4?

6 **(a)** Work with a friend. Choose five different places in your school. Estimate (guess) the distance to them from your classroom door.
(b) Now check your estimate using a metre rule or your piece of string.
(c) Copy and complete the table:

Distance from classroom	Estimated distance	Actual distance
1.		
2.		
3.		
4.		
5.		

Activity

Work with a group of friends. You will need a watch and a metre rule.

(a) Estimate the time it would take to walk 10 m, 20 m, 30 m, 40 m and 50 m.
(b) Using the metre rule to measure the distances and a watch to measure time, check your estimates in (a).
(c) Copy and complete the table:

Distance	Estimated time	Actual time
10 m		
20 m		
30 m		
40 m		
50 m		

The centimetre and millimetre

The metre is a fairly large unit of length.
To measure shorter lengths, we use
the **centimetre** $\frac{1}{100}$ of a metre
the **millimetre** $\frac{1}{1000}$ of a metre

Here is a line 1 centimetre long: ______
Here is a line 1 millimetre long: -

The abbreviation **cm** is used for centimetre.
The abbreviation **mm** is used for millimetre.

A rough estimate of a centimetre is the width of your smallest finger.

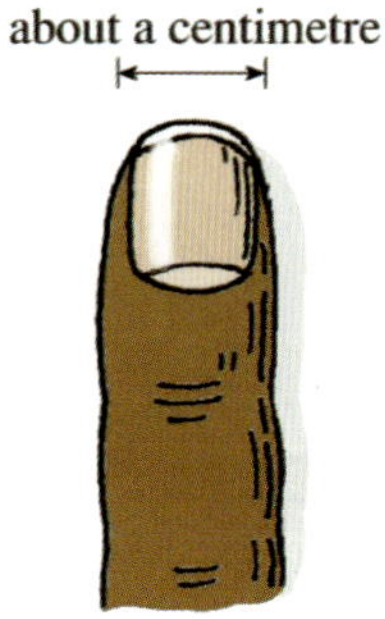

- 100 cm = 1 m
  1 cm = $\frac{1}{100}$ m = 0.01 m
- 10 mm = 1 cm
  1 mm = $\frac{1}{10}$ cm = 0.1 cm
  1 mm = $\frac{1}{1000}$ m = 0.001 m
  1000 mm = 1 m

Exercise 7C

1 Use your smallest finger to estimate the length of:
(a) your exercise book
(b) your desk
(c) your pencil
(d) your geometry set.

2 This line is 5 cm 3 mm or 5.3 cm.

Now measure these lines. Give each answer in two ways.
(a)
(b)
(c)

3 Estimate the length of each line.
(a)
(b)
(c)
(d)
(e)

4 Now measure each line in Question 3.
Were your estimates good ones?

5 Without using a ruler, mark two points that you think are 10 cm apart.
Now measure the distance between them with a ruler. Were you nearly right? If not, try again.

6 Repeat Question 5 for a distance between the points of:
(a) 1 cm (b) 2 cm (c) 5 cm
(d) 15 cm (e) 20 cm (f) 1 mm
(g) 5 mm

7 (a) Estimate the height of this book using cm.
(b) Now measure its height using cm and mm.
Was your estimate a good one?

8 Repeat Question 7 for the width of the book.

9 (a) Estimate **(i)** the length **(ii)** the width of your desk top in cm.
(b) Now measure it, using cm and mm.
Was your estimate a good one?

Activity

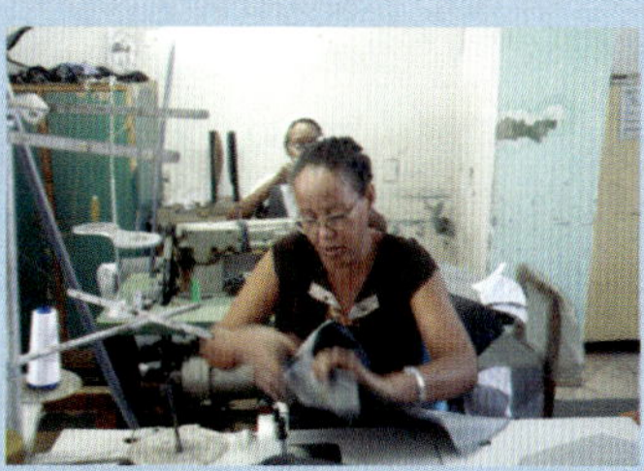

Interview a dressmaker or seamstress.
- Find out what units of measurement they use.
- What do they use to make measurements?
- What measurements do they take?
- Write up and present your findings to the class.

The kilometre

For great distances, a metre is too small a unit to use. Instead, we use the **kilometre**, **km**.

A kilometre is roughly the distance you can walk in 15 minutes.

- 1000 m = 1 km
  1 m = $\frac{1}{1000}$ km = 0.001 km

Exercise 7D

1 (a) Write down five places that are about 15 minutes walk from your school.
(b) How could you check that these places are really 1 km away?

2 (a) How long does it take you to walk to school?
(b) Estimate the distance you walk.

3 Estimate the distance from your school to the nearest post office. How would you measure the distance?

4 Write down the names of four cities or towns in your country. Now find out the km distances between them.

Relationships between metric units

To change lengths in metres to centimetres, or metres to kilometres, you need to remember that

1000 m = 1 km
100 cm = 1 m
10 mm = 1 cm

Sometimes you multiply, sometimes you divide. This diagram can help you decide:

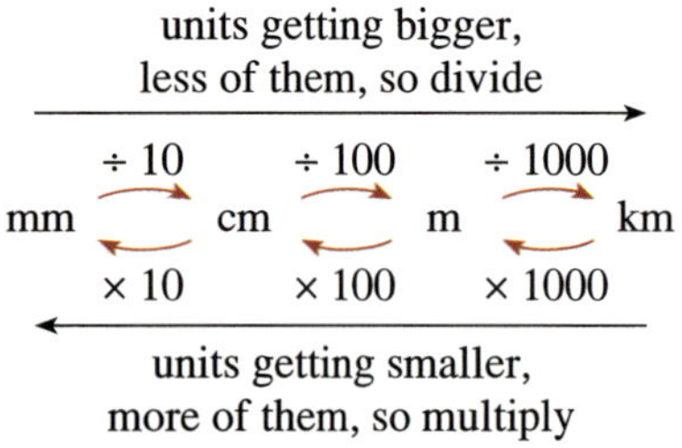

Example 1

Change
(a) 6 cm 5 mm to mm
(b) 5.6 km to m

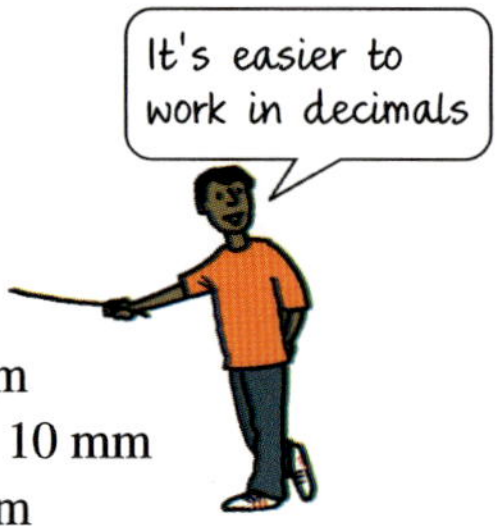

(a) 1 cm = 10 mm
so 6 cm 5 mm = 6.5 cm
= 6.5 × 10 mm
= 65 mm

(b) 1 km = 1000 m
So 5.6 km = 5.6 × 1000 m
= 5600 m

Example 2

Change 6314 m to km.
1000 m = 1 km
So 6314 m = 6314 ÷ 1000 km
= 6.314 km

Exercise 7E

1 Change to mm:
(a) 3 cm **(b)** 16 cm
(c) 3 cm 2 mm **(d)** 5.7 cm

2 Change to cm:
(a) 40 mm **(b)** 120 mm
(c) 58 mm **(d)** 92 mm

3 Write these distances in metres:
(a) 1 km **(b)** 5 km
(c) 3.6 km **(d)** 4.12 km

4 Write these distances in kilometres:
(a) 3000 m **(b)** 12 000 m
(c) 500 m **(d)** 1680 m

5 The table gives the height of five students. Copy and complete the table.

Student	**Height m and cm**	**Height m**	**Height cm**
James	1 m 42 cm		
Anthony		1.56 m	
Garth			145 cm
Albert		1.25 m	
Andy	1 m 70 cm		

6 Peter is 1 m 36 cm tall.
Susan is 18 cm taller.
How tall is Susan?

7 Seta went on a tour of her island. The table shows how far she walked each day.

Day	Mon	Tue	Wed	Thur	Fri
Km travelled	19.5	38.7	24.8	30.1	35.9

(a) Find the total number of km she walked.
(b) Express the answer to part (a) in m.

8 Which distance is greater:
(a) 2000 m or 1 km 571 m
(b) 196 mm or 32 cm 7 mm
(c) 3 km or 30 000 cm?

9 Find the value of the following:
(a) 73.9 cm + 36 mm (answer in cm)
(b) 3.61 m + 58.7 cm (answer in m)
(c) 2531 m + 793 m − 1.7 km (answer in m)
(d) 1.818 km − 972 m (answer in m)
(e) 351.3 m × 5 (answer in (i) m (ii) km)

10 An iron rod is 3.025 m long. It is cut into five pieces of equal length. Find the length of each piece in cm.

Perimeter

Mr Stevens is growing cabbages. He wants to prevent animals from eating them. He decides to put a fence around his garden. How much fencing does he need to purchase?

To answer this he must find the **distance around** the garden. This distance is called the **perimeter**.

- The perimeter of a shape is the total distance around it.

Example 3

Find the perimeter of this shape.

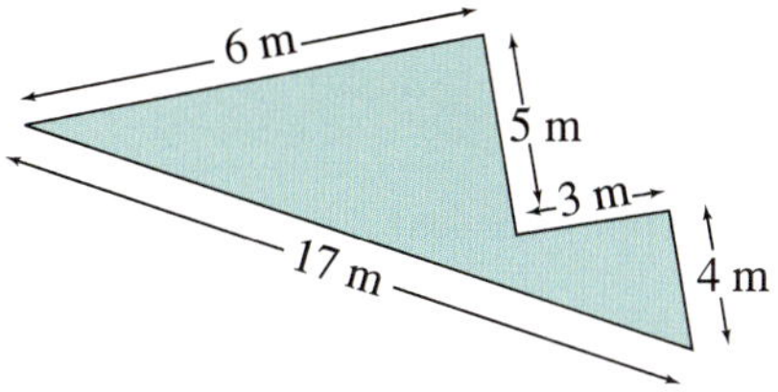

Perimeter = distance around
= 6 m + 5 m + 3 m + 4 m + 17 m
= 35 m

Exercise 7F

1 Find the perimeter of these shapes.

(a)
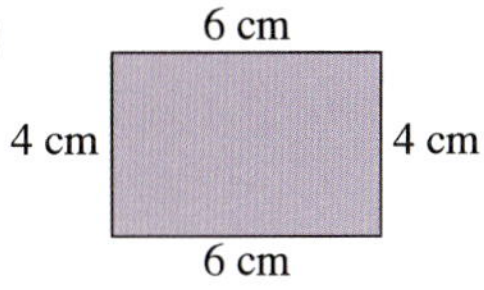

(b)
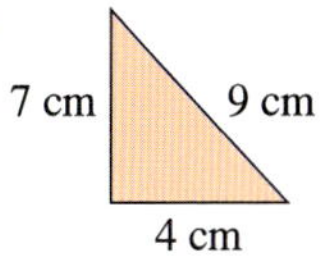

(c)
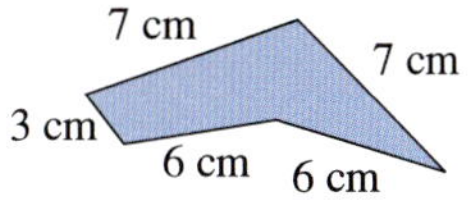

(d)
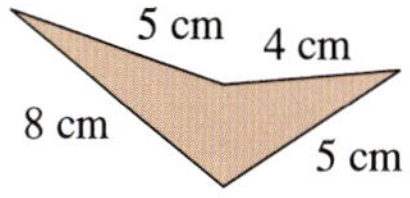

2 Find the length of the unknown sides in these shapes.

(a)
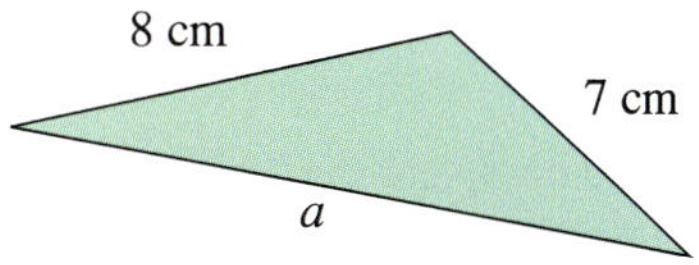

Perimeter = 27 cm

(b)
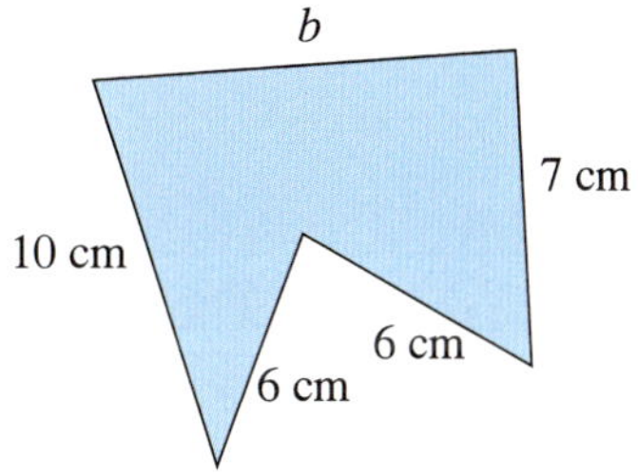

Perimeter = 39 cm

(c)
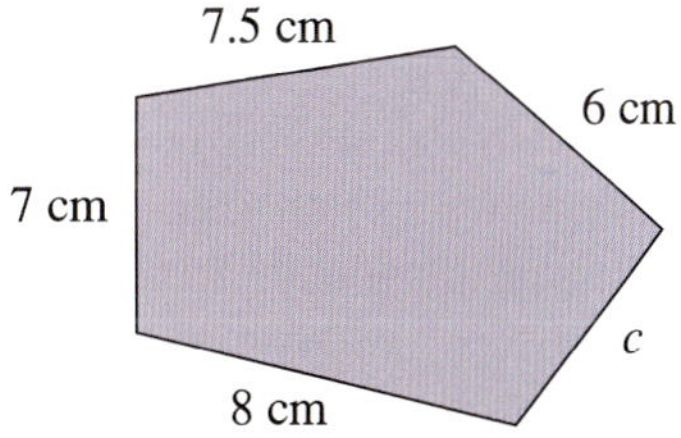

Perimeter = 34 cm

(d)
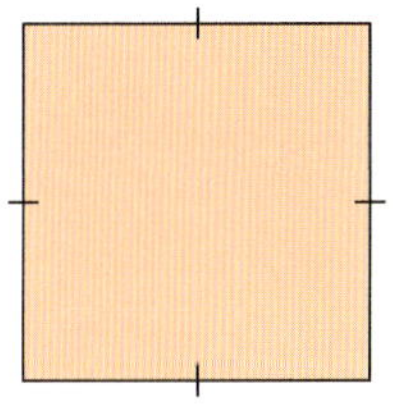

Perimeter = 36 cm

3 Find the perimeter of these rectangles.

(a)

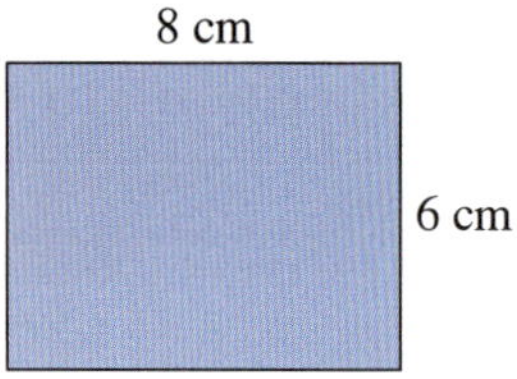

(b)

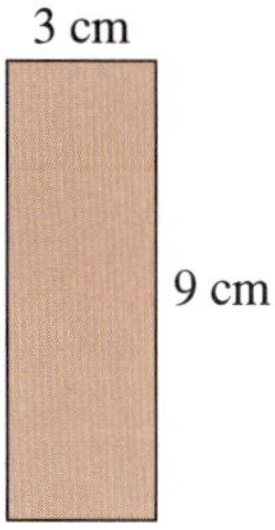

(c)

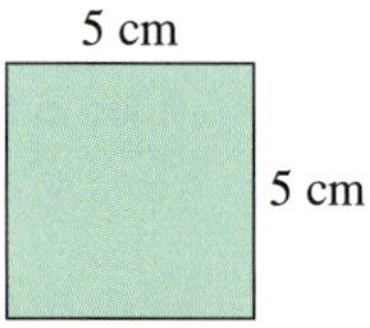

(d)

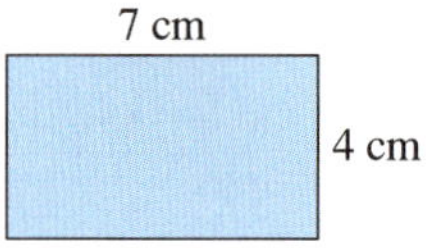

4 **(a)** Copy and complete the table for the rectangles in Question 3.

Rectangle	Length	Width	Length + Width	Perimeter
(a)	8 cm	6 cm	14 cm	

(b) What do you notice about the last two columns?

(c) Copy and complete:

Perimeter of rectangle = □ × (length + width)

5 Use the formula you discovered in Question 4 to calculate the perimeter of these rectangles.

(a) length 6 cm width 4 cm
(b) length 7.5 cm width 3.5 cm
(c) length 8 cm width 7 cm
(d) length 4.3 cm width 6.2 cm
(e) length 9.4 m width 7.9 m

6 A rectangular field has perimeter 210 m. What is the field's width if its length is 75 m?

7 A rectangular garden has length 20 m and width 15 m. What will it cost to fence the garden if fencing costs $43.25 per metre?

8

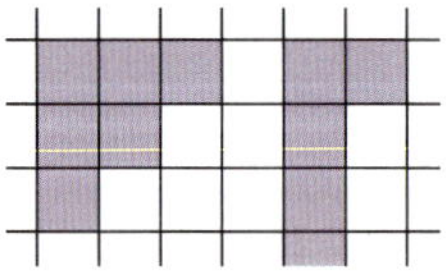

Look at the two shapes above. Both have perimeter 12 units.

(a) Using squared paper, find as many shapes as you can that have perimeter 12 units.

(b) Make a display of your results.

Investigation

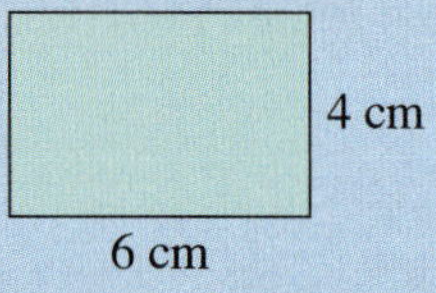

Investigate rectangles that have a perimeter of 20 cm. How many different such rectangles can you draw?

The easiest way to find the perimeter of an irregular shape is to place a piece of string around the shape. Then measure how much string was used with a ruler.

Example 4

To find the distance around the leaf, place string around it.

Stretch out the string.

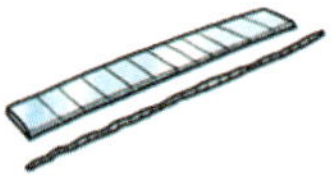

The perimeter of the leaf is ____ cm.

Exercise 7G

1 (a) Find the distance around the necks of ten students.
(b) Repeat part (a) for the distances around their wrists.
(c) Copy and complete the table.

Student	Neck perimeter (cm)	Wrist perimeter (cm)
1		
2		
10		

(d) What do you notice?

2 Repeat Question 1 for ankle perimeter and waist perimeter.

3 (a) Using a piece of string to stretch around your foot, find the distance around your foot.
(b) Repeat part (a) with five other classmates.
(c) Who has the biggest foot?

4 Collect some leaves and find out which has the largest perimeter.

7.2 Mass

Units of mass

Long ago, people measured things like rice in handfuls, or bowlfuls, or gourds.

Exercise 7H

1 Mrs Addy and Mrs Armstrong both sell sugar by the bowlful.

Mrs Addy Mrs Armstrong

They each charge 40 cents for a bowlful.
From which of them would you buy your sugar?
Why?

2 Do you think that measuring in handfuls could cause problems? Why?

3 Look again at the units shown above.
Could you use any of these for measuring meat?

Handfuls, bowlfuls and gourds are not satisfactory units for measuring quantities. Bowls and gourds come in all different shapes and sizes.

You need to use standard sizes so that you know how much you are getting.

First you need to understand the difference between mass and weight.

Mass and weight

Many people might ask 'What is your weight?'
But it is more correct to ask 'What is your mass?'
This is because weight can change from place to place. It depends on how far you are from the centre of the earth.

- The mass of an object is always the same.

An astronaut who weighs 70 kilograms on earth will weigh almost nothing at all when he is in space. He will have to be tied to his spaceship to prevent him floating away.

But the astronaut himself does not change. He is still the same man. The quantity of him is the same. This quantity is his mass. You should begin to use the word 'mass' instead of 'weight'.

The SI unit of mass – the kilogram

The SI unit of mass is the **kilogram** or **kg**. It is the mass of a small block of metal kept in a laboratory near Paris.

- The mass of a bag of sugar is a kilogram.

Exercise 7I

You will need a 1 kg mass, some oranges, grapefruit and bananas.

1 Lift up the 1 kg mass. Feel how heavy it is.
 (a) Write down five objects that are heavier than 1 kg.
 (b) Write down five objects that are lighter than 1 kg.

2 Work with a group of friends.
 (a) Compare the masses of a grapefruit, an orange and a banana with the 1 kg mass.
 (b) How many oranges are needed to make 1 kg? How many bananas? How many grapefruits?

3 **(a)** Find out your own mass in kilograms from a pair of scales.
 (b) Find out if you are above average or below average mass for your age.

4 Here are some approximate masses of everyday objects:

A large pineapple	about 1 kg
7 or 8 medium-sized bananas	about 1 kg
5 or 6 large oranges	about 1 kg
An average 12-year-old boy	about 38 kg
A small car	about 750 kg

Estimate the mass in kilograms of:
 (a) a grown man
 (b) a new-born baby
 (c) a bicycle
 (d) a cat
 (e) a cow.
Find out if your estimates are correct.

The gram

The mass of a biscuit is much much less than 1 kg. For such small masses we need a smaller unit. We use the **gram**, **g**.

- 1000 g = 1 kg
  $1\text{ g} = \frac{1}{1000}\text{ kg} = 0.001\text{ kg}$

Exercise 7J

You will need a balance and 1 g, 10 g and 100 g masses.

1 Lift up the 1 g, 10 g and 100 g masses in turn.
 (a) Write down three objects whose masses are less than 10 g.
 (b) Write down three objects whose masses are less than 100 g but more than 10 g.

2 You will need your pencil, ruler, exercise book, textbook and geometry set. Lift up each object and compare their masses.
 (a) Write down the objects in order of mass, smallest first.
 (b) Guess the masses of each object.

3 **(a)** Find the masses of the objects in Question 2 using a balance. Ask your science teacher to help you.

(b) Copy and complete the table:

Object	Estimated mass	Actual mass
Pencil		
Ruler		
Geometry set		
Exercise book		
Textbook		

(c) Which was your best estimate?

4 Here are some approximate masses:

A postcard	2 g
A new pencil	3 g
A large egg	60 g
This book	350 g
A small loaf of bread	400 g

Estimate the mass of:

(a) a ball-point pen
(b) 1 ten cent coin
(c) a teaspoon
(d) a knitting needle
(e) a letter.

Activity

A very simple balance can be made using your ruler, a pencil and some masses from your science room.

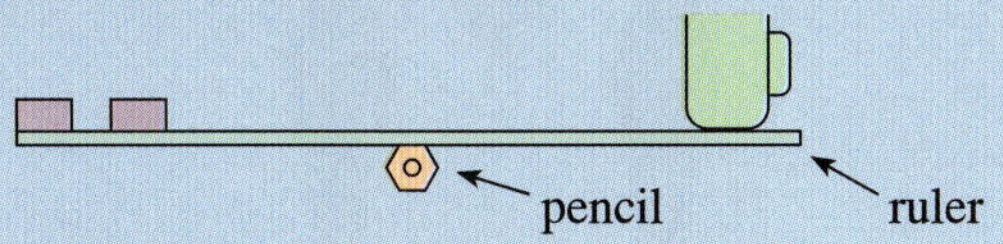

The ruler must first balance on the pencil on its own.

(a) Work with a friend and use the balance to find the masses of five objects in your school bag.
(b) Find out how a spring balance works. In what ways is a spring balance different from the one you made in part (a)?
(c) Ask your science teacher for a spring balance. Use it to check your answers to part (a).

Activity

Work with a group of friends. You will need a metre of thread, a watch and some standard masses.
Tie a 10 g mass to a metre of thread and attach the thread to your desk so it can swing freely.

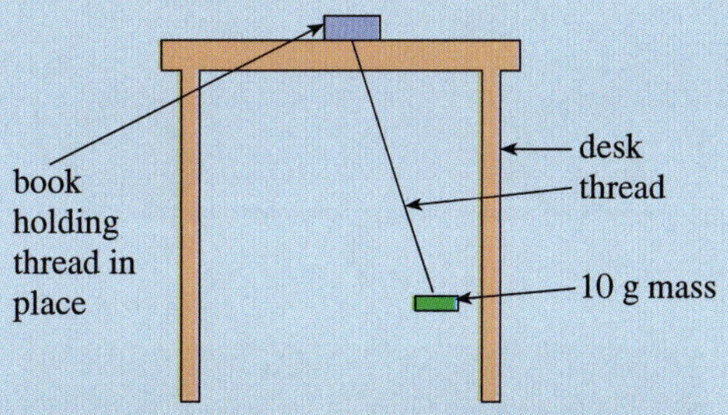

(a) Push the mass slightly, the thread will swing from side to side.
(b) How long does it take to make 20 swings?
(c) Remove the 10 g mass and put on a 50 mass. How long does it take to make 20 swings?
(d) Copy and complete the table:

Mass	Time for 20 swings
10 g	
50 g	
100 g	
200 g	

(e) What do you notice?
(f) Repeat, but this time keep the 10 g mass on the thread. Use only 50 cm of thread and find the time for 20 swings.
(g) Use 30 cm of thread, and find the time for 20 swings.
(h) Copy and complete the table:

Length of thread	Time for 20 swings
1 m	
50 cm	
30 cm	
10 cm	

(i) What do you notice?
(j) Estimate the time for 20 swings if only 20 cm of thread were used.

The tonne

For very large masses, a larger unit is used.
It is the **tonne**, **t**.

- 1 t = 1000 kg

Here are some approximate masses:

Car, about 1 t

Elephant, about 5 t

Exercise 7K

1 Write down five objects with masses greater than 1 t. Try to find out their masses.

2 Copy and complete:
1 kg = □ g   1 t = □ kg
1 g = □ kg   1 kg = □ t

3 Add these masses and give the answer in
(i) grams **(ii)** kilograms.
(a) 972 g, 83 g, 523 g
(b) 323 g, 1.521 kg, 97 g
(c) 2 t, 731 kg, 432 g

4 Give your answers in the most appropriate units.
(a) 734 g + 88 g − 236.7 g
(b) 396 g + 7 kg 86 g − 3 kg 746 g
(c) 45.87 g × 27

5 The total mass of 4 sacks of provisions is 213 kg. The masses of three of the sacks are 51 kg, 47 kg and 63 kg.
What is the mass of the fourth sack?

6 One tin of biscuits has a mass of 0.32 kg.
What is the mass of 7 of these tins in **(i)** kg **(ii)** g?

7 A truck full of sand has a mass of 3.2 t.
What is the mass of the truck if the mass of the sand is 1.875 t?
Give your answer in
(i) tonnes **(ii)** kilograms.

8 Merlene buys a piece of meat with a mass of 4 kg 65 g.
(a) Express the mass in grams.
She divides the piece of meat into 4 equal portions.
(b) Give the mass of each portion in
(i) grams **(ii)** kilograms.

7.3 Time

In the past, people measured time with sand timers or candles.

Today, time is measured most accurately using atomic clocks.

- The SI unit of time is the **second**, **s**.

A second is defined in terms of the vibrations of a caesium atom.

Larger units of time and their relationships are shown in the table.

Unit of time	Relationship
Minute (min)	60 s = 1 min
Hour (h)	60 min = 1 h
Day	24 h = 1 day
Week	7 days = 1 week
Year	52 weeks = 1 year

Exercise 7L

1. Work with a friend. Shut your eyes and tell your friend when you think a minute has passed.
   Get your friend to time you.
   How good was your estimate?

2. Look at the time on a watch or clock.
   Now see if you can count to 60 at a steady rate in 1 minute. Practise this.

3. (a) Write down five activities you take less than 1 minute to do.
   (b) Write down five activities you take less than 10 seconds to do.

4. Estimate the time it takes to:
   (a) read this question
   (b) count to twenty
   (c) open a door
   (d) drink a glass of water.

5. (a) How many seconds make an hour?
   (b) How many minutes make a day?
   (c) How many hours make a week?

6. Estimate the time it takes to:
   (a) cook half a kilogram of rice
   (b) wash up the lunch plates
   (c) bathe in the morning
   (d) walk a kilometre
   (e) multiply 367 by 294.

7. Try and check the times it actually takes you in Question 6.

8. (a) How many days are there in 5 weeks?
   (b) How many hours are there in 2 weeks 5 days?
   (c) How many days are there in 1 year 3 weeks?

Telling the time

Most time is now recorded on digital clocks or watches.

The time on this watch is 9:37 or 37 minutes after 9 o'clock.

Some watches and clocks use hands.

The time on this watch is also 9:37.

To read such clock faces, you need to remember that the face is divided into 60 minutes as shown below.

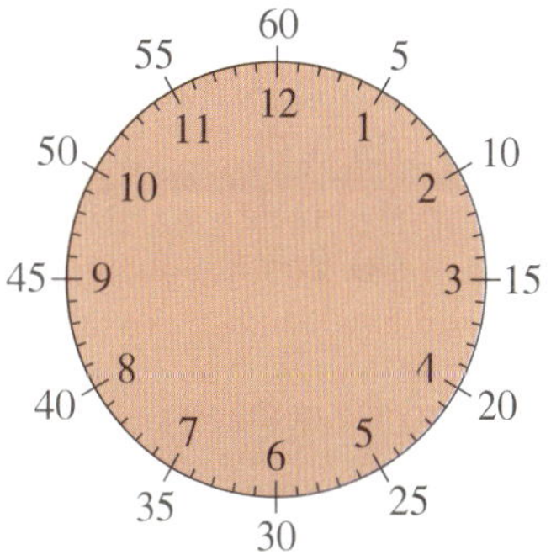

The hour and the minute hand tell the time.

The minute hand points to the 12, that is 0 minutes past the hour. The hour hand points to the 4, so the time is 4:00.

The minute hand points to the 8, that is 40 minutes past the hour. The hour hand points between the 4 and the 5, so the time is 4:40.

Exercise 7M

1 What time is shown on these six clocks?

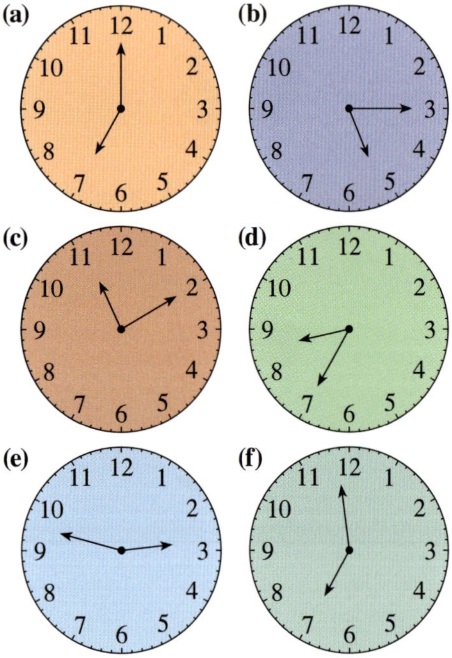

2 Draw clock faces to show these times.

(a) 3:00 **(b)** 3:30 **(c)** 6:40
(d) 8:45 **(e)** 11:05 **(f)** 1:16
(g) 3:54 **(h)** 2:37

3 The number line of times shows how Vincent spends his morning.

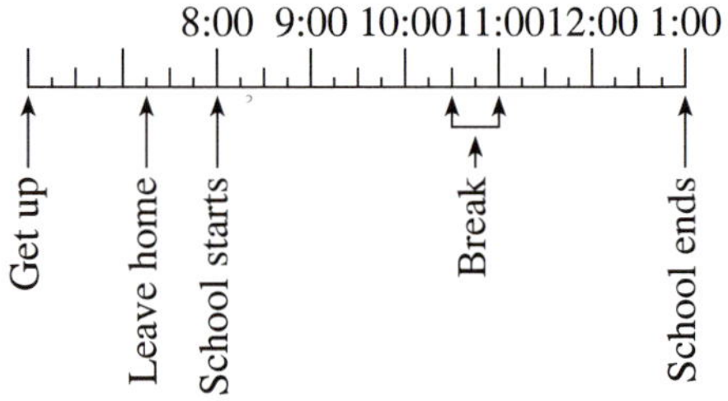

(a) What time does he leave home?
(b) How long is break?
(c) How long does he take to get to school?

4 **(a)** How do you spend your school day?
(b) Write down all the things you do in a normal school day, from getting up in the morning to going to bed at night.
(c) Write down the times you begin each activity.
(d) Draw a time line as in Question 3 from 6 am to 9 pm showing your day.

5 **(a)** Draw a clock face to show the time you start school.
(b) Draw a clock face to show the time you leave school.
(c) How long is your school day?

6 Repeat Question 5 for:
(a) starting and finishing breakfast
(b) going to bed at night and getting up in the morning
(c) starting and finishing your homework.

Technology

Visit the website <u>www.woodlands-junior.kent.sch.uk/maths</u> and try out some of the telling the time games.

Activity

Recovery times

- Using a watch with a second hand or a stop clock, find how many times your pulse beats each minute.
- Run about 100 m as fast as you can.
- Check your pulse rate now.
- Check your pulse rate every minute until it gets back to what it was before you did your run.
- How long was this?

24-hour clock

8 o'clock in the morning is represented by 8 00 am on the 12-hour clock, 08 : 00 on the 24-hour clock.

This time is read as 'zero eight hundred hours'.

7.30 in the evening is represented by 7.30 pm on the 12-hour clock, 19 : 30 on the 24-hour clock.

This time is read as 'nineteen thirty'.

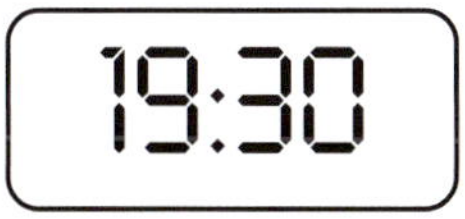

- The 24-hour clock uses all 24 hours in a day to give the time.
  The first two figures give the number of hours after midnight, and the last two figures give the number of minutes past the hour.

Example 5

(a) Writc 8.15 pm in 24-hour clock time.
(b) Write 02.54 in am/pm time.

(a) 8 pm is 8 + 12 = 20 hours after midnight
so 8.15 pm is 20 15
(b) 02 : 00 is 2 am
So 02 : 54 is 2.54 am

Exercise 7N

1 Write in 24-hour clock time:

(a) 4 am	(b) 8.30 am	(c) 11 am
(d) 1 pm	(e) 3.30 pm	(f) 8.45 pm
(g) 9.25 pm	(h) 7.53 pm	(i) 1.52 am

2 Write in am/pm time:

(a) 03 : 00	(b) 05 : 00	(c) 12 : 00
(d) 15 : 00	(e) 19 : 00	(f) 23 : 00
(g) 01 : 05	(h) 04 : 25	(i) 21 : 55

It is easier to find time intervals with the 24-hour clock than the 12-hour clock.

Example 6

(a) A football match kicked off at 15 : 45 and ended at 17 : 25. How long did the game last?
(b) How long is it from 21 : 30 on Tuesday to 03 : 15 on Wednesday?

(a)

6 60
17:25
Time taken = −15:45
1:40

The game lasted 1 hr 40 min

(b)

3 60
24:00
−21:30
2:30

02:30 — time to midnight
+03:15 — time from midnight
05:45

Time span = 5 hr 45 min

Exercise 7O

1 How long is it from:

(a) 06 : 00 to 07:15	(b) 22 : 00 to 23 : 50
(c) 09 : 20 to 13:40	(d) 03 : 15 to 16 : 28
(e) 12 : 25 to 15:10	(f) 19 : 32 to 22 : 17
(g) 18 : 40 to 07:15	(h) 21 : 35 to 02 : 05

2 BWIA flies from Kingston, Jamaica at 14 : 30 and arrives in Antigua at 18 : 10. How long is the flight?

3 Write the times you begin each of today's classes in 24-hour clock time.

4 Look at the LIAT flight timetable below:

Dominica	Arr.	06:30	16:50
	Dep.	06:40	17:00
Martinique	Arr.	07:00	17:20
	Dep.	07:10	17:30
St Lucia	Arr.	07:35	17:55
	Dep.	07:45	18:05
Barbados	Arr.	08:25	18:45

(a) What time does the first flight leave Dominica?
(b) When does the second flight arrive in St Lucia?
(c) What is the flight time from Martinique to St Lucia, ignoring stopover times?
(d) What is the flight time from Dominica to Barbados?
(e) Rewrite the timetable using the 12-hour clock.

5 The 'Late Show' begins at 22:45 and ends at 01:05. How long is the show?

6 Caribbean Airways has three flights daily leaving Part of Spain, Trinidad for New York (JFK). The timetable is shown below.

Flight No.	From	Dep.	To	Arr.
520	POS	00:40	JFK	05:50
522	POS	08:55	JFK	14:05
424	POS	17:30	JFK	22:40

(a) Rewrite the timetable using the 12-hour clock.
(b) What is the flight time for each flight?

7 Passengers should arrive $2\frac{1}{2}$ hours before travelling on international airline flights.
What time should I arrive if my flight leaves at:
(a) 15:30 **(b)** 06:20?

8 A cyclist started a journey at 08:15. She rode for 1 h 25 min, rested for 25 min and then rode for another 1 h 55 min.
At what time did she reach her destination?

Technology

- Compare the 12-hour clock with the 24-hour clock by visiting the following website and looking at the Teachers Toolkit *www./crickweb.co.uk/ks2numeracy.html*
- Did you know that when it is
10.00 am in Trinidad it is
9.00 am in Kingston, Jamaica,
7.00 am in Los Angeles, and
3.00 pm in London?
Visit
www.timeanddate.com/worldclock
to see how time changes around the world.

7.4 Temperature

Temperature is usually measured in degrees (°) using the Celsius (C) temperature scale.

This scale is based on the freezing point of water (0°C) and the boiling point of water (100°C).

The SI unit of temperature is the Kelvin (K). It is related to the Celsius scale as shown:

	Celsius	Kelvin
Freezing point of water	0°C	273 K
Boiling point of water	100°C	373 K

Temperature is normally measured with a thermometer.

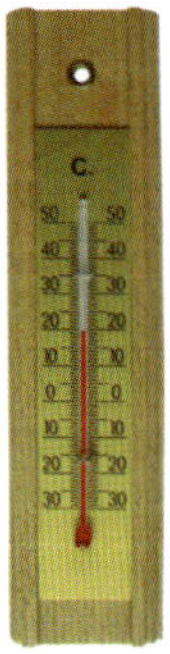

Special thermometers are used to measure the temperature of people.

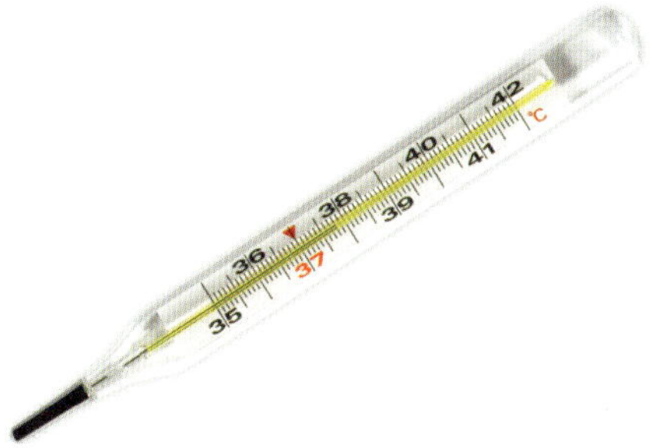

Clinical thermometer

Normal body temperature is 37.0°C. An increase of just a few degrees may indicate a serious fever.

Exercise 7P

1 Make estimates in °C of the temperature of
- **(a)** ice cream
- **(b)** juice taken from a refrigerator
- **(c)** a hot cup of tea
- **(d)** the water you bathe in
- **(e)** the water in a car's radiator after it has travelled 20 km.

2 Research the body temperatures of animals. Make a list of ten animals and their body temperatures.

3 **(a)** Go on the internet to find out more about how temperature is measured and what instruments are used.
- **(b)** Write up your findings as a short report.

4 **(a)** Record the 9.00 am temperature in your classroom over 5 days.
- **(b)** Draw a chart to show how the temperature changes over the 5 days.

5 Use the internet to find the temperatures for ten different places around the world.
- **(a)** Which place is usually the hottest?
- **(b)** Which place is usually the coldest?
- **(c)** In which of these locations would you prefer to live? Give reasons.

Exercise 7Q – mixed questions

1 Use this ruler to answer the question.

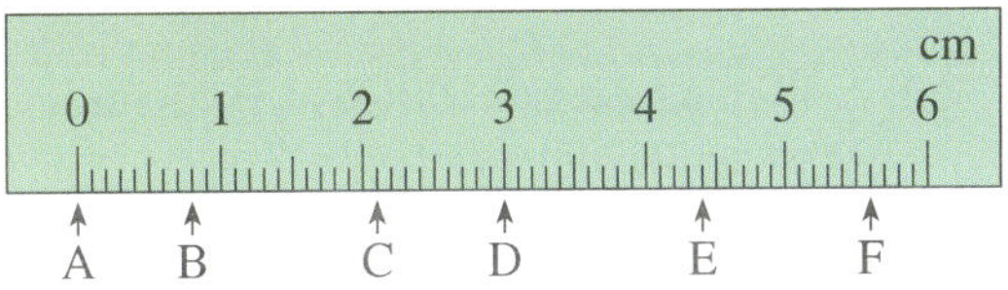

Write down the distances:

(a) AB **(b)** AC **(c)** AD
(d) AE **(e)** AF **(f)** DE
(g) DF **(h)** CF

2 In Question 1, work out the distances:
(a) BC **(b)** CD **(c)** BE **(d)** CE

3 In Question 2 by how much is:
- **(a)** BC longer than CD
- **(b)** BE longer than CE?

4 Look at these rectangles.

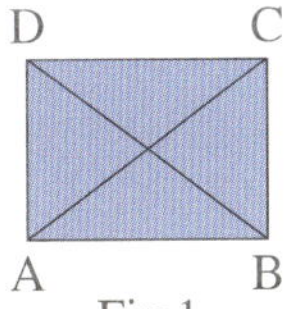

Fig 1

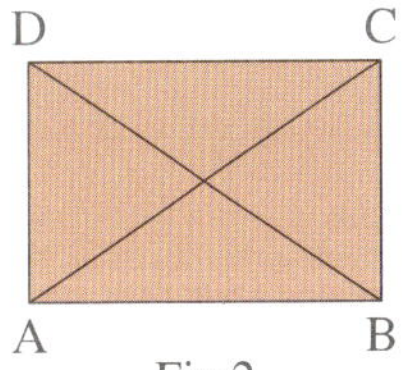

Fig 2

- **(a)** Measure the diagonals AC and BD in Fig. 1.
- **(b)** Measure the diagonals AC and BD in Fig. 2.
- **(c)** Draw two more rectangles of your own. Measure their diagonals. What do you notice?

5 Look at the lines AB, CD and EF.

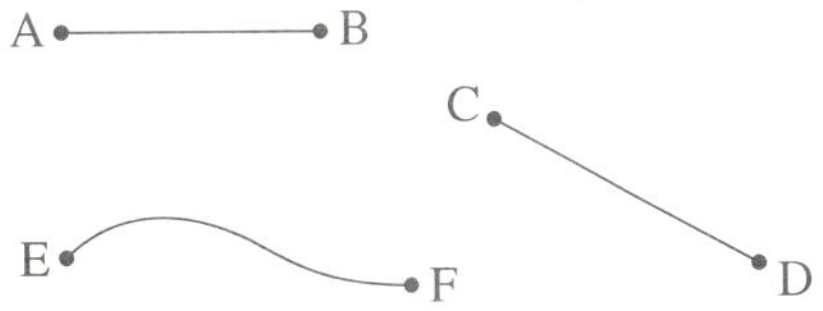

- **(a)** Which of the lines do you think is the longest?
- **(b)** How would you find the length of each line?
- **(c)** Write down the lengths AB, CD and EF.

6 **(a)** What is the thickness of 50 pages of this textbook?
- **(b)** How would you find the width of a single page?

7 Three identical suitcases together weigh 14.1 kg.
(a) How much, in kilograms, does one suitcase weigh?
(b) What is your answer to part (a) in grams?

8 (a) A 40-minute lesson started at 11.15 am. At what time did it end?
(b) A 35-minute lesson finished at 12.40 pm. At what time did it start?
(c) Write the lesson start and finish times as 24-hour clock times.

9 Caribbean Airways flight departures from Bridgetown, Barbados are shown in the timetable below.

Dep.	Arr.	Destination
08:30	09:30	Antigua
18:35	19:55	Georgetown
08:30	11:25	Kingston
22:00	10:10 (next day)	London
08:00	10:45	Miami
18:15	22:20	New York

(a) Which is the shortest flight time?
(b) How long is the longest flight time?
(c) Rewrite the timetable using 12-hour clock times.

7 Consolidation

Example 1

Which unit would you use to measure the

(a) width of your classroom
(b) length of your little finger
(c) distance from London to New York?

(a) Your classroom is a few big strides long, so use metres.
(b) Your little finger is much smaller than a stride, so use centimetres.
(c) London to New York is a great distance, so use kilometres.

Example 2

Convert:

(a) 35 mm to cm
(b) 3.2 km to m

(a) 10 mm = 1 cm
so 35 mm = 35 ÷ 10 cm
= 3.5 cm

(b) 1000 m = 1 km
so 3.2 km = 3.2 × 1000 m
= 3200 m

Example 3

Estimate the mass of

(a) a pen in grams; in kg
(b) a chair in kg; in grams

(a) A pen is very light. Its mass could be 25 g.
1000 g = 1 kg
so 25 g = 25 ÷ 1000 kg
= 0.025 kg

(b) A chair is quite heavy. Its mass could be 25 kg.
1000 g = 1 kg
so 25 kg = 25 × 1000 g
= 25 000 g

Example 4

What time is shown on these clocks?

(a)

(b)

(a) 1:25 **(b)** 7:57

Example 5

What is

(a) 7.40 pm in 24-hour clock time
(b) 13:21 in 12-hour clock time?

(a) 7 pm is 7 + 12 = 19 hours after midnight so 7.40 pm is 19:40.
(b) 13:00 is 13 hours after midnight or 13 − 12 = 1 hour after midday so 13:21 is 1.21 pm.

Exercise 7

1 Which unit would you use to measure

(a) your height
(b) length of your foot
(c) height of your classroom
(d) width of a fly's wing
(e) length of a cricket pitch
(f) distance from Grenada to Jamaica?

2 Estimate the mass of these objects using appropriate units.

(a) a pencil **(b)** a cup
(c) a football **(d)** a table

3 Convert

(a) 23 mm to cm **(b)** 4 cm to mm
(c) 3 km to m **(d)** 2 kg to g
(e) 3.1 kg to g **(f)** 800 g to kg
(g) 6 h to min **(h)** 4200 s to min
(i) 4 weeks to hours

4 Find the perimeter of these shapes.

(a)

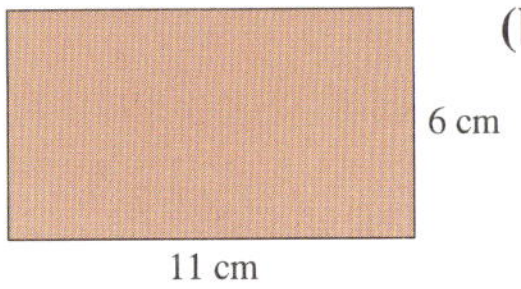

(b)

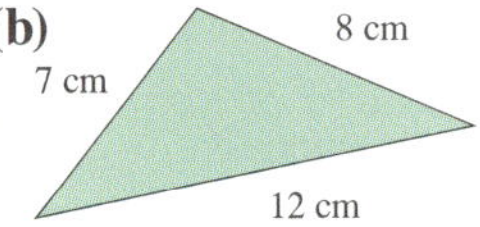

(c)

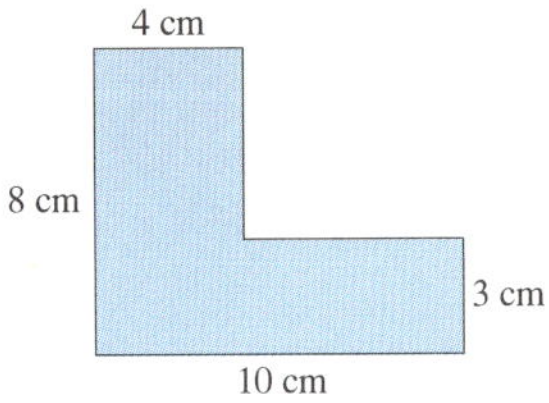

Application 7

5 Tricia Smith of Jamaica won the gold medal for triple jump at the 2005 World Athletics Championships in Helsinki with a leap of 15.11 m.

(a) How far is this in centimetres?
(b) With a metre rule, measure out this distance.
(c) Make a triple jump of your own. How far did you jump?
(d) How far were you from Tricia Smith's winning leap?
(e) Walter Davis of the USA won the men's event with a jump of 17.57 m. How much further did Davis jump than Smith?

6 A fish currently 3 cm long grows 6 mm per year.
(a) How long will it be in:
(i) 2 years time **(ii)** 5 years time?
(b) Use a ruler to find the age of the fish shown below.

7 The Caribbean Star flight schedule from Barbados to Beef Island, Tortola, is

Depart	Arrive
7.30 am	12.30 pm
1.00 pm	6.10 pm
3.30 pm	6.50 pm (Fridays only)

(a) Draw clock faces to show the Friday departure and arrival times.
(b) How long is the Friday flight?
(c) Which is the faster flight, that leaving at 7.30 am or 1.00 pm?
(d) Rewrite the timetable in 24-hour clock times.

Companion CD

Want some extra practice? Go to Chapter 7 on your companion CD for further exercises, animations, and solutions.

Summary

You should know ...

1 The SI unit of length is the metre (m).
Smaller units used are centimetres (cm) or millimetres (mm).

1 m is approximately on long stride.

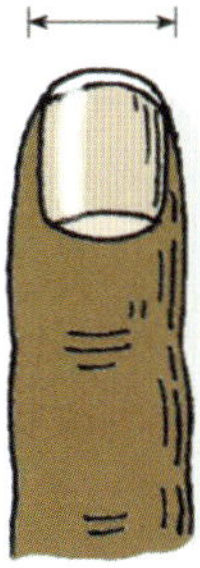

1 cm is approximately the width of your smallest finger.

A larger unit used is the kilometre (km).

2 10 mm = 1 cm
100 cm = 1 m
1000 cm = 1 km

3 The SI unit of mass is the kilogram (kg).
A smaller unit used is the gram (g).
A larger unit used is the tonne (t).

1 kg is approximately the mass of a large pineapple.

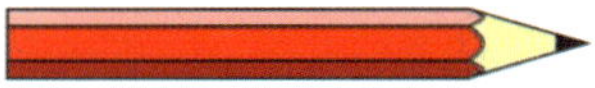

A pencil's mass is about 3 g.

Check out

1 What unit would be most convenient to measure:
(a) the width of a football field
(b) the width of this book
(c) the distance between Kingston and Bridgetown?

2 Express:
(a) 3 m in cm
(b) 270 m in km.

3 What unit would be most convenient to measure:
(a) the mass of a bicycle
(b) the mass of a paint brush
(c) the mass of a bus?

4 1000 g = 1 kg
1000 kg = 1 t

4 **(a)** Add together 2 t, 57 kg and 321 g.
Give your answer in grams.
(b) Find 33.5 g × 32
Give your answer in **(i)** g and **(ii)** kg.

5 How to tell the time.

5 **(a)** What time is shown on this clock?

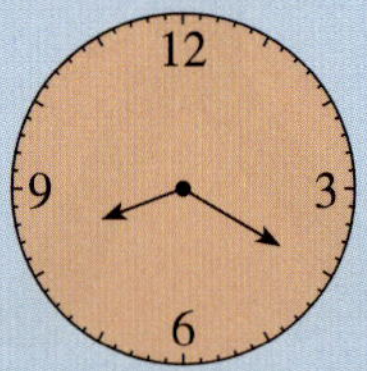

(b) Find the number of hours in 1 week 3 days.
(c) What is 7.46 pm as a 24-hour clock time?

Shapes 8

Objectives

- ✔ sort and classify triangles and quadrilaterals
- ✔ investigate the properties of shapes to solve problems
- ✔ use ruler and compasses to construct shapes accurately
- ✔ create patterns and art using ideas of symmetry and simple transformations

What's the point?

Shapes are all around us. A football pitch is rectangular, the tiles on a floor may be square, earrings may be circular in shape.

Before you start

You should know ...

1 Different types of angle:

less than 90°: acute

between 90° and 180°: obtuse

2 How to measure angles:

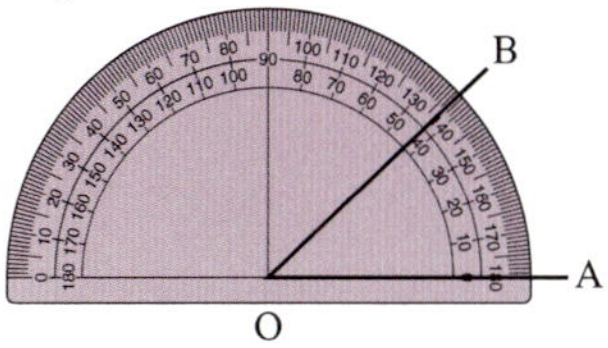

The angle AOB is 43°

3 How to measure lines:

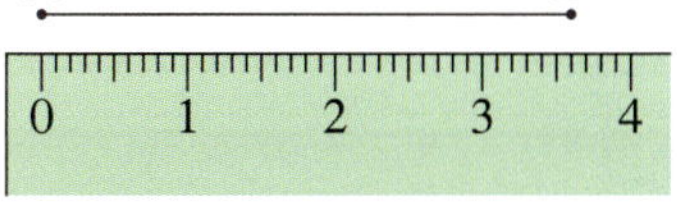

The line AB = 3.6 cm

Check in

1 Which of these angles are acute?

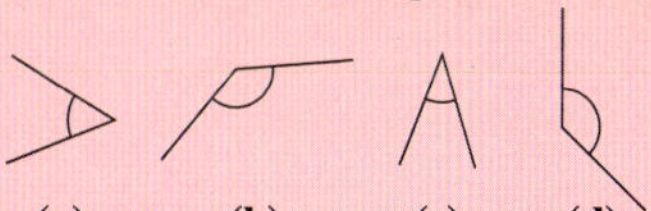

(a) **(b)** **(c)** **(d)**

2 Use your protractor to measure this angle.

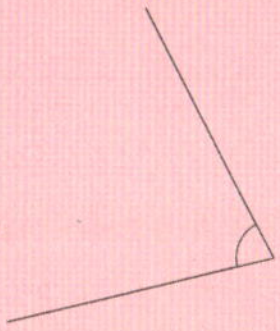

3 **(a)** Measure these lines.

(i) ____________________

(ii) ________

(b) Draw a line 6.2 cm long.

8.1 Looking at triangles

You will need squared paper, a ruler and a protractor.

Measure the sides of each of these triangles.
Write down the measurements.

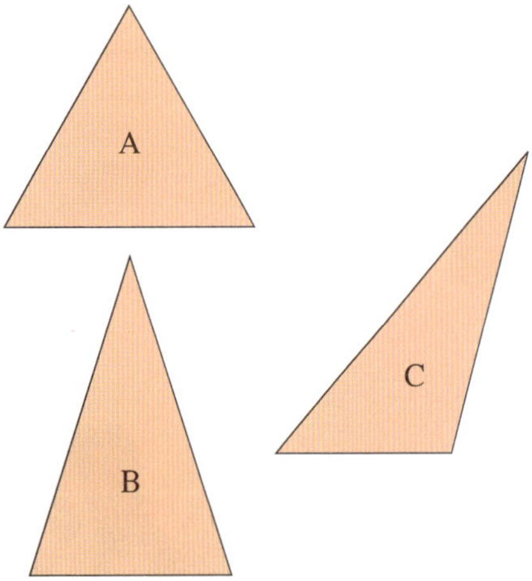

Triangle A has all its sides equal in length. It is called an **equilateral** triangle.

Triangle B has two sides equal. It is an **isosceles** triangle.

In triangle C there are no equal sides.
It is a **scalene** triangle.

Exercise 8A

1 Here are three triangles.

(i)

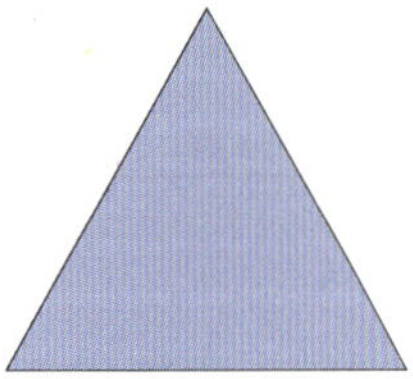

(ii)

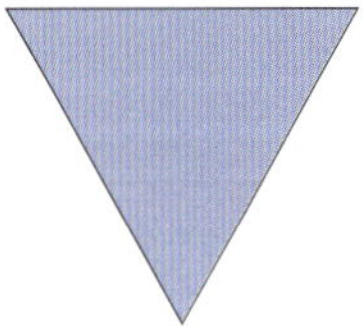

(iii)

For each triangle:

(a) Measure the length of each side.
What sort of triangle is it?

(b) Now measure each angle.
What do you notice?

2 Write down two properties of an equilateral triangle.

3 **(a)** Cut out two triangles like the one shown below:

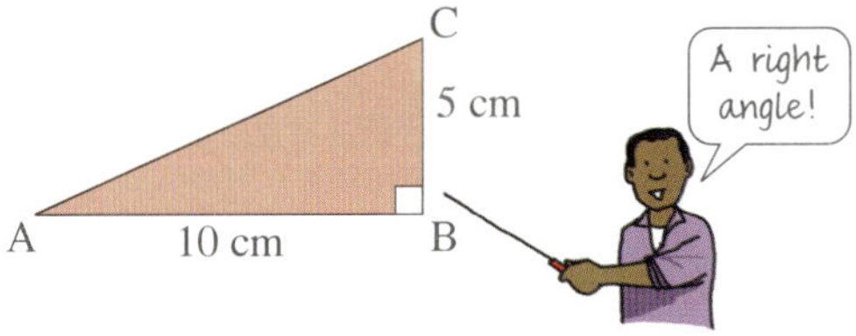

(b) Tape them together carefully along the 10 cm long side.

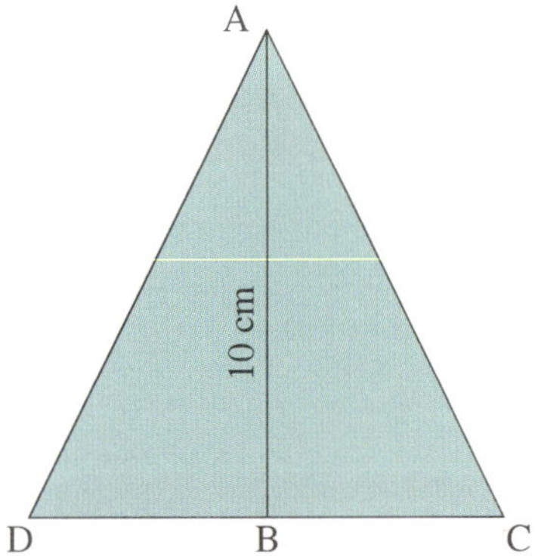

(c) Fold the triangle along AB. What do you notice about AD and AC?
What type of triangle is ACD?

(d) Fold the triangle along AB again.
What do you notice about $A\hat{C}B$ and $A\hat{D}B$?

4 For each of the following triangles:

(a) Measure the sides. What sort of triangle is it?

(b) Now measure the angles with a protractor.
What do you notice?

(i)

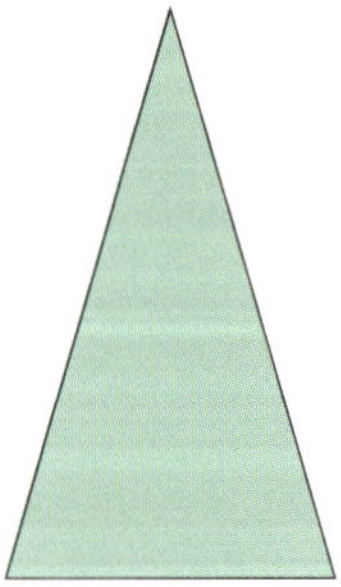

(ii)

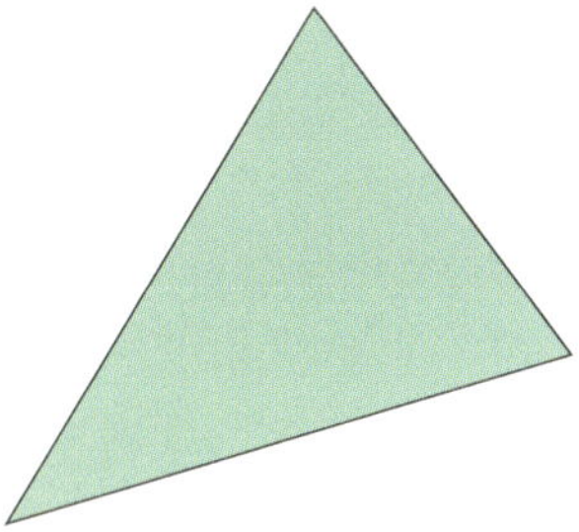

(iii)

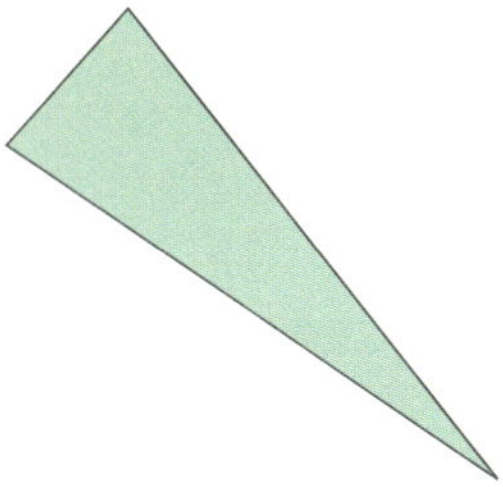

5 Write down the properties you have discovered for an isosceles triangle.

6 For each of the following triangles:

(a) Measure the edges. What sort of triangle is it?

(b) Measure the angles. Are any of them equal?

(i)

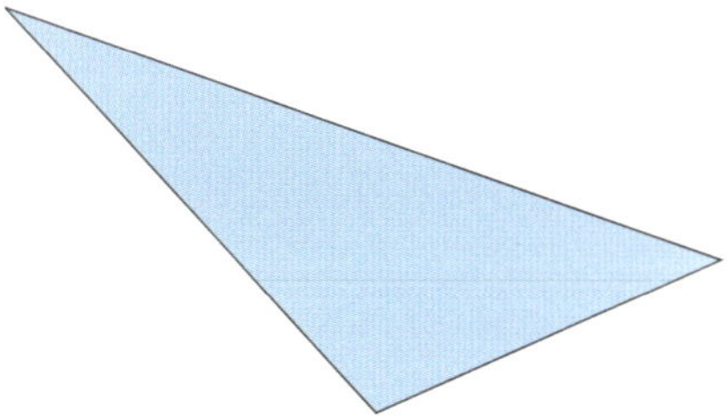

(ii)

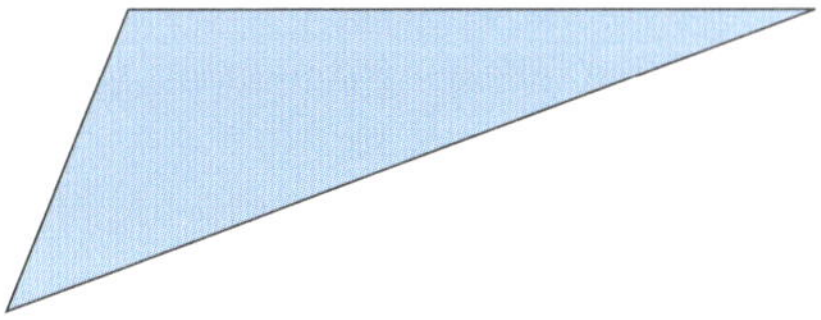

(iii)

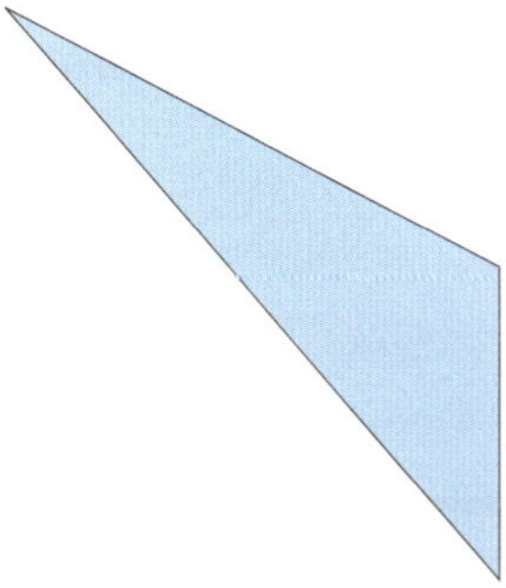

7 Write down two properties of a scalene triangle.

8 **(a)** Look at the triangle below.
It is called a right-angled triangle.
Can you see why?

(b) Measure its angles.

(c) Did you find one of those angles was a right angle?

9 **(a)** Make two copies on card of this right-angled triangle.

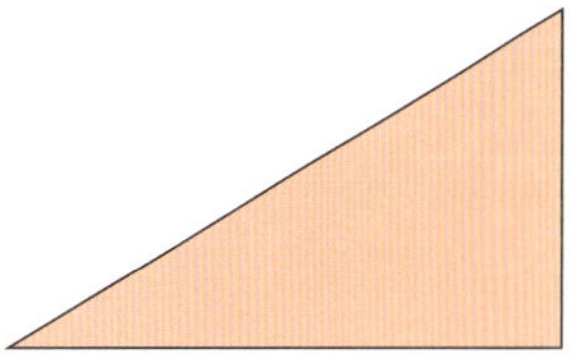

(b) Cut them out.

(c) How many different shapes can you make using your two right-angled triangles?

(d) Make a list of all the things you notice about each shape.

10 Which of these triangles are:

(a) right-angled

(b) isosceles

(c) scalene?

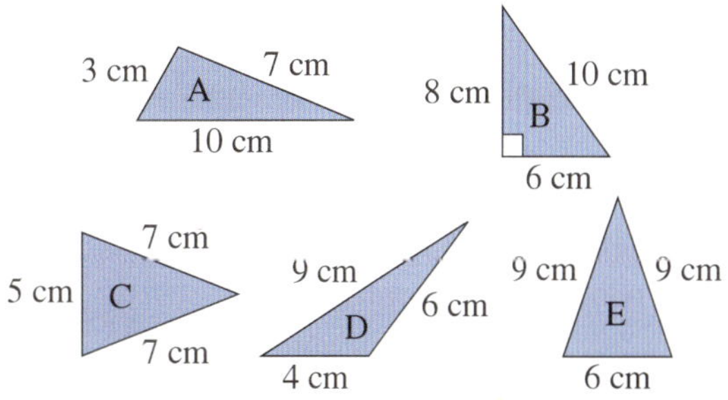

11 Label the sets in the diagram.

12 Label the sets in the diagram.

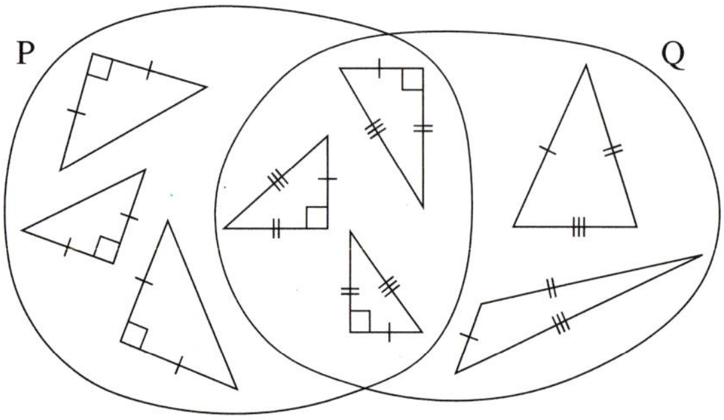

Triangles classified by angles

Obtuse-angled triangles have one obtuse angle and two acute angles.

For example:

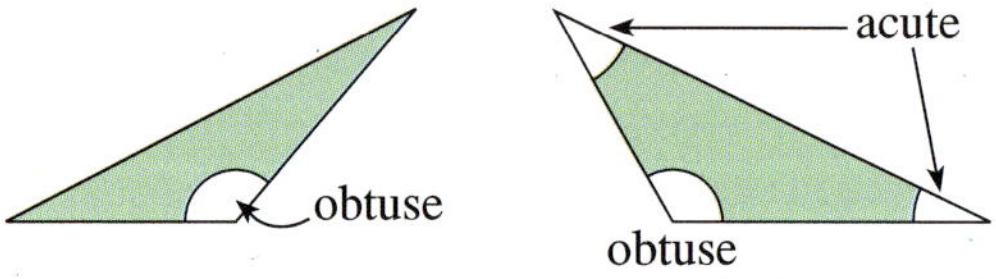

Acute-angled triangles have all three angles acute.

For example:

Right-angled triangles have one angle of 90°.

For example:

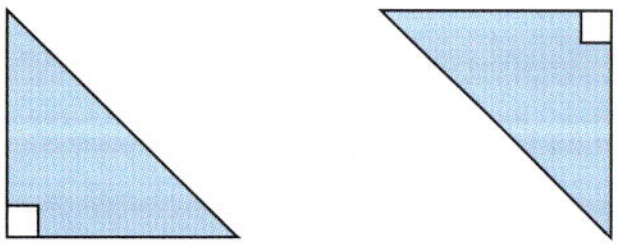

Exercise 8B

1 Label the sets in the diagram.

2 These are acute-angled triangles. What kind of angle is every angle in each triangle?

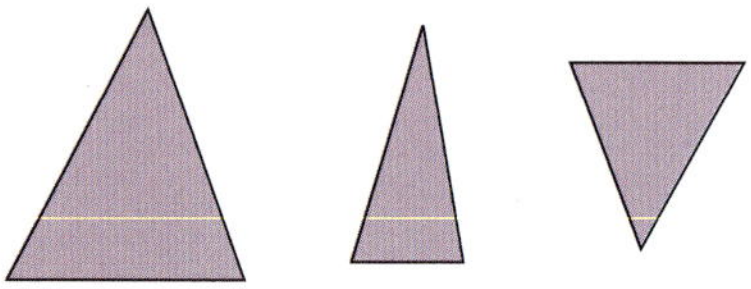

(a) **(b)** **(c)**

3 Label the sets in the diagram.

4 Copy the following statements completing them with 'All', 'Some' or 'No'.

(a) … right-angled triangles are obtuse-angled triangles.

(b) … isosceles triangles are right-angled triangles.

(c) … equilateral triangles are isosceles triangles.

(d) … right-angled triangles are equilateral triangles.

(e) … acute-angled triangles are equilateral triangles.

8.2 Looking at quadrilaterals

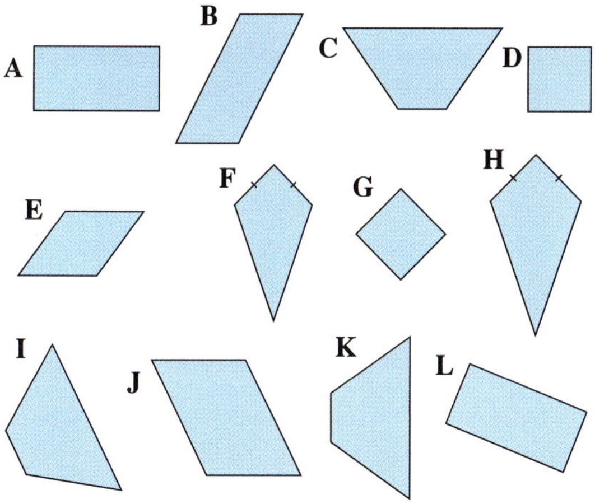

Look at the shapes in the set above. They all have four sides. Four-sided shapes are called **quadrilaterals**.

For this exercise you will need 12 card cut-outs of the shapes shown in the set above.

Exercise 8C

1 (a) Divide your set of quadrilaterals into two groups.
(b) How did you sort them?
(c) Sort your set using a different method.
(d) How did you sort them this time?

2 (a) Sort your quadrilaterals into three groups.
(b) How did you sort them?

3 Which of the shapes have four square corners?

4 Which shapes have just one pair of parallel sides?

5 Which shapes have two pairs of parallel sides?

6 Which shapes have two pairs of parallel sides and four square corners?

7 Which shapes have four sides all equal in length?

8 What is similar about shapes A, B, E and J?

9 What is similar about shapes C and K?

10 What is similar about shapes F and H?

In Exercise 8C you should have found that some quadrilaterals have special properties.

Rectangles and squares

A rectangle has four right angles
So does a square.

How are they different?

Exercise 8D

1 (a) Name five things that are rectangular in shape.
(b) Name five things that are square.

2 (a) Draw three different-sized rectangles and cut them out.
(b) Fold one of your rectangles down the middle.

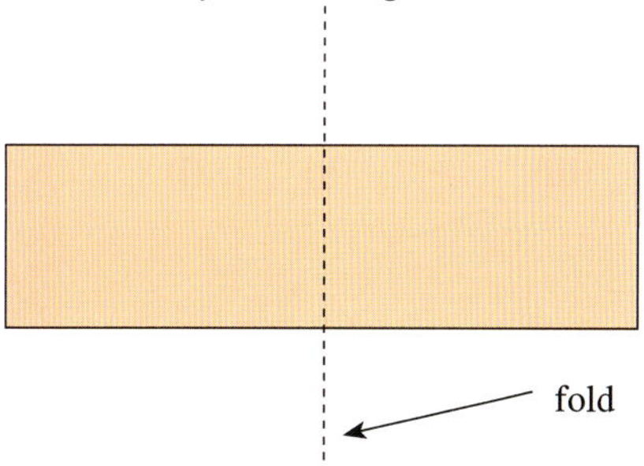

What do you notice?
(c) Repeat for your other rectangles.
What do you notice?
(d) Fold your rectangles along their diagonal.

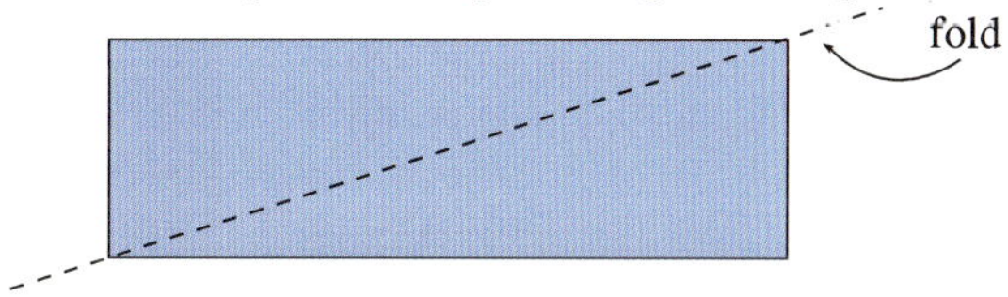

What do you notice?

3 Repeat Question 2 for three different-sized squares.

4 (a) Write down three properties of a rectangle.
(b) Write down three properties of a square.
(c) How does a square differ from a rectangle?

5 (a) Is it true to say that all rectangles are squares? or all squares are rectangles? or some squares are rectangles?
(b) Draw a Venn diagram to show your answer.

Parallelograms and rhombi

A **parallelogram** is a four-sided shape or quadrilateral with opposite sides parallel.

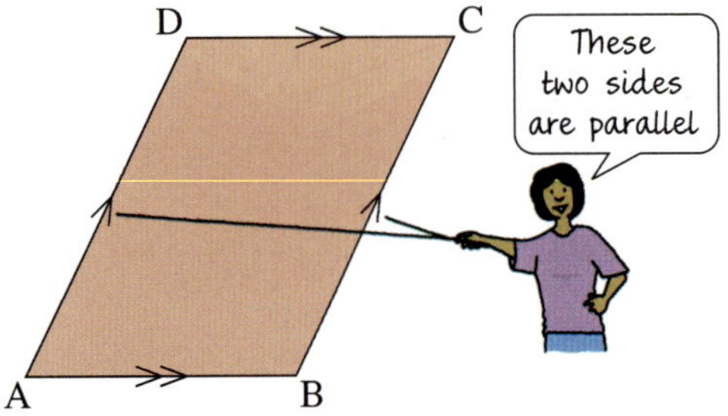

In the diagram, notice
line segment AB is parallel to DC
line segment AD is parallel to BC.

A **rhombus** is a special type of parallelogram.

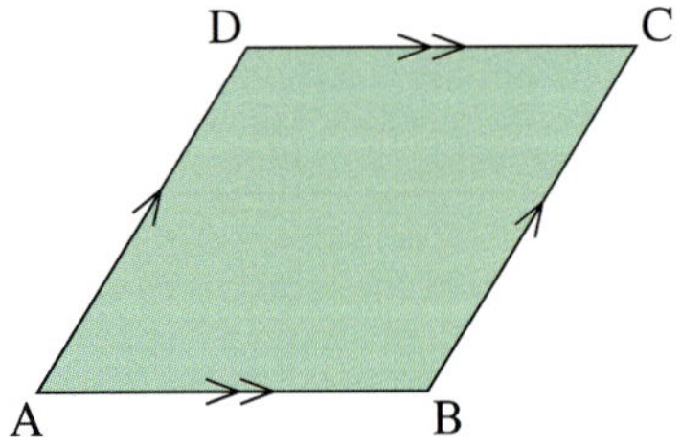

It has all four sides equal in length.

Exercise 8E

1 What type of quadrilateral do you see in the photograph?

2 Give some other examples where you may see parallelograms in or out of the classroom.

3 (a) Draw three different-sized parallelograms and cut them out.
(b) Fold your parallelograms down the middle.

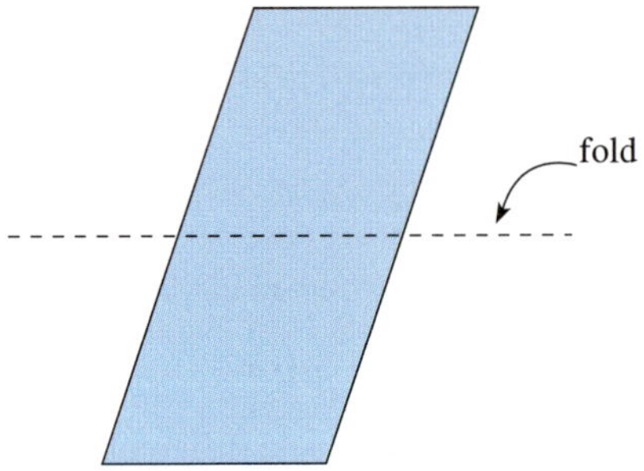

What do you notice?
(c) Fold the parallelograms along a diagonal.

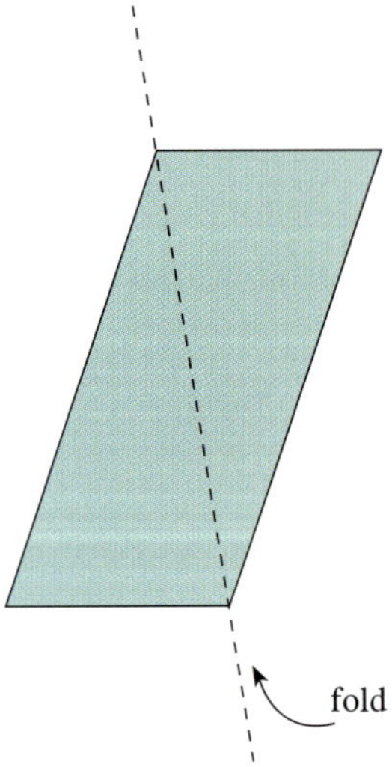

What do you notice?

4 **(a)** Look at these parallelograms.

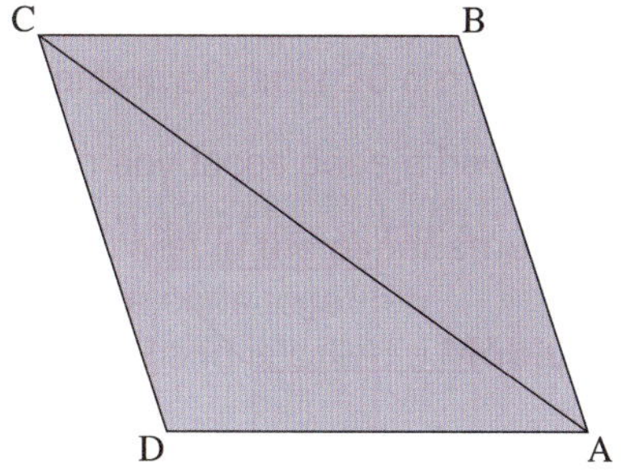

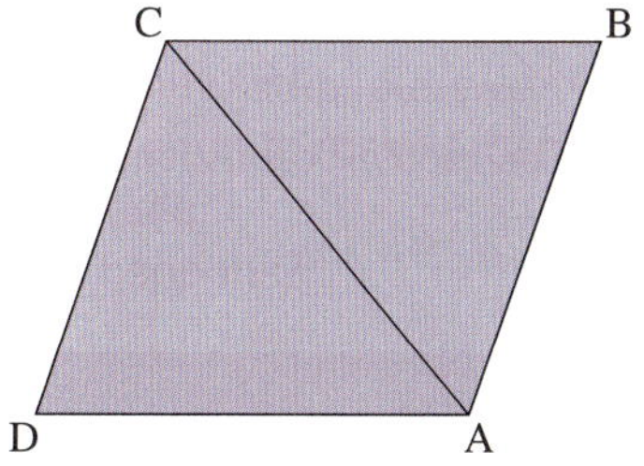

In each case measure the angles

(i) $A\hat{C}B$, $D\hat{A}C$

(ii) $B\hat{A}C$, $D\hat{C}A$

with your protractor.

(b) What do you notice?

5 **(a)** Take a piece of paper and fold it in two.

Fold it in two again.

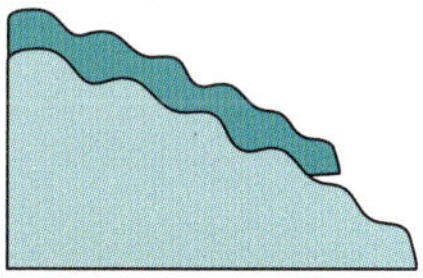

Then cut off a corner …

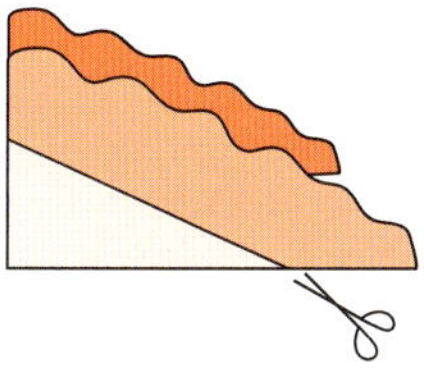

and open it out.

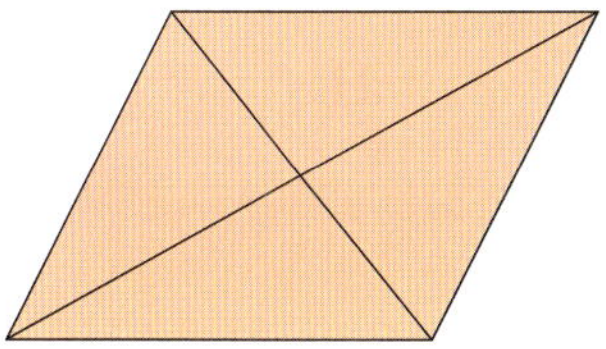

(b) What shape is it?

6 Use your protractor to measure each of the angles you made in Question 5. What do you notice?

7 **(a)** Make two other different-sized rhombi, as in Question 5.

(b) Measure their angles.

(c) Did you get the same result as in Question 6?

8

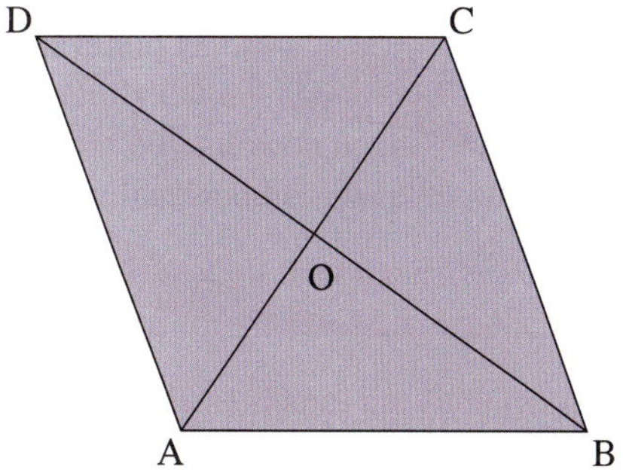

In the rhombus ABCD above:

(a) Measure the length of the diagonals AC and BD.

(b) If the diagonals meet at O, what can you say about

(i) AO and CO

(ii) BO and DO?

(c) Measure the angles $A\hat{O}B$ and $D\hat{O}C$. What do you notice?

9 Repeat Question 8 for other rhombi. Do you get the same answers?

10 Copy the table and complete with ticks where appropriate.

Properties	Parallelogram	Rhombus
Opposite sides parallel		
Opposite sides equal		
All sides equal		
Opposite angles equal		
Diagonals equal		
Diagonals bisect each other		
Diagonals meet at 90°		

11 **(a)** Draw a Venn diagram to show the relationship between

Q = {quadrilaterals}

P = {parallelograms}

R = {rhombi}.

(b) What is $P \cap R$?

Other quadrilaterals

Two other special quadrilaterals are the **trapezium** and the **kite**.

A **trapezium** has just one pair of parallel sides.

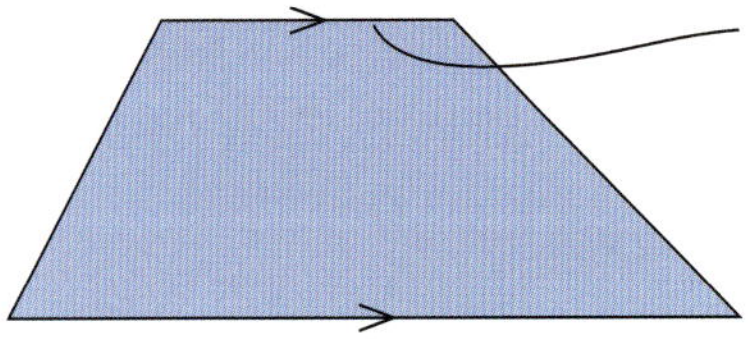

Trapezium

A **kite** has two pairs of adjacent sides that are equal in length.

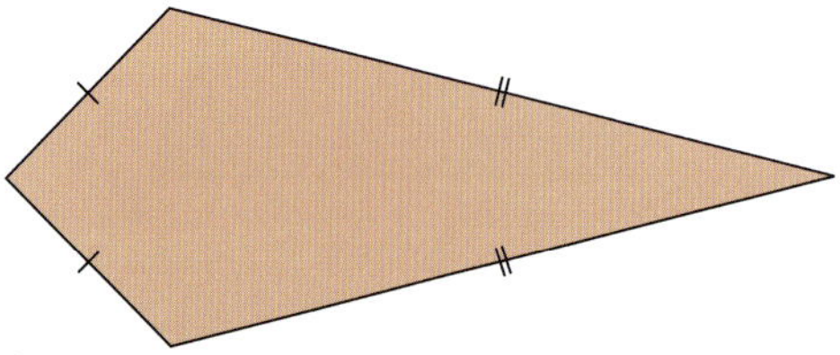

Kite

Exercise 8F

1 **(a)** Take a piece of paper and fold it in two.

(b) With a pair of scissors make two cuts across the fold line.

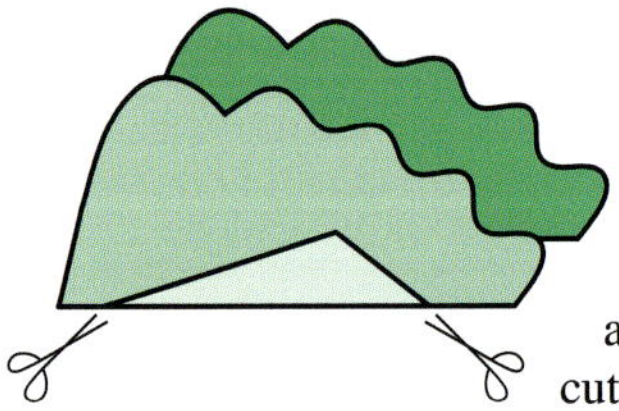

(c) Unfold the triangle.

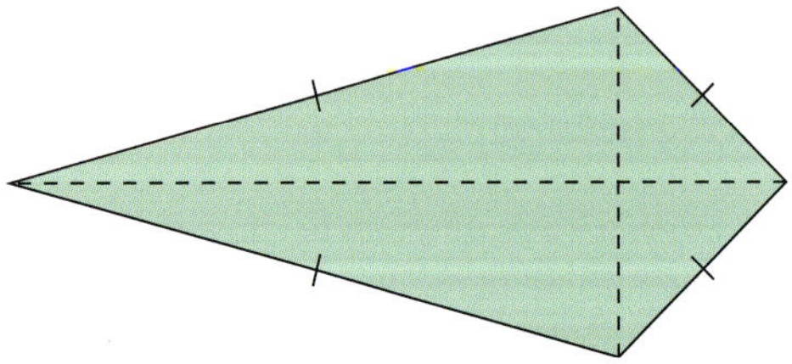

You should get a kite.

2 Take the kite you made in Question 1.

(a) Measure each of the sides.

(b) Measure each of the diagonals.

(c) Do the diagonals cut each other into two equal lengths?

(d) Do the diagonals bisect each other at right angles?

3 Make some more kites and repeat Question 2. Do you get similar answers?

4

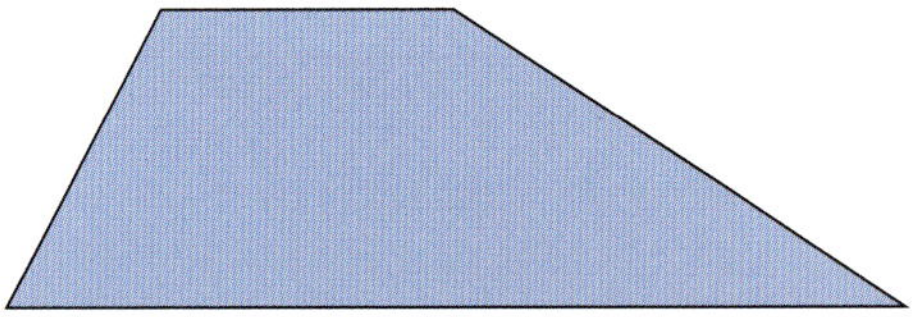

(a) Measure each of the angles in the trapezium ABCD with your protractor.

(b) Measure the length of each side of trapezium ABCD.

(c) Did you notice anything special?

5 **(a)** Draw a Venn diagram to show the relationship between

Q = {quadrilaterals}

T = {trapezia}

K = {kites}.

(b) What is $T \cap K$?

Technology

Need to review all this work about quadrilaterals? Visit
www.mathsisfun.com/geometry
Then try the Quadrilateral Quest in the shape section at
www.woodlands-junior.kent.sch.uk/maths

8.3 Constructions

You will need a protractor and a pair of compasses as well as a ruler.

Some things to remember about constructions

(i) The pencil you use should be sharp.
(ii) Don't press the pencil too heavily on the paper.
(iii) Measure and draw lengths and angles carefully.

Exercise 8G

1 **(a)** Mark two points 7 centimetres apart. Join them with a straight line. Call the line AB.
(b) At A, draw an angle of 50°. At B, draw an angle of 80°. Continue the lines to intersect at the point C, making a triangle ABC, as in the sketch.

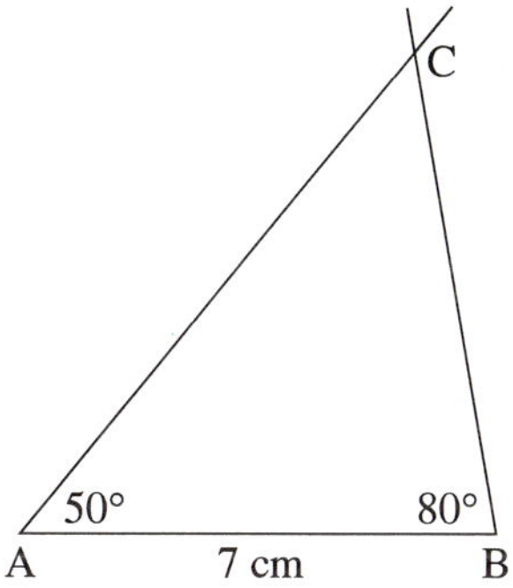

(c) Measure AC and BC. What sort of triangle have you drawn?

2 Make an accurate drawing of each of these triangles.

(a)

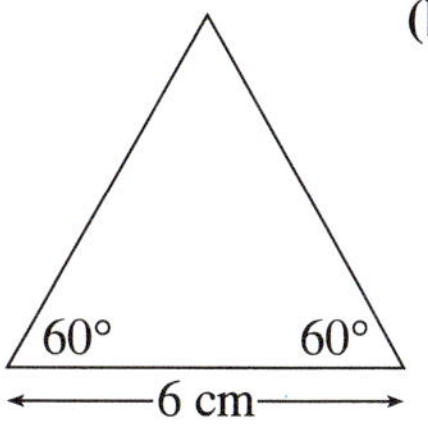

(b)

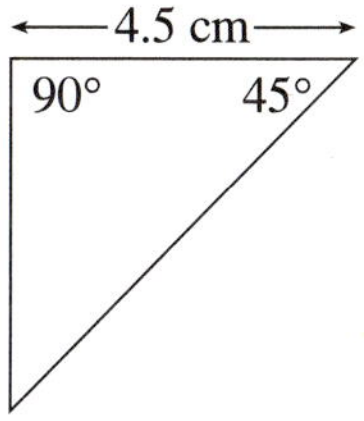

(c)

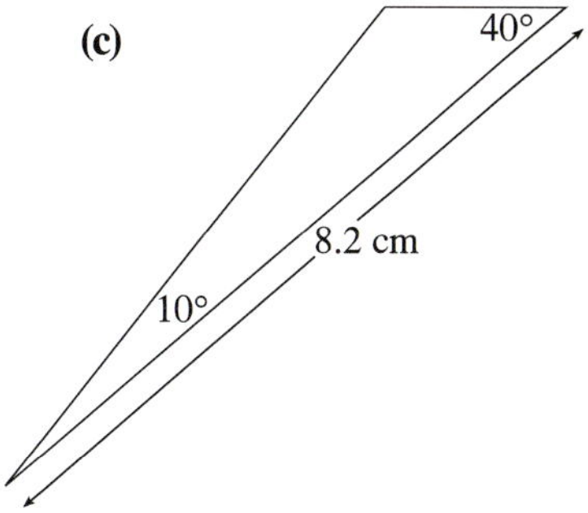

(d)

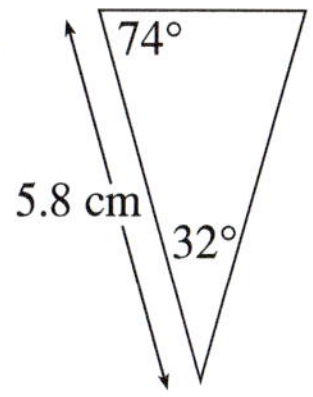

3 **(a)** Measure the unmarked angles in Question 2.
(b) Name the type of each triangle you drew.

Using compasses

To draw other sorts of triangles you will need a pair of compasses.

First you need to know how to draw a line accurately using compasses.

Example 1

Draw the line AB exactly 6 cm long.

(a) First draw a line longer than 6 cm, say about 7.5 cm.
(b) Next, mark a point A near one end.
(c) Open the compasses to exactly 6 cm on your ruler, as in the diagram below.

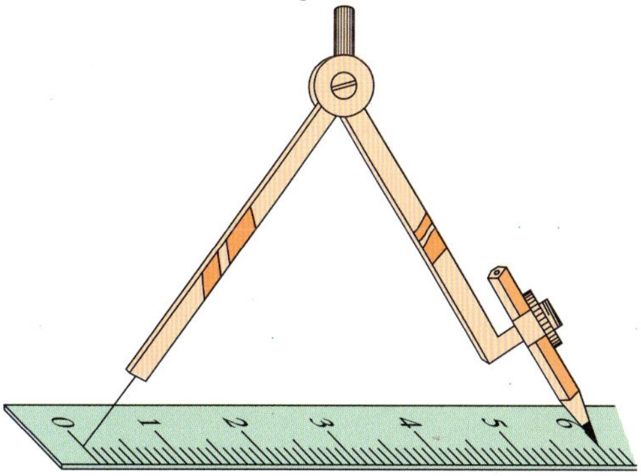

(d) An **arc** is part of a circle. Put the point of the compasses at A, and draw a small arc to cut the line.
Call the point where the arc intersects the line B. You now have a line AB 6 cm long.

Exercise 8H

1 Using compasses, draw the line:

(a) MN, 6 cm **(b)** PQ, 6.5 cm
(c) ST, 5.8 cm **(d)** CD, 7.2 cm
(e) AB, 8.6 cm **(f)** GH, 7.9 cm

2 **(a)** Using compasses, draw the line XY, 6.2 cm.
(b) At X, draw an angle of 50° using your protractor.
(c) Open the compasses to 5.1 cm. With the point of the compasses at X, draw an arc 5.1 cm along the second arm of the angle, as in the drawing below.
Call the point Z.

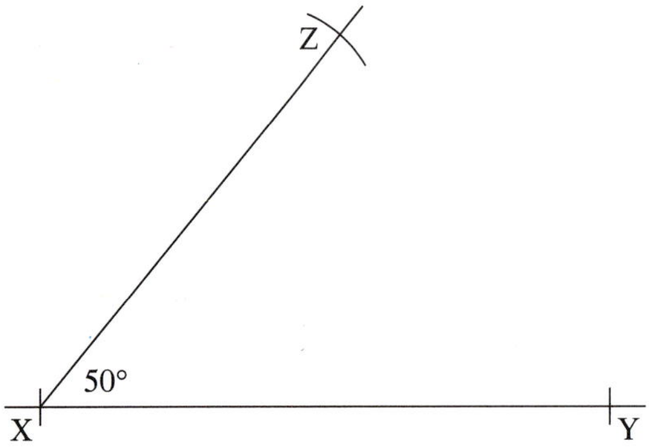

(d) Join YZ. What sort of triangle have you constructed?

3 **(a)** Draw the line AB, 7.3 cm.
(b) At B, draw an angle of 27°.
(c) With the point of the compasses at B, mark a point C, 5.9 cm from B, as in the drawing below.

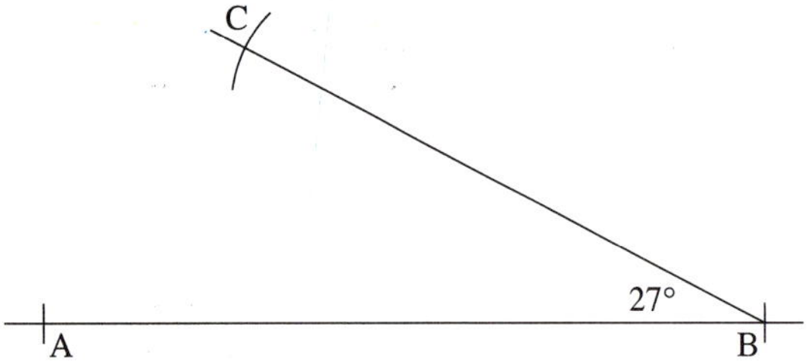

(d) Join AC. What sort of triangle have you constructed?

4 In Questions 2 and 3, you could draw a triangle when you knew just two sides and the angle between them. Use the same method to make an accurate drawing of each of the triangles below.

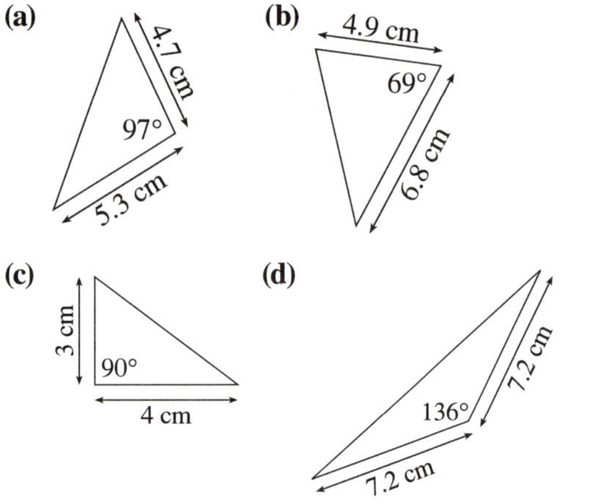

Drawing triangles given three sides

Example 2

Construct triangle ABC, with
AB = 10 cm, AC = 8 cm and BC = 6 cm.

(1)
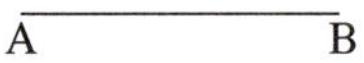

Draw base line AB 10 cm long.

(2)
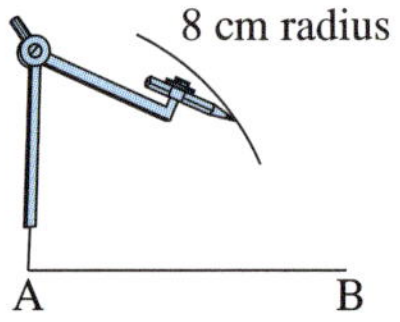

Set the compasses to 8 cm.
Put the point on A.
Draw the arc.

(3)
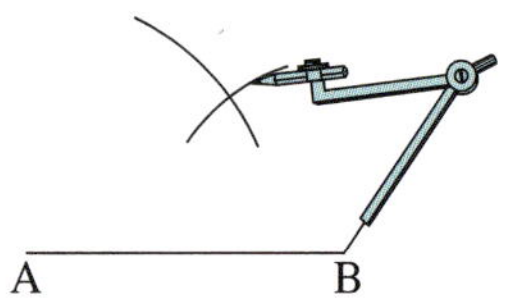

Set the compasses to 6 cm.
Put the point on B.
Draw the arc.

(4)
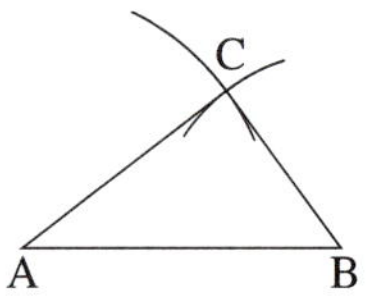

Join C, where the arcs cross, to A and B.

Exercise 8I

1 **(a)** Draw a line PQ, 7.5 cm.

(b) With the point of the compasses at P, draw an arc 6.8 cm from P.

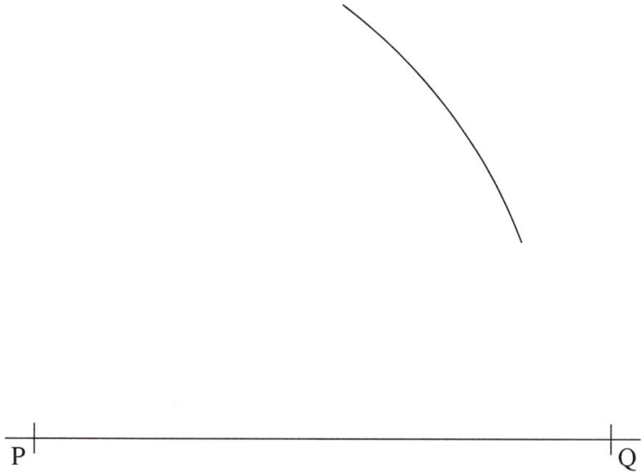

(c) With the point of the compasses at Q, draw an arc 5.4 cm from Q. It should intersect the first arc, as in the drawing below. Call the point of intersection O.

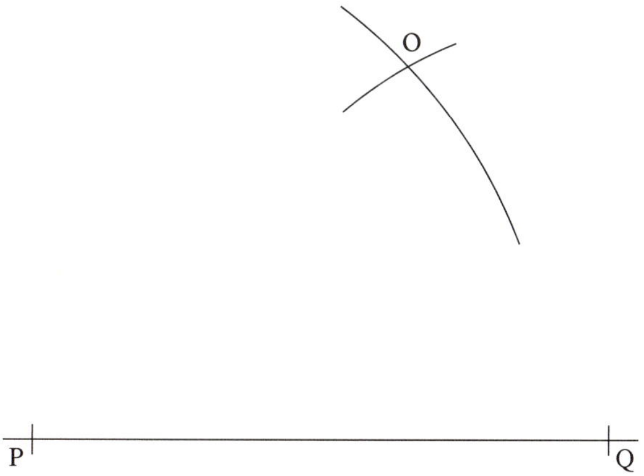

(d) Join OP and OQ.
What sort of triangle is OPQ?

2 **(a)** Draw a line FG, 6.2 cm.

(b) With the point of the compasses at G, draw an arc 6.2 cm from G.

(c) With the point of the compasses at F, draw an arc 6.2 cm from F. It should intersect the first arc as in the drawing that follows.
Call the point of intersection H.
What sort of triangle is FGH?

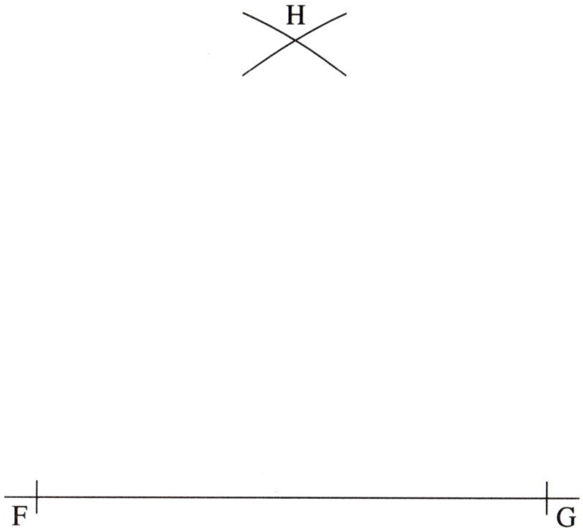

3 Use the method of Example 2 to construct these triangles.

(a) ABC, AB = 9.1 cm, BC = 7.5 cm, AC = 4.1 cm.

(b) DEF, DE = 6.4 cm, DF = 4.3 cm, EF = 6.4 cm.

(c) JKL, JK = 3.5 cm, KL = 10.3 cm, JL = 7.6 cm.

4 Construct a triangle with all three sides of length 6 cm.

(a) What sort of triangle is it?

(b) What is the size of each angle?

5 You are told that two of the sides of an isosceles triangle are of length 4 cm and 7 cm. Construct two *different* isosceles triangles from this information.

6 One side of a triangle is 10 cm long.
Explain why you cannot construct the triangle if the other two sides are given as 5 cm and 4 cm.

7 Set your compasses at 3 cm. Try to draw a circle and a flower pattern like this. How many petals are there?

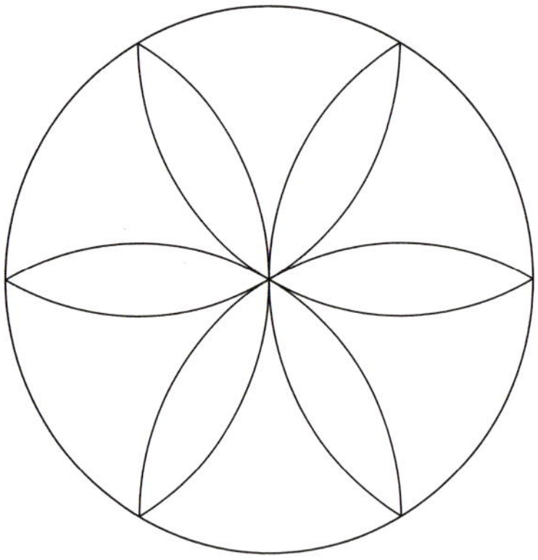

8 Here is part of the pattern in Question 7:

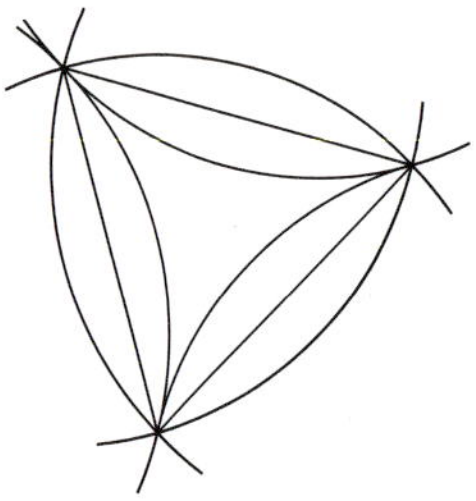

(a) What sort of triangle has been drawn?
(b) Can you say why?

9 Draw another flower pattern and use a ruler to draw six equilateral triangles of the same size.

10 Use your compasses and a ruler to construct the six-sided shape that fits inside a circle.

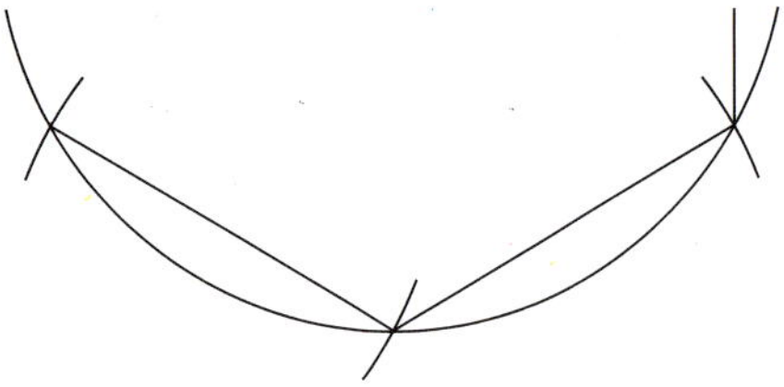

11 The six-sided shape drawn in Question 10 is called a regular **hexagon**. What is the size of each of its angles?

12 **(a)** Construct a regular hexagon of side 6 cm.
(b) Divide up the hexagon into equilateral triangles. How many equilateral triangles make up a regular hexagon?
(c) Can you draw two larger equilateral triangles in your figure?

13 Make up a list of instructions for someone to follow in order to:
(a) construct an equilateral triangle
(b) construct an isosceles triangle
(c) construct a regular hexagon.

14

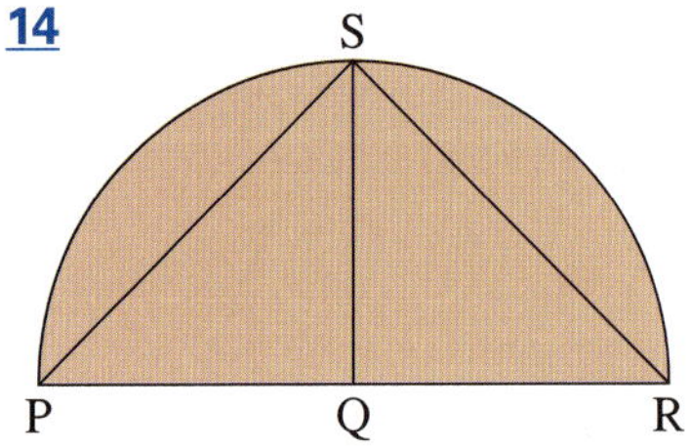

equilateral
scalene
isosceles
obtuse-angled
acute-angled
right-angled

Using words from the list, state what kind of triangles are the following:
(a) PSR **(b)** PQS **(c)** QSR

15 Copy the table, and where possible draw a triangle in each space.

	All sides are of differents lengths	**Two sides are of equal lengths**	**Three sides are of equal lengths**
Acute-angled			
Right-angled			
Obtuse-angled			

Technology

Learn how to bisect a line segment or bisect an angle. Visit the geometry section at the website
www.regentsprep.org
and watch the short video demonstrations.

Draw a triangle and bisect each of its angles. Where do the angle bisectors meet?

8.4 Symmetry

Symmetry is all around us. It occurs in nature and in the physical world.

To investigate the idea of symmetry, you will need some paper, some tracing paper and a pair of scissors.

Activity

Fold a piece of paper in two.

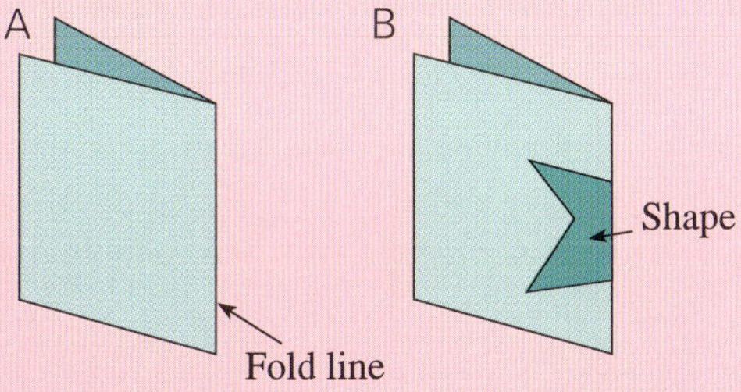

Draw a shape on the folded paper, starting and finishing at the fold line, as in diagram B.

Keeping the paper folded, cut out the shape, as in diagram C. Open out your shape, as in diagram D.

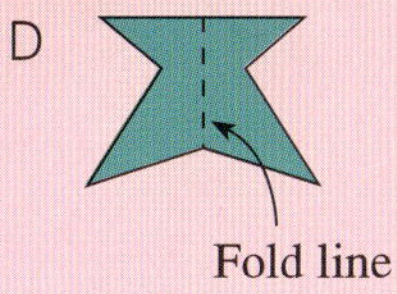

Draw a line along the fold line with a pencil. What do you notice about the parts on each side of the fold line?

Repeat the activity for different shapes.

This shape has been cut from folded paper. Trace the shape, cut out the tracing and find the fold line.

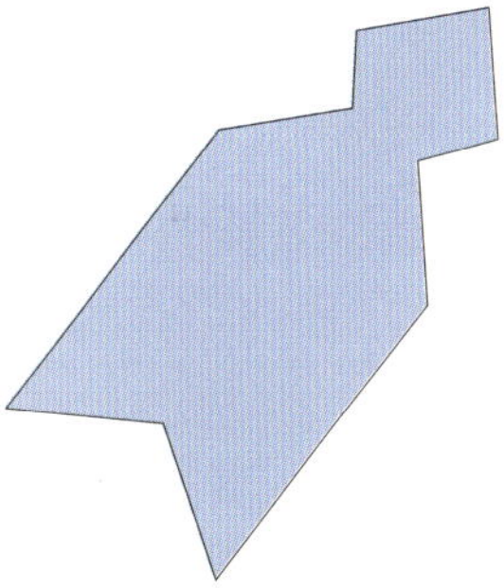

Notice that one half of the shape fits exactly over the other. We say the shape is **symmetrical**. The shapes you cut out in the activity are also symmetrical.

The fold line is called **a line of symmetry**.

A line of symmetry is also called a **mirror line**.

Exercise 8J

1 Which of these shapes have a line of symmetry?

(a)

(b)

(c)

(d)

(e)
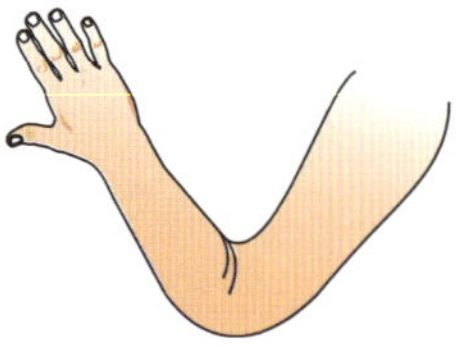
(f)

2 Copy these shapes, drawing the line of symmetry where possible.

(a)
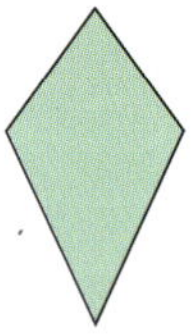
(b)
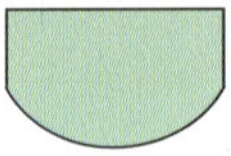
(c)
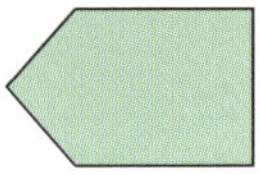
(d)
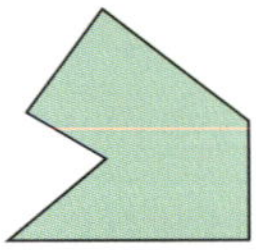
(e)

(f)
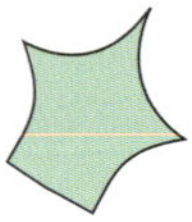
(g)
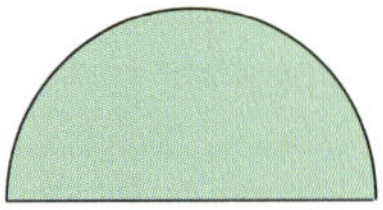
(h)
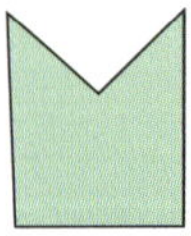
(i)
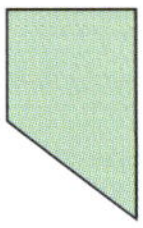

3 These drawings show halves of shapes. In each, the dotted line is a line of symmetry. Trace and complete each shape.

(a)
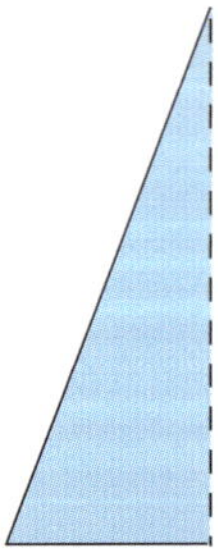
(b)
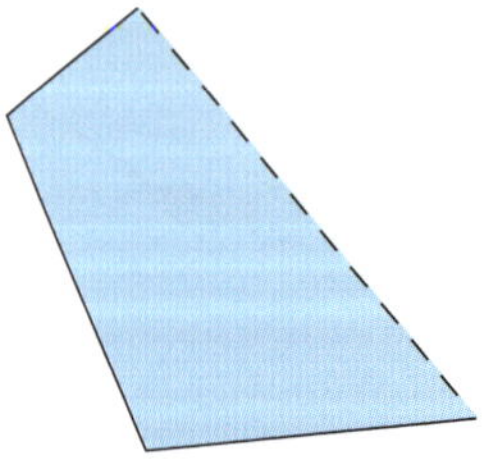
(c)
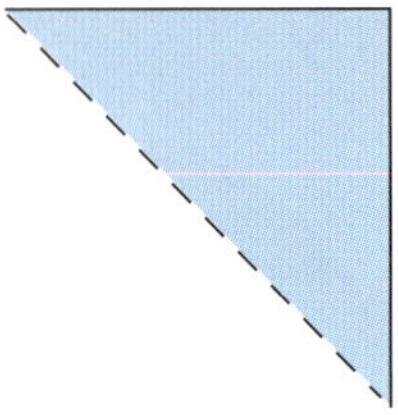
(d)
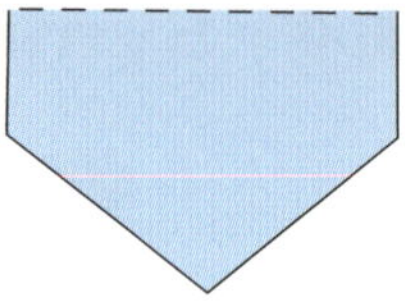
(e)
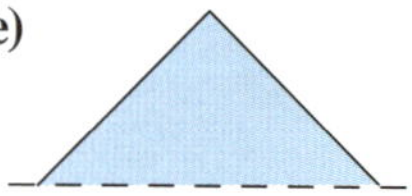
(f)
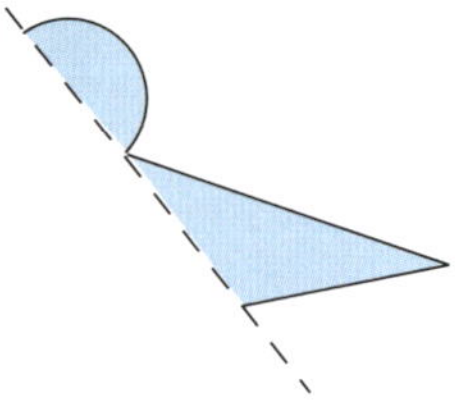
(g)
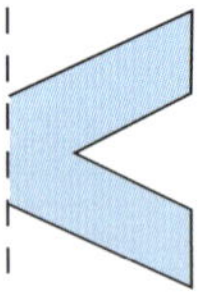
(h)

(i)
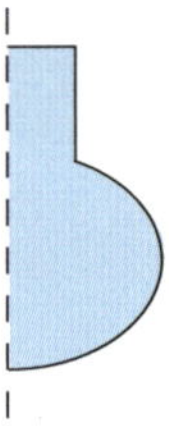
(j)
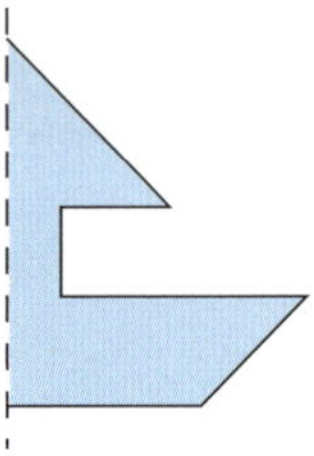
(k)
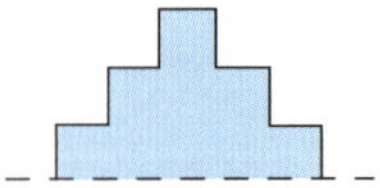
(l)
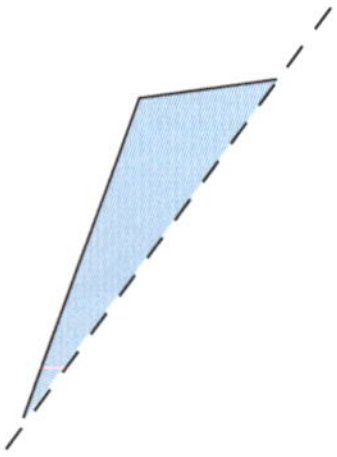

4 Fold a piece of paper, then fold it again as in diagram A.

A
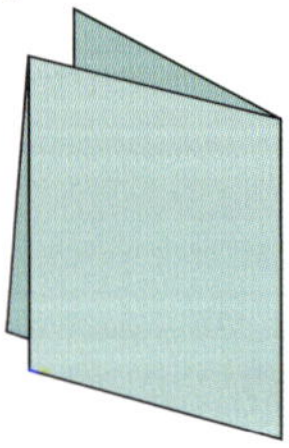
B

Draw a shape at the corner as in diagram B.

C

Cut out the shape at the corner.
Open out your shape as in diagram D.

D

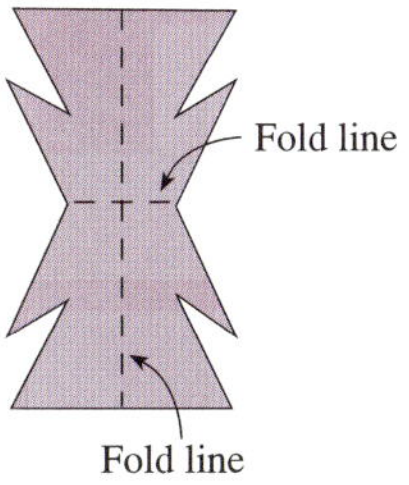

How many fold lines does your shape have?
How many lines of symmetry?

5 Repeat Question 4 for three different shapes.

6 Trace each shape. Cut out your tracing. By folding, find a line of symmetry, and mark it with a pencil. There may be more than one line. See how many you can find.

(a)

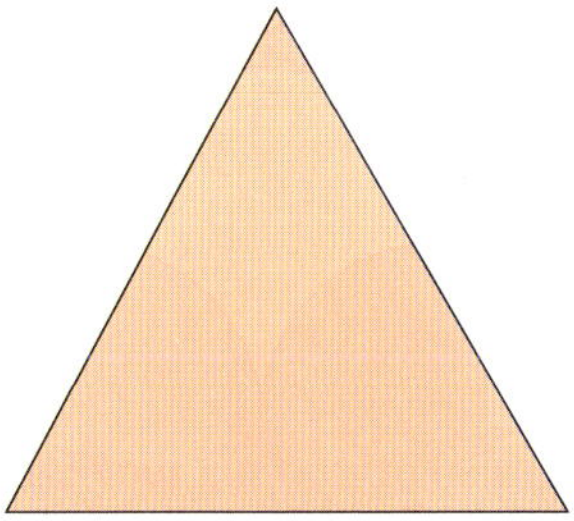

(b)

(c)

7 Repeat Question 6 for this shape. Is there a line of symmetry?

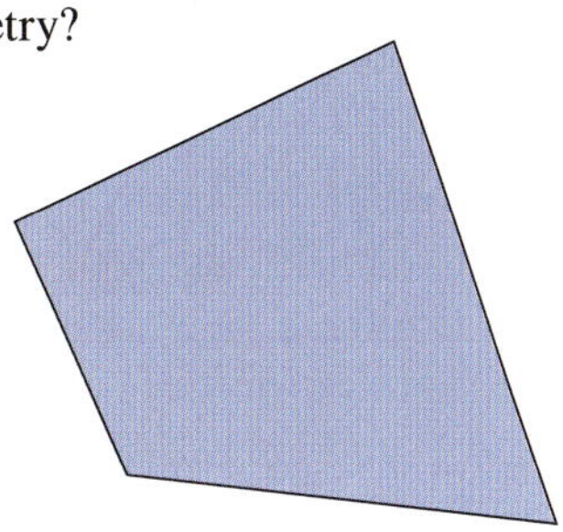

8 Copy and complete the table.

Shape	**Number of lines of symmetry**
Kite	
Trapezium	
Rhombus	
Square	
Parallelogram	

9 How many lines of symmetry do these shapes have?

(a)

(b)

(c)

(d)

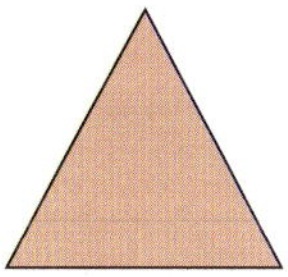

(e)

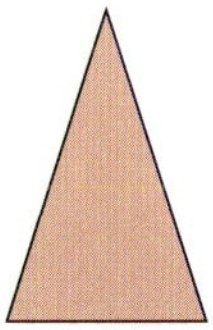

(f)

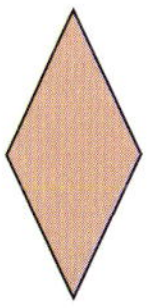

(g)

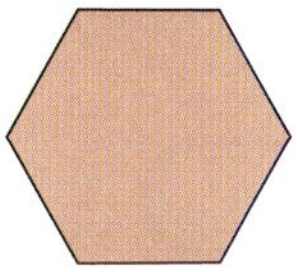

(h)

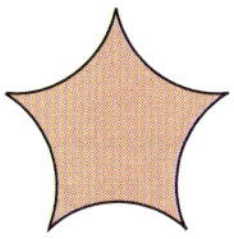

(i)

(j)

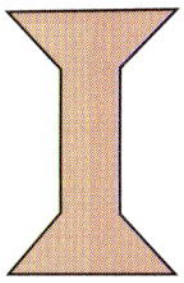

(k) 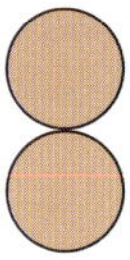

(l) 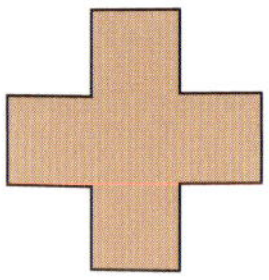

10 **(a)** Write the alphabet in capital letters A B C D E F . . .

(b) Which letters have one line of symmetry?

(c) Which letters have two lines of symmetry?

Technology

You will need a digital camera.

- Take some photos of the faces of your friends.
- Download them and paste them into a word processing program.
- Are your friend's faces symmetrical?

Activity

Make a collection of pictures or photographs which show symmetry in nature.
Display these in your class.
Visit this website for some ideas.
www.misterteacher.com

Investigation

Can you draw a triangle with

(a) no lines of symmetry

(b) one line of symmetry

(c) two lines of symmetry

(d) three lines of symmetry?

Repeat for a quadrilateral.
What about a five-sided shape?

8.5 Reflection

You will need a small straight-edged mirror, squared paper, a little ink or poster paint, some thin paper to draw on, a ruler and a pin.

Place mirror along here

The picture shows the sketch of a carnival queen.

Place a mirror on the line indicated. Look at the carnival queen in your mirror.

You should find that the **reflection** or **mirror image** is exactly the same as is shown in the sketch.

Exercise 8K

1 Use your mirror to read these two sentences:

(a) .ƎGAUGИA⅃ ЯOЯЯIM ƧI ƧIHT

(b) !ʜɔnɘɿꟻ nɒʜɈ ɿɘiƨɒɘ ƨi ƨiʜT

2 Write your name as it would appear if you saw it in a mirror:

(a) using capitals,

(b) using small letters.

3 In the diagram the heavy straight line represents a mirror.
On squared paper, copy and complete each drawing, to show the object and its mirror image.
Use your mirror to help you.

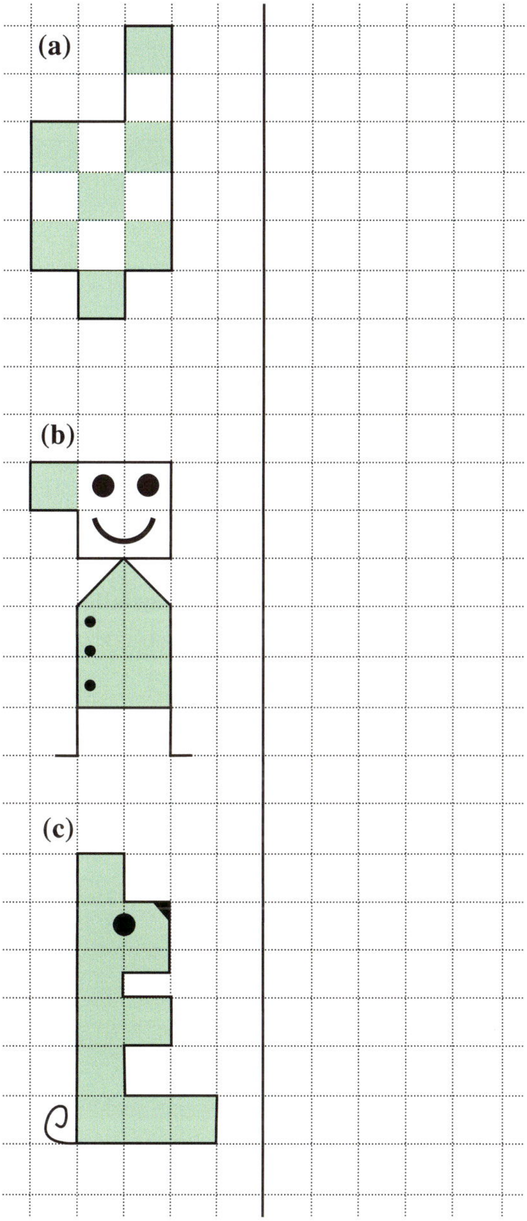

4 Copy the shapes and the mirror lines indicated by dotted lines on to squared paper. Draw the mirror image of each shape.

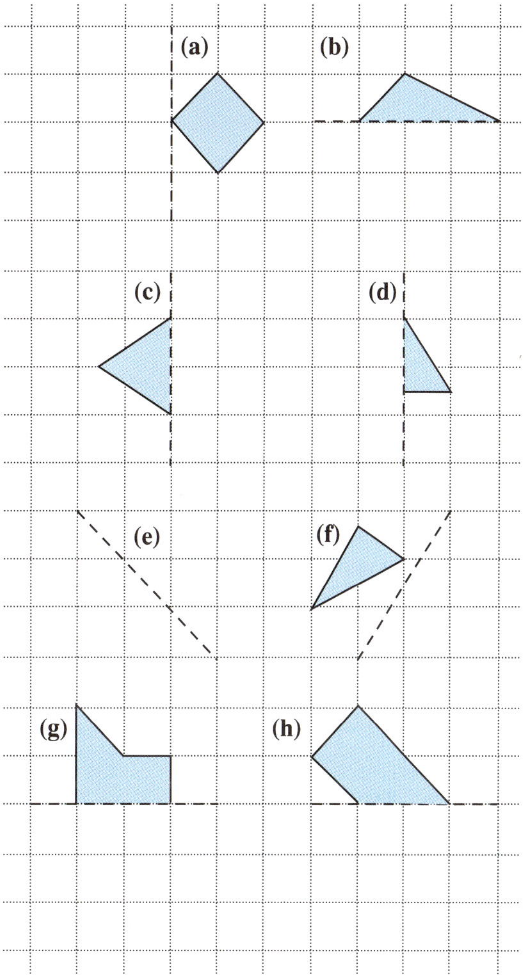

5 Reflect each of the following shapes in the mirror line indicated by a dotted line.

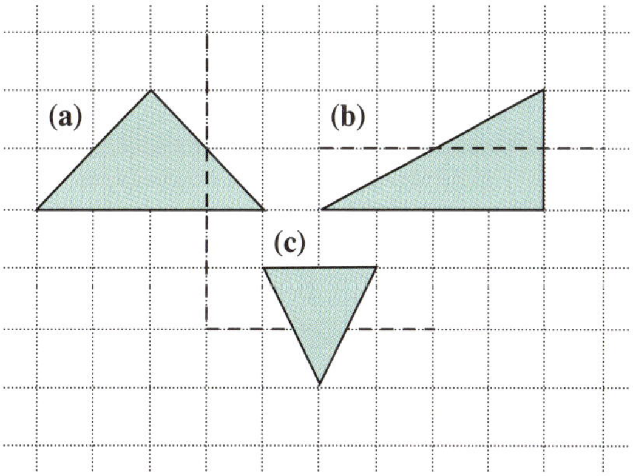

6 Fold a piece of squared paper in two, along a grid line. On the inside surface of one part, put a blob of ink (or paint).

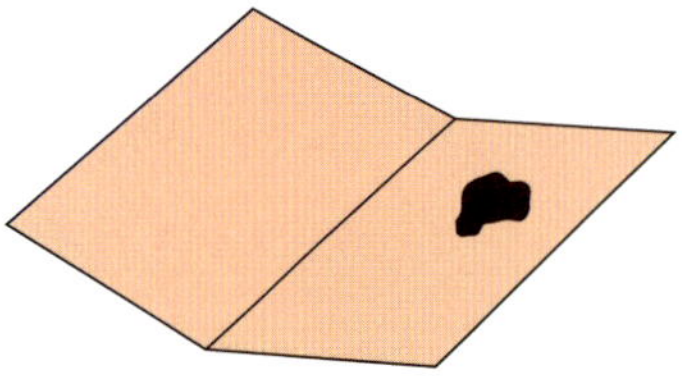

Press hard on the folded paper over the ink blob. Open it out again and let the ink dry. You now have two blobs.
Is each blob a mirror image of the other?
Check by placing a mirror along the fold line.

7 In Question 6 is the fold line acting as a mirror line? Give reasons.

8 **(a)** Fold a piece of paper in two. Draw a straight line on one side.
Pierce both ends of the line with a pin so that the pin goes right through the folded paper.

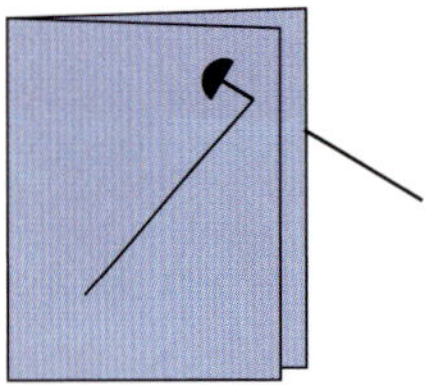

(b) Open out the paper. Join the second set of pin holes to give a straight line. You now have two lines. Call one line AB and the other line A′B′ as in the drawing below. Mark the fold line.

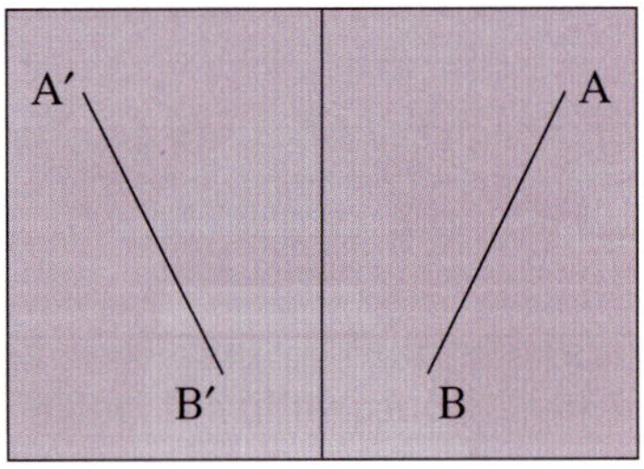

(c) Is one line a mirror image of the other? Check by using a mirror.
(d) Does the fold line act like a mirror line?

8.6 Moving shapes

Objects that have the same size and shape are said to be **congruent** to each other.

A tiled floor

The triangular tiles in this floor are **congruent** to each other.

Notice that the tiling pattern or **tessellation** was made by simply sliding the dark and light blue triangular tiles to a new position.

This sliding movement is called a **translation**.
A translation does not change an object's size, shape or direction.

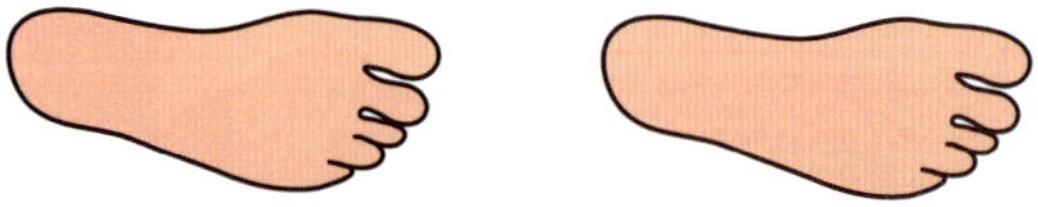

The footprint has been translated to a new position.

Exercise 8L

1 Which of these transformations shows a translation?

(a)

(b)

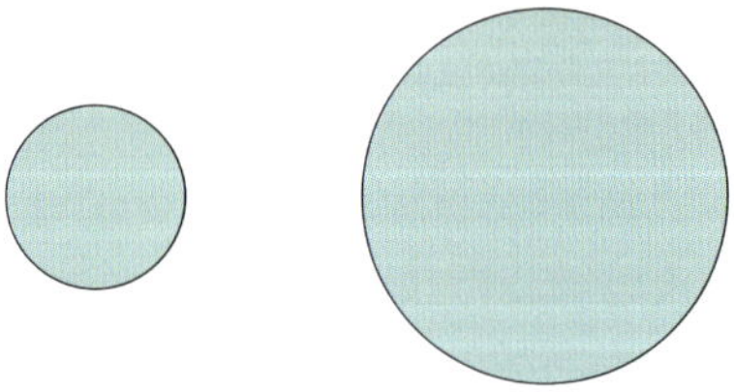

(c)

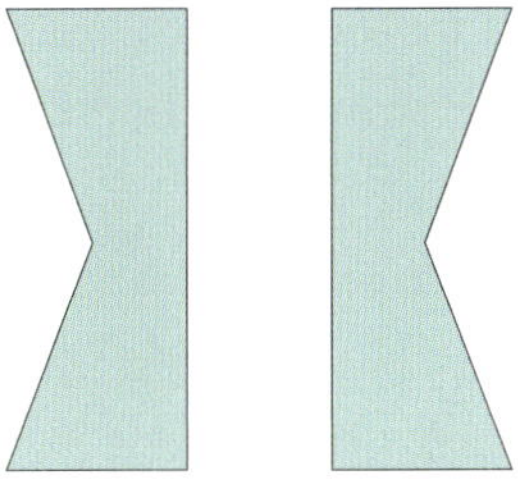

(d)

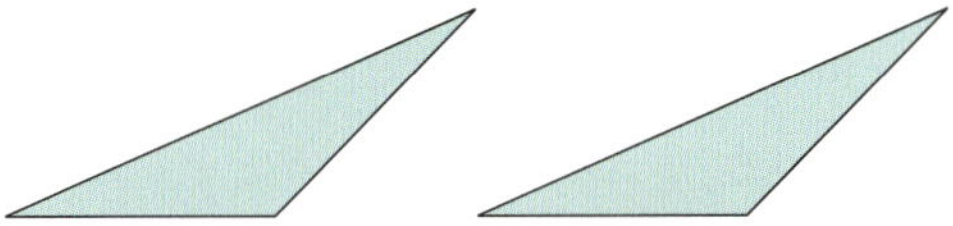

2 Which of these pictures show translations?

(a)

(b)

(c)

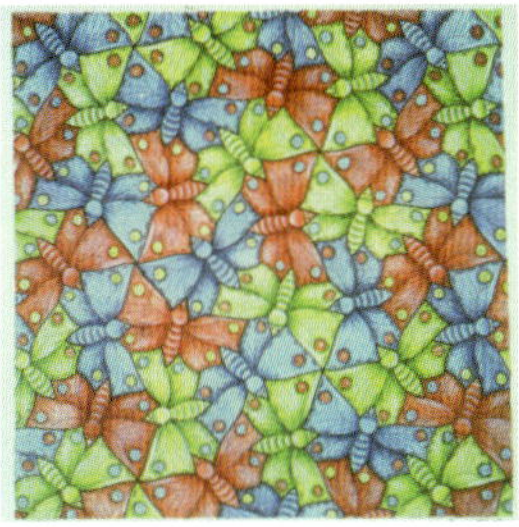

3

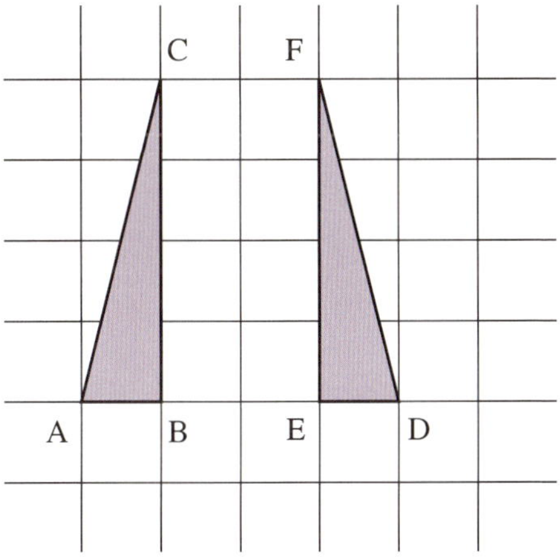

Look at the triangles ABC and DEF.

(a) Is triangle ABC congruent to triangle DEF?

(b) Is triangle DEF the image of triangle ABC under a translation? Give reasons for your answer.

4

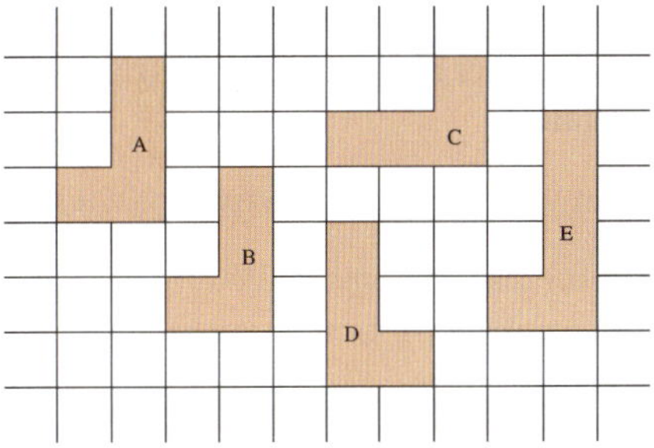

Look at the shapes A, B, C, D and E.

(a) Which of the shapes are congruent to shape A?

(b) Which of the shapes can be translated so that shape B is the image under a translation?

Fitting shapes together

In this section you will make patterns from shapes.

You will need cardboard, a pair of scissors, tracing paper (greaseproof paper) and coloured pencils or crayons.

Activity

Make an exact copy, on cardboard, of this hexagon. Use tracing paper to help you. Cut out your copy very carefully.

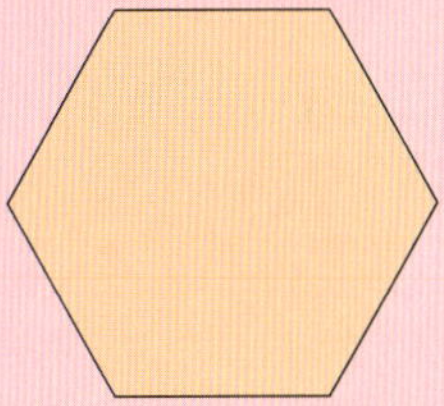

Place your hexagon on a sheet of paper. Draw its outline. Continue drawing outlines to make a larger copy of the pattern below. Colour your pattern with coloured pencils or crayons.

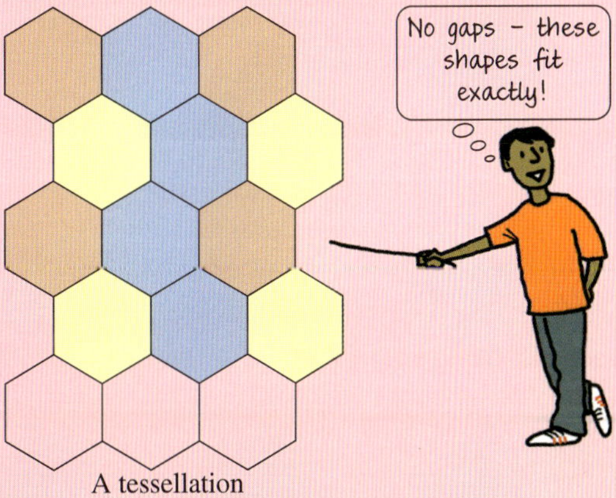

A tessellation

- A pattern made by fitting shapes together, *with no spaces and no overlapping*, is called a **tessellation**.

The pattern you made in the Activity is a tessellation.

You often see tessellations on tiled floors. People have used tessellations for thousands of years.

The photo shows Egyptian floor tiling.

With the use of colour you can make some beautiful tessellations.

Exercise 8M

1 **(a)** Make an exact copy, on cardboard, of this shape.

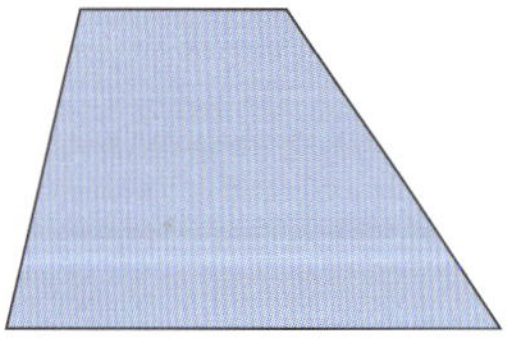

(b) Use your shape to draw a tessellation.

(c) Make sure your tessellation covers at least a quarter of your page.

(d) Colour your pattern.

2 Repeat Question 1 for each of these triangular shapes.

(a)

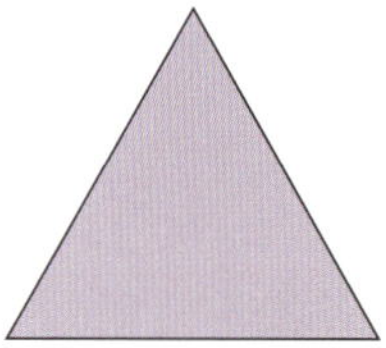

(b)

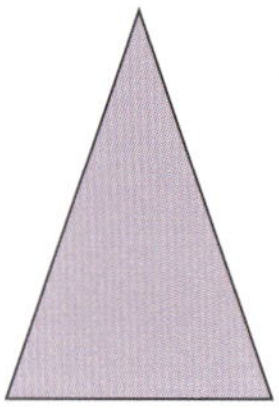

(c)

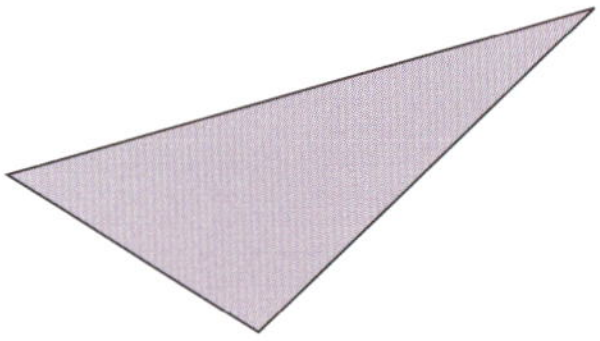

3 Repeat Question 1 for each four-sided shape:

(a)

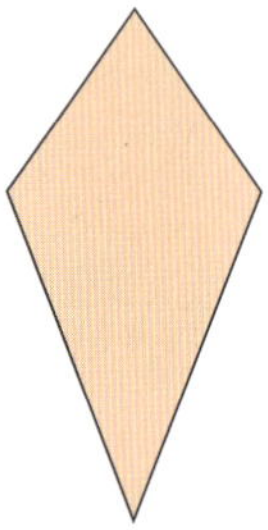

(b)

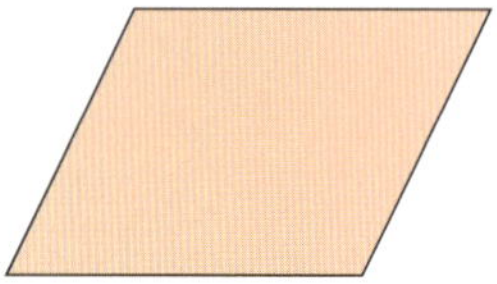

(c)

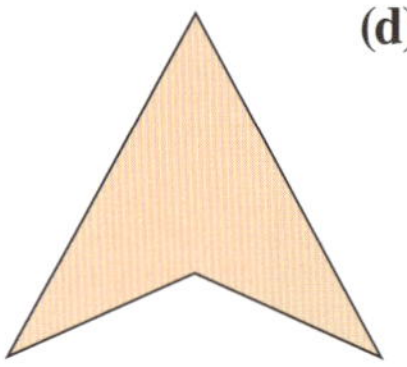

(d)

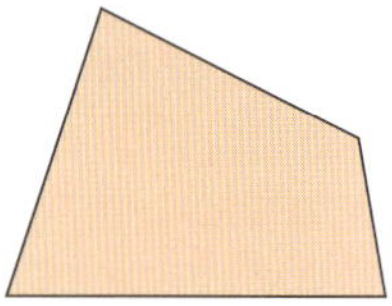

4 Not all shapes tessellate.

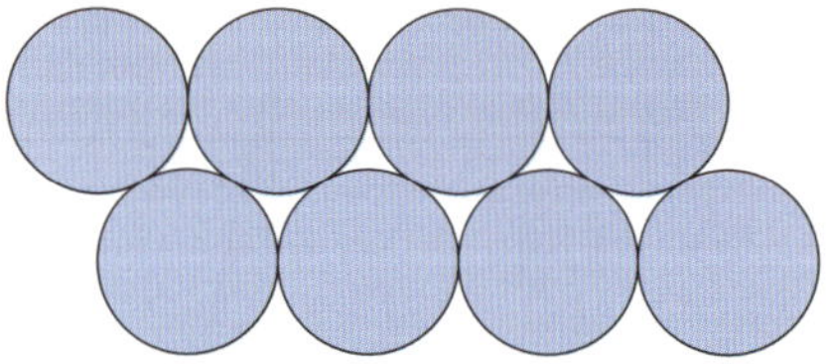

Why is the pattern above not a tessellation?

Investigation

(a) Draw four different types of triangle. Which ones tessellate? Can you find a triangle that does not tessellate?

(b) Repeat your investigation but this time use four-sided shapes.

5 **(a)** Make cardboard cut-outs of each of the four shapes.

(i)

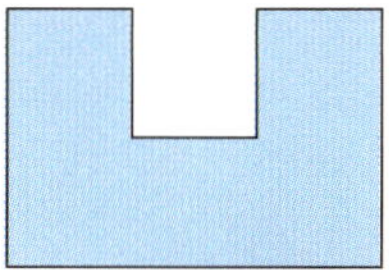

(ii)

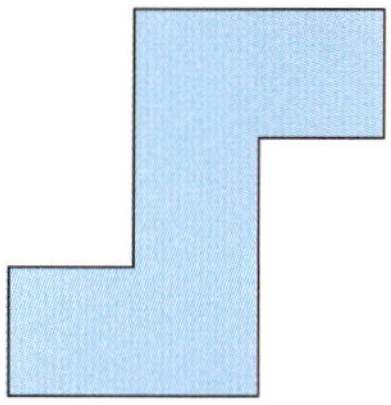

(iii)

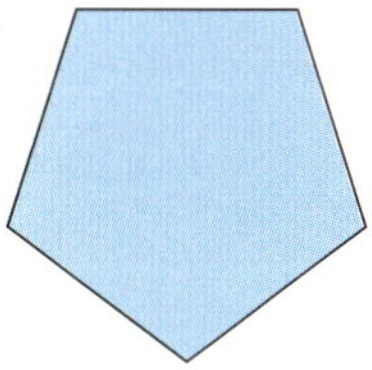

(iv)

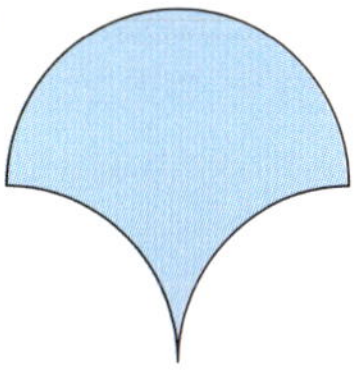

(b) Use your cut-outs to help you decide which of the shapes tessellate.

6 Use dot paper to see if you can make different tessellations with each of these tiles.

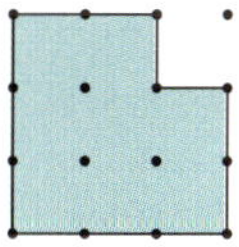

(a)

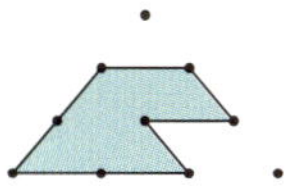

(b)

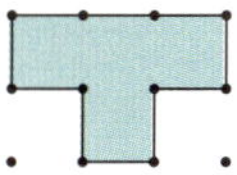

(c)

7 In each of the pictures find the value of the angles marked a, b, c, d, e.

(a)

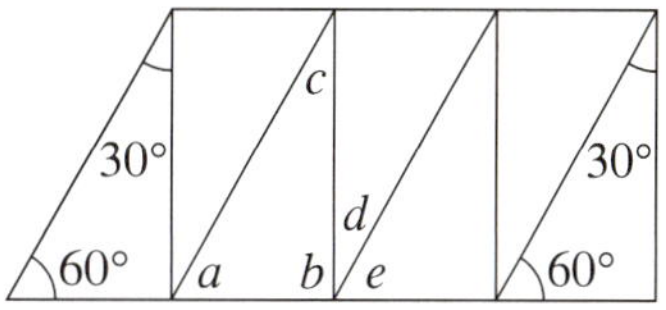

(b)

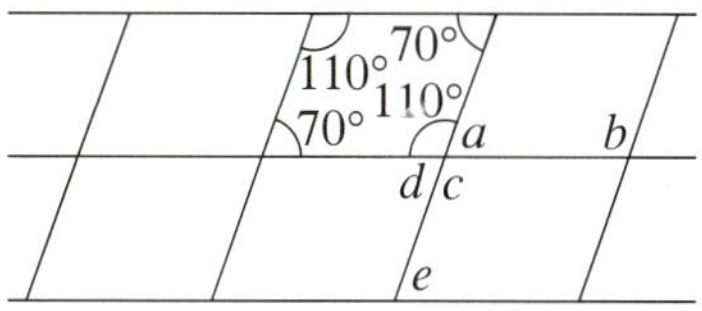

(c)

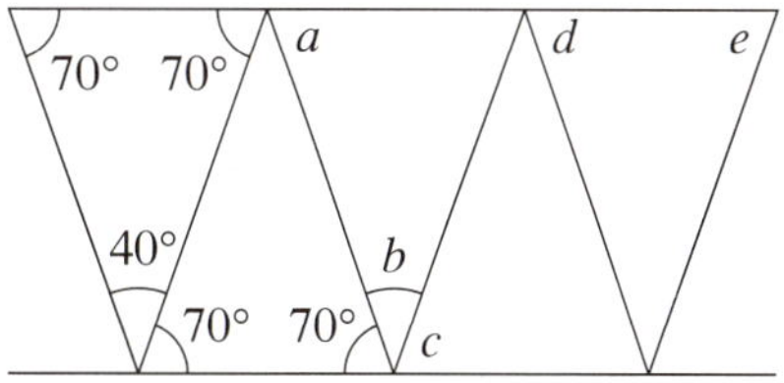

(d)

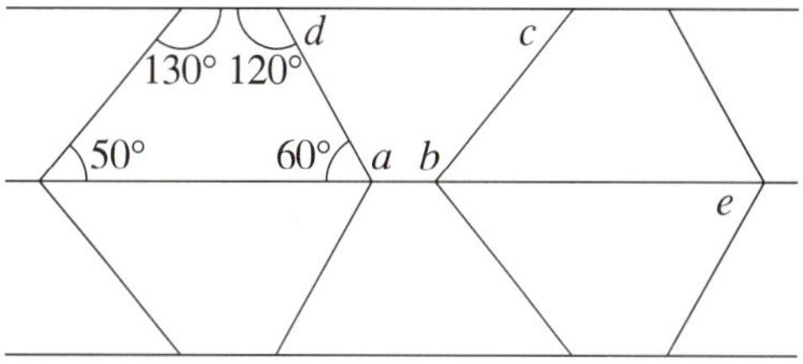

8 Look at this tessellation of an equilateral triangle.

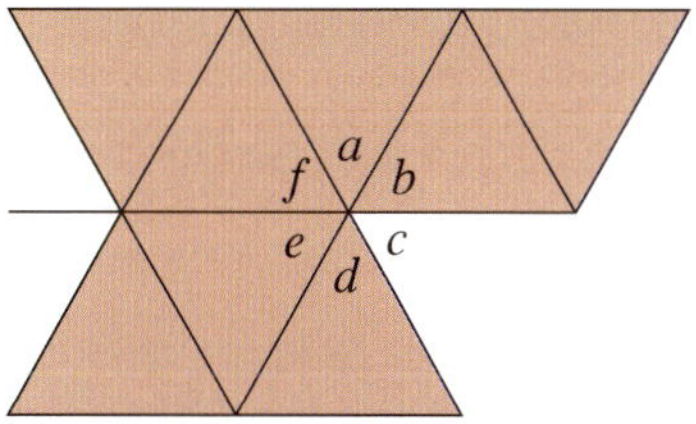

(a) Do you agree that the angles a, b, c, d, e, f are all equal?

(b) What do these six angles add up to?

(c) What is the size of angle a?

9 **(a)** Find the size of angles a, b, c and d in this tessellation:

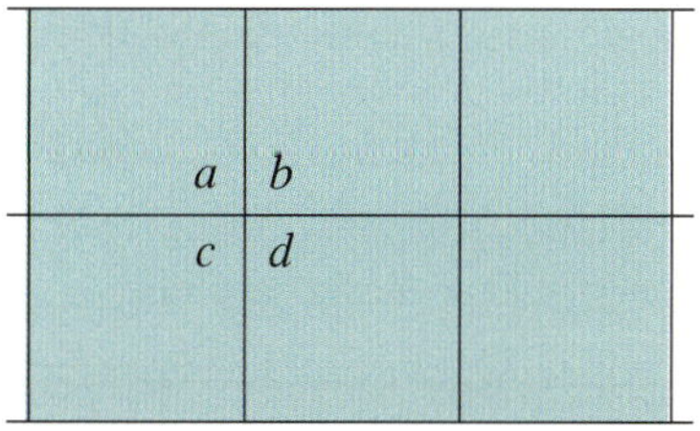

(*Hint*: $a + b + c + d = 360°$)

(b) Find the size of a, b and c in this tessellation.

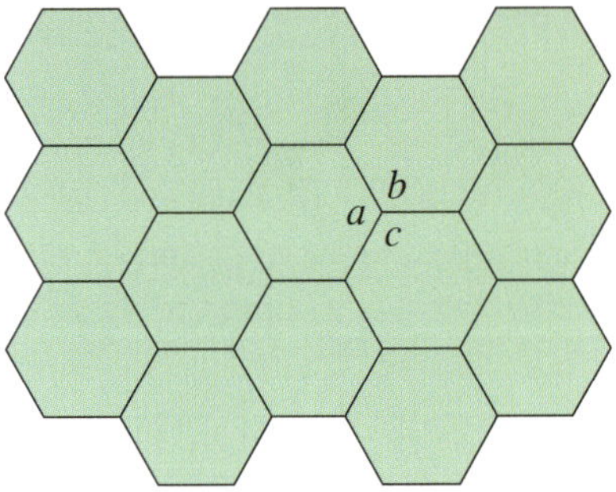

(*Hint*: $a + b + c = 360°$)

Technology

- You can use 'Paint' to make your own tessellations.
  Visit
  www.mathcats.com
  to see how.
- Investigate making your own tessellations using Microsoft Word and the Shape tools.
- Check out the site
  www.tessellations.org
  Have a look at the galleries!
  Click on the 'Do it yourself' section and learn how to make great tessellations of your own.
- Display your tessellations in your classroom.

8.7 Investigating shapes

You will need scissors and card.

Counting shapes

Look at the shape below.

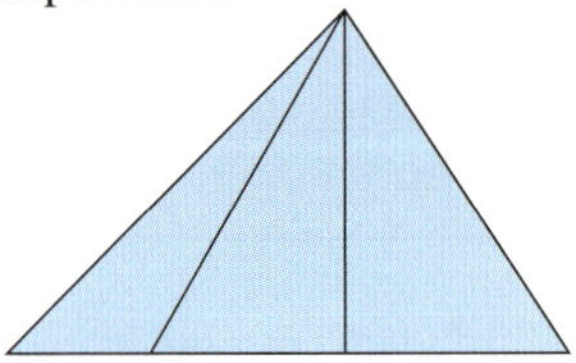

How many triangles do you see?

Was your answer three triangles? If it was, maybe you missed these shaded triangles.

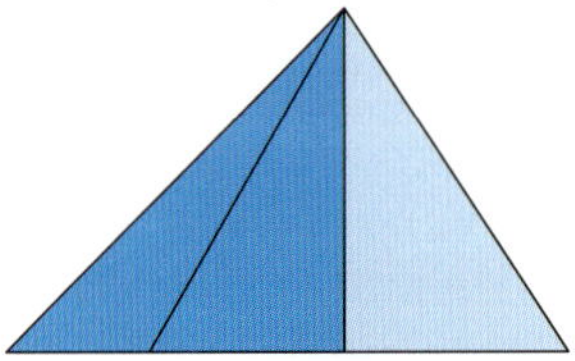

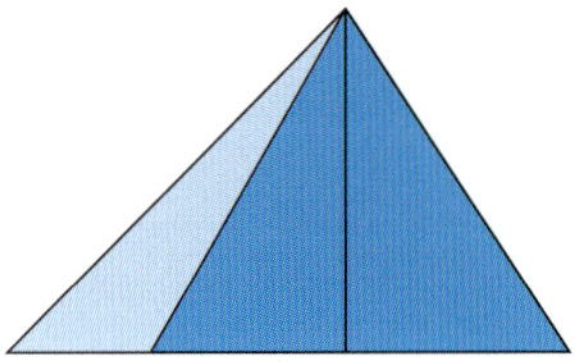

How many triangles do you now see?

You should find there are six different triangles. Draw pictures to show them.

Exercise 8N

1 How many triangles are there in this shape?

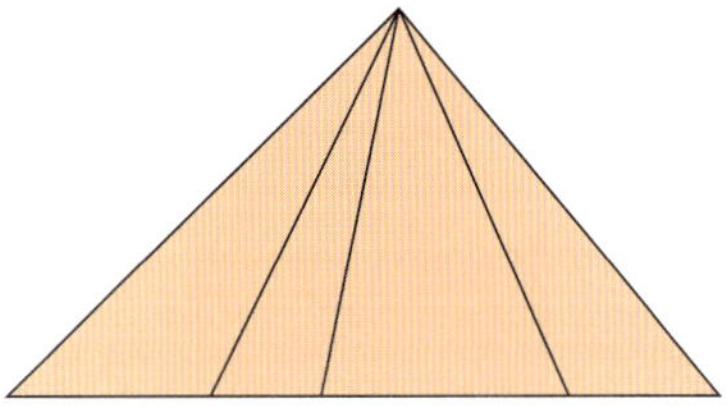

2 How many different rectangles are there in these shapes?

(a)

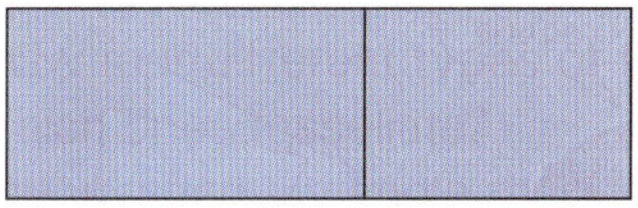

(b)

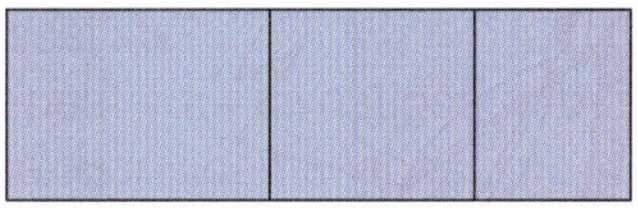

(c)

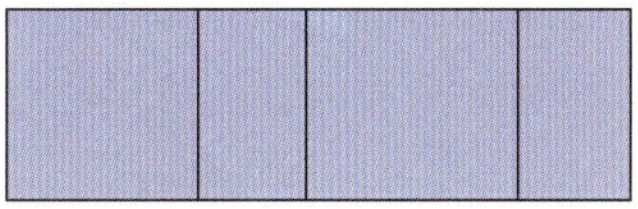

3 How many different triangles are there in these tessellations?

(a)

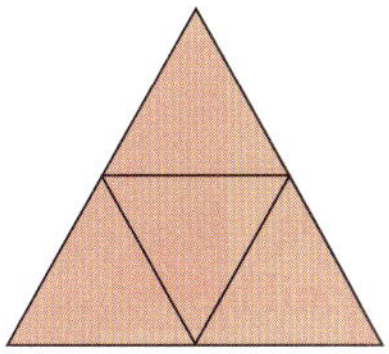

(b)

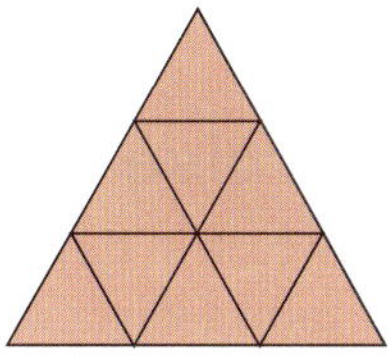

4 **(a)** Draw this square on card.

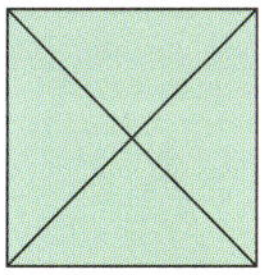

(b) Cut your square out. Now cut it along its diagonals to form four triangles.

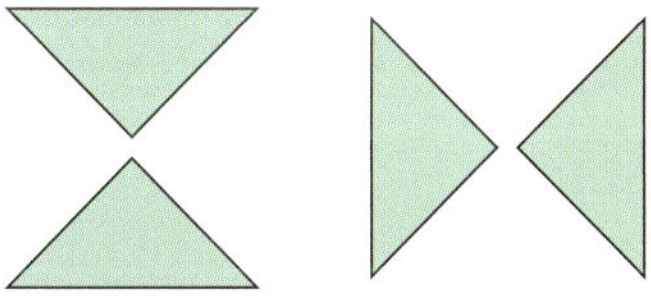

(c) How many different shapes can you make with your four triangles?

5 **(a)** Copy the square below on card.

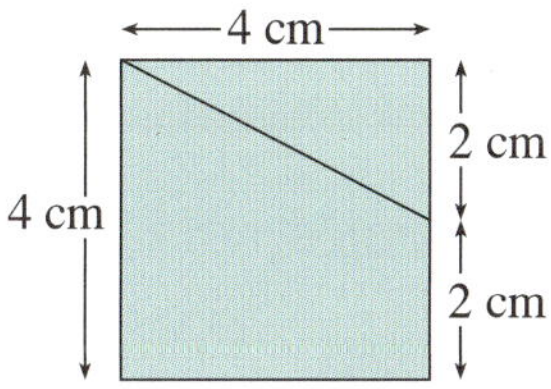

(b) Cut the square out. Now cut the square along the line shown to form a four-sided shape and a triangle.

(c) Use your two shapes to make as many different shapes as you can.

6 Take a strip of paper 9 cm long and 4 cm wide. Cut the paper as shown.

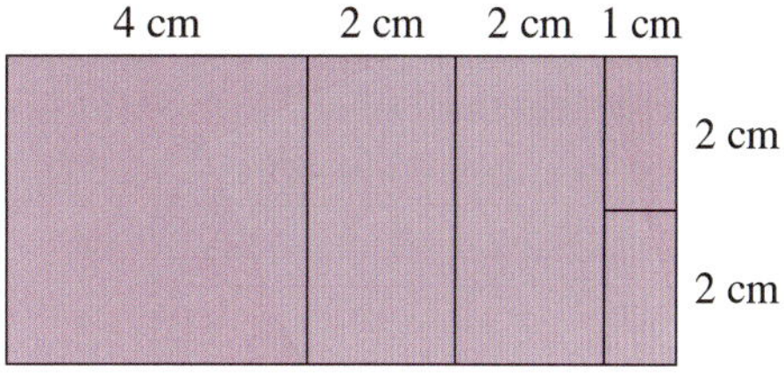

Rearrange the pieces to form a square.

7 **(a)** Copy this shape on card.

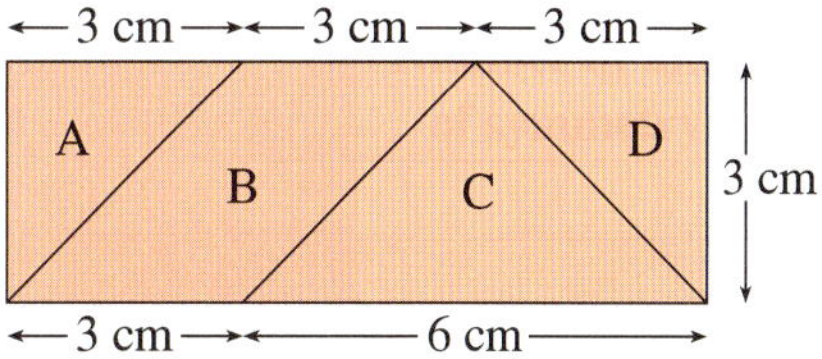

(b) Cut it into the four pieces A, B, C and D.

(c) How many different shapes can you make from A, B, C and D?

Tangrams

Draw this shape on card.

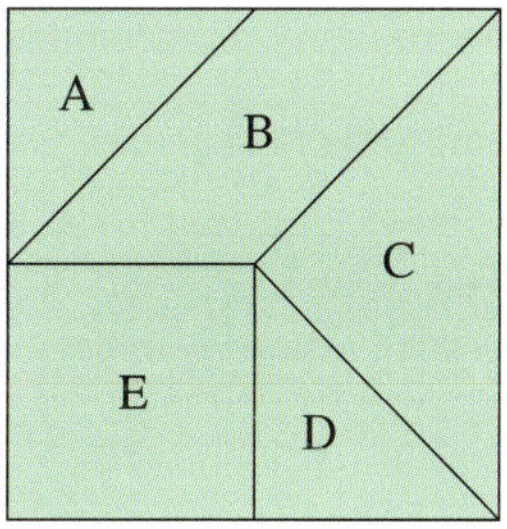

Cut out the five pieces A, B, C, D and E. Your five shapes A, B, C, D and E form a five-piece **tangram**.

Exercise 80

1 **(a)** Make a square from some of your tangram pieces.

(b) How many different ways can you make a square?

2 **(a)** Make rectangles from some or all of your pieces.

(b) Did you find as many as eight different rectangles?

3 How many different triangles can you make with some or all of your pieces?

4 How many different four-sided shapes can you make from some or all of your pieces?

5 The shapes A, B, C, D, E, F and G make up this seven-piece tangram.

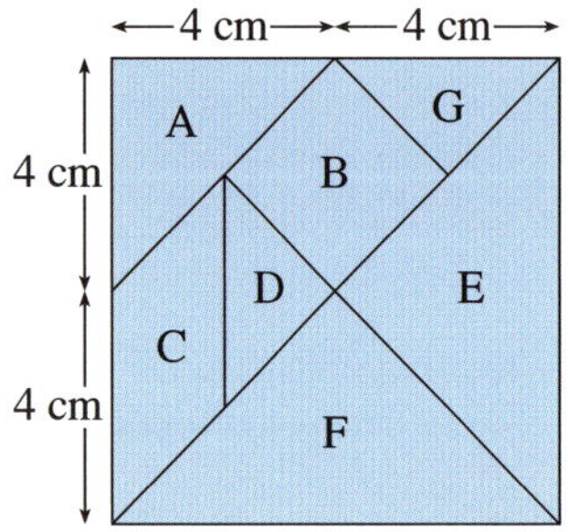

(a) Copy the figure on card and cut out the shapes A, B, C, D, E, F and G.

(b) Use all seven of your shapes to make one large triangle.

6 **(a)** Use all your pieces in Question 5 to make a rectangle.

(b) Can you make a six-sided figure?

7 The seven shapes in Question 5 can be put together to form many picture puzzles.

See if you can make these.

(a)

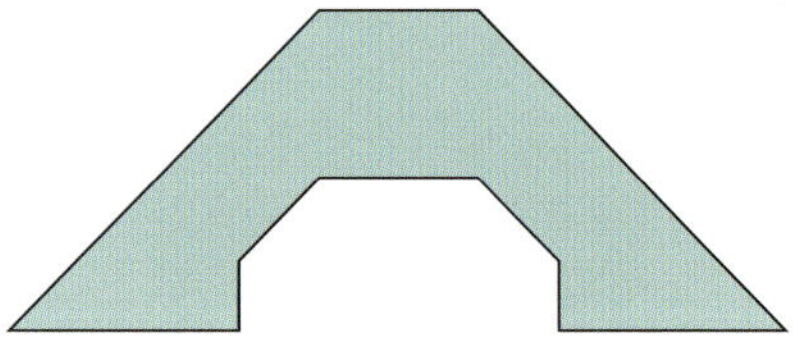

(b)

(c) See if you can make a dog from your shapes, or other pictures.

Rep-tiles

Cut out four identical equilateral triangles.

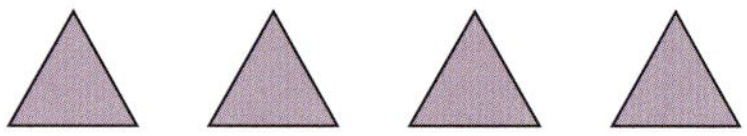

Can you fit these triangles together to make a larger triangle?

A group of shapes that can be fitted together to form a larger version of the original shape is called a rep-tile.

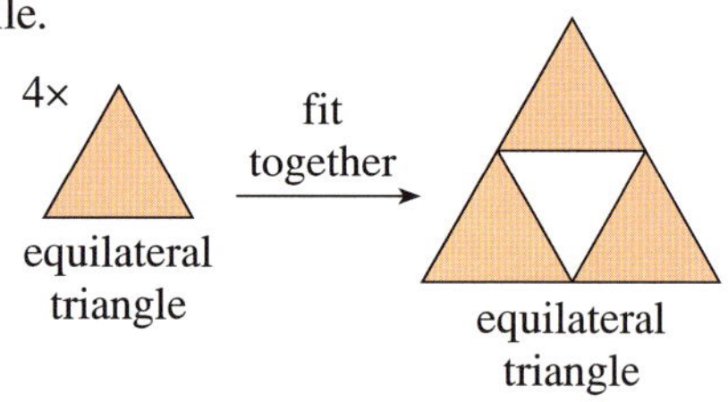

Exercise 8P

1 Which of these shapes can be fitted together to form a larger version of the original shape?

(a)

(b)

(c)

(d)

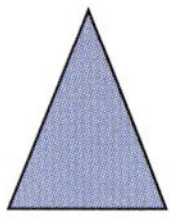

(e)

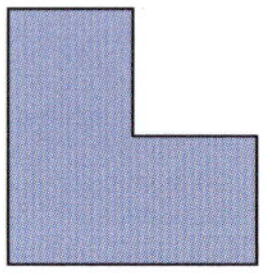

2

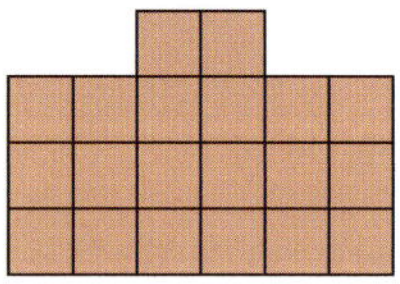

(a) Can you cover the shape above with tiles like this?

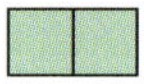

(b) What about this shape?

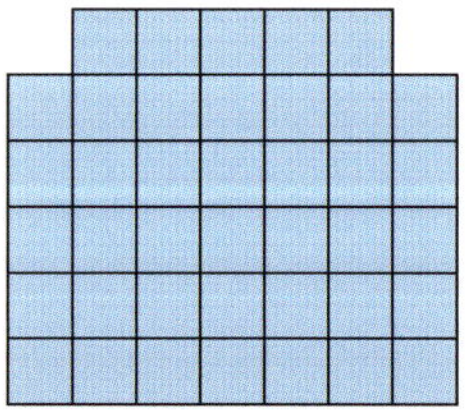

8 Consolidation

Example 1

Describe these triangles and quadrilaterals in terms of their properties.

(a)

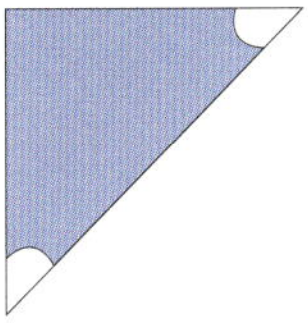

(b)

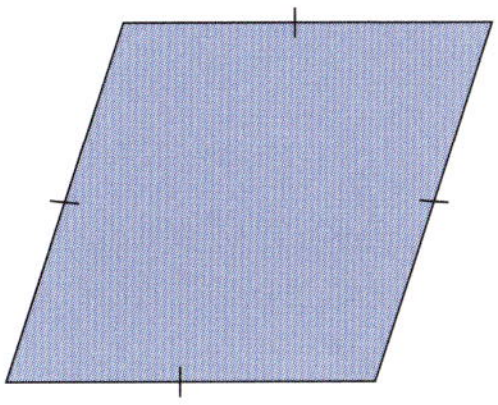

(c)

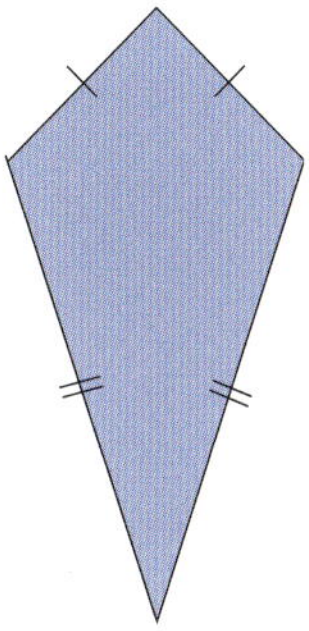

(a) The triangle has two equal acute angles. It is isosceles.

(b) The quadrilateral has two pairs of parallel sides and all sides equal. It is a rhombus.

(c) The quadrilateral has two pairs of adjacent sides equal in length. It is a kite.

Example 2

Construct the triangle XYZ with
XY = 8 cm, XZ = 7 cm and YZ = 6 cm.

1

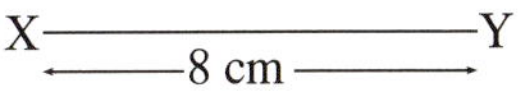

Draw base line XY 8 cm long.

2

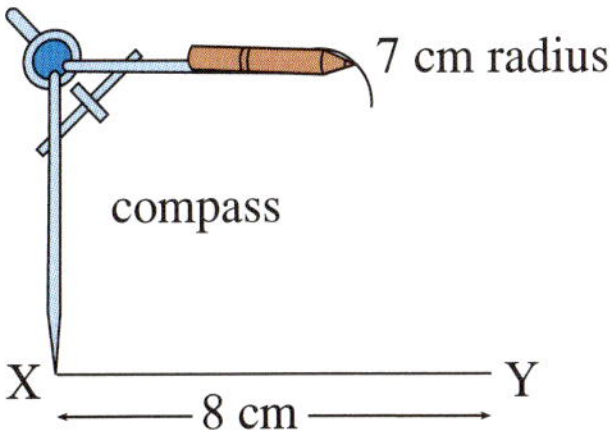

Set compasses to 7 cm.
Put the point on X. Draw the arc.

3 Repeat Step 2 with compass set to 6 cm and point at Y.

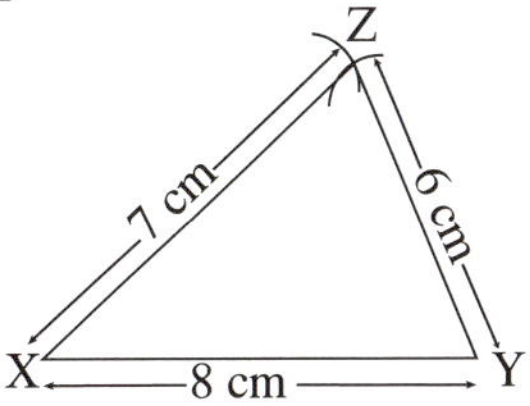

Join XZ and YZ.

Example 3

How many lines of symmetry does this shape have?

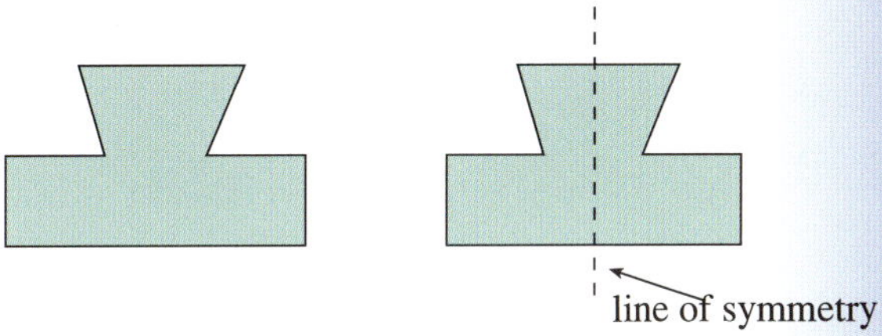

It has one line of symmetry only.

Example 4

Draw the image of the shape in the mirror line.

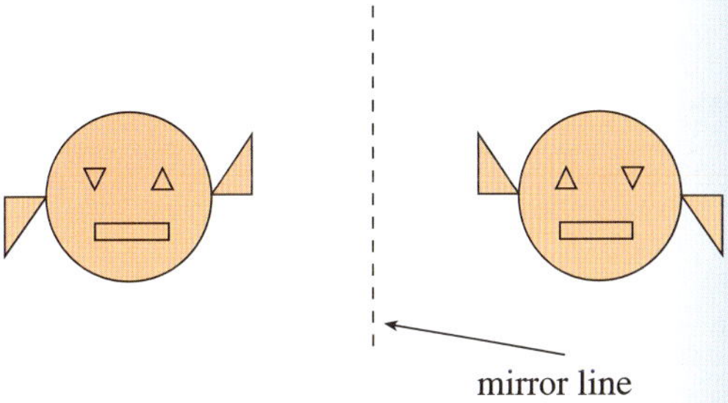

Example 5

Which of these shapes tessellate?

(a)

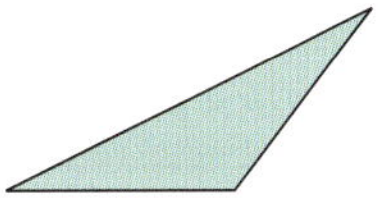

(b)

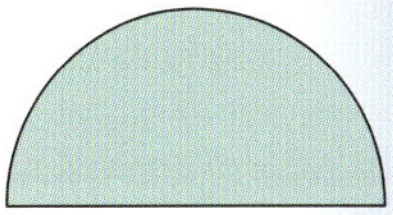

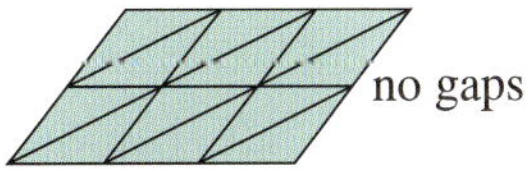

The triangle tessellates.

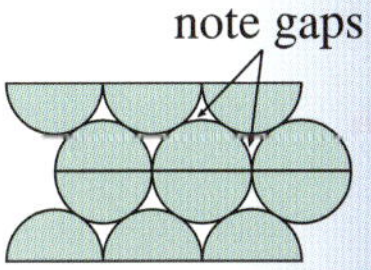

The semicircle does not tessellate.

Exercise 8

1 Name these shapes.

(a)
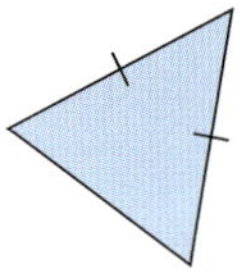

(b)
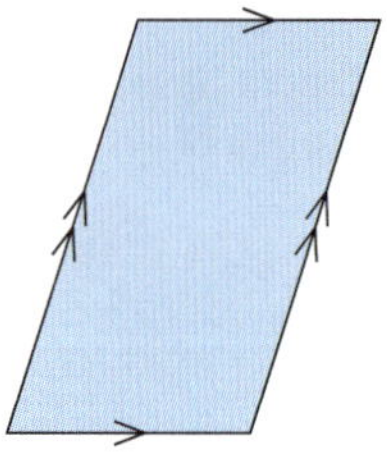

(c)
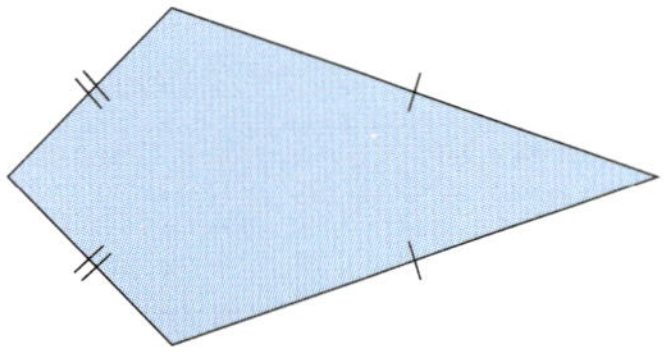

(d)
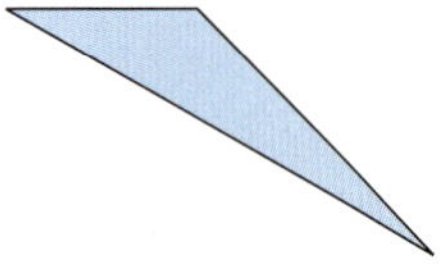

(e)

2 **(a)** If T = {triangles}, I = {isosceles triangles}, E = {equilateral triangles}, draw a Venn diagram to show the relationship between T, I and E.

(b) If Q = {quadrilaterals}, R = {rectangles}, P = {parallelograms}, S = {squares}, draw a Venn diagram to show the relationship between Q, R, P and S.

3 Construct these triangles:

(a) ABC, AB = 7 cm, BC = 5 cm, AC = 8 cm

(b) DEF, DE = 8.4 cm, DF = 9.2 cm, EF = 5.8 cm

(c) GHI, GJ = 9.6 cm, GI = 7.9 cm, HI = 8.7 cm

(d) JKL, JK = 7.5 cm, L$\hat{J}$K = 60°, JL = 6 cm

4 **(a)** Draw four different shapes with exactly two lines of symmetry.

(b) How many lines of symmetry do these shapes have?

(i)
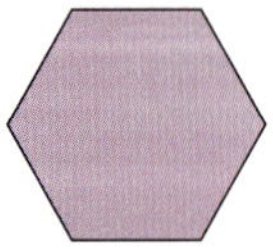

(ii)

(iii)
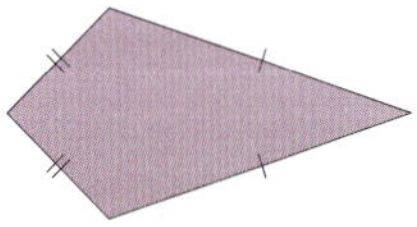

5 Copy the diagram and reflect each shape in the mirror line shown.

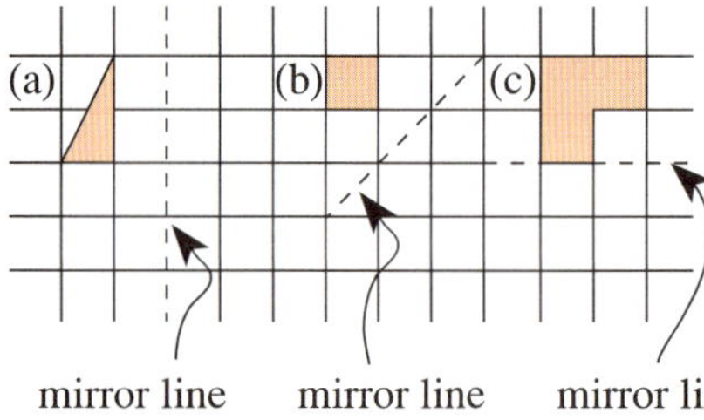

6 Which of these shapes tessellate? Make tiling patterns to find out.

(a)
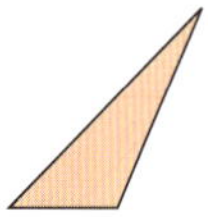

(b)
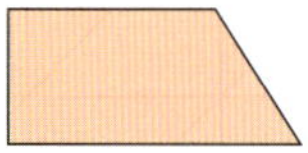

(c)
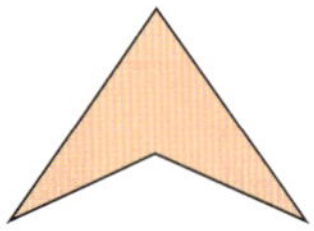

Application 8

7 **(a)** Make an accurate drawing, with lengths in centimetres, of the plan for the side of this house.

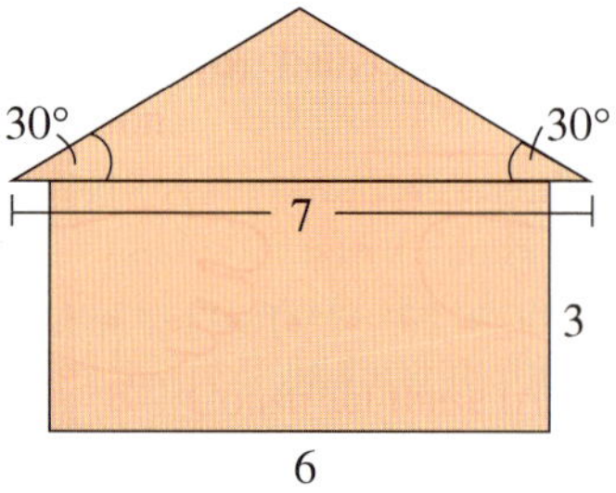

(b) What is the distance from the tallest part of the roof to the ground?

8 Look at some floors and walls in your neighbourhood.

(a) Can you find any tessellation or tiling patterns?

(b) Sketch some of the patterns you find.

Companion CD

Want some extra practice? Go to Chapter 8 on your companion CD for further exercises, animations, and solutions.

Summary

You should know ...

1 Triangles can be classified according to their sides:

(a) An equilateral triangle

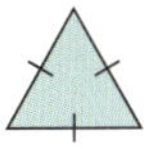

all three sides are equal

(b) An isosceles triangle

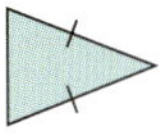

two sides are equal

(c) A scalene triangle

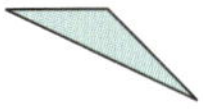

no sides are equal

2 Triangles can also be classified by angles:

(a) acute-angled triangle

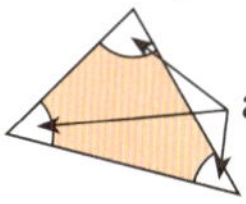

(b) right-angled triangle

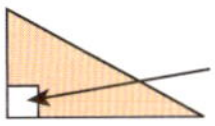

(c) obtuse-angled triangle

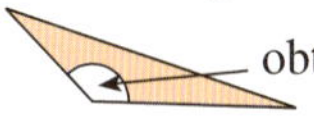

3 Quadrilaterals can be sorted according to their properties:

(a) 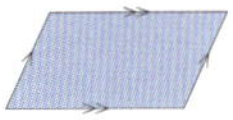 A parallelogram has two pairs of parallel sides.

(b)  A trapezium has one pair of parallel sides.

(c) 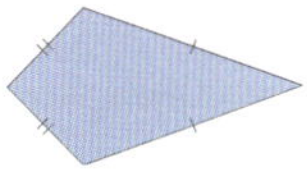 A kite has two pairs of adjacent sides equal in length.

(d) 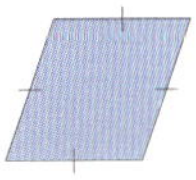 A rhombus has two pairs of parallel sides and all sides equal in length.

Check out

1

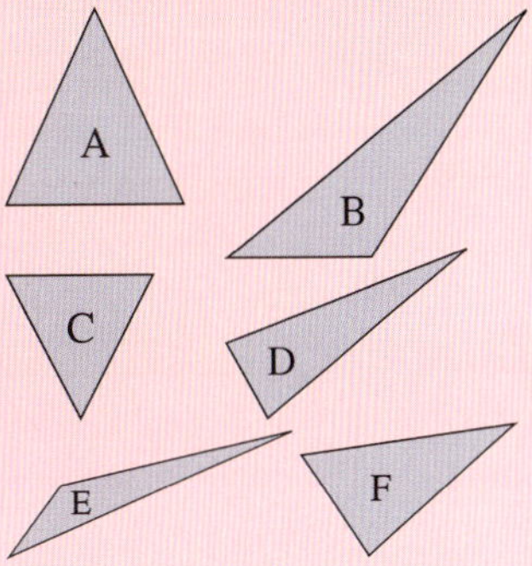

(a) Which triangles are equilateral?

(b) Which triangles are isosceles?

(c) Which triangles are scalene?

2 **(a)** Draw a right-angled triangle.

(b) Draw a right-angled isosceles triangle.

(c) Draw an obtuse-angled isosceles triangle.

3 **(a)** Write down four properties of a square.

(b) Which quadrilateral has diagonals that

(i) are perpendicular

(ii) bisect each other?

4 When a shape is folded so that one half fits exactly over the other half, the fold line is called a line of symmetry or mirror line.
For example:

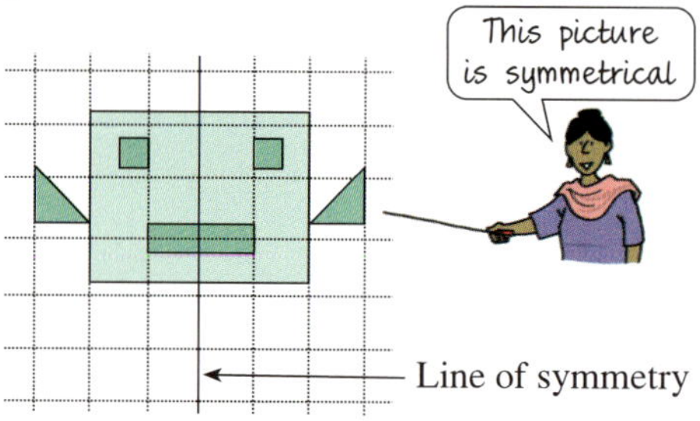

4 Copy these shapes and draw in the lines of symmetry.

(a)  **(b)** 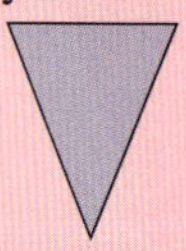

(c) 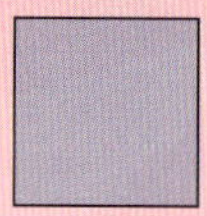 **(d)** 

5 A shape can be reflected in a line.
For example:

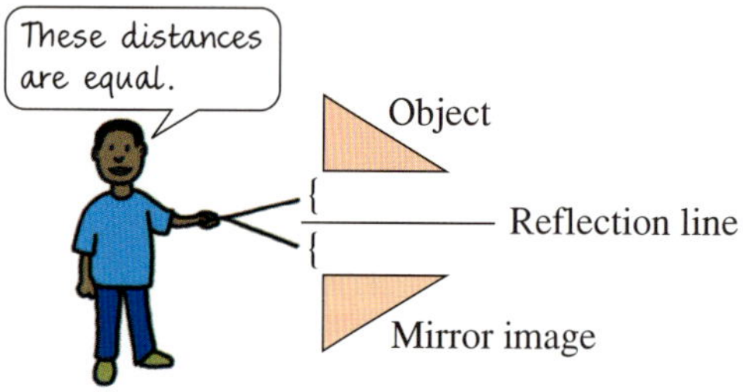

5 Draw the image of the shape after reflection in the mirror line.

(a)

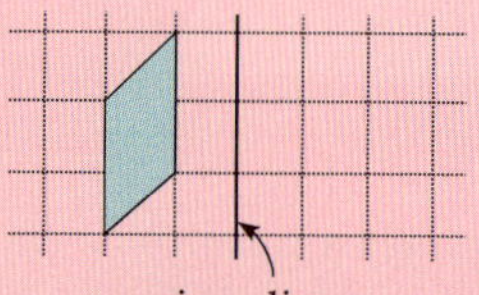

(b)

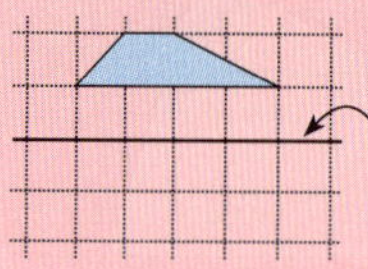

6 How to construct triangles using compasses.

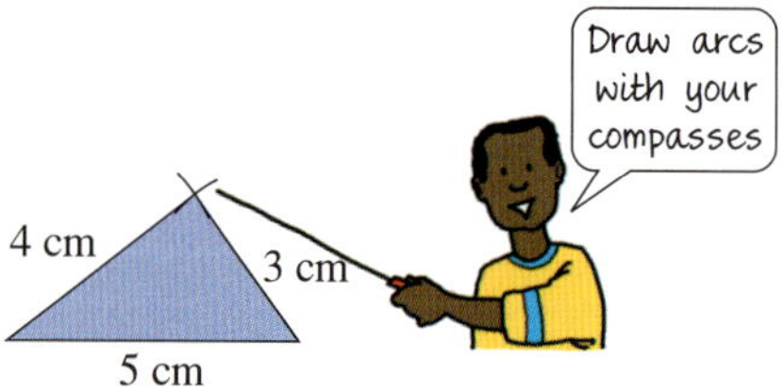

6 Construct these triangles:
(a) AB = 7.5 cm, BC = 4.5 cm, AC = 5.5 cm
(b) AB = 8 cm, AC = 5 cm, $A\hat{B}C = 30°$

7 A tessellation is a tiling pattern of shapes that fit together with no gaps.

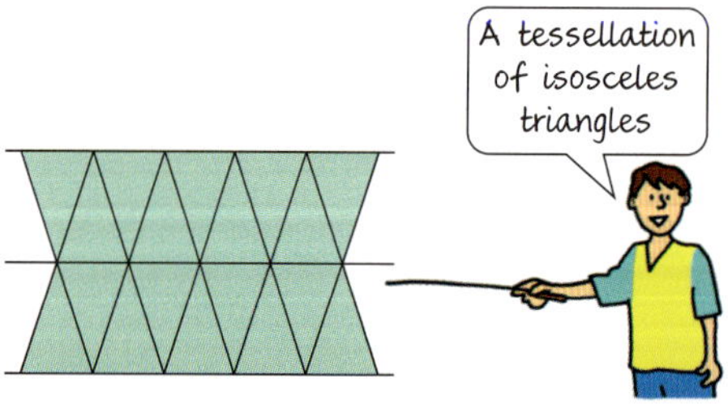

7 **(a)** Trace this shape.

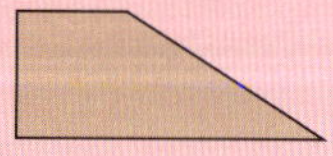

Make a tessellation pattern with it.
(b) Make as many different shapes as you can from four identical equilateral triangles.

Revision exercise 2

Angles

1 Measure the lettered angles shown in each of the following.

(a)

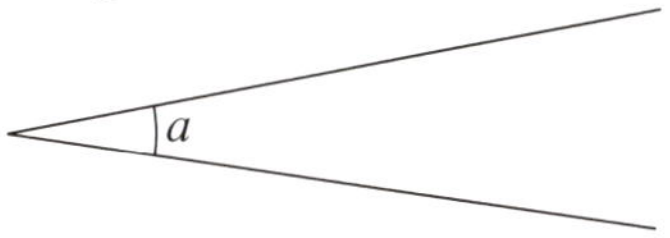

(b)

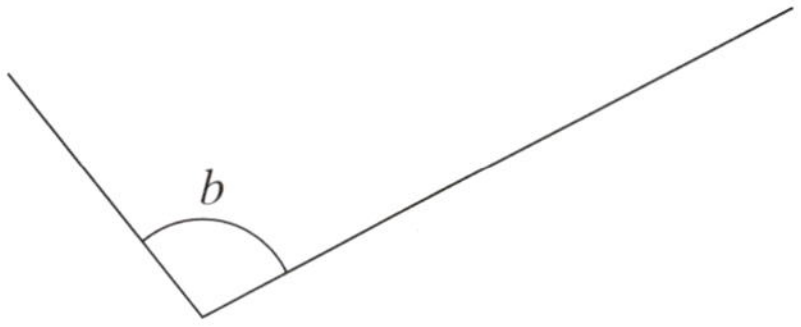

(c)

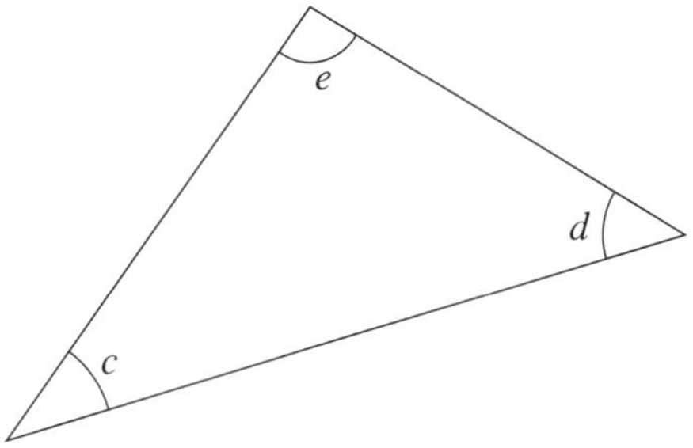

(d)

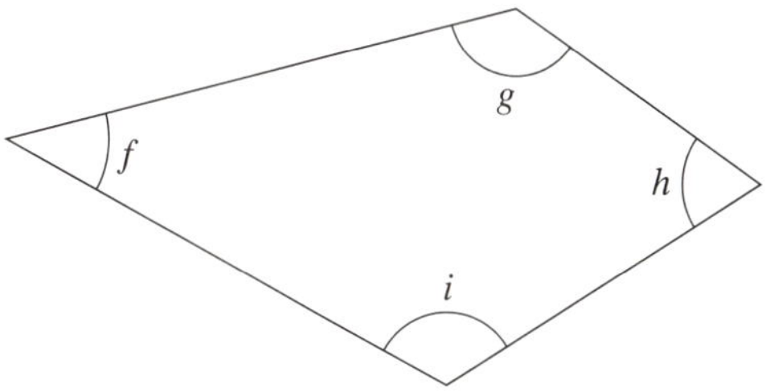

2 Use your ruler and protractor to draw accurately the shapes below.

(a)

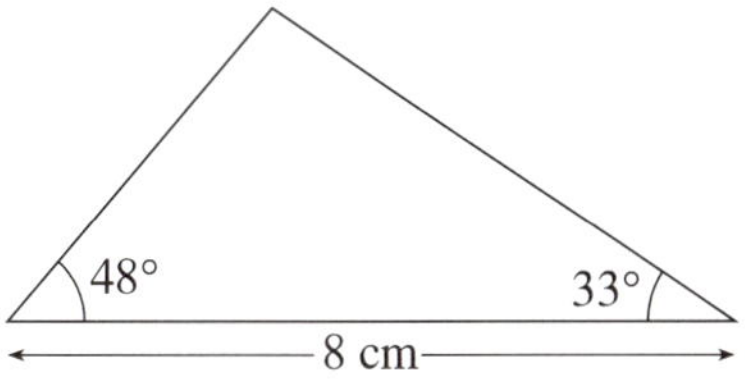

(b)

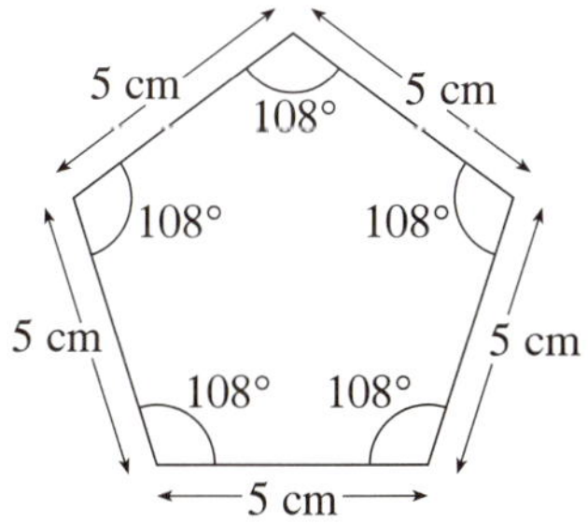

(c)

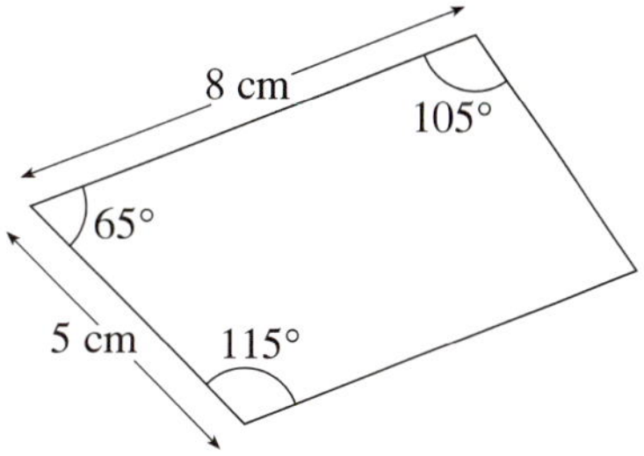

3 Through how many degrees does the minute hand of a clock turn between:

(a) 3 o'clock and 3.15 p.m.

(b) 3.15 p.m. and 3.25 p.m.

(c) 3.25 p.m. and 4.05 p.m.

4 Find the size of the angles marked by the letters.

(a)

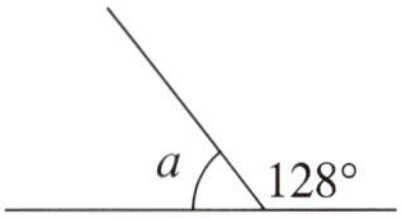

(b)

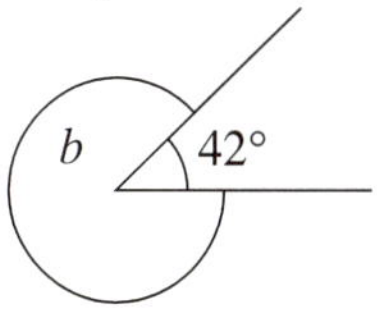

5 Find the size of the angles marked by the letters.

(a)

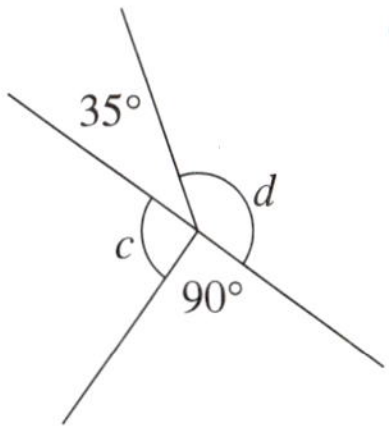

(b)

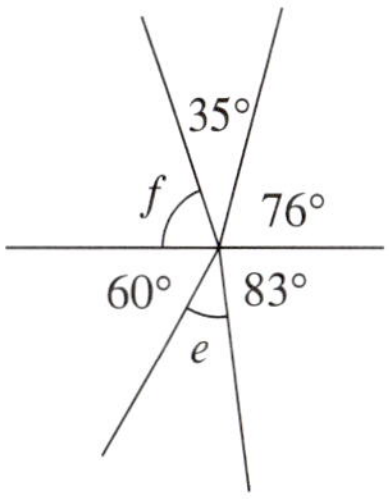

6 Find the angles marked by the letters in these triangles.

(a)

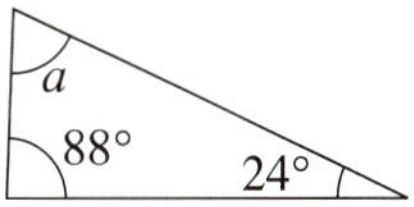

(b)

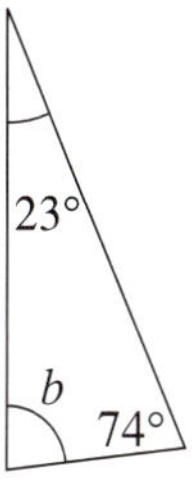

(c)

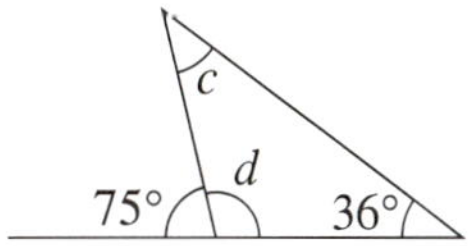

(d)

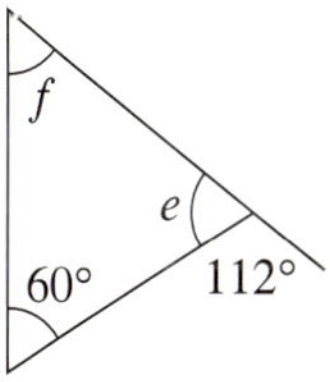

7 Find the angles marked by the letters in these four-sided figures.

(a)

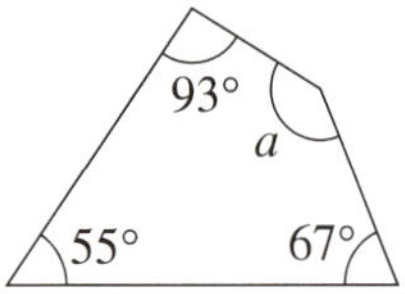

(b)

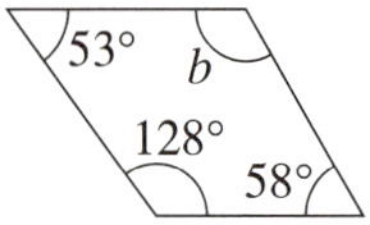

(c)

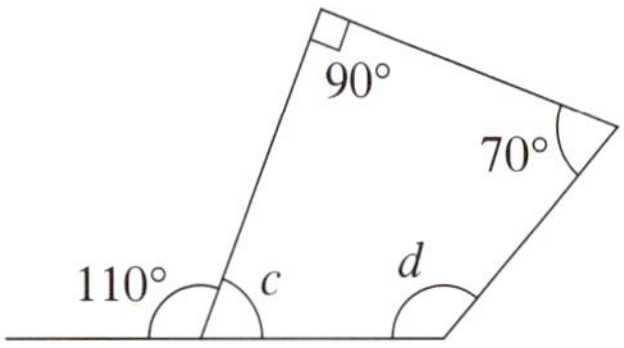

8 **(a)** Draw accurately with your protractor triangle ABC with $\hat{A} = 49°$, $\hat{B} = 70°$ and $\hat{C} = 61°$.

(b) Draw triangle DEF with $\hat{D} = 49°$, $\hat{E} = 70°$ and $\hat{F} = 61°$.

(c) Your two triangles might not be equal in every respect. Why not?

9 Use your ruler and protractor to draw a six-sided shape, with all six sides equal in length. Find the sum of the angles.

10 **(a)** Draw a five-sided shape of your own like the one below.

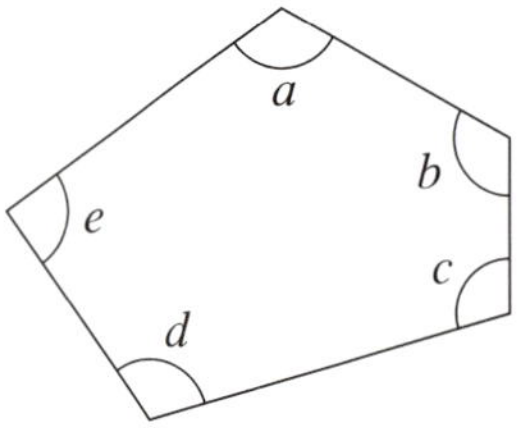

(b) Use a protractor to find the size of each angle.

(c) Find the angle sum $a + b + c + d + e$.

(d) Do all five-sided shapes have the same angle sum?

Solids

11 This cube has been made from 27 smaller cubes.

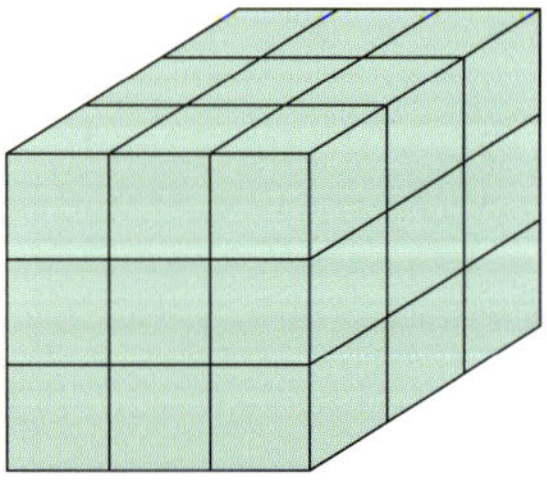

If the outside is painted red, how many small cubes have

(a) 3 red faces **(b)** 2 red faces

(c) 1 red face **(d)** no red faces?

12 How many small cubes are needed to build a larger cube with four along each edge?
If this larger cube is painted red, find the number of small cubes that have:

(a) 3 red faces **(b)** 2 red faces

(c) 1 red face **(d)** no red faces.

13 A cube has the numerals 1, 2, 3, 4, 5, 6 painted on its faces. Here are two views of the cube:

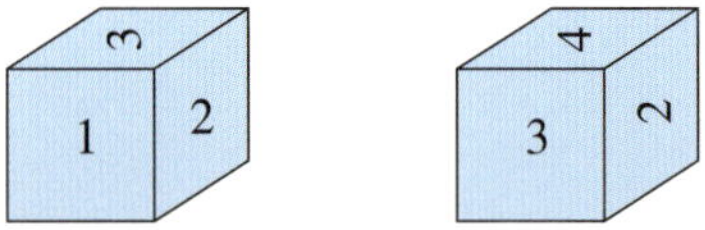

(a) Draw this net of the cube and put in the missing numbers.

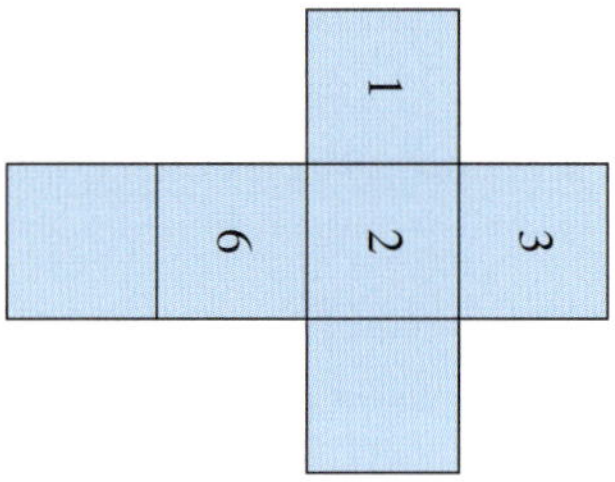

(b) What are the numbers on the faces that touch both 5 and 6?

14 Which, if any, of the following solids are prisms?

(a) cube **(b)** tetrahedron

(c) cylinder **(d)** sphere.

15 A prism has equal triangles at each end.
Sketch the solid and write down its number of:

(a) edges **(b)** faces **(c)** vertices.

16 A cube has 6 faces and 8 vertices. Sketch a solid that has 8 faces and 6 vertices.

17 A student made a prism with hexagon end faces like this.

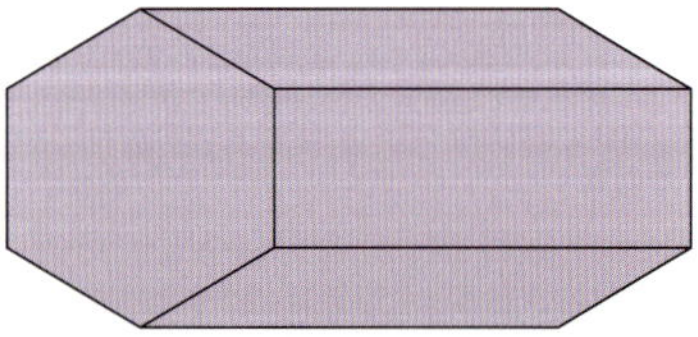

(a) Describe how the prism may be coloured with three colours, red, blue and green, so that touching faces are different colours.

(b) Sketch a prism with pentagon end faces. Can this be similarly coloured using three colours?

18 Use diagrams or models to show that you need four different colours to paint a tetrahedron so that no two touching faces are the same colour but three colours are sufficient to paint a cube.

19 If you looked at a solid and saw a circle, which of the following might it be?

(a) a cylinder (b) a cube

(c) a cone (d) a sphere.

20 Half a sphere is called a hemisphere.

(a) Do you live in the northern hemisphere or the southern hemisphere of the Earth?

(b) What is the name of the circle that separates the two hemispheres?

Measuring

21 Write out these lengths in order starting with the longest:

(a) 23 mm, 2 cm, 3 cm 2 mm

(b) 20 cm, 700 m, 2 km

(c) 6 m, 500 cm, 4 km

(d) 6000 m, 5000 cm, 4 km

22 Write down a pair of lengths that are the same, one from set A, one from set B.

A = {3 cm, 32 mm, 0.32 m, 250 m}

B = {0.25 km, 3.2 cm, 0.03 m, 32 cm}

23 What units would you use to measure:

(a) the height of a tree

(b) the length of your hair

(c) the weight of a banana

(d) the weight of your school bag

(e) the distance to New York?

24 A cricket pitch is 22 yards long or about 20 m. If all eleven of the fielding side lie down in a long line do you think they would stretch:

(a) much shorter than a pitch

(b) much longer than a pitch

(c) about the same length as a pitch?

25 In some countries road distances are measured in miles. 8 km is nearly the same as 5 miles. Which is the larger:

(a) 20 miles or 30 km

(b) 100 miles or 200 km

(c) 85 miles or 130 km?

26 Find out the approximate length of the equator. A car is advertised as being able to go 16 km per litre of petrol. Estimate how much fuel the car would use in travelling that distance.

27 16 sheets of my writing paper have a mass of 70 g. Does a box of 500 sheets have a mass of more or less than 2 kg?

28 A car has a mass of 0.9 t. What is its total mass when carrying four passengers with a mass of 80 kg each?

29 What time is shown on a digital watch when it is:

(a) mid-day

(b) twenty past four in the morning

(c) twenty to three in the morning

(d) five to six in the morning

(e) three o'clock in the afternoon

(f) quarter to seven in the evening

(g) twenty-five minutes before midnight.

30 It is possible to travel from London to Paris by train, boat and train. This is part of a timetable:

London (depart)	Paris (arrive)
0804	1807
0850	1702
1430	2228
2040	0625
2255	0915

(a) Write the timetable using the 12-hour clock.
(b) Which journeys involve travelling at night?
(c) Calculate the total time for each journey.
(d) Which is the shortest journey?

Shapes

31 In this diagram there are five squares:

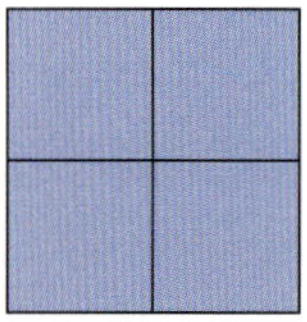

But there are more than ten squares altogether below. How many?

32 How many squares are there altogether when 25 small squares are fitted together to make a large 5×5 square?

33 Use a ruler and compasses to draw these triangles as accurately as you can. Measure the angles of each triangle.
(a) AB = 8 cm, BC = 5 cm, AC = 8 cm
(b) PQ = 8 cm, QR = 8 cm, PR = 8 cm
(c) XY = 8 cm, YZ = 10 cm, XZ = 6 cm

34 For each of the triangles in Question 33, state whether it is equilateral, isosceles or right-angled.

35 Draw a circle radius 5 cm. Use your compasses to mark off the radius 5 cm around the circle from a point P on the circle:

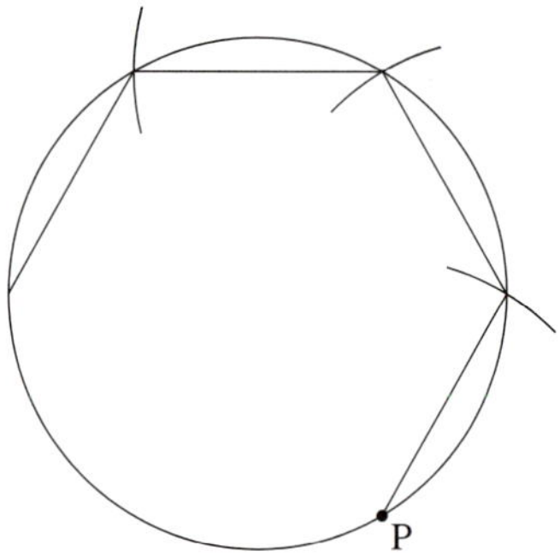

Join up where the arcs cut the circle. What is the name of the shape?

36 P = {parallelograms}
Q = {quadrilaterals}
R = {rectangles}
T = {trapeziums}
(a) Draw a Venn diagram to illustrate the relationship between the sets P, Q, R and T.
(b) Is it true to say that all parallelograms are rectangles? Explain.

37 Look at the capital letters

A B C D E F G H I J K L M
N O P Q R S T U V W X Y Z.

Which of these letters have
(a) no lines of symmetry
(b) one line of symmetry
(c) two lines of symmetry
(d) more than two lines of symmetry?

38 Here is a tessellation using the letter F. Draw it on squared paper to show that you can cover all the paper without leaving gaps.

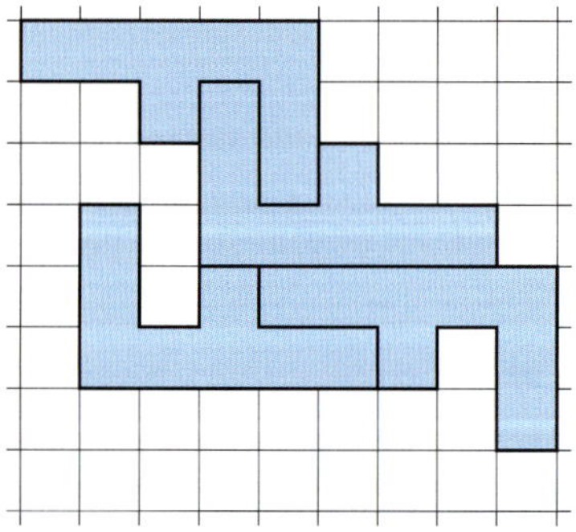

Draw a tessellation using your own design of the letter E.

39 Draw a square side 10 cm. Join up the mid-points of each side. What is the new shape? Now join up the mid-points of the sides of the new shape. Keep going.

40 Draw an equilateral triangle side 10 cm. Join the mid-points of each side. What is the name of the new shape? Keep going.

Mixed questions 2

1 Estimate the size of this angle in degrees.

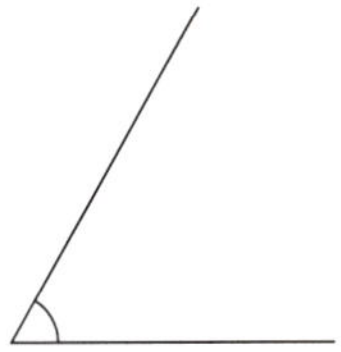

A 120° **B** 90°
C 15° **D** 60°

2 What is the name of this angle?

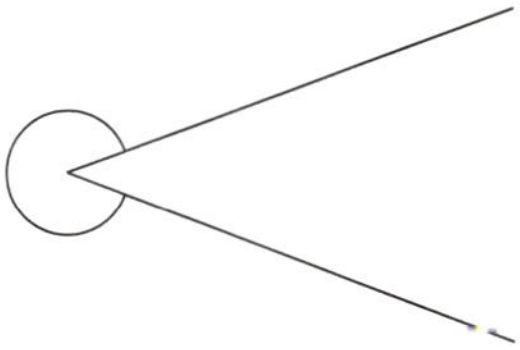

A straight **B** acute
C reflex **D** obtuse

3 How many degrees are there in a right angle?
A 180° **B** 90°
C 60° **D** 360°

4 How many degrees are there clockwise between West and North East?
A 225° **B** 90°
C 135° **D** 180°

5 Find the missing angle:

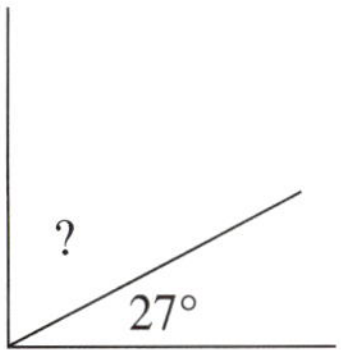

A 27° **B** 143°
C 72° **D** 63°

6 Find the missing angle:

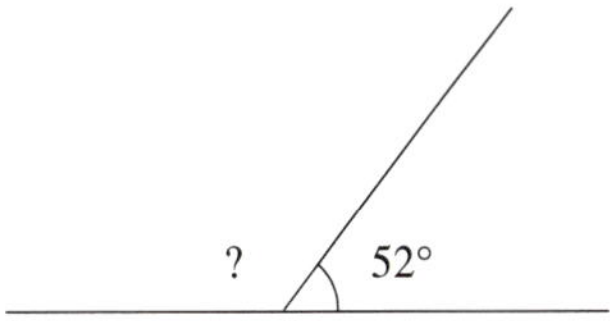

A 152° **B** 128°
C 148° **D** 38°

7 Find the missing angle:

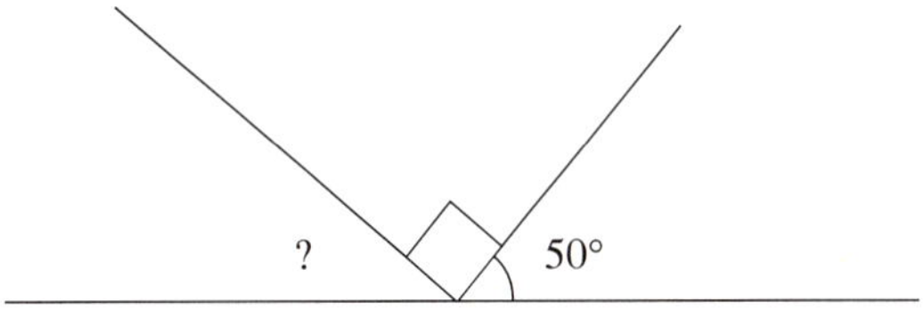

A 50° **B** 90°
C 40° **D** 60°

8 Find the missing angle:

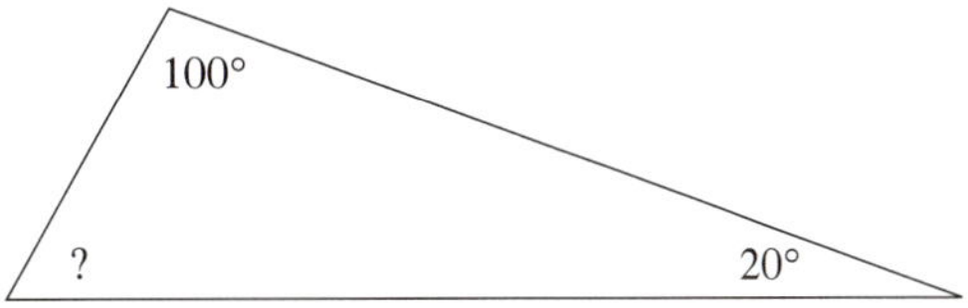

A 60° **B** 70°
C 50° **D** 20°

9 Find the missing angle:

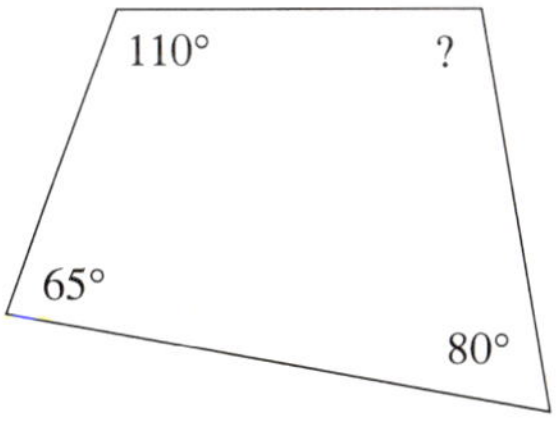

A 105° **B** 65°
C 20° **D** 120°

10 The best unit that could be used to measure the distance around the classroom is
A kilometres **B** metres
C centimetres **D** millimetres

11 0.52 m =
A 0.052 mm **B** 5.2 mm
C 520 mm **D** 5200 mm

12 The number of 25 mg tablets equivalent to 10 g is

A 4000 **B** 400 **C** 40 **D** 4

13 42 kg of rice is divided equally among 8 people. Each person gets

A 5.25 g **B** 52.5 g
C 525 g **D** 5250 g

14 1 km 5 m =

A 15 m **B** 105 m
C 1005 m **D** 10 005 m

15 327 mm =

A 0.0327 m **B** 0.327 m
C 3.27 m **D** 32.7 m

16 What do you call a triangle with no sides the same length?

A equilateral **B** obtuse
C isosceles **D** scalene

17 How many faces does a cuboid have?

A 1 **B** 5
C 12 **D** 6

18 How many minutes are there in 3 hours?

A 120 **B** 180
C 30 **D** 360

19 How long is it between 09:15 and 14:10?

A 5 hours 5 min **B** 7 hours 5 min
C 4 hours 55 min **D** 3 hours 15 min

20 How many mm are there in 1 m 1 cm?

A 1001 **B** 1110
C 1010 **D** 1100

21 What is the value of 1 – 0.05 as a fraction?

A $\frac{1}{20}$ **B** $\frac{9}{10}$ **C** $\frac{19}{20}$ **D** $\frac{5}{100}$

22 One of the angles in an isosceles triangle is 100°. What are the other two angles?

A 100° and 160° **B** 40° and 40°
C 100° and 40° **D** 50° and 50°

23 Add together:

5 cm 2 m 36 mm.

A 25.36 cm **B** 2536 mm
C 2.86 m **D** 2086 mm

24 A shape has 5 faces, 5 vertices and 8 edges. What is the shape?

A cube
B triangular prism
C square-based pyramid
D cylinder

25 What is the cross-section of a cylinder?

A circle **B** triangle
C square **D** rectangle

26

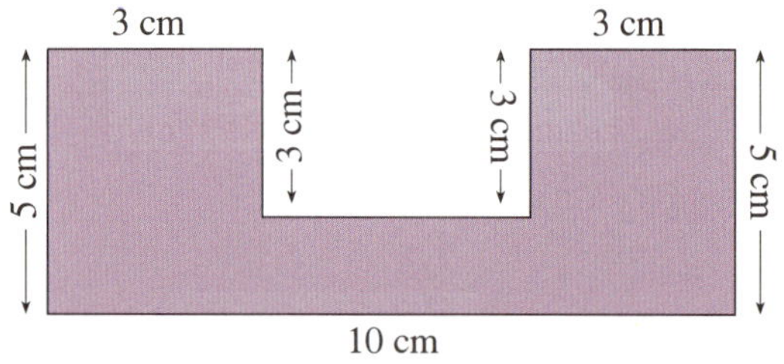

What is the perimeter of this shape?

A 20 cm **B** 32 cm
C 36 cm **D** 50 cm

27 I got on the bus at 5.07 pm and got off it at 6.32 pm. How long was my journey?

A 125 mins **B** 85 mins
C 35 mins **D** 105 mins

28 What is the largest number?

A 0.824 **B** 0.795
C 1.002 **D** 0.999

29 What shape has exactly 4 identical faces?

A triangular
B tetrahedron
C triangle-based prism
D square-based pyramid

30 How many equal angles does an equilateral triangle have?

A 1 **B** 2
C 3 **D** 4

31 How much is this?

\$6.30 + 15 c + \$0.40

A \$21.70 **B** \$670.15
C \$5.25 **D** \$6.85

Consumer arithmetic 9

Objectives

- ✔ calculate bills and find 'best buys'
- ✔ see how percentages are used in everyday life
- ✔ change fractions and decimals to percentages
- ✔ find percentage profit and loss on goods sold
- ✔ calculate savings through discounts
- ✔ find interest on loans and deposits

What's the point?

We use money on a daily basis to buy and sell things. Finding how much you can save when a discount is offered is important if you don't want to end up broke!

Before you start

You should know ...

1 How to simplify fractions.

$$\frac{4}{10} = \frac{2}{5} \quad (\div 2 \text{ top and bottom})$$

2 How to find fractions of a number.
For example:
$\frac{1}{3}$ of $12 = 12 \div 3 = 4$
$\frac{2}{3}$ of $12 = 2 \times \frac{1}{3}$ of $12 = 2 \times 4 = 8$

3 How to write a fraction as a decimal.
For example:
$\frac{3}{10} = 3 \div 10 = 0.3$
$\frac{47}{100} = 47 \div 100 = 0.47$

Check in

1 Simplify:
(a) $\frac{6}{10}$ **(b)** $\frac{6}{9}$ **(c)** $\frac{8}{12}$
(d) $\frac{18}{24}$ **(e)** $\frac{12}{36}$ **(f)** $\frac{26}{39}$

2 Work out:
(a) $\frac{1}{5}$ of 10 **(b)** $\frac{2}{5}$ of 10
(c) $\frac{4}{25}$ of 50 **(d)** $\frac{3}{4}$ of 64
(e) $\frac{14}{20}$ of 80 **(f)** $\frac{10}{25}$ of 75

3 Write as decimals:
(a) $\frac{2}{10}$ **(b)** $\frac{7}{10}$ **(c)** $\frac{16}{100}$
(d) $\frac{82}{100}$ **(e)** $\frac{3}{5}$ **(f)** $\frac{3}{4}$

9.1 Using money

When you go into a supermarket and buy some goods, the cashier will give you a **bill**,

Item description	Qty	Price	Total
RN 1203			
JUICE 250 ml	2	$1.75	$ 3.50
RN 4307			
BALLPOINT PEN	3	$2.95	$ 8.85
TOTAL			$12.35

The bill gives the cost of each item, the number of items purchased and the total cost.

When you pay for the items you will normally receive **change**.

Example 1

Alan buys 4 tins of beans at $5.25 each and 3 boxes of matches at $0.75 each.

How much change will he get from a $100 bill?

4 tins of beans = $5.25 × 4 = $21.00
3 boxes of matches = $0.75 × 3 = $ 2.25
TOTAL $23.25

Change = $100 – $23.25 = $76.75

Exercise 9A

1 What is Chandra's bill if she buys
- **(a)** one portion of wings and a small juice
- **(b)** two portions of legs, one large chips and two large juices
- **(c)** one portion of wings, one portion of legs, two small chips and two small juices
- **(d)** four portions of wings, two large chips, two small chips and four small juices?

2 In Question 1 what is Chandra's change if she has a $100 bill?

3

Belinda has $50. Which of the following can she buy?
- **(a)** 6 teacups and saucers
- **(b)** 4 plates and one jug
- **(c)** 4 teacups and saucers and 2 jugs
- **(d)** 3 plates and 2 jugs

4 Tickets for a test cricket match are priced
Adults $75.00
Children $45.00
What is the cost for
- **(a)** 2 adults
- **(b)** 2 adults and 3 children
- **(c)** 1 adult and 6 children?

5 Jackson buys two magazines for $17.99 each and a newspaper for $1.50.

What change does he get from two $20 bills?

6

Music CDs are priced at \$69.95 and DVDs at \$147.50.
Anton has \$500. How much change will he receive if he buys

(a) 2 DVDs **(b)** 2 DVDs and 1 CD
(c) 5 CDs **(d)** 4 CDs and 1 DVD?

7 David is paid \$9.20 per hour, and \$17.50 per hour for each hour's overtime. What is his weekly pay if he works

(a) 40 hours plus 3 hours overtime
(b) 40 hours plus 7 hours overtime?

8 **(a)** Copy and complete Egbert's payslip:

Egbert Baptiste Basic rate \$16.25 per hour			
Rate	**Number of hours**	**Amount per hour**	**Total**
Basic	35	\$16.25	
Overtime	6	\$25.99	
Total pay			

(b) If he buys a radio for \$137.50, how much does he have left?

Best buys

Have you ever gone into a store and seen two signs like this?

Which is the best buy?

To work this out you need to find the cost of a single pair of socks.

In the first case:
6 socks pairs cost \$43.80
So 1 sock pair costs \$43.80 ÷ 6
= \$7.30

In the second case:
4 sock pairs cost \$28.40
So 1 sock pair costs \$28.40 ÷ 4
= \$7.10

It is cheaper to buy the socks from the second pile.

In some cases you will need to look at the sizes sold.

Example 2

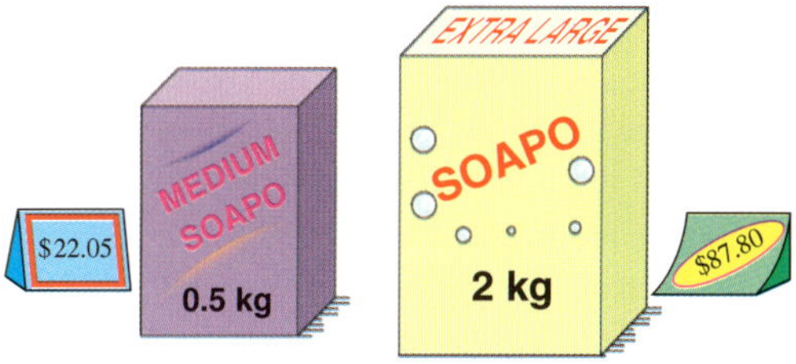

Which soap powder is the better buy?

Extra large size holds 2 kg for \$87.80
So 1 kg costs \$87.80 ÷ 2 = \$43.90

Medium size holds 0.5 kg for \$22.05
So 1 kg costs \$22.05 ÷ 0.5 = \$44.10

Hence, it's cheaper to purchase the extra large size. (If you can afford it!)

Exercise 9B

1 In each case find the unit cost and then state which is the better buy.

(a) 5 oranges for \$4.00 or 4 oranges for \$3.10
(b) 6 eggs for \$8.40 or 12 eggs for \$16.20
(c) 5 exercise books for \$14.50 or 8 exercise books for \$22.80
(d) 7 tins of milk for \$24.50 or 9 tins of milk for \$31.05

2 Which would be the best buy?
5 pens for \$10.00 or
7 pens for \$14.70 or
9 pens for \$15.75?
Give reasons for your answer.

3 Which would be the best buy?
5 kg of oranges for $12.25 or
3 kg of oranges for $7.29 or
4 kg of oranges for $9.56?
Give reasons for your answer.

4 Which is the better buy?
0.36 kg of beef for $7.20 or
0.54 kg of beef for $10.77?
Give reasons for your answer.

5

Which is the better buy?
130 g of toothpaste for $11.70 or
150 g of toothpaste for $13.05?
Give reasons for your answer.

6 Visit a local supermarket. Find the prices of different-sized tubes of toothpaste for a given brand.
(a) Write down the sizes and prices.
(b) Which is the best buy?
(c) Write up your findings and present them to your class.

7 Repeat Question 6 for other items, such as soap powder or bleach.

Profit and loss

If you sell something for more money than it has cost you, you make a profit.

In the picture, Ken bought a bike for $220 and sold it for $300.

Ken's profit = $300 − $220
= $80

- **Profit** = selling price − cost price. If the cost price is more than the selling price a **loss** is made.

Exercise 9C

1 For each item he sold last week, Johnny wrote down how much it cost him **(cost price)** and how much he sold it for **(selling price)**.

For each item:
(a) find the difference between the cost price and the selling price
(b) say whether he made a profit or loss.

Item	*Cost price*	*Selling price*
Table	$320	$365
4 Chairs	$288	$240
Bed	$495	$570
Fridge	$2163	$2437
Gas stove	$1400	$1077

2 Copy and complete this table.

Cost price	Selling price	Profit
$3.00	$5.00	
$1.50		$1.50
	$6.40	$1.40
$3.00	$3.00	
	$6.20	$1.20

3 Copy and complete this table.

Cost price	Selling price	Loss
$4.00		$1.00
$3.50	$3.25	
$1.00		$0.75
	$3.50	$1.20
	$10.00	$3.50

4 Look again at the list in Question 1.
(a) Altogether, by the end of the week, had Johnny made a profit or loss on his sales?
(b) How did you work out the answer?

Some profit and loss problems are more complicated.

Example 3

Kevin bought 150 pairs of shoes for \$6000. He sold 100 of them for \$50 each and the remaining 50 for \$55 each. How much profit did he make altogether?

Kevin sold 100 shoes for

$$100 \times \$50 = \$5000$$

Kevin sold the other 50 for

$$50 \times \$55 = \$2750$$

Selling price of 150 shoes

$$= \$5000 + \$2750$$
$$= \$7750$$

Kevin bought the shoes for \$6000

So Kevin's profit = \$7750 − \$6000
= \$1750

Exercise 9D

1 Ian Wallis bought 200 shirtjacs for \$6000. He sold 120 of them for \$32.50 each. He sold the remaining 80 for \$35 each. How much profit did he make altogether?

2 Albert Toussaint bought 25 calculators for \$1625. He sold them for \$72.50 each.

(a) How much did each calculator cost Albert?

(b) How much profit did Albert make on each calculator?

(c) How much profit did Albert make altogether?

3 Belle Jackson bought 30 pairs of trousers for \$1560. She sold them all at the same selling price and made a profit of \$180.

(a) How much did each pair of trousers cost Belle to buy?

(b) How much profit did she make on each pair of trousers?

(c) What was the selling price of each pair?

4 Belle also bought 12 pairs of men's sandals. She sold them for \$34.95 each and made a total profit of \$51.

(a) How much profit did she make on each pair of sandals?

(b) How much did each pair cost her?

5 Alice bought a bag of 300 mangoes for \$225. When she sorted then she found she had

90 top quality mangoes

186 premium mangoes

and the rest were bad.

She sold the top quality mangoes for \$1.10 each and her premium fruits for 90 cents each. She threw away the bad ones.

What profit, if any, did she make?

6

Belle's brother bought 120 straw hats for \$5.25 each. He sold forty of them to tourists at \$7.30 each, and then sold the rest to Belle for \$350.

(a) For how much did Belle's brother buy the 120 straw hats?

(b) How much money did he get from the sale of the hats to tourists?

(c) How much money did he receive from the sale of all his hats?

(d) Did he make a profit or a loss? How much?

9.2 Understanding percentages

Often you will go into a store and see signs like this:

The sign means that the price of the TV has been reduced by 10%.

The symbol % means per cent or 'out of a 100'.
For example:

In a bag of 100 tomatoes, 6 are bad. $\frac{6}{100}$ or 6 per cent (6%) of the tomatoes are bad.

Example 4

Mrs Brown the fruit vendor bought 200 oranges. She found 8 of the oranges were bad. Find the percentage that were bad.

$$\text{Fraction of bad oranges} = \frac{8}{200}$$

$$= \frac{8 \div 2}{200 \div 2} = \frac{4}{100}$$

4 oranges in 100 were bad.
That is, 4 per cent were bad.

Exercise 9E

1 Write using the symbol %.

(a) 5 per cent **(b)** 14 per cent
(c) 8 per cent **(d)** 20 per cent
(e) 11 per cent **(f)** 25 per cent

2 Write using the symbol %.

(a) 15 in 100 **(b)** 25 in 100
(c) 13 in 100 **(d)** 72 in 100
(e) 32 in 100 **(f)** 99 in 100

3 **(a)** Jan scored 67 out of 100 in a maths exam. What percentage is this?
(b) Her sister got 16 out of 20 in a science test. Who got the higher percentage?

4 Mrs Brown kept a record of the bad oranges she received from the fruit farmer. Using the method of Example 4, copy and complete the table.

Oranges bought from Mr Johnson in 2009				
Month	**Number bought**	**Number bad**	**Fraction bad**	**Percentage bad**
Jan	300	36	$\frac{36}{300} = \frac{12}{100}$	12
Feb	500	40	$\frac{40}{500} = \frac{8}{100}$	8
March	600	54	$\frac{54}{600} = \frac{\square}{100}$	$\square$
April	600	42		
May	800	40		
June	900	45		
July	1200	72		
Aug	1500	75		
Sept	1000	70		
Oct	800	56		
Nov	700	63		
Dec	500	55		

5 What do you think these mean?

(a)

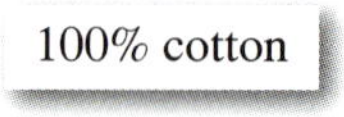

(b)

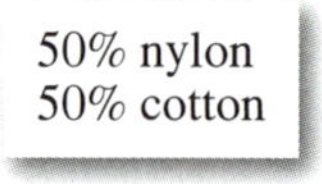

(c)

(d)

9.3 Fractions, decimals and percentages

You will need squared paper.

You can shows percentages, like fractions, on diagrams.

Example 5

What percentage of the square is shaded?

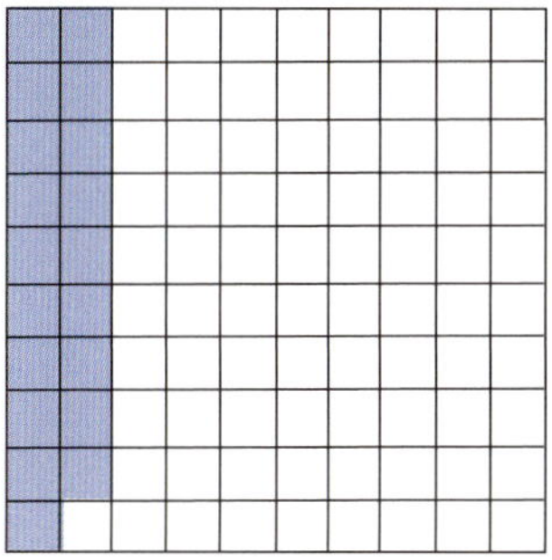

19 out of 100 squares are shaded. That is $\frac{19}{100}$ or 19%.

Exercise 9F

1 What percentage of each shape is shaded?

(a)

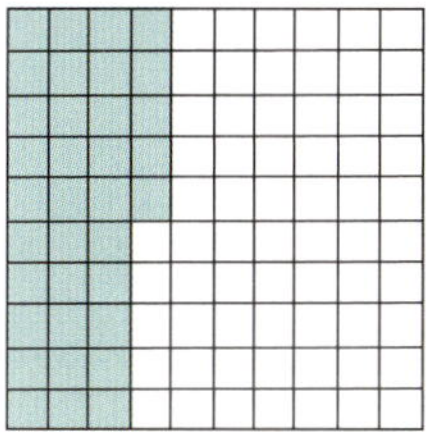

(b)

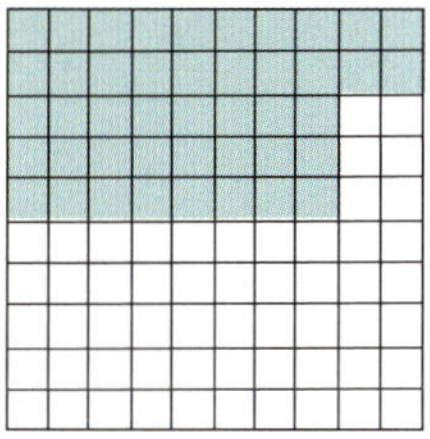

(c)

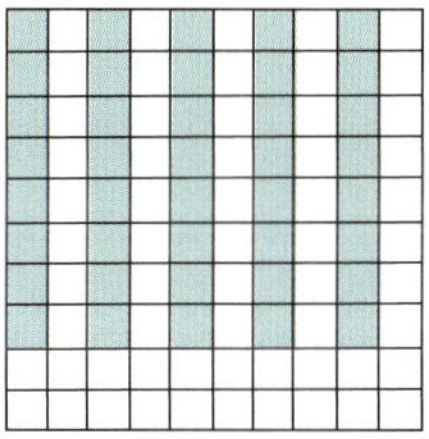

(d)

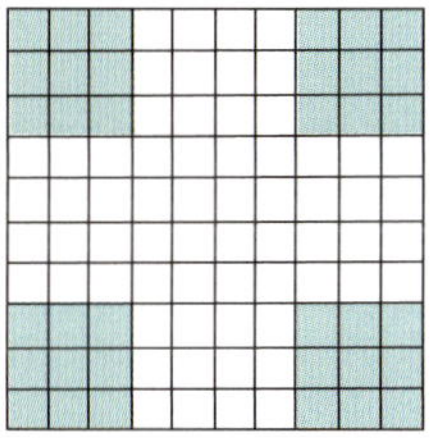

2 Draw pictures on your squared paper to show:

(a) 50% **(b)** 25%
(c) 70% **(d)** 64%

3 1% is the same as $\frac{1}{100}$.
Use the same idea to copy and complete:

(a) 5% is the same as …
(b) 20% is the same as …
(c) 25% is the same as …
(d) 39% is the same as …
(e) 81% is the same as …

4 $22\% = \frac{22}{100}$ as a per cent fraction. Write these as per cent fractions.

(a) 34% **(b)** 11% **(c)** 19%
(d) 20% **(e)** 28% **(f)** 31%
(g) 9% **(h)** 43%

5 Write as a percentage.

(a) $\frac{15}{100}$ **(b)** $\frac{25}{100}$ **(c)** $\frac{17}{100}$
(d) $\frac{33}{100}$ **(e)** $\frac{19}{100}$ **(f)** $\frac{29}{100}$
(g) $\frac{76}{100}$ **(h)** $\frac{97}{100}$

Changing fractions to percentages

It is easy to write a fraction with a denominator of 100 as a percentage.
For example:

$\frac{23}{100} = 23\%$

You can change any fraction to a percentage by writing it with a denominator of 100.

Example 6

Write the fraction $\frac{6}{25}$ as a percentage.

$$\frac{6}{25} \overset{\times 4}{=} \frac{24}{100} = 24\% \quad (\times 4 \text{ top and bottom})$$

A quicker way of changing a fraction to a percentage is to multiply by 100%. Remember $100\% = \frac{100}{100} = 1$

Example 7

Write the fraction $\frac{28}{80}$ as a percentage.

$$\frac{28}{80} = \frac{28}{80} \times 100\%$$

$$= \frac{28}{\cancel{80}_{8}} \times \cancel{100}^{10}\%$$

$$= \frac{\cancel{28}^{7}}{\cancel{8}_{2}} \times 10\%$$

$$= \frac{70}{2}\% = 35\%$$

Exercise 9G

1 Copy and complete, using the method in Example 6.

(a) $\frac{1}{4} = \frac{\square}{100} = \square\%$
(b) $\frac{1}{2} = \frac{\square}{100} = \square\%$
(c) $\frac{3}{4} = \frac{\square}{100} = \square\%$
(d) $\frac{7}{10} = \frac{\square}{100} = \square\%$
(e) $\frac{7}{20} = \frac{\square}{100} = \square\%$

2 Write as a percentage.

(a) $\frac{3}{5}$ **(b)** $\frac{4}{5}$ **(c)** $\frac{11}{20}$
(d) $\frac{9}{15}$ **(e)** $\frac{3}{50}$

3 Write as a percentage.

(a) $\frac{32}{80}$ (b) $\frac{15}{75}$ (c) $\frac{28}{40}$

(d) $\frac{48}{60}$ (e) $\frac{22}{55}$ (f) $\frac{17}{68}$

(g) $\frac{120}{150}$ (h) $\frac{108}{144}$

4 John scored 6 out of 10 in a mathematics test.

(a) Write his score as a fraction.

(b) Write his score as a percentage.

5 David scored 13 out of 20 in an English test.

(a) Write his score as a fraction.

(b) Write his score as a percentage.

6 **(a)** Janice scored 56 out of 80 in a science exam. What is her score as a percentage?

(b) Janice scored 49 out of 70 in a French paper. In which exam did she get a higher percentage?

7 A man uses two bottles of rum to make five bottles of rum punch.

(a) What fraction of the volume of punch is rum?

(b) What percentage of the volume of punch is rum?

8 Six children in a class of forty were absent from school. What percentage were absent?

9 Earl and Eric won the last 6 of their 8 domino matches.

Rennick and Raymond won the last 14 of their 20 domino matches.
Which pair won the higher percentage of matches?

10 Out of the 200 students at Anytimes School, 120 were present today, 50 were late and 30 were absent. Write down the percentage
(a) present **(b)** late **(c)** absent.

11 Copy and complete the table below showing the number of girls at Queenstown School.

Form	No. of girls	Total pupils	% girls
1	75	150	
2	90	120	
3	58	100	
4	66	120	
5	50	80	

Which form has the greatest percentage of girls?

12 At a driving centre in Port-of-Spain last week, 45 people took a driving test. The results are shown below.

	Number tested	Number passed
Men	25	13
Women	20	14

Find the percentage of:

(a) men who passed

(b) women who passed

(c) men who failed

(d) women who failed

(e) people who passed.

Expressing decimals as percentages

To write decimals as percentages you can first write your decimal as a fraction with denominator 100.

Example 8

Write **(a)** 0.3 **(b)** 0.35 as percentages.

(a) $0.3 = \frac{3}{10} = \frac{30}{100} = 30\%$

(b) $0.35 = \frac{35}{100} = 35\%$

As with fractions, a quick way to change a decimal to a percentage is to multiply by 100%.

Example 9

Write 0.316 as a percentage.

$0.316 = 0.316 \times 100\%$

$= 31.6\%$

Exercise 9H

1 Study Example 8. Then copy and complete the table below.

Decimal	Per cent fraction	%
0.5	$\frac{50}{100}$	50%
0.68	$\frac{68}{100}$	68%
0.9		
0.75		
0.25		
0.03		

2 Look at the table in Question 1. Can you see a quick way of changing a decimal to a percentage?

3 Using the pattern you discovered, write each decimal as a percentage.
(a) 0.8 **(b)** 0.41 **(c)** 0.97
(d) 0.06 **(e)** 0.01

4 Write each of these decimals as a percentage.
(a) 0.1 **(b)** 0.134 **(c)** 0.025
(d) 0.796 **(e)** 0.0234 **(f)** 0.8175

Expressing percentages as decimals

Percentages are easily turned back to decimals.

Example 10

Write 45% as a decimal.

$45\% = \frac{45}{100} = 0.45$

Exercise 9I

1 Copy and complete the table.

%	Per cent fraction	Decimal
32	$\frac{32}{100}$	0.32
5	$\frac{5}{100}$	0.05
12	$\frac{12}{100}$	
8		
10		
16		
39		
64		

2 Look at the table you completed in Question 1.
(a) Compare the numbers in the first and third columns.
(b) How many places do the digits move?

3 Write each percentage as a decimal:
(a) 19% **(b)** 29% **(c)** 66%
(d) 3% **(e)** 2% **(f)** 79%
(g) 1%

4 Copy and complete the table.

Fraction	Decimal	%
$\frac{2}{5}$		
	0.8	
		70
$\frac{3}{4}$		
	0.65	
		85
$\frac{6}{25}$		
	0.06	
		4

5 Copy and complete the table.

Fraction	Decimal	%
$\frac{1}{8}$		
	0.375	
		62.5
$\frac{3}{16}$		
		43.75
$\frac{2}{3}$		
	0.1565	
$\frac{3}{7}$		

6 Look at the fractions $\frac{36}{40}$ and $\frac{51}{60}$.
(a) Can you tell quickly which is the larger fraction?
(b) Now express each fraction as a percentage. Which one is larger?
(c) Express each percentage as a decimal.

Technology

Review online what you have learnt. Visit
www.mathsisfun.com/numbers
Then have a go at the conversion game at
www.nrich.maths.org
Can you score 400?

9.4 Finding percentages of amounts

Percentages are often used in everyday transactions. For example,

Discount	5%
Tax	15%

In each case you have to find the percentage of an amount to find the discount or the tax.

Example 11

Find 75% of 20 oranges.

$75\% \text{ of } 20 = \frac{75}{100} \text{ of } 20$
$= \frac{75}{100} \times 20$
$= \frac{3}{4} \times 20$
$= 3 \times \frac{1}{4} \times 20 = 3 \times 5 = 15$

So 75% of 20 oranges is 15 oranges.

Example 12

A 10% cash discount is given on a table priced at $1450.
How much is the discount?

$\text{Discount} = 10\% \text{ of } \$1450$
$= \frac{10}{100} \times \$1450$
$= \frac{1}{10} \times \$1450$
$= \$145$

Exercise 9J

Work out:

1 (a) 15% of 100 soldiers
(b) 15% of 60 sailors
(c) 20% of $35
(d) 35% of 80 eggs
(e) 50% of 120 tigers
(f) 50% of 72 mangoes
(g) 60% of 40 flying fish
(h) 70% of 50 flamingos.

2 Find these percentages:
(a) 50% of $50 (b) 50% of $64
(c) 25% of $64 (d) 75% of $64
(e) 100% of $64 (f) 100% of $40
(g) 50% of $40 (h) 75% of $32

3 There are 25 children in class 2A and 20% wear glasses.
How many wear glasses?

4 There are 60 members of the All Stars club. 50% prefer cricket, 30% football and the rest basketball. How many prefer each game?

5

(a) Find the cash discount for the
(i) blender (ii) stove.
(b) How much would a cash costumer pay for the
(i) blender (ii) stove?

6 Of 80 drivers stopped by police 20% did not have licenses, 30% had defective lights and 5% failed to observe a stop sign. Calculate the number of drivers who committed each offence.

7 The gas tank of a truck holds 8 gallons when it is 40% full. How much does the tank hold when it is full?

9.5 Buying and selling

The profit made when selling something can be written as a percentage. This percentage is called the **percentage profit**.

Example 13

Jim bought a motorbike for $800 and sold it for $1120. Find his percentage profit.

Actual profit = $1120 − $800
= $320

Profit as a fraction of cost price

$= \frac{320}{800} = \frac{40}{100}$

Profit as a percentage = 40%

In general

$$\textbf{Percentage profit} = \frac{\textbf{selling price} - \textbf{cost price}}{\textbf{cost price}} \times 100\,\%$$

Exercise 9K

1 Copy and complete the table.

Item	Cost price	Selling price	Profit	Percentage profit
Shoes	$80	$100		
Table	$600	$750		
Stove	$750	$1000		
Glass	$5	$6		
Mat	$3	$6		
Dish	$7.50	$10		

2 

Jim's friend Tom bought an old van. It cost him $8000. What percentage profit would he make if he sold it again for:

(a) $8800 **(b)** $9600 **(c)** $10 000

3 Sugar can be bought wholesale for $3.60 per kilogram. What is the percentage profit if it is sold for

(a) $4.05 per kg **(b)** $4.50 per kg?

4 Jones Johnson bought a new car for $80 000. He sold it three years later for $20 000.

(a) What was Jones' loss?

(b) Write this loss as a fraction of the cost price.

(c) What was his percentage loss?

5 Alison Abraham bought a refrigerator for $2500. What was her percentage loss if she sold it for:

(a) $2000 **(b)** $1500 **(c)** $2150?

6 Bert bought some furniture for $600 and sold it for $720.

(a) Express his profit as a percentage of the cost price.

(b) Express it as a percentage of the selling price.

(c) Explain why these two answers are different.

7 Would you prefer to make a profit that was 10% of the cost price or 10% of the selling price? Why?

8 Make up a flow chart that shows how to express profit as a percentage of the selling price.

Calculating selling prices

If you know the cost of an item and the percentage profit made by selling it, you can find its selling price.

Example 14

A craftsman makes a chair for \$80 and sells it to make a 20% profit on its cost price. What is his selling price?

$$\begin{aligned}\text{Profit made} &= 20\% \text{ of } \$80\\ &= \tfrac{20}{100} \times \$80\\ &= \tfrac{1}{5} \times \$80\\ &= \$16\end{aligned}$$

$$\begin{aligned}\text{Selling price} &= \text{cost price} + \text{profit}\\ &= \$80 + \$16\\ &= \$96\end{aligned}$$

In general

Selling price = cost price + profit

Exercise 9L

1 Using the method shown in Example 14, copy and complete the table.

Item	Cost price	Profit as % of cost price	Selling price
Iron	\$70	25%	
Chair	\$240	15%	
Mug	\$3.60	10%	
Vase	\$48	8%	
Radio	\$220	9%	

2 

Jason sells his hi-fi for a 20% profit. If he bought it for \$290, what did he sell it for?

3 What is the selling price of a television made for \$1000 and sold at a 25% profit?

4 Workers in a glove factory earn \$150 a week. The management offers them an increase of 10%.
(a) How much would the workers earn if they accepted the management offer?
(b) The workers want an increase of 15%. How much would that give them?

5 A restaurant adds a service charge of 8% on to every bill. What is the total bill if a meal costs:
(a) \$40 (b) \$65 (c) \$9.50

6 Mr Samuel sells his car at a 30% loss. What is his selling price if he bought it for \$30 000?

7 Beverly buys six marbles for 60 cents. She sells them to her friend for a 20% loss.
(a) For how much did she buy each marble?
(b) How much did she lose on each marble she sold?
(c) What did she sell each marble for?

8 

Davina buys a goat for \$75. What is her selling price for the goat if she sells it for:
(a) a loss of 20% (b) a loss of 15%?

9 A car bought for \$50 000 depreciates in value by 20% each year.
(a) What is its value after one year?
(b) What is its value after two years?

10 (a) Find the value of the car in Question 9 after 5 years.
(b) What would be its value after 5 years if the depreciation rate was only 10%?

11 Under a new wage agreement workers of the Technical Services Union will receive a 5% pay rise immediately, a further 4% in one year and a further 3% in two years.
Davidson currently gets \$280 per week.
What will his weekly wage be
(a) immediately after the rise
(b) in two years' time?

Discounts and sales

The amount that you subtract from a bill is called the **discount**.

A discount is usually a percentage of your total bill.

Example 15

A television marked at $1400 is sold at a 15% discount. What is the discount price?

Discount = 15% of $1400

$= \frac{15}{\cancel{100}_1} \times \$\overset{14}{\cancel{1400}}$

= $210

Discount price = cost price − discount

= $1400 − $210

= $1190

Exercise 9M

1 Find the discounted prices of the items shown below.

(a)

(b)

(c)

(d)

(e)

2 What would be the selling prices of the items in Question 1 if the discount was 30%?

3 The sign in Samuel's paint shop reads:

Mr Singh bought some paint and paint brushes in Samuel's shop.
Here is the bill he got.

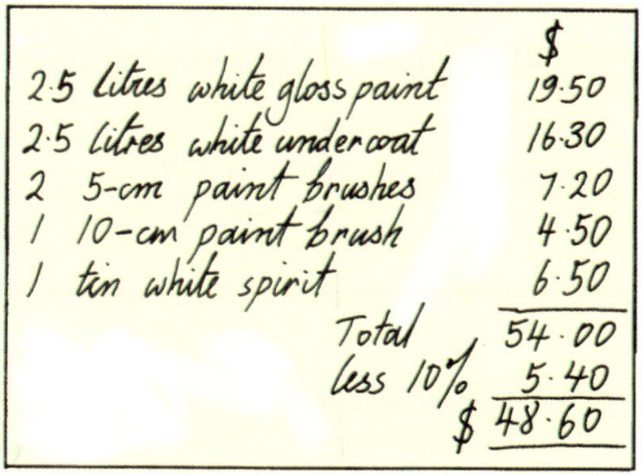

	$
2.5 litres white gloss paint	19.50
2.5 litres white undercoat	16.30
2 5-cm paint brushes	7.20
1 10-cm paint brush	4.50
1 tin white spirit	6.50
Total	54.00
less 10%	5.40
	$ 48.60

(a) What does *less 10%* mean?
(b) Has Samuel calculated the 10% properly?
(c) How much does Mr Singh pay for his brushes and paint?

4 How much would you have to pay at Samuel's paint shop, in Question 3, if your bill total was:
(a) $205 **(b)** $84.15 **(c)** $196.84
(d) $923 **(e)** $303.50 **(f)** $416.03

5 Find how much you would have to pay on a bill of $65 if a discount was given of either:
(a) 7% or **(b)** 9%

6 Here is a bill sent out by the Cool & Casual Clothing Company, to Jane's Shop in Ganges Street.

(a) Copy and complete the bill.

THE COOL & CASUAL CLOTHING CO.

To: Mrs J Akin
Address: 401 Ganges St, Georgetown
Date: 20th January 2010

No.	Article	Price each	Cost
12	Lady's dress	$165.00	$1980.00
10	Evening dress	$315.00	$3150.00
24	Lady's blouse	$115.25	
10	Slacks	$123.75	
		Total	

Note: Customers are reminded that a discount of 10% is allowed for payment within 15 days of the above date.

(b) By what date must Mrs Akin pay this bill, in order to get a discount?
(c) After discount, how much will she have to pay?
(d) Why do you think some companies offer discount if you pay your bill quickly?

7 Copy and complete these bills.

(a)

TIME-OUT FASHIONS

Stock No.	Description	Value
191	1 pants suit	$82.50
167	1 evening dress	$125.00
83	1 swim suit	$37.50
	Total	
	Less 5%	
	Amount due	

(b)

GENUINE AUTO-PARTS LTD.

1 Tyre $150.00
12% discount .... ______
Amount now due .... ______

8 Johnson's sells floor tiles as follows:

13″ × 13″ tiles	$4.95
8″ × 8″ tiles	$1.95

(a) Make a bill for Lambert Peters who buys 220 13″ × 13″ tiles and 60 8″ × 8″ tiles.
(b) Complete the bill if Johnson's gives a 10% discount on all purchases over $200.
(c) How much money should Peters pay if government sales tax is 3%?

Sales

Here is a shop window on Main Avenue. There is a **sale** going on in the shop. This means the shopkeeper is offering a discount on the usual prices.

Exercise 9N

1 Why do shopkeepers have sales? Try to think of three reasons.

2 (a) What is the meaning of *big reductions*?
(b) What is the meaning of *bargains*?

3 Look again at the shop window. A 10% reduction is given on all marked prices. Find the sale prices of all the items in the window.

4 What would be the sale prices of the items in the shop window if the discount given was 30%?

5 Gordon has a man's clothing shop. In his sale, he gives a discount of 22% on all selling prices. Copy and complete the table below, for things on sale in Gordon's shop.

Item	Usual price	Sale price
Shirt jac	\$46.50	
Vest	\$19.00	
Trousers	\$54.00	
Pairs of socks	\$12.50	
Belt	\$14.50	

If the cost price and the sale price are given, you can work out the percentage discount.

- To convert a fraction to a percentage, you multiply the fraction by 100%.

Example 16

Find the percentage discount on the dress shown.

Discount = \$120 – \$80
= \$40

Discount as fraction of cost price

$= \frac{14}{120} = \frac{1}{3}$

Percentage discount $= \frac{1}{3} \times 100\%$
$= 33\frac{1}{3}\%$

Exercise 9O

1 Calculate the percentage discount on these items.

(a)

(b)

(c)

(d)

(e)

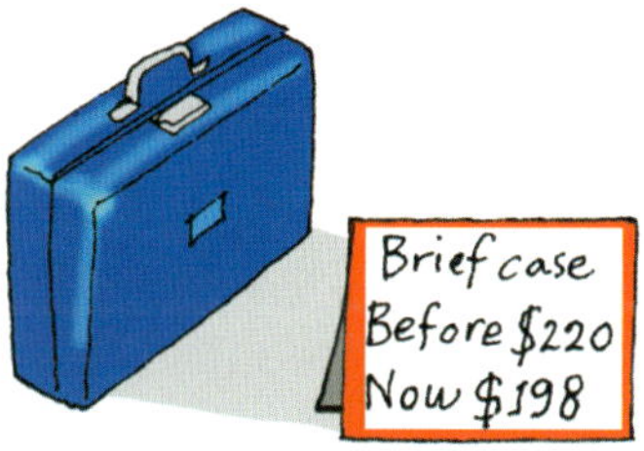

2 Which is the better buy
9 CDs for \$531.00 or
12 CDs for \$768.00 with a 10% discount?

3 An insect spray is sold in 600 ml and 450 ml containers. The 600 ml container costs \$19.50 and has a 10% cash discount. The 450 ml container sells for \$13.22. Which is the better buy? Why?

4 Rampasand's take away offers a 10% discount for senior citizens. If a senior citizen paid \$59.40 for a meal, what would he have paid if there was no discount?

9.6 Loans and deposits

Loans

Andy Paul wants to borrow \$200 from his bank. He has to pay back, though, more than he borrows. The extra money is the fee or **interest** charged for the loan.

The interest is usually a percentage of the loan.

Example 17

Andy borrows $200 from the bank. If the interest is 15% per year, how much interest will he owe at the end of one year?

Loan = $200

Interest = 15% of $200

$= \frac{15}{100} \times \$200$

= $30

So Andy will owe $30 interest.
Altogether he will owe $230.

Exercise 9P

1 How much interest would Andy have to pay at the end of the year, if the interest on his loan of $200 was:
(a) 10% per year **(b)** 20% per year
(c) 7% per year?

2 In Question 1 how much money must be paid back altogether to the bank?

3 If the interest charged is 15% per year, how much interest will Andy pay on year long loans of:
(a) $100 **(b)** $500 **(c)** $5000?

4 Beryl wants to buy a washing machine for $2500. Her bank charges 12% interest on loans. How much will her washing machine cost her if she pays the bank back after one year?

5 Alan needs $8000 to buy a piece of land. If the bank's interest rate is 10%, find the interest payable on his loan
(a) after one year
(b) after two years
(c) after five years.

6 Find the interest on the following loans:
(a) $200 for 4 years at 15% per year.
(b) $500 for 4 years at 15% per year.
(c) $1000 for 2 years at 15% per year.
(d) $3000 for 2 years at 12% per year.
(e) $4500 for 3 years at 9% per year.

7 The interest rate at Scrooge's Bank is 2% per year. George has $1000. How long will he have to keep his money in the bank before he gets $200 in interest?

Investigation

(a) What does a bank do with the extra money it receives as interest on loans?
(b) Who can get loans from a bank? What are the conditions?
Go to a bank or credit union and find out.

Putting money in the bank

Andy's brother Griffin has saved $200. He puts his money in a savings account at his bank. This time Griffin loans the bank $200. Now the bank has to pay Griffin interest on his loan.

To **deposit** money just means to put it in your account at the bank.

The fee that banks pay you when you lend money to them is also called **interest**.

Exercise 9Q

1 How much interest will the bank pay Griffin if he deposits $200 and the interest is:
(a) 3% per year (b) 4% per year
(c) 5% per year?

2 The interest rate at the People's Bank is 4%. How much will Celia have in the bank after one year if she deposits
(a) $50 (b) $200 (c) $250
(d) $500 (e) $10 000 (f) $50 000?

3 Credance Credit Union offers a 5% interest rate on deposits. What interest will be given on a deposit of $400 after
(a) one year
(b) two years
(c) five years?

4 Mr Munroe put $6000 in his bank. He withdraws it all four years later. How much does he withdraw if the interest is 4% per year?

5 (a) Write down two reasons why people save money in banks.
(b) Try to find out how banks use the money that people deposit.

6 Debbie puts $500 in the First Street Bank. Four years later her money is worth $600.
(a) What interest did the bank pay her each year?
(b) What was the bank's interest rate?

Investigation

Find the interest rates on deposits and loans in banks near where you live.
Are they all the same?
Which, do you think, is the best bank?
Explain why.
Discuss your answer with your friends.

Exercise 9R – mixed questions

1 Part of James Khan's annual school report is shown; it was sent to his parents last July. It shows his marks in the tests at the end of each term.

SCHOOL REPORT
NAME: James Khan

Subject	Marks		
	1st. term	2nd. term	3rd. term
English	$\frac{135}{150}$	$\frac{43}{50}$	$\frac{70}{100}$
Spanish	$\frac{38}{40}$	$\frac{89}{100}$	$\frac{166}{200}$
Integrated Science	$\frac{68}{100}$	$\frac{72}{100}$	$\frac{47}{50}$
History	$\frac{108}{150}$	$\frac{96}{120}$	$\frac{84}{100}$

Each mark is shown as a fraction of the full marks for the subject.
(a) Can you tell quickly whether James's History marks improved over the year?
(b) Can you tell quickly which of the subjects he got the highest mark in, during the first term?
(c) Do you think this is a good way to show the marks? Why?

2 Copy the report in Question 1, but this time show all the marks as percentages.

3 Look at the report you completed in Question 2.
(a) Did James's History marks improve over the year?
(b) In the first term, which of his marks was highest?
(c) In which subject and which term did he get his highest mark?

4 Could you answer the parts of Question 3 quickly? Do you think percentages are a good way to show test marks? Why?

5 This notice is displayed in Mr Mulling's shop in Abaco Street.

SALE OF DRESSES!!!
10% off the marked price

Attracted by the notice, Melinda chooses a dress in the shop. The price marked on it is $20.

(a) What does 'off' mean in the notice?
(b) What is 10% of $20?
(c) How much will be taken off the price?
(d) What will Melinda have to pay?

6 Copy and complete the table of sale items in Mr Mulling's shop.

Marked price	10% of marked price	Sale price
$50	$5	$45
$80	$8	$72
$20	$2	
$250		
$180		
$30		
$10		

7 This notice appeared in the Yellow Elder clothing factory where Janice works.

Notice

From April 1st., all wages will be increased by 5%

Janice earns $240 a week for her job there.

(a) What is 5% of $240?
(b) What will be her new wage per week, from 1st April?

8

Civil servants get 7% wage hike

(a) What would be the new monthly salary of these civil servants:
(i) a clerk who earns $900 per month,
(ii) a teacher who earns $2500 each month,
(iii) a permanent secretary who earns $8000 per month?

(b) Who got the biggest dollar increase?

9

A tin of beans normally weighs 450 g.
A new tin holds 20% more.

(a) What is the weight of the new tin?
(b) What should be the price of the new tin if the original tin of beans sold for $4.80?

10 **(a)** What is the cost of a refrigerator priced at $2000 if a sales tax of 3% is charged?
(b) How much would the price rise if the government increased sales tax to 5%?

11 At the Vacation Inn the rates are advertised as:

Double room $150
Single room $120

(a) What would be the bill for Alan St Ville who stays one night only and there is a 10% government room charge and a 5% service charge?
(b) What would be the bill for Mr & Mrs Trotman if they stay for 3 nights and the same charges apply?

12 The value of a car depreciates by 10% each year. James Burton buys a new car for $50 000. What will the value of the car be after:

(a) one year
(b) two years
(c) three years?

9 Consolidation

Example 1

Which is the best buy?

12 oranges for \$7.20
or 8 oranges for \$5.20?

In first case 1 orange costs $\$7.20 \div 12 = \$0.60$
In second case 1 orange costs $\$5.20 \div 8 = \$0.65$
So 12 oranges for \$7.20 is the best buy.

Example 2

Write:

(a) $\frac{3}{8}$ as a percentage
(b) 0.75 as percentage
(c) 65% as a fraction

(a) $\frac{3}{8} = \frac{3}{8} \times 100\% = \frac{300}{8}\%$
$= 37.5\%$

(b) $0.75 = 0.75 \times 100\%$
$= 75\%$

(c) $65\% = \frac{65}{100} = \frac{13}{20}$

Example 3

Find:

(a) 5% of \$40 **(b)** 15% of \$8

(a) $5\% \text{ of } \$40 = \frac{5}{10\not{0}} \times 4\not{0}$
$= \frac{20}{10}$
$= \$2$

(b) $15\% \text{ of } \$8 = \frac{\not{15}^{3}}{\not{100}_{20}} \times 8$
$= \frac{24}{20}$
$= \frac{12}{10}$
$= \$1.20$

Example 4

A new 'Sizzler' CD costs \$70.
If it is sold for an 8% discount, what is its sale price?

Discount = 8% of \$70
$= \frac{8}{100} \times 70$
$= \frac{56}{10}$
$= \$5.60$

Sale price = list price − discount
$= \$70 - \$5.60$
$= \$64.40$

Example 5

What is the interest on a deposit of \$5000 which remains in a bank for 3 years at an interest rate of 4%?

Interest after 1 year = 4% of \$5000
$= \frac{4}{100} \times \$5000 = \$200$

Interest after 3 years $= \$200 \times 3 = \$600$

Exercise 9

1 In each case, identify the better buy and give reasons for your answer.
(a) 60 apples for \$96.60
or 110 apples for \$178.20
(b) 750 g of soap powder for \$24.00
or 1 kg of soap powder for \$31.00

2 Copy and complete the table.

Percentage	Fraction	Decimal
38%		
	$\frac{4}{5}$	
		0.02

3 Find:
(a) 10% of \$50 **(b)** 20% of \$10
(c) 50% of \$8 **(d)** 5% of \$60
(e) 15% of \$80 **(f)** 1% of \$50
(g) 3% of \$50 **(h)** 8% of \$25

4 Copy and complete the table.

Item	Cost price	% profit	Sale price
Iron	\$190	5	
TV	\$1350	8	
Camera	\$850		\$900
Calculator	\$125		\$160

Application 9

5 A government offers its teachers a 3% salary increase. What will be the new salary of a teacher who currently earns
(a) \$20 000 **(b)** \$34 000 **(c)** \$41 500?

6 The Peoples Store has a sale. Find the sale price of the items marked below.

(a)

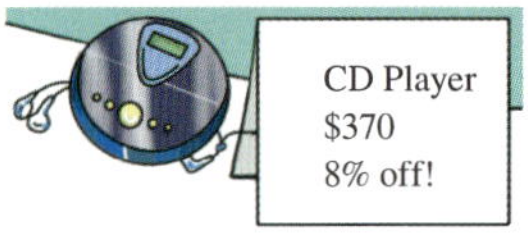

(b) What would be their actual sale price if a 15% value added tax (VAT) had to be added?

7 Stephenson borrows $12 000 from his Credit Union which has an interest rate of 9% on loans. If he intends to pay back the loan over 5 years, find:

(a) his total interest payment

(b) the total amount he has to repay

(c) how much he should pay back each month if he pays in equal installments.

Companion CD

Want some extra practice? Go to Chapter 9 on your companion CD for further exercises, animations, and solutions.

Summary

You should know ...

1 Profit = selling price – cost price

Radio cost price $96 Selling price $120

Profit = $120 – $96
= $24

2 Per cent means out of a hundred.

$\frac{25}{100}$ can be written as 25%

Check out

1 Find the profit or loss.

(a) Car bought for $75 000 sold for $50 000.

(b) 12 bags of sugar bought for $95 each, sold together for $1200.

2 **(a)** David got 85 out of 100 in a test. What is this as a percentage?

(b) 90% of the class were present for their exam. What percentage were absent?

3 How to write percentages as fractions or decimals.

$36\% = \frac{36}{100} = 0.36$

$\frac{3}{5} = \frac{3}{5} \times 100\% = 60\% = 0.6$

3 Copy and complete.

Fraction	Decimal	Percentage
$\frac{4}{5}$		
	0.45	
		70%
$\frac{5}{8}$		

4 How to find a percentage of an amount.

15% of 80 oranges

$= \frac{15}{100} \times 80$

$= \frac{3}{20} \times 80$

$= 3 \times \frac{1}{20} \times 80$

$= 3 \times 4$

$= 12$ oranges

4 **(a)** Find:

(i) 10% of \$600

(ii) 15% of \$20

(b) A radio marked \$95 is reduced by 20% in a sale.

(i) How much was taken off the price?

(ii) What was the sale price?

5 How to find the cost price or selling price if you know the % profit or % loss.

For example:

A salesman buys a watch for \$60 and sells it for a 25% profit. What is his selling price?

Profit $= 25\%$ of \$60

$= \frac{25}{100} \times \$60$

$= \frac{1}{4} \times \$60$

$= \$15$

Selling price = cost price + profit

$= \$60 + \$15$

$= \$75$

5 Copy and complete.

Item	Cost price	Percentage profit	Selling price
Stove	\$1500	10	
Computer	\$6000	15	
Clock	\$75	5	

6 Discount is the amount you subtract from a bill.

Discount on iron $= 20\%$ of \$105

$= \frac{20}{100} \times £105 = \frac{\$210}{10} = \$21$

Sale price = marked price − discount

= \$105 − \$21

= \$84

6 **(a)** A store gives 5% discount on items. What is the cost of a dining set marked at \$1250?

(b) What would be the price of the dining set if a 3% sales tax was then added?

Representing information 10

Objectives

- ✔ learn ways to collect and record data
- ✔ represent data in the form of pictures and charts
- ✔ choose and use scales in your charts
- ✔ interpret charts and graphs
- ✔ summarise data using averages

What's the point?

What is your favourite TV programme? Which foods do you prefer? Which soap powder washes whitest? To answer such questions advertisers and market researchers carry out surveys. To illustrate their results they use graphs and charts.

Before you start

You should know ...

1 How to read information from a table.

Country	Dominica	Grenada	St Lucia	St Kitts
Male lifespan (years)	75	69	67	64
Female lifespan (years)	81	74	74	70

The life span of a St Lucia woman is 74 years.

2 How to find fractions of an amount.

For example:

$\frac{2}{3}$ of 15 = $2 \times \frac{1}{3}$ of 15 = $2 \times 5 = 10$

3 How to plot points on a grid.

For example, you plot the points (0, 2), (1, 3) and (2, 4) and join them up like this:

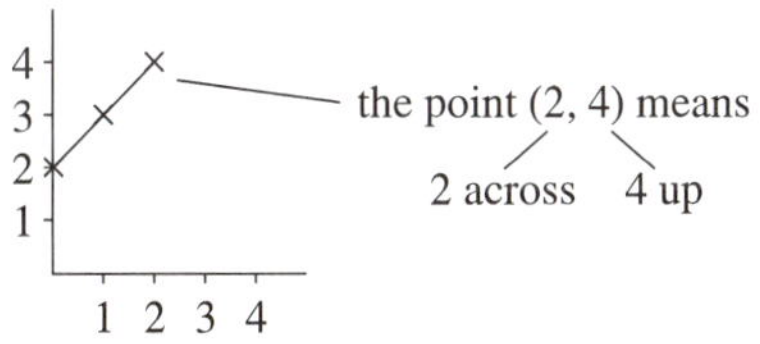

Check in

1 **(a)** What is the lifespan of a Dominican man?

(b) How much longer do Grenadan women live than Grenadan men?

(c) People from which country live longest?

2 Find:

(a) $\frac{1}{4}$ of 12 **(b)** $\frac{2}{3}$ of 12

(c) $\frac{3}{5}$ of 60 **(d)** $\frac{4}{7}$ of 56

3 **(a)** Plot these points on a grid and join them up:

(1, 0) (1, 2) (3, 1) (1, 0)

(b) What shape have you drawn?

10.1 Collecting data

You wish to find out from your classmates which of these traditional Caribbean dishes is their favourite:

Chicken & rice & peas
Curried goat & plain rice
Ackee & cod fish with boiled bananas
Flying fish & cou-cou

How would you obtain the information?

You could:

- ask each classmate individually
- pass around a sheet with the dishes listed and ask each classmate to tick one of them
- ask for a show of hands.

Whichever method is used, data or information is being collected.

There are two basic types of data:

- **discrete** and
- **continuous**.

Discrete data can only take on definite values.
For example:

shoe sizes – size 1, size 2 etc.
gender – male, female
colour – red, yellow, blue etc

Continuous data can take on any numerical value.
For example:

your height
your weight

In this section we will mainly look at ways of showing discrete data.

A useful way of collecting and recording discrete data is to keep a tally.

Look at this frequency table:

Item	Tally	Frequency
Chicken	||||	4
Curried goat	𝍸 ||	7
Ackee	𝍸 𝍸 𝍸 |	16
Flying fish	𝍸 𝍸 |||	13

𝍸 represents 5 classmates.

The frequency column gives the total of the tally marks.

Example 1

Represent the following numbers using tally marks.

(a) 2 **(b)** 9 **(c)** 15 **(d)** 23

(a) 2 — ||
(b) 9 — 𝍸 ||||
(c) 15 — 𝍸 𝍸 𝍸
(d) 23 — 𝍸 𝍸 𝍸 𝍸 |||

Exercise 10A

1 Identify which of these are discrete and which are continuous.
(a) your age
(b) your eye colour
(c) your last test score
(d) the distance around your waist
(e) your favourite drink
(f) the time it takes you to bathe

2 State the numbers represented by each of the following tallies.
(a) |||
(b) 𝍸 𝍸 𝍸 ||||
(c) 𝍸 𝍸
(d) 𝍸 𝍸 𝍸 𝍸 𝍸 𝍸 ||

3 The heights of a group of children are measured in cm.

139	138	142	136	142
142	136	138	139	141
142	136	136	139	143
136	143	138	141	142
141	142	142	138	142
138	142	141	136	139

Copy and complete the frequency table:

Height (cm)	Tally marks	Frequency
136	𝍸 |	6
138		
139		
141		
142		
143	||	2

4 Find out the number of students who were absent from your class each day last week.
Use tally marks to represent the information in a frequency table.

5 Collect information from your classmates about their favourite game out of:
football, cricket, baseball, basketball and hockey.
Record the information in a frequency table.

6 Go to any place where traffic passes. Use tallies to record the number of each type of vehicle

(car, truck, bus, bicycle, taxi, motorbike)

that passes by during 30 minutes.
Record the information in a frequency table.

Investigation

1 Toss a coin 100 times.
Record the number of times it lands either on heads or on tails.
What do you notice?
Compare your results with your friends.

2 Throw a dice 100 times.
Record the number of times each digit appears.
What do you notice?
Compare your results with your friends.

10.2 Pictographs

When people collect information, they try to show it in a way that everyone will easily understand.

Activity

You will need plasticine or crayons or coloured pencils.

The table shows the students absent in David's class at Portsmouth Secondary School last week.

Day	Mon	Tue	Wed	Thur	Fri
Number absent	2	3	5	1	7

On what day were most students absent?
The chart that follows shows some of the information from the table.

(a) On a sheet of paper make a larger copy of the chart below.
If you have plasticine use the plasticine to make the little figures. Stick them on your sheet. If you have no plasticine, draw the figures with coloured pencils or crayons.

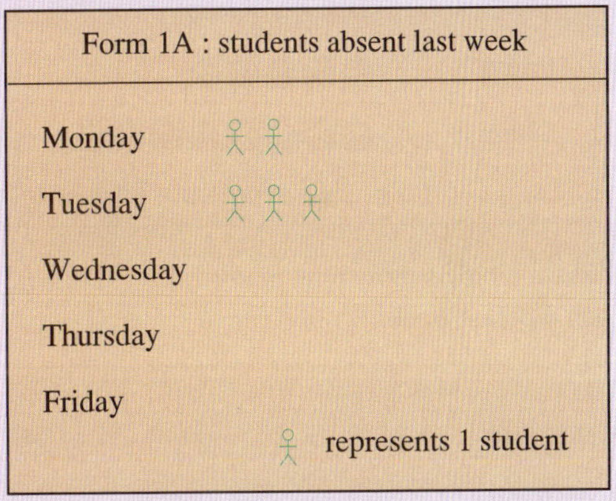

(b) Complete the chart to show the rest of the numbers from the table.

The chart you just made is called a **pictograph**.

- A pictograph uses pictures or drawings to represent discrete data.

Exercise 10B

1 Represent the information from the tables in Questions 3 and 4 of Exercise 10A on a pictograph.

2 The table shows the favourite sports of the students in Form 1B of Portsmouth Secondary School.

Netball	Football	Cricket	Volley-ball
13	10	19	9

Show the information on a pictograph.

Example 2

Make a table to show how many cakes were sold each day last week.

Days	Mon	Tues	Wed	Thur	Fri	Sat
Cakes sold	35	7	28	42	35	56

A drawing of 1 cake represents 7 cakes.
A scale of 1 to 7 has been used.

- A **scale** tells you the number of items each symbol represents.

Every pictograph must have a scale.

Exercise 10C

1 The pictograph shows how the students in Form 1A of Portsmouth Secondary School travel to school every day. The pictograph is not complete because it does not say what each 웃 represents.

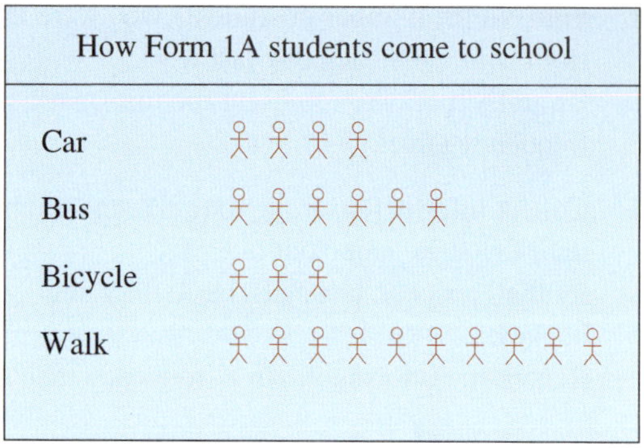

(a) 20 students in Form 1A travel by car every day. What scale has been used in the pictograph?

(b) What should be written at the bottom?

(c) Write down the number of students that walk to school, cycle to school, and go to school by bus every day.

2 The pictograph shows the pets kept by the students of Form 2 at the Little Valley School.

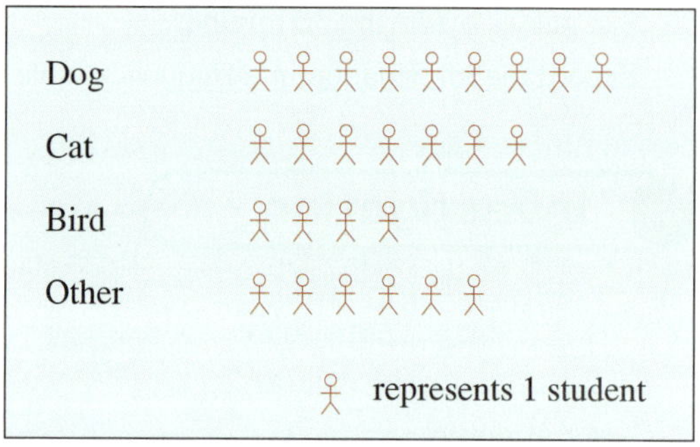

(a) How many students kept a cat as a pet?

(b) How many students were in the survey?

(c) What fraction of the students kept a bird as a pet?

3 The activities chosen by Form 3 students are shown in the pictograph.

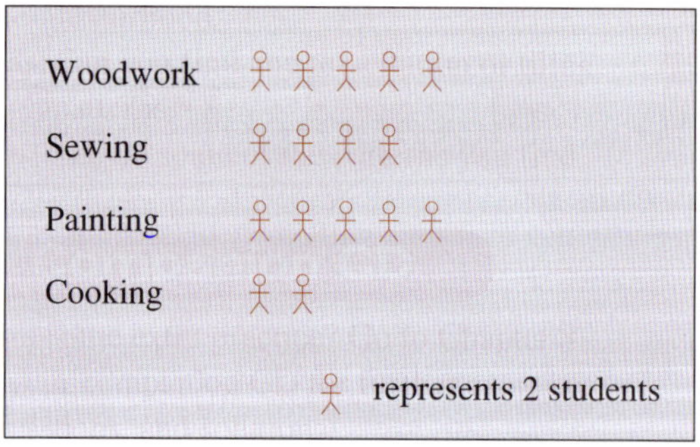

(a) How many students chose painting?

(b) Which was the least popular activity?

(c) How many students were surveyed?

4 The favourite subject of some students is represented in the pictograph:

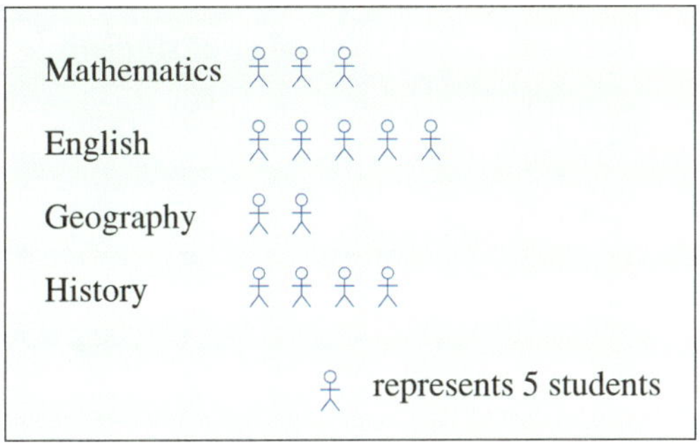

(a) How many students like History the most?
(b) Which is the most popular subject?
(c) Which is the least popular?
(d) How many students were surveyed?

5 Here are the numbers of students in the first two years of Tranquillity School.

Form	1A	1B	1C	2A	2B	2C
Number of students	40	35	45	45	40	40

(a) How many students could a  represent?
(b) Make a pictograph for the table.

6 In a basketball tournament for a special trophy, the scores were:

Eagles	44 goals
Ravens	32 goals
Guynettes	56 goals
Surinayas	48 goals
G.D.F.	52 goals

(a) What object could you use to represent goals in the pictograph?
(b) What scale could you use?
(c) Draw a pictograph to show the scores.

7 Find out the population of each of the following Caribbean territories. Draw a pictograph to show the information.

Trinidad and Tobago	Jamaica
Guyana	Barbados
Grenada	St Lucia

What scale did you use?

8 Tim Bembo is a fisherman. His weekly catch, over six weeks, is shown.

Week	1st	2nd	3rd	4th	5th	6th
Kilograms (kg) of fish caught	150	140	130	110	150	130

(a) What symbol would you use to represent his catch?
(b) Draw a pictograph to show the information.
(c) Can you think of another way you could show the information?

10.3 Bar graphs

Sometimes it takes a lot of time to draw the pictures for a pictograph. A **bar graph** is quicker to draw.
In a bar graph, a small square is used to represent the object, instead of a picture. Bar graphs are sometimes called **bar charts** or **block graphs**.

Activity

You will need squared paper, coloured pencils or crayons, scissors and gum.
Look again at the table in the Activity on page 201.

Day	Mon	Tue	Wed	Thurs	Fri
Number absent	2	3	5	1	7

The bar graph (started below) uses a square to represent each student in the table.

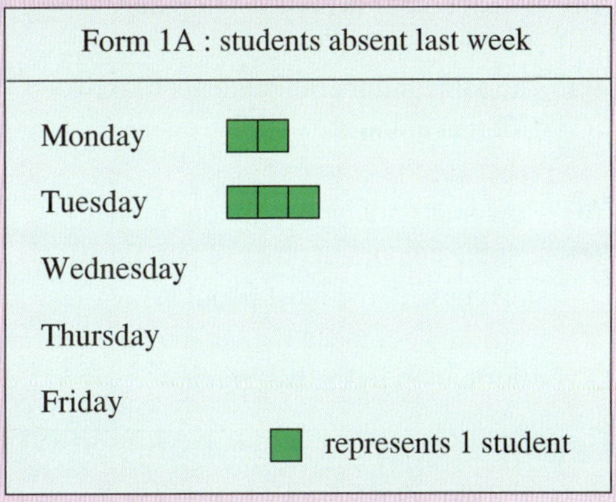

Copy the bar graph. Cut squares from squared paper and use coloured pencils or crayons to colour them. Stick them down on your bar graph to represent the students. Complete the bar graph for the rest of the table.

- A bar graph uses bars of different lengths to represent data.

Exercise 10D

1 The bar graph shows the favourite colours of the students in Form 1A.

Favourite colours of Form 1A

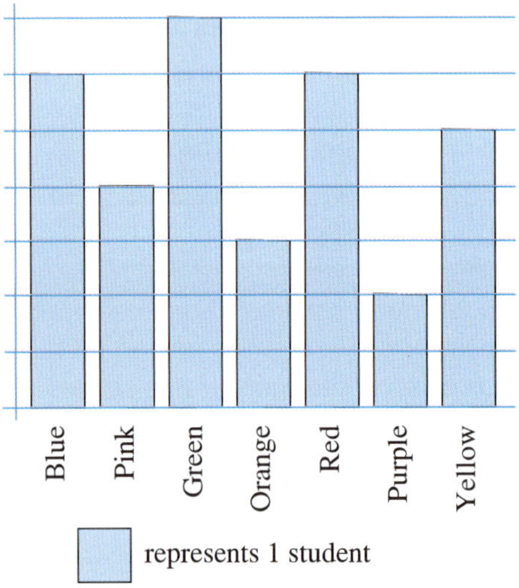

(a) Which colour is the most popular? How can you tell?
(b) Which colour is the least popular? How can you tell?
(c) The same number of students like two different colours. What are the colours?
(d) How many students were questioned?
(e) List the colours in order of popularity, starting with the most popular.
(f) Copy and complete the table below for the information in the bar graph.

Favourite colour	Blue	Pink	Green	Orange	Red		
Number of students							

2 The table shows the subjects that students in Form 1C like the least.

Subject	**Number of students**
English	6
Spanish	7
Maths	10
History	5
Geography	6
P.E.	5
Science	3

(a) On squared paper, draw a bar graph, like the one in Question 1, to show this information. Use a coloured pencil to shade the squares.
(b) Which subject is the most unpopular?

3 The bar graph shows the day of the week on which some students have their birthdays this year.

Some student's birthdays

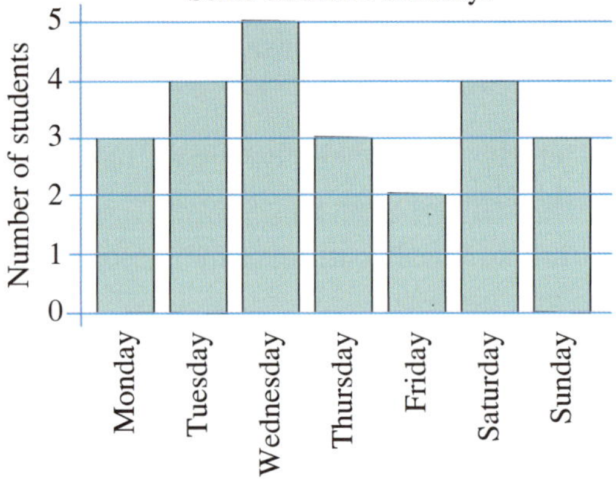

Use the bar graph to answer:
(a) How many students have birthdays on a Saturday this year?
(b) How many students have birthdays on a Sunday?
(c) On which day have most students got a birthday this year?
(d) Can you explain why there is no need to write what each square represents, at the bottom of this graph?

4 (a) Find out the birthday month of each of the students in your class. Fill in a table like this one.

Birthday month	Number of students
January	
February	
March	

(b) Which month is the most popular for your class?

(c) On the squared paper, make a larger copy of the bar graph started below, to show all the months of the year. On your copy, fill in the information from your table.

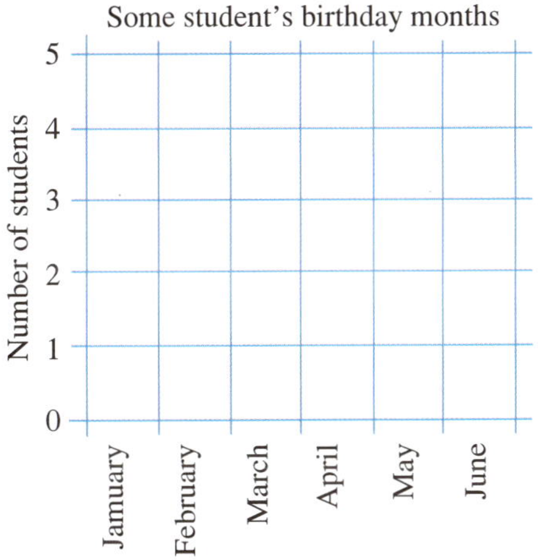

5 Form 3A were asked to choose their favourite radio programme out of:

Record Request, Meet the Stars, Story Time, Sport Special and Reggae Review.

The table below shows how they chose.

Favourite programme	Number of students
Record Request	7
Meet the Stars	5
Story Time	7
Sport Special	9
Reggae Review	8

(a) Which progamme was the most popular?

(b) Use squared paper to show the information in the table as a bar graph.

Example 3

The table shows how the Form 2 students in Radley High School come to school every day.

Means of transport	Number of students
Bus	70
Car	40
Bicycle	20
Walk	80

Draw a bar graph to show this information

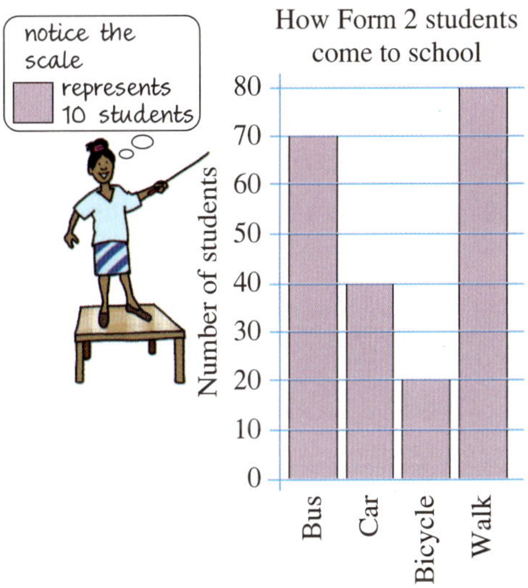

Each square represents 10 students.

Exercise 10E

1 The occupations of mothers of students at Little Rock School are shown in the table.

Occupation	Numbers of mothers
Teacher	70
Farmer	100
Office worker	120
Clerk	80
Housewife	90

What scale should you use to show the data on a bar graph?

2 The table shows the shoe sizes of the Form 1C students in Radley High School.

Shoe size	Number of students
1	6
$1\frac{1}{2}$	12
2	15
$2\frac{1}{2}$	6
3	3
$3\frac{1}{2}$	3

(a) How many students could you represent by each square in a bar graph?
(b) On squared paper, draw a bar graph to show the information in the table.
(c) What scale did you use in your bar graph for the number of students?

3 The table shows the favourite sports of the students of Form 2 in Radley High School.

Favourite Sport	Number of students
Rounders	35
Football	60
Netball	10
Cricket	50
Athletics	25
Basketball	30

(a) On squared paper draw a bar graph to show this information.
(b) What scale did you use in your bar graph for the number of students?
(c) Which sport is the most popular?

4 The bar graph shows the number of cakes sold in the Radley High School kitchen each day.

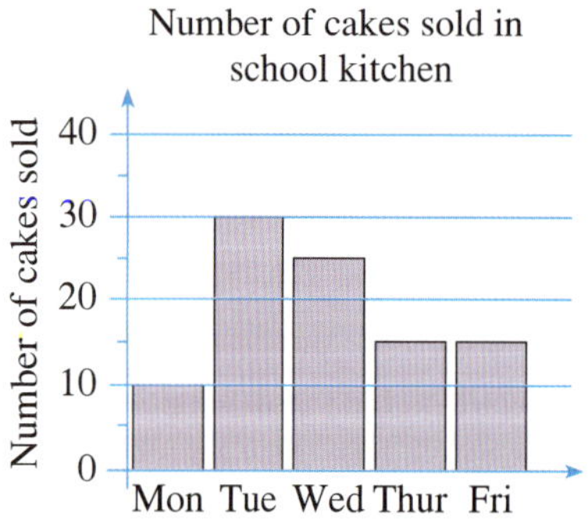

(a) How many cakes were sold on Monday?
(b) How many cakes were sold on Friday?
(c) How many cakes were sold during the week?
(d) If each cake costs 10 cents, how much money was taken in the week?

5 The bar graph shows the approximate population, in millions, of some Caribbean states.

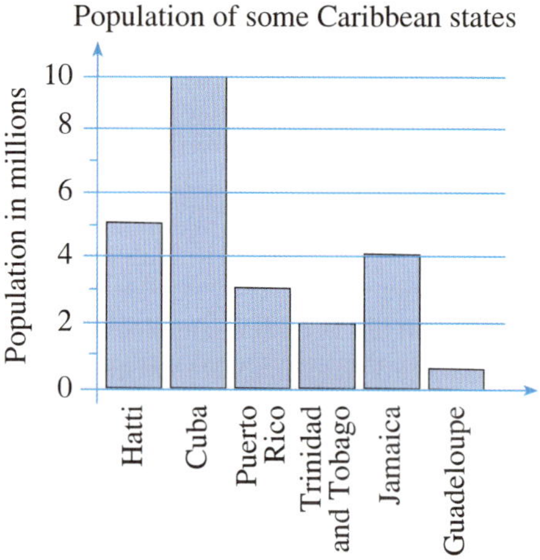

(a) What is the population of Haiti?
(b) What do you think is the population of Guadeloupe?

Technology

You can draw bar charts using Microsoft Word.

Use the data from Question 1 of Exercise 10E.

On the Word menu click on **Insert** then **Chart**.

On the pop-up spreadsheet type the data from Question 1.

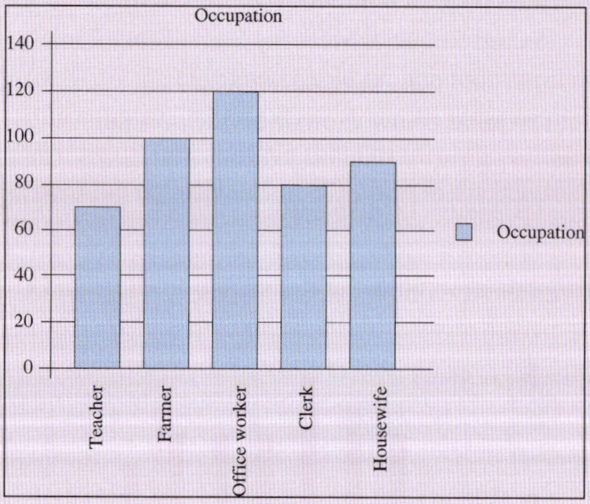

Repeat for other questions in Exercise 10E.

10.4 Pie charts

Another way of showing information is on a **pie chart**.

Example 4

The circle below is a pie chart. It shows how a boy spends $12 pocket money.

Work out how much he spends on each item and how much he saves.

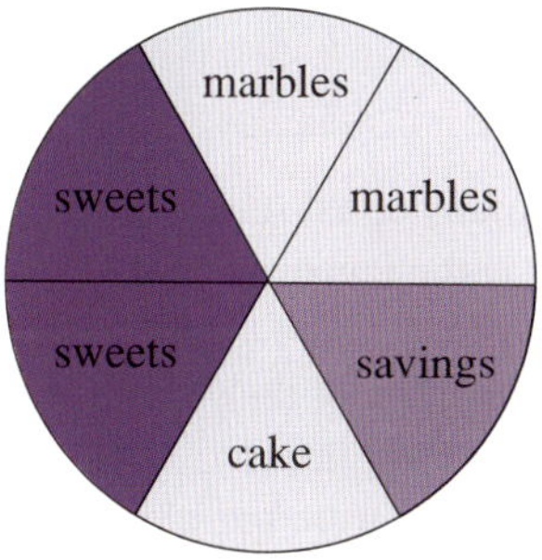

The circle represents the total amount of $12.
It is divided into six equal **sectors**.
So each sector is worth $\frac{1}{6}$ of $12 = $2.

He spends 2 × $2 = $4 on sweets.
He spends 2 × $2 = $4 on marbles.
He spends 1 × $2 = $2 on cake.
He saves $2.

- A pie chart uses a circle divided into sectors to represent discrete data.

Exercise 10F

1 This pie chart shows how a girl spends $16.

(a) How many sectors are in the pie chart?
(b) How much is each sector worth?
(c) Copy and complete the table.

Where money goes	Sweets	Savings	Books
Money spent ($)			

2 This pie chart shows how Susan spends her day.

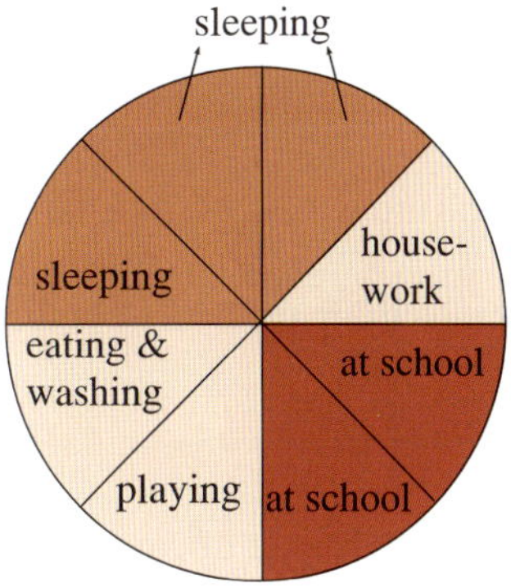

(a) How many equal sectors are in the pie chart?
(b) How many hours does each sector represent?
(c) Copy and complete:

Activity	Sleeping	House work	School	Eating + Washing	Playing
No. of hours					

3 (a) This pie chart shows how Mr Williams spends his weekly wage of $2000.

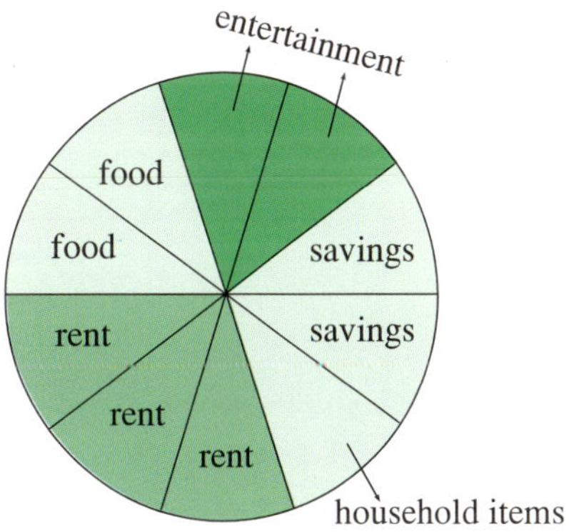

(i) How many sectors are in the pie chart?
(ii) How much is each sector worth?

(b) Copy and complete the table to show how Mr Williams spends his weekly wage of $2000.

Where money goes	Savings	Rent	Food	Household items	Entertainment
Money spent ($)					

(c) Draw a bar graph using the data from the table.

(d) Draw a pictograph using the data from the table.

Drawing pie charts

You will need a protractor and a pair of compasses.

Example 5

The table shows how 80 students travel to school.

Means of transport	Walk	Minibus	Car	Bicycle
Number of students	40	20	10	10

Draw a pie chart to show this information

Fraction of students walking $= \frac{40}{80} = \frac{4}{8} = \frac{1}{2}$

Fraction of students coming by minibus $= \frac{20}{80} = \frac{2}{8} = \frac{1}{4}$

Fraction of students coming by car $= \frac{10}{80} = \frac{1}{8}$

Fraction of students coming by bicycle $= \frac{10}{80} = \frac{1}{8}$

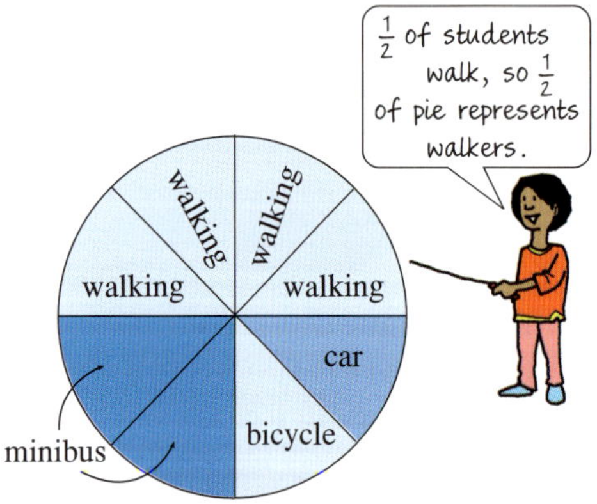

The whole circle represents the 80 students. Divide the circle into 8 equal sectors. Each sector represents $80 \div 8 = 10$ students.

Exercise 10G

1 The pie chart shows the favourite fruits of some students.

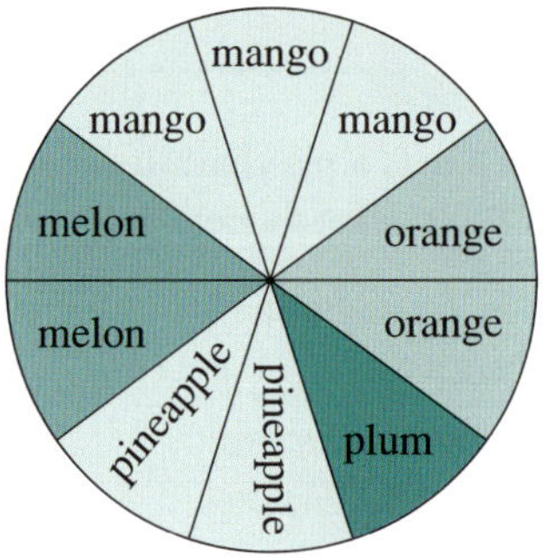

(a) How many equal sectors are in the pie chart?

(b) What is the favourite fruit?

(c) What fruit is liked least?

(d) What fraction of the students chose **(i)** mango **(ii)** plum?

150 students were questioned.

(e) How many students were represented by each sector?

(f) How many students preferred **(i)** pineapple **(ii)** melon **(iii)** orange?

2 The table shows the number of letters a school receives each day.

Day	Mon	Tues	Wed	Thur	Fri
Number of letters	5	10	15	5	5

(a) How many letters does the school receive during the week?

(b) What fraction of letters are received on **(i)** Monday **(ii)** Tuesday **(iii)** Wednesday?

(c) Into how many sectors should you divide a circle in order to draw a pie chart for the information in the table?

(d) How many letters will be represented by each sector?

(e) How many sectors will represent the number of letters received on Wednesday?

(f) Draw a pie chart to show this information.

3 The table shows the number of cars sold each year by Cheap motors.

Year	2005	2006	2007	2008	2009
Number of cars sold	100	200	200	300	400

(a) How many cars were sold between 2005 and 2009?
(b) What fraction of the cars were sold in **(i)** 2005 **(ii)** 2008 **(iii)** 2009?
(c) Into how many sectors should you divide the circle in order to draw a pie chart?
(d) How many cars will each sector represent?
(e) How many sectors will represent the number of cars sold in 2008?
(f) Draw a pie chart to show this information.

4 The table shows the favourite type of music in a class of 24 students.

Type of music	Reggae	Soul	Calypso	Cadance	Soca
Number of students	9	3	6	3	3

(a) Draw a pie chart to show the information in the table.
(b) Draw a bar chart to show the same information.
(c) Draw a pictograph to show the information.
(d) Which method of showing the information is the easiest to read? Why?

5 (a) Which method of showing data do you prefer? Explain why.
(b) When may it be better to use **(i)** a bar chart **(ii)** a pictograph **(iii)** a pie chart to show data?

10.5 Looking at averages

Instead of using pictures or charts to show data, it is often useful to describe the data with a single value. An **average** is a single value that describes a data set.

There are three types of average:

- **mean**
- **mode**
- **median**.

Which one to use depends on the circumstances.

The mean

This is what many people mean by the word average.

To find the mean of a data set add all the values and divide by the number of values.

For example, in the cricket series West Indies against England in the Caribbean in 2009, the batsman Ramnaresh Sarwan scored

107, 94, 106, 291, 14, 14

in six test innings.

$$\text{Sarwan's mean score} = \frac{\text{sum of scores}}{\text{number of scores}}$$
$$= \frac{107 + 94 + 106 + 291 + 14 + 14}{6}$$
$$= \frac{626}{6} = 104.3$$

Exercise 10H

1 Aldie rolled a die four times. His scores were
4, 1, 5, 2
What was his mean score?

2 Aaron picked six pea pods. The numbers of peas in the pods were
7, 8, 10, 5, 6, 6
(a) How many peas did he get altogether?
(b) What was the mean number of peas in the pods?

3 Brenda bought five packets of sweets. The numbers of sweets in each packet were
28, 32, 29, 31, 30
What is the mean number of sweets in a packet?

4

The Super Wood Match Company does a control check of its match boxes. The numbers of matches in eight boxes were found to be
48, 52, 52, 51, 49, 47, 53, 48

What is the mean number of matches per box?

Technology

Which West Indian batsmen would you choose for the next test match?
Go to

www.stats.cricinfo.com

Enter the names of your top West Indian batsmen, and find their last 10 test scores. Based on their averages (means) choose your batting line up!

The mode and median

The **mode** is the data value that occurs most often.

Example 6

In one morning ten pairs of shoes were sold at Better Fit Shoe Shop. The sizes were:

6, 7, 7, 5, 8, 9, 8, 9, 9, 5
What was the modal size?

2 size 5
1 size 6
2 size 7
2 size 8
3 size 9 were sold.

Size 9 is the most common. The modal size is 9.

The **median** is the middle value of a data set.

To find the median you need to put the data in order of size.

Example 7

Find the median of

(a) Test scores 3, 8, 4, 5, 9
(b) Temperatures 16°, 23°, 20°, 18°, 17°, 25°

(a) Test scores in size order are
3, 4, (5,) 8, 9
The middle value is 5.
The median test score is 5.

(b) Temperatures in size order are
16°, 17°, (18°, 20°,) 23°, 25°
The two middle values are 18° and 20°.
The median is half way between: 19°.
Hence median temperature is 19°.

Exercise 10I

1 The heights in centimetres of five flowers were

12 cm, 7 cm, 6 cm, 11 cm, 11 cm

(a) What is the modal height?
(b) What is the median height?

2 The shoe sizes of 8 students were

8, 6, 4, 6, 6, 7, 9, 10

(a) What is the modal size?
(b) What is the median size?
(c) Which of the two results would be more useful for the manager of a shoe store? Why?

3 The temperatures at Piarco Airport in Trinidad on six days were

21°C, 23°C, 19°C, 25°C, 25°C, 24°C

(a) What was the median temperature in that period?
(b) What was the modal temperature?

4 **(a)** In a group of five students, measure their
(i) height
(ii) waist
(iii) head size

(b) In each case find the
(i) median
(ii) mode
(iii) mean
for each measurement.

(c) Write up your results and present them to the class.

Activity

- Make some body measurements for some boys and girls, for example weight, arm length, shoe size.
- Find the mean, mode and median for boys and girls.
- Draw bar charts to illustrate your findings.
- Present your results to the class.

10.6 Coordinate graphs

Another way of showing information is on a coordinate graph, which is drawn on graph paper.

The table shows the cost in dollars of buying T-shirts.

Number of T-shirts	1	2	3	4	5	6	7
Cost in dollars	5	10	15	20	25	30	35

Instead of shading squares and drawing a bar graph you use dots or points.

The points are: (1, 5) (2, 10) (3, 15) (4, 20) (5, 25) (6, 30) (7, 35).

The cost of T-shirts

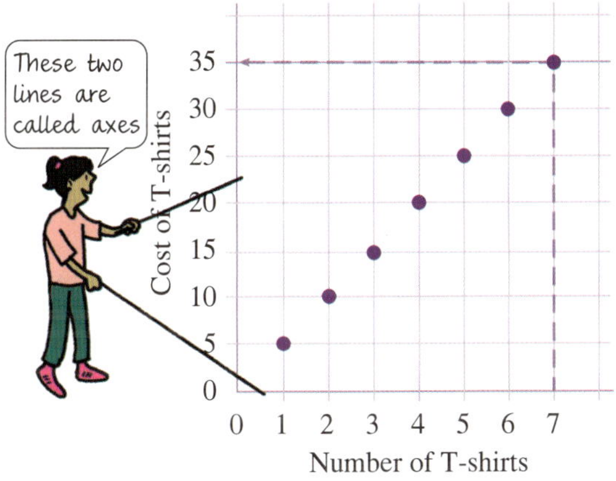

You can see that 7 T-shirts cost $35.

Showing information by points on a graph is often called **plotting a graph**.

- On a coordinate graph the information is represented by a series of dots which connect the number on one axis with the corresponding number on the other axis.

Technology

Practise using coordinates by visiting the Shapes section at the following site

www.woodlands-junior.kent.sch.uk

Try the Billy Bug games, then have a go at the 'Hidden Craft' and 'Bike Hunt Game'.

Exercise 10J

1 The graph shows the total number of students absent in Form 1 each week, for the first ten weeks of term.

Number of students absent in Form One

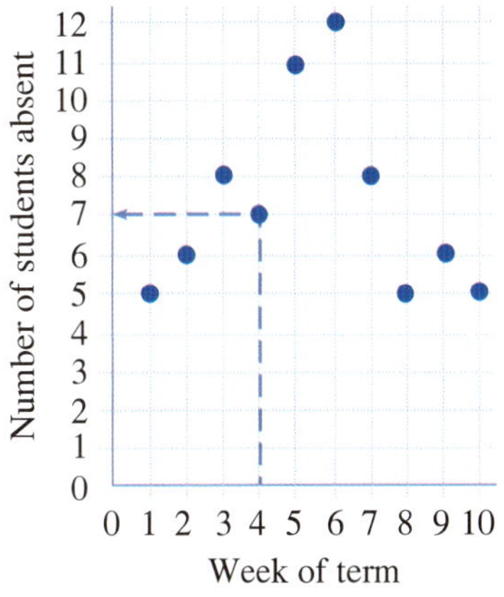

Look at the graph carefully. You will see that in the 4th week of term 7 students were absent.

(a) How many students were absent in the 3rd week?

(b) How many were absent in the 9th week?

(c) In which week were 11 students absent?

(d) Which week had most students absent? Suggest a reason for this.

2 John Manger owns a bicycle shop. The graph shows the number of bicycles he sold in each of the twelve months last year.

Bicycles John Manger sold

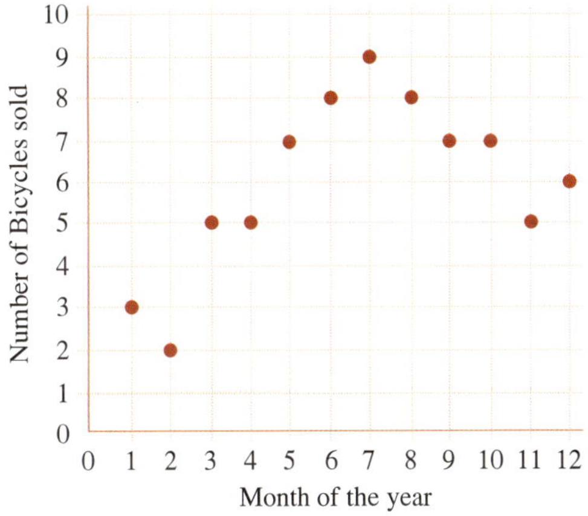

(a) How many bicycles did he sell in the 6th month?

(b) Copy and complete the table, to show the information in the graph.

Month	1	2	3	4	5	6	7	8	9	10	11	12
Number of bicycles sold												

(c) What scale has been used on the vertical axis?

3 Diane is training to be a secretary. She does a typing test every week. The table shows how fast she could type in the first eight tests she took.

Test	1	2	3	4	5	6	7	8
Number of words per minute	10	10	15	20	25	35	45	55

Some of the information from the table is shown on the graph that has been started.

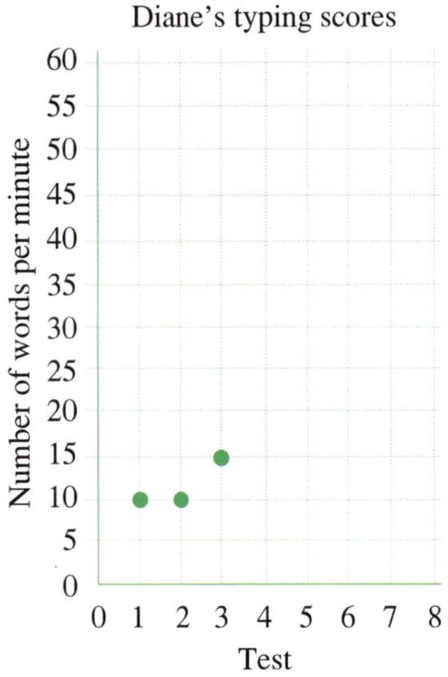

(a) What scale has been used on the vertical axis?

(b) Copy and complete the graph on squared paper.

Scales

In Questions 2 and 3 of Exercise 10J different scales were used on the vertical axes.

In Question 2 one square represents one bicycle, while in Question 3 one square represents 5 words per minute.

You must choose a convenient scale so that the data given can be represented on a graph.

Note that the scale on each axis must be **uniform**.

In a uniform scale the distance between divisions on the scale is unchanged:

For example:

In a non-uniform scale the distance between division varies:

For example:

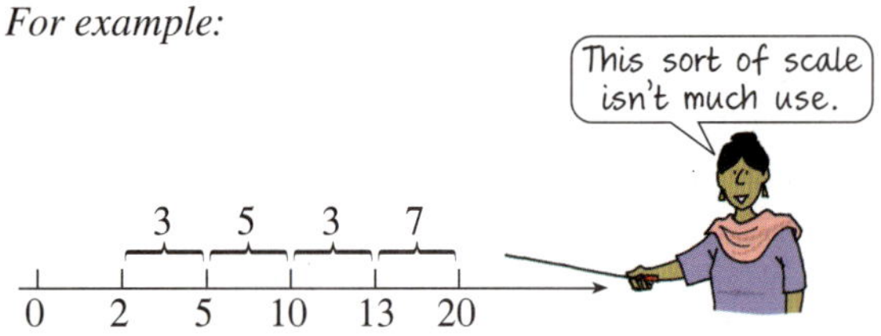

Exercise 10K

1 This table shows the cost of shirts.

Number of shirts	1	2	3	4	5	6	7	8	9	10
Cost in dollars	5	10	15	20	25	30	35	40	45	50

On squared paper, draw a graph to show this information.
Show the number of shirts on the horizontal axis.
Show the cost of the shirts on the vertical axis.
What scale will you use on the vertical axis?

2 A boy's height was measured in cm on each birthday. This table shows the results.

Age in yrs	birth	1	2	3	4	5
Height (cm)	20	40	70	90	100	110

(a) Represent the age on the horizontal axis, and the height on the vertical axis.
What is a suitable scale to use on the vertical axis?
(b) Draw the graph.
(c) Estimate the height of the boy when he was $1\frac{1}{2}$.

3 A car increases its speed steadily over 6 seconds.

Time (s)	0	1	2	3	4	5	6
Speed (km/h)	0	15	30	45	60	75	90

(a) Represent the time on the horizontal axis and the speed on the vertical axis.
Choose a convenient scale for the vertical axis and draw the graph.
(b) From your graph estimate the car's speed after $4\frac{1}{2}$ seconds.

4 Compare the graph you drew in Question 2 with those of Questions 1 and 3.
(a) What differences do you see?
(b) Explain the differences.

5 The growth of a company over a five-year period is shown in the table.

Year	Profit before tax ($m)
2005	6 (A)
2006	9 (B)
2007	18 (C)
2008	23 (D)
2009	30 (E)

(a) Draw a graph to show this data. Plot the year on the horizontal axis and the profit on the vertical axis.
(b) Join the points A and B, B and C, C and D, D and E with straight lines.
(c) What do you notice about the line BC? Can you explain?

Coordinates

Anab, Deo, Ram, Bob, Murray and Geno each took two spelling tests in one week. In the graph, the mark for the first test has been plotted against the mark for the second test.

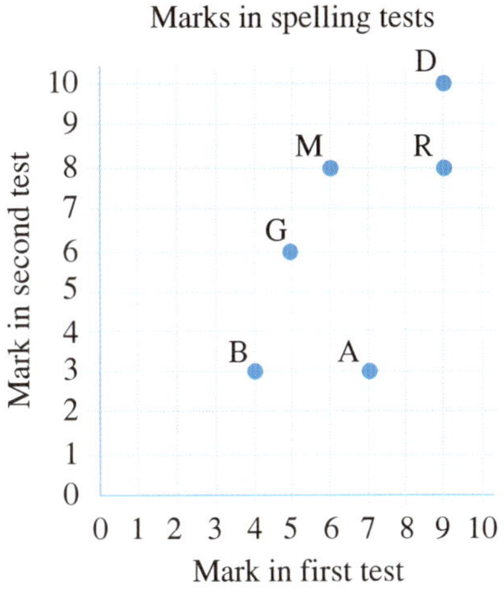

The point marked A represents Anab's marks. It shows he got 7 marks in the first test, and 3 marks in the second test.

To get to A you go across 7 and then go up 3. A is the point (7, 3).
(7, 3) are the **coordinates** of A.

The marks in each test for the others are:

Bob (4, 3), Geno (5, 6), Rani (9, 8), Deo (9, 10) and Murray (6, 8).

- Coordinates tell you exactly where a point is on a graph. The coordinates (3, 1) represent the point 3 across and then 1 up from where the axes meet.

Exercise 10L

1 Are the coordinates (7, 3) the same as (3, 7)? Explain.

2

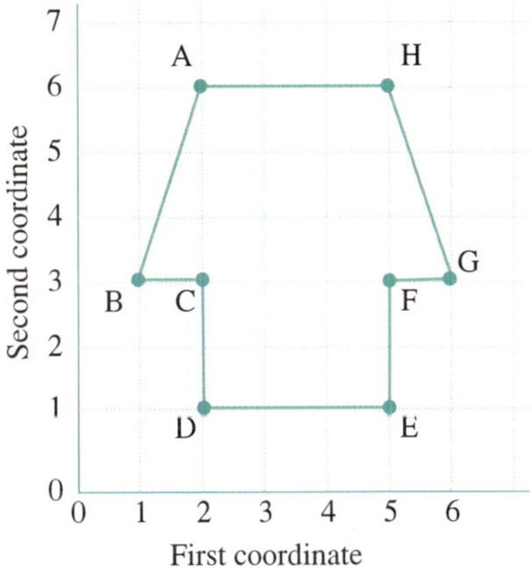

Write down the coordinates of all the marked points on the graph.

3 **(i)** On squared paper, make a larger copy of the graph started below.

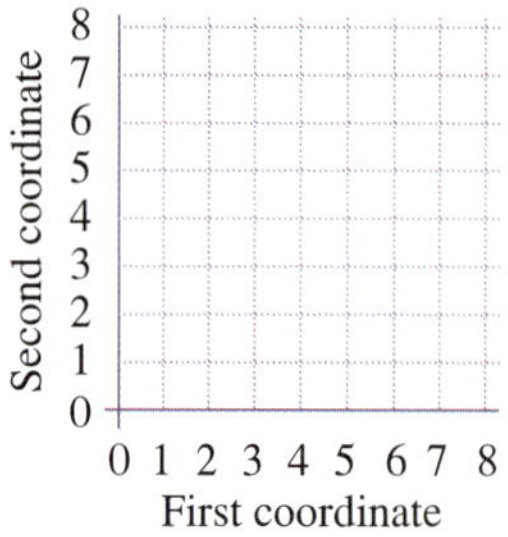

(ii) On your copy, plot the points, using a coloured pencil:

(1, 3) (1, 5) (2, 4) (3, 2) (3, 3)
(3, 6) (3, 7) (4, 2) (4, 3) (4, 6)
(4, 7) (6, 3) (6, 4) (6, 5) (6, 6)
(7, 4)

(iii) Use a ruler and a different coloured pencil to join these points:

(a) (1, 3) to (1, 5) **(b)** (1, 3) to (2, 4)
(c) (1, 5) to (2, 4) **(d)** (2, 4) to (3, 3)
(e) (3, 3) to (6, 3) **(f)** (6, 3) to (7, 4)
(g) (7, 4) to (6, 6) **(h)** (6, 6) to (3, 6)
(i) (3, 6) to (2, 4) **(j)** (6, 4) to (7, 4)
(k) (4, 3) to (4, 2) **(l)** (4, 2) to (3, 2)
(m) (3, 2) to (4, 3) **(n)** (4, 6) to (4, 7)
(o) (4, 7) to (3, 7) **(p)** (3, 7) to (4, 6)

What shape have you drawn?

Exercise 10M – mixed questions

1 The pictograph shows the number of ice-cream cones sold in a canteen during the first week in March

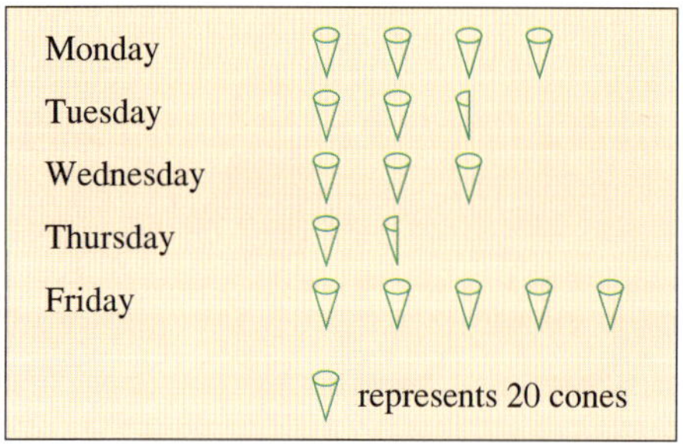

(a) How many cones were sold on Tuesday?

(b) How many cones were sold altogether during this week?

(c) If the cost of a cone was $12, how much money did the canteen make this week?

2 The pictograph shows the number of children in 56 families.

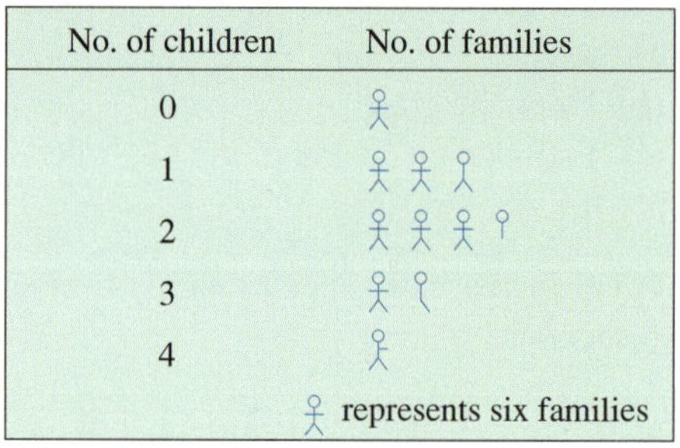

In how many families were there
(a) 4 children **(b)** 3 children **(c)** 2 children?

3 Miss Carty kept a record of the number of students in her class each day for one week.

The results are shown in the table:

Day	Mon	Tues	Wed	Thur	Fri
Number present	27	24	30	25	16

Copy and complete the bar graph below.

4 (0, 3), (6, 3), (3, 6) and (3, 0) are the four corners of a square.
Plot the points and join them to form the square.
State the coordinates of the point in the centre of the square.

5 The results of a class test taken by boys and girls are shown on the bar graph:

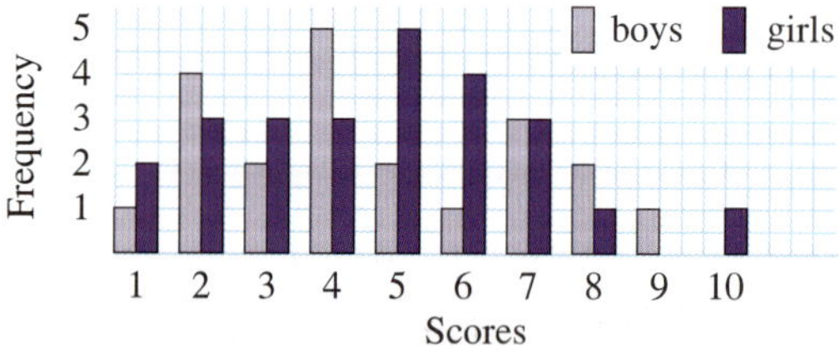

(a) How many **(i)** boys **(ii)** girls were in the class?
(b) If the pass mark is 5, how many **(i)** boys **(ii)** girls passed the test?

6 Every 400 g of dried fish contains about 150 g of water, 50 g of fat, 150 g of protein and 50 g of other substances.
(a) To represent this information, draw a pie chart divided into 8 equal sectors.
(b) How many grams does each sector represent?
(c) How many sectors will represent the amount of protein in dried fish?

7 The table shows a tally of the types of vehicles involved in serious accidents on a busy road.

Vehicle	Taxi	Car	Bus	Truck	Other
Frequency	卌 II	卌	III	I	II

(a) Write the frequencies as numbers instead of tallies.
(b) Which type of vehicle had the least number of accidents?
(c) How many accidents were there altogether?
(d) Which two types of vehicle account for $\frac{2}{3}$ of the total number of accidents?

8 The pie chart shows how Mrs Peters spends her weekly housekeeping money.

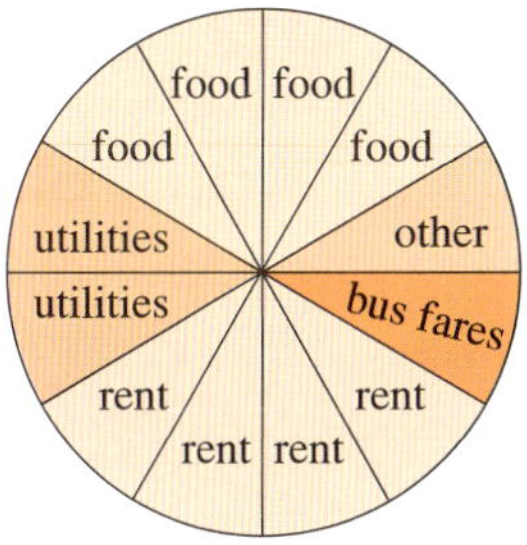

The amount that she spends on rent is $1000. Find
(a) the amount represented by each sector.
(b) the amount spent on
(i) utilities
(ii) bus fares
(c) the total weekly housekeeping money.

9 For each of the following, plot the points given and find the coordinates of the fourth point needed to make the named shape.
(a) (3, 2), (8, 2), (3, 7) square
(b) (6, 1), (6, 10), (3, 10) rectangle
(c) (5, 1), (1, 5), (9, 5) square

Investigation

Measure the distance around your wrist.
Measure the distance around your neck.

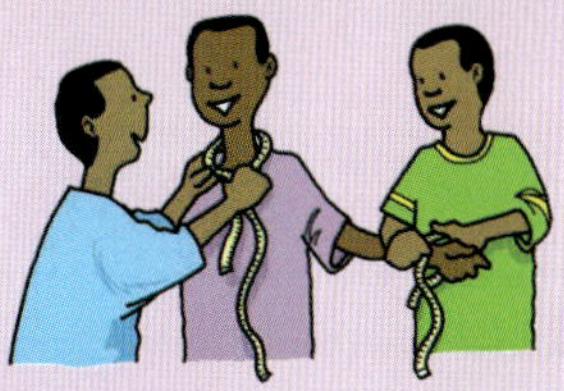

Repeat these measurements for some of your friends.
Copy and complete the table.

Name	Distance around neck (cm)	Distance around wrist (cm)

Do you notice anything?
On suitable axes, draw a graph to show this information.
Can you say anything about the distance around your wrist and the distance around your neck?

Technology

Visit the Graphs Index at the website
www.mathsisfun.com/data
Make bar, line and pie charts and compare them.
Which representation do you prefer? Why?

10 Consolidation

Example 1

This table shows the favourite band of a group of 50 students.

Band	WCK	Kassav	Morgan Heritage	Square One	Steel Pulse
Votes	10	5	15	10	10

Show this as a pictograph.

Favourite band	
WCK	♀♀
Kassav	♀
Morgan Heritage	♀♀♀
Square One	♀♀
Steel Pulse	♀♀
	♀ represents 5 students

Example 2

Use the data in Example 1 to draw a bar chart showing this information.

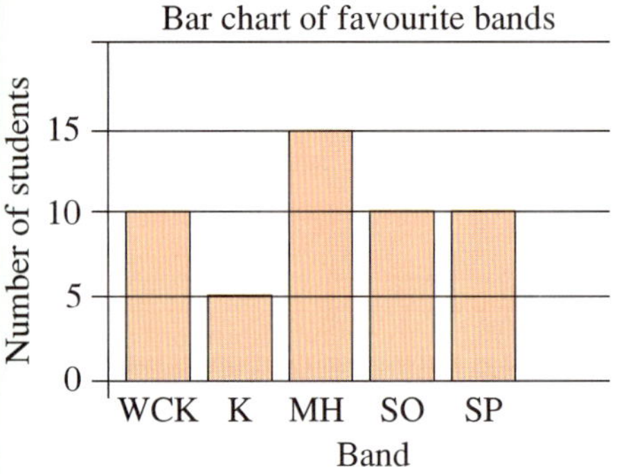

Example 3

Using the data in Example 1, draw a pie chart to show this information.

There are 50 students.

Fraction liking WCK $= \frac{10}{50} = \frac{2}{10}$

Angle for WCK $= \frac{2}{10} \times 360° = 72°$

Fraction liking Kassav $= \frac{5}{50} = \frac{1}{10}$

Angle for Kassav $= \frac{1}{10} \times 360° = 36°$

Fraction liking Morgan Heritage $= \frac{15}{50} = \frac{3}{10}$

Angle for MH $= \frac{3}{10} \times 360° = 108°$

Fraction liking Square One $= \frac{10}{50} = \frac{2}{10}$

Angle for Square One $= \frac{2}{10} \times 360° = 72°$

Fraction liking Steel Pulse $= \frac{10}{50} = \frac{2}{10}$

Angle for Steel Pulse $= \frac{2}{10} \times 360° = \frac{72°}{360°}$

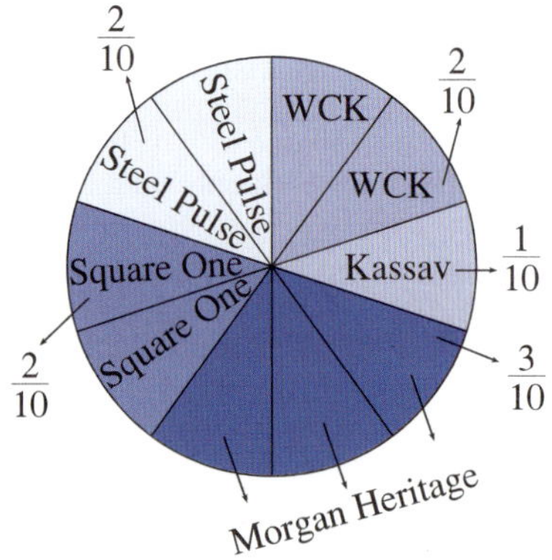

Exercise 10

1 The table shows the colours of fish in Grace's aquarium.

Colour	Gold	Green	Blue	Silver
Number	7	4	2	5

The charts below all represent the data from the table.

Write a paragraph comparing the charts. Explain which features of the data each chart shows most clearly, and comment on how easy each one is to read.

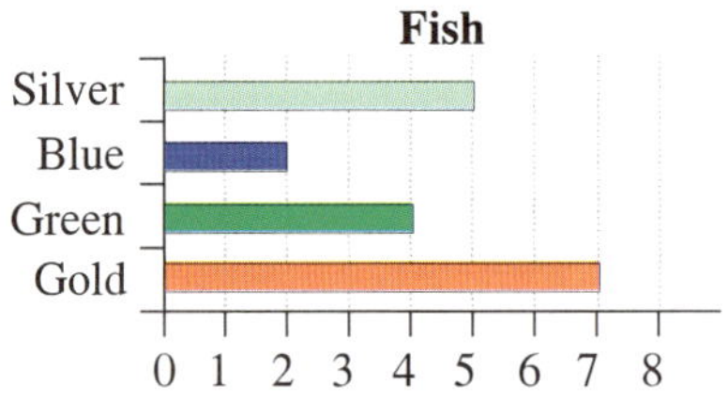

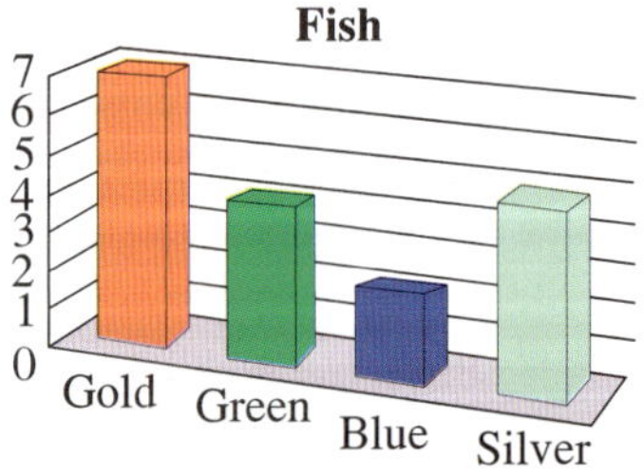

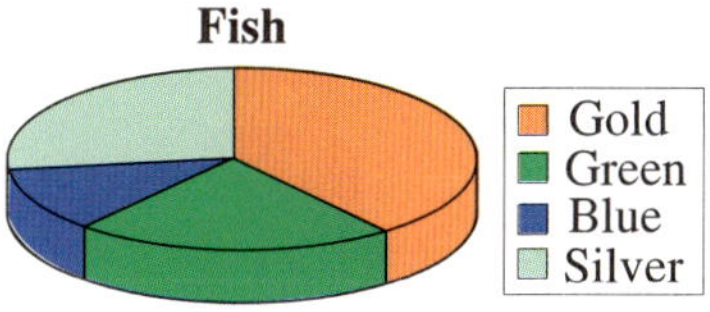

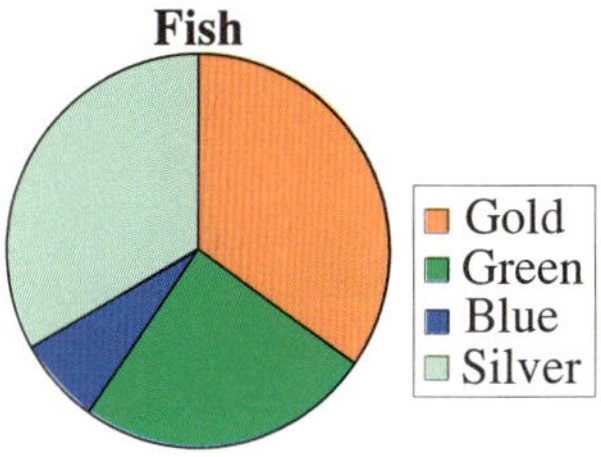

Application 10

2 Carry out a survey in your class to find each student's shoe size.
- **(a)** Make a table of your results.
- **(b)** What is the modal shoe size?
- **(c)** Draw a pictograph to show your findings.
- **(d)** Comment on your results.

3 Is it true that most people have cereal for breakfast?
- **(a)** Carry out a classroom survey to find out.
- **(b)** Draw a bar chart showing breakfast foods eaten by your class.
- **(c)** What do your results show?

4 Is it true that boys have bigger heads than girls?
- **(a)** In groups discuss how you could find this out.
- **(b)** Use the method your group decided to collect data on this.
- **(c)** Show the results of your data on a pictograph or bar chart.
- **(d)** What is the mean head size for **(i)** boys **(ii)** girls?
- **(e)** What did you find out?

Companion CD

Want some extra practice? Go to Chapter 10 on your companion CD for further exercises, animations, and solutions.

Summary

You should know ...

1 A tally helps you count items.
For example:
The votes for favourite singer in a class

Singer	Tally	Frequency
Alison Hinds	𝍸 I	6
Buju Bunton	𝍸 𝍸 II	12
De Brakes	III	3
Gypsy	𝍸 IIII	9

Check out

1 State the numbers represented by the following tallies:
(a) IIII **(b)** 𝍸 𝍸 II
(c) 𝍸 𝍸 𝍸

2 A pictograph uses pictures or drawings to represent data.
For example:

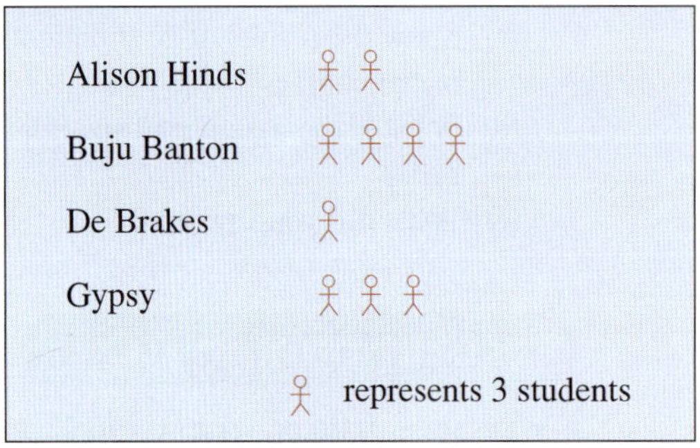

3 A scale can be used when numbers are large.

4 A bar graph uses squares to represent frequencies.
For example:

Bar chart of favourite singers

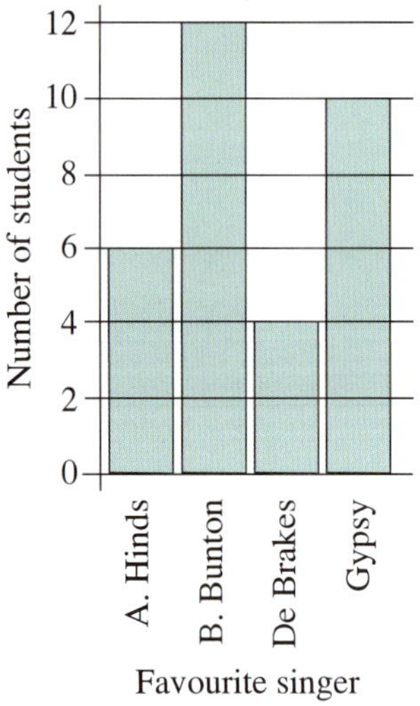

2 The diagram below shows part of a pictograph.

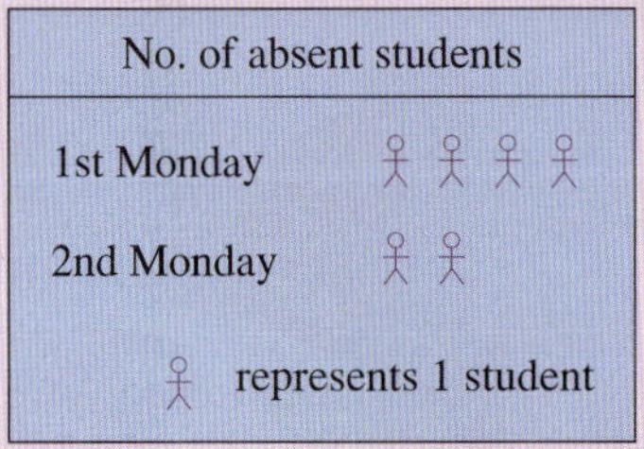

How many students were absent on the 1st Monday?

3 If (symbol) represents 50 students, how many symbols would you use to represent 250 students?

4 The bar graph below shows places visited by Tobias High School students during the holidays.

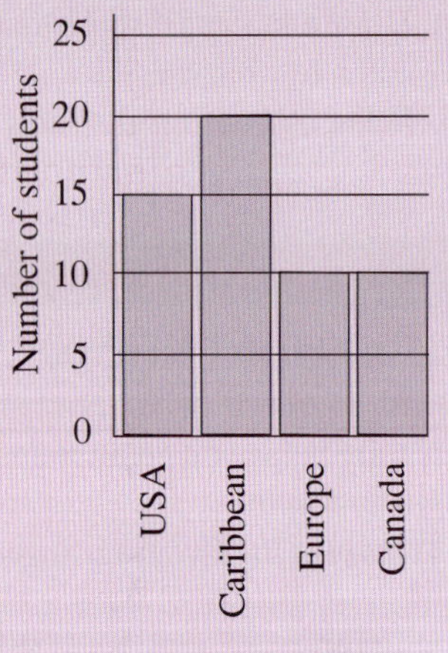

(a) How many students visited **(i)** Canada **(ii)** the Caribbean?

(b) How many students took part in the survey?

5 A pie chart is a circle divided into sectors.
The size of the sector represents the number of items.
For example:

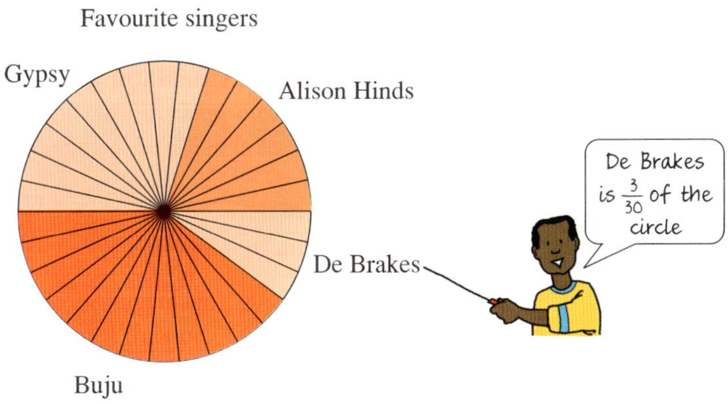

5 A survey showed the ways in which the students in 1T travelled to school.

Bus	Car	Walk	Cycle
20	8	8	4

Draw a pie chart to show this information.

6 Describe data using a single value called an **average**.
There are three types of average: **mean**, **mode** and **median**.
For example:
What is the mean, mode and median of 4, 6, 2, 10, 2?

$$\text{Mean} = \frac{4+6+2+10+2}{5} = \frac{24}{5} = 4.8$$

Mode = most common value = 2
Values in order are 2, 2, 4, 6, 10
Median = middle value = 4

6 Find the mean, mode and median of these test scores.
(a) 6, 6, 10, 8, 4
(b) 17, 14, 13, 12, 13, 18

7 How to plot and read a graph.
For example:
The graph below shows the number of radios sold each week.

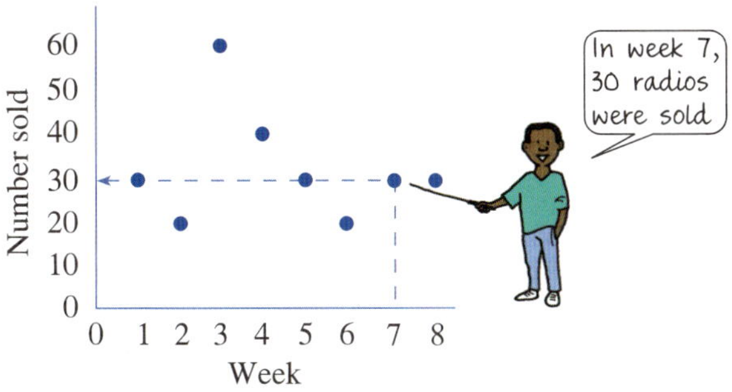

7 The diagram below represents the temperature taken in a village at 9:00 am every day during one week.

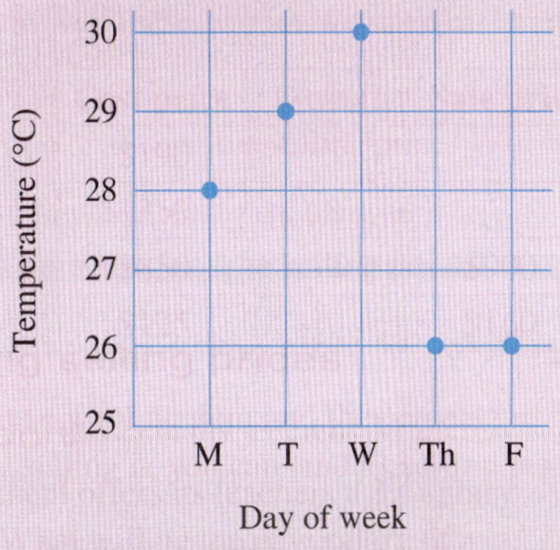

Make a table of values for the information on the graph.

8 How to write coordinates of a point.
For example:
In the graph above the coordinates of the point shown are (7, 30).

8 From the graph, write down the coordinates of A, B and C.

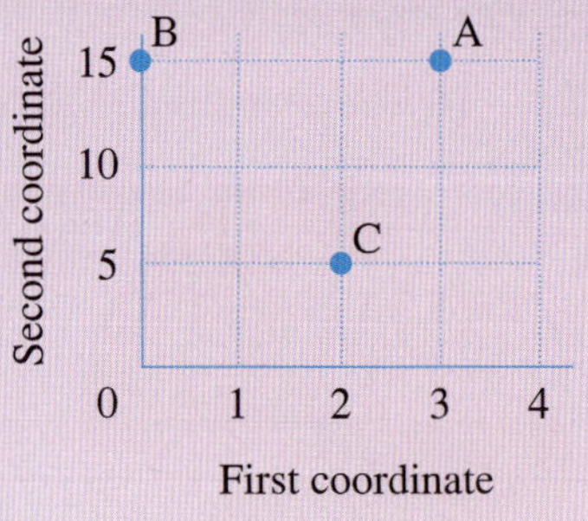

Area 11

Objectives

- ✔ compare areas
- ✔ use standard units of area
- ✔ estimate areas of irregular shapes
- ✔ calculate the areas of rectangles and triangles
- ✔ calculate the perimeters of shapes

What's the point?

How big is your bedroom? How much carpet would you need to buy to put on your bedroom floor? What about your whole house? To answer such questions you need to be able to measure the area of shapes.

Before you start

You should know ...

1 Some shapes fit together in a pattern with no gaps.
For example these triangles form a tessellation.

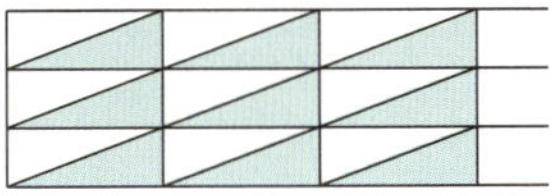

2 The relationship between metres, centimetres and millimetres.
1 m = 100 cm
1 cm = 10 mm

Check in

1 Make a tessellation pattern with these shapes.
(a) **(b)**

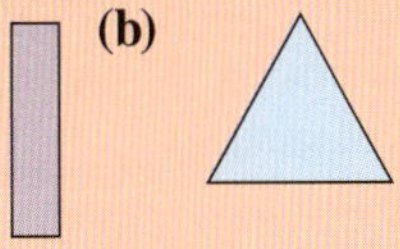

2 **(a)** Write in centimetres:
(i) 6 m **(ii)** 2.4 m
(b) Write in millimetres:
(i) 7 cm **(ii)** 7.3 cm

11.1 What is area?

The top of a desk is a **surface**. The front of a blackboard and the floor of a room are also surfaces.

- The size of a surface is called its **area**.

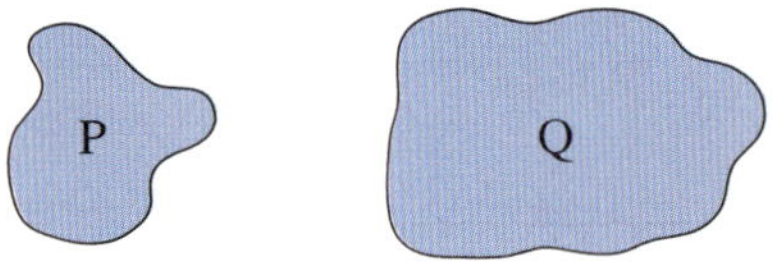

The area of surface Q is bigger than the area of surface P.

Exercise 11A

1 Which is larger, the area of your desk top or the area of this page?

2 Compare the surface areas of three leaves. Can you tell which has the largest area?

3 Write down ten different surfaces that you can see around you.

4 

A milk tin has one curved and two flat surfaces. Write down three objects that have at least one
(a) flat surface
(b) curved surface.

5 How many stamps would fit on the surface of a small envelope?

11.2 Comparing areas

You will need tracing paper and centimetre squared paper.

You can use tessellations to compare the areas of shapes.

Example 1

Which rectangle is larger?

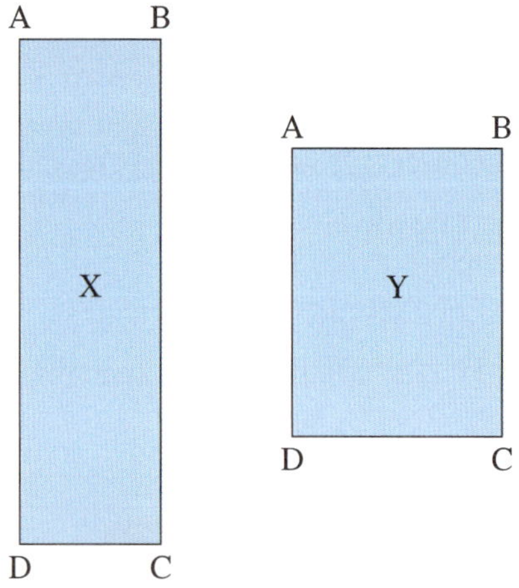

First, cover the rectangles with a tessellation of triangles.

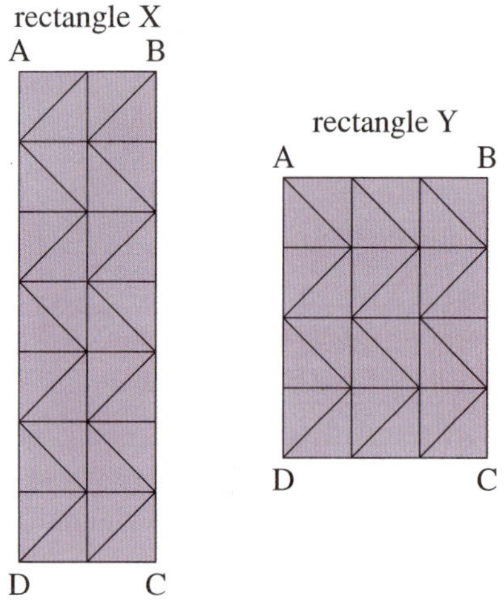

Next, count the triangles in each rectangle. There are 28 triangles in X, but only 24 in Y. So, X is larger.

Exercise 11B

1

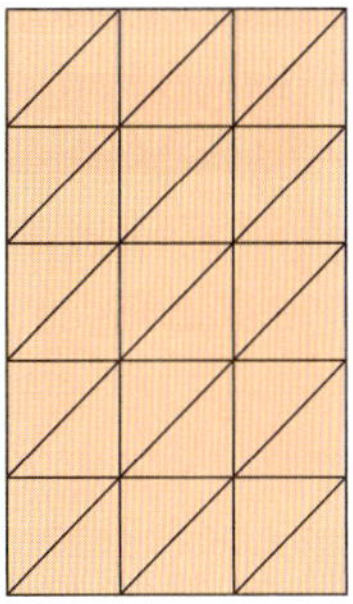

V

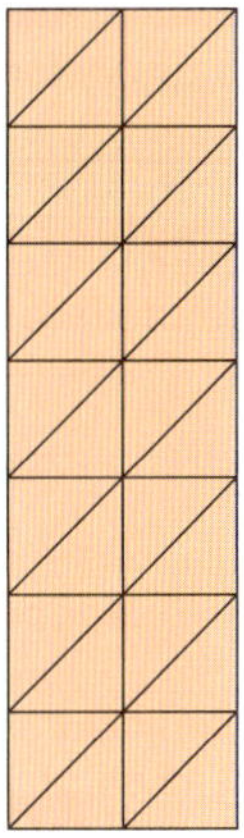

W

Copy and complete for shapes V and W:
The area of rectangle V is ____ triangles.
The area of rectangle W is ____ triangles.
Rectangle ____ is larger than rectangle ____.

2 Count triangles to find which of the two rectangles is larger.

(a)

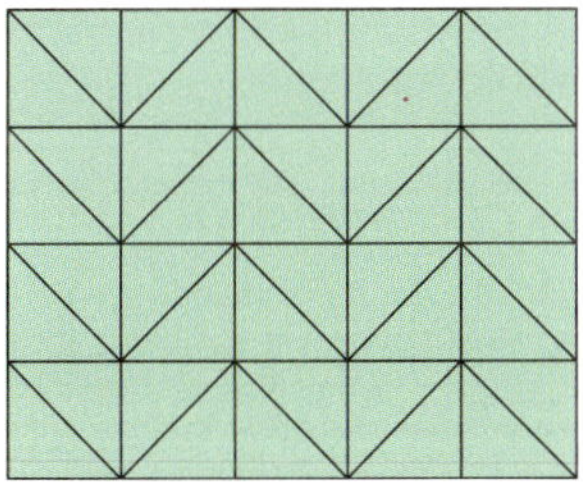

(b)

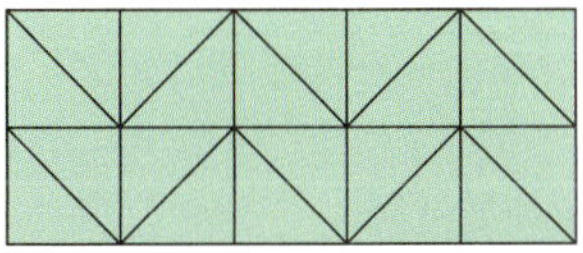

3 Here are the two rectangles from Question 1.

V

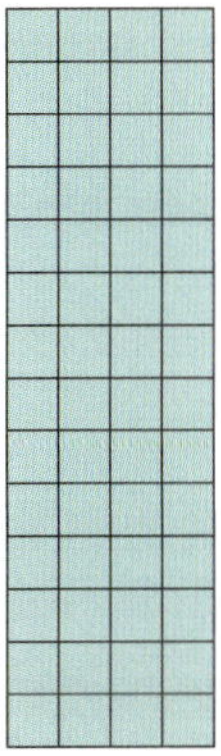

W

(a) Count the number of squares in V.
(b) Count the number of squares in W.
(c) Which rectangle is larger?
(d) Is your answer the same as in Question 1?

Ways to find area

To find the area of the rectangle below. . .

you could fill it with a tessellation of:

(a) squares

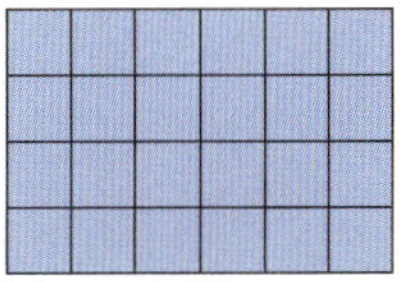

Area = 24 squares

(b) rectangles

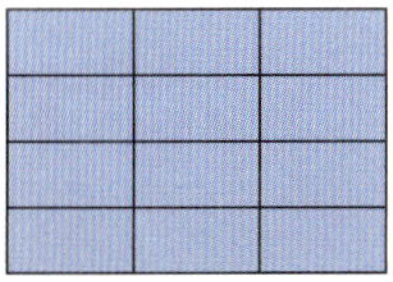

Area = 12 rectangles

(c) triangles

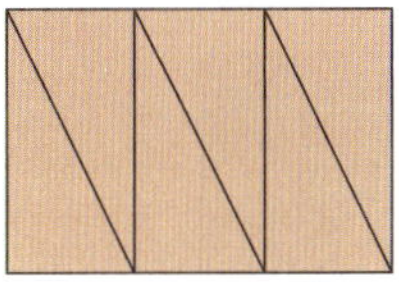

Area = 6 triangles

(d) L-shapes

Area = 8 L-shapes

Exercise 11C

1 **(a)** Would you use squares, rectangles, triangles or L-shapes to find the area of the shape below? Explain why.

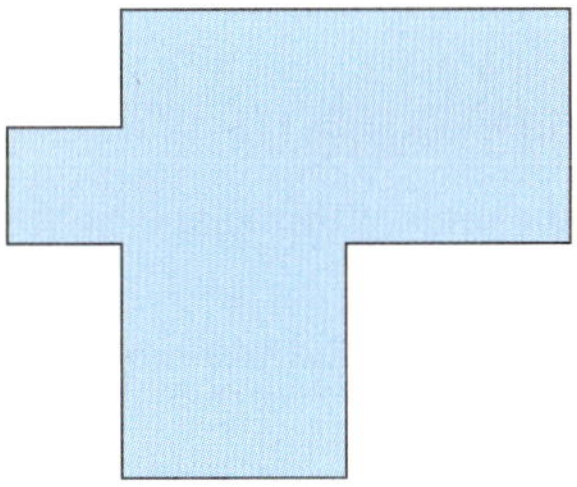

(b) Find its area using the shapes of your choice.

2 **(a)** Would you use squares, rectangles or triangles to find the area of these shapes? Explain why.

(i)

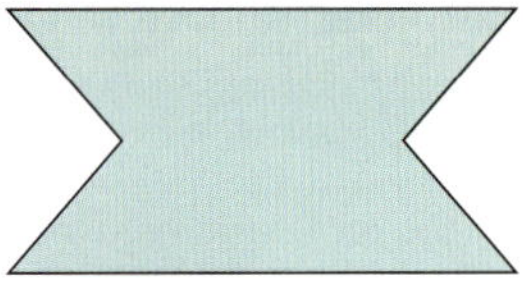

(ii)

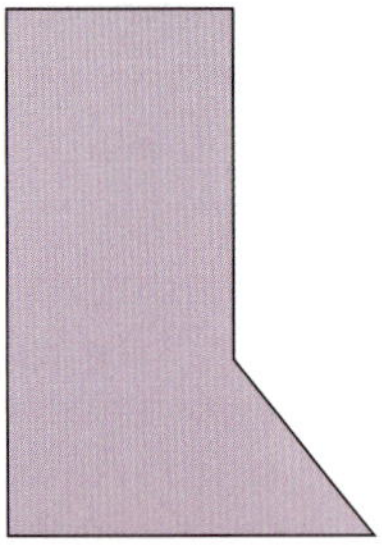

(iii)

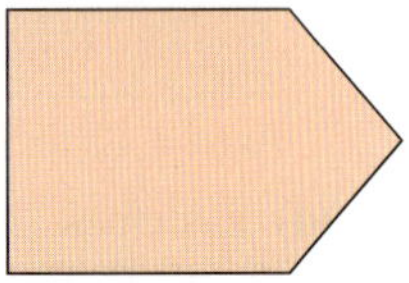

(iv)

(b) Find the area of each shape using the shapes of your choice.

3

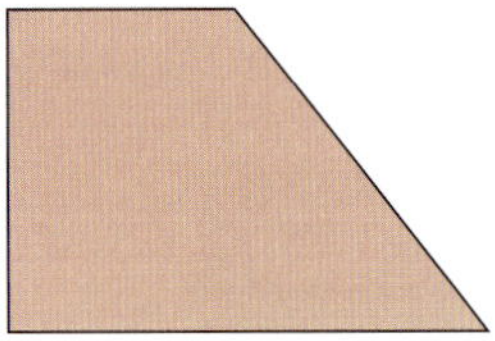

(a) Find the area of this shape by filling it with small squares.

(b) What problems did you have with this method?

Irregular shapes

You can find the areas of irregular shapes using a tessellation.

Example 2

Find the area of the shape below.

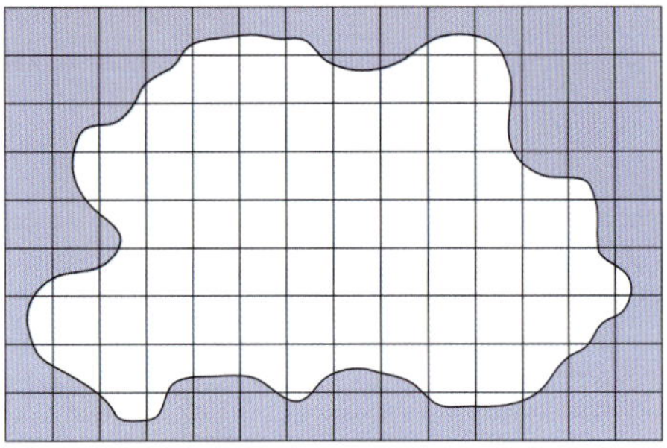

First, lightly shade all the part squares

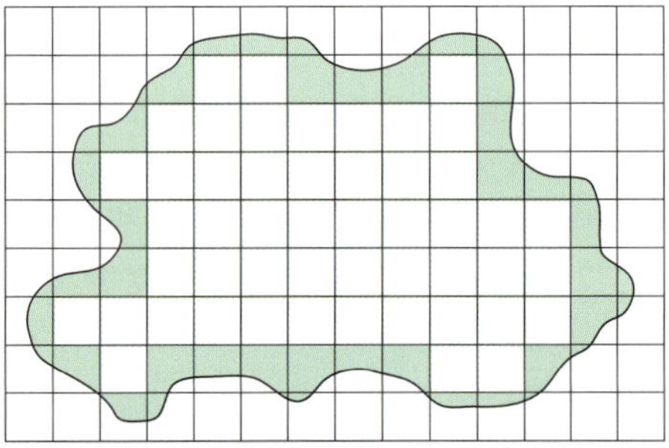

Next count the whole squares.

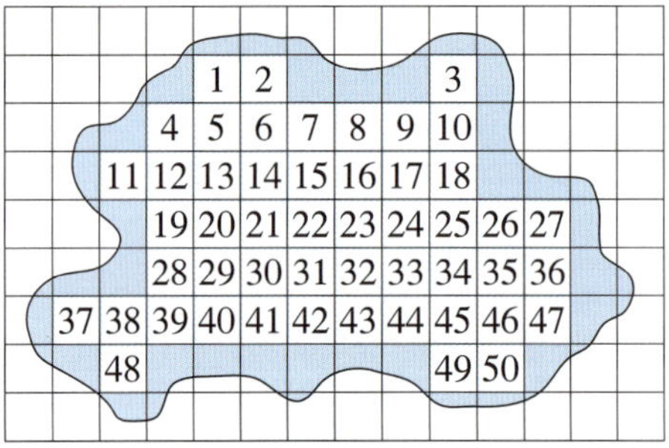

There are 50 whole squares.

Now look at the shaded parts.

If a shaded part is larger than half a square, put a dot in it.

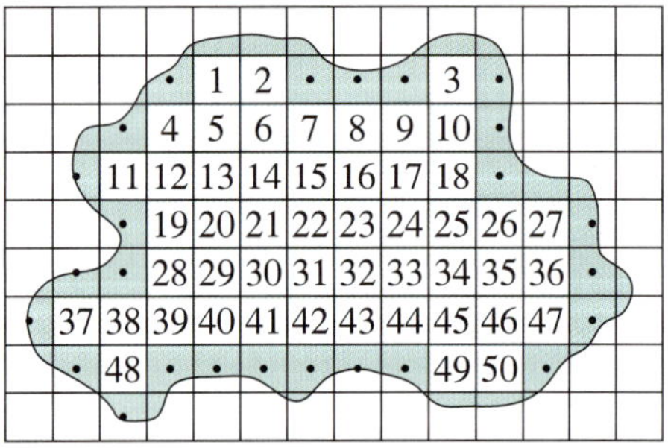

Count the number of dots. There are 25 of them. This is approximately equal to the total area of the shaded area. Can you explain why?

The total area of the shape
= 50 whole squares + 25 shaded squares
= 75 squares.

Exercise 11D

1 Using tracing paper, trace this shape on to centimetre squared paper.

Use the method in Example 2 to find the approximate area of the shape in squares.

2 Put your hand flat on a sheet of centimetre squared paper. Trace round it carefully as far as your wrist. Now find the approximate area of your hand in squares.

3 **(a)** At first glance, which of these shapes do you think is the larger?

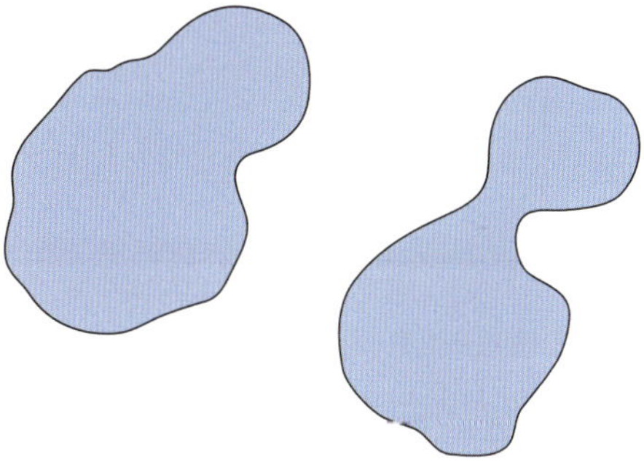

(b) See if you were right by finding their areas using the method of Example 2.

4 Is this pattern of circles a tessellation? Explain your answer.

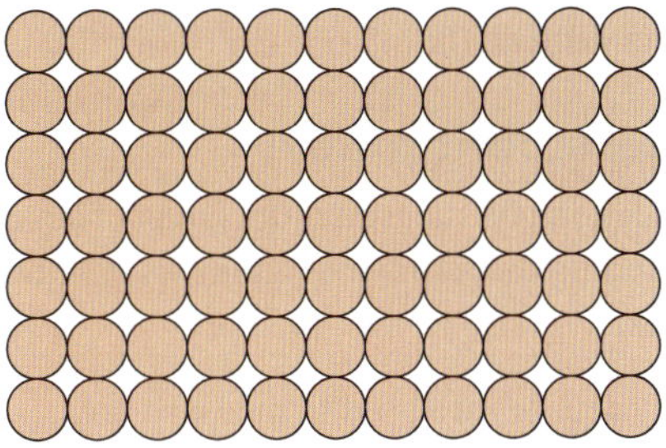

5 Trace this shape on to tracing paper. Put the tracing on to the pattern of circles above. Find the area of the shape in circles.

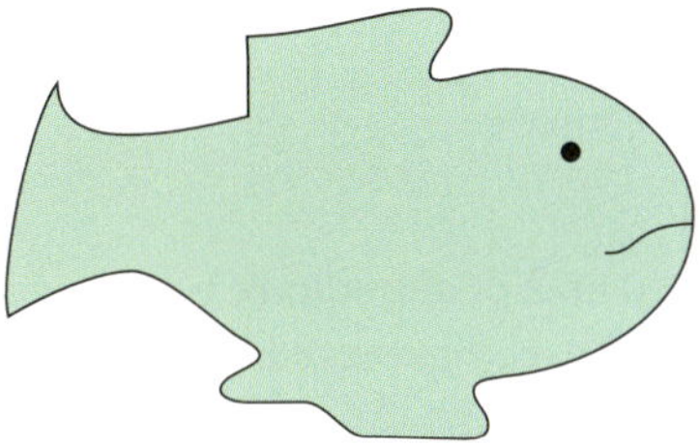

6 Look at the gaps between the circles in Question 4. Do you think these should also be counted when finding the area of the shape? Do you think circles are a good way to measure area? Why?

7 Does the method in Example 2 give the exact area of the shape? Explain why.

Technology

Remember: perimeter is the distance around a shape.
Visit the Area and Perimeter section at the site
www.woodlands-junior.kent.sch.uk/maths
and try

(i) Area Explorer
(ii) Perimeter Explorer
(iii) Compare Area and Perimeter

for further practice.

11.3 Some units of area

You will need tracing paper, centimetre squared paper, scissors and chalk.

The square centimetre

In the last section you measured the areas of several shapes by finding the number of triangles or squares in the shapes.

Usually only squares are used to measure area.
A square centimetre is a square with each edge 1 cm long. Here it is.

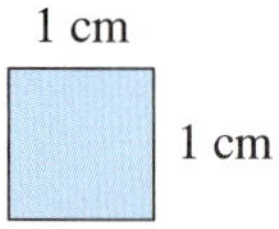

Area = 1 square centimetre
or 1 cm^2

This square has an area of **one square centimetre**. Centimetre squared paper is covered with squares like this.

Exercise 11E

1 Write in a short way:

(a) 5 square centimetres
(b) 16 square centimetres
(c) 42 square centimetres
(d) 13 square centimetres
(e) 57 square centimetres
(f) 110 square centimetres.

2 The shape below is drawn on centimetre squared paper.

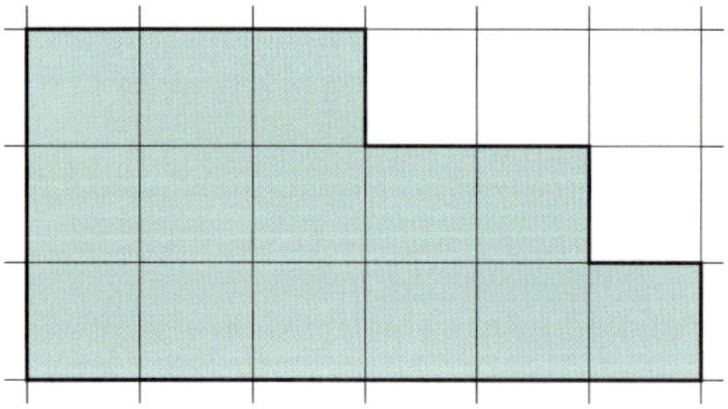

(a) What is the area of each square?
(b) How many squares are in the shaded shape?
(c) What is the area of the shaded shape?

3 Write down the area, in square centimetres, of each of the shaded shapes below.

(a)

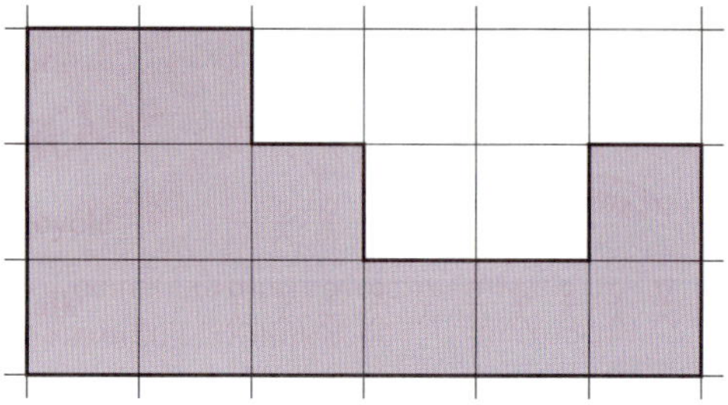

(b)

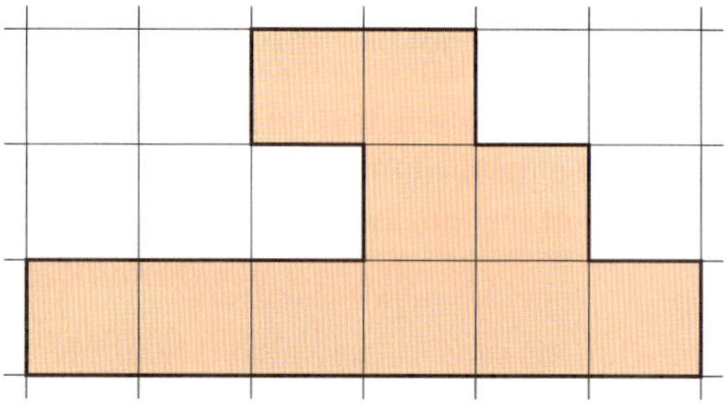

(c)

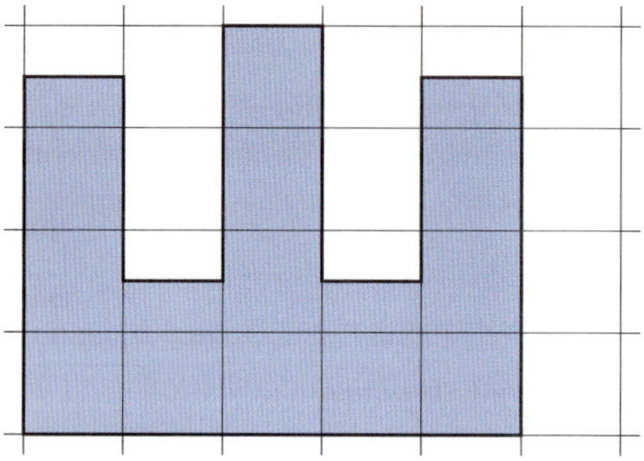

(d)

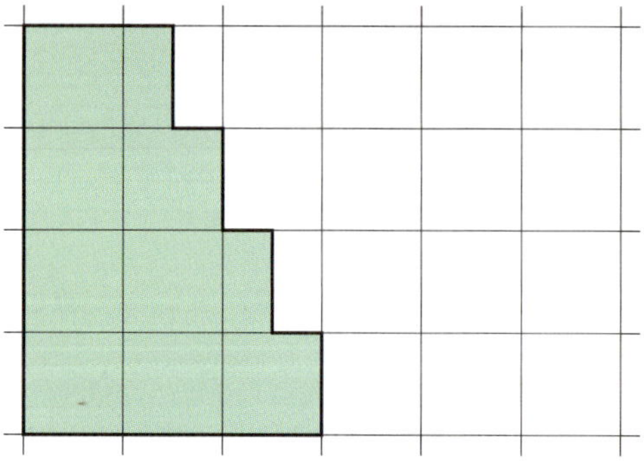

4 Draw accurately, two shapes with an area of 4 square centimetres.

5 Look at the shaded triangles below. Can you find their areas?

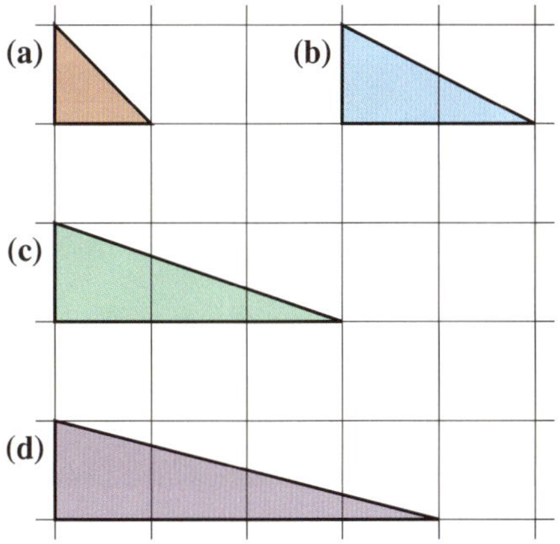

6 Find the area of each of the shapes below:

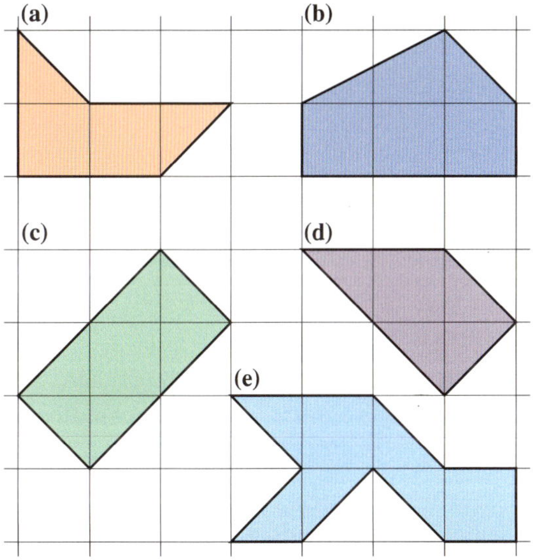

7 Which shapes in Question 6 have the same area?

8 Trace around a leaf from a tree. Use the method of Example 2 on page 224 to find its area in square centimetres.

9 **(a)** Estimate the area of the items in the table:

Object	Estimated Area (cm^2)	Actual Area (cm^2)
1 cent coin		
25 cent coin		
$1 note		
matchbox top		
a postage stamp		

(b) Check your answers by drawing each object on centimetre squared paper.

(c) Copy and complete the table.

10 Estimate the area, in cm^2, of
- **(a)** this page
- **(b)** a page in your exercise book
- **(c)** the top of your geometry set
- **(d)** a newspaper page.

Investigation

Big foot!

Put you shoe or sandal on a sheet of centimetre squared paper.

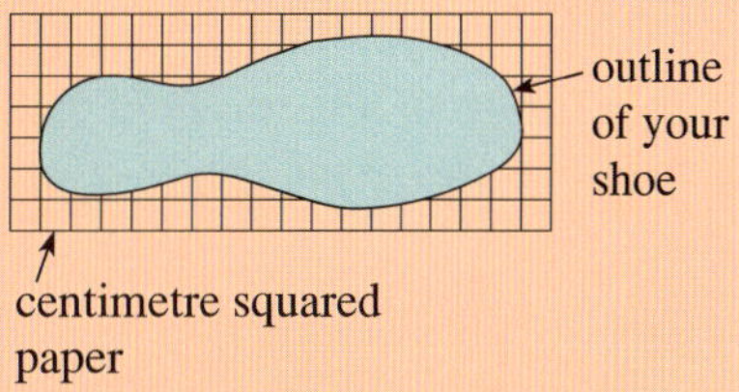

(a) Draw around the outline. Find the approximate area of your foot.

(b) Compare your foot size with other class members. Who has the biggest foot?

(c) Repeat parts (a) and (b) to find the biggest hand.

(d) Do people with big feet have big hands?

The square millimetre

Look at the drawing below of a mosquito's wing and a square centimetre.

Mosquito's wing

1 cm^2

The area of the mosquito's wing is less than 1 cm^2.

You can measure small areas using the square millimetre (mm^2).

A square millimetre is a square with side 1 mm.

Below is a square centimetre divided into 100 square millimetres.

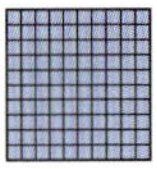

$1\ \text{cm}^2 = 100\ \text{mm}^2$

Exercise 11F

1 The shape below is drawn on cm/mm graph paper. Each small square is $1\ \text{mm}^2$.

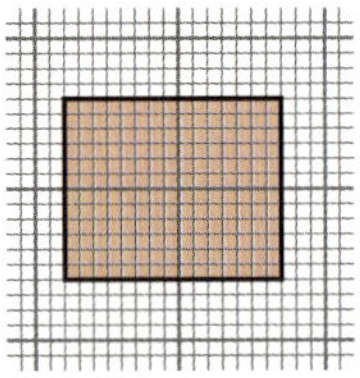

(a) How many small squares are in the shape?
(b) What is the area of the shape?

2 Find the area of each of these shapes in mm^2.

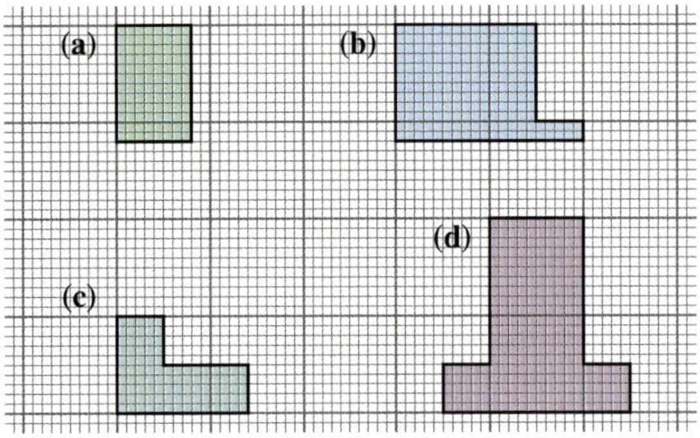

3 Draw accurately shapes with area:
(a) $300\ \text{mm}^2$ **(b)** $450\ \text{mm}^2$

4 Draw around a 25 cent coin. Next to it draw a square with area $100\ \text{mm}^2$.
(a) Which shape has the larger area?
(b) Estimate, in mm^2, the area of the 25 cent coin.

5 Repeat Question 4 for:
(a) a postage stamp
(b) one face of a small dice
(c) a blade of grass
(d) a one cent coin
(e) a ten cent coin.

The square metre

The square centimetre is too small to measure large areas like the area of a football stadium.

For larger areas, the square metre (m^2) is used.

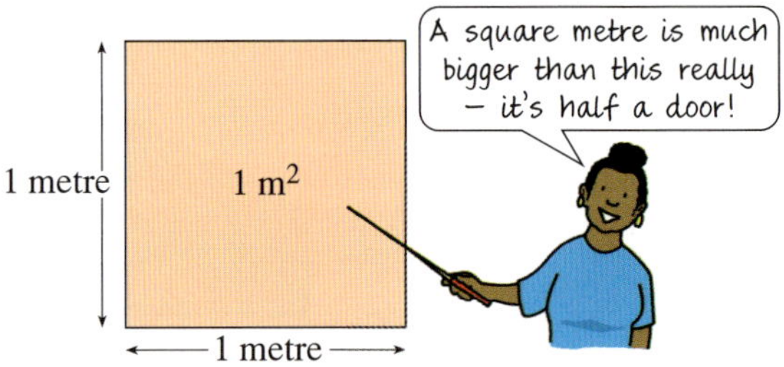

A square metre is a square with side 1 m. It is about half the size of a door.

Exercise 11G

1 Take a piece of chalk and draw a square with edge length 1 metre on the classroom floor. What is the area of your square?

2 Estimate the area, in m^2, of:
(a) your classroom ceiling
(b) the side of a bus
(c) a football field
(d) your bedroom floor
(e) the classroom window.

3 Which unit would you choose for measuring the area of:
(a) the classroom floor
(b) your smallest fingernail
(c) the unsharpened end of your pencil
(d) this page
(e) the school playground
(f) the top of your desk
(g) a handkerchief
(h) a one cent coin
(i) a ten dollar note
(j) a shirt button?

11.4 Areas of rectangles and triangles

Areas of rectangles

These rectangles are drawn on centimetre squared paper. Count squares to find the area of each. Then copy and complete the table.

(a)

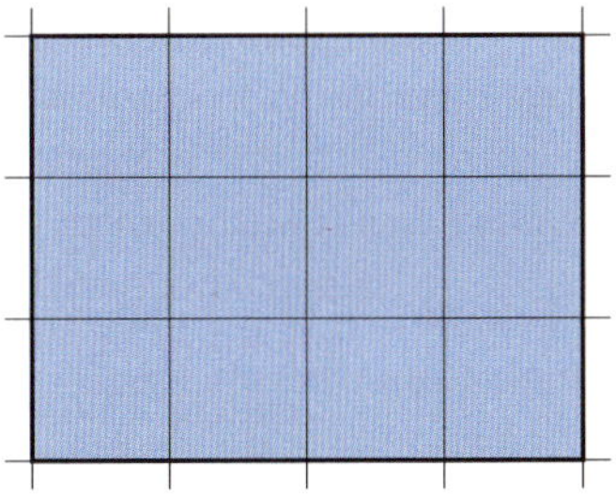

(b)

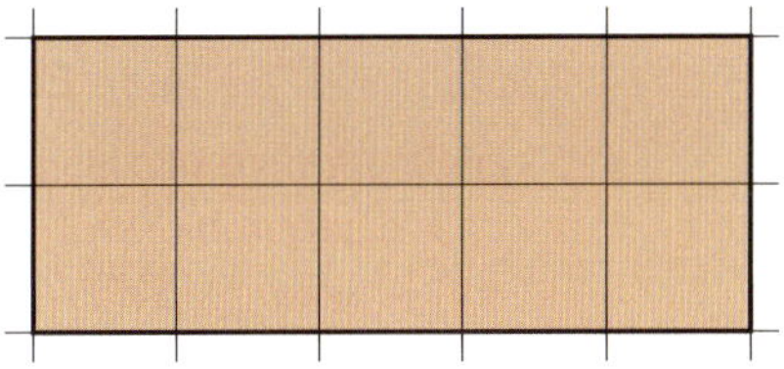

(c)

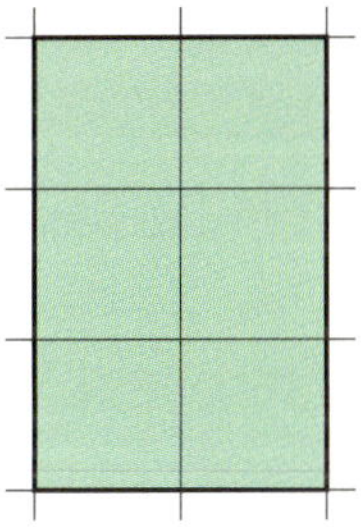

(d)

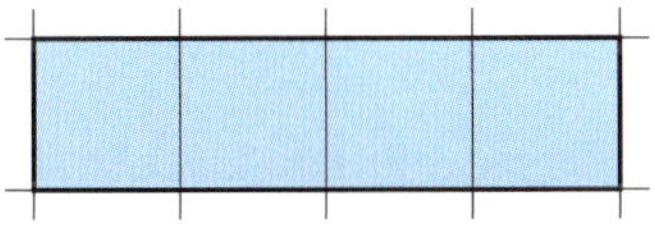

	Area	Length	Width	Length × Width
(a)	12	4	3	12
(b)				
(c)				
(d)				

Compare the first column and the last column of the completed table. What do you notice?
Can you see a quick way to find the area of a rectangle without counting all the squares?

- The area of a rectangle = length × width

Example 3

Find the area of the rectangle below.

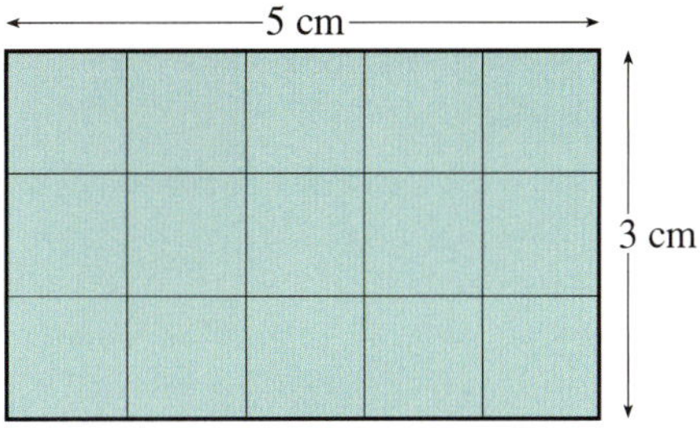

The length of the rectangle = 5 cm
The width of the rectangle = 3 cm
Area of rectangle = length × width
= 5 cm × 3 cm
= 15 cm^2

Exercise 11H

1 Find the area of each rectangle when drawn on centimetre squared paper:

(a)

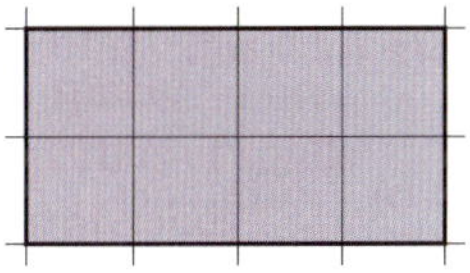

(b)

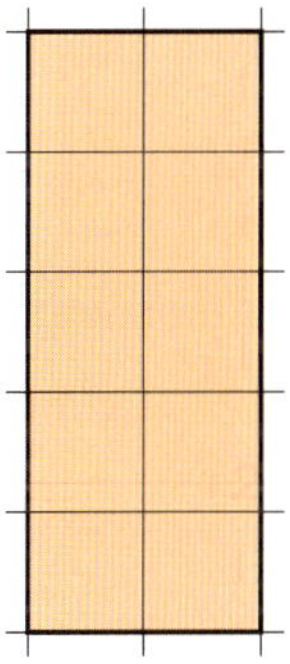

(c)

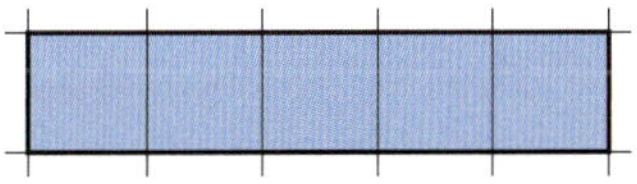

(d)

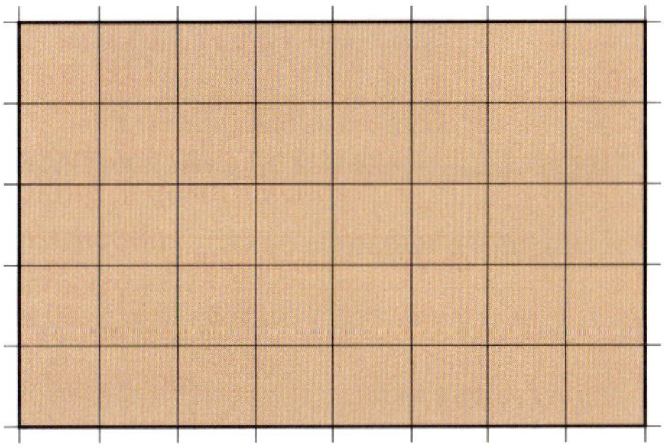

2 Find the area of each rectangle.

(a)

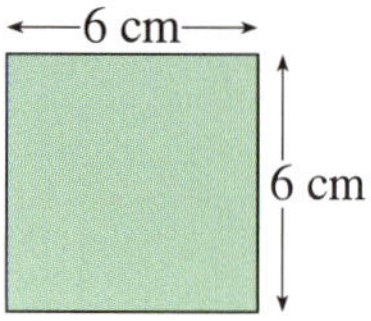

(b)

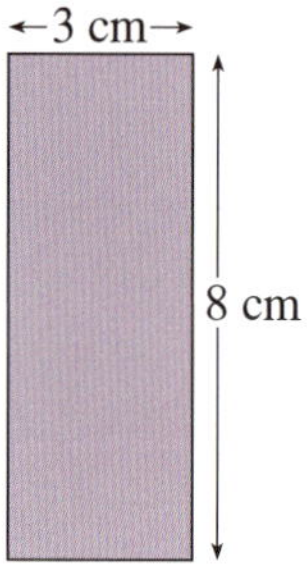

(c)

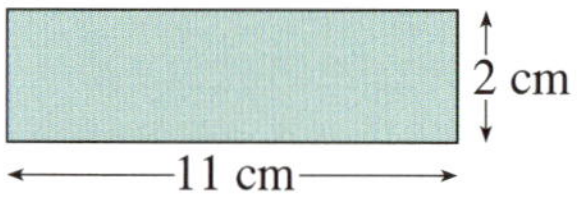

(d)

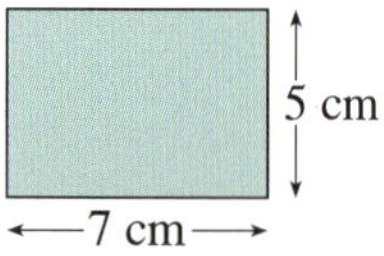

(e)

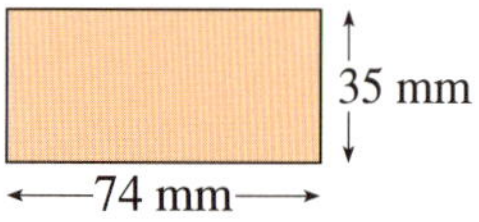

3 Copy and complete the table for rectangles.

Length (in cm)	Width (in cm)	Area (in cm^2)
9	7	
6	3	
6		24
	4	36
	10	110
12		144

4 The rectangle below has length, L, and width W.

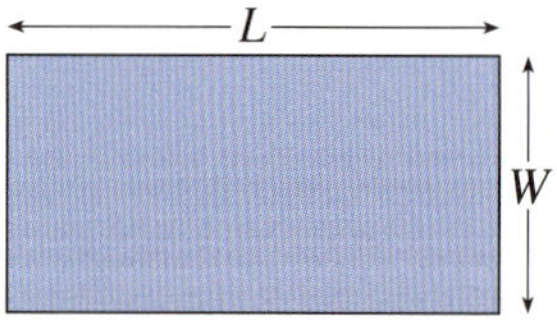

Write down its area, A in terms of L and W.

5 Look at the rectangle below.

(a) Measure, with your ruler, its length and width.

(b) What do you notice about the length and width?

(c) What is the special name for this sort of rectangle?

(d) What is its area?

6 Find the area of the square with each side:

(a) 3 cm **(b)** 5 cm

(c) 4 cm **(d)** 10 cm

7 Fill in the missing measurements:

Rectangle	Length (cm)	Width (cm)	Area (cm^2)
Picture	25 cm	20 cm	
Envelope		25 cm	150
Book	30 cm		600
Poster	50 cm		1200

8 Draw as many rectangles as you can with area 24 cm^2.

9 A square carpet has an area of 36 m^2. What is the length of one side?

10 A rectangle is 40 mm long and 30 mm wide. Find its area in

(a) square millimetres

(b) square centimetres.

11 A school has two football fields. One is 115 m long and 60 m wide and the other is 105 m long and 85 m wide.
Which football field has the larger area and by how much?

12 A carpenter wants to make a rectangular table with an area of 1.8 m^2. The width must be 90 cm.
How long should he make it?

13 The floor of a room 3 m by 4 m is to be covered with tiles. The tiles are 20 cm square.
How many tiles are needed?

14 A rectangular photograph measures 15 cm by 12 cm. It is fixed on to a rectangular piece of cardboard which measures 24 cm by 30 cm.
What area of the cardboard is not covered by the photograph?

15 Mrs Ali decided that she needed 15 m^2 of curtain material. She was shown some materials in three different widths:

(a) 90 cm **(b)** 1.2 m **(c)** 1.5 m

What length of each width would she have to buy?

Areas of triangles

Example 4

Find the area of the triangle below, drawn on centimetre squares.

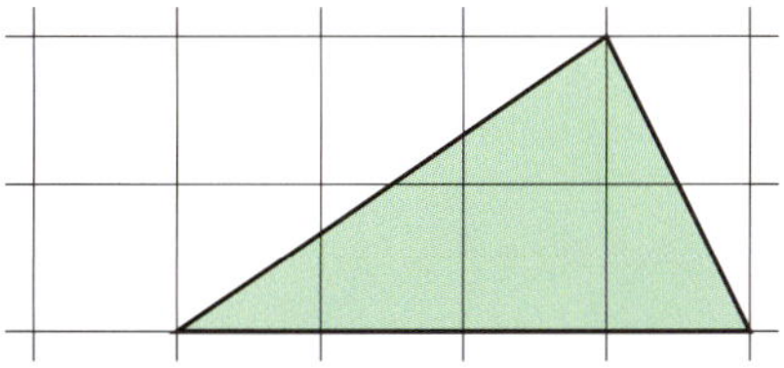

A simple way to find the area is to complete a rectangle surrounding the triangle:

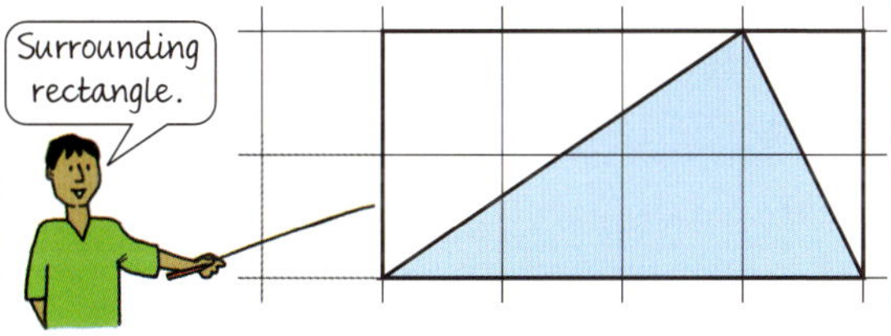

Then divide the triangle into two triangles A and B:

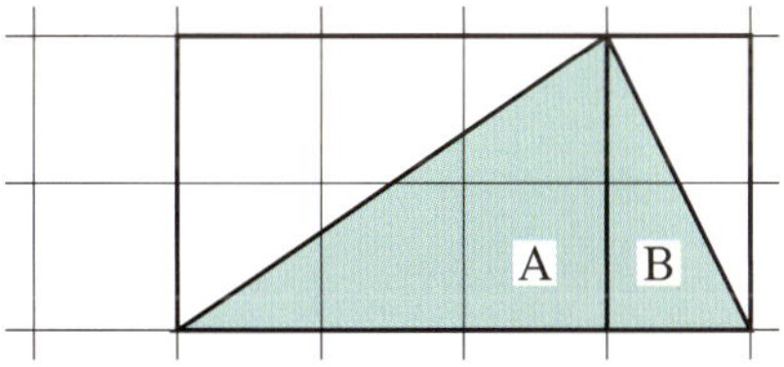

Area of triangle A $= \frac{1}{2}$ of 6 cm^2

$= 3$ cm^2

Area of triangle B $= \frac{1}{2}$ of 2 cm^2

$= 1$ cm^2

Area shaded triangle $= 3$ cm^2 $+ 1$ cm^2

$= 4$ cm^2

Notice area of surrounding rectangle

$= 8$ cm^2

Exercise 11I

1 Using the method of Example 4 find the area of these shaded triangles.

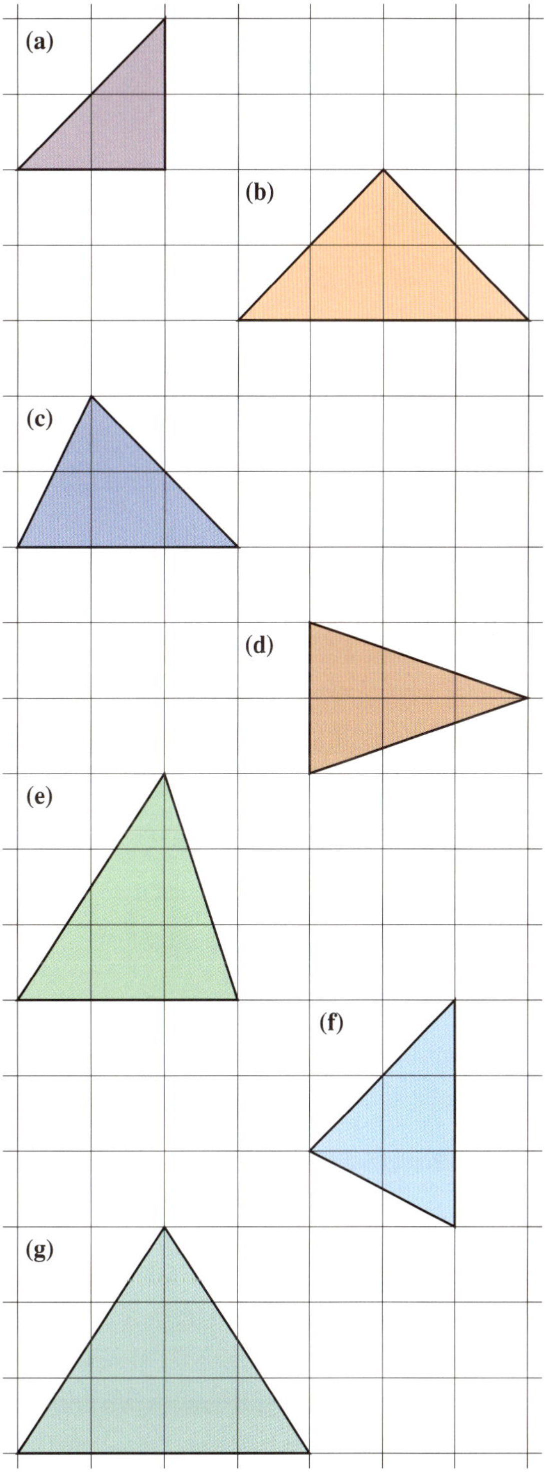

2 **(i)** Using your answers to Question 1 copy and complete the table:

	Area of surrounding rectangle	Area of triangle
(a)		
(b)		
(c)		
(d)		
(e)		
(f)		
(g)		

(ii) What do you notice about the two columns?

(iii) Copy and complete.

Area of triangle = … × area of surrounding rectangle.

3 **(a)** Find the area of this rectangle.

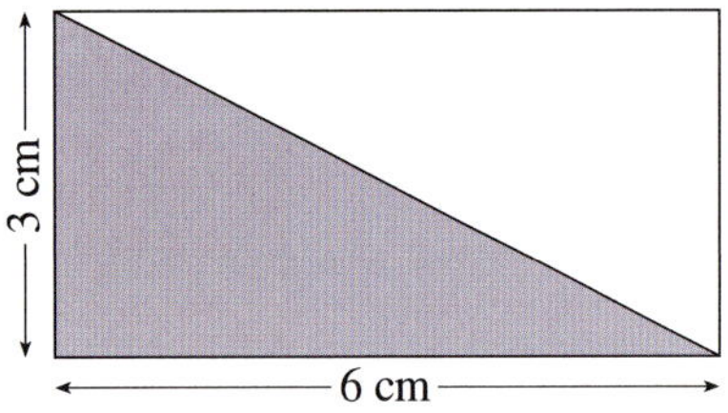

(b) What fraction of the rectangle is the shaded triangle?

(c) What is the area of the shaded triangle?

4 Find the area of the shaded triangle.

(a)

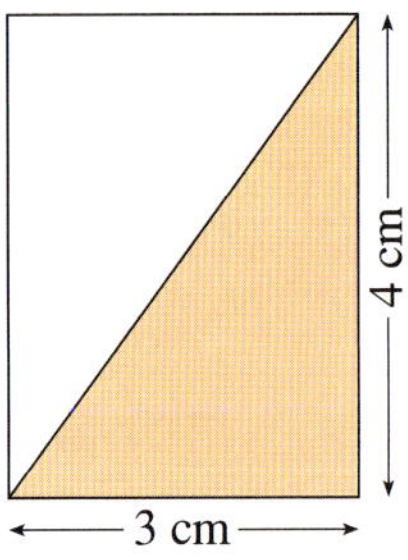

(b)

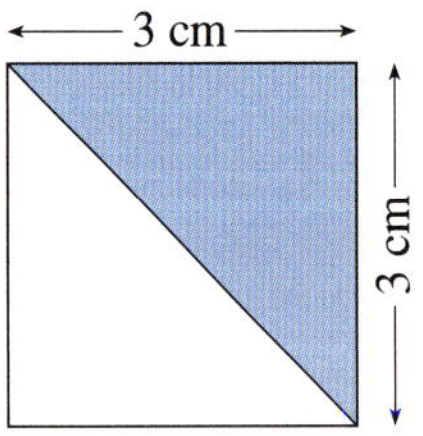

5 Look at this triangle.

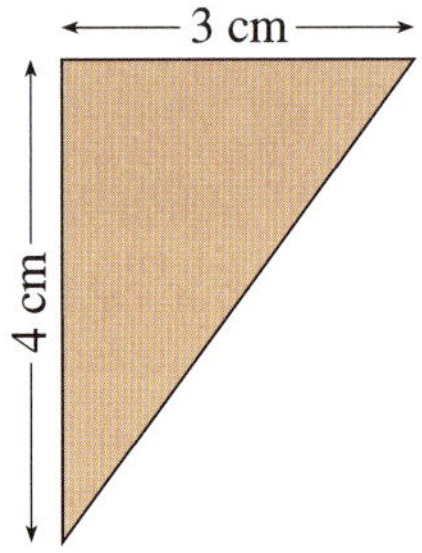

(a) Is the area of the triangle the same as half of a rectangle with sides 3 cm and 4 cm?

(b) Find the area of the triangle.

6 Find the area of these triangles.

(a)

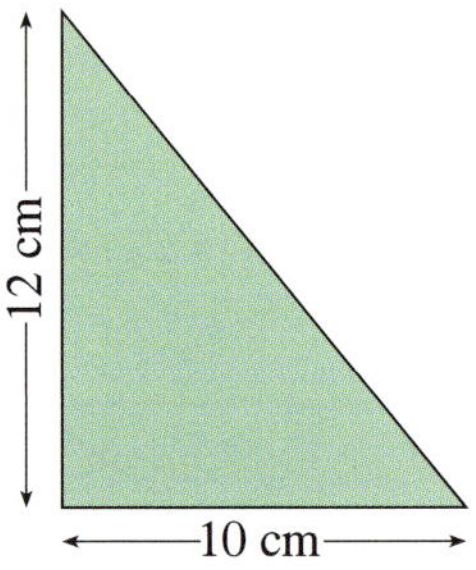

(b)

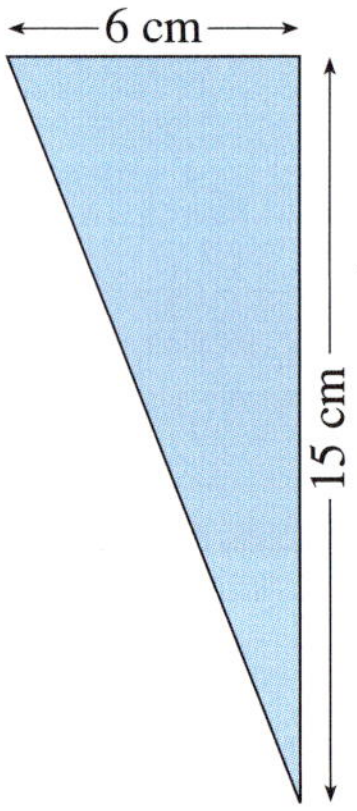

(c)

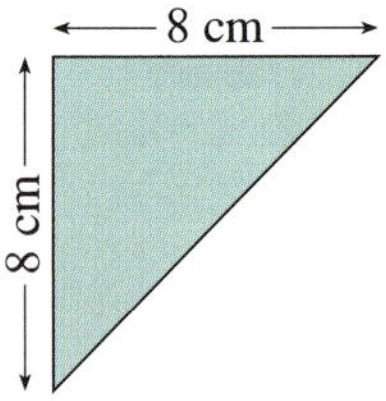

(d)

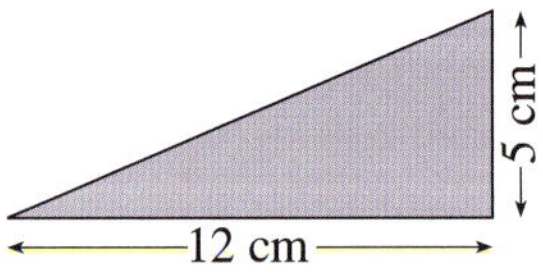

7 Find the areas of these triangles.

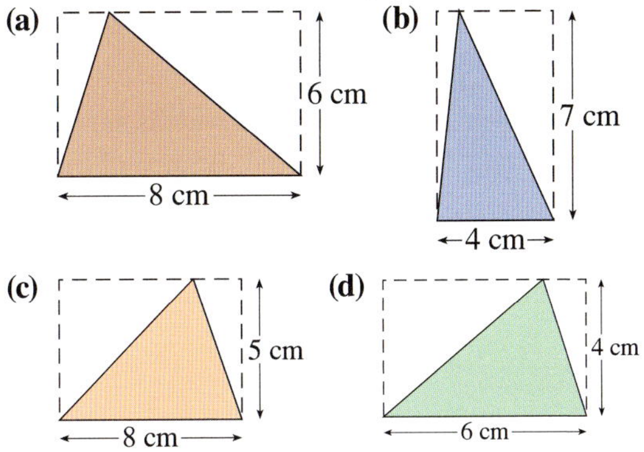

8 What is the area of the shaded part?

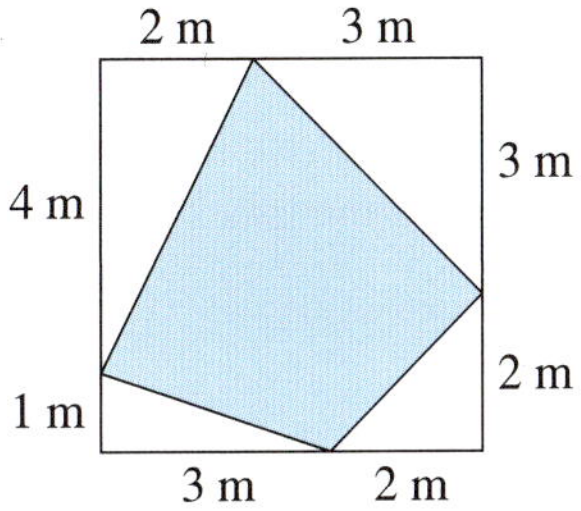

9 Find the area of this shape.

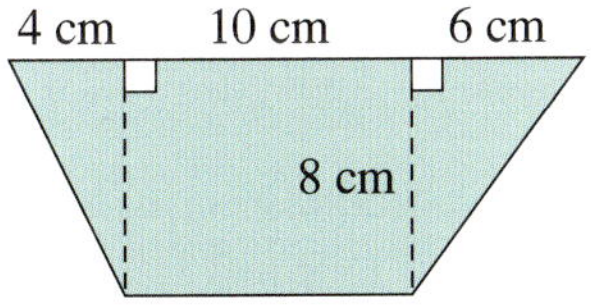

10 Find the area of the quadrilateral.

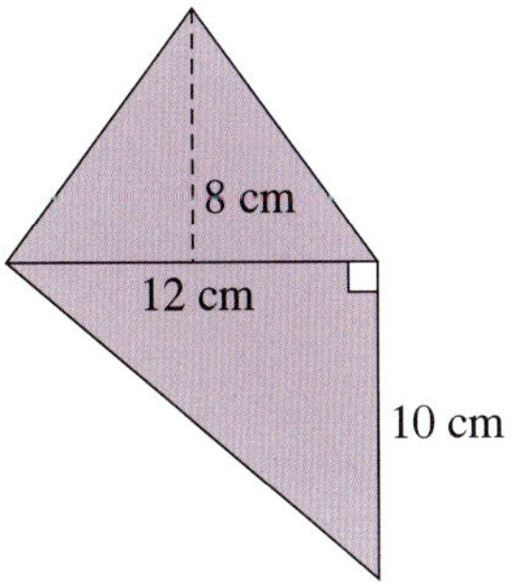

11 What is the area of this field?

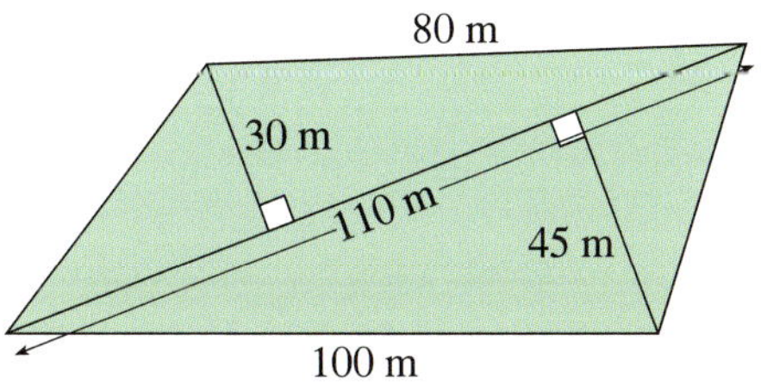

Perimeter

- The distance around the edge of a shape is called its **perimeter**.

Exercise 11J – mixed questions

1 Look at the shape below which is drawn on centimetre squares.

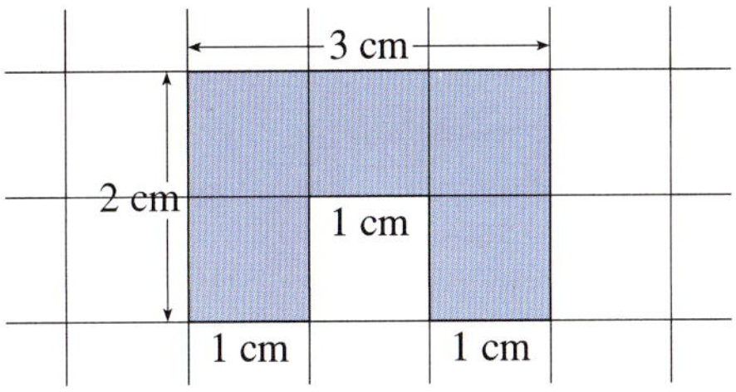

(a) Do you agree that the distance around the edge is 12 cm?

(b) Do you agree that the area of the shape is 5 cm^2?

(c) Draw on centimetre squared paper as many shapes as you can with perimeter 12 cm and area 5 cm^2.

2 **(a)** Cut out eight 1 cm squares.

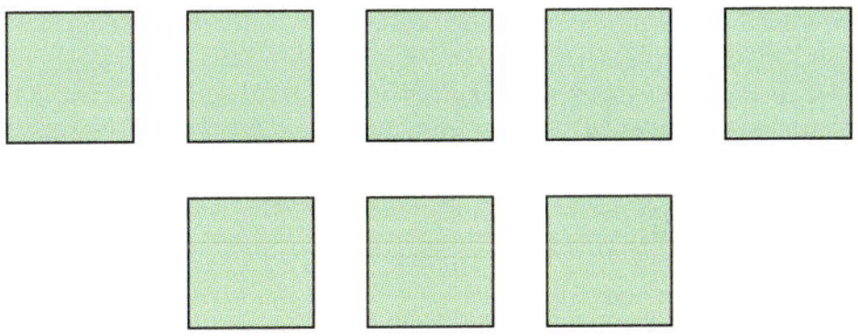

(b) Can you fit all these squares together to make a shape with perimeter 12 cm?

(c) Can you fit 6 of the squares together to make a shape with perimeter 12 cm?

(d) What is the smallest number of squares you can use to make a shape with perimeter 12 cm?

3 Take six of the squares you cut out in Question 2.

(a) What shape can you make which has the smallest perimeter?

(b) What shape can you make which has the largest perimeter?

4 (a) Use an atlas to trace maps of St Vincent and Grenada on to centimetre squared paper. (Make sure they have the same scale—ask your teacher if you are not sure.)
(b) Find the area of the maps in square centimetres.
(c) Which country has the larger area?

5 (a) Estimate the area of your desk top.
(b) Now measure the length and width of your desk top in centimetres.
(c) Calculate its area to the nearest cm^2. Was your estimate a good one?

6 Find the area of one page of your exercise book. What area of paper was needed to make your exercise book?

7 The area of a rectangle is the same as the area of a square of side 12 cm. If the rectangle is 18 cm long, find its width.

8 A rectangular piece of cardboard 160 cm long and 80 cm wide is cut into 8 equal squares. Find the area of each square.

9 A garden 10 m long by 8 m wide is surrounded by a path 1.5 m wide. Find the area of the path.

10 A tray base is cut out a rectangular piece of wood 120 cm by 60 cm.

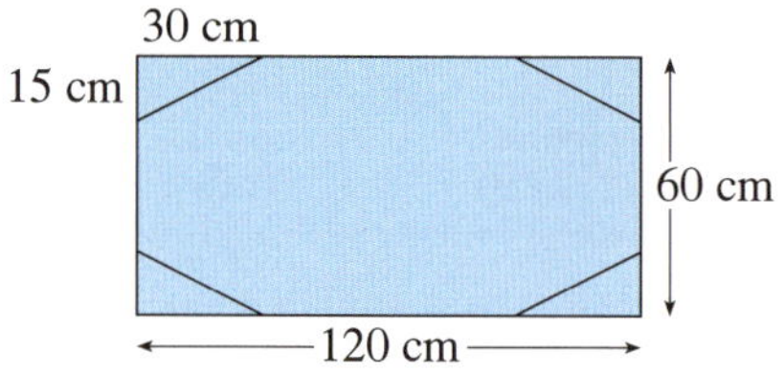

The four corners cut out are right-angled triangles with dimensions as shown.
Find the area of the tray base.

11 Consolidation

Example 1

What is the area of the shaded shape?

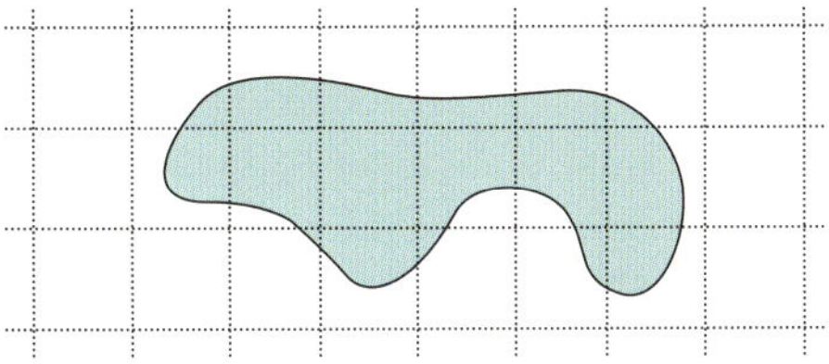

First count the whole squares. Then count all the half or larger squares.

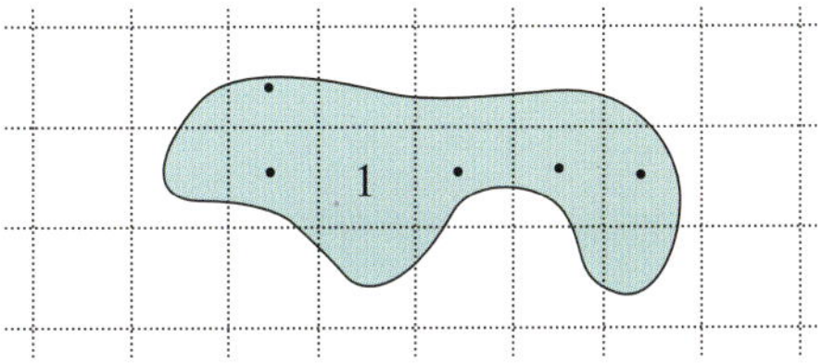

There is one whole square and 5 half sized or larger squares.

Area $\simeq 1 + 5 = 6$ squares

Example 2

Find the area of these rectangles.

(a)

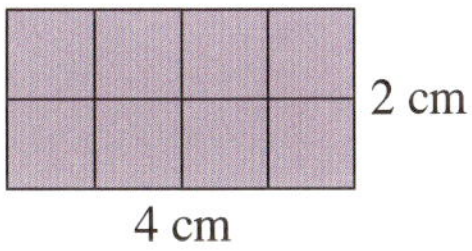

(b)

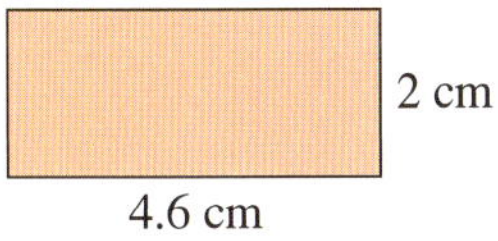

(a) Area of rectangle = length × width

$= 4 \text{ cm} \times 2 \text{ cm}$

$= 8 \text{ cm}^2$

(b) Area of rectangle = length × width

$= 4.6 \text{ cm} \times 2 \text{ cm}$

$= 9.2 \text{ cm}^2$

Example 3

Find the perimeter of these shapes.

(a)

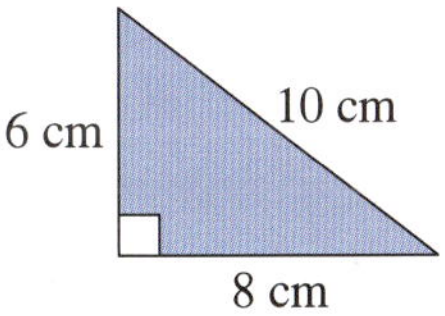

(b)

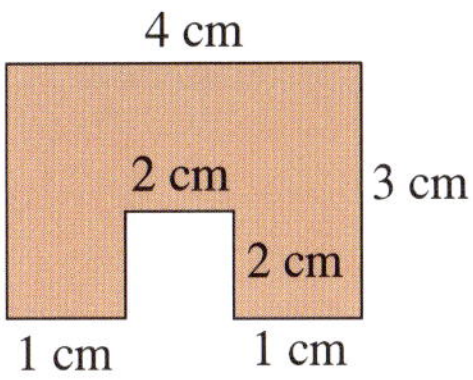

(a) Perimeter = distance around shape

$= 6 \text{ cm} + 8 \text{ cm} + 10 \text{ cm}$

$= 24 \text{ cm}$

(b) Perimeter = distance around shape

$= 4 \text{ cm} + 3 \text{ cm} + 1 \text{ cm} + 2 \text{ cm}$

$+ 2 \text{ cm} + 2 \text{ cm} + 1 \text{ cm} + 3 \text{ cm}$

$= 18 \text{ cm}$

Exercise 11

1 Find the approximate area of these shapes by counting squares.

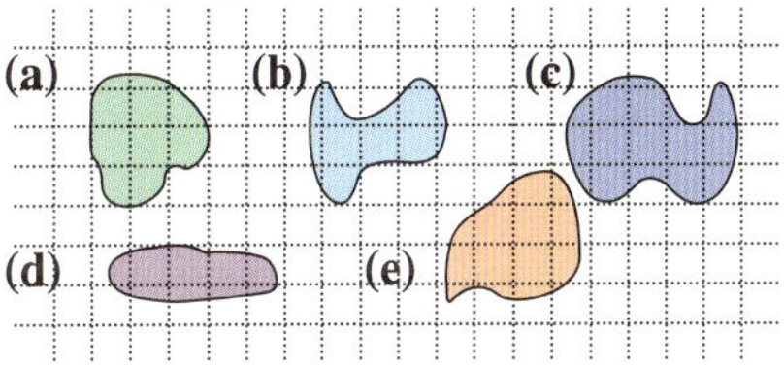

2 Draw five different shapes with area

(a) 6 cm^2 **(b)** 8 cm^2 **(c)** 10 cm^2

(d) 28 mm^2

3 Which metric units of area would you use to measure the area of

(a) your classroom door **(b)** your hand

(c) a computer screen **(d)** a cat's paw

(e) Anguilla **(f)** a blade of grass?

4 Calculate the area of these rectangles.

(a)

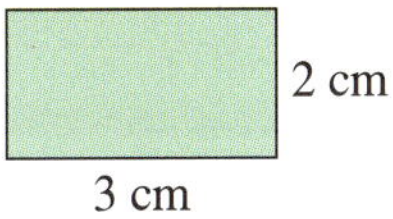

(b)

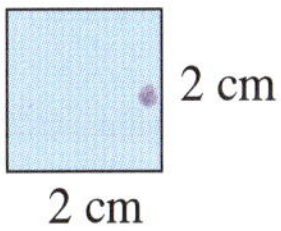

5 A rectangular room is 7 m wide. If its area is 35 m^2, what is the room's length?

6 Find the perimeter of these shapes.

(a)

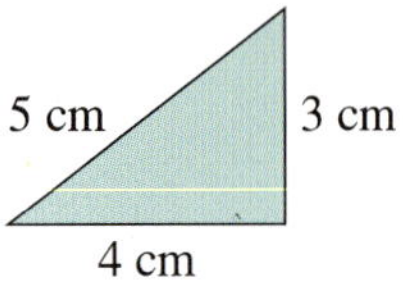

(b)

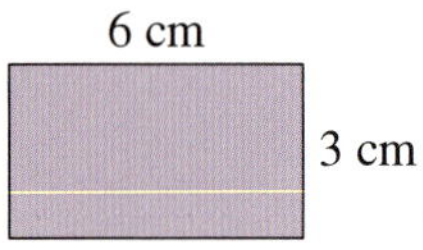

(c)

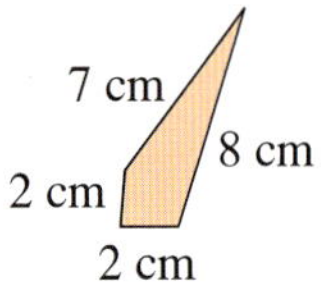

Application 11

7 Place your hand, fingers together, on cm^2 paper and trace.

(a) Count the squares to find the area of your hand.

(b) Draw around your hand again, but this time spread your fingers. What is the area of your hand now?

(c) Compare your two answers. What do you notice?

8 A double page of 'The Chronicle' newspaper is 56 cm wide and 43 cm deep. Find:

(a) the area of a single page

(b) the total area of paper required to produce a newspaper with 32 pages.

9 A wall of a shower in a bathroom is 2 m high and 1.5 m wide.

(a) What is the area of the wall in m^2?

(b) What is the area of the wall in cm^2?

(c) The bathroom tiles are square with a length of 15 cm.
What is the area of such a tile in cm^2?

(d) How many tiles would be needed to tile the shower wall?

(e) What would be the cost of tiling if one tile sold for $3.15?

Companion CD

Want some extra practice? Go to Chapter 11 on your companion CD for further exercises, animations, and solutions.

Summary

You should know ...

1 The size of a surface is called its area.

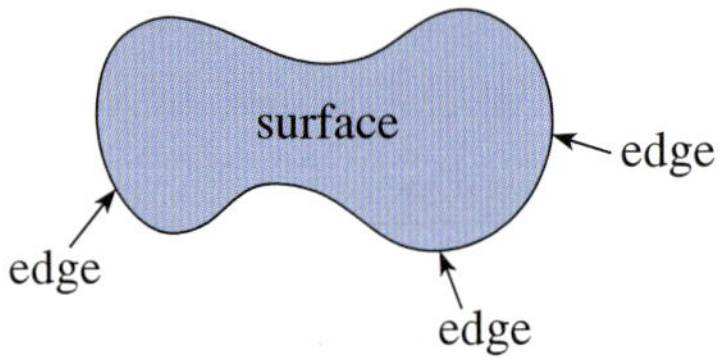

You can compare areas by covering shapes with tesselations.

Check out

1 Which is larger, X or Y?

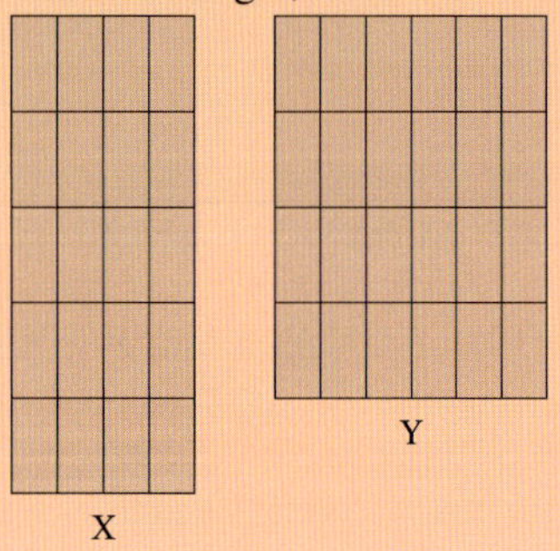

2 How to find areas of shapes by counting triangles or squares.

Area = 11 + 11 = 22 squares

2 Find the area of these shapes.

(a)

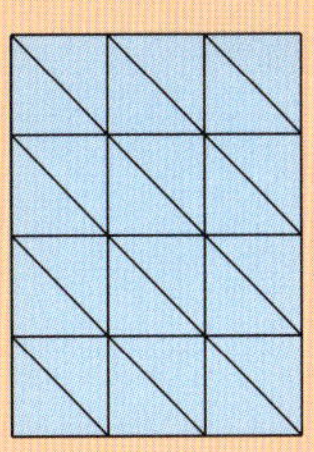

(b)

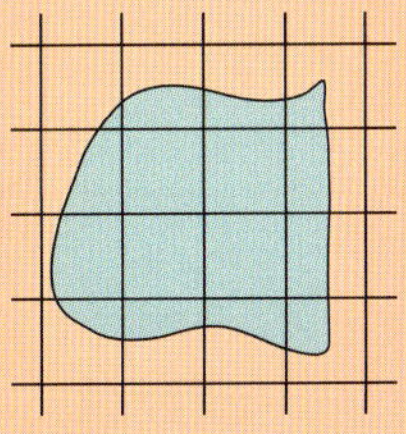

3 Standard units of area are:

One square metre = 1 m^2

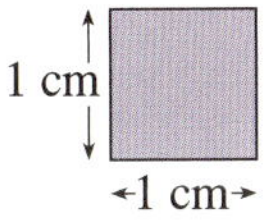

One square centimetre = 1 cm^2

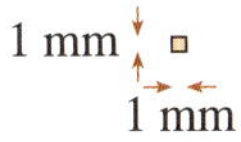

One square millimetre = 1 mm^2

100 mm^2 = 1 cm^2

3 Which unit would you use to find the area of:

(a) your fingernail
(b) an envelope
(c) a cricket pitch
(d) a fly's wing?

4 You can find the area of a shape by counting the number of square centimetres or square millimetres in it.

For example:

(a)

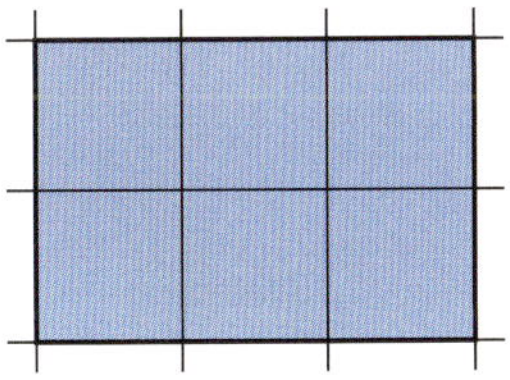

Area = 6 cm^2

(b)

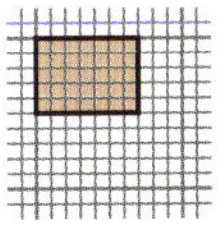

Area = 35 mm^2

4 Find the area of these shapes

(a)

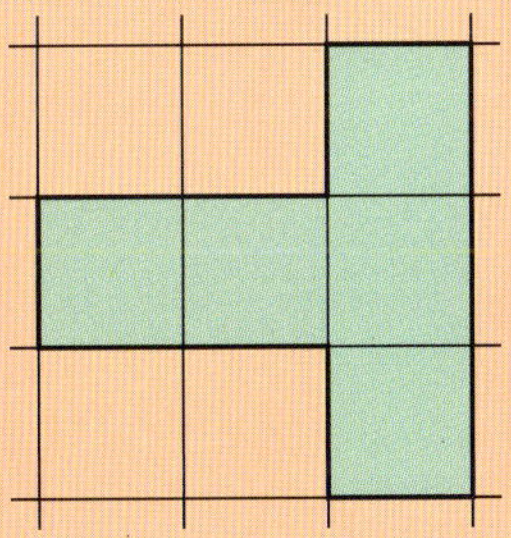

(b)

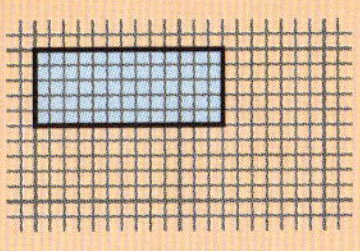

5 The area of a rectangle, A is given by $A = \text{length} \times \text{width}$

For example:

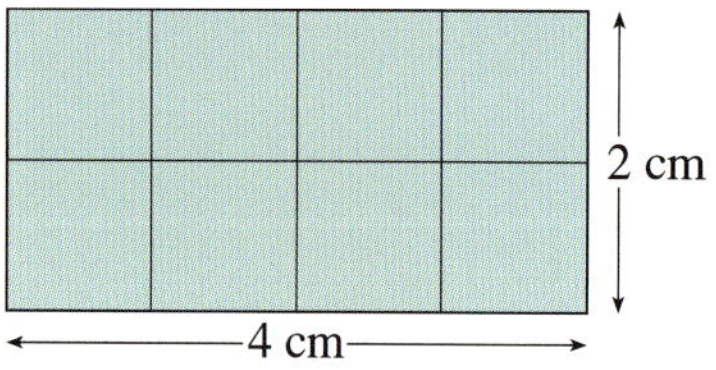

Area of rectangle = length × width

$= 4\text{ cm} \times 2\text{ cm}$

$= 8\text{ cm}^2$

6 How to find the area of a triangle:

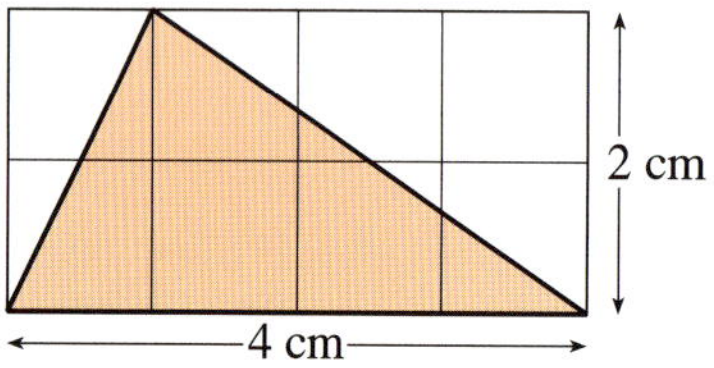

Area of triangle $= \frac{1}{2}$ area of rectangle

$= \frac{1}{2}$ of 8 cm^2

$= 4\text{ cm}^2$

7 The distance around the edge of a shape is called its perimeter.

5 **(a)** Find the area of the rectangle below.

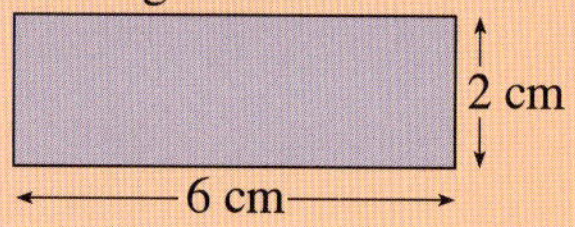

(b) What is the area of a football pitch 80 m long and 50 m wide?

6 What is the area of these triangles?

(a)

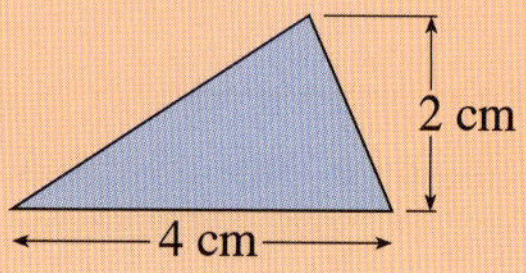

(b)

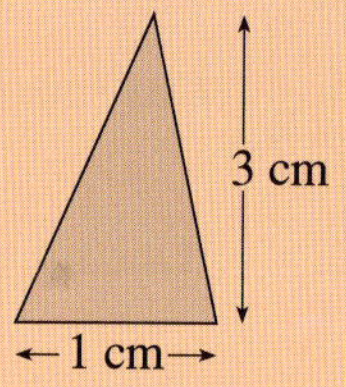

7 What is the perimeter of this shape?

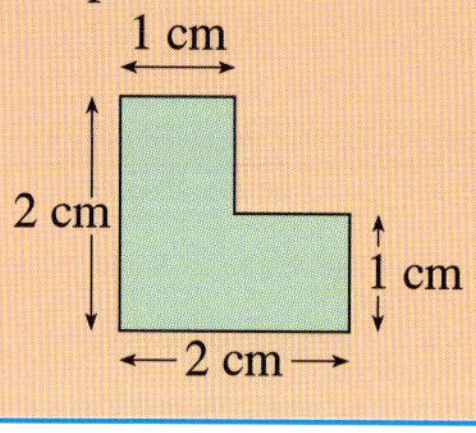

Symbols and patterns 12

Objectives

- ✔ identify constants and variables
- ✔ add, subtract and multiply symbols
- ✔ substitute numbers for letters
- ✔ describe a situation using symbols
- ✔ spot patterns in sequences and add extra terms
- ✔ work out the *n*th term of a sequence
- ✔ solve simple equations

What's the point?

The use of symbols or letters for numbers helps to describe relationships among variables. For example, the speed (v) of a race car is related to the time (t) it takes to travel a particular distance (d) by $v = d \div t$.

Before you start

You should know ...

1 The area of a rectangle is length × width.

2 The perimeter of a shape is the distance around it.

Check in

1 What is the area of a rectangle of length 12 cm and width 8 cm?

2 Find the perimeter of the figure.

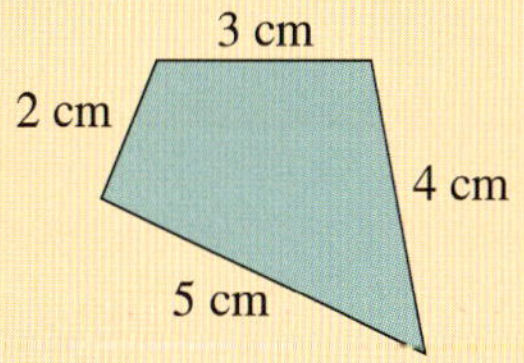

12.1 Symbols

- A symbol is a short way of writing information.

Sometimes you will see a workman holding up a red flag on a busy road which is being repaired.

What does the red flag mean?

What does the sign  mean on an ordinance survey map?

What do you think the sign  means?

Where might you find this sign?

Often, on boxes, you will find the sign 

What would you expect to find in the box?

What does this sign mean?

The red flag, the , the  and the  are all **symbols**. They are used instead of words to tell us something.

Numerals are also symbols. They are used instead of words. *9* is the symbol of *nine*. *106* is the symbol for *one hundred and six*, and so on.

Exercise 12A

1 Write down six more symbols (not numerals) and what they represent. (Think about traffic signs and symbols on maps.)

2 Write down the symbol for:
(a) forty-four **(b)** ninety-five
(c) two hundred and thirty
(d) fifty-seven.

3 In mathematics, letters are often used as symbols for words and numbers. For example:
A is used for area
l is used for length
h is used for height
g could be used for the number of girls in a class
t could be used for the marks in a test.

What letter would you choose to represent
(a) the number of boys in the class
(b) the number of sisters a student has
(c) a student's shoe size
(d) the mass of fish a fisherman catches
(e) the time for the 100 m race on sports day
(f) the distance between two cities
(g) the population of a country
(h) the number of runs in a cricket match?

Constants and variables

- A **constant** is a symbol which always means the same thing. For example, 9 and 7 are constants.
- A **variable** is a symbol which can represent different numbers.

Exercise 12B

1 **(a)** Look up the word 'constant' in the dictionary. Write down its meaning.
(b) Write down six more symbols that are constants.

2 **(a)** If A is the symbol for the area of a rectangle, l is the symbol for its length, and w is the symbol for its width, write an equation for the relationship between A, l and w.

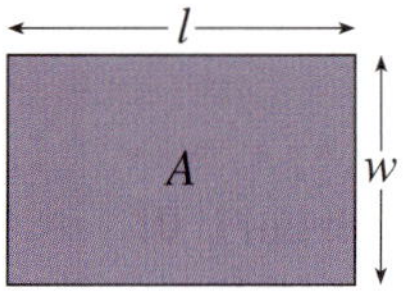

(b) Use the relationship you found to copy and complete the table.

l	5	7	6	8
w	2	3	10	12
A				

(c) Look at the table you completed. Are A, l and w constants?
Why?

3 **(a)** If P is the symbol for the perimeter of an equilateral triangle and a is the symbol for the length of a side, write an equation for the relationship between P and a.

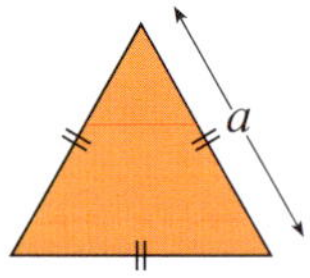

(b) Use the relationship you found to copy and complete the table:

a	4	5	6
P			

In Question 2 above, A, l and w are variables because each of them can be used to represent different numbers.

In the first column, for example, l represents 5.

In the second column it represents 7.

12.2 Adding, subtracting and multiplying symbols

The part of mathematics where letters are used to represent numbers is called **algebra**. In this section we look at the way to add, subtract and multiply using letters.

Adding and subtracting

$7 + 7 + 7 = 3 \times 7$
$23 + 23 + 23 = 3 \times 23$

In the same way

$a + a + a = 3 \times a$

and

$b + b + b - b = 2 \times b$

Example 1

Simplify:
(a) $9 + 9 + 9 + 9 - 5 - 5$
(b) $p + p + p + p - q - q$
(c) $a + a + a + a - a - a + a$

(a) $9 + 9 + 9 + 9 - 5 - 5$
$= 4 \times 9 - 2 \times 5$
$= 36 - 10$
$= 26$

(b) $p + p + p + p - q - q$
$= 4 \times p - 2 \times q$

(c) $a + a + a + a - a - a + a$
$= a + a + a + a + a - a - a$
$= 5 \times a - 2 \times a$
$= 3 \times a$

Exercise 12C

1 Simplify:
(a) $a + a + a + a$
(b) $m + m + m + m + m$
(c) 🍎 + 🍎 + 🍎 + 🍎 + 🍎 + 🍎
(d) $\triangle + \triangle + \triangle + \triangle + \triangle + \triangle + \triangle$
(e) $p + p + p + p + p + p - p - p$
(f) $l + l + l + l + b - b$
(g) $x + x + x + x + y + y + y$
(h) $x + x + y + y + y + y + z + z - z + z$

2 Simplify:
(a) $x + x + x - x - x + x$
(b) $a + a - b + a + b + b$
(c) $p + p - q + p$
(d) $p + p + p + p - p - q - q$

Multiplying

The equation for the area of a rectangle is:

$A = l \times w$.

This is written in a short way as $A = lw$.

The $\times$ sign is left out.

Here are some more multiplications written in a short way.

$3 \times n = 3n$
$5 \times p = 5p$
$8 \times b = 8b$
$a \times b = ab$
$a \times c = ac$

You can also swap the order of multiplication. For example:

$3 \times 5 = 5 \times 3$
$a \times b = n \times a$
$n \times 3 = 3 \times n$

So $n \times 3$ can be written as $3n$.
The numeral should be written before the letter.

Exercise 12D

1 Write the multiplication in a short way.
(a) $5 \times p$ **(b)** $x \times 6$
(c) $3 \times d$ **(d)** $8 \times m$
(e) $g \times 9$ **(f)** $12 \times z$

(g) $b \times c$ **(h)** $x \times y$
(i) $m \times n$ **(j)** $d \times p$
(k) $q \times s$ **(l)** $a \times z$

2 Work out Exercise 12C Question 2 again. This time write the multiplications in a short way.

Algebraic expressions

Your answers to Question 2, such as $3p - 2q$, are called algebraic expressions.

- An **algebraic expression** is one which contains some letters instead of numbers.
  For example,
  $7a$ and $5x - 2y$ are both algebraic expressions.

Example 2

Find the area of the rectangle.

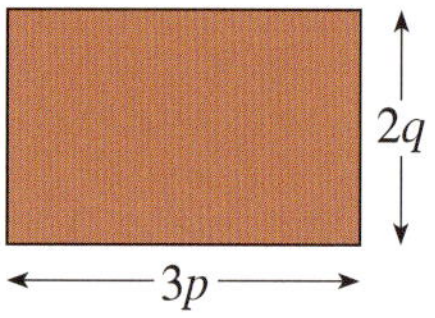

Area = length × width
$= 3p \times 2q$
$= 3 \times p \times 2 \times q$
$= 3 \times 2 \times p \times q$
$= 6pq$

Exercise 12E

1 Find the areas of the following rectangles. All lengths are in centimetres.

(a)
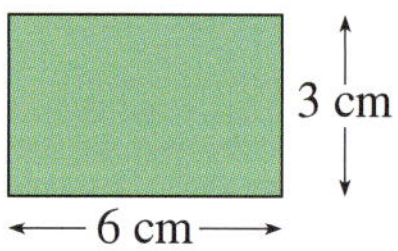

(b)
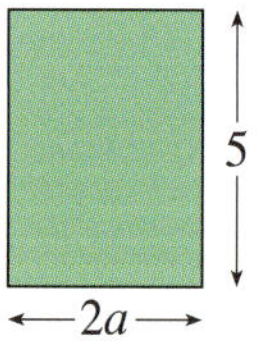

(c)
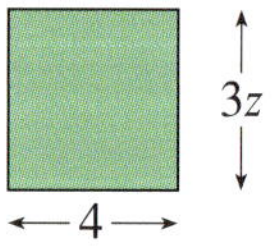

(d)
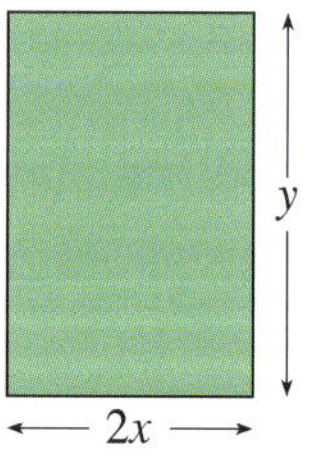

(e)
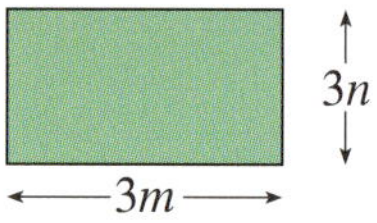

(f)
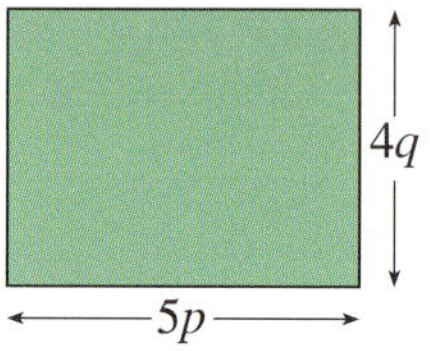

2 Find the perimeter of the following shapes. All lengths are in centimetres.

(a)
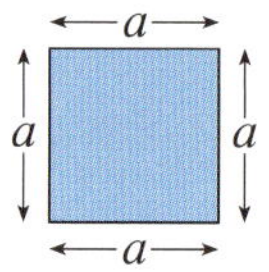

(b)
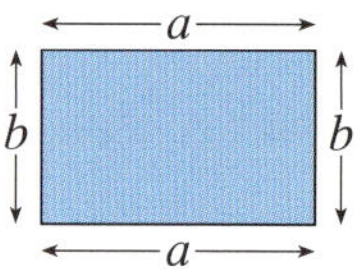

(c)
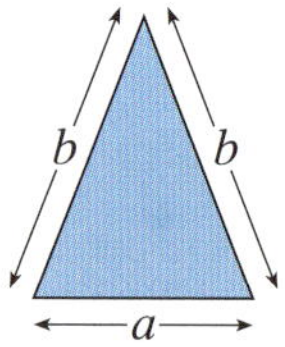

(d)
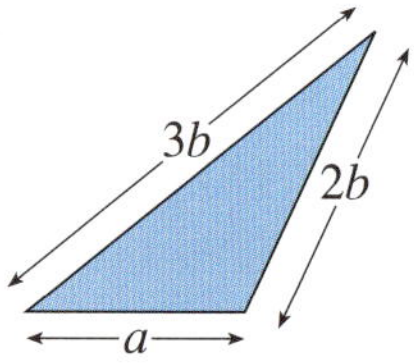

(e)
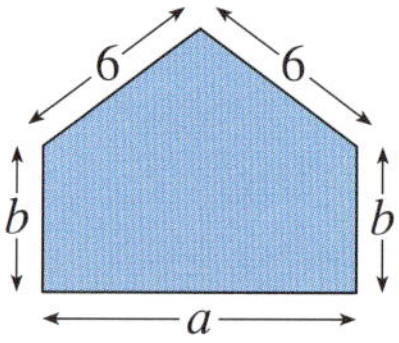

(f)
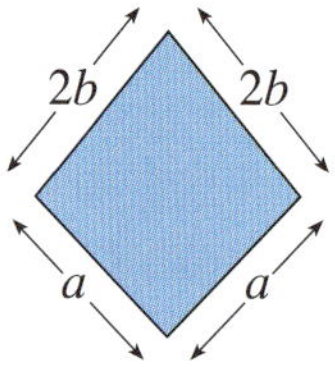

3 In Question 2 what would be the perimeter of the shapes if $a = 5$ and $b = 3$?

Substituting into algebraic expressions

In Question 3 of Exercise 12E you replaced the letters by numbers. This is called **substituting** numbers for letters.

In Question 2 of Exercise 12B you substituted numbers for A, l and w.

Exercise 12F

1 If $x = 4$, find the value of
(a) $2x$
(b) $3x - 6$

2 If $a = 2$ and $b = 5$, find the value of
(a) $2a + b$
(b) $3a - b$
(c) $2b + 6a - 3$

12.3 Writing expressions

Example 3

How many days are there in:
(a) 4 weeks
(b) 9 weeks
(c) x weeks
(d) $5x$ weeks?

(a) In one week there are 7 days
In 4 weeks there are $7 \times 4 = 28$ days
(b) In 9 weeks there are $7 \times 9 = 63$ days
(c) In x weeks there are $7 \times x = 7x$ days
(d) In $5x$ weeks there are $7 \times 5x = 35x$ days

Exercise 12G

1 How many millimetres are there in
(a) 1 cm (b) 6 cm (c) x cm?

2 How many seconds are there in
(a) 1 minute (b) 5 minutes
(c) x minutes?

3 How many legs have
(a) 1 person (b) 7 people
(c) x people

4 How many cents are there in
(a) 4 dollars (b) 15 dollars
(c) x dollars (d) $3x$ dollars?

5 How many players are there in
(a) 2 cricket teams
(b) 5 cricket teams
(c) y teams
(d) $4y$ cricket teams?

6 How many centimetres are there in
(a) 6 metres (b) 16 metres
(c) x metres (d) $8x$ metres?

7 How many days are there in
(a) 2 years (b) 10 years
(c) y years (d) $5y$ years?

8 A week has 7 days. So in x weeks and 3 days there are $7x + 3$ days.
In the same way, write an expression for the number of
(a) days in x weeks and 4 days
(b) days in y weeks – 5 days
(c) days in $2y$ weeks
(d) months in x years – 3 months
(e) months in $2x$ years + 5 months
(f) months in $3x$ years – 11 months
(g) cm in z metres – 30 centimetres
(h) cm in z metres + 40 centimetres.

9 (a) Adam is 7 years old. How old will he be in 3 years' time? How did you get your answer?
(b) Deo is y years old. How old will he be in three years' time?
(c) Johnny is p years old. How old will he be in 5 years' time?
(d) Betty is m years old. How old will she be in n years' time?

10 (a) Angus got \$5 from his father and \$8 from his mother. How much did he get altogether? How did you get your answer?
(b) Caroline got \$10 from her father and \$$d$ from her mother. How much did she get altogether?

11 (a) A car can hold 5 people. How many people can fit in 6 such cars? How did you get your answer?
(b) How many people could you fit into y cars?
(c) If a bus holds 48 people, how many people can fit in z buses?

12 (a) Steve has \$10. He wishes to share it equally between his 5 friends. How much does each friend get? How did you get your answer?
(b) June has \$$d$. She wishes to share it equally between 3 friends. How much does each friend get?

13 (a) Ambrose has \$14. Peter has \$6 less than Ambrose. How many dollars has Peter? How did you get your answer?
(b) How many dollars do Ambrose and Peter have altogether? How did you get your answer?
(c) Len has \$$x$. Tom has 10 dollars less than Len. How many dollars has Tom?
(d) How many dollars have they both together?

12.4 Writing equations

An equation is a statement which contains an equals sign: $E = F + V - 2$ is an equation.

Activity

For this section you will need centimetre squared paper, coloured pencils or crayons and scissors.

(a) From centimetre squared paper, cut out the strips in the list below.
Colour each one as shown in the last column, using coloured pencils or crayons.

Number of strips	Width	Length	Colour
1	1 cm	16 cm	Red
2	1 cm	8 cm	Green
4	1 cm	4 cm	Blue
8	1 cm	2 cm	Yellow

(b) **(i)** You can use the letter R to represent the red strip. Why is it a good letter to use?

(ii) Write down three letters that could be used to represent the green, blue and yellow strips.

(c) Place one of your green strips below the red strip, as in the diagram below.

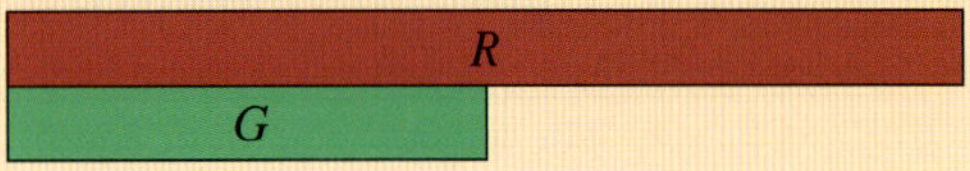

(i) How many blue strips can you add to the green strip to make up the length of the red strip?

(ii) How many yellow strips can you add to a green strip to make the same length as the red strip?

(d) Copy and complete:

(i) $R = G + \square\ B$

(ii) $R = G + \square\ Y$

Exercise 12H

Use the strips that you made for the Activity.

1 **(a)** How many blue strips equal one red strip?

(b) Copy and complete the equation:

$R = \square\ B$

(c) Find an equation connecting

(i) R and G **(ii)** G and B

(iii) R and Y **(iv)** G and Y

2 Find an equation connecting G, B and Y.

3 Find three equations connecting R, B and Y.

4 A bag contains 10 beads. There are g green beads and y yellow beads. Write an equation connecting g, y and 10.

5 **(a)** Look at angles $x°$ and $y°$ below. What do they add up to?

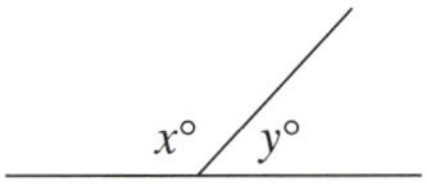

(b) Write an equation connecting $x°$, $y°$ and 180°.

6 Write an equation to show the relation between:

(a) $p°$, $q°$ and 90° in this diagram.

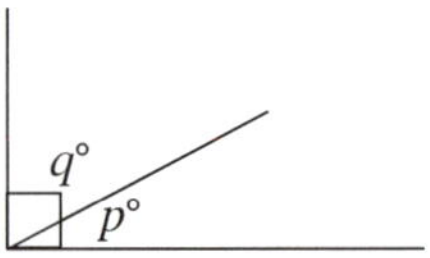

(b) $a°$, $b°$, $c°$, $d°$ and 360° in this diagram.

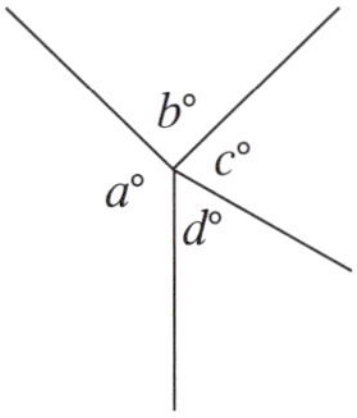

(c) $a°$, $b°$, $c°$ and 180° in this diagram.

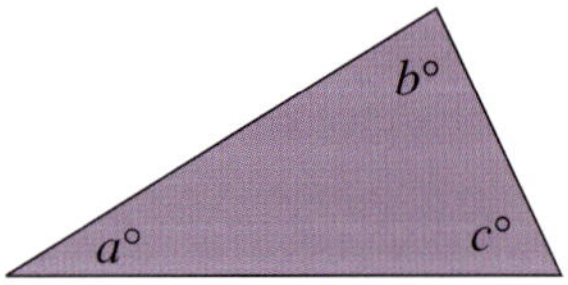

7 The first drawing below shows a cube. The second shows one face of this cube. The face has an area A cm^2.

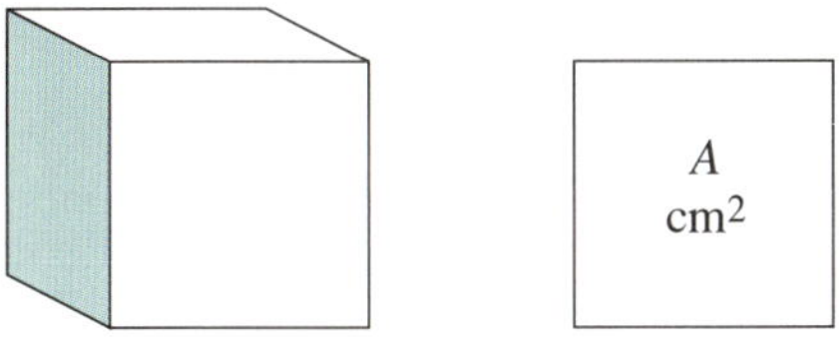

(a) How many faces has a cube?

(b) Is the area of each face of a cube the same?

(c) If T represents the total area of the surface of a cube, copy and complete:

$T = \square\, A$

8 (a) Look at the array of dots below. Without counting every dot, quickly find the number of dots in the array.

(i)  (ii) 

(iii)  (iv) 

(b) If n = number of dots in the array,
d = number of dots in each row,
r = number of rows,
find the equation connecting n, d and r.

9 The drawing shows a cuboid with lengths in centimetres.

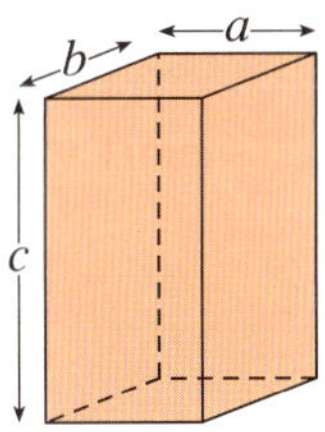

(a) How many faces has a cuboid?

(b) If T represents the total surface area of the cuboid, write an expression for T in terms of a, b, and c.

10 Look at this set of solids.

A set of solids

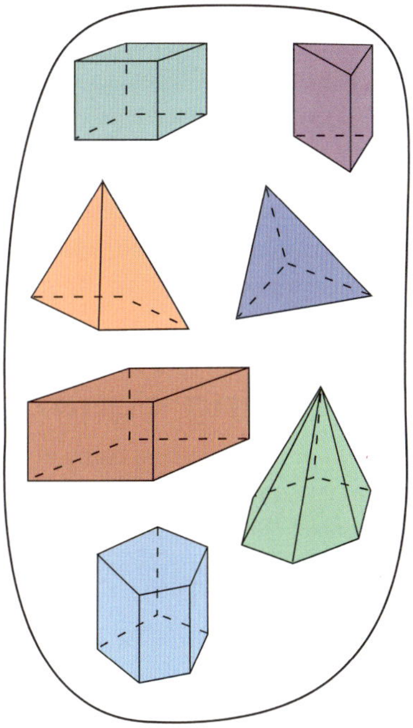

(a) Copy and complete the table, for the solids in the set.

Number of edges	Number of faces	Number of vertices	Number of faces + vertices

(b) Look at the first and last columns of your table. What could you add to each number in the first column to give the corresponding number in the last column?

(c) If E = number of edges
F = number of faces
V = number of vertices
write an equation connecting E, F and V.

The equation that you found in Question 10 is **Euler's relationship** for solids with plane faces. Euler was a famous German mathematician. (His name is pronounced Oil-er.)

12.5 Solving equations

- An *equation* is a statement using algebra that contains an equals sign.
  For example: $b + g = 5$ is an equation.

You can solve an equation using the balance method.

Example 4

Find x if $x + 5 = 7$.

Think of the equation as a balance:

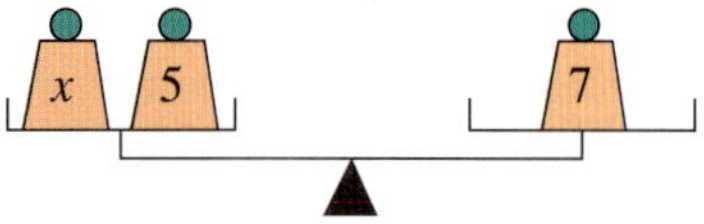

Take 5 from each side (-5).
The scales balance so $x = 2$.

Example 5

Use the balance method to find y if $2y + 1 = 9$.

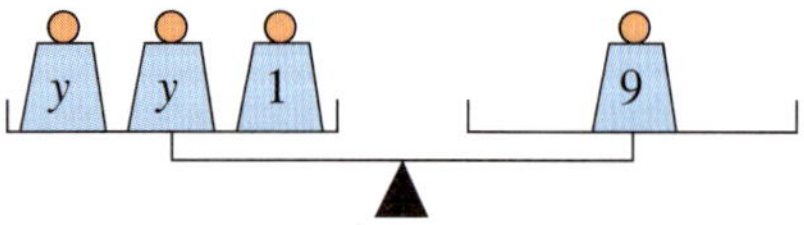

Take 1 from each side.
To make the scales balance $2y$ must be 8.
So $y = 4$.

Exercise 12I

Use the balance method to solve these equations.

1 $a + 6 = 9$

2 $b + 3 = 11$

3 $c + 5 = 6$

4 $8 + d = 12$

5 $2e + 1 = 11$

6 $3f + 4 = 19$

7 $2 + 5g = 17$

8 $h + 7 = 11$

9 $3i + 1 = 10$

10 $10 + 3j = 13$

11 $k + 7 = 7$

12 $2l + 1 = 5$

13 $3 + 2m = 9$

14 $n + 1 = 2n$

15 $2o + 5 = 3o$

16 $p - 1 = 5$

17 $q - 2 = 1$

18 $2r + 4 = 4r$

19 $s + 2 = 2s + 1$

20 $t + 7 = 2t - 1$

21 $3u - 1 = 14$

22 $v + 6 = 2v$

23 $3w - 4 = 17$

24 $4x - 1 = 15$

25 $2y + 3 = y + 7$

26 $3z + 1 = z + 3$

Equations can be used to solve simple word problems.

Example 6

Kisha and Kevin have \$20 altogether. Kisha has \$6. How much has Kevin?

Let k be Kevin's amount, then

$$k + 6 = 20$$

(subtract 6) $k = 14$

Kevin has \$14.

Notice that you need to substitute a letter for the unknown and then try to form an equation.

Example 7

The perimeter of a rectangular field is 80 m. If the field's length is 30 m, what is its width?

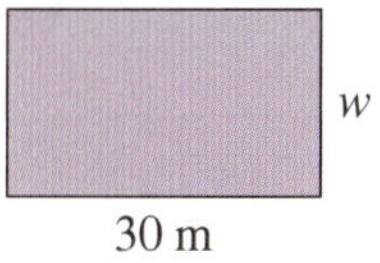

Let width be w, then

$$w + 30 + w + 30 = 80$$
$$2w + 60 = 80$$

(subtract 60) $2w = 20$

(divide by 2) $w = 10$

Width of field is 10 m.

Exercise 12J

1 Three times a certain number is 78. What is the number?

2 Two less than a given number is 29. What is the number?

3 Alison and Anya have 36 mangoes between them. Alison has twice as many mangoes as Anya. How many mangoes does Anya have?

4 Write down and solve an equation for each of these statements.

(a) When x is doubled the result is 24.

(b) When 14 is added to x the result is 30.

(c) When x is divided by 5 the result is 20.

(d) When x is doubled and 3 is added the result is 27.

5

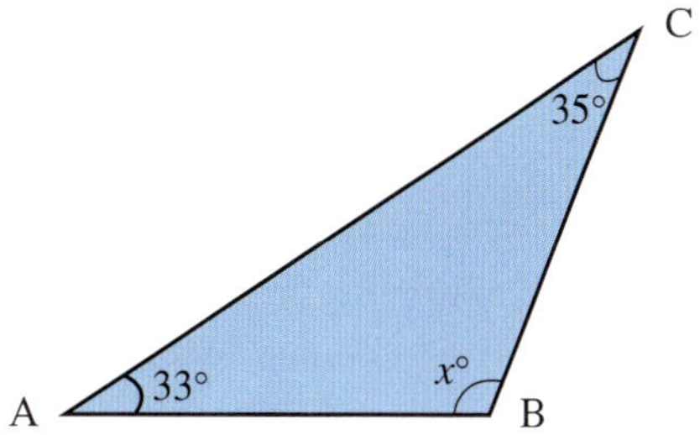

In the triangle ABC

(a) Write down an equation connecting the three angles.

(b) Solve the equation to find the value of x.

6 Stacy has 6 more oranges than Susan. Altogether they have 74 oranges. How many oranges does Stacy have?

7 The area of a rectangle is 24 cm^2. What is its length if its width is 4 cm?

8 The perimeter of a rectangle is 45 cm. What is its width if its length is 12 cm?

9 The sum of \$90 is shared between Pete and Petra so that Petra gets \$15 more than Pete. How much does Pete receive?

10 In Bayview village there are 12 more women than men. If the village's population is 240, how many villagers are men?

12.6 Looking for patterns

Example 8

Look at the pattern made from matchsticks:

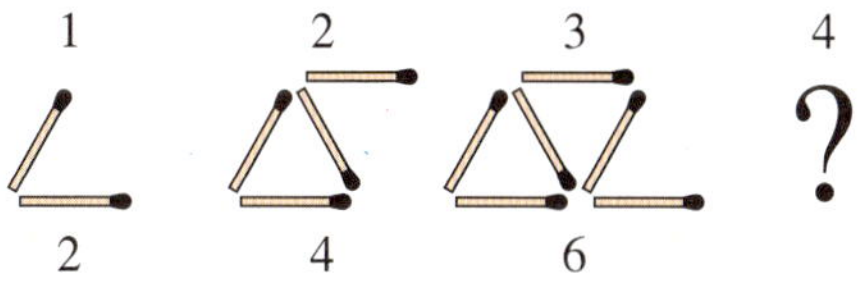

The 1st pattern has 2 matchsticks.
The 2nd pattern has 4 matchsticks.
The 3rd pattern has 6 matchsticks.

You can write a table:

Pattern number	Number of matchsticks
1	2
2	4
3	6

The number of matchsticks is related to the pattern number.

(a) How many matchsticks are needed to make the 4th pattern?
(b) How many to make the 10th pattern?
(c) How many to make the 60th pattern?
(d) How many to make the nth pattern?

(a) $4 \times 2 = 8$
(b) $10 \times 2 = 20$
(c) $60 \times 2 = 120$
(d) $n \times 2 = 2n$

Exercise 12K

1 Look at this pattern:

Pattern No.	1	2	3	4	5
Number of dots	2	3	4	5	? –

(a) How many dots will make the 5th pattern?
(b) How many dots will make the 20th pattern?
(c) How is the pattern number related to the number of dots?
(d) How many dots will make the nth pattern?

2 Repeat Question 1 for each of the following patterns:

(a)

Pattern No.	1	2	3	4	5
Number of dots	3	6	9	12	?

(b)

Pattern No.	1	2	3	4	5
Number of dots	3	4	5	6	?

(c)

Pattern No.	1	2	3	4	5
Number of dots	0	1	2	3	?

(d)

Pattern No.	1	2	3	4	5
Number of dots	3	5	7	9	?

In Question 2(d), did you find the number of dots for the 5th pattern was $5 \times 2 + 1 = 11$?

Flow charts

- A flow chart is a diagram that shows a series of steps that need to be carried out in a certain order. For example:

Choose any number from 1 to 9.
↓
Multiply it by 5.
↓
Add 3.
↓
Multiply the result by 2.
↓
Remove the last digit from your answer.
↓
Write down this result.

Exercise 12L

1 **(a)** Carry out the instructions in the flow chart above. What do you notice about the number you start with and the number you finish with?
(b) Use the flow chart again for another number between 1 and 9. What do you notice?
(c) Is your answer always the same as your starting number, for this flow chart?

2 **(a)** Carry out the instructions in this flow chart. What do you notice about the number you start with and the number you finish with?

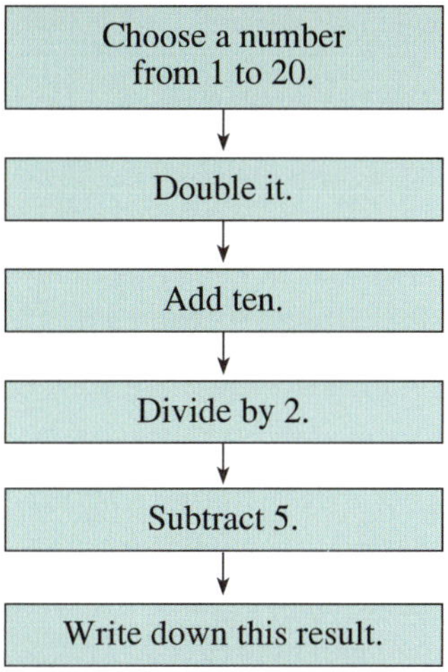

(b) Use the flow chart again for another number. What do you notice?

(c) Do you think that the answer will always be the same as the starting number for this flow chart? Can you explain why?

3 **(a)** Using this flow chart, what is the answer when you start with 5?

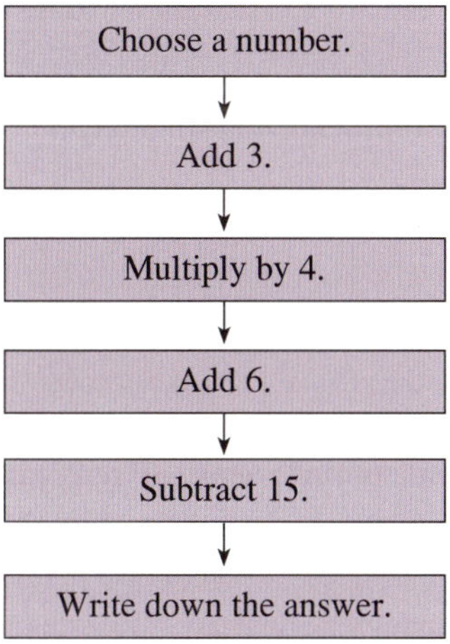

(b) Copy and complete the table for this flow chart.

Number chosen	1	2	3	4	5	6	7	8	9	10
Answer										

(c) Can you see a pattern in the answers? Without working through the flow chart, use the pattern to write down the answer when the starting number is:
(i) 11 **(ii)** 12 **(iii)** 15 **(iv)** 20

4 Copy and complete the flow chart below, so that it gives the same results as the flow chart in Question 3.

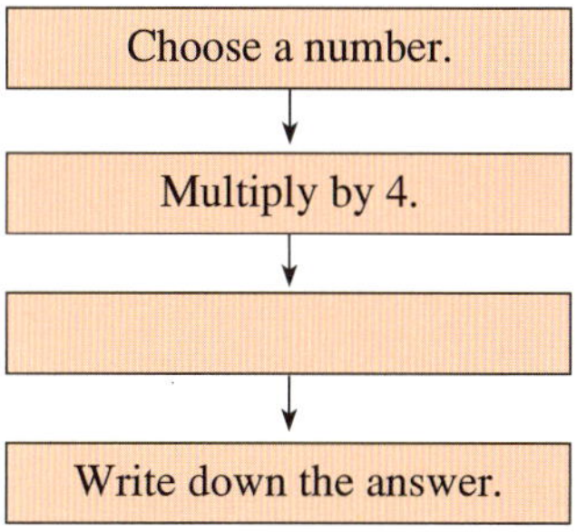

5 **(a)** Look at this flow chart, then copy and complete the table that follows.

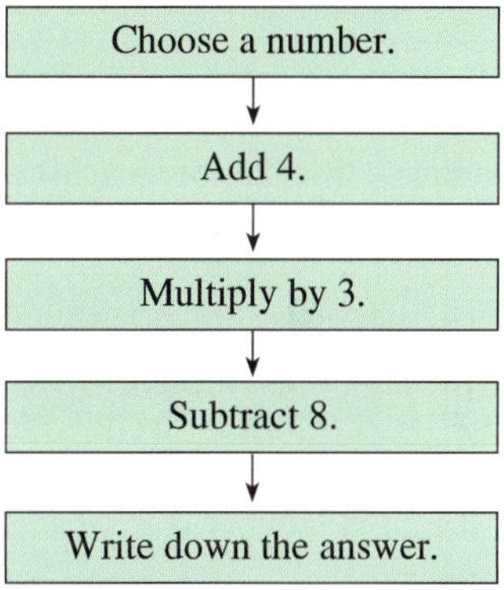

Number chosen	1	2	3	4	5	6	7	8	9	10
Answer										

(b) Find the pattern in your answers. Use the pattern to write down the answer if the starting number is:
(i) 11 **(ii)** 12 **(iii)** 15 **(iv)** 20

6 The drawing below shows a **number machine**. A number machine is a type of flow chart.

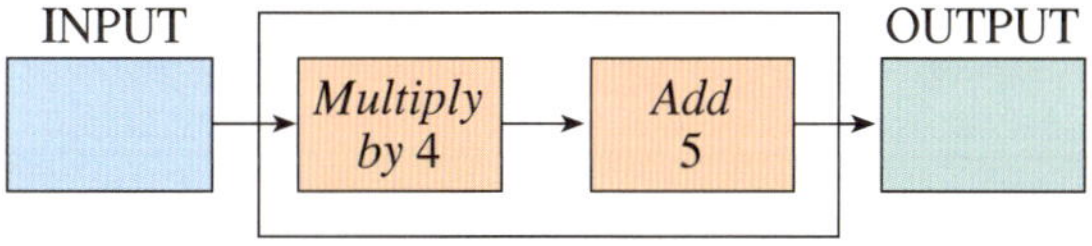

Suppose you put a 3 in the input box. The machine carries out the instructions *Multiply by 4* followed by *Add 5*. The answer in the output box is 17.

(a) Copy and complete the table below for the number machine above.

Input	1	2	3	4	5	6	7	8	9	10
Output			17							

(b) What is the difference between each output number and the next?

(c) With which instruction in the number machine is this difference connected?

(d) Write down the output number when the input number is n.

7 Look at the table you completed in Question 3(b).

(a) Fill in the correct number in the boxes below so that the answers are the same as those in Question 3(b).

1	2	3
$(1 \times \square) + 3$	$(2 \times \square) + 3$	$(3 \times \square) + 3$

(b) Complete this number machine to fit the table.

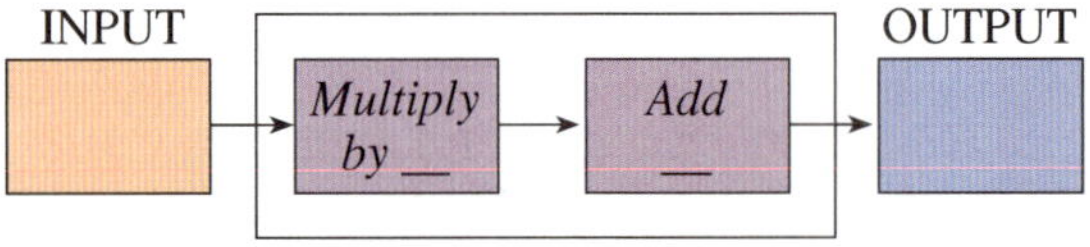

(c) If the input number is n, what is the output number?

8 Look at the table you completed in Question 5(a).

(a) Fill in the correct number in the boxes below so that the answers are the same as those in Question 5(a).

1	2	3
$(1 \times \square) + 4$	$(2 \times \square) + 4$	$(3 \times \square) + 4$

(b) Complete this number machine to fit the table.

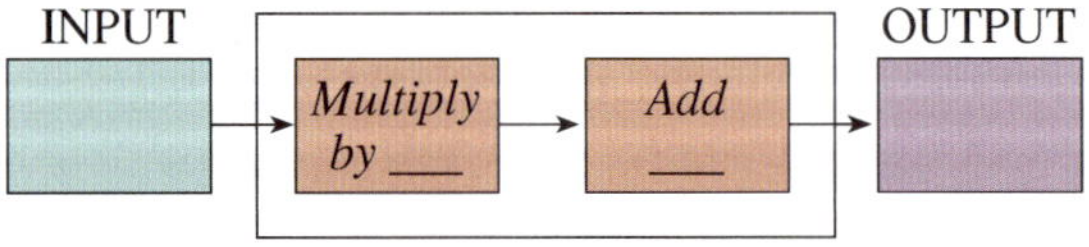

(c) If the input number is n, what is the output number?

9

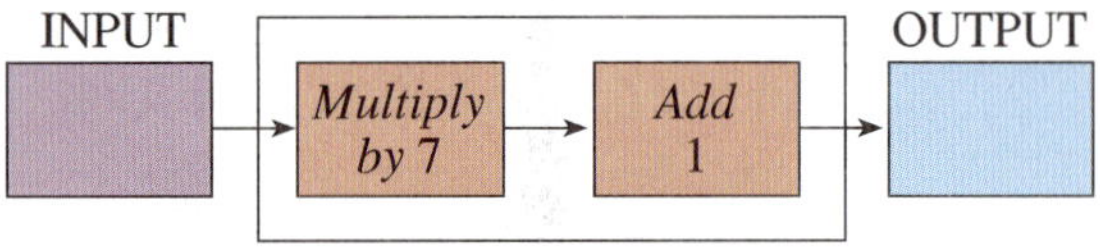

(a) Use the number machine to fill in the correct numbers in the boxes below.

1	2	3
$1 \times \square + \Delta$	$2 \times \square + \Delta$	$3 \times \square + \Delta$

(b) Copy and complete the table:

Input	1	2	3	4	5	6
Output						

(c) If the input number is $n + 1$ what is the output number?

10 Look at the number machine.

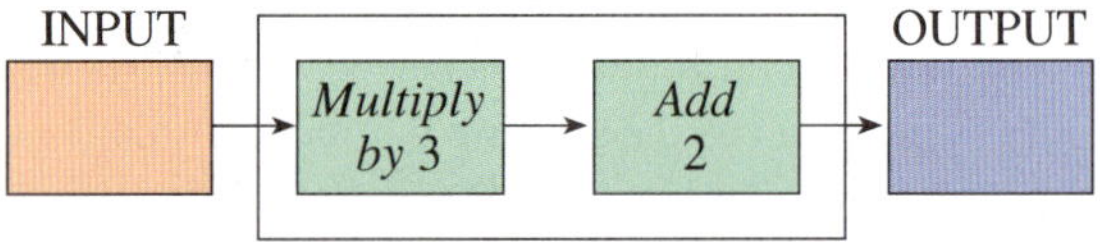

(a) Do you agree that 5, 8, 11, 14, 17, 20, … are output numbers for your machine?

(b) What is the pattern for these numbers?

Number sequences

The numbers 5, 8, 11, 14, 17, 20, … follow a pattern.

You can add 3 to each number to get the next number. ($5 + 3 = 8$, $8 + 3 = 11$ and so on.)

- A **sequence** is a set of numbers that follows a pattern.
- Each number in a sequence is called a **term**. For example, the third term in the sequence 5, 8, 11, 14, 17, 20, … is 11.

Exercise 12M

1 **(a)** Write down the next three terms in the sequence:

(i) 6, 12, 18, 24, 30, …

(ii) 2, 4, 6, 8, 10, …

(iii) 1, 3, 5, 7, 9, …

(iv) 4, 7, 10, 13, 16, …

(v) 6, 9, 12, 15, 18, …

(vi) 5, 11, 17, 23, 29 …

(b) For each sequence in part (a), draw a number machine that will produce the sequence when the whole numbers, starting from 1, are put in.

2 Look at this table.

Input	1	2	3	4	5	6	7	8	9	10
Output	8	14	20	26	32	38	44	50	56	62

(a) Do you agree that the sequence of output numbers could also be written as:
$(1 \times 6) + 2,\ (2 \times 6) + 2,$
$(3 \times 6) + 2,\ (4 \times 6) + 2 \ldots$?

(b) Using this pattern, find the 12th, 20th and nth terms in the sequence.

3 **(a)** Write each term of the sequence using brackets, as in Question 2(a).

(i) 4, 8, 12, 16, …
(ii) 5, 10, 15, 20, …
(iii) 11, 22, 33, 44, …
(iv) 4, 7, 10, 13, …
(v) 9, 11, 13, 15, …
(vi) 12, 14, 16, 18, …
(vii) 1, 4, 7, 10, …
(viii) 2, 7, 12, 17, …

(b) Write down the 10th, 12th and nth term of each sequence.

4 A number is added to each term in the sequence below, to give the next term. The number added may be the same each time or it may be different. If different, there is still a pattern.
Find the pattern, then write down the next three terms of each sequence.

(a) 1, 7, 13, 19, 25, 31, …
(b) 1, 11, 21, 31, 41, 51, …
(c) 1, 9, 17, 25, 33, 41, …
(d) 1, 6, 11, 16, 21, 26, …
(e) 1, 2, 4, 7, 11, 16, …
(f) 1, 2, 5, 10, 17, 26, …
(g) 1, 2, 3, 5, 7, 10, …
(h) 1, 11, 31, 61, 101, 151, …
(i) 1, 4, 10, 19, 31, 46, …
(j) 0, 1, 5, 14, 30, 55, …

5 **(a)** What does **random** mean?

(i) Mark two points on a sheet of paper. Join them with a straight line.

(ii) Mark three points at random on a sheet of paper. How many straight lines are needed to join each point to all the others?

(iii) Mark four points at random on a sheet of paper. How many straight lines are needed, to join each point to all the others?

(iv) Repeat for five points and six points.

(b) **(i)** Copy and complete this table.

Number of points	2	3	4	5	6
Number of lines joining them					

(ii) Express the sequence of numbers in the bottom row of the table using brackets as in Question 2(a).

(iii) How many lines do you think you would need to join nine points to each other? Check by drawing.

12.7 Arrow diagrams

An **arrow diagram** is another way of showing simple relationships.

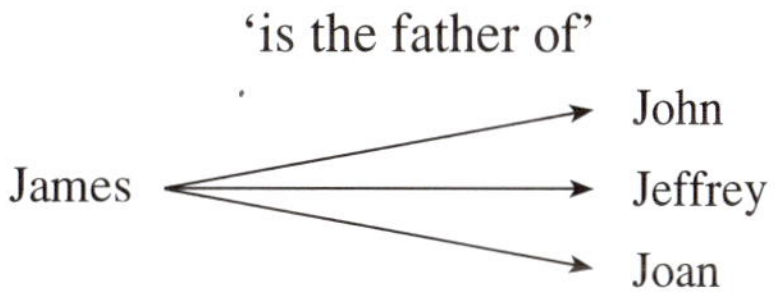

They can also show relationships between numbers

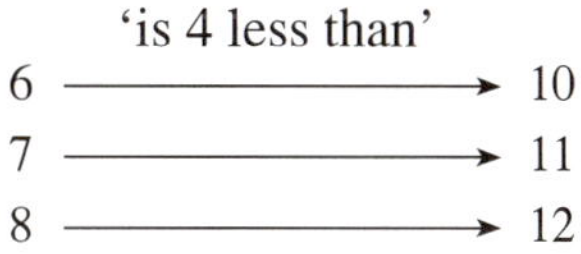

You can use the language of sets to show arrow diagrams.
For example,

$A = \{1, 2, 3, 4\}$
$B = \{4, 5, 6, 7\}$

The relation 'add 3' can be drawn as

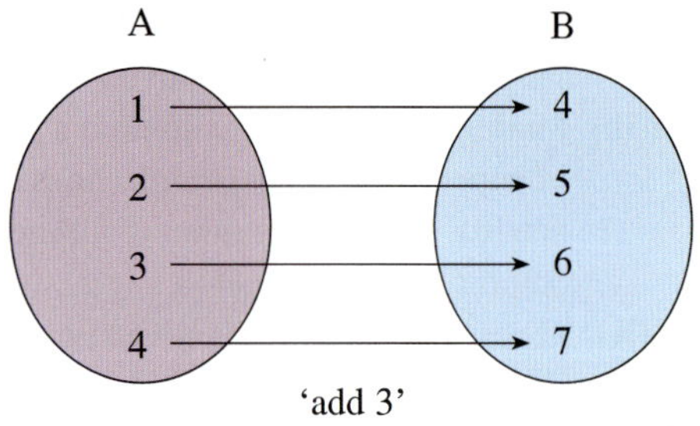

Given two sets, you can usually figure out the relationship.

Example 9

Describe the relationship between sets A and B.

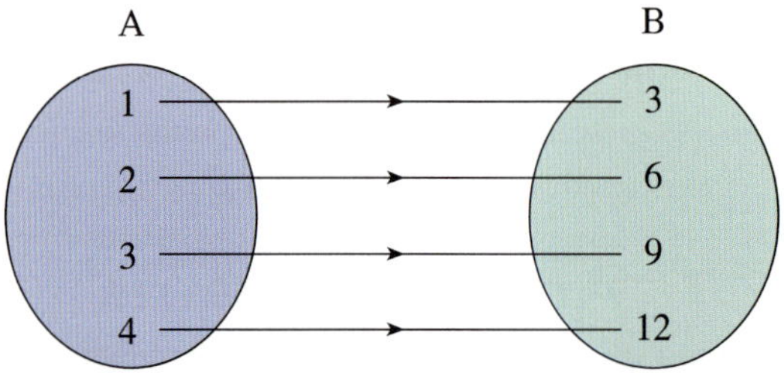

The arrow diagram shows the relation 'multiply by 3'.

Exercise 12N

1 Find out the year in which ten of your classmates were born. Draw an arrow diagram to show the relation 'was born in'.

2 Find out the favourite sporting activity of six of your friends. Draw an arrow diagram to show the relation 'favourite sporting activity is'.

3 What are the favourite meals of members of your family? Draw an arrow diagram to show this information.

4 Draw arrow diagrams to illustrate the relationships:

(a) is the mother of
(b) is the father of
(c) is a sister of
(d) is a brother of
(e) is a cousin of

for members of your family.

5 Copy and complete the arrow diagrams.

(a)

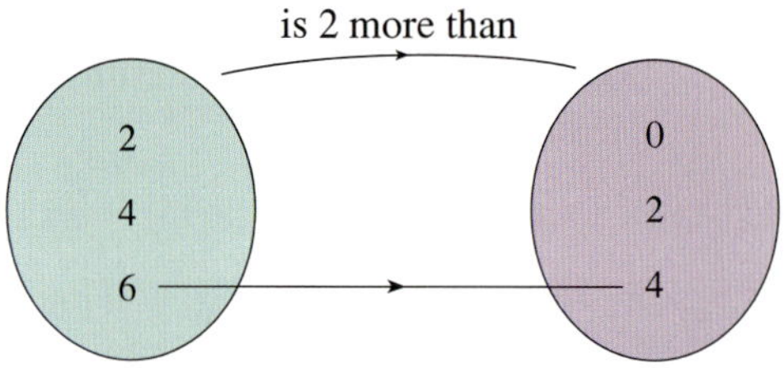

(b)

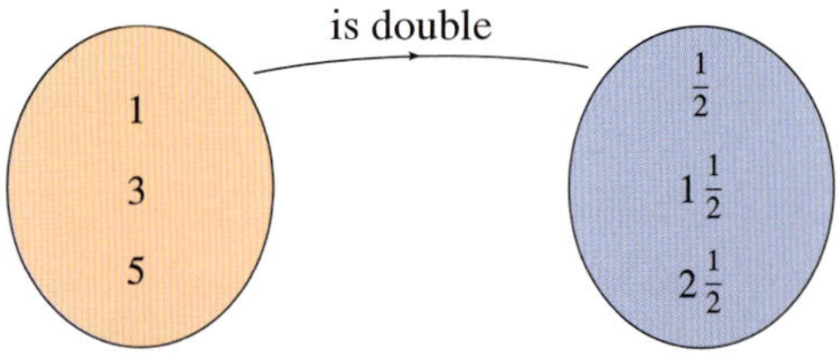

(c)

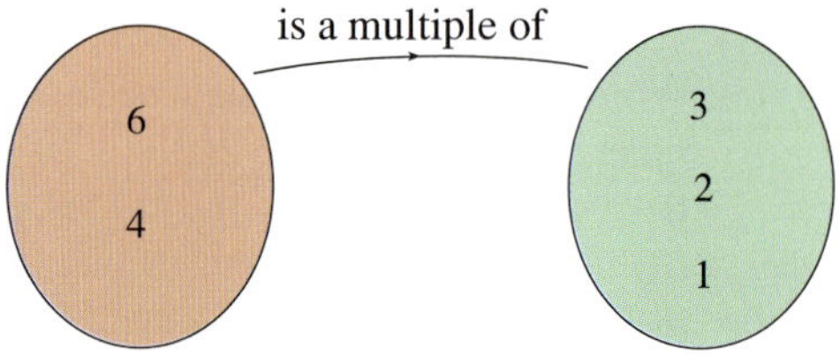

6 Look at these arrow diagrams. In each case try to identify the relationship.

(a)

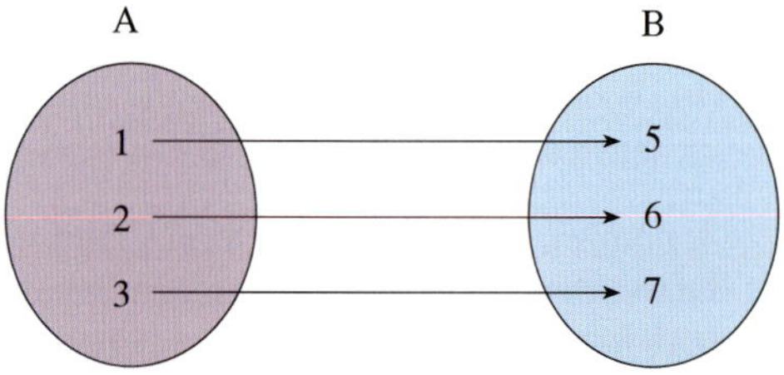

(b)

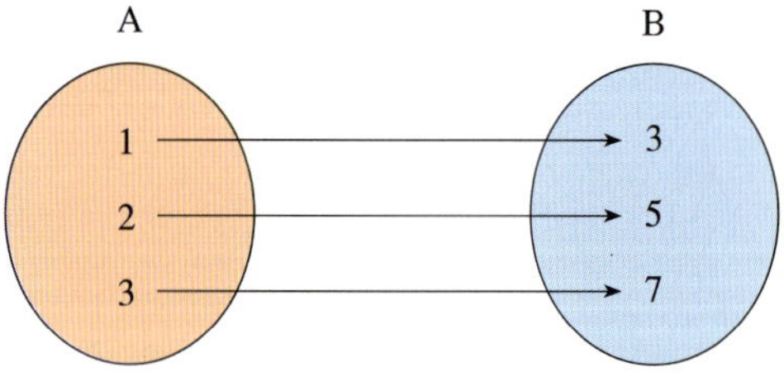

(c)

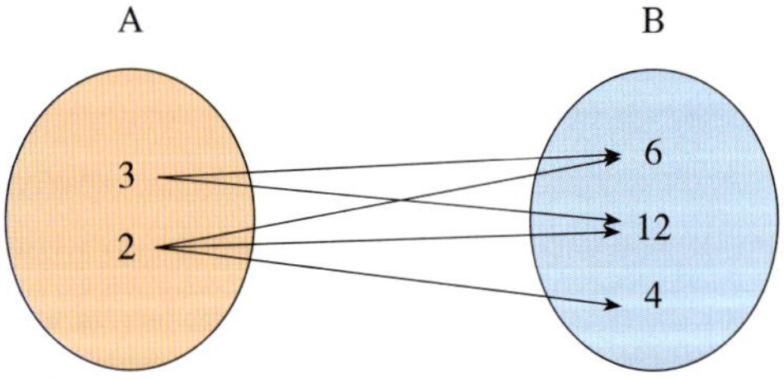

7 A = {2, 4, 6, 8, 10}, B = {1, 4, 8}
Draw arrow diagrams to show the relationships:
(a) is equal to
(b) is less than
(c) is a factor of

8 A = {1, 2, 3, 4}, B = {3, 6, 9, 12}
Draw arrow diagrams to show:
(a) is one third of **(b)** is three times
(c) is less than **(d)** is greater than

9 A = {1, 2, 3, 4, 6}, B = {2, 4, 6, 12}
Draw arrow diagrams to show:
(a) is a factor of **(b)** is a multiple of
(c) is equal to **(d)** is not equal to

Types of arrow diagram

Look at this arrow diagram.

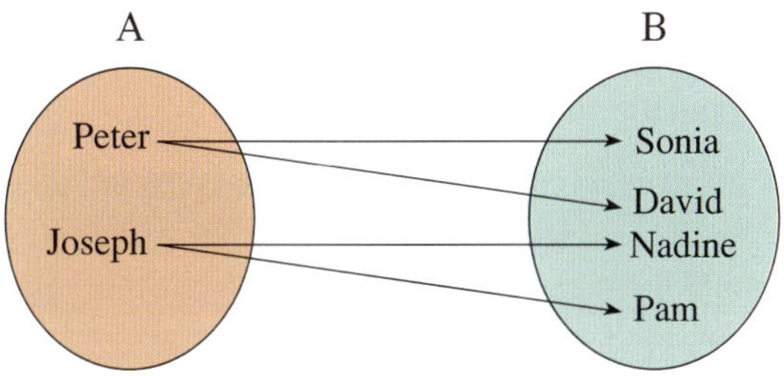

'is the uncle of'

This arrow diagram illustrates a relation that is **one-to-many**. Each member in the set A is related to more than one member of set B.

Relations can be:

- one-to-one
- many-to-one
- one-to-many
- many-to-many.

For example:

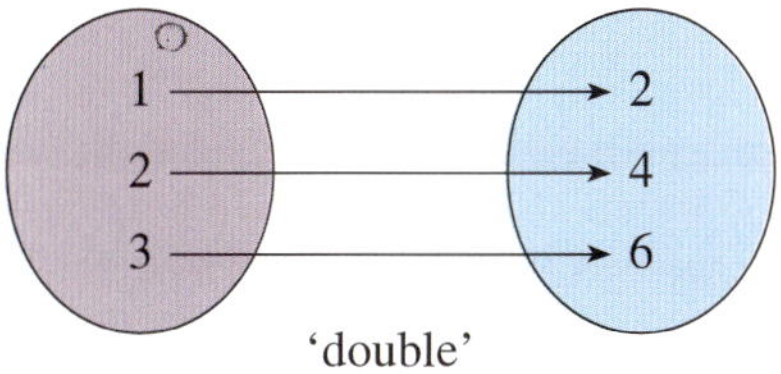

'double'

A **one-to-one** relation

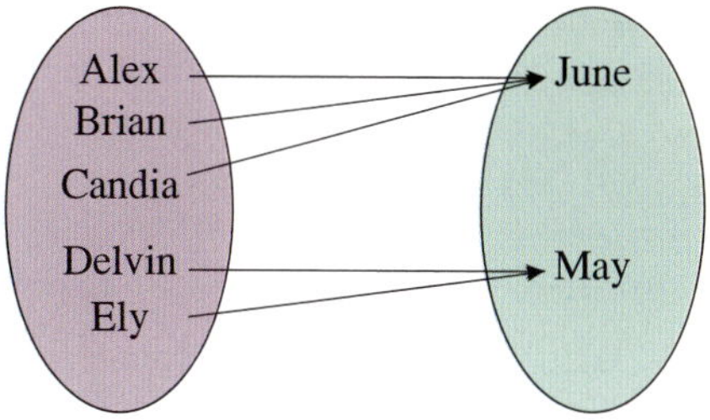

'was born in'

A **many-to-one** relation

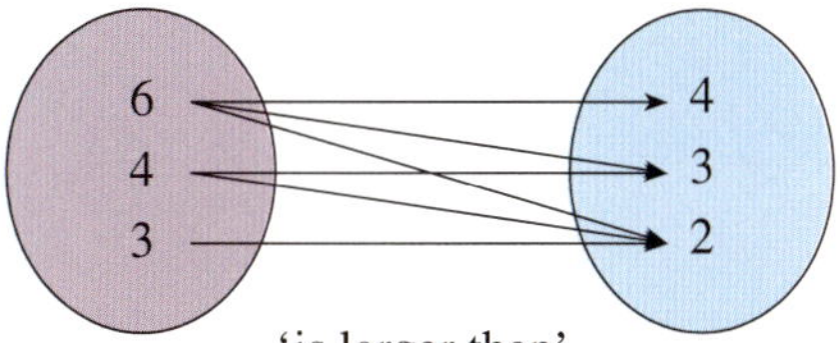

'is larger than'

A **many-to-many** relation

Exercise 12O

1 Look at the arrow diagrams you draw for Questions 1–4 of Exercise 12N.

Identify the type of relation in each case.

2 A = {1, 2, 3, 4}, B = {5, 6, 7, 8}
(a) Draw arrow diagrams to show the relations:
  (i) is 3 less than
  (ii) is a factor of
  (iii) is not equal to
(b) Identify the relation type in each case.

3 Using the sets
A = {1, 2, 3, 4}, B = {3, 6, 9, 12}
(a) Draw arrow diagrams to illustrate
  (i) a one-to-one relation
  (ii) a many-to-one relation
  (iii) a many-to-many relation
(b) In each case state the relation you used.

Exercise 12P – mixed questions

1 Simplify:
(a) $3x + 7x + 5x$
(b) $9x + 3y + y - 2x$
(c) $10n + 8 + 2m - 3n - 1$
(d) $5x \times 3y$

2 If $x = 3$ and $y = 4$ find the value of
(a) $x + y + 5$
(b) $5x + 3y$
(c) $7x - 2y$

3 Write an expression for the number of
(a) cents in \$$d + p$ cents
(b) days in $3x$ weeks + 5 days
(c) metres in k kilometres + s metres.

4 (a)

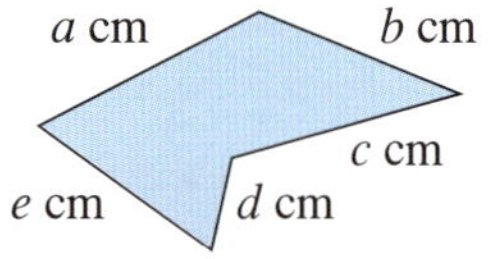

The perimeter of this figure is 31 cm.
Write an equation linking a, b, c, d, e and 31.

(b)

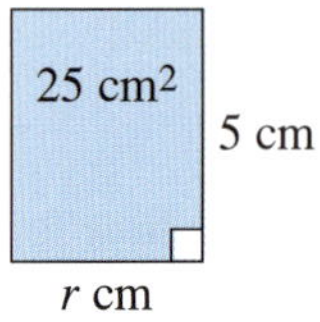

The area of the rectangle with sides of length 5 cm and r cm is 25 cm^2.
Write an equation linking 5, r and 25.

5 A man walks $2z$ km on the first day, 8 km on the second day and $(z + 3)$ km on the third day.
How far does he walk in three days?

6 In a test Matt got 15 more marks than Nana who got x marks.
(a) How many marks did Matt get?

Percy got y marks more than Matt.
(b) How many marks did Percy get?
(c) How many marks did the three have altogether?

7 Lorne buys 5 books at x dollars each, and y books at 7 dollars each.
How much does she spend altogether?

8

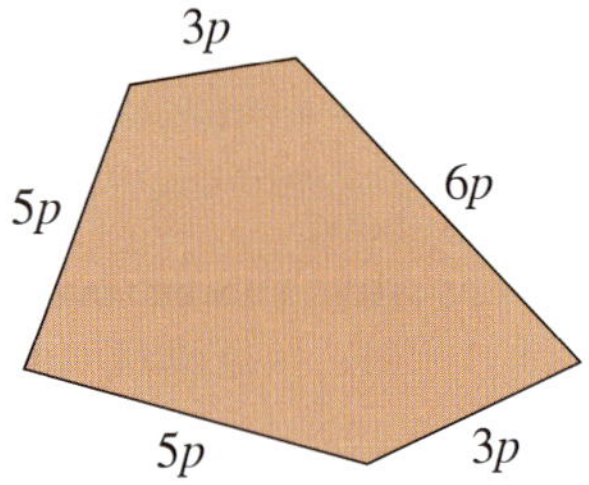

The perimeter of the shape above is 66 cm.
What is the value of p?

9 Rectangles A and B have the same area.

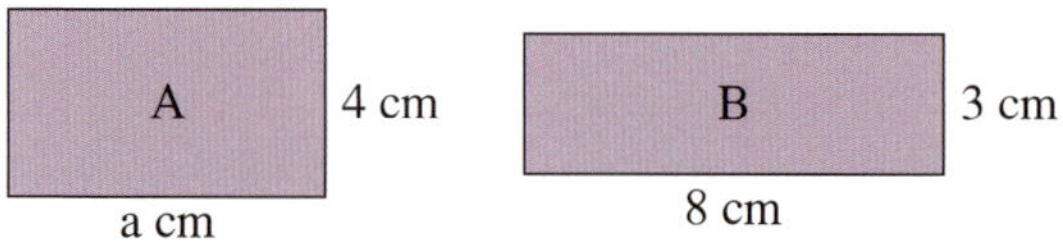

Find the value of a.

10 Write down the next two terms and the nth term in the sequence:
(a) 7, 14, 21, 28 …
(b) $1\frac{1}{2}$, 3, $4\frac{1}{2}$, 6 …
(c) $\frac{1}{2}$, $\frac{1}{4}$, $\frac{1}{6}$, $\frac{1}{8}$ …

11 (a) Copy and complete:

$$1 = 1$$
$$1 + 3 = 4$$
$$1 + 3 + 5 = \square$$
$$1 + 3 + 5 + 7 = \square$$
$$1 + 3 + 5 + 7 + 9 = \square$$

(b) Write down the next four terms of this sequence.
(c) Without adding, can you work out
(i) $1 + 3 + 5 + 7 + \cdots + 21$?
(ii) $1 + 3 + 5 + 7 + \cdots + 99$?

12 Consolidation

Example 1

Simplify the algebraic expressions

(a) $3a + b + b - a + 4b$ **(b)** $6a \times 4b$

(a) $3a + b + b - a + 4b$
$= 3a + 2b - a + 4b$
$= 3a - a + 2b + 4b$
$= 2a + 6b$

(b) $6a \times 4b$
$= 6 \times a \times 4 \times b$
$= 24 \times a \times b$
$= 24ab$

Example 2

How many hours are there in

(a) x days **(b)** p weeks q days?

(a) There are 24 hours in 1 day so there are $24 \times x$ hours $= 24x$ hours in x days.

(b) Number of hours in a day $= 24$

Number of hours in a week $= 24 \times 7$
$= 168$

Hours in p weeks q days $= 168 \times p + 24 \times q$
$= 168p + 24q$

Example 3

Write equations to represent these situations.

(a) Rhoda scored 17 marks on her first maths test and x marks on her second test. Her total score for the two tests was 39.

(b) A rectangle has length 5 cm and width y cm. The perimeter of the rectangle is 2 cm.

(a) $17 + x = 39$

(b) Perimeter = distance around
$24 \text{ cm} = 5 \text{ cm} + y \text{ cm} + 5 \text{ cm} + y \text{ cm}$
$24 = 10 + 2y$

Example 4

Solve these equations.

(a) $17 + x = 39$ **(b)** $2y + 10 = 24$

(a) $17 + x = 39$
Take 17 from both sides.
$x = 39 - 17$
$= 22$

(b) $2y + 10 = 24$
Take 10 from both sides.
$2y = 24 - 10$
$2y = 14$
$y = 7$

Exercise 12

1 Simplify:

(a) $a + a + a + a$ **(b)** $b + b - a + a + b$
(c) $3a - 2b + 4a + 6b$ **(d)** $2a \times 2b$
(e) $3a \times 2b$ **(f)** $6a \times 12b$

2 How many minutes in

(a) 3 hours **(b)** x hours
(c) 1 day **(d)** y days
(e) 2 days x hours **(f)** y days 14 hours
(g) y days x hours?

3 What is the total value of

(a) 6 \$5 notes **(b)** x \$5 notes **(c)** y \$20 notes
(d) y \$20 notes, 6 \$5 notes
(e) x \$5 notes, y \$20 notes?

4 Write down the perimeter of these shapes.

(a)

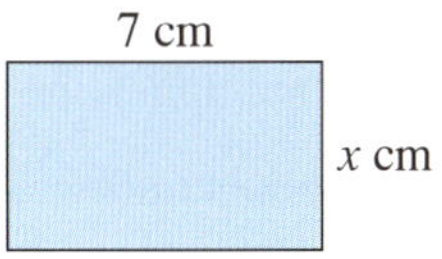

(b)

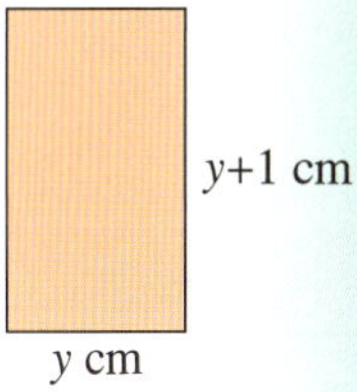

(c)

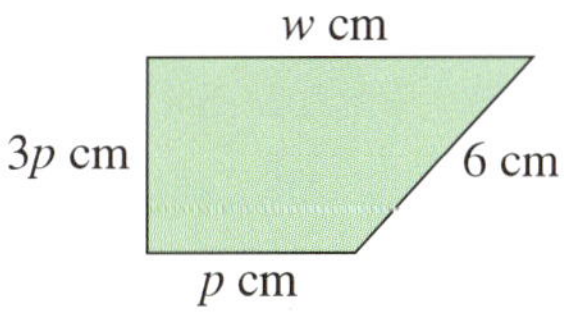

5 Write down the area of these rectangles.

(a)

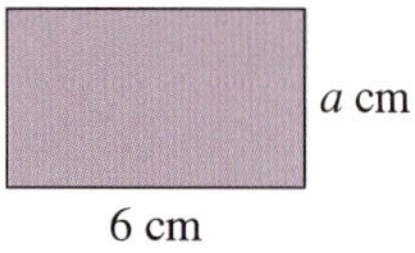

(b)

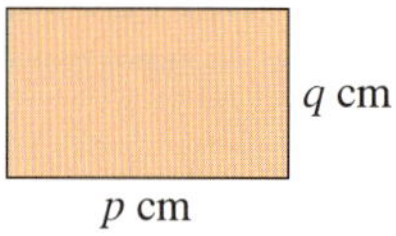

(c)

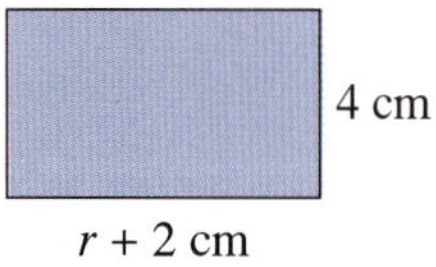

6 Solve these equations.

(a) $x + 2 = 5$ **(b)** $x - 2 = 7$ **(c)** $x + 11 = 24$

(d) $11 + x = 23$ **(e)** $2x + 3 = 7$ **(f)** $2x - 3 = 7$

Application 12

7 The bus fare from Coast Town to the city is \$9 for adults and \$5 for children.

(a) What is the bus fare for 3 adults and 2 children?

(b) What is the bus fare for d adults and c children?

(c) The bus fare for 5 passengers was \$29. How many were adults?

8 Taxi rates on Grand Island consist of a \$5 flat charge and a payment of \$4 for each kilometre travelled.

(a) What is the cost for a passenger who travels one kilometre?

(b) A passenger pays a taximan \$39 for a journey. If the passenger travels x km, write down an equation linking x with the charges.

(c) Solve the equation in part (b) to find out how far the passenger went.

9 Ken has \$8. His brother Claude has \$$x$ more than Ken. If they have \$32 altogether, how much do they each have?

Companion CD

Want some extra practice? Go to Chapter 12 on your companion CD for further exercises, animations, and solutions.

Summary

You should know ...

1 A symbol is a sign, a numeral or a letter used to give information.

× is a symbol—it means multiplication.

9 is a symbol—it is the number nine.

Check out

1 Give examples of three symbols.

2 A constant is a symbol which always means the same thing.

A variable is a symbol that can represent different numbers.

2 Which of the following symbols are constants?
A, ÷ , 5, 7, d

3 You can add, subtract and multiply symbols.
For example: $x + x + x + y + y = 3 \times x + 2 \times y$
$= 3x + 2y$

3 Simplify
(a) $2a + 3a - 2b$
(b) $5x \times 2y$

4 You can substitute numbers for letters.
For example: if $a = 3$, $b = 5$ then
$2a + 3b = 2(3) + 3(5)$
$= 6 + 15 = 21$

4 If $x = 7$ and $y = 3$ find
(a) $2x + 3y$
(b) $3xy$

5 You can write an algebraic expression to describe a situation.
For example: John is 4 years old. In d years time, John will be $4 + d$ years old.

5 **(a)** Mary has \$$2x$ and Lilly has 7 dollars more. How much money does Lilly have?
(b) Susie shares t tarts among her four friends.
How many tarts does each child receive?

6 A sequence is a set of numbers that follow a pattern.
For example: 3, 6, 9, 12, …
The pattern is: add 3 to each number to get the next number.

6 Find the next two terms in the following sequences:
(a) 6, 13, 20, 27, …
(b) 7, 14, 21, 28, …

7 How to find the nth term of a sequence:
For example: 3, 6, 9, 12, …
The 1st term is $3 \times 1 = 3$
The 2nd term is $3 \times 2 = 6$
The 3rd term is $3 \times 3 = 9$
The 4th term is $3 \times 4 = 12$
So the nth term is $3 \times n = 3n$

7 Write down the nth term in the following sequences:
(a) 3, 6, 9, 12, …
(b) 3, 5, 7, 9, …

8 Showing relationships using arrow diagrams.
For example: the arrow diagram shows the relation 'is a third of'.

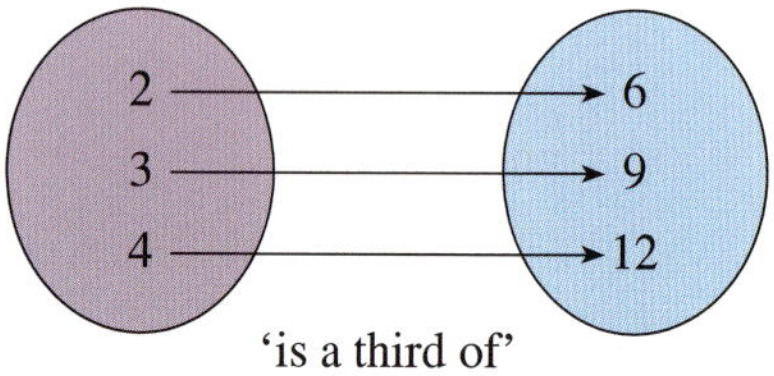

'is a third of'

8 $A = \{2, 3, 4, 5\}$, $B = \{7, 8, 9, 10\}$
Draw an arrow diagram to show:
(a) is two less than
(b) is a factor of

Revision exercise 3

Percentages

1 Write as a per cent:
(a) 20 in 100 (b) 20 in 200
(c) 20 in 500 (d) 20 in 1000

2 In a survey, 100 shoppers were asked their favourite fruit, the results were:

Oranges	28	Apples	12
Bananas	26	Pineapples	34

Write out the popularity of each fruit as a per cent.

3 Change these fractions to a per cent.
(a) $\frac{1}{4}$ (b) $\frac{3}{10}$ (c) $\frac{6}{25}$ (d) $\frac{17}{20}$
(e) $\frac{64}{80}$ (f) $\frac{12}{75}$ (g) $\frac{80}{125}$ (h) $\frac{36}{60}$

4 Calculate:
(a) 10% of 200 men
(b) 5% of 60 girls
(c) 75% of 140 car drivers
(d) 32% of 5000 voters
(e) 35% of 2400

5 Copy and complete this table.

Fraction	%	Decimal
$\frac{1}{4}$		
$\frac{1}{5}$		
	75	
		0.2
	16	
	8	
		0.8
		0.08
	100	
$\frac{13}{20}$		

6 How much do you save if a shop offers:
(a) 10% reduction off a $175 dress?
(b) 20% reduction off a $3.40 tie?

7 Find the cost of:
(a) Coat at $210 less 5%
(b) Bicycle at $150 less 15%
(c) Car at $7600 plus 8% local tax
(d) TV at $540 plus 12% import tax.

8 Ahab Wilson borrows $2000 from his bank at 12% p.a. (per annum or each year) interest. How much does he have to pay back at the end of the year?

9 Dona Masters puts her money in a savings account. How much interest does she gain when she has $460 in the account for six months if the rate is 9% p.a.?

10 Half of $\frac{1}{4}$ is $\frac{1}{8}$. What is $\frac{1}{4}$ as a per cent?
Do you agree that $\frac{1}{8}$ must be $12\frac{1}{2}\%$?
Complete the following table:

Fraction	%
$\frac{1}{8}$	$12\frac{1}{2}$
$\frac{1}{4}$	25
$\frac{3}{8}$	
$\frac{1}{2}$	
$\frac{5}{8}$	
$\frac{3}{4}$	
$\frac{7}{8}$	
1	

You can change per cents containing fractions like this: $17\frac{1}{2}\% = 17\frac{1}{2}$ in 100
= 35 in 200
$= \frac{35}{200}$

Now try these, changing the per cents to fractions and cancelling down:
(a) $27\frac{1}{2}\%$ (b) $33\frac{1}{3}\%$ (c) $6\frac{1}{4}\%$

Representing information

11 This pictogram shows the number of PCs in Latin America and the Caribbean to the nearest 5 million.

Year	
1990	□□
1995	□□□
2000	□□□□□
2005	□□□□□□□
2008	□□□□□□□□

□ represents 5 million PCs

(a) How many PCs are shown for 2005?

(b) In 2000 there were 27 million TVs but only 25 million is shown in the pictogram. Show a way of improving the representation.

12 The total number of cell phones in use in Latin America and the Caribbean is given by this table:

Year	1990	1995	2000	2005	2008
Cell phones (millions)	34	51	81	100	127

Design a pictogram to represent this information.

13 The estimated world primary energy production is shown on this pie chart:

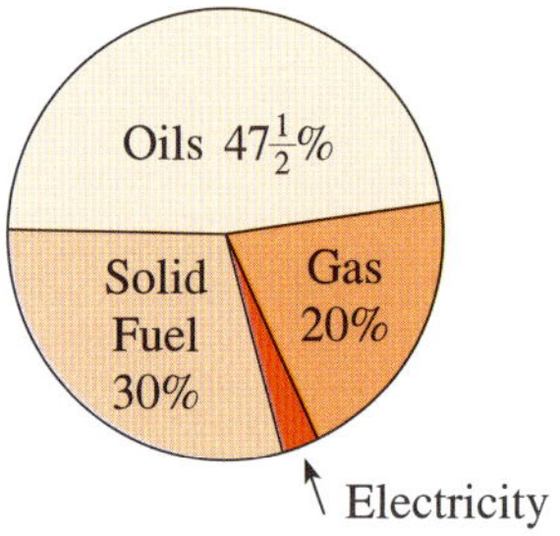

(a) What percentage of the total energy is represented by electricity?

(b) What is the size of the angle of the sector representing electricity?

(c) Calculate the sizes of the angles of the other sectors.

14 The estimated percentage of total world energy production in 2009 is given in this table:

Region	%
North America	30
Asia	$22\frac{1}{2}$
USSR	$22\frac{1}{2}$
Europe	15
Africa	5
South America	5

Construct a pie chart to show the information.

15 This bar chart shows the recorded sugar production of Trinidad and Tobago from 2000 to 2004. The production is shown to the nearest 10 million tonnes.

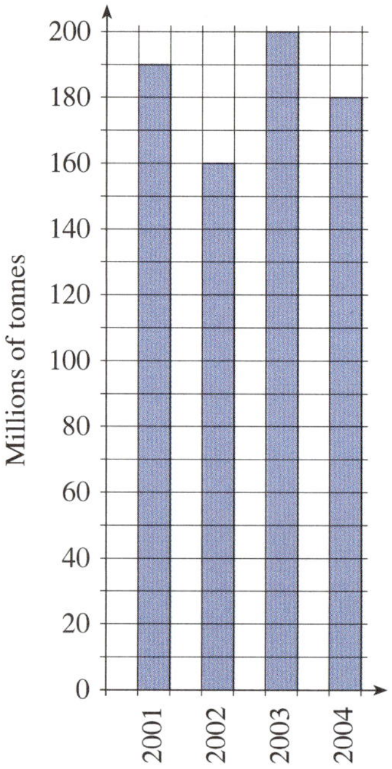

(a) What was the approximate tonnage of sugar production in 2004?

(b) What is the difference between the greatest and least years' production shown?

16 The sugar production for Trinidad and Tobago from 2005 to 2009 is given by this table:

Year	2005	2006	2007	2008	2009
Million tonnes	150	140	110	90	80

Copy the bar chart shown in Question 15 and extend it to 2009. What do you notice?

17 The sugar production for Barbados from 2000 to 2009 is given in this table:

Year	Million tonnes	Year	Million tonnes
2000	113	2005	117
2001	102	2006	135
2002	106	2007	97
2003	120	2008	88
2004	104	2009	

Construct a bar chart to show this information.

18 Wilson Smith works for a workshop producing sewing machines. He has to keep a record of sales which he plots on a graph. So far his graph looks like this:

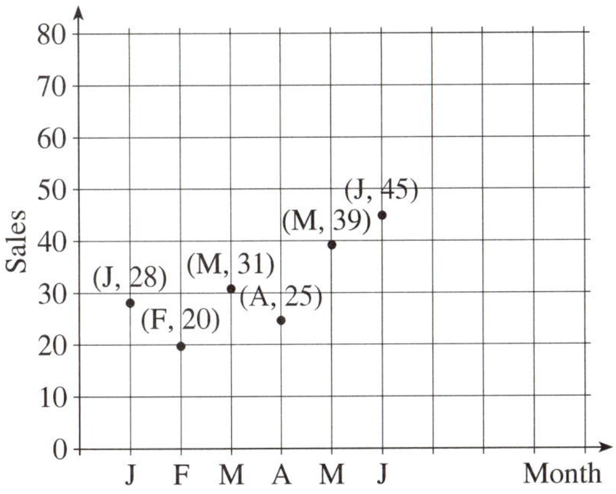

Wilson can record the result for January as (J, 28). In the same way, write down the results for the other five months.

19 Wilson records the sales for the last six months of the year as:
(J, 50), (A, 50), (S, 54), (O, 62), (N, 60), (D, 65).
Draw a graph like the one shown in Question 18 for the whole year's sales.
What do you notice?

20 Draw a coordinate graph to show these points:
(a) (2, 1), (3, 2), (4, 3), (5, 4)
(b) (1, 5), (2, 4), (3, 3), (6, 0)
(c) (0, 4), (3, 4), (4, 4), (6, 4)

In each case, what can you say about the points?

Area

21 Here is a rectangle with a perimeter of 24 cm.

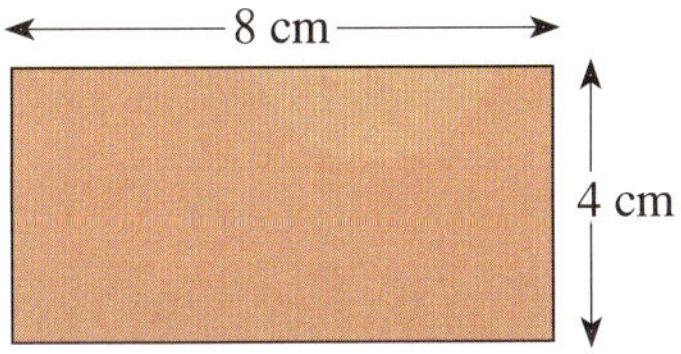

(a) Draw two different rectangles each with a perimeter of 24 cm.
(b) Calculate the area of each rectangle.

22 On squared paper, construct
(a) a square of side 4.5 cm
(b) an equilateral triangle of side 6 cm
(c) a regular hexagon of side 3 cm.

What is the perimeter in each case?
By counting squares, estimate the area of each shape.

23 A rectangle is 3 cm long and 2 cm wide.
(a) What is its area using cm^2?
(b) What is the length and breadth using mm?
(c) What is the area using mm^2?

24 The sides of a rectangle are 10 cm and 4.3 cm.
(a) What are the sides using mm?
(b) What is the area using mm^2?
(c) What is the area using cm^2?

25 Calculate the area of the triangles:

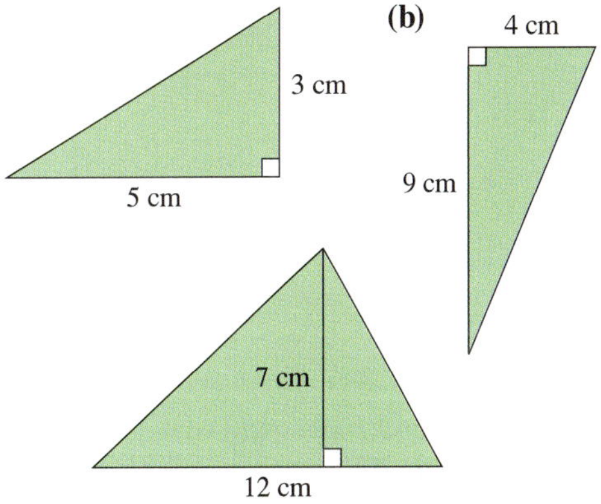

26 In the diagram, X lies on one side of the rectangle.

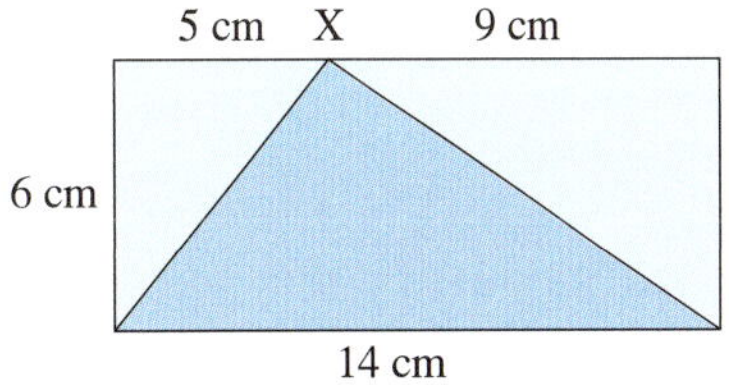

Calculate the area of each of the triangles.
What do you notice?

27 Calculate the area of the shapes drawn on cm squared paper.

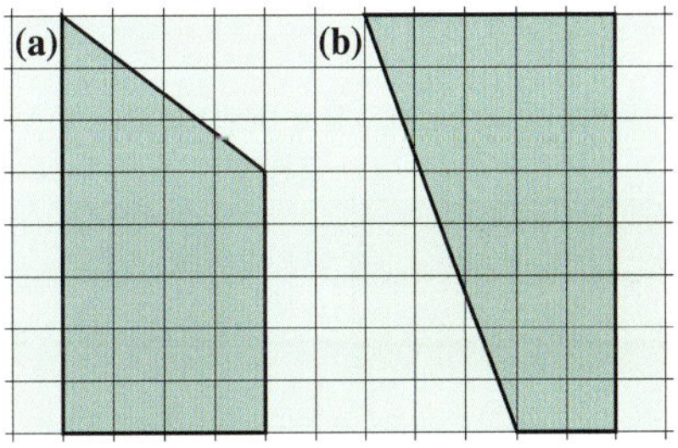

28 The side wall of a swimming pool is shown in this diagram.

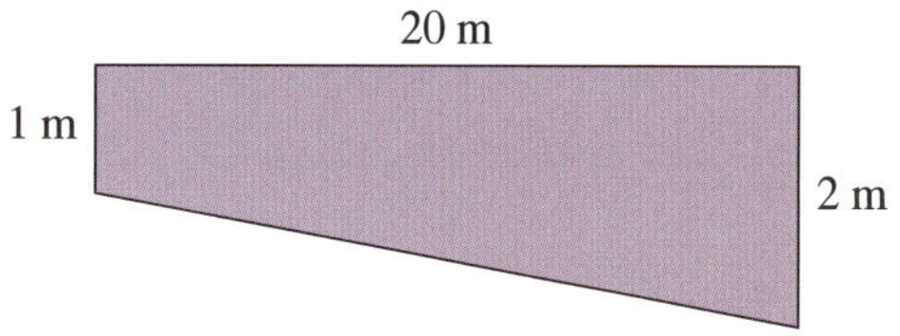

Calculate the area of the wall.

29 In these diagrams, ABYX is a rectangle and C is a point on the line through X and Y. In each case calculate the area of the triangle ABC.

(a)

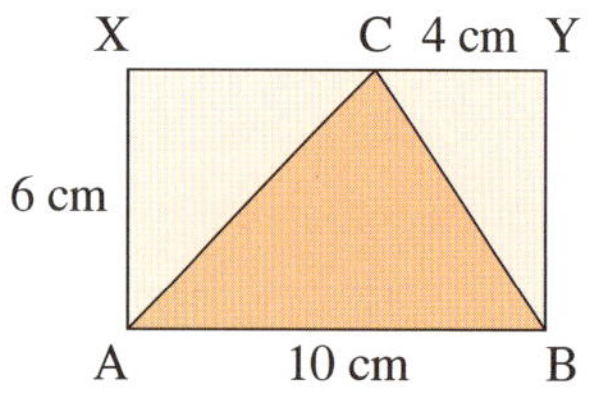

(b)

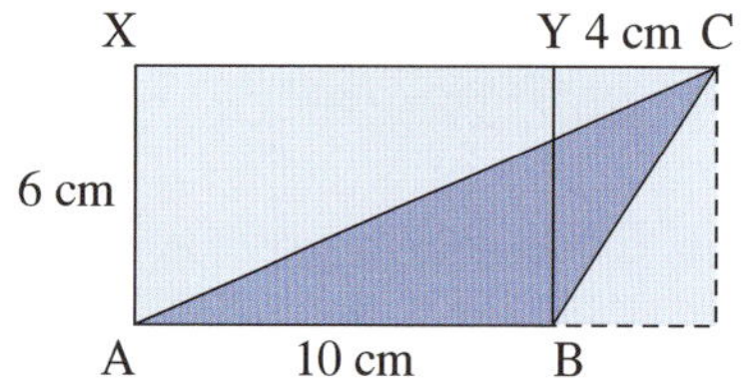

30 In Question 29, C is a point on the line XY. Find the area of triangle ABC with C in another position on XY.

Symbols and patterns

31 Simplify:

(a) $x + y + 2x$

(b) $a + 2a + b + a$

(c) $p + q + q + q + p$

(d) $3s + 2t + s$

32 Simplify:

(a) $2x + y - x$

(b) $3a + 2b - 2a$

(c) $2p + q - p + q - p$

(d) $3s - 2t + t + s + 4t$

33 Write down the area and the perimeter of.

(a)

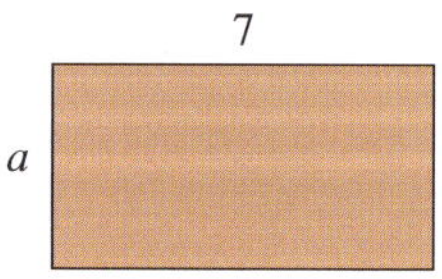

(b)

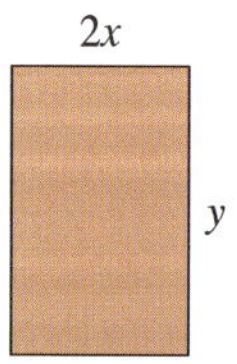

34 Write down:

(a) the number of days in w weeks

(b) the number of hours in d days

(c) the number of minutes in h hours.

35 Write an expression that states:

(a) Sarah has \$$a$ and Ruth has \$$b$ and they have \$10 together.

(b) Eli has \$$c$ and Tom has \$$d$ but Eli has \$10 more than Tom.

36 My age is x years and my son's age is y years. Write down an expression that states:

(a) The total of our ages is 72.

(b) I am twice as old as my son.

What is my age?

37 Bricks are built up to make a pattern like this:

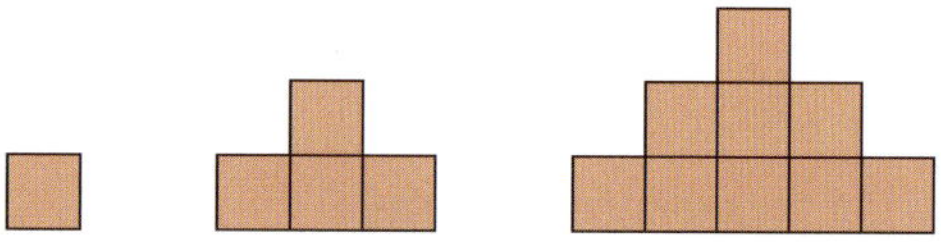

If the pattern is continued, how many bricks will there be:

(a) in the fourth building

(b) in the tenth building

(c) in the nth building?

38 The drawing shows a number machine.

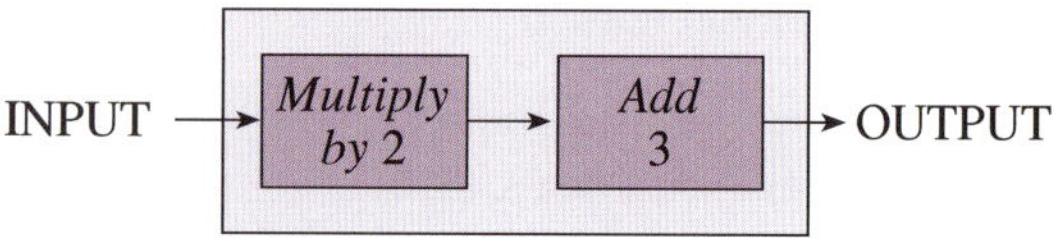

Find the output when the input is:

(a) 5 **(b)** 7 **(c)** 10 **(d)** x

39 Draw a number machine that, given an input x, produces an output

(a) $2x$ **(b)** $3x + 1$ **(c)** $4x + 5$

40 The square grid problem. Imagine a grid made of straight lines forming squares like this.

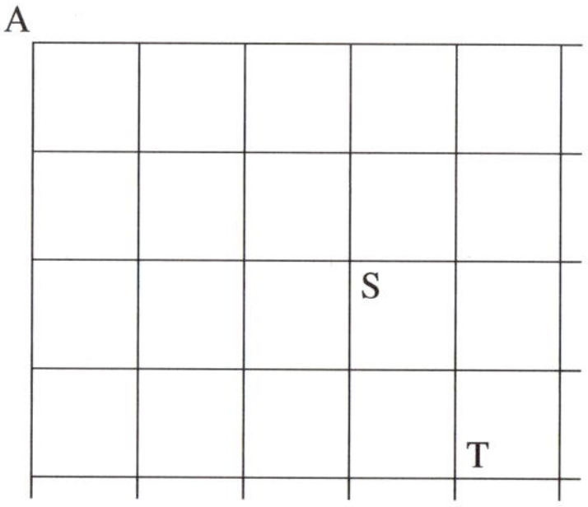

If you start at corner A and can only travel along the edges of the squares, how many different shortest ways are there to reach each corner?

Start like this:

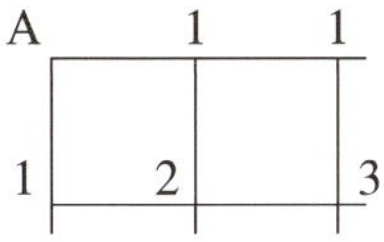

Can you find two ways of going from A to the corner marked 2? And can you find three ways of going from A to the corner marked 3? And do you agree that there is only one way of reaching each of the corners marked 1?

Now try some more corners and look for any patterns. Can you find the total number of ways from A to S and from A to T?

Mixed questions 3

1 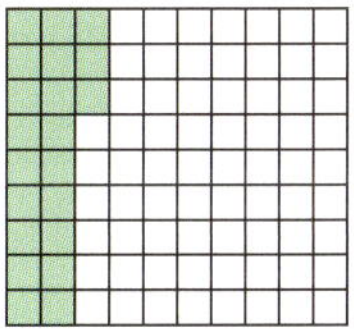

What percentage of the shape is shaded?
A 2.3% **B** 7.7% **C** 23% **D** 77%

2 The fraction $\frac{17}{20}$ written as a percentage is
A 3.4% **B** 8.5% **C** 34% **D** 85%

3 A school has 250 children. 40% are boys. How many are girls?
A 16 **B** 100 **C** 150 **D** 234

4

Red	Green	Yellow	Blue
5	7	9	4

The table shows the favourite colour of a class of children. What percentage like yellow?
A 9% **B** 36% **C** 45% **D** 90%

5 What is the cost of a vase priced at $30 if a sales tax of 3% is charged?
A $0.90 **B** $9 **C** $30.90 **D** $39

6 What is 45% as a fraction in its simplest form?
A $\frac{4}{5}$ **B** $\frac{45}{100}$ **C** $\frac{9}{20}$ **D** $1\frac{11}{20}$

7 Which is the largest number?
A 65% **B** 0.6 **C** $\frac{4}{5}$ **D** 0.79

8 A bottle holds 3 litres when it is 75% full. How much does the bottle hold?
A 4 litres **B** 25 litres
C 40 litres **D** 225 litres

9 What is 1% of $1?
A $0.01 **B** $0.10 **C** $1 **D** $10

10 In a carton of 36 eggs, 25% are broken. What percentage are not broken?
A 9% **B** 27% **C** 75% **D** 125%

11 Using tally strokes, the number 10 is represented by
A
B 
C
D

12 On a pictograph  represents 6 students.
 would represent
A 2 students **B** 3 students
C 4 students **D** 5 students

13 A family spends $8100 per month as follows

Food	$2700	Clothing	$1350
Mortgage	$2430	Fuel	$540
Electricity	$1080.		

On a pie chart, the angle representing the amount spent on clothing is
A 30° **B** 60° **C** 90° **D** 120°

14 In a school canteen the number of bottles of soft drinks consumed by pupils each day is recorded below.

Day	Mon	Tues	Wed	Thur	Fri
Number of bottles	150	130	90	130	90

If  represents 10 bottles the total number of  in the pictograph would be
A 9 **B** 13 **C** 15 **D** 59

15 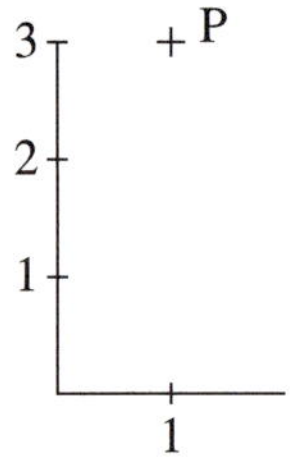

The point P has coordinates

A (1, 3) **B** (1, 1) **C** (3, 1) **D** (3, 3)

16 The results of a class test in mathematics are recorded in the bar graph below.

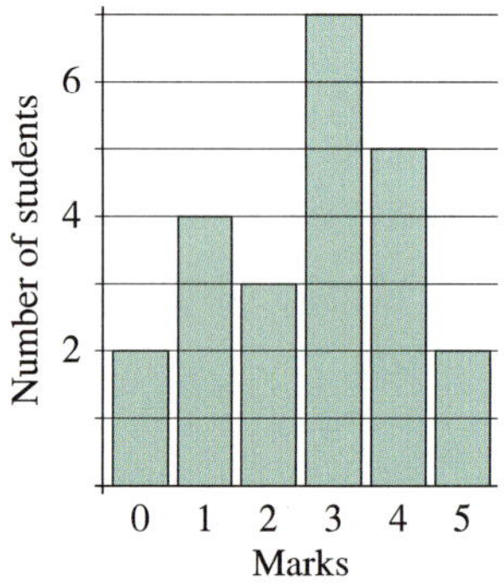

The number of students doing the test is

A 15 **B** 19 **C** 23 **D** 30

17 What is the area of a square with a side of 4 cm?

A 16 cm^2 **B** 4 cm^2
C 8 cm^2 **D** 2 cm^2

18 What is the area of this triangle?

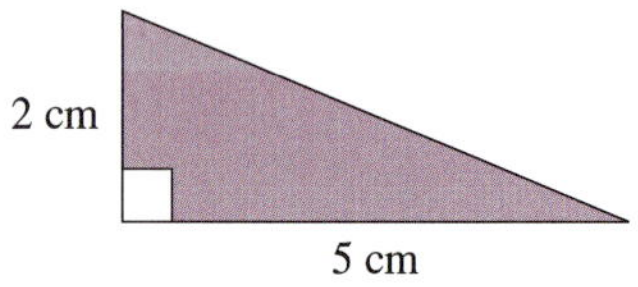

A 10 cm^2 **B** 5 cm^2
C 2 cm^2 **D** 7 cm^2

19 What is the perimeter of a square with a side of 3 cm?

A 3 cm **B** 9 cm
C 6 cm **D** 12 cm

20 What units would you use to measure the area of the top of your table?

A mm^2 **B** cm^2
C m^2 **D** km^2

21 Find the area of this triangle:

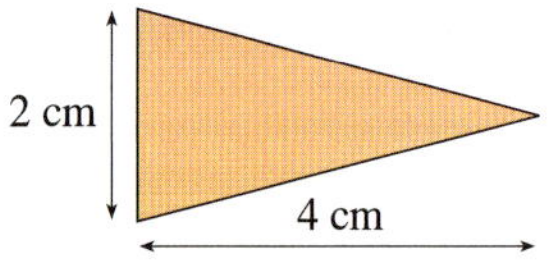

A 6 cm^2 **B** 8 cm^2
C 4 cm^2 **D** 2 cm^2

22 What is the perimeter of this shape?

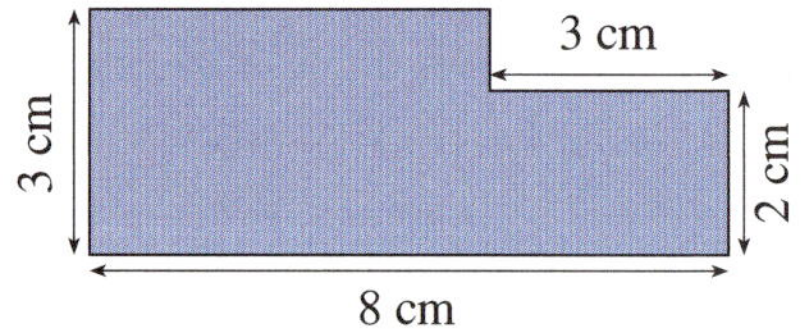

A 18 cm **B** 22 cm
C 16 cm **D** 24 cm

23 What is the next number in this sequence: 1, 3, 6, 10, . . .

A 13 **B** 15
C 17 **D** 19

24 If $x = 6$ and $y = 2$ find $2x + 3y$

A 5 **B** 58
C 22 **D** 18

25 If $a = 6$ and $b = 3$ find $3a - 2b$

A 13 **B** 24
C 12 **D** 1

26 Simplify $3x + 2y - x + 3y$

A $2x + 5y$ **B** $4x + y$
C $8xy$ **D** $2x - y$

27 Which of these symbols are constants?

A x **B** +
C 7 **D** cm

28 What is the next number in this sequence? 1, 4, 9, 16, 25, __

A 41 **B** 34
C 36 **D** 38

29 $\frac{1}{4}$ of students surveyed walk to school. What angle would they be represented by in a pie chart?

A 180° **B** 40°
C 25° **D** 90°

30 What is the area of this shape?

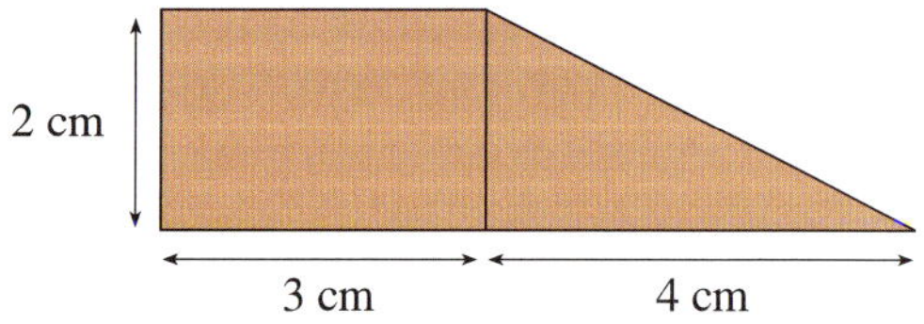

A 14 cm^2 **B** 7 cm^2
C 10 cm^2 **D** 12 cm^2

Glossary

1 Number

Place value Number system in which the position of the digit affects the value of the number.

Face value The numerical value of the digit, e.g. the face value of the digit 2 in 7284 is 2.

Value The actual value of the digit, e.g. the value of the digit 2 in 7284 is 200.

Factor The factors of a number are the whole numbers that divide into it, e.g. factors of 6 are 1, 2, 3, 6.

Multiple The multiples of a number are formed from its times table, e.g. multiples of 6 are 6, 12, 18, 24, …

Composite A composite number has three or more factors.

Prime A prime number has only two factors.

Prime factors The prime factors of a number are the factors of a number that are prime numbers.

HCF The highest common factor of two or more numbers is the largest number that can divide into those numbers without remainder.

LCM The lowest common multiple of two or more numbers is the smallest number into which those numbers can divide without remainder.

2 Sets

Set A collection of things with a common feature.

Empty set A set with no members.

Venn diagram A pictorial way of showing sets.

Subset A set which contains part or all of another set.

3 Fractions

Equivalent fractions Two or more different fractions that are equal in value, e.g. $\frac{2}{3}, \frac{4}{6}, \frac{6}{9}$.

Improper fraction A fraction in which the numerator is greater than the denominator, e.g. $\frac{7}{4}, \frac{5}{2}$.

Proper fraction A fraction in which the numerator is less than the denominator, e.g. $\frac{2}{3}, \frac{7}{15}$.

Mixed number A number made up of a whole number and a proper fraction, e.g. $2\frac{1}{3}, 7\frac{14}{17}$.

5 Angles

Ray A straight line that extends from a point.

Line segment A line joining two points.

Angle An angle is made when two rays extend from the same point. An angle is a measure of turn.

Right angle An angle made by a quarter of a full turn or 90°.

Straight angle An angle made by half a full turn or 180°.

Complete turn (or full turn) A measure of the angle made when the line which is turning has moved right around to its starting point.

Parallel Two rays that do not meet are called parallel rays.

Acute angle An acute angle is less than a right angle.

Obtuse angle An obtuse angle is more than a right angle but less than a straight angle.

Reflex angle A reflex angle is more than a straight angle but less than a complete turn.

Complementary angles A pair of angles that sum to 90°.

Supplementary angles A pair of angles that sum to 180°.

6 Solids

Cuboid A box-like solid. It has six rectangular faces.

Vertex A vertex or corner of a solid is formed where two edges or sides of the solid meet.

Prism A solid shape with a regular cross-section.

Net A flat shape that folds to make a solid.

7 Measuring

SI units Units of measure based on the metric system. The principal units are the metre (m) for length, kilogram (kg) for mass, second (s) for time and kelvin (K) for temperature.

Mass The quantity of matter in a body.

Weight The force of gravitational attraction on a body.

8 Shapes

Perimeter The distance around a closed shape.

Triangle A three-sided shape.

Equilateral triangle A triangle with all three sides equal in length.

Isosceles triangle A triangle with two sides equal in length or two equal angles.

Scalene triangle A triangle with all three sides different in length.

Quadrilateral A four-sided shape.

Parallelogram A quadrilateral with two pairs of parallel sides.

Rhombus A quadrilateral with two pairs of parallel sides and all sides equal in length.

Trapezium A quadrilateral with one pair of parallel sides.

Kite A quadrilateral with two pairs of adjacent sides equal in length.

Line of symmetry A line along which a shape is folded so that one half of the shape fits exactly on the other half.

Reflection A transformation that gives the mirror image of a shape.

Tessellation A pattern made by fitting shapes together without overlapping and without spaces.

Translation A transformation that moves a shape into a new position.

Congruent Two shapes are congruent to each other if they have the same size and shape.

9 Consumer arithmetic

Cost price The amount an item cost.

Selling price The amount an item is sold for.

Profit Selling price – cost price if the selling price is greater than the cost price.

Percentage profit $\dfrac{\text{Selling price} - \text{cost price}}{\text{cost price}} \times 100\%$

Discount The amount taken off the price of an item.

Interest The amount of extra paid or the fee charged for the use of someone's money.

10 Representing information

Discrete data Data that can only take on definite values, e.g. eye colour, shoe size.

Continuous data Data that can take on any numerical value, e.g. height, weight.

Mean The mean of a set of data is found by adding all the separate values of the data and dividing the sum by the number of data values.

Mode The mode of a set of data is the value that occurs most frequently.

Median The median of a set of data is the middle value after arranging the data set in order of size.

12 Symbols and patterns

Constant A constant is a symbol that always has the same value, e.g. 6, 18.

Variable A variable is a symbol that can take any value.

Algebra A part of mathematics where letters are used to represent numbers.

Algebraic expression A collection of constants and variables, e.g. $7a + 4b$, $6ab - 7c + 2d$.

Equation A statement showing the equality of two expressions, e.g. $7a + 2c = 6$, $4a - 2b = 6c - 4$.

Flow chart A diagram showing a series of steps to be carried out.

Sequence A set of numbers following a particular pattern, e.g. 2, 4, 6, 8, …

Arrow diagram A way of showing a simple relationship between two sets.

Answers

1 Number

Check in

1 (a) 100 (b) 5 (c) 7

2 (a) 14 (b) 18 (c) 32 (d) 20 (e) 63 (f) 72

Exercise 1A

1 (a) four (b) forty (c) four hundred
(d) forty (e) four thousand (f) forty thousand
(g) four thousand

2 (a) 2, 9, 16, 27, 81 (b) 0, 29, 99, 111, 308
(c) 41, 268, 401, 999, 1001 (d) 1234, 2134, 2413, 4132, 4321
(e) 3, 610, 6002, 8109, 71 506

3 (a) 2500 (b) 1100 (c) 900 (d) 11 000
(e) 2499 (f) 991 (g) 1992 (h) 7099

4 3100

5 6789

6 (a) 3 (b) 8 (c) 13

7 (a) 4.10 (b) 5.2 (c) 5.6 (d) 6.6 (e) 3.6

8 (b) (i) XXIX (ii) XCII (iii) CDXLIX

Exercise 1B

1 (a) 20 + 7 (b) 100 + 6 (c) 200 + 70 + 1
(d) 900 + 10 + 4 (e) 1000 + 100 + 30 + 7
(f) 10 000 + 3000 + 600 + 10 + 9

2 (a) 6 (b) 24

3 (a) 67 (b) 167 (c) 640 (d) 836 (e) 434

5 (a) 3 \$100 bills, 4 \$10 bills and 5 \$1 coins

6 (a) one 16 g, one 4 g and one 2 g weight
(b) all weights to 32 g (c) objects over 32 g

Exercise 1C

1 (a) 34 (b) 101 (c) 633 (d) 1328
(e) 390 (f) 1234

2 (a) 51 (b) 64 (c) 38 (d) 46 (e) 95
(f) 92 (g) 189 (h) 376 (i) 1015 (j) 889

3 445

4 \$176

5 2012

6 467

7 2856

8 39

9 (a)

5	3	7
7	5	3
3	7	5

(b)

4	9	2
3	5	7
8	1	6

10 (a) 12, 36, 48 (b) 18

Exercise 1D

1 4, 8, 12, 16, 20, 24, 28, 32, 36

2 (a) 5, 10, 15, 20, 25, 30 (b) 7, 14, 21, 28, 35, 42

3 (a) 48 (b) 60 (c) 90

4 (a) 24, 28 (b) 54, 63 (c) 72, 84
(d) 96, 112 (e) 98, 105

5 (a) 6, 12 (b) 15, 30 (c) 12, 24

6 It ends in either 0 or 5

7 (a) The sum of the digits in each multiple is 9.
(b) The sum of the digits in each multiple makes the pattern 6, 3, 9 repeated.

Investigation page 5

(a) It is a diagonal pattern.
(b) The diagonals slope the opposite way with 5 columns, and straight down with 3.

Exercise 1E

1 (a) 1, 3 (b) 1, 2, 4, 8 (c) 1, 3, 5, 15 (d) 1, 2, 4, 5, 10, 20

2

Number	Factors	Number of different factors
1	1	1
2	1, 2	2
3	1, 3	2
4	1, 2, 4	3
5	1, 5	2
6	1, 2, 3, 6	4
7	1, 7	2
8	1, 2, 4, 8	4
9	1, 3, 9	3
10	1, 2, 5, 10	4
11	1, 11	2
12	1, 2, 3, 4, 6, 12	6
13	1, 13	2
14	1, 2, 7, 14	4
15	1, 3, 5, 15	4
16	1, 2, 4, 8, 16	5
17	1, 17	2
18	1, 2, 3, 6, 9, 18	6
19	1, 19	2
20	1, 2, 4, 5, 10, 20	6

3 (a) 2, 3, 5, 11, 13, 17, 19 **(b)** 2

4 23, 29, 31

5 1

Investigation page 6

60, 72, 84, 90 and 96 all have 12 factors

Exercise 1F

1 (a) (i) 1, 5, 7, 35 **(ii)** no **(b) (i)** 1, 37 **(ii)** yes

2 (a) 23, 29, 31, 37, 41, 43, 47
(b) 2, 3, 5, 7, 11, 13, 17, 19, 23, 29, 31, 37, 41, 43, 47

3 No, it has only one factor.

4 (a) prime **(b)** composite

6 (a) 2, 3, 5, 7, 11, 13, 17, 19, 23, 29, 31, 37, 41, 43, 47, 53, 59, 61, 67, 71, 73, 79, 83, 89, 97 **(b)** yes

7 (a) Once: 2 and 3
(b) Never, because at least one of three consecutive numbers must be an even number, and all even numbers greater than 2 are not prime.

8 (a) 5 and 7 **(b)** 8

9 (a) 613 is prime **(b)** 4999 is prime
(c) 30 031 is not prime, 59 is a factor.

Investigation page 8

(a) No **(b)**

Number	Two primes equal to number
5	2 + 3
6	3 + 3
7	2 + 5
8	3 + 5
9	2 + 7
10	5 + 5
11	not possible
12	5 + 7
13	2 + 11
14	3 + 11
15	2 + 13
16	3 + 13
17	not possible
18	5 + 13
19	2 + 17
20	3 + 17

Exercise 1G

1 (a) $2^2 \times 3$ **(b)** 2^4 **(c)** $2^3 \times 3$ **(d)** $2^2 \times 3^2$ **(e)** 2×23
(f) $2^4 \times 3$ **(g)** 2^6 **(h)** 5×13 **(i)** $2^3 \times 3^2$
(j) $2^2 \times 3 \times 7$ **(k)** $2^3 \times 17$ **(l)** $2^2 \times 7^2$

3 6, 12, 18, 24, 30

4 (a) 6 **(b)** 30

5 210

Exercise 1H

1 (b) (i) 4 **(ii)** 6 **(iii)** 12 **(iv)** 12 **(v)** 5 **(vi)** 36

2 (b) (i) 15 **(ii)** 14 **(iii)** 24 **(iv)** 36 **(v)** 108 **(vi)** 24

4 (a) 6, 252 **(b)** 3, 126 **(c)** 5, 350 **(d)** 13, 390
(e) 24, 288 **(f)** 20, 2520

5 (a) after 15 min 10 s **(b)** 14

Exercise 1I

1 (a) 60 **(b)** 160 **(c)** 230 **(d)** 230 **(e)** 690 **(f)** 880
(g) 2140 **(h)** 2140

2 (a) 120 **(b)** 480 **(c)** 1480 **(d)** 1530 **(e)** 1920
(f) 7830 **(g)** 2100 **(h)** 5280

3 2350

Exercise 1J

2 (a) 310 **(b)** 210 **(c)** 810 **(d)** 2050 **(e)** 560
(f) 2310 **(g)** 5720 **(h)** 9300

3 46 800

Exercise 1K

1 (a) $5 \times (4+2) = 5 \times 4 + 5 \times 2$ **(b)** 30

2 (i) $4 \times (3+2) = 4 \times 3 + 4 \times 2$
(ii) $6 \times (5+3) = 6 \times 5 + 6 \times 3$

Exercise 1L

1 (a) 168 **(b)** 208 **(c)** 252 **(d)** 972 **(e)** 1632 **(f)** 2940

3 Yes, both sides 12

4 (a) $6 \times (8-4) = 6 \times 8 - 6 \times 4$
(b) $10 \times (4-3) = 10 \times 4 - 10 \times 3$
(c) $12 \times (8-5) = 12 \times 8 - 12 \times 5$
(d) $15 \times (12-7) = 15 \times 12 - 15 \times 7$
(e) $16 \times (8-2) = 16 \times 8 - 16 \times 2$

5 Yes, it does

6 323

7 (a) 133 **(b)** 162 **(c)** 429 **(d)** 776 **(e)** 513 **(f)** 1056

8 221

9 7200

Exercise 1M

1 **(c)** ends in 0

2 **(c)** ends in 0 or 5

3 **(b)** even numbers **(c)** gives even number when divided by 2

4 **(b)** digit sums are 3, 6 or 9 **(d)** sum of digit is divisible by 3

5 **(d)** sum of digits is divisible by 9

6 divisible by 2 and by 3

Exercise 1N

1 **(a)** yes **(b)** yes **(c)** yes **(d)** yes **(e)** yes **(f)** no

3 **(a)** no **(b)** yes **(c)** yes **(d)** no **(e)** no **(f)** no

4 **(a)** $2^6 \times 7$ **(b)** 3^6 **(c)** $3^3 \times 5 \times 47$ **(d)** 2^{10}
(e) $2^5 \times 5 \times 79$ **(f)** $2^4 \times 3^3 \times 167$

Exercise 1O

1 **(a)** 3 **(b)** 3 **(c)** 4 **(d)** 6 **(e)** 2 **(f)** 4 **(g)** 3
(h) 6

3 **(a)** 11 **(b)** 16 **(c)** 14 **(d)** 26 **(e)** 16 **(f)** 27
(g) 11 **(h)** 12

Exercise 1P

1 **(a)** 18 **(b)** 32 **(c)** 17 **(d)** 23 **(e)** 45 **(f)** 82
(g) 64 **(h)** 57 **(i)** 102 **(j)** 109

2 34

3 41

4 **(a)** 39r5 **(b)** 43r7 **(c)** 25r10 **(d)** 62r2 **(e)** 77r12
(f) 76r23 **(g)** 94r21 **(h)** 65r5 **(i)** 136r28 **(j)** 172r30

5 717

6 29

Exercise 1Q

1 **(c)** **(i)** 10 **(ii)** 30 **(iii)** 40 **(iv)** 60 **(v)** 90

2 **(c)** **(i)** 280 **(ii)** 260 **(iii)** 290 **(iv)** 310 **(v)** 320

3 **(c)** **(i)** 200 **(ii)** 400 **(iii)** 600 **(iv)** 400 **(v)** 800

4 **(c)** **(i)** 2000 **(ii)** 1900 **(iii)** 2200 **(iv)** 2400 **(v)** 2200

5 **(a)** 1000 **(b)** 4000 **(c)** 6000 **(d)** 1000 **(e)** 34 000
(f) 45 000

6 **(a)** 80 **(b)** 110 **(c)** 850 **(d)** 1050 **(e)** 6140
(f) 7620 **(g)** 11 310 **(h)** 12 950

7 **(a)** 100 **(b)** 100 **(c)** 800 **(d)** 1000 **(e)** 6100
(f) 7600 **(g)** 11 300 **(h)** 13 000

8 **(a)** 0 **(b)** 0 **(c)** 1000 **(d)** 1000 **(e)** 6000
(f) 8000 **(g)** 11 000 **(h)** 13 000

9 **(a)** 8500 **(b)** 8500 **(c)** 9000 **10** 550

Exercise 1R

2 **(a)** 240 **(b)** 1000 **(c)** 600 **(d)** 200 **(e)** 1000
(f) 3000 **(g)** 2100 **(h)** 8000 **(i)** 40 **(j)** 50

3 no **4** 5 **5** $500

Exercise 1S

1 **(a)** 81 **(b)** 610 **(c)** 799 **(d)** 1005 **(e)** 6234 **(f)** 24
(g) 2961 **(h)** 36 036 **(i)** 40 824 **(j)** 86

4 **(a)** × **(b)** + **(c)** − **(d)** ÷ **(e)** ÷
(f) − **(g)** × **(h)** × **(i)** × **(j)** −

Exercise 1T

1 232, 134, 213, 32, 3120, 9408, 42, 53, 5291, 45

2 **(a)** 4 **(b)** 15 **(c)** 4 **(d)** 9 **(e)** 17 **(f)** 24 **(g)** 23
(h) 14 **(i)** 42 **(j)** 27

3 **(a)** 15 **(b)** 18 **(c)** 19 **(d)** 23 **(e)** 23 **(f)** 35
(g) 13 **(h)** 15 **(i)** 102 **(j)** 100

4 **(d)** Same number as in (a) **(e)** yes

Investigation page 18

(a) 49 ways (assuming that 12 × 34 is the same as 34 × 12)
(c) 41 × 32

Exercise 1U

1 **(a)** 34 560 **(b)** 10 minutes 25 seconds

2 39

3 146

4 20, 20

5 **(a)** 83 + 29 = 112 **(b)** 92 − 67 = 25
(c) 23 × 7 = 161 **(d)** 417 ÷ 3 = 139 **(e)** 209 ÷ 11 = 19

6 4 × 5 + 3 − 6 = 17

7 **(a)** 12321, 1234321 **(b)** 9, 98, 987, 9876

8 27 and 28

9 26

10 3 × (3 + 3) − (3 ÷ 3) + 3

11 153 + 351 = 504, 252 + 252 = 504

Consolidation exercise 1

1 **(a)** 48 **(b)** 42 **(c)** 73 **(d)** 67 **(e)** 222 **(f)** 6251 **(g)** 106
(h) 1133 **(i)** 1885

2 **(a)** 6, 12, 18, 24 **(b)** 13, 26, 39, 52 **(c)** 23, 46, 69, 92
(d) 37, 74, 111, 148 **(e)** 48, 96, 144, 192

3 **(a)** {1, 2, 3, 4, 6, 8, 12, 24} **(b)** {1, 2, 3, 4, 6, 9, 12, 18, 36}
(c) {1, 3, 9, 27} **(d)** {1, 2, 3, 6, 9, 18, 27, 54}
(e) {1, 2, 4, 7, 8, 14, 16, 28, 56, 112}
(f) {1, 2, 3, 4, 6, 8, 12, 16, 24, 32, 48, 96}
(g) {1, 2, 3, 4, 6, 9, 12, 18, 27, 36, 54, 108}
(h) {1, 2, 3, 4, 6, 8, 9, 12, 16, 18, 24, 36, 48, 72, 144}
(i) {1, 2, 4, 8, 16, 32, 64, 128, 256}
(j) {1, 2, 4, 8, 16, 32, 64, 128, 256, 512, 1024}

4 **(a)** 8, 16 **(b)** 7, 14 **(c)** 4, 120 **(d)** 2, 180
(e) 8, 48 **(f)** 5, 100 **(g)** 5, 150 **(h)** 6, 252
(i) 2, 756 **(j)** 8, 360

5 **(a)** 221 **(b)** 462 **(c)** 864 **(d)** 522 **(e)** 702
(f) 729 **(g)** 1786 **(h)** 12654

6 **(a)** 18 **(b)** 18 **(c)** 15 **(d)** 36 **(e)** 14
(f) 16 **(g)** 17 **(h)** 24

7 **(a)** **(i)** 20 **(ii)** 0 **(b)** **(i)** 40 **(ii)** 0
(c) **(i)** 140 **(ii)** 100 **(d)** **(i)** 210 **(ii)** 200
(e) **(i)** 310 **(ii)** 300 **(f)** **(i)** 750 **(ii)** 700
(g) **(i)** 810 **(ii)** 800 **(h)** **(i)** 1320 **(ii)** 1300
(i) **(i)** 1070 **(ii)** 1100 **(j)** **(i)** 1870 **(ii)** 1900

8 **(a)** 423 mm **(b)** 190 mm 9 **(a)** 392 **(b)** 78.4

10 **(a)** 651 **(b)** 21 **(c)** \$4725 **(d)** \$7.26

Check out

1 **(a)** six **(b)** sixty **(c)** six hundred **(d)** six thousand

2 **(a)** 3, 6, 9, 12, 15 **(b)** 11, 22, 33, 44, 55

3 **(a)** 1, 2, 7, 14 **(b)** 1, 2, 3, 4, 6, 8, 12, 24

4 **(a)** prime **(b)** composite **(c)** prime **(d)** composite

5 **(a)** $2^3 \times 3$ **(b)** $2^3 \times 3^2$ **(c)** $2^3 \times 3 \times 7$ **(d)** $3 \times 5 \times 17$

6 **(a)** 4, 80 **(b)** 9, 54 **(c)** 4, 360 **(d)** 5, 105

7 **(a)** 224 **(b)** 234 **(c)** 378 **(d)** 2160

8 **(a)** 4 **(b)** 8 **(c)** 43r5 **(d)** 103

9 **(a)** **(i)** 720 **(ii)** 700 **(b)** **(i)** 610 **(ii)** 600
(c) **(i)** 1110 **(ii)** 1100 **(d)** **(i)** 1250 **(ii)** 1200

10 **(a)** 8 **(b)** 11 **(c)** 25

2 Sets

Check in

1 **(a)** 17, 215, 7 **(b)** 28, 116, 30

2 15, 60, 95

3 1, 2, 3, 4, 6, 12

4 **(a)** 11, 13 **(b)** 15, 8, 20

Exercise 2A

3 **(a)** 9 **(b)** 4 **(c)** 6 **(d)** 4

Exercise 2B

1 **(a)** {January, February, March, April, May, June, July, August, September, October, November, December}
(b) {Trindad, Tobago, Tortola, Turks & Caicos}
(c) {11, 12, 13, 14, 15, 16, 17, 18, 19} **(d)** {12}
(e) {27, 29, 31, 33}

2 **(b)** {Mon, Tues, Weds, Thurs, Fri, Sat, Sun}
(d) {3, 5, 7, 9} **(e)** {82, 84, 86, 88, 90, 92, 94, 96, 98}

3 Question 1:
(a) 12 **(b)** 4 **(c)** 9 **(d)** 1 **(e)** 4

Question 2:
(b) 7 **(d)** 4 **(e)** 9

5 **(a)** methods of transportation **(b)** odd numbers less than 12
(c) multiples of 10 from 10 to 100 **(d)** rivers

Exercise 2C

2 **(a)** $36 \in \{6, 16, 26, 36\}$ **(b)** $A \in \{A, B, C\}$
(c) St Lucia ∈ {Grenada, St. Lucia, St. Kitts, Trindad, Puerto Rico} **(d)** $16 \in \{10, 12, 14, 16, 18, 20\}$

3 **(a)** {whole numbers from 0 to 20}
(b) {odd numbers from 1 to 31}
(c) {multiples of 3 from 3 to 51}

4 **(a)** {10, 20, 30, 40, 50, 60, 70, 80, 90, 100}
(b) 6, 9, 12, 15, 18, 21, 24, 27, 30, 33, 36, 39, 42, 45, 48, 51, 54, 57, 60, 63, 66, 69, 72, 75, 78} **(c)** { }

5 **(a)**, **(b)**, **(e)**, **(g)**, **(i)** and **(j)** are empty sets

Exercise 2D

2 **(a)** {London, New York, Cairo, Paris, Delhi, Bangkok, Georgetown, Port of Spain, Bridgetown, Kingston}
(b) {Georgetown, Port of Spain, Bridgetown, Kingston}

3 subset = {2, 4, 6, 8, 10}

4 **(a)** {3, 6, 9, 12, 15, 18} **(b)** {4, 8, 12, 16, 20}
(c) {5, 10, 15, 20} **(d)** {1, 2, 4, 5, 10, 20}
Multiples of 5 has fewest members.

5 **(a)** {Hugh, Mohamed, Michael, Morris, Lawrence}
(b) {Donald, Michael, Greg, Morris, Winston}
(c) {Donald} **(d)** {Morris} **(e)** {Michael} **(f)** { }
(g) {Hugh, Mohamed, Donald, Michael, Greg, Morris, Winston, Lawrence}

Exercise 2E

1 **(b)** {lion, tiger, rhino, cheetah} ⊂ {dog, horse, camel, cow, sheep, cat, lion, tiger, rhino, cheetah}
(c) $\{7, 8, 9, 10\} \subset \{1, 2, 3, 4, 5, 6, 7, 8, 9, 10\}$

2 **(a)** odd numbers **(b)** even numbers **(c)** less than 10

Exercise 2F

1 **(a)** {Janet, Raquel, Ratna, Regina, Rose, Shirley}
(b) {Ratna, Rose, Regina, Robert, Ramsingh, Roland, Rocky, Raquel}

2 **(a)** {Ratna, Raquel, Regina, Rose}
(b) R only: {Rocky, Robert, Ramsingh, Roland} R and Girl: {Raquel, Ratna, Regina, Rose} Girl only: {Janet, Shirley}

3 yes

4 **(a)** {Deo, Wendy, Ali, Addie, Shirley, Janice}
(b) {Deo, Ramsingh, Bob, Janice, Rani}
(c) {Deo, Janice}
(d) Maths onlyl: {Wendy, Ali, Addie, Shirley} Maths and swim: {Deo, Janice} Swim only: {Ramsingh, Bob, Rani}
(e) She does not like maths and cannot swim

5 **(a)** **(i)** {Deo, Ramsingh, Bob, Janice, Rani}
(ii) {Wendy, Ramsingh, Bob, Shirley}
(b) {Ramsingh, Bob} **(c)** {Ali, Lorna, Addie}
(d) {Wendy, Shirley}

6 **(a)** {2, 4, 6, 8, 10, 12, 14, 16, 18, 20} **(b)** {3, 6, 9, 12, 15, 18} **(c)** {6, 12, 18} **(d)** {2, 4, 8, 10, 14, 16, 20} **(e)** {3, 9, 15} **(f)** {1, 5, 7, 11, 13, 17, 19}

7 **(b)** **(i)** {1, 3, 5, 7, 9, 11, 13, 15, 17, 19, 21, 23, 25, 27, 29} **(ii)** {5, 10, 15, 20, 25, 30} **(iii)** {5, 15, 25} **(iv)** {1, 3, 7, 9, 11, 13, 17, 19, 21, 23, 27, 29} **(v)** {10, 20, 30} **(vi)** {2, 4, 6, 8, 12, 14, 16, 18, 22, 24, 26, 28}

8 **(a)** Prime: {2, 3, 5, 7, 11, 13, 17, 19, 23} Composite: {4, 6, 8, 9, 10, 12, 14, 15, 16, 18, 20, 21, 22, 24, 25} **(b)** none **(c)** none

Exercise 2G

1 **(a)** {1, 2, 4, 8} **(b)** {1, 2, 3, 4, 6, 12} **(d)** {1, 2, 4}

2 **(a)** {1, 3, 9} **(b)** {1, 2, 3, 4, 6, 12} **(d)** {1, 3)

3 **(a)** {1, 5} **(b)** {1, 2} **(c)** {1, 2} **(d)** {1, 2} **(e)** {1, 2} **(f)** {1, 3}

Exercise 2H

1 **(a)** 5 **(b)** 2 **(c)** 2 **(d)** 2 **(e)** 2 **(f)** 3

2 **(a)** 3 **(b)** 5 **(c)** 4 **(d)** 6 **(e)** 5 **(f)** 14 **(g)** 8 **(h)** 18

3 **(a)** {1, 2, 3, 4, 6, 8, 12, 24} **(b)** {1, 2, 3, 4, 6, 9, 12, 18, 36} HCF is 12.

Exercise 2I

1 **(a)** {2, 4, 6, 8, 10, 12, 14, 16, 18, 20} **(b)** {5, 10, 15, 20} **(d)** {10, 20}

2 **(a)** {2, 4, 6, 8, 10, 12} **(b)** {3, 6, 9, 12, 15, 18} **(d)** {6, 12}

3 **(a)** {15, 30, ... } **(b)** {6, 12, 18, ... } **(c)** {14, 28, ... } **(d)** {20, 40, ... } **(e)** {8, 16, ... } **(f)** {12, 24, 36, ... }

Exercise 2J

1 **(a)** 15 **(b)** 6 **(c)** 14 **(d)** 20 **(e)** 8 **(f)** 12

2 **(a)** 6 **(b)** 8 **(c)** 12 **(d)** 4 **(e)** 18 **(f)** 10 **(g)** 35 **(h)** 24

Exercise 2K – mixed questions

1 **(a)** physics ∈ {science subjects} **(b)** {April} ⊂ {months of the year} **(c)** {knife, fork, spoon} ⊂ {kitchen utensils} **(d)** 15 ∈ {multiples of 5} **(e)** {3, 6, 12} ⊂ {factors of 24}

2 **(b)**, **(c)** and **(e)**

3 $a = 3$

4 **(a)** **(i)** {Cyril, Jan, Ron, Sheila, Mark} **(ii)** {Mara, Vivia} **(iii)** {Susan, Paul} **(iv)** {Jan, Sheila} **(b)** 7

5 **(a)** {2, 6}

6 **(a)** {1, 2, 3, 6} **(b)** {1, 2, 3, 4, 6, 8, 12, 24}

7 **(a)** HCF = 2, LCM = 48 **(b)** HCF = 3, LCM = 84 **(c)** HCF = 3, LCM = 45

Consolidation Exercise 2

1 **(a)** odd numbers from 7 to 17 **(b)** prime numbers from 2 to 17 **(c)** islands in the West Indies

3 **(a)**

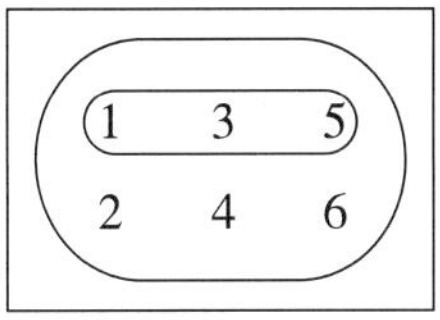

(b)

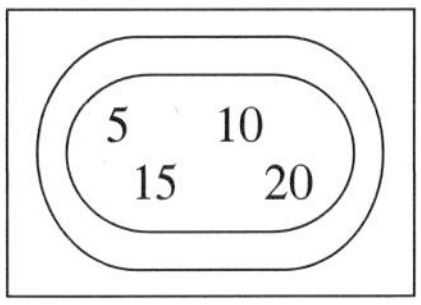

(c)

4 **(a)** {1, 2}

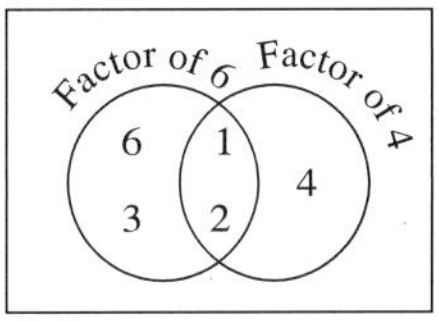

(b) {1, 2, 3, 4, 6, 12}

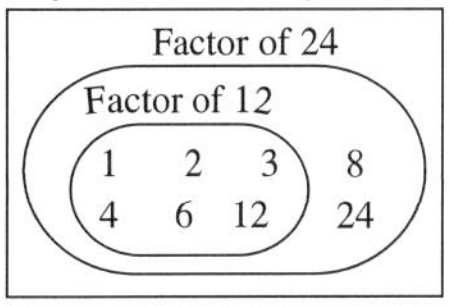

(c) {1, 3}

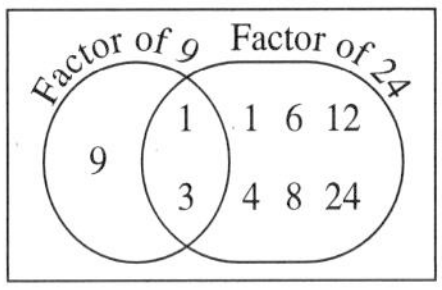

(d) {1, 3}

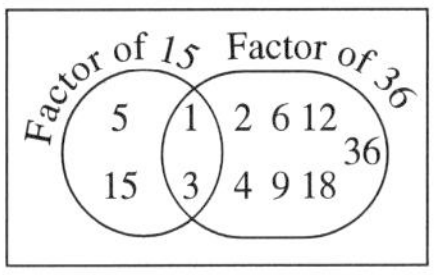

5 **(a)**

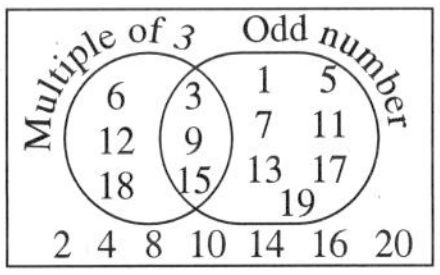

(b) **(i)** {3, 6, 9, 12, 15, 18} **(ii)** {1, 3, 5, 7, 9, 11, 13, 15, 17, 19} **(iii)** {3, 9, 15} **(iv)** {1, 5, 7, 11, 13, 17, 19} **(v)** {6, 12, 18} **(vi)** {2, 4, 8, 10, 14, 16, 20}

6 **(a)**

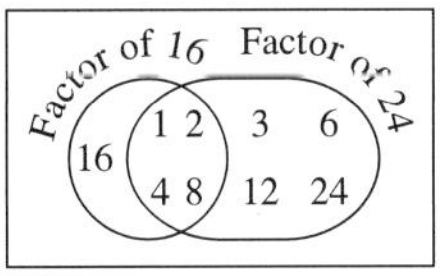

(b) 1, 2, 4, 8 **(c)** 1, 2, 4, 8 **(d)** 8

7 **(a)** 6 **(b)** 9 **(c)** 12

8 **(a)** 15 **(b)** 6 **(c)** 105

Check out

1 **(a)** {7, 9, 11, 13, 15} **(b)** {Tuesday, Thursday}

2 **(a)** cod ∈ {fish} **(b)** {birds with two heads} = { }

3 **(a)** {2, 3, 5, 7} **(b)** {Mary, Liz} ⊂ {girls names}

5 **(b)** 7 **(d)** 12

3 Fractions

Check in

1 (a) $\frac{1}{2}$ **(b)** 5

2 (a) numerator = 3, denominator = 4
(b) numerator = 2, denominator = 3
(c) numerator = 5, denominator = 7
(d) numerator = 2, denominator = 10

3 (a) $\frac{3}{4}$ **(b)** $\frac{2}{5}$ **(c)** $\frac{5}{6}$

Exercise 3A

1 (a) $\frac{1}{2}$ **(b)** $\frac{1}{4}$ **(c)** $\frac{1}{5}$ **(d)** $\frac{1}{6}$ **(e)** $\frac{1}{8}$ **(f)** $\frac{1}{11}$

Exercise 3B

1 (a) $\frac{3}{4}$ **(b)** $\frac{5}{6}$ **(c)** $\frac{3}{20}$ **(d)** $\frac{3}{8}$ **(e)** $\frac{7}{15}$ **(f)** $\frac{12}{28}$

4 (a) $\frac{2}{8}$ **(b)** $\frac{3}{8}$ **(c)** $\frac{2}{8}$ **(d)** $\frac{1}{8}$

5 (a) (i) $\frac{4}{9}$ **(ii)** $\frac{2}{9}$ **(iii)** $\frac{1}{9}$ **(iv)** $\frac{1}{9}$ **(b)** $\frac{1}{9}$

6 (a) 17 hectares

7 (a) 10 **(b) (i)** $\frac{3}{10}$ **(ii)** $\frac{1}{10}$ **(iii)** $\frac{2}{10}$ **(iv)** $\frac{4}{10}$

Exercise 3C

1 (a) 5 **(b)** 5 **(c)** 3 **(d)** 3 **(d)** 5 **(f)** 6

2 \$9

3 24

4 \$75 600

Exercise 3D

1 (a) 3 **(b)** 9 **(c)** 7 **(d)** 28 **(e)** 6 **(f)** 36 **(g)** 7
(h) 35 **(i)** 5 **(j)** 35

3 (a) 12 centimetres **(b)** 18 students **(c)** 56 fishing boats
(d) 40 lemons **(e)** 33 exercises
(f) 60 minutes **(g)** 45 soldiers **(h)** 35 robbers

4 (a) (i) $\frac{3}{8}$ **(ii)** $\frac{4}{8}$ **(iii)** $\frac{1}{8}$ **(b) (i)** 18 **(ii)** 24 **(iii)** 6

5 (a) $\frac{1}{5}$ **(b)** $\frac{3}{5}$ **(c)** 20 **(d)** 60

6 Super Wash

Exercise 3E

1 (a) 60 litres **(b)** 64 litres **(c)** 36 litres

2 (a) $\frac{3}{8}$ **(b)** 5 **(c)** 8 equal parts, 40 students

3 (a) 6 **(b)** 72

4 63 litres

5 (a) 9 litres **(b)** 27 litres **(c)** 45 litres

6 (b) 12 **(c)** 3 **(d)** 27

Exercise 3F

1 (a) 2 **(b)** 2 **(c)** 6 **(d)** 2 **(e)** 6 **(f)** 12 **(g)** 8

3 (a) yes **(b) (i)** 2 **(ii)** 4 **(iii)** 6 **(iv)** 8 **(v)** 10
(c) $\frac{1}{2}=\frac{2}{4}=\frac{3}{6}=\frac{4}{8}=\frac{5}{10}$

Exercise 3G

1 (a) $\frac{4}{6}, \frac{8}{12}$ **(b)** $\frac{1}{3}, \frac{4}{12}$

2 (a) $\frac{2}{4}, \frac{3}{6}$ **(b)** $\frac{2}{6}$

3 (a) $\frac{1}{3}=\frac{2}{6}=\frac{4}{12}$ **(b)** $\frac{1}{4}=\frac{2}{8}=\frac{3}{12}$ **(c)** $\frac{3}{4}=\frac{6}{8}=\frac{9}{12}$
(d) $\frac{3}{6}=\frac{4}{8}=\frac{6}{12}$ **(e)** $\frac{9}{12}=\frac{6}{8}=\frac{3}{4}$ **(f)** $\frac{4}{12}=\frac{2}{6}=\frac{1}{3}$

Exercise 3H

1 (b) $\frac{1}{12}$ **(c)** $\frac{1}{3}$ **(d)** 4 **(e)** $\frac{1}{3}=\frac{4}{12}$

2 (d) $\frac{4}{6}=\frac{8}{12}$

3 (e) $\frac{5}{6}=\frac{10}{12}$

6 (a) $\frac{2}{3}=\frac{16}{24}$ **(b)** $\frac{4}{6}=\frac{16}{24}$ **(c)** $\frac{6}{12}=\frac{12}{24}$ **(d)** $\frac{3}{8}=\frac{9}{24}$
(e) $\frac{6}{8}=\frac{18}{24}$ **(f)** $\frac{3}{4}=\frac{18}{24}$

Investigation page 46

(a) multiply the numerator and denominator by 2 **(b)** multiply the numerator and denominator by 3
(c) multiply the numerator and denominator by 4
(d) $\frac{1}{3}=\frac{5}{15}=\frac{6}{18}=\frac{7}{21}\cdots$

Exercise 3I

1 (a) $\frac{1}{2}=\frac{2}{4}$ **(b)** $\frac{2}{3}=\frac{4}{6}$ **(c)** $\frac{3}{4}=\frac{9}{12}$ **(d)** $\frac{3}{8}=\frac{9}{24}$ **(e)** $\frac{5}{6}=\frac{20}{24}$
(f) $\frac{5}{8}=\frac{20}{32}$ **(g)** $\frac{4}{7}=\frac{8}{14}$ **(h)** $\frac{3}{11}=\frac{15}{55}$ **(i)** $\frac{6}{13}=\frac{24}{52}$

2 $\frac{6}{15}=\frac{2}{5}$

3 (a) $\frac{4}{8}=\frac{1}{2}$ **(b)** $\frac{12}{24}=\frac{4}{8}$ **(c)** $\frac{6}{9}=\frac{2}{3}$ **(d)** $\frac{5}{15}=\frac{1}{3}$ **(e)** $\frac{35}{40}=\frac{7}{8}$
(f) $\frac{32}{40}=\frac{8}{10}$ **(g)** $\frac{56}{84}=\frac{8}{12}$ **(h)** $\frac{54}{63}=\frac{6}{7}$ **(i)** $\frac{65}{91}=\frac{5}{7}$

4 (a) $\frac{40}{100}=\frac{20}{50}=\frac{10}{25}=\frac{2}{5}$ **(b)** $\frac{75}{90}=\frac{50}{60}=\frac{25}{30}=\frac{5}{6}$
(c) $\frac{72}{84}=\frac{36}{42}=\frac{12}{14}=\frac{6}{7}$ **(d)** $\frac{81}{189}=\frac{27}{63}=\frac{9}{21}=\frac{3}{7}$ **(e)** $\frac{105}{135}=\frac{21}{27}=\frac{7}{9}$

Exercise 3J

1 (a) $\frac{1}{3}$ **(b)** $\frac{1}{4}$ **(c)** $\frac{2}{5}$ **(d)** $\frac{5}{7}$ **(e)** $\frac{2}{3}$ **(f)** $\frac{1}{3}$ **(g)** $\frac{1}{3}$
(h) $\frac{7}{9}$ **(i)** $\frac{6}{11}$ **(j)** $\frac{3}{29}$

2 (a) $\frac{20}{72}$ **(b)** $\frac{8}{98}$ **(c)** $\frac{14}{45}$

3 65 and 78 are both divisible by 13, simplest form is $\frac{5}{6}$

4 (a) $\frac{9}{11}$ **(b)** $\frac{4}{9}$ **(c)** $\frac{144}{361}$ **(d)** $\frac{7}{9}$

5 (a) (i) $\frac{5}{18}$ **(ii)** $\frac{1}{10}$ **(b) (i)** $\frac{31}{127}$ **(ii)** $\frac{49}{127}$

6 (b) $\frac{2}{3}=\frac{8}{12}, \frac{3}{4}=\frac{9}{12}$ **(c)** $\frac{3}{4}$ is larger

Exercise 3K

1 (a) 12 **(b)** $\frac{5}{6}$ **(c)** $\frac{1}{12}$

2 (a) $\frac{1}{3}$ is larger by $\frac{1}{21}$ **(b)** $\frac{2}{7}$ is larger by $\frac{1}{28}$
(c) $\frac{4}{5}$ is larger by $\frac{1}{20}$ **(d)** $\frac{3}{7}$ is larger by $\frac{1}{35}$
(e) $\frac{7}{10}$ is larger by $\frac{1}{30}$ **(f)** $\frac{8}{11}$ is larger by $\frac{2}{33}$
(g) $\frac{7}{9}$ is larger by $\frac{5}{99}$ **(h)** $\frac{11}{14}$ is larger by $\frac{17}{84}$
(i) $\frac{17}{20}$ is larger by $\frac{1}{30}$

3 (a) $\frac{1}{3}<\frac{1}{2}$ **(b)** $\frac{1}{6}<\frac{5}{18}$ **(c)** $\frac{3}{4}=\frac{9}{12}$ **(d)** $\frac{23}{24}>\frac{11}{12}$ **(e)** $\frac{5}{6}>\frac{7}{9}$
(f) $\frac{4}{15}<\frac{3}{10}$ **(g)** $\frac{3}{7}<\frac{4}{9}$ **(h)** $\frac{7}{12}<\frac{9}{15}$ **(i)** $\frac{20}{100}=\frac{5}{25}$

4 (a) $\frac{2}{3}$ **(b)** $\frac{7}{10}$ **(c)** $\frac{17}{20}$

Activity page 48

You can make 1 complete circle from 7 quarter-circles, with $\frac{3}{4}$ of a circle left over.

Exercise 3L

1

Number of quarter-circles	As a fraction	As a mixed number
1	$\frac{1}{4}$	—
2	$\frac{2}{4}$	—
3	$\frac{3}{4}$	—
4	$\frac{4}{4}$	—
5	$\frac{5}{4}$	$1\frac{1}{4}$
6	$\frac{6}{4}$	$1\frac{1}{2}$
7	$\frac{7}{4}$	$1\frac{3}{4}$
8	$\frac{8}{4}$	2
9	$\frac{9}{4}$	$2\frac{1}{4}$
10	$\frac{10}{4}$	$2\frac{1}{4}$
11	$\frac{11}{4}$	$2\frac{3}{4}$
12	$\frac{12}{4}$	3

2 **(a)** $\{\frac{1}{3}, \frac{4}{11}, \frac{1}{9}, \frac{2}{7}\}$ **(b)** $\{\frac{13}{2}, \frac{18}{5}, \frac{5}{2}, \frac{10}{3}, \frac{3}{2}\}$ **(c)** $\{\frac{3}{3}, \frac{6}{6}, \frac{8}{8}, \frac{10}{10}\}$

3 **(a)** $\{\frac{1}{5}, \frac{3}{11}, \frac{2}{9}, \frac{4}{15}\}$ **(b)** $\{\frac{7}{3}, \frac{10}{7}, \frac{6}{5}, \frac{8}{5}\}$ **(c)** $\{2\frac{1}{3}, 3\frac{1}{2}, 2\frac{1}{5}, 4\frac{1}{3}, 1\frac{1}{4}\}$

4 $2\frac{5}{6}$

5 **(a)** $1\frac{2}{3}$ **(b)** $2\frac{1}{3}$ **(c)** $1\frac{2}{3}$ **(d)** $4\frac{1}{4}$ **(e)** $2\frac{6}{11}$

6 **(d)** **(i)** $2\frac{3}{7}$ **(ii)** $3\frac{1}{5}$ **(iii)** $9\frac{1}{3}$ **(iv)** $7\frac{1}{4}$ **(v)** $6\frac{1}{6}$
(vi) $5\frac{1}{9}$ **(vii)** $8\frac{3}{11}$ **(viii)** $8\frac{7}{10}$ **(ix)** $10\frac{1}{12}$ **(x)** $7\frac{13}{20}$

7 **(d)** **(i)** $\frac{5}{2}$ **(ii)** $\frac{13}{4}$ **(iii)** $\frac{22}{5}$ **(iv)** $\frac{39}{8}$ **(v)** $\frac{17}{3}$
(vi) $\frac{71}{11}$ **(vii)** $\frac{59}{10}$ **(viii)** $\frac{43}{9}$ **(ix)** $\frac{77}{12}$ **(x)** $\frac{149}{20}$

Exercise 3M

1 **(a)** 3 **(b)** $\frac{1}{4} + \frac{2}{4} = \frac{3}{4}$

2 **(a)** $\frac{5}{8}$ **(b)** $\frac{3}{8} + \frac{2}{8} = \frac{5}{8}$

3 **(a)** $\frac{8}{10} = \frac{4}{5}$ **(b)** $\frac{5}{12}$ **(c)** $\frac{14}{16} = \frac{7}{8}$

4 **(a)** $\frac{9}{10}$ **(b)** $\frac{6}{6} = 1$ **(c)** $\frac{8}{9}$ **(d)** $\frac{19}{20}$ **(e)** $\frac{15}{32}$ **(f)** $\frac{43}{50}$

5 To add fractions with the same denominator, you add the numerators and put the answer over the original denominator.

6 **(a)** $\frac{6}{4} = 1\frac{1}{2}$ **(b)** $\frac{4}{3} = 1\frac{1}{3}$ **(c)** $\frac{6}{6} = 1$ **(d)** $\frac{16}{12} = 1\frac{1}{3}$
(e) $\frac{9}{8} = 1\frac{1}{8}$ **(f)** $\frac{27}{16} = 1\frac{11}{16}$

Exercise 3N

1 **(a)** $\frac{3}{5} + \frac{3}{10} = \frac{6}{10} + \frac{3}{10} = \frac{9}{10}$ **(b)** $\frac{1}{6} + \frac{2}{3} = \frac{1}{6} + \frac{4}{6} = \frac{5}{6}$
(c) $\frac{3}{4} + \frac{1}{8} = \frac{6}{8} + \frac{1}{8} = \frac{7}{8}$ **(d)** $\frac{5}{6} + \frac{1}{12} = \frac{10}{12} + \frac{1}{12} = \frac{11}{12}$
(e) $\frac{3}{8} + \frac{5}{16} = \frac{6}{16} + \frac{5}{16} = \frac{11}{16}$

2 **(a)** $\frac{1}{2}$ **(b)** $\frac{1}{2}$ **(c)** $\frac{9}{10}$ **(d)** $\frac{7}{12}$ **(e)** $\frac{11}{12}$ **(f)** $\frac{8}{9}$
(g) $\frac{11}{16}$ **(h)** $\frac{2}{3}$ **(i)** $\frac{8}{9}$ **(j)** $\frac{5}{6}$

3 **(a)** $\frac{2}{3} + \frac{1}{2} = \frac{4}{6} + \frac{3}{6} = \frac{7}{6}$ **(b)** $\frac{4}{5} + \frac{3}{8} = \frac{32}{40} + \frac{15}{40} = \frac{47}{40}$
(c) $\frac{3}{8} + \frac{9}{12} = \frac{9}{24} + \frac{18}{24} = \frac{27}{24}$

4 **(a)** $\frac{5}{6}$ **(b)** $\frac{33}{40}$ **(c)** $1\frac{1}{24}$ **(d)** $\frac{17}{18}$ **(e)** $\frac{31}{35}$ **(f)** $1\frac{1}{45}$
(g) $\frac{27}{28}$ **(h)** $\frac{29}{33}$ **(i)** $\frac{35}{36}$

5 **(a)** $\frac{7}{12}$ **(b)** 140

6 **(a)** $\frac{9}{10}$ **(b)** $\frac{1}{10}$

Exercise 3O

1 **(a)** $\frac{3}{5} - \frac{3}{10} = \frac{6}{10} - \frac{3}{10} = \frac{3}{10}$ **(b)** $\frac{2}{3} - \frac{1}{6} = \frac{4}{6} - \frac{1}{6} = \frac{3}{6}$
(c) $\frac{3}{4} - \frac{3}{8} = \frac{6}{8} - \frac{3}{8} = \frac{3}{8}$ **(d)** $\frac{5}{6} - \frac{5}{12} = \frac{10}{12} - \frac{5}{12} = \frac{5}{12}$
(e) $\frac{5}{8} - \frac{3}{16} = \frac{10}{16} - \frac{3}{16} = \frac{7}{16}$

2 **(a)** $\frac{1}{2}$ **(b)** $\frac{5}{8}$ **(c)** $\frac{2}{9}$ **(d)** $\frac{3}{8}$ **(e)** $\frac{1}{2}$ **(f)** $\frac{1}{8}$ **(g)** $\frac{1}{3}$
(h) $\frac{1}{2}$ **(i)** $\frac{1}{4}$ **(j)** $\frac{3}{10}$

3 **(a)** 12 **(b)** $\frac{4}{12}$ and $\frac{9}{12}$ **(c)** $\frac{5}{12}$

4 **(a)** $\frac{1}{2} - \frac{1}{3} = \frac{3}{6} - \frac{2}{6} = \frac{1}{6}$ **(b)** $\frac{2}{3} - \frac{1}{2} = \frac{4}{6} - \frac{3}{6} = \frac{1}{6}$
(c) $\frac{1}{3} - \frac{1}{4} = \frac{4}{12} - \frac{3}{12} = \frac{1}{12}$ **(d)** $\frac{3}{4} - \frac{2}{3} = \frac{9}{12} - \frac{8}{12} = \frac{1}{12}$
(e) $\frac{5}{6} - \frac{3}{4} = \frac{10}{12} - \frac{9}{12} = \frac{1}{12}$

5 **(a)** $\frac{1}{6}$ **(b)** $\frac{1}{8}$ **(c)** $\frac{1}{36}$ **(d)** $\frac{1}{6}$ **(e)** $\frac{13}{40}$ **(f)** $\frac{7}{12}$
(g) $\frac{5}{24}$ **(h)** $\frac{17}{40}$ **(i)** $\frac{23}{42}$

6 $\frac{2}{15}$

7 $2\frac{5}{6}$

8 4

Investigation page 52

Any unit fraction can be written as the sum of two other different unit fractions. If you divide the larger of the two new denominators by the smaller one, you always get the original denominator.

$$\frac{1}{n} = \frac{1}{n+1} + \frac{1}{n(n+1)}$$

Exercise 3P

1 **(a)** 6 **(b)** $2 \times \frac{3}{4} = \frac{6}{4}$

2 **(a)** 12 **(b)** $4 \times \frac{3}{4} = \frac{12}{4}$

3 **(a)**

Number of $\frac{3}{4}$-circles made	Number of $\frac{1}{4}$-circles used	The multiplication
1	3	$1 \times \frac{3}{4} = \frac{3}{4}$
2	6	$2 \times \frac{3}{4} = \frac{6}{4}$
3	9	$3 \times \frac{3}{4} = \frac{9}{4}$
4	12	$4 \times \frac{3}{4} = \frac{12}{4}$
5	15	$5 \times \frac{3}{4} = \frac{15}{4}$
6	18	$6 \times \frac{3}{4} = \frac{18}{4}$
7	21	$7 \times \frac{3}{4} = \frac{21}{4}$
8	24	$8 \times \frac{3}{4} = \frac{24}{4}$

(c) $3 \times$ (the number of $\frac{3}{4}$-circles made) **(d)** they are the same

(e) multiply the numerator by the whole number

Exercise 3Q

1 (a) $1\frac{1}{3}$ (b) $1\frac{3}{4}$ (c) $1\frac{4}{5}$ (d) $2\frac{1}{3}$ (e) $1\frac{1}{5}$ (f) $1\frac{1}{4}$ (g) $1\frac{1}{5}$ (h) $3\frac{1}{3}$ (i) $2\frac{5}{8}$

2 (a) $2\frac{1}{6}$ (b) $2\frac{1}{2}$ (c) $1\frac{1}{3}$ (d) $2\frac{2}{11}$ (e) $4\frac{1}{5}$ (f) $4\frac{1}{6}$ (g) $5\frac{3}{5}$ (h) $11\frac{2}{3}$ (i) $57\frac{3}{5}$ (j) $22\frac{10}{17}$

3 (a) 10 (b) $15\frac{1}{6}$ (c) $16\frac{1}{4}$ (d) 20 (e) $73\frac{1}{3}$ (f) $82\frac{1}{4}$

4 $5\frac{1}{4}$ hours **5** $10\frac{1}{2}$ kg **6** $13\frac{1}{5}$ lb **7** 1200

8 $31\frac{1}{4}\,m^2$ **9** 4 **10** (a) 240 (b) 180

Exercise 3R

1 (a) $\frac{1}{4}$ (b) $\frac{1}{6}$ (c) $\frac{2}{9}$ (d) $\frac{9}{20}$ (e) $\frac{3}{10}$

Exercise 3S

1 (a) $\frac{2}{19}$ (b) $\frac{1}{6}$ (c) $\frac{4}{15}$ (d) $\frac{22}{51}$ (e) $\frac{2}{57}$ (f) $\frac{3}{7}$

2 (a) $\frac{5}{6}$ (b) $\frac{3}{4}$ (c) $2\frac{8}{9}$ (d) $\frac{18}{35}$ (e) $1\frac{3}{32}$ (f) $4\frac{4}{5}$ (g) $3\frac{1}{8}$ (h) $9\frac{4}{5}$

3 (a) $\frac{5}{9}$ (b) $\frac{72}{77}$ (c) $1\frac{3}{5}$ (d) $\frac{5}{6}$ (e) $\frac{19}{40}$ (f) $\frac{1}{2}$

4 $1\frac{4}{5}$ m **5** $2\frac{1}{2}$ hours

6 $2\frac{1}{2}$ km (if he goes to school 5 times a week)

Investigation page 55

(a) yes (b) yes (c) For example, $7 - \frac{7}{8} = 7 \times \frac{7}{8}$

Exercise 3T

1 (a) 24, $6 \div \frac{1}{4} = 24$ (b) 8, $6 \div \frac{3}{4} = 8$

2 (a) 36, $9 \div \frac{1}{4} = 36$ (b) 12, $9 \div \frac{3}{4} = 12$

3 (a) $6 \div \frac{1}{4} = 6 \times 4 = 24$ (b) $6 \div \frac{3}{4} = 6 \times \frac{4}{3} = 8$

4 (a) $9 \div \frac{1}{4} = 9 \times 4 = 36$ (b) $9 \div \frac{3}{4} = 9 \times \frac{4}{3} = 12$

Exercise 3U

1 (a) $4 \div \frac{2}{3} = 4 \times \frac{3}{2} = \frac{4 \times 3}{2} = \frac{12}{2} = 6$
(b) $10 \div \frac{2}{5} = 10 \times \frac{5}{2} = \frac{50}{2} = 25$ (c) $10 \div \frac{4}{5} = 10 \times \frac{5}{4} = \frac{50}{4} = 12\frac{1}{2}$
(d) $5 \div \frac{3}{4} = 5 \times \frac{4}{3} = \frac{20}{3} = 6\frac{2}{3}$ (e) $8 \div 1\frac{3}{4} = 8 \div \frac{7}{4} = 8 \times \frac{4}{7} = 4\frac{4}{7}$

2 (a) 45 (b) $5\frac{1}{3}$ (c) 9 (d) $9\frac{3}{5}$ (e) 12 (f) 9

3 (a) $4\frac{4}{5}$ (b) $2\frac{2}{3}$ (c) $4\frac{10}{11}$ (d) $2\frac{18}{19}$ (e) $2\frac{12}{19}$ (f) $3\frac{7}{27}$

4 21 bottles **5** 18 people **6** $2\frac{1}{2}$ weeks **7** same value

Exercise 3V

1 (a) $\frac{2}{3}$ (b) $\frac{33}{50}$ (c) $\frac{15}{16}$ (d) $1\frac{1}{15}$ (e) $\frac{4}{21}$
(e) $\frac{4}{21}$ (f) $2\frac{2}{7}$

2 (a) $2\frac{2}{9}$ (b) 8 (c) $4\frac{2}{5}$ (d) $1\frac{7}{20}$ (e) $4\frac{2}{9}$ (f) $\frac{7}{10}$ (g) $\frac{1}{8}$ (h) $\frac{13}{56}$ (i) $\frac{1}{2}$

3 (a) 10 (b) 30 (c) 8 (d) 2 (e) 6 (f) 14

4 (a) $2\frac{2}{3}$ (b) $5\frac{1}{3}$ (c) 2 (d) 7 (e) $7\frac{1}{5}$ (f) $3\frac{1}{3}$

5 (a) (i) $\frac{15}{16}$ (ii) 4 (iii) $\frac{32}{35}$ (iv) $2\frac{3}{16}$ (v) $\frac{35}{36}$ (vi) $\frac{17}{30}$

6 $\frac{5}{26}$ **7** 30 **8** $8\frac{1}{4}$ **9** 3 **10** (a) $\frac{13}{34}$ (b) $\frac{21}{34}$ **11** $280

Exercise 3W – mixed questions

4 (a) $1\frac{4}{10}, 1\frac{1}{2}, 1\frac{2}{3}, 1\frac{7}{10}, 1\frac{3}{4}$ (b) $1\frac{13}{20}$ is greater

6 14 out of 20

7 $\frac{5}{7}$

8 12

9 27

10 (a) $\frac{5}{12}$ (b) $144

11 $5\frac{5}{6}$ cm **12** 66 **13** $37\frac{1}{2}$ cm **14** $\frac{1}{20}$ mm

15 $506\frac{2}{3}$ kg

Consolidation exercise 3

1 (a) $\frac{2}{4}$ (b) $\frac{3}{4}$ (c) $\frac{1}{2}$ **2** (a) $36 (b) 21 gallons (c) 49 students (d) 44 days

3 (a) $\frac{9}{12}$ (b) $\frac{12}{30}$ (c) $\frac{60}{100}$ (d) $\frac{16}{100}$

4 (a) $1\frac{1}{2}$ (b) $1\frac{3}{20}$ (c) $2\frac{5}{8}$ (d) $4\frac{5}{8}$ (e) $\frac{4}{15}$ (f) $\frac{11}{40}$ (g) $\frac{1}{6}$ (h) $\frac{7}{12}$

5 (a) $\frac{2}{5}$ (b) $1\frac{1}{5}$ (c) $8\frac{1}{4}$ (d) 10 (e) $\frac{1}{2}$ (f) $\frac{5}{7}$ (g) $\frac{8}{9}$ (h) $2\frac{1}{28}$

6 (a) 160 (b) 78 (c) 292 (d) 174 (e) 55

7 $4\frac{2}{5}$ km per h **8** (a) 90 litres (b) 30 litres

Check out

1 (a) $\frac{3}{8}$ (b) $\frac{1}{4}$

2 (a) 10 (b) 21 (c) 240 ml

3 (a) $\frac{3}{4} = \frac{9}{12}$ (b) $\frac{2}{3} = \frac{16}{24}$ (c) (i) $\frac{2}{3}$ (ii) $\frac{5}{9}$

4 (a) (i) $3\frac{2}{3}$ (ii) $3\frac{2}{5}$ (b) (i) $\frac{5}{2}$ (ii) $\frac{22}{5}$

5 (a) 1 (b) $\frac{1}{2}$ (c) $\frac{1}{3}$

6 (a) (i) $1\frac{1}{2}$ (ii) 4 (iii) 6 (iv) $\frac{1}{2}$ (v) $\frac{9}{20}$ (vi) $1\frac{1}{2}$ (b) 38 g

7 (a) 1 (b) $\frac{1}{2}$ (c) $\frac{3}{8}$ (d) $8\frac{1}{2}$

8 (a) (i) 12 (ii) 7 (iii) $\frac{8}{9}$ (iv) $1\frac{17}{40}$ (b) 12

4 Decimals

Check in

1 (a) (i) $\frac{4}{10}$ (ii) $\frac{8}{20}$

2 (a) $\frac{2}{5} = \frac{4}{10}$ (b) $\frac{9}{10} = \frac{90}{100}$

3 (a) $\frac{8}{10}$ (b) $\frac{37}{100}$

Exercise 4A

1 (a) 0.3 (b) 0.6 (c) 0.9 (d) 1.2 (e) 2.8 (f) 3.4 (g) 12.1 (h) 132.5

2 (a) $\frac{6}{10} = 0.6$ (b) $\frac{5}{10} = 0.5$ (c) $\frac{3}{10} = 0.3$ (d) $\frac{8}{10} = 0.8$

3 (a) 0.2, 0.3, 0.6, 0.8 (b) 0, 0.5, 0.9, 1 (c) 0.6, 0.9, 1.8, 2.1 (d) 0.2, 6.9, 9, 13.2

4 (a) 0.4 (b) 0.8 (c) 1.0 (d) 1.1 (e) 3.0 (f) 6.1

5 (a) Earlson (b) 12.1 seconds

Exercise 4B

2 (a) 0.2 (b) 0.5 (c) 0.7 (d) 1.1 (e) 1.4 (f) 1.8

3 (a) 2.6 (b) 52.4 (c) 26.6

4 (a) 37.8 °C (b) 38.3 °C

Activity page 65

(a) 10 (b) 100 (c) $\frac{1}{10}$ (d) $\frac{1}{100}$

Exercise 4C

2 (a) 0.3 (b) 0.06 (c) 0.26 (d) 0.47 (e) 1.2 (f) 1.4 (g) 1.32 (h) 1.04 (i) 2.1 (j) 1.01

Exercise 4D

1 (a) 0.5 (b) 0.7 (c) 0.06 (d) 0.45 (e) 0.4 (f) 0.1 (g) 1.2 (h) 1 (i) 1.3 (j) 2

Exercise 4E

1 0.94

2 A = 0.1, B = 0.25, C = 0.45, D = 0.79, E = 0.56, F = 0.64, G = 0.94, H = 0.04

3 Points in order: F, A, B, E, D, C

4 A = 0.35, B = 0.51, C = 0.63, D = 0.97, E = 0.18

Exercise 4F

1 (a) 300 (b) 30 (c) 3 (d) $\frac{3}{10}$ (e) $\frac{3}{100}$ (f) $\frac{3}{10}$ (g) $\frac{3}{100}$ (h) $\frac{3}{10}$

2 (a) two hundreds or 200 (b) two units or 2
(c) two tenths or $\frac{2}{10}$ (d) two thousands or 2000
(e) two hundredths or $\frac{2}{100}$ (f) two tens or 20

3 (a) 1 unit or 1 (b) three tenths or $\frac{3}{10}$ (c) six tenths or $\frac{6}{10}$
(d) two hundredths or $\frac{2}{100}$ (e) one hundredth or $\frac{1}{100}$
(f) two hundredths or $\frac{2}{100}$ (g) five tenths or $\frac{5}{10}$
(h) four hundredths or $\frac{4}{100}$

Exercise 4G

1 (a) two tenths or $\frac{2}{10}$ or 0.2 (b) eight hundredths or $\frac{8}{100}$ or 0.08
(c) five tenths or $\frac{5}{10}$ or 0.5 (d) one ten or 10
(e) two units or 2 (f) four hundredths or $\frac{4}{100}$ or 0.04
(g) two thousandths or $\frac{2}{1000}$ or 0.002
(h) five thousandths or $\frac{5}{1000}$ or 0.005 (i) four tenths or $\frac{4}{10}$ or 0.4
(j) three thousands or 3000 (k) zero hundredths or $\frac{0}{100}$ or 0.00
(l) four tenths or $\frac{4}{10}$ or 0.4

2 (a) 0.006, 0.02, 0.3, 0.4 (b) 0.003, 0.3, 3, 30
(c) 0.036, 0.36, 3.6, 36 (d) 0.008, 0.8, 8, 800

4 Gamber, Ponting, Tendulkar, Kallis, Hussey

Exercise 4H

1 (a) $\frac{5}{10}$ (b) $\frac{7}{10}$ (c) $\frac{15}{100}$ (d) $\frac{34}{100}$ (e) $\frac{72}{100}$ (f) $\frac{699}{1000}$ (g) $\frac{708}{1000}$ (h) $\frac{94}{1000}$

2 (a) 10 (b) 100 (c) 1000
(d) The number of zeros in the denominator is always the same as the number of digits after the decimal point.

3 (a) $\frac{3}{10}$ (b) $\frac{8}{10}$ (c) $\frac{15}{100}$ (d) $\frac{37}{100}$

4 (a) $\frac{9}{10}$ (b) $\frac{4}{10}$ (c) $\frac{14}{100}$ (d) $\frac{46}{100}$ (e) $\frac{7}{100}$ (f) $\frac{5}{100}$
(g) $\frac{4}{100}$ (h) $\frac{149}{1000}$ (i) $\frac{237}{1000}$ (j) $\frac{97}{1000}$ (k) $\frac{62}{1000}$ (l) $\frac{51}{1000}$

5 (a) $1\frac{7}{10}$ (b) $2\frac{5}{10}$ (c) $3\frac{54}{100}$ (d) $9\frac{27}{100}$ (e) $5\frac{114}{1000}$
(f) $11\frac{438}{1000}$ (g) $8\frac{5}{1000}$ (h) $21\frac{9}{1000}$ (i) $9\frac{442}{1000}$ (j) $14\frac{803}{1000}$
(k) $16\frac{2}{1000}$ (l) $15\frac{77}{1000}$

7 (a) $\frac{1}{5}$ (b) $\frac{3}{5}$ (c) $\frac{4}{5}$ (d) $\frac{1}{2}$ (e) $\frac{1}{4}$ (f) $\frac{3}{4}$ (g) $\frac{1}{8}$
(h) $\frac{3}{8}$ (i) $\frac{5}{8}$

8 (a) 0.2 (b) 0.6 (c) 0.9 (d) 0.65 (e) 0.28 (f) 0.56
(g) 0.06 (h) 0.82

Exercise 4I

1 (a) 100 (b) $\frac{1}{100}$ (c) 0.01

2 (a) $\frac{15}{100}$ (b) 0.15

3 (a) \$1.10 (b) \$2.25 (c) \$3.55 (d) \$5.05 (e) \$10.09
(f) \$100.05 (g) \$54.13 (h) \$1.50

Exercise 4J

1 (a) 4.9 (b) 4.0 (c) 9.9 (d) 10.1 (e) 11.0 (f) 4.72
(g) 3.23 (h) 4.05 (i) 6.4 (j) 5.46

2 20.29

3 (a) 3.84 (b) 8.42 (c) 217.38 (d) 11.14 (e) 10.11

4 (a) She has forgotten to write 7 as 7.0 (b) 10.28

5 \$6.25

6 (a) Antoine (b) 50.03 seconds

7 (a) 5.0 (b) 7.44 (c) 6.53 (d) 11.07

Exercise 4K

1 (a) 1.2 (b) 0.9 (c) 2.6 (d) 0.3 (e) 4.2 (f) 2.87
(g) 6.75 (h) 1.63 (i) 1.44 (j) 93.2

2 (a) He should have written 6 as 6.0 and taken 1.87 away from it.
(c) 4.13

3 \$15.05

4 (a) Gretta (b) 2.89 seconds

5 (a) Johnson 10.3, Davis 10.39 seconds, Roberts 10.41 seconds
(b) 10.25 seconds
(c) Johnson beat Davis by 0.09 seconds

Exercise 4L

3 (a) 73.2 (b) 63.8 (c) 84 (d) 10.7 (e) 8.25
(f) 60.45

4 (a) 732 (b) 638 (c) 840 (d) 107 (e) 82.5
(f) 604.5

5

Number	Number × 10	Number × 100
7.32	73.2	732
6.38	63.8	638
8.4	84	840
1.07	10.7	107
0.825	8.25	82.5
6.045	60.45	604.5

6 Each digit moves one place to the left when you multiply by 10 and two places to the left when you multiply by 100.

7 **(a)** 74.5 **(b)** 89 **(c)** 3.4 **(d)** 30.4 **(e)** 0.6 **(f)** 10.06 **(g)** 184 **(h)** 216.3

8 **(a)** 745 **(b)** 890 **(c)** 34 **(d)** 304 **(e)** 6 **(f)** 100.6 **(g)** 1840 **(h)** 2163

9 **(a)** 0.76 **(b)** 0.43 **(c)** 2.61 **(d)** 4.8 **(e)** 52.3 **(f)** 6.87 **(g)** 94.3 **(h)** 9.9

10 **(a)** 0.076 **(b)** 0.043 **(c)** 0.261 **(d)** 0.48 **(e)** 5.23 **(f)** 0.687 **(g)** 9.43 **(h)** 0.99

11

Number	Number ÷ 10	Number ÷ 100
7.6	0.76	0.076
4.3	0.43	0.043
26.1	2.61	0.261
48	4.8	0.48
523	52.3	5.23
68.7	6.87	0.687
943	94.3	9.43
99	9.9	0.99

12 Each digit moves one place to the right when you divide by 10 and two places to the right when you divide by 100.

13 **(a)** 0.78 **(b)** 0.92 **(c)** 2.73 **(d)** 5.9 **(e)** 94.7 **(f)** 3.15

14 **(a)** 0.078 **(b)** 0.092 **(c)** 0.273 **(d)** 0.59 **(e)** 9.47 **(f)** 0.315

15 **(d)** 6.6

16 5.2, 4.75, 4.5, 7.125, 9.6, 6.5, 1.2, 2.333 …, 5.666 …, 0.25

Exercise 4M

1 **(a)** 63.5 **(b)** 635 **(c)** 714 **(d)** 7140 **(e)** 3.18 **(f)** 31.8 **(g)** 0.76 **(h)** 7.6

2 **(i)** **(a)** 98.43 **(b)** 160.4 **(c)** 1.4 **(d)** 79.6 **(e)** 1032 **(f)** 841.9
(ii) **(a)** 984.3 **(b)** 1604 **(c)** 14 **(d)** 796 **(e)** 10 320 **(f)** 8419
(iii) **(a)** 9843 **(b)** 16 040 **(c)** 140 **(d)** 7960 **(e)** 103 200 **(f)** 84 190

3 **(a)** 0.81 **(b)** 0.081 **(c)** 5.37 **(d)** 0.537 **(e)** 0.0014 **(f)** 0.000 14 **(g)** 0.0176 **(h)** 0.001 76

4 **(i)** **(a)** 4.62 **(b)** 0.708 **(c)** 0.0314 **(d)** 7.69 **(e)** 24.01 **(f)** 2.304
(ii) **(a)** 0.462 **(b)** 0.0708 **(c)** 0.003 14 **(d)** 0.769 **(e)** 2.401 **(f)** 0.2304
(iii) **(a)** 0.0462 **(b)** 0.007 08 **(c)** 0.000 314 **(d)** 0.0769 **(e)** 0.2401 **(f)** 0.023 04

5 **(a)** 642¢ **(b)** 1906¢ **(c)** 24 711¢

6 **(a)** \$0.45 **(b)** \$0.06 **(c)** \$1.37

Exercise 4N

1 **(a)** 15.6 **(b)** 15.6 **(c)** 1.56 **(d)** 1.56 **(e)** 1.56 **(f)** 0.156 **(g)** 0.0156 **(h)** 0.001 56

2 **(a)** 14.094 **(b)** 140.94 **(c)** 140.94 **(d)** 14.094 **(e)** 14.094 **(f)** 1.4094 **(g)** 0.140 94 **(h)** 0.014 094

3 **(a)** 2.4 **(b)** 0.24 **(c)** 0.15 **(d)** 0.8 **(e)** 3.2 **(f)** 0.14 **(g)** 0.7 **(h)** 0.3 **(i)** 2.52 **(j)** 2.24

4 **(a)** \$44.10 **(b)** \$283.50 **(c)** \$10.80 **(d)** \$9.75 **(e)** \$31.50

5 119.28 km **6** \$8.18 **7** 6.91 seconds **8** 1.3 and 1.4

Exercise 4O

1 **(a)** 0.4 **(b)** 0.9 **(c)** 0.04 **(d)** 0.08 **(e)** 0.32 **(f)** 0.016 **(g)** 0.75 **(h)** 0.016 **(i)** 0.19 **(j)** 0.084

2 **(a)** 1.49 **(b)** 0.142 **(c)** 1.801 25 **(d)** 0.0605 **(e)** 4.55 **(f)** 0.148 33 …

3 \$17.28 **4** 4.35 km h^{-1} **5** \$2.46 **6** \$14.13 **7** \$8.90

Exercise 4P

1 **(a)** 40 **(b)** 40 **(c)** 24 **(d)** 30 **(e)** 2.4 **(f)** 3 **(g)** 30 **(h)** 90

2 **(a)** 3.6 **(b)** 36 **(c)** 36 **(d)** 360 **(e)** 0.36 **(f)** 3.6

3 **(a)** 50 **(b)** 12 **(c)** 24 **(d)** 160 **(e)** 600 **(f)** 3.2

4 \$32.41 **5** **(b)** 30 **6** 41 **7** 16

Exercise 4Q

1 \$157.55 **2** **(a)** \$7.69 **(b)** \$12.31

3 **(a)** 43 **(b)** \$1.10

4 \$0.74 million or \$740 000

5 \$328.52

6 \$3158.40

7 **(a)** \$281.85 **(b)** 47 hours

8 33.5 kilometres per hour

Consolidation exercise 4

1 **(a)** 0.3 **(b)** 0.7 **(c)** 0.49 **(d)** 1.6 **(e)** 13.9

2

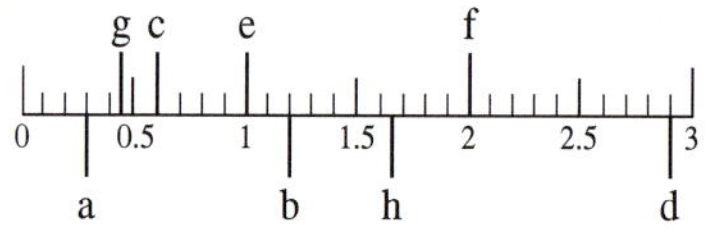

3 **(a)** 0.2 **(b)** 0.4 **(c)** 0.1

4 **(a)** 0.17, 0.2, 0.3, 3 **(b)** 0.07, 0.8, 1.6, 15 **(c)** 0.48, 0.5, 1, 8.02

5 **(a)** $\frac{5}{10}$ **(b)** $\frac{8}{10}$ **(c)** $1\frac{4}{10}$ **(d)** $3\frac{8}{10}$ **6** **(a)** \$63.89 **(b)** \$36.11

7 **(a)** 1.3 **(b)** 38.3 **(c)** 2.04

8 **(a)** Campbell **(b)** Oyepitan and Lee **(c)** 0.13 sec **(d)** 0.96 sec

9 The first piece of cheese. It sells for \$19.80 per kg, the second sells for \$19.82 per kg.

Check out

1 **(a)** $\frac{6}{10}$ **(b)** 2 **(c)** $\frac{7}{100}$ **(d)** 400 **(e)** $\frac{2}{1000}$

2 A = 1.62, B = 1.65, C = 1.66. D = 1.72

3 **(a)** 0.3 **(b)** 0.06 **(c)** 2.5 **(d)** 13.07 **(e)** 9.17

4 **(a)** $\frac{75}{100}$ **(b)** $\frac{8}{10}$ **(c)** $\frac{3}{10}$ **(d)** $\frac{225}{100}$ **(e)** $\frac{1368}{100}$

5 **(a)** 0.5 **(b)** 3 **(c)** 0.3 **(d)** 1

6 **(a)** 7.36 **(b)** 14.08 **(c)** 9.7

7 **(a)** 4.34 **(b)** 0.0392 **(c)** 190 **(d)** 1200

Revision exercise 1

1 **(a)** 66, 77, 88 **(b)** 102, 119, 136 **(c)** 138, 161, 184
(d) 171, 190, 209

2 **(a)** 1378 **(b)** 2312 **(c)** 10 044 **(d)** 27 636, 20 076

3 **(a)** 782 **(b)** 23

4 806

5 **(a)** 896 **(b)** 69

6 216

7 **(a)** 290 **(b)** 1479

8 **(a)** 49 **(b)** $16\frac{1}{3}$

9 997

10 **(a)** 36 **(b)** 312 **(c)** 283

12 **(a)** {a, e, i, o, u}
(b) {b, c, d, f, g, h, j, k, l, m, n, p, q, r, s, t, v, w, x, y, z}
(c) {a, c, e, h, i, m, s, t}

13 **(a)** 20 **(b)** 8
(c) Paul, Mary, Tony, Carol, George,David, Frances, Jennifer
(d) Martin, Delbert, Ann-Marie, Donald, Alicia, James, Cuthbert
(e) Paul, Mary, Tony **(f)** Carol, George, David, Frances, Jennifer
(g) They like science but do not like English.

14 **(a)** 7 **(b)** 6 **(c)** 8 **(d)** 4

15 **(a)** 45 **(b)** 72 **(c)** 78 **(d)** 60

16 **(a)** 23, 29, 31, 37 **(b)** yes: 21, 25, 27, 33, 35, 39
(c) even numbers between 20 and 40

17 **(a)** no **(b)** {factors of 6} ⊂ {factors of 24}

19 **(a)** { }, {1}, {2}, {1,2}
(b) { }, {a}, {b}, {c}, {a, b}, {a, c}, {b, c}, {a, b, c}
(c) { }, {2}, {4}, {6}, {8}, {2, 4}, {2, 6}, {2, 8}, {4, 6}, {4, 8}, {6, 8}, {2, 4, 6}, {2, 4, 8}, {2, 6, 8}, {4, 6, 8}, {2, 4, 6, 8}

20 **(a)** tall and wears glasses **(b)** tall and no glasses
(c) short and no glasses **(d)** short and wears glasses

21 **(a)** $\frac{3}{4} = \frac{6}{8} = \frac{12}{16} = \frac{21}{28} = \frac{63}{84}$ **(b)** $\frac{4}{7} = \frac{12}{21} = \frac{24}{42} = \frac{48}{84} = \frac{36}{63}$
(c) $\frac{12}{18} = \frac{14}{21} = \frac{10}{15} = \frac{28}{42} = \frac{42}{63}$ **(d)** $\frac{5}{6} = \frac{25}{30} = \frac{20}{24} = \frac{35}{42} = \frac{60}{72}$

22 **(a)** $\frac{2}{9}, \frac{5}{18}, \frac{1}{3}$ **(b)** $\frac{7}{12}, \frac{2}{3}, \frac{3}{4}$ **(c)** $\frac{7}{12}, \frac{9}{15}, \frac{13}{18}$

23 1280 litres

24 36 litres

25 **(a)** $\frac{4}{7}$ **(b)** $9\frac{1}{3}$ **(c)** $9\frac{1}{2}$ **(d)** $\frac{6}{7}$ **(e)** $4\frac{4}{7}$ **(f)** $12\frac{3}{4}$

26 $\frac{11}{15}$ m

27 $\frac{5}{7}$ m or $71\frac{3}{7}$ cm

28 $\frac{5}{24}$

29 9 hours

30 54 km

31 **(a)** 0.6 **(b)** 0.45 **(c)** 0.95 **(d)** 0.08 **(e)** 0.13
(f) 0.03 **(g)** 0.66 **(h)** 0.012

32 **(a)** $\frac{4}{5}$ **(b)** $\frac{1}{5}$ **(c)** $\frac{1}{4}$ **(d)** $\frac{3}{20}$ **(e)** $\frac{1}{8}$ **(f)** $\frac{37}{100}$

33 **(a)** $\frac{1}{2}$ **(b)** 0.4 **(c)** 0.5 **(d)** $\frac{3}{4}$

34 **(a)** 0.05 **(b)** 0.05 **(c)** 0.2 **(d)** 0.025

35 Points in order: 0.06, 0.15, 0.3, 0.43, 0.75, 0.8

36 Points in order: 1.25, 3.5, 4.8, 5.99, 6.4, 9.1

37 **(a)** \$6.50 **(b)** \$6.95 **(c)** \$9.65 **(d)** \$9.97

38 **(a)** 8.0 **(b)** 8.1 **(c)** 1.9 **(d)** 2.54 **(e)** 7.68
(f) 4.9 **(g)** 0.112 **(h)** 1.2 **(i)** 12 **(j)** 12

40 no; 96, yes; 1.12, yes; 0.17

Mixed questions 1

1 B 2 D 3 D 4 B 5 C 6 C 7 C 8 D
9 D 10 B 11 B 12 B 13 A 14 D 15 D 16 C
17 C 18 C 19 A 20 C 21 B 22 C 23 C 24 B
25 D 26 B 27 B 28 B 29 C 30 D 31 C
32 A 33 B 34 C 35 C 36 C 37 C
39 A 40 C

5 Angles

Check in

1 **(a)** R **(b)** **(i)** Q **(ii)** P **(iii)** S

2 **(a)** and **(d)** contain right angles

3 **(a)** 50 **(b)** 20

Exercise 5A

1 **(a)** yes **(b)** no **(c)** no **(d)** yes

2 **(a)** 3 **(b)** 4 **(c)** 4 **(d)** 0 **(e)** 4 **(f)** 6 **(g)** 0
(h) 10

Exercise 5B

1 **(b)** and **(d)**

2 **(a)** CD, DE, $C\hat{D}E$ **(b)** LM, MN, $L\hat{M}N$ **(c)** XZ, ZY, $X\hat{Z}Y$
(d) RQ, QP, $R\hat{Q}P$ **(e)** GH, HF, $G\hat{H}F$ **(f)** RS, ST, $R\hat{S}T$
(g) BD, DC, $B\hat{D}C$ **(h)** LM, MK, $L\hat{M}K$
(i) MN, NO, $M\hat{N}O$ **(j)** UV, VW, $U\hat{V}W$

Exercise 5C

1 **(a)** **(ii)** is larger **(b)** **(i)** is larger **(c)** **(ii)** is larger
(d) **(ii)** is larger

Exercise 5D

3 **(a)** 4 **(b)** 1 **(c)** 5 **(d)** 6

6 **(a)** **(i)** AD, AB; CB, AB; DC, CB; DC, AB **(ii)** none
(iii) IN, NM; NM, ML; ML, LK; LK, KJ; IJ, JK; IJ, IN
(b) **(i)** AD, BC; AB, DC **(ii)** HG, EF
(iii) NM, LK, IJ; NI, ML, KJ

7 **(a)** (vi), (ix) **(b)** (viii), (x) **(c)** (i), (ii), (xi) **(d)** (iii), (iv)
(e) (v), (vii), (xii)

8 **(b)** right angles and straight angles

Exercise 5E

1 **(a)** about half of a right angle **(b)** about two thirds of a right angle **(c)** about $1\frac{1}{3}$ right angles **(d)** about $2\frac{1}{2}$ right angles **(e)** about $1\frac{1}{3}$ right angles **(f)** about $3\frac{2}{3}$ right angles

Exercise 5F

1 **(a)** 90° **(b)** 180° **(c)** 270° **(d)** 45° **(e)** 30°

3 **(a)** 90°, right angle **(b)** 135°, obtuse **(c)** 45°, acute **(d)** 315°, reflex **(e)** 180°, straight angle **(f)** 270°, reflex **(g)** 135°, obtuse **(h)** 225°, reflex **(i)** 315°, reflex

Exercise 5G

1 **(a)** **(i)** 70° **(ii)** 45° **(iii)** 85° **(iv)** 120°

2 **(i)** 134° **(ii)** 72° **(iii)** 138° **(iv)** 168°

Exercise 5H

1 **(b)** If you put the protractor at X, use the anticlockwise scale. If you put the protractor at Y, use the clockwise scale

2 **(a)** acute **(b)** acute **(c)** acute **(d)** right angle **(e)** obtuse **(f)** acute

3 **(a)** obtuse **(b)** acute **(c)** acute **(d)** obtuse **(e)** obtuse **(f)** obtuse

Exercise 5I

1 **(a)** 55° **(b)** 35° **(c)** 90° **(d)** 90° **(e)** complementary

2 **(a)** 74° **(b)** 106° **(c)** 180° **(d)** supplementary

3 **(a)** **(i)** 115°, 65°, 180°, supplementary **(ii)** 100°, 80°, 180°, supplementary

Exercise 5J

1 **(a)** 57° **(b)** 67° **(c)** 22° **(d)** 57°

2 **(a)** 47° **(b)** 77° **(c)** 48° **(d)** 43°

3 **(a)** 32° **(b)** 63°

Exercise 5K

1 $\hat{A} = 45°$, $\hat{B} = 60°$, $\hat{C} = 75°$, $\hat{A} + \hat{B} + \hat{C} = 180°$

3 **(d)** 180°

4 $\hat{A} = 56°$, $\hat{B} = 85°$, $\hat{C} = 100°$, $\hat{D} = 119°$, $\hat{A} + \hat{B} + \hat{C} + \hat{D} = 360°$

6 **(d)** 360°

Exercise 5L – mixed questions

2 **(a)** 35° **(b)** 80° **(c)** 132°

4 **(a)** 69° **(b)** 135° **(c)** 62° **(d)** 65°

5 **(a)** 150°, 130°, 20° **(b)** 60°, 35°

Consolidation exercise 5

1 **(b)** **(i)** 35° **(ii)** 128° **(iii)** 108° **2** students' drawings

3 **(a)** 32° **(b)** 76° **(c)** 47° **(d)** 96° **(e)** 82°

4 **(a)** 55° **(b)** 119° **(c)** 91°

5 **(a)** students' drawings **(b)** 23° **6** 30°

Check out

1 **(a)** $Q\hat{P}Z$ or $Z\hat{P}Q$ **(b)** $S\hat{T}U$

2 **(a)** obtuse **(b)** reflex **(c)** straight angle **(d)** right angle

4 **(a)** 54° **(b)** 125°

5 **(a)** 30° **(b)** 20° **(c)** 140° **(d)** 20°

6 **(a)** 50° **(b)** 30° **(c)** 130°

6 Solids

Check in

1 **(a)** **(i)** cylinder **(ii)** cone **(iii)** cuboid **(b)** **(i)** sphere **(ii)** cylinder **(iii)** cuboid

2 **(a)** 8 **(b)** 6 **(c)** 12

3 **(a)** **(ii)**, **(iv)** **(b)** **(iii)**

4 **(a)**, **(b)** and **(c)**

Exercise 6A

1 **(b)** rectangle

3 6

Exercise 6B

1 **(a)** 8 **(b)** 8 **(c)** 8

2 **(a)** 8 **(b)** 8

3 **(a)** 12 **(b)** 12

4 3 pairs

7 **(b)**, **(c)** and **(e)**

8 **(a)** no **(b)** yes

9 All cubes are cuboids, but not all cuboids are cubes.

Exercise 6D

2 **(a)** 2 **(b)** 1 **(c)** yes

3 A cylinder has three faces.

4 none

5 **(a)** 2 **(b)** curved **(c)** circular

6 circular

10 **(a)** and **(b)** are cylinders

Exercise 6E

1 cuboids are 1, 2, 5, 6; triangular prisms are 4, 7

2 **(a)** yes **(b)** yes **(c)** no

3 **(a)** yes **(b)** no

4 (a)

Shape	Number of vertices	Number of faces	Number of edges
1. Cuboid	8	6	12
2. Cuboid	8	6	12
3. Pentagonal prism	10	7	15
4. Triangular prism	6	5	9
5. Cuboid	8	6	12
6. Cuboid	8	6	12
7. Triangular prism	6	5	9
8. Heptagonal prism	14	9	21
9. Hexagonal prism	12	8	18

(b) number of vertices + number of faces = number of edges + 2

Exercise 6F

1 1

2 circular

3 (a) 1 (b) 1 (c) 1

5 (a) Both can stand upright on a circular base.
(b) They do not both have an opposite pair of faces.

Exercise 6G

1 (a) B, F, G (b) A, C, D, E

2 (b) (i) no (ii) no

3 (a) A, B (b) A, B, C, D, E (c) E, F, G (d) E
(e) B, E, F, G (f) C

4 (a)

Shape	Number of vertices	Number of faces	Number of edges
A	12	8	18
B	7	7	12
C	8	6	12
D	8	6	12
E	6	6	9
F	4	4	6
G	5	5	8

(b) number of vertices + number of faces = number of edges + 2

Exercise 6H

1 (a) circular (b) yes

3 (a) 0 (b) 1 (c) 0 (d) 0

Exercise 6I

1 (a) cube, cuboid, cylinder, triangular prism, cone, square-based pyramid (b) cylinder, cone, sphere
(c) cylinder, cone (d) cube, cuboid, cylinder, triangular prism

2 (a) cylinder (b) sphere (c) cylinder (d) cylinder
(e) cuboid (f) cylinder (g) truncated cone
(h) sphere (i) cylinder (j) sphere

3 (a) cone (b) sphere (c) cone (d) cylinder
(e) cylinder (f) cylinder (g) cone (h) cylinder

4 (a) cone (b) cube (c) sphere (d) triangular-based prism
(e) cylinder

Exercise 6J

2 (a) square-based prism (b) triangular-based prism

Investigation page 116

(a) (i) it only has 4 faces (ii) and (iii) the faces would overlap
(b) (i) and (iii) are nets of cubes

Investigation page 116

(a) There are eight different shapes that can be made using four cubes.

Activity page 117

(a) 2 (b) 1 (c) You should get a longer strip, with four twists, joined in the middle.

(d) You should get two inter-linked bands each with two twists.

Consolidation exercise 6

1 (a) sphere (b) square-based pyramid (c) pentagonal prism

2 (a)
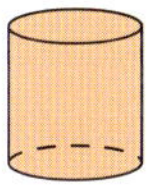
(b)
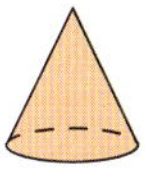
(c)
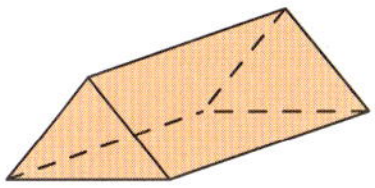
(d)
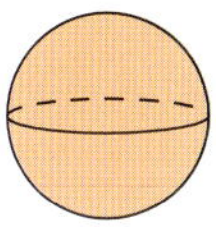
(e)
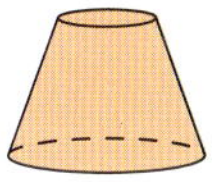
(f)
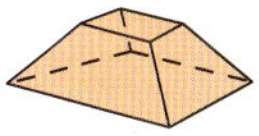

4 (a) 6 rectangular faces, 8 vertices, 12 edges
(b) 2 square faces, 4 rectangular faces, 8 vertices, 12 edges
(c) 2 circular faces, 1 curved face, 0 vertices, 2 edges
(d) 2 triangular faces, 3 rectangular faces, 6 vertices, 9 edges
(e) 4 triangular faces, 1 square face, 5 vertices, 8 edges
(f) 1 hexagonal face, 6 triangular faces, 7 vertices, 12 edges

7 (b) 3

Check out

1 (c) Both have six faces, eight vertices and 12 edges.
(d) All the faces of a cube must be square.

2 (b) (i) and (ii)

3 (a) (i) and (iii) (b) (i) triangular-based pyramid (ii) pentagonal-based pyramid

4 one face, no edges and no corners

5 (c) and (d)

7 Measuring

Check in

1 (a) 60 (b) 60 (c) 7 (d) 24 (e) 12

2 (a) morning (b) evening (c) afternoon (d) morning

3 (a) 37 (b) 430 (c) 18 000 (d) 0.233 (e) 14.24 (f) 1.424

Exercise 7A

1 (a) a stride (b) a palm, hand or span (c) a stride or foot (d) a stride (e) a palm, hand or span (f) an arm (g) a palm, hand or span

2 Deo, because his stretch is longer.

3 Slim, because his strides are longer.

4 Yes, because the units vary from one person to another.

5 millimetre, centimetre, metre, kilometre

Exercise 7C

2 (a) 5 cm 4 mm or 5.4 cm (b) 6 cm 3 mm or 6.3 cm (c) 1 cm 3 mm or 1.3 cm

4 (a) 5.3 cm (b) 2.3 cm (c) 6.1 cm (d) 0.8 cm (e) 1.3 cm

Exercise 7E

1 (a) 30 mm (b) 160 mm (c) 32 mm (d) 57 mm

2 (a) 4 cm (b) 12 cm (c) 5.8 cm (d) 9.2 cm

3 (a) 1000 m (b) 5000 m (c) 3600 m (d) 4120 m

4 (a) 3 km (b) 12 km (c) 0.5 km (d) 1.68 km

5

Student	Height m and cm	Height m	Height cm
James	1 m 42 cm	1.42 m	142 cm
Anthony	1 m 56 cm	1.56 m	156 cm
Garth	1 m 45 cm	1.45 m	145 cm
Albert	1 m 25 cm	1.25 m	125 cm
Andy	1 m 70 cm	1.70 m	170 cm

6 1 m 54 cm

7 (a) 149 km (b) 149 000 m

8 (a) 2000 m (b) 32 cm 7 mm (c) 3 km

9 (a) 77.5 cm (b) 4.197 m (c) 1624 m (d) 846 m (e) (i) 1756.5 m (ii) 1.7565 m

10 60.5 cm

Exercise 7F

1 (a) 20 cm (b) 20 cm (c) 29 cm (d) 22 cm

2 (a) 12 cm (b) 10 cm (c) 5.5 cm (d) 9 cm

3 (a) 28 cm (b) 24 cm (c) 20 cm (d) 22 cm

4 (c) Perimeter of rectangle = 2 × (length + width)

5 (a) 20 cm (b) 22 cm (c) 30 cm (d) 21 cm (e) 34.6 m

6 30 m 7 $3027.50

Exercise 7H

1 Mrs Armstrong, because her bowl is bigger.

2 Yes, people's hands are different sizes.

3 No

Exercise 7K

2 1 kg = 1000 g, 1 t = 1000 kg, 1 g = 0.001 kg, 1 kg = 0.001 t

3 (a) (i) 1578 g (ii) 1.578 kg (b) (i) 1941 g (ii) 1.941 kg (c) (i) 2 731 432 g (ii) 2731.432 kg

4 (a) 585.3 g (b) 3.736 kg (c) 1.23849 kg

5 52 kg

6 (i) 2.24 kg (ii) 2240 g

7 (i) 1.325 t (ii) 1325 kg

8 (a) 4065 g (b) (i) 1016.25 g (ii) 1.01625 kg

Exercise 7L

5 (a) 3600 (b) 1440 (c) 168

Exercise 7M

1 (a) 7:00 (b) 5:15 (c) 11:10 (d) 8:35 (e) 2:48 (f) 6:59

3 (a) 7:15 (b) 30 minutes (c) 45 minutes

Exercise 7N

1 (a) 04:00 (b) 08:30 (c) 11:00 (d) 13:00 (e) 15:30 (f) 20:45 (g) 21:25 (h) 19:53 (i) 01:52

2 (a) 3 am (b) 5 am (c) 12 noon (d) 3 pm (e) 7 pm (f) 11 pm (g) 1.05 am (h) 4.25 am (i) 9.55 pm

Exercise 7O

1 (a) 1 h 15 min (b) 1 h 50 min (c) 4 h 20 min (d) 13 h 13 min (e) 2 h 45 min (f) 2 h 45 min (g) 12 h 35 min (h) 4 h 30 min

2 3 h 40 min

4 (a) 06:40 (b) 17:55 (c) 25 min (d) 1 h 45 min

5 2 h 20 min 6 (b) 4 h 10 min; 5 h 10 min; 5 h 10 min

7 (a) 13:00 (b) 03:50 8 12:00

Exercise 7Q – mixed questions

1 (a) 8 mm (b) 2.1 cm (c) 3 cm (d) 4.4 cm (e) 5.6 cm (f) 1.4 cm (g) 2.6 cm (h) 3.5 cm

2 (a) 1.3 cm (b) 9 mm (c) 3.6 cm (d) 2.3 cm

3 **(a)** 4 mm **(b)** 1.3 cm

4 **(a)** AC = BD = 2 cm **(b)** AC = BD = 2.9 cm

5 **(a)** EF **(c)** AB ≃ 1.8 cm, CD ≃ 2.0 cm, EF ≃ 2.5 cm

7 **(a)** 4.7 kg **(b)** 4700 g

8 **(a)** 11.55 am **(b)** 12.05 pm

9 (a) Babados–Antigua flight **(b)** 12 h 10 min

Consolidation Exercise 7

1 **(a)** cm **(b)** cm **(c)** m **(d)** mm **(e)** m **(f)** km

2 **(a)** 2.3 cm **(b)** 40 mm **(c)** 3000 m **(d)** 76 mm
(e) 0.35 km **(f)** 600 m

3 **(a)** 2.3 cm **(b)** 40 mm **(c)** 3000 m **(d)** 2000 g
(e) 3100 g **(f)** 0.8 kg **(g)** 360 min **(h)** 70 min **(i)** 672 h

4 **(a)** 34 cm **(b)** 27 cm **(c)** 36 cm

5 **(a)** 1511 cm **(e)** 2.46 m

6 **(a)** **(i)** 4.2 cm **(ii)** 6 cm **(b)** $6\frac{1}{3}$ years old

7 **(a)**

(b) 3 hours 20 mins

(c) the 7.30 am flight

Check out

1 **(a)** metre **(b)** centimetre **(c)** kilometre

2 **(a)** 300 cm **(b)** 0.27 km

3 **(a)** kilogram **(b)** gram **(c)** tonne

4 **(a)** 2 057 321 g **(b)** **(i)** 1072 g **(ii)** 1.072 kg

5 **(a)** 8:20 **(b)** 240 hours **(c)** 19:46

8 Shapes

Check in

1 **(a)** and **(c)**

2 75°

3 **(a)** **(i)** 3.1 cm **(ii)** 1.3 cm

Exercise 8A

1 **(a)** They are all equilateral triangles.
(b) All the angles are 60°.

2 The sides are all the same length and the angles are all equal.

3 **(c)** AD and AC are the same length. Triangle ACD is isosceles.
(d) Angles ACB and ADB are equal.

4 **(a)** The triangles are all isosceles.
(b) Two angles are equal in each triangle.

5 Two sides and two angles are equal.

6 **(a)** They are scalene triangles.
(b) In each triangle, none of the angles are equal.

7 All three sides are different lengths and all three angles are different sizes.

8 **(a)** one angle is 90° **(c)** yes

10 **(a)** B **(b)** C, E **(c)** A, D

11 Set A: right-angled triangles. Set B: isosceles triangles.

12 Set P: right-angled triangles. Set Q: scalene triangles.

Exercise 8B

1 Set A: obtuse-angled triangles. Set B: isosceles triangles.

2 Every angle is an acute angle.

3 Set P: scalene triangles. Set Q: acute-angled triangles.

4 **(a)** No right-angled triangles are obtuse-angled triangles.
(b) Some isosceles triangles are right-angled triangles.
(c) All equilateral triangles are isosceles triangles.
(d) No right-angled triangles are equilateral triangles.
(e) Some acute-angled triangles are equilateral triangles

Exercise 8C

3 A, D, G, L **4** C, I, K **5** A, B, D, E, G, J, L **6** A, D, G, L

7 D, E, G **8** All have two pairs of parallel sides.

9 Both have one pair of parallel sides.

10 Both have two pairs of adjacent sides equal in length.

Exercise 8D

5 **(a)** All rectangles are not squares, but all squares are rectangles.
(b)

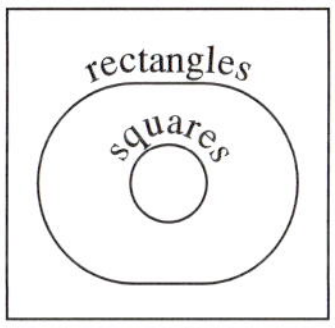

Exercise 8E

1 parallelograms **4** **(b)** all are 35°

5 **(b)** rhombus

8 **(b)** **(i)** AO = CO **(ii)** BO = DO **(c)** AÔB = DÔC = 90°

10

Properties	Parallelogram	Rhombus
Opposite sides parallel	✓	✓
Opposite sides equal	✓	✓
All sides equal	✗	✓
Opposite angles equal	✓	✓
Diagonals equal	✗	✗
Diagonals bisect each other	✓	✓
Diagonals meet at 90°	✗	✓

11 (a)

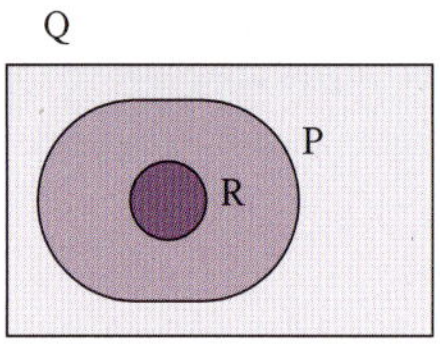

(b) R

Exercise 8F

2 (c) no **(d)** yes

5 (a)

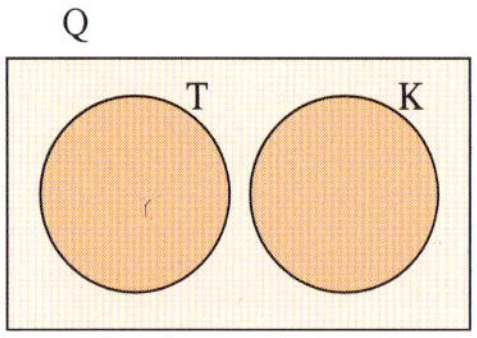

(b) { }

Exercise 8G

1 (c) You have drawn an isosceles triangle.

3 (a) The unmarked angles are: 60°, 45°, 130°, 74°
(b) equilateral, isosceles, scalene, isosceles

Exercise 8I

4 (a) equilateral **(b)** 60°

5 One triangle has 2 sides of length 4 cm, the other has two sides of length 7 cm.

6 The total length of the 5 cm and 4 cm sides would be less than the length of the third side, so they would never meet.

7 6

8 (a) equilateral
(b) Two sides are radii and so are the same length, making the triangle at least isosceles. This means the angles at the circle edge must be equal. As there are 6 triangles, the angle at the circle centre is 60°, which means the other two angles must also be 60°. Hence the triangle is equilateral.

11 120°

12 (b) 6

14 (a) isosceles **(b)** right-angled **(c)** right-angled

Exercise 8J

4 2 fold lines, 2 lines of symmetry

6 (a) 3 lines of symmetry
(b) 4 lines of symmetry
(c) 2 lines of symmetry

7 There are no lines of symmetry.

8

Shape	Number of lines of symmetry
Kite	1
Trapezium	0
Rhombus	2
Square	4
Parallelogram	0

9 (a) 2 **(b)** 2 **(c)** 4 **(d)** 3 **(e)** 1 **(f)** 2 **(g)** 6 **(h)** 5 **(i)** 4 **(j)** 2 **(k)** 2 **(l)** 4

10 (b) A, B, C, D, E, K, M, T, V, W **(c)** H, I, X

Exercise 8K

1 (a) THIS IS MIRROR LANGUAGE.
(b) This is easier than French!

6 Each blob is the mirror image of the other.

7 yes **8 (c)** yes **(d)** yes

Exercise 8L

1 (a), (d) **2 (a), (b), (c)** **3 (a)** yes **(b)** no

4 (a) B and D **(b)** A

Exercise 8M

4 There are gaps between the circles.

5 (b) (i), (ii) and **(iv)** tessellate

7 (a) $a = e = 60°$, $b = 90°$, $c = d = 30°$
(b) $a = d = e = 70°$, $b = c = 110°$
(c) $a = c = d = e = 70°$, $b = 40°$
(d) $a = 120°$, $b = 130°$, $c = 50°$, $d = e = 60°$

8 (a) yes **(b)** 360° **(c)** 60°

9 (a) all angles 90° **(b)** all angles 120°

Exercise 8N

1 10

2 (a) 3 **(b)** 6 **(c)** 10

3 (a) 5 **(b)** 13

Exercise 8P

1 (a), (b), (d) and **(e)**

2 (a) yes **(b)** no

Consolidation Exercise 8

1 (a) isosceles triangle **(b)** parallelogram **(c)** kite
(d) scalene triangle **(e)** rectangle

2 (a)

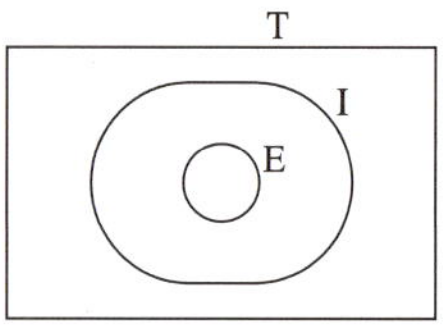

(b)

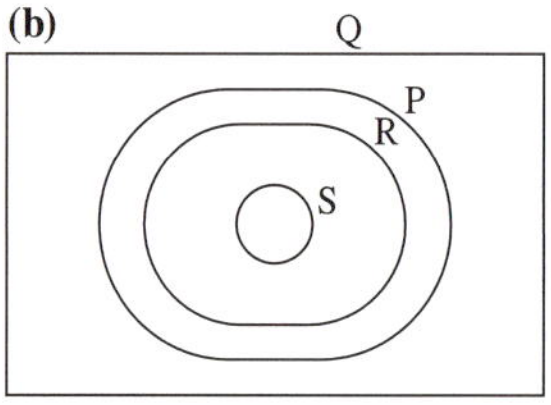

4 (b) (i) 6 **(ii)** 4 **(iii)** 1

6 (a) and **(b)** **7 (b)** 5 cm

Check out

1 (a) C **(b)** A and D **(c)** B, E and F

3 (b) rhombus

Revision exercise 2

1 **(a)** $a = 19°$ **(b)** $b = 102°$ **(c)** $c = 38°, d = 74°, e = 95°$
(d) $f = 43°, g = 130°, h = 67°, i = 120°$

3 **(a)** 90° **(b)** 60° **(c)** 240°

4 **(a)** 52° **(b)** 318°

5 **(a)** $c = 90°, d = 145°$ **(b)** $e = 37°, f = 69°$

6 **(a)** $a = 68°$ **(b)** $b = 83°$ **(c)** $c = 39°, d = 105°$
(d) $e = 68°, f = 52°$

7 **(a)** $a = 145°$ **(b)** $b = 121°$ **(c)** $c = 70°, d = 130°$

8 **(c)** The lengths of the sides could be different.

9 720°

10 **(c)** 540° **(d)** yes

11 **(a)** 8 **(b)** 12 **(c)** 6 **(d)** 1

12 64 **(a)** 8 **(b)** 24 **(c)** 24 **(d)** 8

13 **(b)** 1 and 4

14 **(a)** and **(c)**

15 **(a)** 9 **(b)** 5 **(c)** 6

16 octahedron

19 **(a)**, **(c)** or **(d)**

20 **(b)** Equator

21 **(a)** 3 cm 2 mm, 23 mm, 2 cm **(b)** 2 km, 700 m, 20 cm
(c) 4 km, 6 m, 500 cm **(d)** 6000 m, 4 km, 5000 cm

22 32 mm and 3.2 cm; 3 cm and 0.03 m; 0.32 m and 32 cm; 250 m and 0.25km

23 **(a)** m **(b)** cm **(c)** g **(d)** kg **(e)** km

24 **(c)**

25 **(a)** 20 miles **(b)** 200 km **(c)** 85 miles

26 40 000 km, 2500 litres

27 more

28 1.22 t

29 **(a)** 12:00 **(b)** 4:20 **(c)** 2:40 **(d)** 5:55 **(e)** 15:00
(f) 18:45 **(g)** 23:35

30 **(b)** depart 2040 and depart 2255
(c) 10 hours 3 minutes, 8 hours 12 minutes, 7 hours 58 minutes, 9 hours 45 minutes, 10 hours 20 minutes
(d) depart 1430

31 14

32 55

33 **(a)** 72°, 72°, 36° **(b)** 60°, 60°, 60° **(c)** 90°, 37°, 53°

34 **(a)** isosceles **(b)** equilateral **(c)** right-angled

36 **(a)**

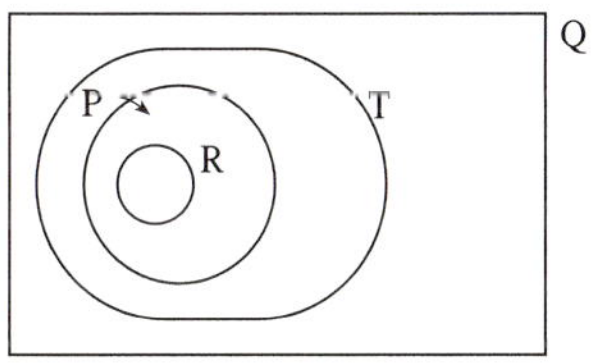

(b) no

37 **(a)** F, G, J, L, N, P, Q, R, S, U, Y, Z
(b) A, B, C, D, E, K, M, T, V, W **(c)** H, I, X **(d)** O

39 All shapes are squares.

40 All shapes are equilateral triangles.

Mixed questions 2

1 D **2** C **3** B **4** C **5** D **6** B **7** C **8** A
9 A **10** B **11** C **12** B **13** D **14** C **15** B
16 D **17** D **18** B **19** C **20** C **21** C **22** B
23 D **24** C **25** A **26** C **27** B **28** C **29** B
30 C **31** D

9 Consumer arithmetic

Check in

1 **(a)** $\frac{3}{5}$ **(b)** $\frac{2}{3}$ **(c)** $\frac{2}{3}$ **(d)** $\frac{3}{4}$ **(e)** $\frac{1}{3}$ **(f)** $\frac{2}{3}$

2 **(a)** 2 **(b)** 4 **(c)** 8 **(d)** 48 **(e)** 56 **(f)** 30

3 **(a)** 0.2 **(b)** 0.7 **(c)** 0.16 **(d)** 0.82 **(e)** 0.6 **(f)** 0.75

Exercise 9A

1 **(a)** $11 **(b)** $40.50 **(c)** $33.50 **(d)** $63

2 **(a)** $89 **(b)** $59.50 **(c)** $66.50 **(d)** $37

3 none of these

4 **(a)** $150 **(b)** $285 **(c)** $345

5 $2.52

6 **(a)** $205 **(b)** $135.05 **(c)** $150.25 **(d)** $72.70

7 **(a)** $420.50 **(b)** $490.50

8 **(a)** $568.75, $155.94, $724.69 **(b)** $587.19

Exercise 9B

1 **(a)** 80¢, 78¢; 4 oranges **(b)** $1.40, $1.35, 12 eggs
(c) $2.90, $2.85; 8 exercise books
(d) $3.50, $3.45; 9 tins of milk

2 9 pens

3 4 kg oranges

4 0.54 kg beef

5 150 g toothpaste

Exercise 9C

1 Table $45 profit, 4 Chairs $48 loss, Bed $75 profit, Fridge $274 profit, Gas stove $323 loss

2

Cost price	Selling price	Profit
$3.00	$5.00	$2.00
$1.50	$3.00	$1.50
$5.00	$6.40	$1.40
$3.00	$3.00	$0
$5.00	$6.20	$1.20

3

Cost price	Selling price	Loss
\$4.00	\$3.00	\$1.00
\$3.50	\$3.25	\$0.25
\$1.00	\$0.25	\$0.75
\$4.70	\$3.50	\$1.20
\$13.50	\$10.00	\$3.50

4 **(a)** profit

Exercise 9D

1 \$700 **2** **(a)** \$65 **(b)** \$7.50 **(c)** 187.50

3 **(a)** \$52 **(b)** \$6 **(c)** \$58

4 **(a)** \$4.25 **(b)** \$30.70 **5** \$410.40 profit

6 **(a)** \$630 **(b)** \$292 **(c)** \$642 **(d)** \$12 profit

Exercise 9E

1 **(a)** 5% **(b)** 14% **(c)** 8% **(d)** 20% **(e)** 11% **(f)** 25%

2 **(a)** 15% **(b)** 25% **(c)** 13% **(d)** 72% **(e)** 32% **(f)** 99%

3 **(a)** 67% **(b)** Jan's sister

4

Fraction bad	Percentage bad
$\frac{12}{100}$	12
$\frac{8}{100}$	8
$\frac{9}{100}$	9
$\frac{7}{100}$	7
$\frac{5}{100}$	5
$\frac{5}{100}$	5
$\frac{6}{100}$	6
$\frac{5}{100}$	5
$\frac{7}{100}$	7
$\frac{7}{100}$	7
$\frac{9}{100}$	9
$\frac{11}{100}$	11

Exercise 9F

1 **(a)** 35% **(b)** 44% **(c)** 40% **(d)** 36%

3 **(a)** 5% is the same as $\frac{5}{100}$ **(b)** 20% is the same as $\frac{20}{100}$ **(c)** 25% is the same as $\frac{25}{100}$ **(d)** 39% is the same as $\frac{39}{100}$ **(e)** 81% is the same as $\frac{81}{100}$

4 **(a)** $\frac{34}{100}$ **(b)** $\frac{11}{100}$ **(c)** $\frac{19}{100}$ **(d)** $\frac{20}{100}$ **(e)** $\frac{28}{100}$ **(f)** $\frac{31}{100}$ **(g)** $\frac{9}{100}$ **(h)** $\frac{43}{100}$

5 **(a)** 15% **(b)** 25% **(c)** 17% **(d)** 33% **(e)** 19% **(f)** 29% **(g)** 76% **(h)** 97%

Exercise 9G

1 **(a)** $\frac{1}{4} = \frac{25}{100} = 25\%$ **(b)** $\frac{1}{2} = \frac{50}{100} = 50\%$ **(c)** $\frac{3}{4} = \frac{75}{100} = 75\%$ **(d)** $\frac{7}{10} = \frac{70}{100} = 70\%$ **(e)** $\frac{7}{20} = \frac{35}{100} = 35\%$

2 **(a)** 60% **(b)** 80% **(c)** 55% **(d)** 60% **(e)** 6%

3 **(a)** 40% **(b)** 20% **(c)** 70% **(d)** 80% **(e)** 40% **(f)** 25% **(g)** 80% **(h)** 75%

4 **(a)** $\frac{6}{10}$ **(b)** 60% **5** **(a)** $\frac{13}{20}$ **(b)** 65%

6 **(a)** 70% **(b)** She scored the same percentage in both.

7 **(a)** $\frac{2}{5}$ **(b)** 40% **8** 15%

9 Earl and Eric **10** **(a)** 60% **(b)** 25% **(c)** 15%

11 50%, 75%, 58%, 55%, 62.5%; Form 2

12 **(a)** 52% **(b)** 70% **(c)** 48% **(d)** 30% **(e)** 60%

Exercise 9H

1

Decimal	Per cent fraction	%
0.5	$\frac{50}{100}$	50%
0.68	$\frac{68}{100}$	68%
0.9	$\frac{90}{100}$	90%
0.75	$\frac{75}{100}$	75%
0.25	$\frac{25}{100}$	25%
0.03	$\frac{3}{100}$	3%

2 Multiply by 100%

3 **(a)** 80% **(b)** 41% **(c)** 97% **(d)** 6% **(e)** 1%

4 **(a)** 10% **(b)** 13.4% **(c)** 2.5% **(d)** 79.6% **(e)** 2.34% **(f)** 81.75%

Exercise 9I

1

%	Per cent fraction	Decimal
32	$\frac{32}{100}$	0.32
5	$\frac{5}{100}$	0.05
12	$\frac{12}{100}$	0.12
8	$\frac{8}{100}$	0.08
10	$\frac{10}{100}$	0.1
16	$\frac{16}{100}$	0.16
39	$\frac{39}{100}$	0.39
64	$\frac{64}{100}$	0.64

2 **(b)** two places to the right

3 **(a)** 0.19 **(b)** 0.29 **(c)** 0.66 **(d)** 0.03 **(e)** 0.02 **(f)** 0.79 **(g)** 0.01

4

Fraction	Decimal	%
$\frac{2}{5}$	0.4	40%
$\frac{4}{5}$	0.8	80%
$\frac{7}{10}$	0.7	70%
$\frac{3}{4}$	0.75	75%
$\frac{13}{20}$	0.65	65%
$\frac{17}{20}$	0.85	85%
$\frac{6}{25}$	0.24	24%
$\frac{3}{50}$	0.06	6%
$\frac{1}{25}$	0.04	4%

5

Fraction	Decimal	Percentage
$\frac{1}{8}$	0.125	12.5
$\frac{3}{8}$	0.375	37.5
$\frac{5}{8}$	0.625	62.5
$\frac{3}{16}$	0.1875	18.75
$\frac{7}{16}$	0.4375	43.75
$\frac{2}{3}$	0.6666 ...	66.67
$\frac{3}{7}$	0.4285 ...	42.86

6 (b) 90%, 85%, $\frac{36}{40}$ **(c)** 0.9, 0.85

Exercise 9J

1 (a) 15 soldiers **(b)** 9 sailors **(c)** $7 **(d)** 28 eggs **(e)** 60 tigers **(f)** 36 mangoes **(g)** 24 flying fish **(h)** 35 flamingos

2 (a) 25 **(b)** 32 **(c)** 16 **(d)** 48 **(e)** 64 **(f)** 40 **(g)** 20 **(h)** 24 **3** 5

4 30 cricket, 18 football, 12 basketball

5 (a) (i) $21 **(ii)** $231.50 **(b) (i)** $399 **(ii)** $2083.50

6 16 no licences, 24 defective lights, 4 did not observe stop sign

7 20 gallons

Exercise 9K

1

Item	Cost price	Selling price	Profit	Percentage profit
Shoe	$80	$100	$20	25%
Table	$600	$750	$150	25%
Stove	$750	$1000	$250	33%
Glass	$5	$6	$1	20%
Mat	$3	$6	$3	100%
Dish	$7.50	$10	$2.50	$33\frac{1}{3}$%

2 (a) 10% **(b)** 20% **(c)** 25%

3 (a) 12.5% **(b)** 25%

4 (a) $30 000 **(b)** $\frac{3}{4}$ **(c)** 75%

5 (a) 20% **(b)** 40% **(c)** 14%

6 (a) 20% **(b)** 16.7%

Exercise 9L

1

Item	Cost price	Profit as % of cost price	Selling price
Iron	$70	25%	$87.50
Chair	$240	15%	$276
Mug	$3.60	10%	$3.96
Vase	$48	8%	$51.84
Radio	$220	9%	$239.80

2 $348 **3** $1250 **4 (a)** $55 **(b)** $57.50

5 (a) $43.20 **(b)** $70.20 **(c)** $10.26

6 $21 000 **7 (a)** 10 cents **(b)** 2 cents **(c)** 8 cents

8 (a) $60 **(b)** $63.75 **9 (a)** $40 000 **(b)** $32 000

10 (a) $16 384 **(b)** $29 524.50 **11 (a)** $294 **(b)** $314.93

Exercise 9M

1 (a) $100.40 **(b)** $68 **(c)** $73.20 **(d)** $154 **(e)** $56

2 (a) $87.85 **(b)** $59.50 **(c)** $64.05

3 (a) take off 10% **(b)** yes **(c)** $48.60

4 (a) $62.55 **(b)** $34.02 **(c)** $39.41 **(d)** $78.30 **(e)** $88.74 **(f)** $119.97

5 (a) $60.45 **(b)** $59.15

6 (a) Lady's blouse $2766, Slacks $1237.50, Total $9133.50 **(b)** 4th February 2000 **(c)** $8220.15

7 (a) Total $245, Less 5% $12.25, Amount due $232.75 **(b)** 12% discount $18, Amount now due $132

8 (a) Total $1206 **(b)** Amount due $1085.40 **(c)** $1117.96

Exercise 9N

5

Item	Usual price	Sale price
Shirtjac	$46.50	$36.27
Vest	$19.00	$14.82
Trousers	$54.00	$42.12
Pair of socks	$12.50	$9.75
Belt	$14.50	$11.31

Exercise 9O

1 (a) 30% **(b)** 25% **(c)** 25% **(d)** 12.5% **(e)** 10%

2 12 CDS **3** 600 ml container **4** $66

Exercise 9P

1 **(a)** $20 **(b)** $40 **(c)** $14

2 **(a)** $220 **(b)** $240 **(c)** $214

3 **(a)** $15 **(b)** $75 **(c)** $750 **4** $2800

5 **(a)** $800 **(b)** $1600 **(c)** $4000

6 **(a)** $120 **(b)** $300 **(c)** $300 **(d)** $720
(e) $1215 **7** 10 years

Exercise 9Q

1 **(a)** $6 **(b)** $8 **(c)** $10

2 **(a)** $52 **(b)** $208 **(c)** $260 **(d)** $520
(e) $10 400 **(f)** $52 000

3 **(a)** $20 **(b)** $40 **(c)** $100 **4** $6960

6 **(a)** $25 **(b)** 5%

Exercise 9R

1 **(c)** No, because the marks are not out of the same total

2

English	90%	86%	70%
Spanish	95%	89%	83%
Integrated Science	68%	72%	94%
History	72%	80%	84%

3 **(a)** yes **(b)** Spanish, 95% **(c)** Spanish, first term, 95%

5 **(a)** discount **(b)** $2 **(c)** $2 **(d)** $18

6

Marked price	10% of marked price	Sale price
$50	$5	$45
$80	$8	$72
$20	$2	$18
$250	$25	$225
$180	$18	$162
$30	$3	$27
$10	$1	$9

7 **(a)** $3 **(b)** $63 per week

8 **(a)** **(i)** $963 **(ii)** $2675 **(iii)** $8560
(b) The permanent secretary

9 **(a)** 540 g **(b)** $5.76

10 **(a)** $2060 **(b)** From $2000 to $2100

11 **(a)** $138 **(b)** $517.50

12 **(a)** $45 000 **(b)** $40 500 **(c)** $36 450

Consolidation exercise 9

1 **(a)** 60 apples **(b)** 1 kg soap powder

2

Percentage	Fraction	Decimal
38%	$\frac{19}{50}$	0.38
80%	$\frac{4}{5}$	0.8
2%	$\frac{1}{50}$	0.02

3 **(a)** $5 **(b)** $2 **(c)** $4 **(d)** $3 **(e)** $12
(f) $0.50 **(g)** $1.80 **(h)** $2

4

Item	Cost price	% Profit	Sale price
Iron	$190	5	$199.50
TV	$1350	8	$1458
Camera	$850	5.9	$900
Calculator	$125	28	$160

5 **(a)** $20 600 **(b)** $35 020 **(c)** $42 745

6 **(a)** $80.75 (iron); $103.50 (chair); $340.40 (CD player)
(b) $92.86; $119.03; $391.46

7 **(a)** $5400 **(b)** $17 400 **(c)** $290

Check out

1 **(a)** $25 000 loss **(b)** $60 profit

2 **(a)** 85% **(b)** 10%

3

Fraction	Decimal	Percentage
$\frac{4}{5}$	0.8	80%
$\frac{9}{20}$	0.45	45%
$\frac{5}{8}$	0.625	62.5%

4 **(a)** **(i)** $60 **(ii)** $3 **(b)** **(i)** $19 **(ii)** $76

5

Item	Cost price	Percentage profit	Selling price
Stove	$1500	10	$1650
Computer	$6000	15	$6900
Clock	$75	5	$78.75

6 **(a)** $1187.50 **(b)** $1223.13

10 Representing information

Check in

1 **(a)** 75 **(b)** 5 years **(c)** Dominica

2 **(a)** 3 **(b)** 8 **(c)** 36 **(d)** 32

3 **(b)** isosceles triangle

Exercise 10A

1 (a) continuous (b) discrete (c) discrete (d) continuous (e) discrete (f) continuous

2 (a) 3 (b) 19 (c) 10 (d) 32

3

Height (cm)	Frequency
136	6
138	5
139	4
141	4
142	9
143	2

Investigation page 201

1 The coin should land on heads roughly half the time.

2 The dice should land on each digit roughly 17 times.

Activity page 201

Most students were absent on Friday.

(b)

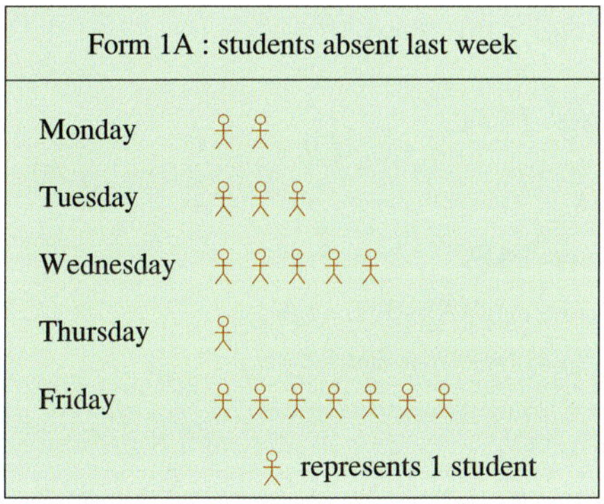

Exercise 10C

1 (a) Each figure represents 5 students. (b) represents 5 students (c) 50 walk, 15 cycle and 30 go by bus every day

2 (a) 7 (b) 26 (c) $\frac{4}{26} = \frac{2}{13}$

3 (a) 10 (b) cooking (c) 32

4 (a) 20 (b) English (c) Geography (d) 70

Activity page 203

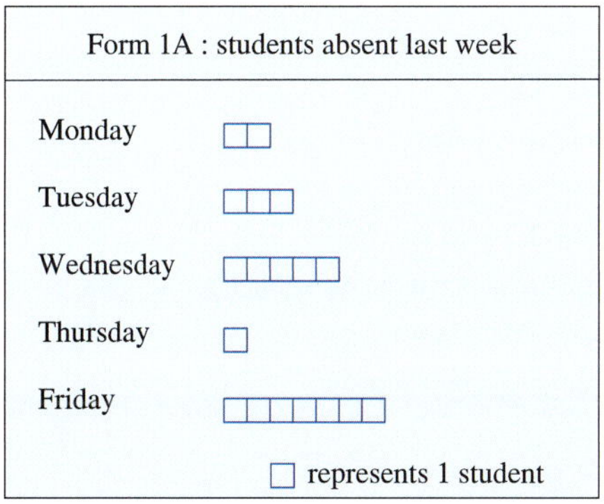

Exercise 10D

1 (a) green, it has the tallest bar (b) purple, it has the shortest bar (c) blue and red (d) 33
(e) green, blue, red, yellow, pink, orange, purple
(f)

Favourite colour	Blue	Pink	Green	Orange	Red	Purple	Yellow
Number of students	6	4	7	3	6	2	5

2 (b) Maths

3 (a) 4 (b) 3 (c) Wednesday
(d) The vertical axis is labelled.

5 (a) Sport Special

Exercise 10E

1 Each square represents 20 mothers

2 (a) 3

3 (c) Football

4 (a) 10 (b) 15 (c) 95 (d) \$9.50

5 (a) 5 million (b) 0.5 million

Exercise 10F

1 (a) 4 (b) \$4
(c)

Where money goes	Sweets	Savings	Books
Money spent \$	\$4	\$4	\$8

2 (a) 8 (b) 3
(c)

Activity	Sleeping	Housework	School	Eating + Washing	Playing
No. of hours	9	3	6	3	3

3 (a) (i) 10 (ii) \$200
(b)

Where money goes	Savings	Rent	Food	Household items	Entertainment
Money spent \$	400	600	400	200	400

Exercise 10G

1 (a) 10 (b) mango (c) plum (d) (i) $\frac{3}{10}$ (ii) $\frac{1}{10}$ (e) 15 (f) (i) 30 (ii) 30 (iii) 30

2 (a) 40 (b) (i) $\frac{1}{8}$ (ii) $\frac{1}{4}$ (iii) $\frac{3}{8}$ (c) 8 (d) 5 (e) 3
(f) 8-sector pie chart with 1 sector each for Monday, Thursday and Friday, 2 sectors for Tuesday and 3 for Wednesday

3 (a) 1200 (b) (i) $\frac{1}{12}$ (ii) $\frac{1}{4}$ (iii) $\frac{1}{3}$ (c) 12 (d) 100
(e) 3 (f) 12-sector pie chart with 1 sector for 1995, 2 for 1996 and 1997, 3 for 1998 and 4 for 1999

5 (b) It is best to use a pictograph when the data can be illustrated with a small number of symbols, otherwise a bar chart is more appropriate. Use a pie chart if you want to show relative amounts rather than actual amounts.

Exercise 10H

1 3 **2 (a)** 42 **(b)** 7 **3** 30 **4** 50

Exercise 10I

1 (a) 11 cm **(b)** 11 cm **2 (a)** 6 **(b)** $6\frac{1}{2}$ **3 (a)** 23.5°C **(b)** 25°C

Exercise 10J

1 (a) 8 **(b)** 6 **(c)** week 5 **(d)** week 6

2 (a) 8 **(b)**

Month	1	2	3	4	5	6	7	8	9	10	11	12
Number of bicycles sold	3	2	5	5	7	8	9	8	7	7	5	6

(c) Each square represents 1 bicycle.

3 (a) 1 square = 5 words per minute

Exercise 10K

2 (a) 1 square = 10 cm **(c)** 55 cm

3 (b) 67.55 km/h

4 (a) The graphs for questions 1 and 3 are straight lines.
(b) In question 1, cost is directly proportional to the number of shirts. Similarly, in question 3 the speed increases steadily with time. In question 2, height does not increase at a steady rate.

5 (c) BC is the steepest part of the graph. Profit doubles between 1997 and 1998.

Exercise 10L

1 no

2 A (2, 6), B (1, 3), C (2, 3), D (2, 1), E (5, 1), F (5, 3), G (6, 3), H (5, 6)

3 (iii) fish

Exercise 10M – mixed questions

1 (a) 50 **(b)** 320 **(c)** $3840

2 (a) 5 **(b)** 9 **(c)** 20

4 (3, 3)

5 (a) (i) 21 **(ii)** 25 **(b) (i)** 9 **(ii)** 14

6 (a) 8-sector pie chart with 3 sectors for water, 1 for fat, 3 for protein and 1 for other substances
(b) 50 g **(c)** 3

7 (a) 7, 5, 3, 1, 2 **(b)** truck **(c)** 18 **(d)** taxi and car

8 (a) $250 **(b) (i)** $500 **(ii)** $250 **(c)** $3000

9 (a) (8, 7) **(b)** (3, 1) **(c)** (5, 9)

Investigation page 215

The bigger the distance around the wrist, the bigger the distance around the neck.

Check out

1 (a) 4 **(b)** 12 **(c)** 15

2 4

3 5

4 (a) (i) 10 **(ii)** 20 **(b)** 55

5 10-sector pie chart with 5 sectors representing bus, 2 representing car, 2 for walk and 1 for cycle

6 (a) mean = 6.8, mode = 6, median = 6
(b) mean = 14.5, mode = 13, median = 13.5

7

Day	M	T	W	Th	F
Temperature (°C)	28	29	30	26	26

8 A (3, 15), B (0, 15), C (2, 5)

11 Area

Check in

2 (a) (i) 600 cm **(ii)** 240 cm
(b) (i) 70 mm **(ii)** 73 mm

Exercise 11A

1 desk top

Exercise 11B

1 The area of rectangle V is 30 triangles.
The area of rectangle W is 28 triangles.
Rectangle V is larger than rectangle W.

2 (a) is larger

3 (a) 60 **(b)** 56 **(c)** V is larger **(d)** yes

Exercise 11C

1 (a) Squares the same size as the one that sticks out on the left. The right number of these squares will fit the shape exactly.
(b) 13 squares

2 (a) (i) triangles **(ii)** triangles **(iii)** triangles **(iv)** squares.

3 (b) It is not possible to fill the shapes entirely with whole squares.

Exercise 11D

1 Approx. 22 centimetre squares

3 (b) The shapes have roughly the same area.

4 No, there are gaps between the circles.

5 Approximately 34 circles, not the including gaps.

6 Yes; No, because of the gaps.

7 No, it just gives a good approximation.

Exercise 11E

1 **(a)** 5 cm^2 **(b)** 16 cm^2 **(c)** 42 cm^2 **(d)** 13 cm^2
(e) 57 cm^2 **(f)** 110 cm^2

2 **(a)** 1 cm^2 **(b)** 14 **(c)** 14 cm^2

3 **(a)** 12 cm^2 **(b)** 10 cm^2 **(c)** 14 cm^2 **(d)** 9 cm^2

5 **(a)** $\frac{1}{2}$ cm^2 **(b)** 1 cm^2 **(c)** $1\frac{1}{2}$ cm^2 **(d)** 2 cm^2

6 **(a)** 3 cm^2 **(b)** $4\frac{1}{2}$ cm^2 **(c)** 4 cm^2 **(d)** 3 cm^2
(e) $4\frac{1}{2}$ cm^2

7 **(a)** and **(d)**, **(b)** and **(e)**

Exercise 11F

1 **(a)** 180 **(b)** 180 mm^2

2 **(a)** 96 mm^2 **(b)** 190 mm^2 **(c)** 95 mm^2 **(d)** 250 mm^2

Exercise 11G

1 1 m^2 **3** **(a)** m^2 **(b)** mm^2 **(c)** mm^2 **(d)** cm^2
(e) m^2 **(f)** cm^2 **(g)** cm^2 **(h)** mm^2 **(i)** cm^2 **(j)** mm^2

Exercise 11H

1 **(a)** 8 cm^2 **(b)** 10 cm^2 **(c)** 5 cm^2 **(d)** 40 cm^2

2 **(a)** 36 cm^2 **(b)** 24 cm^2 **(c)** 22 cm^2 **(d)** 35 cm^2
(e) 2590 mm^2

3

Length (in cm)	Width (in cm)	Area (in cm^2)
9	7	63
6	3	18
6	4	24
9	4	36
11	10	110
12	12	144

4 $A = L \times W$

5 **(a)** both 2.5 cm
(b) The length and width are equal.
(c) square **(d)** 6.25 cm^2

6 **(a)** 9 cm^2 **(b)** 25 cm^2 **(c)** 16 cm^2 **(d)** 100 cm^2

7

Rectangle	Length (cm)	Width (cm)	Area (cm^2)
Picture	25	20	500
Envelope	6	25	150
Book	30	20	600
Poster	50	24	1200

9 6 cm **10** **(a)** 1200 mm^2 **(b)** 12 cm^2

11 105 m long and 85 m wide is larger by 2025 m^2

12 2 m or 200 cm **13** 6000 tiles **14** 540 cm^2

15 **(a)** $16\frac{2}{3}$ m **(b)** 12.5 m **(c)** 10 m

Exercise 11I

1 **(a)** 2 cm^2 **(b)** 4 cm^2 **(c)** 3 cm^2 **(d)** 3 cm^2
(e) $4\frac{1}{2}$ cm^2 **(f)** 3 cm^2 **(g)** 6 cm^2

2 **(i)**

Area of surrounding rectangle (cm^2)	Area of triangle (cm^2)
4	2
8	4
6	3
6	3
9	$4\frac{1}{2}$
6	3
12	6

(ii) The values in the second column are half the values in the first column.
(iii) Area of triangle = $\frac{1}{2}$ × area of surrounding rectangle

3 **(a)** 18 cm^2 **(b)** $\frac{1}{2}$ **(c)** 9 cm^2 **4** **(a)** 6 cm^2 **(b)** $4\frac{1}{2}$ cm^2

5 **(a)** yes **(b)** 6 cm^2 **6** **(a)** 60 cm^2 **(b)** 45 cm^2
(c) 32 cm^2 **(d)** 30 cm^2 **7** **(a)** 24 cm^2 **(b)** 14 cm^2
(c) 20 cm^2 **(d)** 12 cm^2 **8** 13 m^2 **9** 120 cm^2

10 108 cm^2 **11** 4125 m^2

Exercise 11J – mixed questions

2 **(d)** 5 **3** **(a)** 3 × 2 rectangle **(b)** 6 × 1 rectangle

7 8 cm **8** 1600 cm^2 **9** 63 m^2 **10** 6300 cm^2

Consolidation Exercise 11

1 **(a)** 8 squares **(b)** 6 squares **(c)** 11 squares
(d) 4 squares **(e)** 8 squares

3 **(a)** m^2 **(b)** cm^2 **(c)** cm^2 **(d)** mm^2 **(e)** km^2 **(f)** mm^2

4 **(a)** 6 cm^2 **(b)** 4 cm^2 **5** 5 m

6 **(a)** 12 cm **(b)** 18 cm **(c)** 19 cm

8 **(a)** 1204 cm^2 **(b)** 38,528 cm^2

9 **(a)** 3 m^2 **(b)** 30,000 cm^2 **(c)** 225 cm^2 **(d)** 134
(e) $422.10

Check out

1 Y is larger

2 **(a)** 24 triangles **(b)** 9 squares approx.

3 **(a)** mm^2 **(b)** cm^2 **(c)** m^2 **(d)** mm^2

4 **(a)** 5 cm^2 **(b)** 65 mm^2

5 **(a)** 12 cm^2 **(b)** 4000 m^2

6 **(a)** 4 cm^2 **(b)** $1\frac{1}{2}$ cm^2

7 8 cm

12 Symbols and patterns

Check in

1 96 cm^2

2 14 cm

Exercise 12A

2 **(a)** 44 **(b)** 95 **(c)** 230 **(d)** 57

Exercise 12B

2 **(a)** $A = l \times w$

(b)

l	5	7	6	8
w	2	3	10	12
A	10	21	60	96

(c) A, l and w are not constants because they can take different values.

3 **(a)** $P = 3a$

(b)

a	4	5	6
P	12	15	18

Exercise 12C

1 **(a)** $4 \times a$ **(b)** $5 \times m$ **(c)** $6 \times$  **(d)** $7 \times \triangle$
(e) $4 \times p$ **(f)** $4 \times l$ **(g)** $4 \times x + 3 \times y$
(h) $2 \times x + 4 \times y + 2 \times z$

2 **(a)** $2x$ **(b)** $3 \times a + b$ **(c)** $3 \times p - q$ **(d)** $3 \times p - 2 \times q$

Exercise 12D

1 **(a)** $5p$ **(b)** $6x$ **(c)** $3d$ **(d)** $8m$ **(e)** $9g$ **(f)** $12z$
(g) bc **(h)** xy **(i)** mn **(j)** dp **(k)** qs **(l)** az

2 **(a)** $2x$ **(b)** $3a + b$ **(c)** $3p - q$ **(d)** $3p - 2q$

Exercise 12E

1 **(a)** 18 cm^2 **(b)** $10a\text{ cm}^2$ **(c)** $12z\text{ cm}^2$ **(d)** $2xy\text{ cm}^2$
(e) $9mn\text{ cm}^2$ **(f)** $29pq\text{ cm}^2$

2 **(a)** $4a$ cm **(b)** $(2a + 2b)$ cm
(c) $(a + 2b)$ cm **(d)** $(a + 5b)$ cm
(e) $(a + 2b + 12)$ cm **(f)** $(4a + 2b)$

3 **(a)** 20 cm **(b)** 16 cm **(c)** 11 cm **(d)** 20 cm
(e) 23 cm **(f)** 26 cm

Exercise 12F

1 **(a)** 8 **(b)** 6

2 **(a)** 9 **(b)** 1 **(c)** 19

Exercise 12G

1 **(a)** 10 **(b)** 60 **(c)** $10x$

2 **(a)** 60 **(b)** 300 **(c)** $60x$

3 **(a)** 2 **(b)** 14 **(c)** $2x$

4 **(a)** 400 **(b)** 1500 **(c)** $100x$ **(d)** $300x$

5 **(a)** 22 **(b)** 55 **(c)** $11y$ **(d)** $44y$

6 **(a)** 600 **(b)** 1600 **(c)** $100x$ **(d)** $800x$

7 **(a)** 730 **(b)** 3650 **(c)** $365y$ **(d)** $1825y$

8 **(a)** $7x + 4$ **(b)** $7y - 5$ **(c)** $14y$ **(d)** $12x - 3$
(e) $24x + 5$ **(f)** $36x - 11$ **(g)** $100z - 30$
(h) $100z + 40$

9 **(a)** 10 years old; $7 + 3$ **(b)** $(y + 3)$ years old
(c) $(p + 5)$ years old **(d)** $(m + n)$ years old

10 **(a)** \$13; $5 + 8$ **(b)** $\$(10 + d)$

11 **(a)** 30; 5×6 **(b)** $5y$ **(c)** $48z$

12 **(a)** \$2; $10 \div 5$ **(b)** $\$\frac{d}{3}$

13 **(a)** \$8; $14 - 6$ **(b)** \$22; $14 + 8$ **(c)** $\$(x - 10)$
(d) $\$(2x - 10)$

Activity page 244

(b) **(i)** R is the first letter of the word red. **(ii)** G, B, Y
(c) **(i)** 2 **(ii)** 4 **(d)** **(i)** $R = G + 2B$ **(ii)** $R = G + 4Y$

Exercise 12H

1 **(a)** 4 **(b)** $R = 4B$ **(c)** **(i)** $R = 2G$
(ii) $G = 2B$ **(iii)** $R = 8Y$ **(iv)** $G = 4Y$

2 $G = B + 2Y$

3 $R = B + 6Y$, $R = 2B + 4Y$, $R = 3B + 2Y$

4 $g + y = 10$

5 **(a)** 180° **(b)** $x + y = 180°$

6 **(a)** $p + q = 90°$ **(b)** $a + b + c + d = 360°$
(c) $a + b + c = 180°$

7 **(a)** 6 **(b)** yes **(c)** $T = 6A$

8 **(a)** **(i)** 40 **(ii)** 56 **(iii)** 24 **(iv)** 36 **(b)** $n = d \times r$

9 **(a)** 6 **(b)** $T = 2ab + 2ac + 2bc$

10 **(a)**

Number of edges	Number of faces	Number of vertices	Number of faces + vertices
12	6	8	14
9	5	6	11
8	5	5	10
6	4	4	8
12	6	8	14
12	7	7	14
15	7	10	17

(b) 2 **(c)** $E = F + V - 2$

Exercise 12I

1 $a = 3$ 2 $b = 8$ 3 $c = 1$ 4 $d = 4$ 5 $e = 5$
6 $f = 5$ 7 $g = 3$ 8 $h = 4$ 9 $i = 3$

10 $j = 1$ **11** $k = 0$ **12** $l = 2$ **13** $m = 3$
14 $n = 1$ **15** $o = 5$ **16** $p = 6$ **17** $q = 3$
18 $r = 2$ **19** $s = 1$ **20** $t = 8$ **21** $u = 5$
22 $v = 6$ **23** $w = 7$ **24** $x = 4$ **25** $y = 4$ **26** $z = 1$

Exercise 12J

1 26 **2** 31 **3** 12
4 **(a)** $2x = 24, x = 2$ **(b)** $x + 14 = 30, x = 16$
(c) $\frac{x}{5} = 20, x = 100$ **(d)** $2x + 3 = 27, x = 12$
5 **(a)** $33° + 35° + x° = 180°$
(b) $x = 112$
6 40
7 8 cm
8 10.5 cm
9 $37.50
10 114

Exercise 12K

1 **(a)** 6 **(b)** 21
(c) The number of dots is one more than the pattern number.
(d) $n + 1$
2 **(a)** 15; 60; $3n$ **(b)** 7; 22; $n + 2$ **(c)** 4; 19; $n - 1$
(d) 11; 41; $2n + 1$

Exercise 12L

1 **(a)** They are the same. **(b)** They are the same again.
(c) yes
2 **(a)** They are the same. **(b)** They are the same again.
(c) Yes, because the multiplication and division, and the addition and subtraction 'cancel'.
3 **(a)** 23
(b)

Number chosen	1	2	3	4	5	6	7	8	9	10
Answer	7	11	15	19	23	27	31	35	39	43

(c) Answer = 4 × Number chosen + 3: **(i)** 47
(ii) 51 **(iii)** 63 **(iv)** 83
4 Add 3
5 **(a)**

Number chosen	1	2	3	4	5	6	7	8	9	10
Answer	7	10	13	16	19	22	25	28	31	34

(b) Answer = 3 × Number chosen + 4: **(i)** 37
(ii) 40 **(iii)** 49 **(iv)** 64
6 **(a)**

Input	1	2	3	4	5	6	7	8	9	10
Output	9	13	17	21	25	29	33	37	41	45

(b) 4 **(c)** multiply by 4 **(d)** $4n + 5$
7 **(a)**

1	2	3
$(1 \times 4) + 3$	$(2 \times 4) + 3$	$(3 \times 4) + 3$

(b) Multiply by 4; add 3 **(c)** $4n + 3$
8 **(a)**

1	2	3
$(1 \times 3) + 4$	$(2 \times 3) + 4$	$(3 \times 3) + 4$

(b) Multiply by 3; add 4 **(c)** $3n + 4$
9 **(a)**

1	2	3
$(1 \times 7) + 1$	$(2 \times 7) + 1$	$(3 \times 7) + 1$

(b)

Input	1	2	3	4	5	6
Answer	8	15	22	29	36	43

(c) $7(n + 1) + 1$ or $7n + 8$
10 **(b)** 3 is added each time.

Exercise 12M

1 **(a)** **(i)** 36, 42, 48 **(ii)** 12, 14, 16 **(iii)** 11, 13, 15
(iv) 19, 22, 25 **(v)** 21, 24, 27 **(vi)** 35, 41, 47
(b) **(i)** multiply input by 6
(ii) multiply input by 2
(iii) multiply input by 2 and subtract 1
(iv) multiply input by 3 and add 1
(v) multiply input by 3 and add 3
(vi) multiply input by 6 and subtract 1
2 **(b)** 74, 122, $6n + 2$
3 **(a)** **(i)** $(4 \times 1), (4 \times 2), (4 \times 3), (4 \times 4), \ldots$
(ii) $(5 \times 1), (5 \times 2), (5 \times 3), (5 \times 4), \ldots$
(iii) $(11 \times 1), (11 \times 2), (11 \times 3), (11 \times 4), \ldots$
(iv) $(3 \times 1) + 1, (3 \times 2) + 1, (3 \times 3) + 1, (3 \times 4) + 1, \ldots$
(v) $(2 \times 1) + 7, (2 \times 2) + 7, (2 \times 3) + 7, (2 \times 4) + 7, \ldots$
(vi) $(2 \times 1) + 10, (2 \times 2) + 10, (2 \times 3) + 10, (2 \times 4) + 10, \ldots$
(vii) $(3 \times 1) - 2, (3 \times 2) - 2, (3 \times 3) - 2, (3 \times 4) - 2, \ldots$
(viii) $(5 \times 1) - 3, (5 \times 2) - 3, (5 \times 3) - 3, (5 \times 4) - 3, \ldots$
(b) **(i)** 40, 48, $4n$ **(ii)** 50, 60, $5n$ **(iii)** 110, 132, $11n$
(iv) 31, 37, $3n + 1$ **(v)** 27, 31, $2n + 7$
(vi) 30, 34, $2n + 10$ **(vii)** 28, 34, $3n - 2$
(viii) 47, 57, $5n - 3$
4 **(a)** add 6; 37, 43, 49 **(b)** add 10; 61, 71, 81
(c) add 8; 49, 57, 65 **(d)** add 5; 31, 36, 41
(e) add 1, 2, 3, … ; 22, 29, 37 **(f)** add 1, 3, 5, … ; 37, 50, 65
(g) add 1, 1, 2, 2, … ; 13, 17, 21
(h) add 10, 20, 30, … ; 211, 281, 361
(i) add 3, 6, 9, … ; 64, 85, 109
(j) add $1^2, 2^2, 3^2, \ldots$; 91, 140, 204
5 **(a)** **(ii)** 3 **(iii)** 6 **(iv)** 10, 15
(b) **(i)**

Number of points	2	3	4	5	6
Number of lines joining them	1	3	6	10	15

(ii) $\frac{2 \times 1}{2}, \frac{3 \times 2}{2}, \frac{4 \times 3}{2}, \frac{5 \times 4}{2}, \frac{6 \times 5}{2}$ **(iii)** 36

Exercise 12N

5 **(a)**

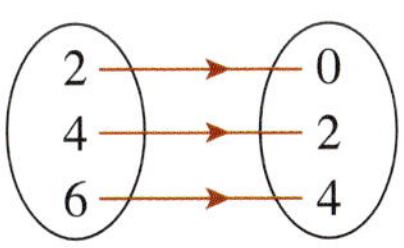

is 2 more than

(b)

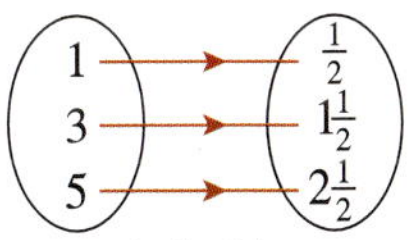

is double

(c)

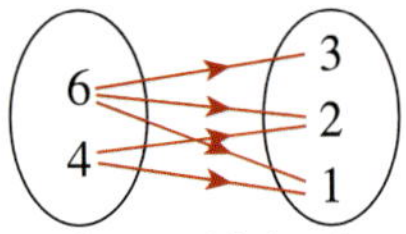

is a multiple of

6 (a) add 4 **(b)** double, then add 1 **(c)** is a factor of

7 (a) A is equal to B

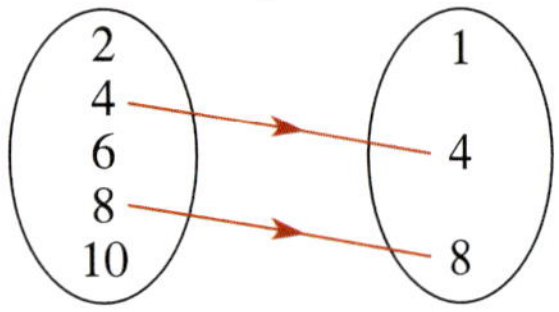

(b) A is less than B

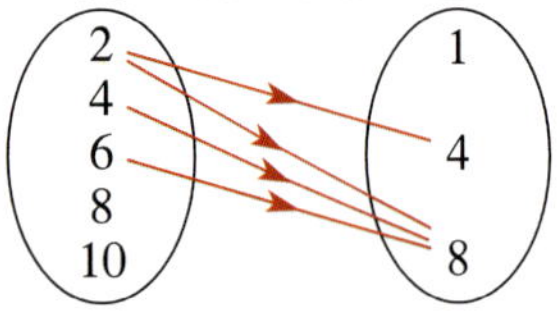

(c) A is a factor of B

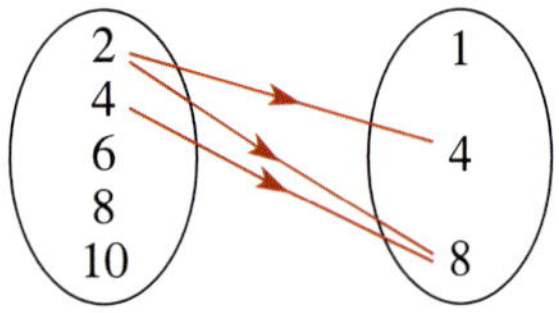

8 (a) A is one third of B

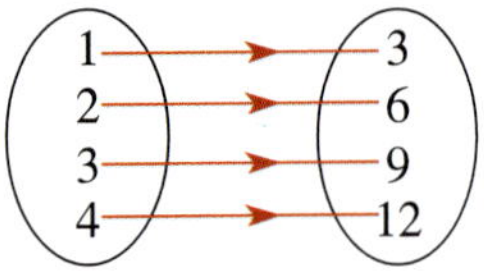

(b) B is three times A

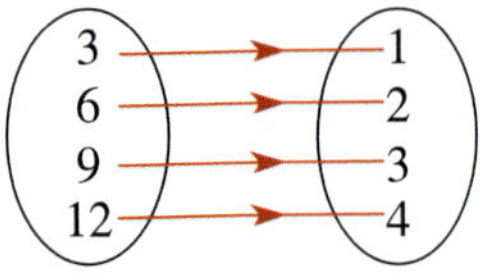

(c) A is less than B

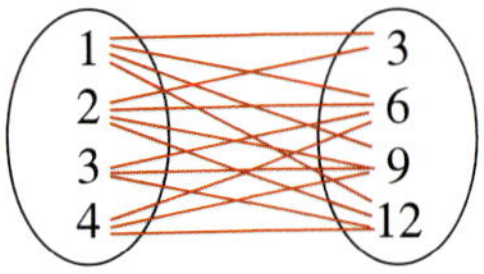

(d) B is greater than A

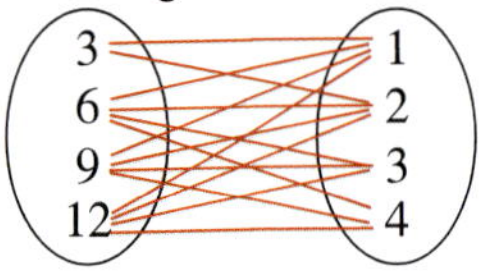

9 (a) A is factor of B

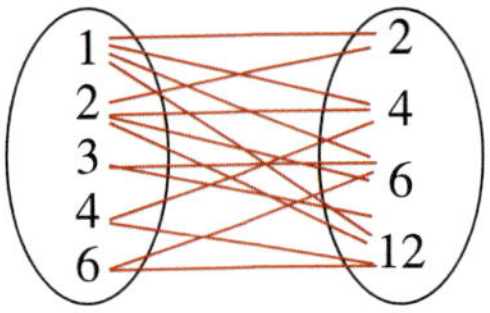

(b) B is a multiple of A

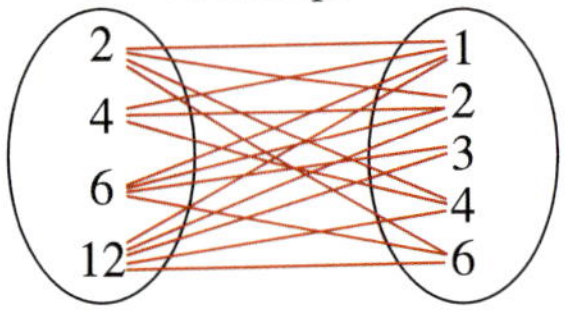

(c) A is equal to B

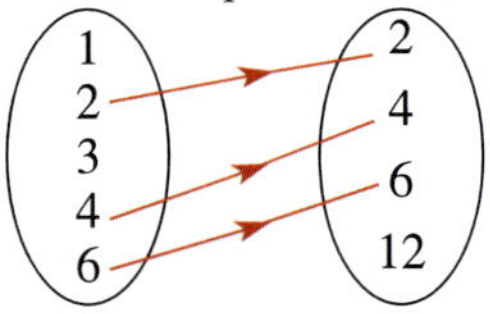

(d) A is not equal to B

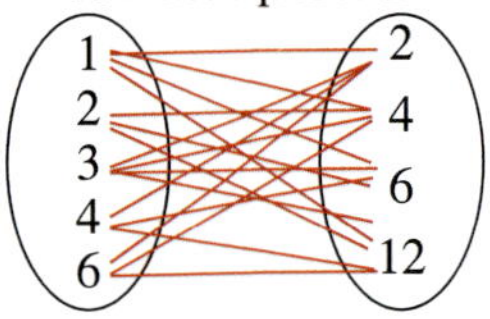

Exercise 12O

2 (a) (i) A is 3 less than B

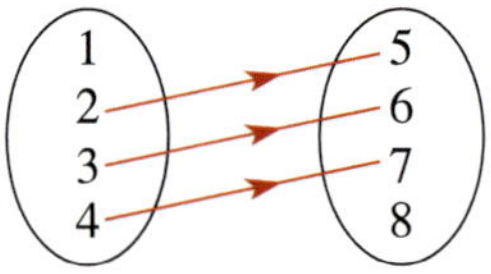

(ii) A is a factor of B

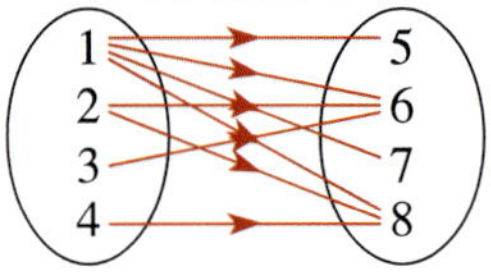

(iii) A is not equal to B

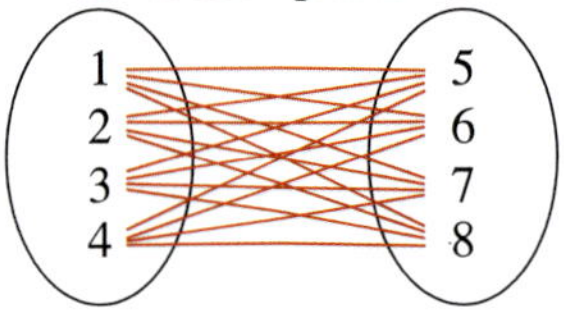

Exercise 12P – mixed questions

1 (a) $15x$ **(b)** $7x + 4y$ **(c)** $2m + 7n + 7$ **(d)** $15xy$

2 (a) 12 **(b)** 27 **(c)** 13

3 **(a)** $100d + p$ **(b)** $21x + 5$ **(c)** $1000k + s$

4 **(a)** $a + b + c + d + e = 31$ **(b)** $5r = 25$

5 $(3z + 11)$ km

6 **(a)** $x + 15$ **(b)** $x + y + 15$ **(c)** $3x + y + 30$

7 $\$(5x + 7y)$

8 3 cm

9 6 cm

10 **(a)** 35, 42, $7n$ **(b)** $7\frac{1}{2}$, 9, $1\frac{1}{2}n$ **(c)** $\frac{1}{10}, \frac{1}{12}, \frac{1}{2n}$

11 **(a)** $1 + 3 + 5 = 9$, $1 + 3 + 5 + 7 = 16$, $1 + 3 + 5 + 7 + 9 = 25$
(b) $1 + 3 + 5 + 7 + 9 + 11 = 36$, $1 + 3 + 5 + 7 + 9 + 11 + 13 = 49$,
$1 + 3 + 5 + 7 + 9 + 11 + 13 + 15 = 64$,
$1 + 3 + 5 + 7 + 9 + 11 + 13 + 15 + 17 = 81$
(c) **(i)** 121 **(ii)** 2500

Consolidation Exercise 12

1 **(a)** $4a$ **(b)** $3b$ **(c)** $7a + 4b$ **(d)** $4ab$ **(e)** $6ab$ **(f)** $72ab$

2 **(a)** 180 **(b)** $60x$ **(c)** 1440 **(d)** $1440y$ **(e)** $2880 + 60x$
(f) $1440y + 840$ **(g)** $1440y + 60x$

3 **(a)** \$30 **(b)** $\$5x$ **(c)** $\$20y$ **(d)** $\$(20y + 30)$
(e) $\$(5x + 20y)$

4 **(a)** $14 + 2x$ cm **(b)** $4y + 2$ cm
(c) $(4p + w + 6)$ cm

5 **(a)** $6a$ cm^2 **(b)** pq cm^2 **(c)** $4(r + 2)$ cm^2

6 **(a)** $x = 3$ **(b)** $x = 9$ **(c)** $x = 13$ **(d)** $x = 12$
(e) $x = 2$ **(f)** $x = 5$

7 **(a)** \$37 **(b)** $\$(9d + 5c)$ **(c)** 1 adult

8 **(a)** \$9 **(b)** $4x + 5 = 39$ **(c)** 8.5 km

9 Ken \$8, Claude \$24

Check out

2 ÷ , 5, 7

3 **(a)** $5a - 2b$ **(b)** $10xy$

4 **(a)** 23 **(b)** 63

5 **(a)** $\$(2x + 7)$ **(b)** $\frac{t}{4}$

6 **(a)** 34, 41 **(b)** 35, 42

7 **(a)** $3n$ **(b)** $2n + 1$

Revision exercise 3

1 **(a)** 20% **(b)** 10% **(c)** 4% **(d)** 2%

2 Oranges 28%, Apples 12%, Bananas 26%, Pineapples 34%

3 **(a)** 25% **(b)** 30% **(c)** 24% **(d)** 85%
(e) 80% **(f)** 16% **(g)** 64% **(h)** 60%

4 **(a)** 20 men **(b)** 3 girls **(c)** 105 car drivers
(d) 1600 voters **(e)** 840

5

Fraction	%	Decimal
$\frac{1}{4}$	25	0.25
$\frac{1}{5}$	20	0.2
$\frac{3}{4}$	75	0.75
$\frac{1}{5}$	20	0.2
$\frac{4}{25}$	16	0.16
$\frac{2}{25}$	8	0.08
$\frac{4}{5}$	80	0.8
$\frac{2}{25}$	8	0.08
1	100	1
$\frac{13}{20}$	65	0.65

6 **(a)** \$17.50 **(b)** 68 cents

7 **(a)** \$199.50 **(b)** \$127.50 **(c)** \$8208 **(d)** \$604.80

8 \$2240

9 \$20.70

10 25%

Fraction	%
$\frac{1}{8}$	$12\frac{1}{2}$
$\frac{1}{4}$	25
$\frac{3}{8}$	$37\frac{1}{2}$
$\frac{1}{2}$	50
$\frac{5}{8}$	$62\frac{1}{2}$
$\frac{3}{4}$	75
$\frac{7}{8}$	$87\frac{1}{2}$
1	100

(a) $\frac{11}{40}$ **(b)** $\frac{1}{3}$ **(c)** $\frac{1}{16}$

11 **(a)** 35 million

13 **(a)** $2\frac{1}{2}$% **(b)** 9° **(c)** Oils 171°, Gas 72°, Solid Fuel 108°

14 Sector angles are: 108°, 81°, 81°, 54°, 18°, 18°

15 **(a)** 190 million tonnes **(b)** 40 million tonnes

16 Sugar production is reducing

18 (F, 20), (M, 31), (A, 25), (M, 39), (J, 45)

19 There is an upward trend at the end of the year.

20 Each set of points lies on a straight line.

22 **(a)** 18 cm, 20 cm^2 **(b)** 18 cm, 16 cm^2 **(c)** 18 cm, 23 cm^2

23 **(a)** 6 cm^2 **(b)** 30 mm, 20 mm **(c)** 600 mm^2

24 **(a)** 100 mm, 43 mm **(b)** 4300 mm^2 **(c)** 43 cm^2

25 **(a)** $7\frac{1}{2}$ cm^2 **(b)** 18 cm^2 **(c)** 42 cm^2

26 15 cm^2, 42 cm^2, 27 cm^2; The area of the largest equals the total area of the other two.

27 **(a)** 26 cm^2 **(b)** 28 cm^2

28 30 m^2

29 **(a)** 30 cm^2 **(b)** 30 cm^2

30 30 cm^2

31 **(a)** $3x + y$ **(b)** $4a + b$ **(c)** $2p + 3q$ **(d)** $4s + 2t$

32 **(a)** $x + y$ **(b)** $a + 2b$ **(c)** $2q$ **(d)** $4s + 3t$

33 **(a)** $7a$, $2a + 14$ **(b)** $2xy$, $4x + 2y$

34 **(a)** $7w$ **(b)** $24d$ **(c)** $60h$

35 **(a)** $a + b = 10$ **(b)** $c = d + 10$

36 **(a)** $x + y = 72$ **(b)** $x = 2y$ 48 years old

37 **(a)** 16 **(b)** 100 **(c)** n^2

38 **(a)** 13 **(b)** 17 **(c)** 23 **(d)** $2x + 3$

39 **(a)** multiply input by 2 **(b)** multiply input by 3 then add 1 **(c)** multiply input by 4 then add 5

Mixed questions 3

1 C	**2** D	**3** C	**4** B	**5** C	**6** C
7 C	**8** A	**9** A	**10** C	**11** A	**12** C
13 B	**14** D	**15** A	**16** C	**17** A	**18** B
19 D	**20** C	**21** C	**22** B	**23** B	**24** D
25 C	**26** A	**27** C	**28** C	**29** D	**30** C

Index

acute angles, 91
acute-angled triangles, 146
addition
  decimals, 70–1
  fractions, 50–1
  numbers, 4
  symbols, 241
algebraic expressions, 242
  substitutions, 242
angles, 87–106
  acute, 91
  comparing, 89–91
  complementary, 97, 98–9
  drawing, 96–7
  and lines, 88–92
  measuring, 93–6
  naming, 88–9
  obtuse, 91
  in quadrilaterals, 99–100
  reflex, 91
  relations between, 97–101
  right, 91
  special, 91
  straight, 91
  supplementary, 97, 98–9
  in triangles, 99–100
  vertically opposite, 98
approximations, 15–17
area, 221–38
  comparing, 222–5
  rectangles, 229–31
  triangles, 231–4
  units, 226–8
arrow diagrams, 251–3
  types of, 253
averages, 209–10
bar charts, 203–6
bar graphs, 203–6
basc 10, 3
binary numbers, 3
block graphs, 203–6
boxes, 108–10
buying, 187–91
calculators
  and decimals, 72–3
  using, 17–19
Celsius, 136
centimetres, 124–5
change, 178
charts
  bar, 203–6
  pie, 207–9
  see also diagrams; graphs
clocks, 24-hour, 135
common denominators, 48
common factors, 9, 32–4
common multiples, 32–4
compasses, 151
complementary angles, 97, 98–9
composite numbers, 7
cones, 112
  truncated, 112
congruent shapes, 160
constants, 240
constructions, 151–4
consumer arithmetic, 177–98
continuous data, 200
coordinate graphs, 211–14
coordinates, 213–14
corners, 97
cross-sections, 111
cubes, 109
cuboids, 108–10
  drawing and making, 109–10
cylinders, 110–11
data
  continuous, 200
  discrete, 200
data collection, 200–1
decimal form, 64
decimal places, two, 65–7
decimal point, 64
decimal system, 3

decimals, 63–80
  addition, 70–1
  and calculators, 72–3
  division, 74–7
    by decimals, 75–6
    by powers of ten, 73–4
    by whole numbers, 75
  and fractions, 69, 182–6
  and money, 70
  multiplication, 74–7
    by powers of ten, 73–4
  on number lines, 64–5
  and percentages, 182–6
  and place value, 68–70
  subtraction, 71–2
degrees, 93
denary numbers, 3
denominators, common, 48
deposits, 191–3
diagrams
  arrow, 251–3
  Venn, 28–9
  see also charts; graphs
discounts, 188–90
discrete data, 200
distributive law, 11
divisibility test, 13
division, 12–15
  decimals, 74–7
    by powers of ten, 73–4
  fractions, 55–7
  long, 14–15
dodecahedrons, 116
edges, 109
empty sets, 27
equations
  solving, 246–7
  writing, 244–6
equilateral triangles, 144
equivalent fractions, 43–8
  calculating, 46–7
estimations, 15–17
Euler's relationship, 246
even numbers, 12
expanded form, 3
expressions
  algebraic, 242
  writing, 243
face value, 2
faces, 109
factors, 5–10
  common, 9, 32–4
  prime, 8–9
fraction walls, 44–5
fractions, 39–62
  addition, 50–1
  calculating, 41–3
  comparing, 48
  and decimals, 69, 182–6
  division, 55–7
    into fractions, 56–7
    into whole numbers, 55–6
  greater than 1, 48–50
  improper, 49
  multiplication, 52–5
    by fractions, 53–5
    by whole numbers, 52–3
  and percentages, 182–6
  problem solving, 57–8
  proper, 49
  of shapes, 45–6
  showing, 40–1
  simplifying, 47–8
  subtraction, 51–2
  of a whole, 41
  whole from, 43
  see also equivalent fractions
frequency tables, 200
grams, 130–1
graphs
  block, 203–6
  coordinate, 211–14
  plotting, 211
  see also charts; diagrams
HCF (highest common factor), 9
highest common factor (HCF), 9
hundredths, 65–6
  on number lines, 66–7
icosahedrons, 116
images, mirror, 158
improper fractions, 49
information, representing, 199–220
information matrices, 29
intersections, sets, 30–2
isosceles triangles, 144
Kelvin, 136
kilograms, 130
kilometres, 125
kites, 150

LCM (lowest common multiple), 9
length, 122–9
  units, 122–7
lines
  and angles, 88–92
  mirror, 155
  of symmetry, 155
  see also number lines
loans, 191–3
long division, 14–15
losses, 180–1
lowest common multiple (LCM), 9
mass, 129–32
  SI units, 130
  units, 129
  and weight, 129–30
matrices, information, 29
means, 209–10
measuring, 121–42
median, 210
metres, 123–4
metric units, 123–7
  relationships between, 126–7
millimetres, 124–5
mirror images, 158
mirror lines, 155
mixed numbers, 48
Möbius strips, 117
mode, 210
money
  and decimals, 70
  using, 178–81
multiples, 5–10
  common, 32–4
multiplication
  decimals, 74–7
    by powers of ten, 73–4
  fractions, 52–5
  shortcuts, 10
  symbols, 241–2
nets, 110
  of solids, 114–17
number lines
  decimals on, 64–5
  hundredths on, 66–7
number sequences, 250–1
number systems, 3, 10–12
numbers, 1–24
  addition, 4
  binary, 3
  composite, 7
  denary, 3
  even, 12
  mixed, 48
  odd, 12
  prime, 6–8
  story of, 2–3
  subtraction, 4
  see also whole numbers
obtuse angles, 91
obtuse-angled triangles, 146
octahedrons, 115
odd numbers, 12
parallel rays, 88
parallelograms, 148–9
patterns, 239–58
  looking for, 247–51
percentage profits, 187
percentages
  of amounts, 186–7
  and decimals, 182–6
  and fractions, 182–6
  understanding, 181–2
perimeters, 127–9, 233
pictographs, 201–3
pie charts, 207–9
place value, 2
  and decimals, 68–70
points, 88
prices, selling, 187–8
prime factors, 8–9
prime numbers, 6–8
prisms, 111–12
problem solving, 19–20
  fractions, 57–8
profits, 180–1
  percentage, 187
proper fractions, 49
protractors, 94–6
pyramids, 112–13
  square-based, 113
quadrilaterals, 147–50
  angles, 99–100
  see also rectangles
rays, parallel, 88
recovery times, 135
rectangles, 147–8
  area, 229–31
reflections, 158–60
reflex angles, 91

rep-tiles, 166
rhombi, 148–9
right angles, 91
right-angled triangles, 146
rounding off, 15
sales, 188–91
scalene triangles, 144
scales, 212–13
  uniform, 212
seconds, 133
selling, 187–91
selling prices, 187–8
sequences, number, 250–1
sets, 25–38
  describing, 26–8
  empty, 27
  intersections, 30–2
  loops, 26
  members, 26
  universal, 28
shapes, 143–70
  congruent, 160
  counting, 164–5
  fractions of, 45–6
  investigating, 164–6
  irregular, 224–5
  moving, 160–4
SI units, 123
  mass, 130
  temperature, 136
  time, 133
solids, 107–20
  nets, 114–17
  properties, 114
spheres, 113–14
square centimetres, 226–7
square metres, 228
square millimetres, 227–8
square-based pyramids, 113
squares, 147–8
straight angles, 91
subsets, 28
  symbols, 29
substitutions, algebraic expressions, 242
subtraction
  decimals, 71–2
  fractions, 51–2
  numbers, 4
  symbols, 241
supplementary angles, 97, 98–9
surfaces, 222
symbols, 239–58
  addition, 241
  multiplication, 241–2
  subsets, 29
  subtraction, 241
  using, 27
symmetry, 155–8
  lines of, 155
Système International d'Unités (SI) *see* SI units
tables, frequency, 200
tangrams, 165–6
temperature, 136–7
  SI units, 136
terms, 250
tessellations, 160, 162
thousandths, 68
time, 132–6
  SI units, 133
  telling the, 133–4
tonne, 132
translations, 160
trapeziums, 150
triangles, 144–6
  acute-angled, 146
  angles, 99–100
  area, 231–4
  classification, 146
  equilateral, 144
  isosceles, 144
  obtuse-angled, 146
  right-angled, 146
  scalene, 144
truncated cones, 112
24-hour clocks, 135
uniform scales, 212
units
  area, 226–8
  length, 122–7
  see also metric units; SI units
universal sets, 28
variables, 240
Venn diagrams, 28–9
vertically opposite angles, 98
vertices, 109
weight, and mass, 129–30
whole numbers
  dividing by fractions, 55–6
  dividing decimal by, 75
  multiplying fractions by, 52–3